Children's Literature Review

Guide to Gale Literary Criticism Series

When you need to review criticism of literary works, these are the Gale series to use:

If the author's death date is: **You should turn to:**

After Dec. 31, 1959 (or author is still living)

CONTEMPORARY LITERARY CRITICISM

for example: Jorge Luis Borges, Anthony Burgess, William Faulkner, Mary Gordon, Ernest Hemingway, Iris Murdoch

1900 through 1959

TWENTIETH-CENTURY LITERARY CRITICISM

for example: Willa Cather, F. Scott Fitzgerald, Henry James, Mark Twain, Virginia Woolf

1800 through 1899

NINETEENTH-CENTURY LITERATURE CRITICISM

for example: Fedor Dostoevski, Nathaniel Hawthorne, George Sand, William Wordsworth

1400 through 1799

LITERATURE CRITICISM FROM 1400 TO 1800 (excluding Shakespeare)

for example: Anne Bradstreet, Daniel Defoe, Alexander Pope, François Rabelais, Jonathan Swift, Phillis Wheatley

SHAKESPEAREAN CRITICISM

Shakespeare's plays and poetry

Antiquity through 1399

CLASSICAL AND MEDIEVAL LITERATURE CRITICISM

for example: Dante, Homer, Plato, Sophocles, Vergil, the Beowulf poet

(Volume 1 forthcoming)

Gale also publishes related criticism series:

CHILDREN'S LITERATURE REVIEW

This ongoing series covers authors of all eras. Presents criticism on authors and author/illustrators who write for the preschool through high school audience.

CONTEMPORARY ISSUES CRITICISM

This two volume set presents criticism on contemporary authors writing on current issues. Topics covered include the social sciences, philosophy, economics, natural science, law, and related areas.

ISSN 0362-4145

volume 12

Children's Literature Review

Excerpts from Reviews,
Criticism, and Commentary
on Books for Children
and Young People

Guest Essay, "Internationalism and
Children's Literature,"
by Anne Pellowski

Gerard J. Senick
Editor

Melissa Reiff Hug
Associate Editor

Gale Research Company
Book Tower
Detroit, Michigan 48226

STAFF

Gerard J. Senick, *Editor*

Melissa Reiff Hug, *Associate Editor*

Susan Miller Harig, *Senior Assistant Editor*

Motoko Fujishiro Huthwaite, *Assistant Editor*

Sharon R. Gunton, *Contributing Editor*

Jeanne A. Gough, *Permissions & Production Manager*
Lizbeth A. Purdy, *Production Supervisor*
Denise Michlewicz Broderick, *Production Coordinator*
Eric Berger, *Assistant Production Coordinator*
Kathleen M. Cook, Maureen Duffy, Sheila J. Nasea, *Editorial Assistants*

Victoria B. Cariappa, *Research Coordinator*
Maureen R. Richards, *Assistant Research Coordinator*
Daniel Kurt Gilbert, Kent Graham, Michele R. O'Connell, Keith E. Schooley,
Filomena Sgambati, Vincenza G. Tranchida, Mary D. Wise, *Research Assistants*

Linda M. Pugliese, *Manuscript Coordinator*
Donna Craft, *Assistant Manuscript Coordinator*
Jennifer E. Gale, Maureen A. Puhl, Rosetta Irene Simms, *Manuscript Assistants*

Janice M. Mach, *Permissions Coordinator, Text*
Patricia A. Seefelt, *Permissions Coordinator, Illustrations*
Susan D. Battista, Margaret A. Chamberlain,
Sandra C. Davis, Kathy Grell, *Assistant Permissions Coordinators*
Mabel Gurney, Josephine Keene, Mary M. Matuz, *Senior Permissions Assistants*
Margaret Carson, H. Diane Cooper, Colleen M. Crane, *Permissions Assistants*
Eileen H. Baehr, Anita Ransom, Kimberly Smilay, *Permissions Clerks*

Arthur Chartow, *Art Director*

Frederick G. Ruffner, *Publisher*
Dedria Bryfonski, *Editorial Director*
Ellen T. Crowley, *Associate Editorial Director*
Laurie Lanzen Harris, *Director, Literary Criticism Division*
Dennis Poupard, *Senior Editor, Literary Criticism Series*

Library of Congress Catalog Card Number 75-34953
ISBN 0-8103-0344-2
ISSN 0362-4145

Computerized photocomposition by
Typographics, Incorporated
Kansas City, Missouri

Printed in the United States

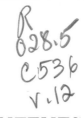
CONTENTS

Preface   5

Authors to Appear in Future Volumes   9

**Guest Essay, "Internationalism and Children's Literature,"
by Anne Pellowski   11**

Appendix   243

Cumulative Index to Authors   255

Cumulative Index to Nationalities   263

Cumulative Index to Titles   265

Isaac Asimov   1920- 21

Margot Benary-Isbert
    1889-1979 65

Marcia Brown   1918- 79

Robert Cormier   1925- 114

Jane Gardam   1928- 156

Ann Jonas   1932- 172

Christine Nöstlinger   1936- 179

Bill Peet   1915- 190

Ann Petry   1908- 209

Ellen Raskin   1928-1984 213

José María Sánchez-Silva   1911-   ...230

John Steptoe   1950- 234

PREFACE

As children's literature has evolved into both a respected branch of creative writing and a successful industry, literary criticism has documented and influenced each stage of its growth. Critics have recorded the literary development of individual authors as well as the trends and controversies that resulted from changes in values and attitudes, especially as they concerned children. While defining a philosophy of children's literature, critics developed a scholarship that balances an appreciation of children and an awareness of their needs with standards for literary quality much like those required by critics of adult literature. *Children's Literature Review* (*CLR*) is designed to provide a permanent, accessible record of this ongoing scholarship. Those responsible for bringing children and books together can now make informed choices when selecting reading materials for the young.

Scope of the Series

Each biannual volume contains excerpts from published criticism on the works of authors and author/illustrators who create books for children from preschool through high school. The author list for each volume is international in scope and represents the variety of genres covered by children's literature—picture books, fiction, folklore, nonfiction, poetry, and drama. The works of approximately fifteen to forty authors of all eras are represented in each volume. Although earlier volumes of *CLR* emphasized critical material published after 1960, successive volumes have expanded their coverage to encompass criticism written before 1960. Since many of the authors included in *CLR* are living and continue to write, it is necessary to update their entries periodically. Thus, future volumes will supplement the entries of selected authors covered in earlier volumes as well as present criticism on the works of authors new to the series.

Organization of the Book

An author section consists of the following elements: author heading, author portrait, author introduction, excerpts of criticism (each followed by a bibliographical citation), and illustrations, when available.

- The **author heading** consists of the author's full name followed by birth and death dates. The portion of the name outside the parentheses denotes the form under which the author is most frequently published. If the majority of the author's works for children were written under a pseudonym, the pseudonym will be listed in the author heading and the real name given on the first line of the author introduction. Also located at the beginning of the introduction are any other pseudonyms used by the author in writing for children and any name variations, including transliterated forms for authors whose languages use nonroman alphabets. Uncertainty as to a birth or death date is indicated by question marks.

- An **author portrait** is included when available.

- The **author introduction** contains information designed to introduce an author to *CLR* users by presenting an overview of the author's themes and styles, occasional biographical facts that relate to his or her literary career, a summary of critical response to the author's works, and information about major awards and prizes the author has received. Where applicable, introductions conclude with references to additional entries in biographical and critical reference series published by Gale Research Company. These sources include past volumes of *CLR* as well as *Contemporary Authors, Something about the Author, Something about the Author Autobiography Series, Yesterday's Authors of Books for Children, Contemporary Literary Criticism, Twentieth-Century Literary Criticism, Nineteenth-Century Literature Criticism, Dictionary of Literary Biography,* and *Authors in the News.*

- **Criticism** is located in three sections: **author's commentary** and **general commentary** (when available) and within individual **title entries,** which are preceded by **title entry headings.** Criticism is arranged chronologically within each section. Titles by authors being profiled are highlighted in boldface type within the text for easier access by readers.

The **author's commentary** presents background material written by the author or by an interviewer. This commentary may cover a specific work or several works. Author's commentary on more than one work appears after the author introduction, while commentary on an individual book follows the title entry heading.

The **general commentary** consists of critical excerpts that consider more than one work by the author being profiled. General commentary is preceded by the critic's name in boldface type or, in the case of unsigned criticism, by the title of the journal.

Title entry headings precede the criticism on a title and cite publication information on the work being reviewed. Title headings list the work's title as it appeared in its country of origin; titles in languages using nonroman alphabets are transliterated. If the original title is in a language other than English, the title of the first English-language translation follows in brackets. The work's first publication date is listed in parentheses following the title. Differing U.S. and British titles of works originally published in English follow the publication date within the parentheses.

Title entries consist of critical excerpts on the author's individual works, arranged chronologically by publication date. The entries generally contain two to six reviews per title, depending on the stature of the book and the amount of criticism it has generated. The editors select titles that reflect the entire scope of the author's literary contribution, covering each genre and subject. An effort is made to reprint criticism that represents the full range of each title's reception —from the year of its initial publication to current assessments. Thus, the reader is provided with a record of the author's critical history.

Beginning with *CLR*-12, entries on author/illustrators will occasionally feature commentary on selected works illustrated but not written by the author being profiled. These works are strongly associated with the illustrator and have received critical acclaim for their art. By including critical comment on works of this type, the editors wish to provide a more complete representation of the author/illustrator's total career. Criticism on these works has been chosen to stress artistic, rather than literary, contributions. Title entry headings for works illustrated by the author being profiled are arranged chronologically within the entry by date of publication and include notes identifying the author of the illustrated work. In order to provide easier access for users, all titles illustrated by the author/illustrator will be boldfaced.

• Selected excerpts are preceded by **explanatory notes,** which provide information on the critic or work of criticism to enhance the reader's understanding of the excerpt.

• A complete **bibliographical citation** designed to facilitate the location of the original book or article follows each piece of criticism.

• Numerous **illustrations** are featured in *CLR*. For entries on author/illustrators, an effort has been made to include illustrations that reflect the author's styles as discussed in the criticism. Entries on major authors who do not illustrate their own works may also include photographs and other illustrative material pertinent to the authors' careers.

Other Features

• A list of **authors to appear in future volumes** follows the preface.

• A **guest essay** appears before the first author entry. These essays are written specifically for *CLR* by prominent critics on subjects of their choice. Past volumes have included essays by John Rowe Townsend, Zena Sutherland, Sheila A. Egoff, Rudine Sims, and Marcus Crouch. Volume 12 contains Anne Pellowski's "Internationalism and Children's Literature." The editors are honored to feature Ms. Pellowski in this volume.

• An **appendix** lists the sources from which material has been reprinted in the volume. It does not, however, list every book or periodical consulted for the volume.

• *CLR* volumes contain **cumulative indexes** to authors, nationalities, and titles.

The **cumulative index to authors** lists authors who have appeared in *CLR* and includes cross-references to *Contemporary Authors, Something about the Author, Something about the Author Autobiography Series, Yesterday's Authors of Books for Children, Contemporary Literary Criticism, Twentieth-Century Literary Criticism, Nineteenth-Century Literature Criticism, Dictionary of Literary Biography,* and *Authors in the News.*

The **cumulative nationality index** lists authors alphabetically under their respective nationalities. Author names are followed by the volume number(s) in which they appear. Authors who have changed citizenship or whose current citizenship is not reflected in biographical sources appear under both their original nationality and that of their current residence.

The **cumulative title index** lists titles covered in *CLR* followed by the volume and page number where criticism begins.

Acknowledgments

No work of this scope can be accomplished without the cooperation of many people. The editors especially wish to thank the copyright holders of the criticism included in this volume, the permissions managers of many book and magazine publishing companies for assisting us in securing reprint rights, and the staffs of the Kresge Library at Wayne State University, the University of Michigan Library, the Detroit Public Library, and the Wayne Oakland Library Federation (WOLF) for making their resources available to us. We are also grateful to Carole McCollough, Coordinator of Children's and Young Adults' Services for WOLF, to her successor, Sylvia Makowski, and to Anthony J. Bogucki for his assistance with copyright research.

Suggestions Are Welcome

In response to various suggestions, several features have been added to *CLR* since the series began:

- Since Volume 3—**Author's commentary,** when available, which presents the viewpoint of the author being profiled.

  —An **appendix** listing the sources of criticism in each volume.

- Since Volume 4—**Author portraits** as well as **illustrations** from works by author/illustrators, when available.

  —**Title entries** arranged chronologically according to the work's first publication; previous volumes listed titles alphabetically.

- Since Volume 5—A **guest essay,** when available, written specifically for *CLR* by a prominent critic on a subject of his or her choice.

- Since Volume 6—**Explanatory notes** that provide information on the critic or work of criticism to enhance the usefulness of the excerpt.

  —A **cumulative nationality index** for easy access to authors by nationality.

- Since Volume 8—Author entries on retellers of traditional literature as well as those who have been the first to record oral tales and other folklore.

  —More extensive illustrative material, such as holographs of manuscript pages and photographs of people and places pertinent to the authors' careers.

- Since Volume 10—Entries devoted to criticism on a major work by a single author.

Readers are cordially invited to write the editor with comments and suggestions for further enhancing the usefulness of the *CLR* series.

AUTHORS TO APPEAR IN FUTURE VOLUMES

Aardema, Verna (Norberg) 1911-
Adams, Adrienne 1906-
Adams, Harriet S(tratemeyer)
  1893?-1982
Adams, Richard 1920-
Adler, Irving 1913-
Aesop 620?BC-564?BC
Anderson, C(larence) W(illiam)
  1891-1971
Arnosky, Jim 1946-
Arundel, Honor (Morfydd) 1919-1973
Asbjörnsen, Peter Christen 1812-1885
  and Jörgen Moe 1813?-1882
Asch, Frank 1946-
Avery, Gillian 1926-
Avi 1937-
Aymé, Marcel 1902-1967
Bailey, Carolyn Sherwin 1875-1961
Ballantyne, R(obert) M(ichael)
  1825-1894
Banner, Angela 1923-
Bannerman, Helen 1863-1946
Barrett, Judi(th) 1941-
Barrie, J(ames) M(atthew) 1860-1937
Baum, L(yman) Frank 1856-1919
Baumann, Hans 1914-1985
BB 1905-
Beatty, Patricia 1922- and John
  1922-1975
Behn, Harry 1898-1973
Belloc, Hilaire 1870-1953
Benchley, Nathaniel 1915-1981
Berenstain, Stan(ley) 1923- and
  Jan(ice) 1923-
Berger, Melvin 1927-
Berna, Paul 1910-
Beskow, Elsa 1874-1953
Bianco, Margery Williams 1881-1944
Bishop, Claire Huchet
Blades, Ann 1947-
Blake, Quentin 1932-
Blos, Joan W(insor) 1928-
Blumberg, Rhoda 1917-
Blyton, Enid 1897-1968
Bodecker, N(iels) M(ogens) 1922-
Bødker, Cecil 1927-
Bonham, Frank 1914-
Brancato, Robin F(idler) 1936-
Branley, Franklyn M(ansfield) 1915-
Branscum, Robbie 1937-
Brazil, Angela 1869-1947
Breinburg, Petronella 1927-
Bridgers, Sue Ellen 1942-
Bright, Robert 1902-
Brink, Carol Ryrie 1895-1981
Brooke, L(eonard) Leslie 1862-1940
Brown, Marc 1946-

Browne, Anthony (Edward Tudor)
  1946-
Bryan, Ashley F. 1923-
Buff, Mary 1890-1970 and Conrad
  1886-1975
Bulla, Clyde Robert 1914-
Burch, Robert 1925-
Burchard, Peter 1921-
Burgess, Gelett 1866-1951
Burgess, Thornton W(aldo) 1874-1965
Burnett, Frances Hodgson 1849-1924
Butterworth, Oliver 1915-
Caines, Jeannette
Caldecott, Randolph (J.) 1846-1886
Carlson, Natalie Savage 1906-
Carrick, Carol 1935-
Chambers, Aidan 1934-
Childress, Alice 1920-
Chönz, Selina
Christopher, Matt(hew) 1917-
Ciardi, John 1916-1986
Clapp, Patricia 1912-
Clark, Ann Nolan 1896-
Clarke, Pauline 1921-
Cleaver, Elizabeth (Mrazik) 1939-1985
Cohen, Barbara 1932-
Colby, C(arroll) B(urleigh) 1904-1977
Colman, Hila
Colum Padraic 1881-1972
Cone, Molly 1918-
Coolidge, Olivia 1908-
Coolidge, Susan 1835-1905
Cooney, Barbara 1917-
Courlander, Harold 1908-
Cox, Palmer 1840-1924
Cresswell, Helen 1934-
Crompton, Richmal 1890-1969
Cunningham, Julia 1916-
Curry, Jane L(ouise) 1932-
Dalgliesh, Alice 1893-1979
Daly, Maureen 1921-
Daugherty, James 1889-1974
D'Aulaire, Ingri 1904-1980 and Edgar
  Parin 1898-1986
De la Mare, Walter 1873-1956
De Regniers, Beatrice Schenk 1914-
Dickinson, Peter 1927-
Dillon, Eilís 1920-
Dodge, Mary Mapes 1831-1905
Domanska, Janina
Drescher, Henrik
Duncan, Lois S(teinmetz) 1934-
Duvoisin, Roger 1904-1980
Eager, Edward 1911-1964
Edgeworth, Maria 1767-1849
Edmonds, Walter D(umaux) 1903-
Ende, Michael 1930(?)-

Epstein, Sam(uel) 1909- and Beryl 1910-
Ets, Marie Hall 1893-
Ewing, Juliana Horatia 1841-1885
Farber, Norma 1909-1984
Farjeon, Eleanor 1881-1965
Field, Eugene 1850-1895
Field, Rachel 1894-1942
Fisher, Dorothy Canfield 1879-1958
Fisher, Leonard Everett 1924-
Flack, Marjorie 1897-1958
Forbes, Esther 1891-1967
Forest, Antonia
Freeman, Don 1908-1978
Fujikawa, Gyo 1908-
Fyleman, Rose 1877-1957
Galdone, Paul 1914-1986
Gantos, Jack 1951-
Garfield, Leon 1921-
Garis, Howard R(oger) 1873-1962
Garner, Alan 1935-
Gates, Doris 1901-
Gerrard, Roy 1935-
Giblin, James Cross 1933-
Giff, Patricia Reilly 1935-
Ginsburg, Mirra 1919-
Goble, Paul 1933-
Godden, Rumer 1907-
Goodrich, Samuel G(riswold) 1793-1860
Gorey, Edward 1925-
Goudge, Elizabeth (de Beauchamp)
  1900-1984
Gramatky, Hardie 1907-1979
Greene, Constance C(larke) 1924-
Grimm, Jacob 1785-1863 and Wilhelm
  1786-1859
Gruelle, Johnny 1880-1938
Guillot, René 1900-1969
Guy, Rosa (Cuthbert) 1928-
Hader, Elmer 1889-1973 and Berta
  1891?-1976
Hale, Lucretia Peabody 1820-1900
Haley, Gail E(inhart) 1939-
Harnett, Cynthia 1893-1981
Harris, Christie 1907-
Harris, Joel Chandler 1848-1908
Harris, Rosemary (Jeanne) 1923-
Haywood, Carolyn 1898-
Heide, Florence Parry 1919-
Highwater, Jamake 1942-
Hill, Eric
Hoban, Tana
Hoberman, Mary Ann 1930-
Hoff, Syd(ney) 1912-
Hoffman, Heinrich 1809-1894
Holland, Isabelle 1920-
Holling, Holling C(lancy) 1900-1973
Howker, Janni 1957-

Hughes, Langston 1902-1967
Hughes, Shirley 1929-
Hunter, Mollie 1922-
Ipcar, Dahlov 1917-
Iwasaki, Chihiro 1918-1974
Jackson, Jesse 1908-1983
Jacobs, Joseph 1854-1916
Janosch 1931-
Jeschke, Susan 1942-
Johnson, Crockett 1906-1975
Johnson, James Weldon 1871-1938
Jones, Diana Wynne 1934-
Judson, Clara Ingram 1879-1960
Juster, Norton 1929-
Keith, Harold 1903-
Kelly, Eric P(hilbrook) 1884-1960
Kennedy, Richard 1932-
Kent, Jack 1920-1985
Kerr, Judith 1923-
Kerr, M. E. 1927-
Kettelkamp, Larry 1933-
King, Clive 1924-
Kipling, Rudyard 1865-1936
Kjelgaard, Jim 1910-1959
Kraus, Robert 1925-
Krauss, Ruth 1911-
Krumgold, Joseph 1908-1980
La Farge, Oliver 1901-1963
La Fontaine, Jean de 1621-1695
Lang, Andrew 1844-1912
Langton, Jane 1922-
Latham, Jean Lee 1902-
Lauber, Patricia 1924-
Lavine, Sigmund A(rnold) 1908-
Leaf, Munro 1905-1976
Lenski, Lois 1893-1974
Levy, Elizabeth 1942-
Lewis, Elizabeth Foreman 1892-1958
Lightner, A(lice) M. 1904-
Linklater, Eric 1899-1974
Locker, Thomas 1937-
Lofting, Hugh 1866-1947
Lunn, Janet 1928-
MacDonald, George 1824-1905
MacGregor, Ellen 1906-1954
MacLachlan, Patricia
Mann, Peggy
Marshall, James 1942-
Martin, Patricia Miles 1899-
Masefield, John 1878-1967
Mayer, Marianna 1945-
Mayne, William 1928-
Mazer, Harry 1925-
Mazer, Norma Fox 1931-
McCaffrey, Anne (Inez) 1926-
McGovern, Ann

McKillip, Patricia A(nne) 1948-
McNeer, May 1902-
Meader, Stephen W(arren) 1892-1977
Means, Florence Crannell 1891-1980
Meigs, Cornelia 1884-1973
Meltzer, Milton 1915-
Merriam, Eve 1916-
Merrill, Jean 1923-
Miles, Betty 1928-
Milne, Lorus 1912- and Margery 1915-
Minarik, Else Holmelund 1920-
Mizumura, Kazue
Molesworth, Mary Louisa 1842-1921
Moore, Lilian
Morey, Walt(er) 1907-
Naylor, Phyllis Reynolds 1933-
Neufeld, John (Arthur) 1938-
Neville, Emily Cheney 1919-
Nic Leodhas, Sorche 1898-1969
Nichols, Ruth 1948-
North, Sterling 1906-1974
Ofek, Uriel 1926-
Olney, Ross R(obert) 1929-
Oneal, Zibby 1934-
Ormondroyd, Edward 1925-
Ottley, Reginald
Oxenbury, Helen 1938-
Parish, Peggy 1927-
Peck, Richard (Wayne) 1934-
Peck, Robert Newton 1928-
Perl, Lila
Perrault, Charles 1628-1703
Petersham, Maud 1890-1971 and Miska 1888-1960
Picard, Barbara Leonie 1917-
Platt, Kin 1911-
Politi, Leo 1908-
Prelutsky, Jack
Price, Christine 1928-1980
Pyle, Howard 1853-1911
Reeves, James 1909-1978
Richards, Laura E(lizabeth) 1850-1943
Richler, Mordecai 1931-
Robertson, Keith 1914-
Rockwell, Anne 1934- and Harlow
Rodgers, Mary 1931-
Rollins, Charlemae Hill 1897-1979
Ross, Tony 1938-
Rounds, Glen 1906-
Rylant, Cynthia 1954-
Sandburg, Carl 1878-1967
Sandoz, Mari 1896-1966
Sawyer, Ruth 1880-1970
Scarry, Huck 1953-
Scott, Jack Denton 1915-
Sebestyen, Ouida 1924-

Seton, Ernest Thompson 1860-1946
Sharmat, Marjorie Weinman 1928-
Sharp, Margery 1905-
Shotwell, Louisa R(ossiter) 1902-
Sidney, Margaret 1844-1924
Silverstein, Alvin 1933- and Virginia 1937-
Sinclair, Catherine 1800-1864
Skurzynski, Gloria 1930-
Sleator, William 1945-
Slobodkin, Louis 1903-1975
Smith, Doris Buchanan 1934-
Snyder, Zilpha Keatley 1927-
Spence, Eleanor 1928-
Sperry, Armstrong W. 1897-1976
Spykman, E(lizabeth) C. 1896-1965
Spyri, Johanna 1827-1901
Steele, William O(wen) 1917-1979
Stevenson, James 1929-
Stolz, Mary 1920-
Stratemeyer, Edward L. 1862-1930
Streatfeild, Noel 1897-1986
Taylor, Sydney 1904?-1978
Taylor, Theodore 1924-
Ter Haar, Jaap 1922-
Titus, Eve 1922-
Tolkien, J(ohn) R(onald) R(euel) 1892-1973
Treadgold, Mary 1910-
Trease, Geoffrey 1909-
Tresselt, Alvin 1916-
Treviño, Elizabeth Borton de 1904-
Tudor, Tasha 1915-
Turkle, Brinton 1915-
Twain, Mark 1835-1910
Udry, Janice May 1928-
Unnerstad, Edith 1900-
Uttley, Alison 1884-1976
Ventura, Piero 1937-
Vincent, Gabrielle
Vining, Elizabeth Gray 1902-
Voigt, Cynthia 1942-
Waber, Bernard 1924-
Wahl, Jan 1933-
Walter, Mildred Pitts
Ward, Lynd 1905-1985
Wells, Rosemary 1943-
Westall, Robert (Atkinson) 1929-
Wiese, Kurt 1887-1974
Wilkinson, Brenda 1946-
Williams, Barbara 1925-
Yates, Elizabeth 1905-
Yonge, Charlotte M(ary) 1823-1901
Zemach, Harve 1933-1974 and Margot 1931-
Zion, Gene 1913-1975

Readers are cordially invited to suggest additional authors to the editors.

GUEST ESSAY

Internationalism and Children's Literature
by Anne Pellowski

Like most children who are raised in a very homogeneous environment, when I was young I thought the world consisted mostly of persons like myself and my extended family. It was mostly from reading books that I began to find out that there was a wider world out there, full of interesting and different people, speaking other languages and living their lives in ways that seemed very strange to me, yet intriguing. At first, I equated stories and novels set in other lands or times (or among people different from my own) with fairy tales. They were all equally fantastic to me.

This was also true for stories describing behavior of children that now seems to me quite universal but that at the time I could not see in those who lived around me. For example, I remember so clearly reading stories about naughty children who had temper tantrums. The descriptions were usually very graphic, telling of children who screamed and stamped their feet, or writhed on the floor, kicking their legs and waving their arms about. I had never seen such extreme behavior among my siblings, nor had I noticed it among the other children who went to the same parish church and school that our family did. It was obviously not condoned in the social milieu to which I belonged, and thus was never visible.

How astonished I was, then, on a trip to the public library in the city where my cousins lived, to observe a child having a full-fledged tantrum there on the library floor. Like a doctor realizing she is seeing the disease whose symptoms she has read about in countless texts, I remember consciously telling myself: "So this is what a real temper tantrum is like. It matches the description exactly."

It was in little bits and pieces such as these that I began to perceive the outside world. Most often it was in reading that I encountered something different. I would then look for this new idea or thing in the places I went and among the new people I met, trying to locate the "reality" of it. It was as though I always had to verify my observations again and again, like a scientist, before I could come to the conclusion that this was indeed the way life was in some families.

I remember holding the book *The Good Master* (1935) by Kate Seredy and staring for long minutes at the color frontispiece portraits of Kate and Jansci, the boy and girl who are the main characters. I would stroke them, perhaps hoping that this would bring them to life. In fact, I am sure I even secretly kissed them! Their emotional lives seemed similar to mine, yet it frustrated me to realize I could not actually go and check to see if girls like Kate in Hungary really did wear eighteen petticoats on holidays, and if boys like Jansci wore divided pants that looked like skirts.

We had only one set of twins in our entire school, but I surmised that Dutch, Spanish, Chinese, French and other foreign families almost always had twins among their members, because I had read many of the Lucy Fitch Perkins books, whose protagonists were always twins. However, I was not entirely convinced and wanted to confirm this by seeing it with my own eyes.

Another book that I read, but somewhat later, when I was fourteen or fifteen, was *Daughter of the Mountains* (1948) by Louise Rankin. This book was set in Tibet, and while the adventures of the little girl who goes in search of her stolen pet Lhasa Apso puppy are full of excitement, many of them could have taken place anywhere. In fact, I had read of such things happening in the United States, because occasionally the newspaper would report on the unusual methods some young pet owners would resort to in order to find their lost dogs. What really impressed me about this book was not so much the general action of it, but rather the manner in which the little Tibetan girl, a Buddhist, prayed so that she would get her dog back. I thought I knew a lot about prayer, because we had morning and evening prayers, prayers to start each class period and end it, prayers before and after meals, prayers for special feast days and, of course, Mass every Sunday. Many of these prayers were exceedingly repetitious.

I was thunderstruck, reading *Daughter of the Mountains,* to find out that somewhere there was a people who were clever enough to have invented the prayer wheel. You simply wrote the prayer you wanted to say many times on a scroll, put it inside the wheel, and then you whirled the wheel around and around, and that prayer went up to God, multiplied by the number of times it was written and then times the number of whirls you had given the wheel. This struck me as a most efficient way of praying! I wanted to see for myself how it worked.

I am convinced it was my early reading about foreign places and peoples and my desire to see in person how they really looked that influenced me in my career and led to my extensive travels. And I cite myself as an example, because I believe my reading was fairly typical of the avid child reader from 1938 to 1950.

Although many of the books I read about other lands and peoples did contain stereotypes, they were, for the most part, very positive rather then negative in the presentation of other customs. Furthermore, they were almost always adventuresome, rather than problematic. There are almost no such books published in the United States today. The few books set in foreign environments that present-day American children read are perhaps less stereotypical, but because they focus on only a small area of reality (usually a problem such as poverty, disease, divorce, a physical handicap, single-parent families, etc.) they often give a negative general impression of life in other areas of the world. Also, there is very little sense of adventure in them. I refer here to contemporary stories; those set in historical periods, particularly of the Second World War, are often filled with perilous escapes.

In the U.S., as in many other countries, there is right now a strongly prevailing "me first" or "we first" attitude. This has been building up for at least a decade. I could see this quite clearly during my last five years of service as director of the Information Center on Children's Cultures, when I carried out a research project that attempted to assess the views our children have of other peoples, and to determine how and when these views are formed. My usual optimism was somewhat daunted, I must admit, when I encountered the overwhelmingly negative attitudes our average child has toward other peoples.

The Information Center on Children's Cultures is an educational service of the U.S. Committee for UNICEF. Founded in 1967, the Center is a research and reference collection of materials by, about, and for children all over the world, with emphasis on children of the developing countries. It answers reference questions related to the cultural and social lives of children, publishes such materials as an annual calendar which features children's art from around the world, arranges exhibitions, and occasionally does research related to these areas.[1]

I was director of the Center from 1967 to 1982. From autumn 1977 to spring 1982 I carried out a research project called "Children's Attitudes Towards Other Peoples—When Are They Formed? Do They Change? How Do They Change?" The project involved approximately 140 children who entered first grade in 1977 and 1978, and about sixty children who entered third grade at the same time. As an interview instrument, we used a questionnaire developed by Wallace E. Lambert and Otto Klineberg in their *Children's Views of Foreign Peoples: A Cross-National Study* (1967).[2]

The 200 children we interviewed at age six, as they were beginning first grade, were quite vocal in expressing the prejudices and stereotypes they had picked up from family members or from television: Germans were all Nazis, Africans were all poor and starving, Russians were all our enemies, etc. When asked about Indians from India, most gave instead their perception of Native Americans; for little children in the United States it seems there is only one kind of Indian—the "savages" seen on television in old movies or Western serials.

For 100 of the children in the research project, our control group, we had no more contact until five years later, when we conducted the final interview.[3] But for the other 100, our initial interview was followed by a weekly visit to their classes, for the purpose of bringing a program of books, storytelling, films, recordings, games and the like, all from or about other countries. We concentrated especially on the countries and peoples about whom the children seemed to have the strongest prejudices. We tried to select only materials that gave a positive image of those peoples, or some aspect of their culture.

This was not too difficult in the first two years of the project, when we could locate a sufficient number of picture books, films, and other material, especially in the genre of folklore. These were generally very much liked by the children, and certainly contributed to their changing perceptions. Since we had access to quite a number of books from other countries, we often used them, even though they were not usually translated into English. A few had been translated and published in English, but in the country of origin, rather than by a U.S. publisher. In spite of their poor quality (in terms of paper and design), these were well received by the children, especially if the story was a good one.

However, for the final three years of the project, we found it ever more difficult to locate materials that we were willing to use. There was a complete lack of both books and other media depicting ordinary, everyday children in story situations set in present-day Russia, Germany, Japan, China, France, African countries and other places that was suited for use in third through fifth grade. There were neither translations nor books of this category written by

Americans who might have experienced life in one of those countries, nor even stories by recent immigrants from those areas.

The nonfiction, informational types of books and materials were occasionally successful, especially if they focused on an individual child or family doing interesting things. But many of them were little more than poorly conceived travelogue geographies, or series books published to satisfy a social studies curriculum.

We also noticed that there were fewer folk tales, legends, and myths being published from other cultures. The only kind that continue to be published with some regularity are the individual illustrated folk tales culled from Grimm, Andersen, Jacobs, and other standard European sources.

Editors and publishers defend the paucity of such publications by saying they are not economically viable. However, we have had isolationism prevalent among our general population before, and there were always writers, translators, editors, librarians, teachers, booksellers, and parents promoting international books because they believed in them. We just happen to have fewer such persons now who are willing to act on their beliefs.

A few editors and translators have consistently continued to bring foreign children's books to U.S. readers, most notably Margaret McElderry, through her own imprint at Atheneum; Susan Pearson, formerly at Carolrhoda Books; and Maria Polushkin and Mirra Ginsburg, both translators. Over the years, McElderry has introduced a steady stream of the best Northern and Central European writers to American audiences and continues to do so, although, as she points out, the numbers have decreased dramatically. Twenty years ago, she used to be able to publish any translation that got good reports from her editorial readers; now, she feels lucky to be able to do one or two picture books and one novel or fictional book for older children each year. Pearson has concentrated on bringing books from Third World countries. Some have been translations; others were U.S. editions of books originally published in English, but in other countries. Polushkin and Ginsburg both translate primarily from the Russian, and both have attempted to bring unusual novels and folk literature, as well as picture book texts, to the attention of young American readers.

To return for a moment to the content of both translated books and books written by Americans but set in other countries, it is timely to question whether editors, librarians, and teachers are selecting the best and most appropriate books, in terms of the reading interests of children as well as the quality of the author's work. We have heard so much in recent years about the fact that children want to read only two kinds of books: those that are pure escapism and those that deal with some problem, preferably in urban American life, and "tell it like it is."

This does not appear to be the case, however, in quite a few places. Since 1968, the Mildred L. Batchelder Award has been given annually by the Association for Library Service to Children, ALA, to recognize the U.S. publisher of the most outstanding children's book originally published in a foreign language in another country, then subsequently translated into English and published in the U.S. Carol Lynch-Brown and Carl M. Tomlinson, in "Batchelder Books: International Read-Alouds," their recent article on field-testing the reading aloud of some of the books nominated for or awarded the Batchelder Award, found that in the fifty classes they surveyed, the children did not like the books from other countries that were too introspective or that had sad endings or harsh realism. However, they *were* prepared to listen to and enjoy serious or thoughtful books, provided the ending was upbeat or held out some hope. The key to their enjoyment seems often to have been the enthusiasm of the individual teacher reading aloud to the class.[4]

In the informal discussions I have held over the past four years with several thousand children, the question I ask each time is: "What are some of the books you have read recently that you have enjoyed?" The replies are most often quite predictable and generally fall heavily into the categories of popular, escapist fiction or books by well-known writers such as Beverly Cleary. But there are always a few children in each area who seem to be reading books not mentioned by the majority.

Once in a while a translated book will come up. In my notes for the past year, I have one citation (from children) for each of two books on the Lynch-Brown and Tomlinson recommended list: *Don't Take Teddy* (1967) by Babbis Friis-Baastad and *Konrad* (1977) by Christine Nöstlinger [see entry on Nöstlinger beginning on p. 179 of this volume]. Nöstlinger seems to have taken over the small niche once held by Margot Benary-Isbert [see entry on Benary-Isbert beginning on p. 65 of this volume]. Benary-Isbert, in her subdued, restrained style, dealt with the fears, privations, and small joys of young people growing up in Germany right after World War Two. In spite of the depressing conditions, these stories are filled with hope. Nöstlinger has her child protagonists facing up to the complications and idiosyncracies of life in Europe in the nuclear age, but her style is much more lighthearted; yet there is also almost always a tinge of cynicism underlying the handling of her themes.

The reason for the continuing popularity of *Don't Take Teddy* is, I believe, due to two main factors: it is a well-written book and, because it received so much attention in the reviewing journals and selective lists, it was given a paperback as well as hardcover edition. Thus, it has had a much wider availability, and a much greater promotion on the part of teachers and librarians, than is usual with translated books. It remains one of the best proofs we have that foreign books, when well-translated, attractively presented, and introduced by many teachers and librarians, will do well with our younger readers. The two main characters, twelve-year-old Mikkel and his older, retarded brother, Teddy, are very well-realized. The resolution to the family's dilemma as to what to do with Teddy now seems a bit dated: virtually all Norwegian communities, just like American ones, now have special classes for such children. But this does not take away from the suspense built up as Mikkel runs away with Teddy, because he fears his brother will be put in prison.

It was interesting to note that at the recent conference of the International Board on Books for Young People in Tokyo, a panel of young readers spoke of their frustrations: they were tired of reading books about peace or with other heavy messages. They simply wanted more good stories, from all over the world, and believed this would make them feel more peaceful toward other peoples than many of the books they were being given, which dealt directly with peace or nonviolence.[5]

In the following week, at a conference in Oita Prefecture[6] on the island of Kyushu, a seventh-grade girl spoke passionately of her love of reading. The books she cited were like a catalogue of the best-written fantasy and fiction of the past thirty years. Some of her particular favorites were *Tom's Midnight Garden* (1958) and *A Dog So Small* (1962) by Philippa Pearce; *The Borrowers* (1953) by Mary Norton; the *Little House* books of Laura Ingalls Wilder—*Little House in the Big Woods* (1932), *Little House on the Prairie* (1935), *On the Banks of Plum Creek* (1937), *The Long Winter* (1940), *Little Town on the Prairie* (1941), and *These Happy Golden Years* (1943); and the more recent books of Ursula K. Le Guin. However, she bemoaned the fact that teachers were forever asking her to analyze this or that in the books she read, instead of letting her get on with her reading. "Parents and teachers all talk about how Japanese children don't read any more," she wailed, "but how can we enjoy our reading if we have to be thinking of all those picky examination questions." This took great courage to say, because the girl's father was a teacher, and he was in the audience!

While her complaint was similar to what I have heard sometimes from American children, I found in private discussions with her after she made her astonishing little speech that the range of her reading experience was much wider than that of any seventh-grader I have encountered recently in the United States. She was familiar with the best works translated from most of the major publishing areas of the world. I was amazed to find that she even knew firsthand *The Day Lasts More Than a Hundred Years* (1983) by Chingiz Aitmatov, which was not published as a children's book in the U.S., unlike his *The White Ship* (1972). Both of these books combine fantasy, science fiction, and down-to-earth realism in a most unusual way. In Japan, it is not uncommon to have books such as these published in a children's line.

Is there somewhere in the United States an equivalent seventh-grader who has read all of the above works, as well as virtually every major Japanese, American, and British fantasy and science fiction writer, plus the works of Astrid Lindgren of Sweden, Patricia Wrightson of Australia, Michael Ende of Germany, Gianni Rodari of Italy, Stanislaw Lem of Poland, and a host of others, cited by the young readers at the Tokyo and Oita Conferences? Does such a list of reading indicate that we are dealing here with very gifted children? Perhaps. But it also indicates a willingness on the part of Japanese publishers to translate and promote these books from all around the world and an openness on the part of young readers in Japan to give them a chance (despite the fact that economic constraints of publishing exist there in much the same way they do in the U.S.).

Or is it the homogeneous quality of Japanese society that allows children there to break away, symbolically, from their world and enter such a variety of unusual worlds through their reading? Perhaps they are so sure of their national and personal identity that they are not threatened by these outsider views. However, this does not prove to be the case when one looks at research on the subject. Also, one has only to take a look at the reading habits of Western European children. These children live in societies that are far from homogeneous, although they are not as diverse as those in the U.S. However, European children read many of the same books that Japanese children do, and there are roughly the same percentages of translations vis-a-vis books of national origin.

Where do we place the responsibility for broadening and increasing the international component of our U.S. children's literature? Is it really economics that dictates Beverly Cleary can be translated and loved by Japanese children, but Miyoko Matsutani, whose Momo-chan stories are close equivalents to the ups and downs of Ramona Quimby's life, should remain unknown and unread by American children? If Japanese children can understand and identify with a big family of children growing up on a farm in Wisconsin, as in my family series—*Willow Wind Farm:*

Betsy's Story (1981), *Stairstep Farm: Anna Rose's Story* (1981), *Winding Valley Farm: Annie's Story* (1982), *First Farm in the Valley: Anna's Story* (1982), and *Betsy's Up-and-Down Year* (1983), why is it deemed unlikely that American children would respond as well to Shigeo Watanabe's *Teramachi 3-chome, 11-banchi (3-11 Temple Street)*, a modern Japanese classic published in 1969 that depicts the lively goings-on in the large (9 children!) Watanabe family during the late 1930s? Mr. Watanabe's picture books for very young children have been translated and are doing very well in the U.S. market. But when it comes to his books for slightly older readers, his Japanese publisher reports that there is virtually no interest on the part of U.S. editors.

Still another example of a writer of the first rank from Japan whose works have not yet been translated into English is Nobuo Ishimori. His children's books have been extremely influential, dealing as they often do with the Ainu minority in northern Japan and the prejudice they face in the homogeneous society that surrounds them.

One could go on, citing other important writers, not only in Japanese but in many of the other major languages of the world, all of whom are totally inaccessible to the American reader. On the other hand, one can also point to a few dozen works that are translated each year, but that invariably fade quickly from the scene, often being declared out-of-print before they have had even a sprinkling of reviews.

Ann Tracy, a doctoral candidate at Michigan State University, has tried to update the various lists of children's books available in translation in the U.S.[7] She wished to use a number of them in her doctoral dissertation. To her dismay, she found it difficult to identity fifty from those published within the past five years that were still in print. And, as she reported in a personal conversation, the range of themes and styles was very limited.

Although their views are often narrow, incomplete, or incorrect, very young American children are as interested in other peoples as children in Europe or Asia or Latin America or Africa. This was one of the conclusions of the Lambert and Klineberg study on which we based our research, and it was confirmed in our results. I find further direct evidence of this in almost every school or library visit I make, in the U.S. and in other countries. It is only as the American children grow older that they begin to exclude or reject as inferior the books from or about other countries that show a different way of looking at life. Parental influence and television are certainly most responsible for this hardening of attitudes, but children's books, especially those used in schools, come in for their share of the blame.

It is the adults who create, translate, publish, distribute, review, purchase, and promote children's books who are most responsible for the narrowness of world view found in U.S. children's literature. It is often these same adults who travel to conferences all over the world, taking an educational tax write-off for their expenses but rarely bringing back a firsthand story to share, or a book to read aloud, or a description of an encounter with a child different from the ones with whom they work in the U.S. It is these adults who support such causes as peace, nuclear disarmament, and sanctions against human rights violations, but who fail to see that it is our lack of reciprocity in the cultural area, especially in the media, that creates many of the misunderstandings in the first place.

We in the field of children's literature and other media have perhaps the most crucial role to play in the development of a global view in our children, if we are to survive in harmony with the universe and those who inhabit it. I personally would like to see some of the following take place:

1. That every parent read aloud each year to their children at least one book that originated in another country, and then talk informally about that country, perhaps speculating how much fun it would be to visit. They would be picture books at first, then folk tales and short novels of everyday life that stressed the more positive aspects of life in other places, and finally, more complex novels and nonfiction of greater depth.

2. That every teacher do the same in the classroom, at every level through high school.

3. That every librarian and book reviewer read at least ten books each year that originated in other countries, making a conscious effort to understand the backgrounds, so as to judge them in the context of the original culture, and not that of the U.S. The editors of review journals should make an extra effort to call to the attention of children's librarians those important works published in English that are often the key to understanding whole areas of children's literature and folklore from another country. Two recent examples were the publication of D. O. Fagunwa's *The Forest of a Thousand Daemons* (1968) and *Journey to the West* (1977-84), newly edited and translated by Anthony Yu. The former, translated from the Yoruba, is so influential in West African life that it is crucial to an understanding of written and oral literature coming from that region. The latter is a Chinese classic that, while not written specifically for children, is frequently cited as being the favorite work read by Chinese children, even in the twentieth

century. It, too, is essential reading if one is to understand the backgrounds of Chinese folklore and contemporary writing. Both of these works were reviewed widely in general book-review journals, but they were hardly mentioned in children's literature periodicals.

4. That every teacher of children's literature include a requirement that five percent of the books read by students for any course they teach should be books originating in other countries.

5. That every editor in children's book publishing develop an ongoing relationship with at least two foreign authors, one from an industrialized country and one from a developing country, and that they consistently advise on and critique the work of these writers, publish it regularly when it reaches their standards, and then promote it consistently, giving it the same treatment as U.S. authors. This would include arranging for occasional author visits to schools and libraries in the U.S.

6. That every successful children's book writer in the U.S. serve as mentor to one writer from another country, establishing a long-term relationship that would help to introduce the foreign writer to U.S. publishing procedures, and give advice and encouragement in an informal way. (This might be done by arranging for writers to meet at such conferences as the recent IBBY Congress.)

Should even a few of these take effect, I believe we would see a decided improvement in our perception of the day-to-day realities, the once-in-a-lifetime dreams, of all the world's peoples.

Footnotes

1. The Information Center on Children's Cultures is located at 331 East 38th Street, New York, New York 10016. Its present director is Melinda Greenblatt.

2. Wallace E. Lambert and Otto Klineberg, *Children's Views of Foreign Peoples: A Cross-National Study* (New York: Appleton-Century-Crofts, 1967).

3. The data from this project has not yet been published.

4. Carol Lynch-Brown and Carl M. Tomlinson, "Batchelder Books: International Read-Alouds," *Top of the News,* 42, no. 3 (Spring 1986): 260-66.

5. "Why Do You Write for Children?" "Children, Why Do You Read?" (Proceedings of the 20th Congress of the International Board on Books for Young People, Tokyo, Japan, 18-23 August 1986, forthcoming from the Japanese Board on Books for Young People).

6. "What Shall We Give Our Children to Read?" (Conference in Oita Prefecture, Japan, 25-27 August 1986).

7. Elana Rabban, comp. *Books from Other Countries,* 1968-1971 (Chicago: American Association of School Librarians, 1972); and Anne McConnell, comp. *Books from Other Countries,* 1972-1976 (Chicago: American Association of School Librarians, 1978).

Bibliography

Aitmatov, Chingiz. *The Day Lasts More Than a Hundred Years.* Translated from the Russian by John French. Bloomington, Ind.: Indiana University Press, 1983.

Aitmatov, Chingiz. *The White Ship.* Translated from the Russian by Mirra Ginsburg. New York: Crown, 1972.

Fagunwa, D. O. *The Forest of a Thousand Daemons: A Hunter's Saga.* Translated from the Yoruba by Wole Soyinka. Illustrated by Bruce Onabrakpeya. London: Nelson, 1968.

Friis-Baastad, Babbis. *Don't Take Teddy.* Translated from the Norwegian by Lise Somme McKinnon. New York: Scribner, 1967.

McConnell, Anne, comp. *Books from Other Countries, 1972-1976.* Chicago: American Association of School Librarians, 1978.

Matsutani, Miyoko. *Chiisai Momo-chan.* Tokyo: Kodansha, 1964.

Norton, Mary. *The Borrowers.* Illustrated by Beth and Joe Krush. New York: Harcourt, 1953.

Nöstlinger, Christine. *Konrad.* Translated from the German by Anthea Bell. Illustrated by Carol Nicklaus. New York: Watts, 1977.

Pearce, Philippa. *A Dog So Small.* Illustrated by Antony Maitland. London: Constable, 1962.

Pearce, Philippa. *Tom's Midnight Garden.* Illustrated by Susan Einzig. London: Oxford University Press, 1958.

Pellowski, Anne. *Betsy's Up-and-Down Year.* Illustrated by Wendy Watson. New York: Philomel, 1983.

Pellowski, Anne. *First Farm in the Valley: Anna's Story.* Illustrated by Wendy Watson. New York: Philomel, 1982.

Pellowski, Anne. *Stairstep Farm: Anna Rose's Story.* Illustrated by Wendy Watson. New York: Philomel, 1981.

Pellowski, Anne. *Willow Wind Farm: Betsy's Story.* Illustrated by Wendy Watson. New York: Philomel, 1981.

Pellowski, Anne. *Winding Valley Farm: Annie's Story.* Illustrated by Wendy Watson. New York: Philomel, 1982.

Rabban, Elana, comp. *Books from Other Countries, 1968-1971.* Chicago: American Association of School Librarians, 1972.

Rankin, Louise. *Daughter of the Mountains.* Illustrated by Kurt Wiese. New York: Viking, 1948.

Seredy, Kate. *The Good Master.* New York: Viking, 1935.

Watanabe, Shigeo. *Teramachi 3-chome, 11-banchi.* Tokyo: Fukuinkan, 1969.

Wilder, Laura Ingalls. *By the Shores of Silver Lake.* Illustrated by Helen Sewell and Mildred Boyle. New York: Harper, 1939.

Wilder, Laura Ingalls. *Farmer Boy.* Illustrated by Helen Sewell. New York: Harper, 1933.

Wilder, Laura Ingalls. *Little House in the Big Woods.* Illustrated by Helen Sewell. New York: Harper, 1932.

Wilder, Laura Ingalls. *Little House on the Prairie.* Illustrated by Helen Sewell. New York: Harper, 1935.

Wilder, Laura Ingalls. *Little Town on the Prairie.* Illustrated by Helen Sewell and Mildred Boyle. New York: Harper, 1941.

Wilder, Laura Ingalls. *The Long Winter.* Illustrated by Helen Sewell and Mildred Boyle. New York: Harper, 1940.

Wilder, Laura Ingalls. *On the Banks of Plum Creek.* Illustrated by Helen Sewell and Mildred Boyle. New York: Harper, 1937.

Wilder, Laura Ingalls. *These Happy Golden Years.* Illustrated by Helen Sewell and Mildred Boyle. New York: Harper, 1943.

Yu, Anthony C., ed. and trans. *Journey to the West.* 4 vols. Chicago: University of Chicago Press, 1977-84.

Anne Pellowski is an American author, critic, librarian, teacher, consultant, lecturer, and storyteller. A recognized authority on international literature and media for children, Pellowski is the author of *The World of Children's Literature* (1968), *The World of Storytelling* (1977), *Made to Measure: Children's Books in Developing Countries* (1980), *The Story Vine: A Source Book of Unusual and Easy-to-Tell Stories from around the World* (1984), and *The Family Storytelling Handbook* (forthcoming). A fourth-generation Polish-American, she uses the history of her family as the background for her series of farm novels for children: *Willow Wind Farm: Betsy's Story* (1981), *Stairstep Farm: Anna Rose's Story* (1981), *Winding Valley Farm: Annie's Story* (1982), *First Farm in the Valley: Anna's Story* (1982), and *Betsy's Up-and-Down Year* (1983); she is also the author of *The Nine Crying Dolls: A Story from Poland* (1979). In 1967, Pellowski founded the Information Center on Children's Cultures, U.S. Committee for UNICEF, and acted as its director until 1982. She has also served on several ALA and ALSC committees for the American Library Association, and has been a member of the Hans Christian Andersen Award Jury for the International Board on Books for Young People (IBBY). From 1957 to 1966 Pellowski served as a storyteller and group work specialist for the New York Public Library. She received the Grolier Foundation Award from the American Library Association in 1979 and was presented with the Constance Lindsay Skinner Award from the Woman's National Book Association in 1980. A visiting lecturer at more than fifty universities, Pellowski is currently acting as a consultant on children's books and library projects in Egypt, Lebanon, Senegal, Venezuela, and Zimbabwe.

Children's
Literature
Review

Isaac Asimov

1920-

(Also writes as Paul French) Russian-born American author of nonfiction, fiction, and short stories, and editor.

A prolific and respected author of adult science fiction and nonfiction, Asimov has also written over one hundred books for children and young adults in the realm of science fiction and in such fields as astronomy, chemistry, biology, history, and etymology. Known for his clear, readable explanations of complex material, Asimov characteristically presents accurate, largely nontechnical information in a casual and enthusiastic writing style which often reflects a playful sense of humor. His ability to synthesize vast amounts of factual material into a logical, condensed, and comprehensible format has made him a noted popularizer of nonfiction subjects. Asimov is the creator of many informational series. Foremost among them are the *How Did We Find Out About* books, which consist of approximately thirty volumes covering the history of scientific discovery on topics ranging from dinosaurs to computers. Other series include the *Realm* trio which centers on mathematics, the *ABC's* and *Word* books which explain the derivation and meaning of words in several subject areas, and two history series on ancient civilizations and the United States. A doctor of biochemistry, Asimov began his career as a children's writer in the 1950s with the *Lucky Starr* books, six science fiction novels for teenagers which relate the adventures of youthful scientist David "Lucky" Starr and his partner Bigman Jones as they save various planets from their enemies in the galaxy. Together with his wife, psychiatrist Janet Jeppson Asimov, he recently introduced another science fiction series which is directed to younger readers and features Norby, a gifted robot.

Reviewers praise Asimov for his skill in translating detailed, often dull scientific facts into entertaining, noncondescending language. While some critics find that his books are too general and that Asimov's simplifications lead to occasional inaccuracies, the majority admire the range and depth of his works and acclaim him as a writer of authoritative, always interesting books that are both appealing and instructive.

In 1985, Asimov received the *Washington Post*/Children's Book Guild Nonfiction Award for his total contribution to the quality of nonfiction for children.

(See also *Contemporary Literary Criticism*, Vols. 1, 3, 9, 19, 26; *Something about the Author*, Vols. 1, 26; *Contemporary Authors New Revision Series*, Vol. 2; *Contemporary Authors*, Vols. 1-4, rev. ed.; and *Dictionary of Literary Biography*, Vol. 8: *Twentieth-Century American Science Fiction Writers*.)

AUTHOR'S COMMENTARY

[The following excerpt is taken from an editorial originally published in the August, 1979 issue of Isaac Asimov's Science Fiction Magazine.*]*

[In] the good old days there was nothing as evanescent as a science fiction story. Here today and gone next month forever, except in the yellowing files of the more ardent science fiction

Photograph by Alex Gotfryd

fans. If you made a mistake, it was quickly gone, and the damage was fleeting.

Nowadays, on the other hand, science fiction stories can live on for many years. My *Foundation* stories, for instance, have been before the public and readily available in book form for nearly thirty years now, more or less continuously, and bear considerable promise of outliving their author.

There are sins of omission in it that become more glaring by the decade. My *Foundation* stories span the galaxies in detail and yet nowhere do I mention quasars, pulsars, or black holes. To be sure, none of these objects was known in the 1940s when I wrote the stories, but I'm still uneasy about it.

As for sins of commission, consider my six books about Lucky Starr. Each of them is set in a different world of the Solar system and I did my best to describe those worlds accurately. Those books were written in the 1950s, however, and I described them accurately only as far as the astronomers of the 1950s knew.

Unfortunately for me, the 1950s saw us on the verge of the Space Age and, what with radar astronomy, satellites, and space probes, there was a revolution in our knowledge of the Solar system and virtually every world in it turned upside down and inside out.

Until the 1950s, as an example, it was taken for granted, and was virtually a science fictional convention, that Venus was a warm, waterlogged primitive planet, similar to Earth in its dinosaur-ridden Mesozoic age. Why not? According to the nebular hypothesis of the origin of the Solar system, which held sway throughout the nineteenth century, the planets were formed from the outside in, so that Mars was considered older than Earth, and Venus was considered younger than Earth.

It made for excellent science fiction. If you wanted an advanced, decadent, dying civilization, you went to Mars. If you wanted a primitive dangerous world, you went to Venus. In *David Starr: Space Ranger,* I used the former; in *Lucky Starr and the Oceans of Venus,* I used the latter.

In the Venus book, particularly, I went to town. I had a world-wide ocean filled with all kinds of interesting creatures, and Lucky had terrific adventures there with something that was rather like a mile-wide jellyfish.

Within just a few years after the appearance of the book in 1954, it turned out our notions of Venus were all wrong. It proved to be a nearly red-hot planet without a drop of surface water, with poisonous clouds, with virtually no rotation, but with gale winds, and so on.

Well, the Lucky Starr books are still in print . . . ; but in recent editions, I've had to insist on the publishers including introductory notes in which I bring the readers up-to-date on planetary conditions and explain that the books were written before present-day knowledge of the planets was established. . . . I can't mislead young readers; nor can I have them think I am a quarter century behind in my knowledge of the Solar system.

Am I saying, then, that science fiction is useless as an educational device?

It may sound like it, so far, but I am not. All I am saying is that it is untrustworthy as a source of "facts," since these may be wrong, or at least out-of-date. There is nothing wrong, however, with science fiction as a way of arousing interest in science.

There, at least, it doesn't matter whether the scientific background of a science fiction story is accidentally wrong through ignorance, deliberately wrong through the exigencies of the plot, or simply out-of-date through the progress in science. If the story is *interesting,* it can be used.

Let us suppose, for instance, that you have a junior high-school class, or a young boy-scout troop, to whom, for some reason, you want to transmit an understanding of the planet, Venus. You may feel that they are not particularly interested in learning about Venus.

You therefore give them *Lucky Starr and the Oceans of Venus* to read, and we can suppose, for the purpose of argument, that they find it interesting and are enthusiastic about it. You may then pose them questions like:

Do you think it makes sense to suppose that Venus has a world-wide ocean? Why?

Scientists have found that Venus has a surface temperature of over 600° F. What do you suppose causes that? How do you suppose they found out? What happens to the ocean Asimov said Venus had?

—And so on.

I'm quite willing to bet that youngsters would be far more eager to talk about Venus after they have enjoyed a story about it—even a story about an out-of-date Venus—than before.

And *that's* the educational value of science fiction; that is what makes it a learning device. It stimulates curiosity and the desire to know. (pp. 52-5)

Isaac Asimov, "Learning Device," in his Asimov on Science Fiction, *Doubleday & Company, Inc., 1981, pp. 51-5.*

[The following excerpt is from an interview by Susan Hood, associate editor of Instructor *magazine.]*

It has been said that you can explain anything, even the most complicated scientific concepts, in language Dick and Jane can follow. How do you do it?

Asimov: For one thing, I like to begin at the beginning, and for another, I'm terribly secure. All the indications from my teachers that I was bright finally convinced me. There's no doubt in my mind that I'm bright. Nor is there any fear that anything I say or do is going to reveal me as not being bright. So I don't have to labor to be very erudite in my writing in order to convince people. I can be very simple without risking my reputation. So I am. I am clear and simple and I don't worry about writing for children.

Why do you write for children?

Asimov: Because I'm asked to, for one thing. And as I said, I really enjoy starting at the beginning and working my way up. For instance, I'd never start with a discussion of uranium. If I ever got to it, I'd go through radioactivity first and before I got to radioactivity, I'd talk about atoms. So in the end, If I'm asked to discuss some small point, I'm quite likely to write an entire book. That's one of the reasons I've written 222 books!

Out of all those books, you are most acclaimed for your science fiction. How did you get hooked on sci-fi?

Asimov: I was nine years old when I started reading science fiction. I thought it was simply fascinating. Besides, it was the only kind of cheap literature my father would let me read. He saw the word *science* on the cover and thought it had to be something somewhat scholarly.

Why should children read science fiction?

Asimov: Because science fiction is the subject that's bound to interest most. If they are not very thoughtful kids and they just like excitement, science fiction is modern fairy tales. Kids today may think giants, ogres, and wicked witches are babyish, but not Darth Vader!

Children who are the least bit thoughtful, though, must realize that times are changing, and that the world they'll live in as adults will be completely different from the world of today. The best way they can prepare for it is to read science fiction. Not that science fiction will tell them for sure what's going to happen, but science fiction will get them used to the idea that there will be a change. They must realize that they will have to accept and guide that change. (p. 33)

Susan Hood, in an interview with Isaac Asimov, in Instructor, *Vol. XC, No. 7, February, 1981, pp. 32-5.*

GENERAL COMMENTARY

NEW YORK HERALD TRIBUNE BOOK REVIEW

Isaac Asimov has written *Words of Science: And the History Behind Them* . . . , offering an enormous amount of most interesting information in connection with his explanations of the roots and origins of scientific terms. The words or phrases are arranged alphabetically from Absolute Zero to Yttrium and Zero followed by an index to the 1,500 terms covered, in a fairly large book that is made as attractive as the text deserves— . . . . His also is *Realm of Numbers* . . . , an invaluable, brilliantly clear presentation of basic concepts of mathematics from finger counting to transfinite numbers that shames textbook explanations.

> *"Facts Presented Clearly and Well," in* New York Herald Tribune Book Review, *November 1, 1959, p. 30.*

ROGER JELLINEK

Isaac Asimov is the author of more than 60 books, mostly on science. He has written down 500 years of Greek history in one of them, labeling that story "a great adventure." A similar sense of purpose informs [*The Roman Republic* and *The Roman Empire*]. Asimov sets himself to relate the evolution of Rome from a few hilltop hamlets to an Empire whose laws and traditions still live in the modern West. His method is quite as clear; he states at the outset that he will concentrate on war and politics. So Asimov is not so much a historian as chronicler, a man with a certain story to tell. It is a story combining all the stories he has heard, each connected to the next by some anecdote, aside or moral, and told with suitable and idiomatic analogies to the present day.

If one accepts this idea of history, Asimov the chronicler has managed quite well. He has organized a great mass of readable detail. He is at his best in sorting out the mechanics of battle tactics—he could probably write an excellent history of warfare. The Punic Wars against Carthage and Julius Caesar's civil wars are the best part of the first book, though one winces on reading that "Fabius, by his tactics, was slowly rubbing out Hannibal's army. . . ." Asimov the scientist, however, does have his difficulties. He is unable to fit into his scheme the early Roman myths and legends, which he dismisses as fanciful tales and superstitious nonsense. Consequently, he finds himself ridiculing his own sources, and this cuts him, and his reader, off from much of the richness of his subject.

The second book, on the Empire, is the better of the two. There is much more material to work from, and the roots of the modern West are more evident: sophisticated administration and communication, a legal code, the *Pax Romana*. Asimov is good on the politics of Judaism and its offshoot, Christianity, showing how the stubborn independence of the one led to isolation and permanent exile, while the flexibility of the other won it the pagan Empire. But again, Asimov's chronicle of Western evolution is led astray by recalcitrant history. He has to record the recurring waves of barbarian invasions and the incessant dynastic squabbles, as Greco-Roman civilization deserted Rome for Constantinople in the East. (At an earlier point he mentions that "that [German] region fell into inferior hands with dire results for Rome and the world . . . an expensive matter for everyone, then and now.") Ironically, Asimov's grandparents probably regarded the Russian Czars, their Empire and their Orthodox Church as the logical heirs to ancient Rome.

> *Roger Jellinek, "Men and Events: 'The Roman Republic' and 'The Roman Empire',"in* The New York Times Book Review, *Part II, May 7, 1967, p. 20.*

PHYLLIS COHEN

[*The Roman Empire*] picks up where *The Roman Republic* . . . leaves off. It is every bit as good as its predecessor and by far the most interesting book on the Roman Empire for youngsters I've read. Again, a sweep of centuries is treated, from Augustus to the end of the West Roman Empire. The strong emperors, and the weak, the humane and the cruel, the wise and the foolish—all are discussed. Isaac Asimov, in his thumb nail sketches, can make the characters more understandable than many authors can manage in entire books. And he is continually reminding his readers that pronunciations on historical characters depend on who is doing the pronouncing. Tiberius, for instance, comes across as not such a horror as he was said to be by the Senators; Caligula was not a monster from birth. . . .

Mr. Asimov's three volumes, *The Greeks: A Great Adventure, The Roman Republic,* and *The Roman Empire,* are a marvellous survey. Every young person should have access to them. They will probably become the standard works in the field for the junior high age, and deservedly so. But they should not be limited to this age group—much older people will find them as entertaining as they are informative. Mr. Asimov's breadth of view, tremendously varied interests, and storytelling ability combine to make these books unusual in every way. (Mr. Asimov, you have my nomination for "Renaissance Man of the year award.")

> *Phyllis Cohen, in a review of "The Roman Empire," "The Roman Republic," and "The Greeks: A Great Adventure," in* Young Readers Review, *Vol. III, No. 10, June, 1967, p. 1.*

ROSE HENNINGE

[*Galaxies* and *Stars*] offer up-to-date, sophisticated astronomy for elementary grade children, augmented with . . . vocabulary lists and "Things to Do."

[The] text, unfortunately, tends to skip abruptly from one subject to another, *Galaxies* offers a useful repetition of basic astronomical concepts, the use of common analogies which establish believably the immensity of the universe, and a clear explanation of the big bang theory. Astronomical history is briefly treated in each book.

> *Rose Henninge, in a review of "Galaxies" and "Stars," in* School Library Journal, *an appendix to* Library Journal, *Vol. 15, No. 3, November, 1968, p. 82.*

MAY HILL ARBUTHNOT

Dr. Asimov's scientific facts never cripple his style. His books for all their carefully authenticated information are as spellbinding as fiction. . . . (p. 284)

[Isaac Asimov] speaks with authority in the science field, writes with clarity and compelling interest, and with refreshing flashes of humor. His own books or his recommendations of other books can be relied upon. His *Realm of Numbers* and *Realm of Measure* are fascinating accounts of the history and advancement of these sciences and of man's gradual development of tools and theories. These are so well written they would interest the most science-resistant readers. *The Kingdom of the Sun* tells of the development of knowledge of the solar system, from earliest records to modern times. This book is superbly written. *The Human Body: Its Structure and Operation* is an authoritative treatment of man's place in the scale of living creatures, his bodily structure, and his various systems such as circulatory, digestive, and reproductive. The AAAS recommends this book not only for adolescents but for elementary-school libraries and for a teacher's reference, which means that it is also an exceedingly valuable book for the whole family. (p. 291)

For mature readers of thirteen upwards, Isaac Asimov's two books on *The Roman Republic* and *The Roman Empire* are good reading for the whole family. . . . The story in both books is told with such clarity that centuries, movements, laws, emperors, philosophies are made understandable and fall into logical sequence. The scholarship is sound and the otherwise oppressive weight of facts is enlivened with characteristic flashes of humor, homely details, and a superb sense of the dramatic pageant of events and human beings that make history. But it must be admitted that political and military exploits over centuries, especially in the second book, make heavy reading. These are fine reference books for the family library to be supplemented at the adult and young adult levels with Edith Hamilton's *The Greek Way* and *The Roman Way*. (pp. 302-03)

May Hill Arbuthnot, "Informational Books," in her Children's Reading in the Home, *Scott, Foresman and Company, 1969, pp. 279-308.*

JOSEPH F. PATROUCH, JR.

Writing under the pseudonym Paul French, Asimov produced during the seven years 1952 through 1958 six juvenile novels featuring David "Lucky" Starr and his pint-sized companion John "Bigman" Jones. In *Opus 100* Asimov gives the following account of the genesis of the Lucky Starr series and of his reasons for and choice of a pseudonym:

It was Walter I. Bradbury of Doubleday who first suggested the idea that I write them. The intention was that of supplying a serial hero for television, so that both the publishers and I, myself, could make an honest dollar.

But I hesitated. I don't object to money, in principle, but I have a set of hang-ups about what I'm willing to do in exchange. I said, "But the television people may ruin the stories and then I would be ashamed to have my name identified with them."

So Brad said, "Use a pseudonym."

And I did. I chose Paul French and wrote all my Lucky Starr books under that name.

As it turned out, television turned out to be utterly uninterested in the Lucky Starr stories and the precaution was unnecessary. . . .

I have been asked a thousand times, by the way, why I picked that particular pseudonym. . . . At the time . . . I heard that the suspense writer, Cornell Woolrich, deliberately chose a nationality as his—William Irish. So I chose Paul French. (p. 151)

The series is set "ten thousand years after the pyramids were built and five thousand years after the first atom bomb had exploded". . . . The physical location of each of the stories is somewhere inside the solar system, depending on which novel one is reading, though we are to assume a Galactic civilization of uncertain extent "out there." For example, in the fourth

novel, *Lucky Starr and the Big Sun of Mercury,* we find a reference to "this age of Galactic civilization, with humanity spread through all the planets of all the stars in the Milky Way". . . . Despite a certain discrepancy in the timing, then—the Galactic Empire of *Pebble in the Sky* and the Foundation Series is hundreds of thousands of years in the future, that of the Lucky Starr series only five thousand—the Galactic setting of all these stories seems to be the same, until, that is, the last few stories of the Lucky Starr series. In them, the Galactic Empire seems to fade and to be replaced by a much smaller colonized volume. For example, in the last novel in the series, *Lucky Starr and the Rings of Saturn,* an interstellar conference is held at which a vote is taken: four planetary systems vote one way and over fifty the other. It is Earth versus the Outer Worlds, and no indication is given that human civilization is Galactic in extent.

To put all this in a slightly different way: As Asimov worked on the Lucky Starr series over a period of seven years, its background unobtrusively shifted from that of the Galactic Empire of *Triangle* and the Foundation Series to that of the Earth versus the Outer Worlds of *The Caves of Steel* and *The Naked Sun,* which novels were being conceived and written during this same period. Asimov started writing the series against a background he had previously worked out for earlier stories and novels, and he ended the series against a background he was developing for two novels he was working on at the same time.

This shift in background is not the only development that took place as the Lucky Starr series unfolded. In the first novel, *David Starr: Space Ranger,* Lucky stumbles across a lost race of disembodied Martians who give him "a strip of gauze". . . . to wrap around his head. Basically, it is "a personal force-shield" . . . which renders him invulnerable to attack and which has certain awe-inspiring side effects like making him appear to others like a shimmering ghost and like giving his voice a deep resonance. Without his mask he is David Starr, ordinary (though extremely intelligent) human being; with it he becomes the mysterious and invulnerable "Space Ranger," righter of wrongs, enemy of evil, and distributor of justice. The parallel with a certain Masked Rider of the Plains is clear. Wisely, Asimov drops this whole incredibly childish business by the third novel in the series, and Lucky Starr settles down to become a human being who solves crimes with rational thought and action rather than a nearly supernatural being who goes around scaring clues and confessions out of people. This change from Lucky Starr, Space Ranger, to Lucky Starr, scientific detective, is a second major development in the series.

The first novel was set on Mars, and in it Lucky acquired a friend named John "Bigman" Jones. Bigman is 5'2" tall (or short) and feisty. He is unbelievably sensitive about his height or lack thereof, and he is incredibly willing to assault physically anyone who makes any chance remark that violates that sensitivity. He is an extreme and melodramatic character, and wherever he goes, exclamation marks trail along. I am aware that Sherlock Holmes had his Dr. Watson and that Gene Autry had his Smiley Burnett. But Bigman is so overdone that it leaves the unfortunate impression that Asimov is writing down to his young audience. As the series develops, Bigman's character is somewhat tempered (if I may be excused a pun), and the series improves as a result. (pp. 152-53)

It is not Bigman's emotionalism in itself that is objectionable: that fits into the pattern of reason versus emotion that Asimov uses so well. It is the pugnacious extremes to which Asimov has Bigman go. In the best Lucky Starr stories Asimov does not have Bigman overdo it.

Getting rid of Lucky's "Space Ranger" role and calming down Bigman's anger contribute to another major change in the series, this one a change in tone. From melodramatic, over-emotional, over-exclamation-pointed silliness, the stories evolve into excellent science fiction detective stories. From the childish action-adventure of *Lucky Starr and the Pirates of the Asteroids* they develop into the tense intellectual puzzles of the two best novels in the series, *Lucky Starr and the Big Sun of Mercury* and *Lucky Starr and the Moons of Jupiter*.

In summary, four major changes took place in the seven years of the series: (1) the background shifted from the Galactic Empire of the Foundation Series to the relatively newly colonized Outer Worlds of *The Caves of Steel*, (2) Lucky Starr stopped being a masked Space Ranger and became a scientific detective, (3) Bigman Jones got better control of his temper, and (4) the stories became less melodramatic and more intellectual, less action-adventure and more detective, less extreme and more realistic. (pp. 153-54)

[In the Foundation Series] Asimov liked to hide his characters' planning and actions so he could spring them on us at the end. The whole of *Lucky Starr and the Rings of Saturn* is ruined (for me at least) because Lucky has a plan from the very beginning, because some selected characters in the story are allowed to share in it and its execution, but it is so well hidden from us the readers that we don't even know it's there. As a result, Lucky is allowed to appear too passive and the novel too structureless—until the end, and by then it's too late.

In *Lucky Starr and the Big Sun of Mercury* Bigman interprets one of Lucky's silences as follows: "He knew what that silence meant. Lucky had thoughts which later he would claim had been too vague to talk about". . . . Lucky is not made to speak these thoughts aloud to Bigman so we can overhear them, nor are we allowed inside Lucky's head to share them. Instead, we get mysterious remarks like "Lucky nodded thoughtfully. It all fit well," and "It was as he thought". . . . We are not told what fit well or what was as he thought. The disease even spreads to Bigman: "And because Bigman had to make arrangements about the gravity, he explained some of his plan" to one of the other characters. . . . But the scene ends without our hearing that explanation, so we don't know what the plan is. Asimov loves to look up from the pot on the stove and mutter promisingly, "Oh what I've got cooking for you! Are you going to like this!" without telling us either the ingredients or the dish.

Another connection with Asimov's other works is that the Lucky Starr series includes two mystery stories based on the Three Laws of Robotics. In this way both *Big Sun of Mercury* (which is very reminiscent of "Runaround") and *Moons of Jupiter* are obviously related to the Robot Stories. The discipline involved in constructing mysteries around the Three Laws may contribute to the extraordinary success of these two novels. I do not find the mystery stories themselves in these two novels in any way inferior to those in the more famous (and perhaps more respectable because not labeled *juveniles*) *The Caves of Steel* and *The Naked Sun*. I would hope that no one deprives himself of the pleasure of reading these two novels simply because they feature Lucky Starr and Bigman Jones instead of Lije Baley and Daneel Olivaw.

One of the strongest points of any Asimov story or novel is the detailed way Asimov works out his settings and the care with which he presents those settings to us. Each novel in the Lucky Starr series is set in a different part of the solar system. Each of these locales has its own well-researched environment and its own human organization specifically tailored to fit that environment. Mercury had been a mining center and is now the location of an experimental station using the huge energies of the sun to do research into the driving of energy through hyperspace to specific destinations. Venus has gigantic, domed, underwater cities specializing in yeast products—i.e., food—for the rest of the solar system. Mars has huge farming combines. Jupiter's moons are a base for research into a new kind of space drive. And Saturn's moons are in the process of being colonized for the first time. Each of these environments has attracted people for different reasons, and as a result, different kinds of human organizations have been set up. Asimov has thought out these new organizations in some detail, giving them sights, technologies, social patterns, and habits of mind of their own. Each novel becomes a little experiment in the relationship between man and environment, and Asimov sets up and performs each experiment with meticulous control of detail.

In one way his insistence on being scientifically accurate has gotten him into what he believes to be trouble. Since the novels were written in the fifties, they make use of the scientific knowledge of the fifties. His Mercury keeps one face to the sun, whereas we now know Mercury rotates. His Venus is a waterworld, whereas we now know that Venus has no water. His Mars has a breathable atmosphere, whereas we now know that the atmosphere of Mars is too thin to support human life. What was the best science could offer in the fifties is not the best it can offer in the seventies. As a result, Asimov is concerned that his Lucky Starr series is popularizing scientific inaccuracies, especially among the young. . . . He also fears that these new scientific discoveries have ruined the series. While the first fear, that of misleading his readers, is certainly valid, just as certainly the second, that of advances in science ruining works of fiction, is not. A work of fiction stands or falls on its internal consistency. A novel is ruined not when its givens turn out to be wrong, but when its givens are mishandled. Asimov does not mishandle his givens, and therefore this bit of Asimovian self-criticism seems to me to be beside the point.

One unusual thing about the Lucky Starr stories is that Asimov does admit aliens into them. It was ancient and disembodied Martian intelligences who gave Lucky that strip of gauze in *David Starr: Space Ranger*. Asimov conjures up some rather awe-inspiring creatures with which to populate the oceans of Venus. There are sea ribbons "of different lengths, varying from tiny threads two inches long to broad and sinuous belts that stretched a yard or more from end to end. They were all thin, thin as a sheet of paper. They moved by rippling their bodies into a series of waves that rippled down their full length. And each one fluoresced, each one sparkled with colored light". . . . At one point Lucky and Bigman are trapped in the ocean under "a two-mile-wide inverted bowl of rubbery flesh" weighing 200 million tons. And the story hinges on the telepathic V-frogs that live by the hundreds of thousands in the tangled seaweed atop the ocean and that raise and lower themselves by unfolding long legs like carpenter's rules. *Big Sun of Mercury* features a creature made of rock that lives in abandoned mine shafts and absorbs heat from any source, including space-suited humans it wraps its tentacles around.

These aliens supply some of science fiction's fabled sense of wonder to the series, but what awes us most often is effects that grow out of the scientific background of the stories. Jules Verne's *Twenty Thousand Leagues Under the Sea* is carried along by an interest in the submarine and in what the submarine enables its occupants to see. It is a series of wonders with little or no story line. Asimov's Lucky Starr stories are first and foremost *stories*. Yet more than once—and with telling effect—the story is set aside so its characters and its readers can simply stand in awe before some natural wonder that space flight has made available. (pp. 154-57)

Most of us like to read series in their proper sequence. This means that the first Lucky Starr stories one is likely to read are the first two in the series. After reading them, one probably is tempted to put the whole thing aside as an aberration on Asimov's part. Even Homer nods, etc. But two thirds of the way through *Oceans of Venus,* the third in the series, something happens. One becomes aware that this rather silly kid's story has somehow become an absorbing mystery story. *Big Sun of Mercury* and *Moons of Jupiter* are first-rate science fiction mystery stories that anyone—science fiction fan or mystery fan—can enjoy reading. (pp. 158-59)

> *Joseph F. Patrouch, Jr., in his* The Science Fiction of Isaac Asimov, *Doubleday & Company, 1974, 283 p.*

D. A. YOUNG

It is not unknown for writers of science fiction to turn their attention to historic fact. These two volumes [*The Shaping of North America* and *The Birth of the United States (1763-1816)*] are to be followed by two more.... Dr. Asimov starts with the first hunters who found their way across the land bridge which at one time linked Asia with North America, traces their defeat by the invaders from Europe who came by the sea and ends the second volume with the treaty of Ghent and the acceptance by Britain that her turbulent colonies were a collection of independent but federated states.

Unlike Alistair Cooke, Dr. Asimov deals with history as the saga of political and military conflict. It is plainly factual and presents people, places and things in great detail, has a fourteen page Table of Dates and a ten page index for each volume. Specialists in American history will be interested to have so much detail at their fingertips, although there does not seem much material for the more speculative historian. (pp. 207-08)

> *D. A. Young, in a review of "The Shaping of North America" and "The Birth of the United States (1763-1816)," in* The Junior Bookshelf, *Vol. 39, No. 3, June, 1975, pp. 207-08.*

MARGARET COUGHLAN

One of the questions historians attempt to answer is how the past has shaped the present. It is not dealt with in Isaac Asimov's *The Shaping of North America* and *The Birth of the United States,* the first two volumes in a series intended to present the history of the United States to 12-15 year-olds. Dr. Asimov has an enormous capacity for the absorption and marshalling of facts in a lucid, orderly pattern; however, he appears to lack the ability to analyze them. Both books are simplistic and contain conclusions that could be considered misleading, if not erroneous, in the light of today's scholarship. They are weakened further by the apparent lack of a theme. Thus, they do little more than the encyclopedia and are on a par with the average highschool American history text.

The Shaping of North America covers a vast expanse of time and a multitude of events culminating in the expulsion of the French from the North American continent and the establish-

ment of British control. All the highpoints are here: voyages, familiar and unfamiliar; Cathay; the Northwest Passage; the explorers; settlements, such short-lived ones as those of the Huguenots in northern Florida and South Carolina in 1562 and 1564 as well as those of the Spanish, Dutch, Swedish, French and English. Here are accounts of the colonies from their beginnings, the coming of the blacks, the invention of the log cabin, the Indians, King Philip's War, Bacon's Rebellion, and the French and Indian Wars beginning in 1689 and ending with the Treaty of Paris in 1763. Nor is the European scene forgotten. However, all this welter of fact leaves no room for social and cultural developments, nor, unfortunately, for perceptive comment. A chronology and index are appended. There is no bibliography.

In *The Birth of the United States* Dr. Asimov continues to deliver a battery of clearly ordered, condensed facts. Emphasis here is on political and military events through the War of 1812 when the young United States became free from British interference. The account is packed with events: those leading up to the War of Independence, military campaigns, the Constitution, the War in the West, the struggle between Federalist and Anti-Federalist, and foreign policy. Important issues such as the constitutional debate over states' rights and slavery, Hamilton's financial policies, and Jay's Treaty are summarized. In this work the British are the villains; little attention is given to the problems the mother country faced and which contributed to her difficulties with the colonies. Over-simplification has lessened the value of the book considerably: contrary to the author's statement, the colonists did not immediately see themselves as "Americans" after the Treaty of Paris, and they were by no means united in their opposition to Great Britain. And there is no discussion of such matters as Canada's relationship with the United States, the complexities of westward expansion, the Indian problem, the social scene, and slavery. Thus this work resembles an encyclopedia or supplementary highschool text, leaving the need for a thoughtful treatment of United States history for young people unfulfilled. There is a chronology and index but no bibliography. (pp. 2703-04)

> *Margaret Coughlan, "American History," in* Growing Point, *Vol. 14, No. 3, September, 1975, pp. 2703-04.*

SARAH-WARNER J. PELL

If learning to read with facility and pleasure is among the most important basic skills, then students must be provided with books and stories they can read easily and enjoy. Isaac Asimov's writings fulfill both requirements. They have a lyrical flow, and each story or novel has a beginning, a middle or climax, and an end, with meaningful interlacing of components. Asimov's style is historical, sequential, personalized, and instructive. He adroitly presents major themes of human concern—political, social and scientific—in a style that is clear, straightforward and unpretentious.

Asimov's specialties are popular science and, more important to the student reader, science fiction. His writing is scientifically accurate and invites logical extrapolation. It can withstand student evaluation in various areas of scholarly concern.

Asimov's works are no stranger to the classroom. He has written at least ten volumes of science for the teenage audience, two works of science for children, and has edited an instruction-oriented science fiction anthology for juveniles—the *Lucky Starr* collection. (pp. 258-59)

Asimov was one of the first writers to transform science fiction from the ridiculous to the respectable. . . . Science fiction has been accepted as a legitimate literary form and has found its way into the classroom, and to quote Frederick Pohl (1955), "In the alphabet of science fiction, 'A' is for Asimov. . . ." (p. 259)

Many attributes of Asimov's works make them adaptable to ethnic and socioeconomic groups. During the period of the U.S. manned space program, some teachers in Alaska noticed that Alaskan Indians and Eskimos with access to television were fascinated by activities in space. As a result, teachers in both urban and rural schools introduced science fiction to students. It was accepted and gained popularity as no traditional language arts or literature form had before. . . .

Students who had had little or no experience with telephones, coin laundries or traffic lights prior to coming to the regional dormitory read eagerly about robots and the future. Asimov seems to be able to transcend ethnic bounds, socioeconomic strata and cultural deprivation and yet maintain ties with reality. Further, it seems that space travel and similar stories have great appeal for students who are closely bound to nature for survival or to whom nature is a threat.

Why should teachers use Asimov in fourth through twelfth grade reading, language arts, social studies and science courses? Poor readers can comprehend Asimov's works. The plots have logical sequence; the writing is clear, straightforward and personalized; the language is understandable; and explanations are extraordinarily clear.

Within the context of the story, the poor reader can be given a relatively painless dose of science within the context of science fiction: for example, "it takes radiation from ten to twenty-two minutes to make the round trip between Mercury and Earth, depending on where each is in its orbit." . . .

The works of Asimov allow the student to consider the present in light of the future. Asimov is a master of creating utopian societies. (p. 260)

In conclusion, schools should include the short stories and novels of Isaac Asimov in the curriculum. They appeal to children of all ages and abilities. They are of high interest and students can read them easily.

These books have the additional distinction of meeting good literary standards and achieving scholarly aims. They present major areas of concern for students who may spend the better part of their lives in the twenty-first century.

Asimov's books encourage students to be creative and imaginative. They transcend cultural and socioeconomic bounds and provide a common denominator across the spectrum of humanity. (p. 261)

> *Sarah-Warner J. Pell, "Asimov in the Classroom," in* Journal of Reading, *Vol. 21, No. 3, December, 1977, pp. 258-61.*

SHERRI BUSH

Since there are clearer, more thorough texts on solar energy, [*How Did We Find Out about Solar Power?*] is a recommended but not an essential addition to a school- or public-library collection. Asimov provides an enlightening historical perspective not only about solar energy rooted in Greek and Roman times but also about current energy shortages and climbing fuel consumption. Unfortunately, Asimov's enthusiasm about the applications of solar energy often turns into difficult technical

reading. Kids might become confused and frustrated with so few illustrations and diagrams.

Primarily [*How Did We Find Out about Volcanoes?*] is a fascinating historical overview of volcanoes—Pompeii to Mt. St. Helens—including the mythology and biblical legends behind volcanic formations. The secondary focus is on the geological formation of volcanic explosions. If Asimov had provided more painstakingly detailed diagrams and close-up photos, this series would provide more balance and clarity.

> *Sherri Bush, in a review of "How Did We Find Out about Solar Power?" and "How Did We Find Out about Volcanoes?" in* School Library Journal, *Vol. 28, No. 3, November, 1981, p. 87.*

KIRKUS REVIEWS

These latest additions to Asimov's science-history series [*How Did We Find Out about Volcanoes?* and *How Did We Find Out about Solar Power?*] don't explain their scientific subjects with any flair or special care. Rather, his historical approach sees him, in the volcano book, ticking off major eruptions from Thera in Cretan times to Mt. St. Helens in 1980; and, in the solar book, describing gadgets and devices from an experimental paraboloid mirror to focus sunlight, devised in 230 B.C. This latter survey, which leads up to solar cells, is better integrated with explanations than is the volcano history, but still cursory; and as for future possibilities of solar power, Asimov ignores all small-scale and local uses of wind, tide, and so on, and discusses only the "hundreds of billions of dollars" project of lining up enormous areas of solar cells in space. Both books contain the odd interesting item, but *Solar Power* has at best a skimpy utility and *Volcanoes* less.

> *A review of "How Did We Find Out about Solar Power?" and "How Did We Find Out about Volcanoes?" in* Kirkus Reviews, *Vol. XLIX, No. 24, December 15, 1981, p. 1522.*

JEAN FIEDLER and JIM MELE

Considering all the attention normally received by Asimov's work, it is surprising to note that he has written another series, roughly equivalent to the Foundation Trilogy, which in critical reviews is mentioned only in passing, if at all. Asimov's name is always linked with the Foundation and his robots, but even his fans are not always aware of his "juvenile" novels, the six Lucky Starr books. (p. 81)

With a television audience in mind from the inception, an audience which seemed to love horse operas like "The Lone Ranger" and "The Cisco Kid," he created a space opera whose hero was a Space Ranger.

David Starr, called Lucky by all who know him, is everything a space opera hero should be: he is tall, good-looking, thin but muscular, intelligent, athletic, has a well-developed sense of right and wrong, and is the man to call upon when the situation seems hopeless. The fact that Lucky was orphaned when his parents were killed by space pirates is also well-calculated. There is no concerned family to encumber his wanderings through space, and he has a justifiable motive for his struggles against evil. (pp. 81-2)

Although he relies on a stock plot—the hero saving our solar system from its enemies in the Galaxy—Asimov typically puts his individual stamp on the stories; the physical setting of each story is, given the knowledge of the time, accurate. (p. 82)

Feeling that the name, David, was too "pedestrian," Asimov changed it to Lucky in his second book, *Lucky Starr and the Pirates of the Asteroids*. Published in 1953, this is the only one in the series that remains scientifically accurate. (p. 83)

During his battle with the pirates [in *Lucky Starr and the Pirates of the Asteroids*], Lucky has occasion to use his Martian shield. Perhaps Asimov was growing weary of overloading his series with stereotypical elements, because this is the last time the shield is mentioned; also, the title "Space Ranger" is never alluded to again.

The most interesting element of *Lucky Starr and the Oceans of Venus* is another of Asimov's alien creations—the V-Frogs. V-Frogs are cute little aquatic oddities that inspire affection through a crude type of emotional control over those who come in contact with them. Since all of Venus is covered by a single ocean, these frogs are quite common and almost everyone living in the planet's domed cities has one as a pet. When a mad genius invents a machine that allows him to control huge numbers of these frogs, and through them, human beings, the colony on Venus is threatened. Lucky discovers the method by which the V-Frogs are being used to manipulate people and puts an end to the mad scientist's dictatorial ambitions.

Although the plot does not withstand critical scrutiny, and even though we now know that there is no ocean on Venus, Asimov's description of aquatic animal and plant forms, as well as human life in underwater cities, is so graphic that the book is often engrossing.

The weakest of the six books is *Lucky Starr and the Big Sun of Mercury*. Here the mechanics of the plot are visible to the most superficial reader. Puppet-like characters react predictably, and by now the limitations of the Bigman character—his stock response to insulting references to his size, his mother-like concern for Lucky's safety—have become grating. The only thing of interest in this book is the introduction of robots and the Three Laws of Robotics to the series. While he continued to write as Paul French, his mention of the Three Laws was as good as a personal signature.

Written in 1957 and 1958 respectively, *Lucky Starr and the Moons of Jupiter* and *Lucky Starr and the Rings of Saturn* both reflect the political insecurities engendered by the Cold War. Sirius bears more than a superficial resemblance to the then-current American view of Russia as it constantly maneuvers to gain both scientific and military advantage over Earth. The weapons here are spies and sabre-rattling, operating in an atmosphere of thinly veiled hostility.

In *The Moons of Jupiter*, Sirian spies have infiltrated one of Earth's most important research projects—the development of an anti-gravity propulsion system. Situated on one of Jupiter's outer moons, the project has been the subject of repeated security checks. Yet no leaks have been uncovered, and the Sirians continue to receive up-to-date information on all areas of the project, areas that no single man has access to. As the first prototype of the system is being prepared for testing, Lucky is sent to the site in a last-ditch effort to destroy the spy ring.

Lucky soon realizes that the spy must be a robot and attempts to discover which of the suspects is governed by the Three Laws. Only at the very end does he realize that he has been tricked by his own preconceptions; like most readers of Asimov's robot fiction, Lucky has expected the robot to be humanoid. When the evidence becomes so overwhelming that

the possibility can no longer be overlooked, he identifies a blind man's Seeing-Eye dog as the robot.

Characteristically Asimovian is the utilization of the unexpected in a plot twist. In this case, Asimov takes advantage of the fact that the word robot connotes mechanical man. It is true that any perceptive reader immediately becomes suspicious when he introduces for the first time in any of his books a handicapped character who is in on all the action. If this is not enough, the blind engineer has a Seeing-Eye dog, an obvious anachronism in such a highly technical environment.

Yet Asimov's description of the anti-gravity system, whether it is used to propel an elevator or a ship, is so plausible and so graphically explained that it draws the reader into the story. We begin to react to the characters as people, and Asimov's moons of Jupiter take on an enjoyable appearance of reality. The book easily overcomes the weak mystery element.

The situation in the last and best book of the series, *Lucky Starr and the Rings of Saturn,* is one in which Earth is threatened by Sirian encroachment on our solar system—Sirius has set up a military base on Titan, Saturn's largest moon. As the birthplace of humanity, Earth is resented by the other worlds of the Galaxy, all former colonies. Earth's leaders know that if they declare war on the Sirians, the majority of the other worlds will side with the enemy. In an attempt to avoid such a war, Earth calls an intergalactic conference. Here in the book's dramatic high point, Lucky, against all odds, engineers a coup. The unallied worlds censure Sirius and order them to abandon Titan.

This novel goes a great deal beyond space opera. It goes far beyond simple action to deal with social, ethical, and political motives. For the first time in the series we see the enemy face to face, and he is no less intelligent nor less honorable than we are. Our strengths lie in what other societies have labeled weaknesses: suspicion of the overuse of technology; the belief that individuality and variety are positive traits; and that the goals of genetic superiority and social conformity are destructive ones.

The label "juvenile" does not seem to fit this novel, nor, in fact, any of the series. That some of the Lucky Starr books are more interesting than others has nothing to do with the audience for whom they were intended. Had Asimov given the concept of juvenile writing the careful thought that is so apparent in his other writing, he would have realized that the tag "juvenile" means much more than simple characters carrying out a simple plot with bits of action thrown in to keep the story going for the required hundred and fifty pages or so. Some of the best juvenile books have become classics that defy age group classification. Perhaps because the Lucky Starr books were not aimed at Asimov's usual readers—they were much simpler and far more action-oriented—Asimov's publishers attempted to sidestep any adverse fan reaction by the disclaimer, "juvenile." The most juvenile aspects of the series are the titles and the packaging.

This is not to say that all the Lucky Starr books will satisfy even the most devoted Asimov fan. Had *David Starr, The Pirates of the Asteroids,* and *The Big Sun of Mercury* actually been written by someone named Paul French, the likelihood is that they would be long forgotten. It's a safe bet that Asimov's name is the only thing that keeps them in print. Still, the entire series cannot be summarily dismissed. The description of underwater life is, in itself, sufficient reason for reading *The Oceans of Venus*. The final two books—*The Moons of*

Jupiter and *The Rings of Saturn*—easily stand on their own, outdistancing the earlier books in conception, characterization, subtlety, and, simply, interest. (pp. 84-7)

Jean Fiedler and Jim Mele, in their Isaac Asimov, *Frederick Ungar Publishing Co., 1982, 122 p.*

JAMES GUNN

Asimov's juvenile novels added little to the development of science fiction, or to Asimov's reputation, or even to the development of the science-fiction juvenile. They were largely scientific exposition with a frosting of narrative to keep the youthful reader involved between discussions. In contrast, Robert A. Heinlein's juveniles, once he developed his skills at the genre beginning with *Red Planet* in 1949, were so thoroughly science-fiction novels that most were serialized in adult magazines. One might speculate that the Heinlein juveniles lead young readers to read more science fiction; those by Asimov, to read more science. Nevertheless, the Lucky Starr books were successful juveniles and have remained in print.

The typical Asimov juvenile opens with a scientific mystery that Starr and Jones are sent to investigate. At their best the novels develop with the skill of Asimov's mysteries: the puzzles are fascinating and the solutions are ingenious. In between, the reader is presented with a great deal of information about the nature of the universe and the laws that govern its behavior. It is ironic that the facts known about several of the planets have changed since the novels were written. In *Opus 100* . . . Asimov noted this fact with embarrassment and speculated that the novels, then out of print, might have to stay out of print. The Mars book might be reprinted (all that had then been discovered was that Mars was cratered, and craters were not difficult to insert), but the Venus and Mercury books "cannot be patched; they can only be scrapped." Nevertheless, at least the latter two were put back into print with 1970 Asimov forewords explaining that Venus has no oceans and that Mercury does not keep one side perpetually toward the sun so that there is a bright side and a dark side. Typically, Asimov used the forewords to explain how the new information was obtained and what the new understanding revealed.

The novels probably did for their young readers what they were intended to do: made the readers think and value the intellectual process and sometimes made them marvel at the wonders of the universe and even sometimes experience what is still beyond our abilities to experience. Those things all are important to Asimov. (pp. 167-68)

James Gunn, in his Isaac Asimov: The Foundations of Science Fiction, *Oxford University Press, 1982, 236 p.*

KLIATT YOUNG ADULT PAPERBACK BOOK GUIDE

[*How Did We Find Out about Atoms? . . . Dinosaurs? . . . Life in the Deep Sea? . . . Our Human Roots? . . . Solar Power?* and . . . *Volcanoes?* present] straightforward explanations of some important scientific principles and discoveries. The format is similar in each, with the text frequently broken up by drawings and other illustrations. The reading level is 6th grade (Fry Readability Scale), and the sometimes difficult concepts are presented clearly, often with a single paragraph per sentence/concept. In this way, the reader is not faced with dense text full of difficult scientific data.

The book about atoms describes how scientists discovered the atom—it does not continue with information about the parts of an atom. The volcano book does include Mt. St. Helens;

the human roots book does not include the very latest discoveries such as Lucy. In each, important scientists who contributed to the knowledge in the field are illustrated [by David Wool], and their contribution described. Each subject is made interesting, with frequent anecdotes.

These are excellent introductions to science at the older elementary and 7th and 8th grade levels. However, even older people who find scientific principles difficult to grasp would benefit from these extremely clear, basic texts.

A review of "How Did We Find Out about Atoms?" & others, in Kliatt Young Adult Paperback Book Guide, *Vol. XVII, No. 1, January, 1983, p. 63.*

FRANCES E. MILLHOUSER

[In *How Did We Find Out About the Beginning of Life?* and *How Did We Find Out About the Universe?*] Asimov continues to explore scientific investigations. In each book, Asimov's writing is easy to follow and interesting to read; there is never a wasted word. . . . [Diagrams] help to clarify the text. Good indexes are in each book. In . . . *The Beginning of Life,* Asimov takes readers from the idea of spontaneous generation to current theories. Especially interesting is his chronological discussion of each scientist's theories and the experiments used to prove or disprove them. His book differs from other good introductions to this field, in particular, *The Origin of Life* (Van Nostrand, 1968) by Alvin and Virginia Silverstein and Marshall's *The Story of Life* (Holt, 1981) in that Asimov provides an historical perspective. In . . . *The Universe,* Asimov traces scientists' questions and discoveries, as well as their mistakes along the way. By limiting the scope somewhat he provides an in-depth explanation of such complicated concepts as how scientists discerned our own Milky Way's existence and its place in the universe, the presence and location of other galaxies, why some galaxies are speeding away from us faster than others and what the Big Bang Theory means. Asimov's chapter arrangement is logical and easy to follow. (pp. 168-69)

Frances E. Millhouser, in a review of "How Did We Find Out about the Beginning of Life?" and "How Did We Find Out about the Universe?" in School Library Journal, *Vol. 29, No. 7, March, 1983, pp. 168-69.*

PHILIP HŸTCH

The history of science has its own fascination, and who better to unfold the story than Isaac Asimov, that well known wizard of science fiction and lewd limericks. In these four examples from the "How we found out about" series [*Dinosaurs, Germs, Energy,* and *Antarctica*], Asimov displays his considerable gifts in locating and exploiting the truly dramatic elements in the development of science without at any time distorting the facts. Indeed he is able, through clever use of the storyteller's art, to present phenomena of considerable complexity in such a way as to facilitate understanding. Which, after all, is what a good story can do. I particularly admired *Germs* and *Dinosaurs,* in both of which I was absorbed from the very first page. These little books (around 50 pages) will make an attractive addition to a school reference library, since despite the "story" format, each contains an excellent index. One point worth noting is that despite the clarity and simplicity with which events are described and explained, Asimov does not "talk down" to his reader. Which means that all but fluent readers will have to struggle with some of the language.

Philip Hÿtch, "Sampling Science," in The Times Educational Supplement, *No. 3485, April 15, 1983, p. 33.*

ZENA SUTHERLAND, MAY HILL ARBUTHNOT, AND DIANNE L. MONSON

Biochemist Isaac Asimov has written his own reference book, *Asimov's Biographical Encyclopedia of Science and Technology,* and his writing covers a wide range of subjects, from authoritative discussions of astronomy in books like *Mars, the Red Planet* (1977) and distinctive science fiction to a story for the preschool child, *The Best Thing* (1971).

Words from History (1968) is a good example of Asimov's work in a field outside his own. Like all of his other books, it is distinguished for a witty, informal style and smoothly carries authoritative information. Using one page of text for each word, he gives its etymology and sets it in historical perspective.

Among his other "Word" books are *Words on the Map* (1962) and *Words of Science: and the History Behind Them* (1959). Each of these books follows the same format as *Words from History,* that is, one word and its explanation on one page. *Words from the Exodus* (1963) and *Words in Genesis* (1962) show how much of our everyday speech comes from the Bible.

The Shaping of North America (1973) and its sequel, *The Birth of the United States 1763-1816* (1974), are two of several Asimov books about the formative years of a country; his fresh viewpoint and easy, informal style make history interesting even when he covers familiar information. All of Asimov's history books, despite his tendency to crowd the pages with names and dates, have a breadth and sweep that give readers perspective on events, personalities, and factions.

Building Blocks of the Universe (1957) is an excellent book on chemistry and contains little sidelights which make the scientific words come alive for young people. *How Did We Find Out About Oil?* (1980) gives information on the topic and also shows how individuals contribute to a body of scientific or technological knowledge. *Realm of Numbers* (1959) is a popularizing of arithmetic for those who don't have a knowledge of algebra, geometry, and calculus. A useful series of books on astronomy includes *How Did We Find Out About Atoms?* (1976) and *How Did We Find Out About Black Holes?* (1978). This format was also used for *How Did We Find Out About the Beginning of Life?* (1982) and *How Did We Find Out About Genes?* (1983). One of the most successful of Asimov's many books about space is *ABC's of Space* (1969), which is illustrated with photographs and drawings from the space program, with short paragraphs for each item. This may be used with very young children, despite the fact that the terminology is sometimes complex. (pp. 488-89)

Zena Sutherland, May Hill Arbuthnot, and Dianne L. Monson, "Informational Books: 'Words from History',' in their Children and Books, *seventh edition, Scott, Foresman and Company, 1986, pp. 488-89.*

DAVID STARR, SPACE RANGER (1952)

Now that the plunge has been taken into juvenile science fiction, . . . rocket operas have become steadily fancier in vocabulary and fabulous in story. Only slightly less spectacular than the scientists of giant brain and noble vision are the detective heroes who shuttle back and forth. In this incredible yarn, David Starr, youngest member of the Earth's Council of Science betakes himself to Mars to investigate Mars' farms as possible sources of poisoned food being shipped to Earth. He masquerades as a farm hand, pursues his investigations, and visits some incorporeal subterranean Martians on the side. An attempted murder, clever sleuthing, and an excited unveiling of the guilty parties provide ample thriller action. Standard Buck Rogers. And doubtless headed for popular favor.

A review of "David Starr, Space Ranger," in Virginia Kirkus' Bookshop Service, *Vol. XIX, No. 24, December 15, 1951, p. 705.*

In this tale of the seventieth century Paul French ingeniously combines mystery with science fiction. His inventiveness and his use of picturesque details remind one of Robert Heinlein's books and, though his characters are not so fully developed as are Heinlein's, they are for the most part more individualized than in the usual story of this kind. There are moments, to be sure, when David Starr suggests the comic-strip hero, but he is convincing enough for the purposes of the story. . . .

This makes fast-moving, imaginative reading.

Ellen Lewis Buell, "Martian Mystery," in The New York Times Book Review, *February 17, 1952, p. 34.*

LUCKY STARR AND THE PIRATES OF THE ASTEROIDS (1953)

David, for some ridiculous reason now called "Lucky," is called upon to free space of the asteroid pirates. With occasional aid from his right-hand man, Bigman, Lucky is captured by the pirates, has a push-tube fight in space, discovers a Sirian plot against the Terrestrial Empire, and captures the man who had killed his father. Chapters are reminiscent of a continued-next-week serial. Gadgets and gimmicks, adventure and excitement will help fill demand for S-F. (pp. 1700-01)

Learned T. Bulman, in a review of "Lucky Starr and the Pirates of the Asteroids," in Library Journal, *Vol. 78, No. 17, October 1, 1953, pp. 1700-01.*

[*Lucky Starr and the Pirates of the Asteroids* is] a story so pack-jammed with thrills that there is not room for one wasted word.

Fantastic as all such yarns are, this is especially well written, particularly the conversation. Whether the characters are leap-frogging planets or shooting through the sun's corona on a forty-five-trillion-mile jaunt they talk as naturally as the folks next door. For those who like space stories here is a good one.

Merritt P. Allen, in a review of "Lucky Starr and the Pirates of the Asteroids," in The Saturday Review, *New York, Vol. XXXVI, No. 46, November 14, 1953, p. 66.*

Lucky Starr And the Pirates of the Asteroids is, as its title indicates, much closer to a TV serial than to such books as Heinlein's. The astronomy and astrogation are noticeably better than in most such space operas, with one really thrilling scene of a spaceflight almost too close to the Sun; but characterization, mystery plot and prose are on the most elementary level.

H. H. Holmes, "Stories of the Space Men Surveyed by a Specialist," in New York Herald Tribune Book Review, *November 15, 1953, p. 30.*

THE CHEMICALS OF LIFE: ENZYMES, VITAMINS, HORMONES (1954)

This is a sound introduction to bio-chemistry, that infant science that is making a revolution in our understanding of how our bodies function. This book deals with those "chemicals that control the workings of living tissue"—the catalysts that make other chemicals function. . . . While the presentation has somewhat the flavor of text book material, it is text book in the modern sense of direct, undramatized factual data. The audience interested in the subject—and their number is growing—wants it that way.

> *A review of "The Chemicals of Life: Enzymes—Vitamins—Hormones," in* Virginia Kirkus' Bookshop Service, *Vol. XXII, No. 20, October 15, 1954, p. 712.*

[This book presents] a new approach to physiology that will be useful to both health and chemistry classes. The up-to-date and detailed information on vitamins will be especially valuable. A complex subject is treated in simple non-technical language but will be difficult for younger students. More advanced students, particularly those taking chemistry, will find it excellent supplementary reading.

> *Dorothy Schumacher, in a review of "The Chemicals of Life," in* Junior Libraries, *an appendix to* Library Journal, *Vol. 1, No. 6, February 15, 1955, p. 24.*

In this account [of enzymes, vitamins, and hormones], the author avoids actual formulae (except that of cane sugar), but by means of diagrams and many apt analogies he gives a good notion of their structures and reactions. He is an American biochemist who writes simply but sensibly, and it would be difficult to better his treatment of such topics as catalysis, hydrolysis, equilibrium and the function of high energy bonds. Enough is provided of cell structure and division to help a young (or not so young) reader to understand how the body works, in health and disease. (p. 284)

> *A review of "The Chemicals of Life," in* The Junior Bookshelf, *Vol. 20, No. 5, November, 1956, pp. 283-84.*

LUCKY STARR AND THE OCEANS OF VENUS (1954)

The third in the adventures of David "Lucky" Starr is Paul French's best juvenile science fiction book to date. Crackling with suspense, lit by humor, sparkling with complexities of plot, and alive with interest, it is a tasty deep-sea dish for every reader who is young at heart.

The great underwater cities which harbor Earth's settlers on Venus are threatened with destruction by a hidden enemy who can control men's minds. Lucky Starr, youngest member of Earth's Council of Science, hurries to Venus with his friend, "Bigman" Jones, to discover why the Council's agent on Venus has turned traitor. Following a trail which grows increasingly complex, Starr and Bigman find themselves in fantastic danger, developed by the author both cunningly and scientifically. The identity of the book's villains is as surprising as it is inevitable. Here is a s-f juvenile guaranteed to keep young people away from the TV set—and, incidentally, to teach them facts about their solar system.

> *Villiers Gerson, "Hidden Enemy," in* The New York Times Book Review, *November 14, 1954, p. 10.*

It seems to be an open secret that "Paul French" is Isaac Asimov; and the latest adventure of Lucky Starr is the first in this series to deserve comparison with Asimov's often admirable adult science fiction. Here he has dropped the foolish trappings which made earlier books seem like a blend of Space Patrol, Superman and the Lone Ranger, and devoted himself to a straightforward, near-Heinlein adventure on Venus—a tight, fast story, including a well plotted detective puzzle and some excellent xenobiology—which, for the uninitiated, means the study of possible non-Earthly life forms.

> *H. H. Holmes, in a review of "Lucky Starr and the Oceans of Venus," in* New York Herald Tribune Book Review, *November 28, 1954, p. 16.*

Mr. French again offers imagination, excitement, a good plot, and an interesting, sustained story that will thrill any adventure or mystery lover whether S-F fan or not. We would be happier if Lucky were not a series hero, but that does not deter us from wholeheartedly recommending this to seventh-graders and older ages.

> *Learned T. Bulman, in a review of "Lucky Starr and the Oceans of Venus," in* Junior Libraries, *an appendix to* Library Journal, *Vol. 1, No. 4, December 15, 1954, p. 32.*

INSIDE THE ATOM (1956)

[*Inside the Atom*] is the best exposition of atomic chemistry we have seen. It is intended for the intelligent reader over thirteen to whom the subject is new. With amazing clarity Mr. Asimov gives the information that an advanced high school or easy college text would offer, from the structure of the atom to atomic dangers and atomic hope. It is clearly the work of some one who has learned to build up concepts for students slowly, effectively and interestingly. Good reading if you are not studying chemistry, a boon if you are.

> *"Some of Man's Tools through the Ages: From Axes to Atoms," in* New York Herald Tribune Book Review, *May 13, 1956, p. 29.*

The author of this book has a real gift for rendering complex information in simple language. The ground covered is familiar, for it has been treated in many other books for general readers. Consequently the book has little to offer (except perhaps a lesson in popular science writing) to readers already acquainted with the elementary facts of atomic energy, but it is an excellent book for high school students and general readers making their first exploration of knowledge about the atom. The following passage may cause readers to question the author's knowledge of everyday mechanics, but it was the only slip detected: ". . . a steel piston ring is bombarded by neutrons until radioactive isotopes have formed on it. A lubricated cylinder is then moved up and down *within* the ring just as it is in an automobile engine." The italics are mine. There is an adequate index but no suggestions for further reading.

> *R. R. Hawkins, in a review of "Inside the Atom," in* Library Journal, *Vol. 81, No. 15, September 1, 1956, p. 1929.*

LUCKY STARR AND THE BIG SUN OF MERCURY (1956)

[*Lucky Starr and the Big Sun of Mercury*] is much the best of the Space Patrol genre this spring. It's an interplanetary detective story of sabotage on a mysterious project on Mercury, with well constructed deduction, exciting action and accurate astronomical information.

> *H. H. Holmes, in a review of "Lucky Starr and the Big Sun of Mercury," in* New York Herald Tribune Book Review, *May 13, 1956, p. 37.*

In much the same pattern as the earlier stories about this hero, David Starr and Bigman Jones are off to settle a new trouble spot in the galaxy. This time the setting is Mercury, the planet nearest the sun. Once again Bigman is led astray by the red herrings that never once fool Lucky; both Bigman and Lucky are almost killed, and the villain is uncovered in a melodramatic, emotion packed climax. An oft-told tale, with nothing new but the setting.

> *A review of "Lucky Starr and the Big Sun of Mercury," in* Bulletin of the Children's Book Center, *Vol. X, No. 1, September, 1956, p. 5.*

BUILDING BLOCKS OF THE UNIVERSE (1957)

The Chemicals of Life and *Inside the Atom* were Mr. Asimov's first ventures into non-fiction for the teen ages after his firm establishment as an s-f writer. This third volume maintains the balance of accuracy and simplicity which marked the other two and presents a fascinating chapter by chapter explanation of the elements, as one learns about them in a high school chemistry course, only in condensed and very readable form. Oxygen, hydrogen, nitrogen, helium, carbon, silicon, the halogens and so on—by weight, family, relative prevalence, social importance and special characteristics—up to yttrium and uranium, all are explained and accounted for. Though the book suggests nothing of method and gives its facts away free, without payment exacted by lab work, it makes a definitely satisfying review and may serve as a stimulus to students who are having a hard time with their class work. (pp. 280-81)

> *A review of "Building Blocks of the Universe," in* Virginia Kirkus' Service, *Vol. XXV, No. 7, April 1, 1957, pp. 280-81.*

With *Building Blocks of the Universe* Isaac Asimov makes a welcome contribution to the scientific book shelf for young people. Here the story of the chemical elements is unfolded easily, entertainingly and informatively. Formulas are not used, and the book can be read by 12-year-olds with profit. Mr. Asimov is particularly successful in his use of everyday allusions to point up his remarks and to add sparkle to his paragraphs. (pp. 8, 12)

> *Robert E. K. Rourke, "Mind and Matter," in* The New York Times Book Review, *November 17, 1957, pp. 8, 12.*

This fascinating book about the chemical elements should be available for reference wherever elementary chemistry or general science are studied. . . .

The author's popular, non-technical phraseology enables him to introduce the different chemical terms, like ''acid'' and ''base,'' easily and naturally, and the derivation of such terms is used to make their meaning abundantly clear. . . .

A wealth of useful information is available here in so readable a form that anyone interested in this subject can appreciate it without previous study. American phraseology and spelling are seldom disturbing and the only minor irritation lies in the use

of a few extremely popular and therefore misleading descriptions of one or two physical phenomena such as magnetism and electrical conductivity.

> *B. J. Hopper, in a review of "Building Blocks of the Universe," in* The School Librarian and School Library Review, *Vol. 9, No. 3, December, 1958, p. 224.*

LUCKY STARR AND THE MOONS OF JUPITER (1957)

Fifth in the series about the efforts of Lucky, young member of the Council of Science, and Bigman Jones to thwart the enemies of Earth. Here Sirians, probably robots, are spying on the construction of [the] first Agrav ship. Lucky and Bigman identify and foil the spy after a succession of exciting and near-fatal adventures. French . . . , improving as a writer of juvenile S-F, is more than just acceptable.

> *Elaine Simpson, in a review of "Lucky Starr and the Moons of Jupiter," in* Junior Libraries, *an appendix to* Library Journal, *Vol. 4, No. 2, October 15, 1957, p. 154.*

This season's crop of science fiction novels for the mid-teens is small, but comes from the three leading specialists in the field: Robert A. Heinlein [with *Citizen of the Galaxy*], André Norton [with *Sea Siege*] and Paul French. Of these leaders, however, only French is in top form. *Lucky Starr and the Moons of Jupiter* . . . sets up the classic puzzle of discovering which of a small group is no true man but a humanoid robot spy and produces a surprising answer by means of brilliant fair-play detection, while giving the reader an accurate and visually exciting tour of Jupiter's satellite system.

> *H. H. Holmes, in a review of "Lucky Starr and the Moons of Jupiter," in* New York Herald Tribune Book Review, *November 17, 1957, p. 20.*

LUCKY STARR AND THE RINGS OF SATURN (1958)

In the sixth and latest Lucky Starr adventure, Lucky and Bigman thwart a Sirian attempt to colonize the Saturnian system. With an abundance of action and political intrigue, this is another competent, well-written story by a top-notch science fiction author. On a par with the previous Lucky Starr stories.

> *Albert Monheit, in a review of "Lucky Starr and the Rings of Saturn," in* Junior Libraries, *an appendix to* Library Journal, *Vol. 5, No. 4, December 15, 1958, p. 41.*

The swashbuckling science-fiction hero, Buck Rogers style, can be a pretty depressing fellow. In *Lucky Starr and the Rings of Saturn* . . . Paul French tells us how Lucky spoils the Sirians' plans to colonize one of our sun's planets. Studded with what one supposes are spaceman epithets, such as ''Great Galaxy!'' and ''Sands of Mars!'', this is a good guy vs. bad guy situation in which neat plotting is the saving grace of an otherwise ordinary effort.

> *Robert Berkvist, "Teen-Age Space Cadets," in* The New York Times Book Review, *December 14, 1958, p. 18.*

[In *Lucky Starr and the Rings of Saturn*] French-Asimov has fun with fresh variations on the Three Laws of Robotics (which are to him what locked rooms are to John Dickson Carr). . . .

The novel's a mite short on plot, and much of its banter seems more childish than youthful; but like all Asimov it is ingenious and carefully credible.

> *H. H. Holmes, "Three, Two, One, Zero and a Space Suit," in* New York Herald Tribune Book Review, *May 10, 1959, p. 27.*

___

WORDS OF SCIENCE, AND THE HISTORY BEHIND THEM (1959)

An excellent encyclopedia of scientific terms, the articles in this alphabetically arranged text are written with that same verve, lucidity, and concentration of knowledge which characterize Isaac Asimov's other books.... *Words of Science* defines everything from "Absolute Zero" to "Zero". No term, animal, mineral, gas, or abstract escapes definition, and with more than 1500 terms considered, each paragraph manages to contain much interesting material on historical usage and derivation. An imperative book for the student of science and one written with such clarity that any reader possessed of intellectual curiosity or love of language will enjoy turning—and returning—to its pages.

> *A review of "Words of Science," in* Virginia Kirkus' Service, *Vol. XXVII, No. 14, July 15, 1959, p. 499.*

A fascinating book, both for the reader interested in science and the reader interested in language and words. Two hundred and fifty words are given one-page explanations, but each word is used as a starting point for giving the histories and derivations of other words related by concept or etymology. The choice of words is, of necessity, rather arbitrary, but the selection is well-balanced and comprehensive; the author has defined his field broadly and includes "grammar" and "liberal arts" as words of science. The material will be of greatest interest to those with a background in science, although the simplified explanations may seem inadequate to serious students; the clarity of writing and the interest of the words themselves should carry the non-scientific reader. Useful for class work in science and in English.... [The] excellent index includes all names and words explained in the text.

> *Zena Sutherland, in a review of "Words of Science, and the History behind Them," in* Bulletin of the Center for Children's Books, *Vol. XIII, No. 3, November, 1959, p. 41.*

At first glance this offering from the prolific Dr Asimov has the look of a mere potboiler, as a series of articles on alphabetically arranged terms, extensive but not exhaustive, must tend to do. But it is written from a position of some depth of understanding, and the author is clearly aware of what he is writing throughout. Everything is always in focus. Most detail is so set in meaningful context as to make this an exceptionally nourishing source of browsing.

> *H. M. Thomas, in a review of "Words of Science and the History behind Them," in* The School Librarian, *Vol. 22, No. 4, December, 1974, p. 387.*

___

REALM OF NUMBERS (1959)

Once more Isaac Asimov takes the venom out of abstract study, presenting the theory of numbers on which mathematics are based in a lucid and entertaining manner. Numbers, their meaning and evolution, alternatives to our number system, their application in multiplication, addition, subtraction, division, decimals, fractions are discussed, not as formidable laws, but as a meaningful system, evolving logically from a coherent basis.... [For] the intellectually curious student, long baffled by the apparent dogmatism of arithmetic by rote, [the text] should prove an inviting welcome into the realm of mathematical investigation.

> *A review of "Realm of Numbers," in* Virginia Kirkus' Service, *Vol. XXVII, No. 16, August 15, 1959, p. 602.*

There are some explanations which are not completely clear, and may therefore be misleading; for example, the reference to an "equilateral right triangle" or "In a sense, all decimals can be considered repeating decimals." On the whole, the text is lucid; it is well organized and it has the combination of information, informality and enthusiasm that make all of Mr. Asimov's books enjoyable.

> *Zena Sutherland, in a review of "Realm of Numbers," in* Bulletin of the Center for Children's Books, *Vol. XIII, No. 7, March, 1960, p. 109.*

___

THE CLOCK WE LIVE ON (1959)

A comprehensive consideration of time, motion, clocks and calendars; written with Asimov's usual happy combination of competence, lucidity and humor. Covers much the same areas as do Zarchy's *Wheel of Time* and *Understanding Time* by Tannenbaum and Stillman, but gives much more material on motion and rotation of the earth, and on lunar variations. Historical development of timepieces is more briefly discussed than is the evolution of the present-day calendar.

> *Zena Sutherland, in a review of "The Clock We Live On," in* Bulletin of the Center for Children's Books, *Vol. XIII, No. 5, January, 1960, p. 77.*

[In *The Clock We Live On* the] reader learns how to construct the primitive sun dial and then discovers how the clock, based on the movement of atoms, was finally derived under the pressure of our ever expanding culture. The hour, the day and the terms describing longer unities are dealt with in a sophisticated manner and yet explained competently and simply.

Many young people, especially those with a bent for science, will find this challenging and exciting. Valuable, too, for the parent or teacher looking for accurate and clear explanations.

> *Janet Miller, in a review of "The Clock We Live On," in* English Journal, *Vol. 54, No. 5, May, 1965, p. 459.*

[This is a] topic book which relates facts consistently to ideas.... Dr. Asimov relates man's thinking to his mechanical inventions clearly and with confidence. There is no ambiguity in his explanation of how man *decided* to measure time, and the actual time-keepers he describes (sundials, water-clocks, zonal time) are used to illustrate this decision. For example, when he discusses sundials he also discusses the multi-divisible number twelve and how it was used for the dividing of days and hours. When dealing with time zones he starts with the Greek idea of dividing the world, and works from this point to a lucid explanation of why time must differ in various places. Brilliant in simplification, his book is direct and clear, with a careful arrangement of chapters stressing earth, sun, moon and stars as man's means of measuring time. Here is one aspect of time excellently portrayed; time as a biological rhythm, historicity, relativity are not discussed. (p. 183)

> *Margery Fisher, "Foundations: Time," in her Matters of Fact: Aspects of Non-Fiction for Children, Thomas Y. Crowell Co., 1972, pp. 165-91.*

THE KINGDOM OF THE SUN (1960)

Dr. Asimov, always a lucid and persuasive guide through fields of science, here takes us through the history of man's understanding of the solar system. We start the tour in ancient Babylonia, seeing the sky as it appears to an attentive but unsophisticated observer. We end the tour with an account of the 1919 total eclipse that verified Einstein's prediction that light rays are bent by the sun's gravitational field. On the way, we are introduced to the men who changed the world's understanding; through simple charts we are led to see what they saw, as they saw it; through Dr. Asimov's explanations we come to the higher level of science to which these men brought the world. The index is excellent; there is an extensive table of dates, with capsule comments. *The Kingdom of the Sun* should be in all science libraries.

> *Arthur A. Brown, in a review of "The Kingdom of the Sun," in The Horn Book Magazine, Vol. XXXVI, No. 4, August, 1960, p. 305.*

This is a most lucid and closely reasoned approach to astronomy for young high-school readers, for as each bit of information is discovered and explained the bits of information that do not fit in serve as an introduction to the next discovery.

> *A review of "The Kingdom of the Sun," in New York Herald Tribune Book Review, November 13, 1960, p. 39.*

BREAKTHROUGHS IN SCIENCE (1960)

In the lucid and information packed style that has rendered the author outstanding in the juvenile science field, Isaac Asimov describes twenty-six men and the moments at which they reversed the course of scientific thought. From Archimedes to Robert Hutchings Goddard, these men accomplished a major breakthrough by establishing original and hitherto unrevealed laws.... Embracing every area of science, this is a readable text which should interest even the most reluctant student, and is therefore recommended to school libraries.

> *A review of "Breakthroughs in Science," in Virginia Kirkus' Service, Vol. XXVIII, No. 19, October 1, 1960, p. 869.*

Collection of brief (1,500 words) essays on the life and work of nearly 30 important scientists and technologists, including Archimedes, Gutenberg, Galileo, Newton, Lavoisier, Henry, Bessemer, Mendel, Carver, Langmuir, and Goddard.... Style is odd: paragraphs and sentences seem often to have been artificially shortened and most unlike Asimov's usual excellent, smooth-flowing exposition. The essays themselves seem far too short for the amount of ground covered. The whole project bears a most un-Asimov-like air, and the result is an inferior work from an author whose true excellence can usually be taken for granted. The general juvenile encyclopedias give far better coverage of the subjects treated here. Not recommended.

> *Theodore C. Hines, in a review of "Breakthroughs in Science," in Junior Libraries, an appendix to Li-*

brary Journal, *Vol. 7, No. 5, December 15, 1960, p. 58.*

REALM OF MEASURE (1960)

Struggling against almost insuperable odds (his subject matter), this versatile scientist-author provides the wherewithal for understanding the origins, development, and use of contemporary systems of measurement and their relationships not only to each other but also to certain basic scientific concepts. Some lay readers may wonder whether the numerous conversion tables might not have been part of a reference section while specialists may chafe at the amount of the author's interjected exposition.

> *A review of "Realm of Measure," in Saturday Review, Vol. XLIII, No. 46, November 12, 1960, p. 101.*

Clearly and interestingly Dr. Asimov has told the story of measure and explained the underlying theories from the most basic measurements of length to the complex measurements of force, energy, and viscosity. Dr. Eleanor Johnson, head of the science department of the Gamaliel Bradford High School in Wellesley, Massachusetts, read the book with interest and added the following comment:

> I regret the choice of the pound as the unit of mass and the poundal as the unit of force, with no mention of the usage which employs the pound as the unit of force, and the 'slug' as the unit of mass. This latter is the usage adopted in some high schools, in the belief that it will ultimately be the most helpful for our future scientists and engineers. However, perhaps Dr. Asimov felt that there was a limit to the amount of confusion he could, with impunity, reveal to his readers. I should also like to see the book go a little further into relativity as it affects measurement and even into the Uncertainty Principle in measurement; however, as the book is now, I believe it well merits a place on the high school reading list.

Also, as it stands, it will probably be inviting to some scientific-minded seventh and eighth graders.

> *Ruth Hill Viguers, in a review of "Realm of Measure," in The Horn Book Magazine, Vol. XXXVII, No. 1, February, 1961, p. 65.*

THE DOUBLE PLANET (1960)

"Double planet" is the author's name for the earth-moon system. He compares the earth and the moon as to size, movement, mass, structure, etc., and explains their relationship to each other and the ways in which the moon affects the earth. He also traces the steps by which scientists throughout history have obtained this information. Appendix tabulates useful information in convenient form and lists important discoveries in chronological order; also has index. As in other books by this author, the material is accurate and presented in simple, graphic style. This information can be found in other books, but this brings together the most significant facts about earth and moon with more detail than in other books at this reading level. Recommended as a useful supplement to the astronomy collection.

Dorothy Schumacher, in a review of "The Double Planet," in Junior Libraries, *an appendix to* Library Journal, *Vol. 7, No. 5, January 15, 1961, p. 68.*

The shape and substance of the earth and moon, the atmosphere, cislunar space, Van Allen radiation belts, and the motion of all of these are discussed in Dr. Asimov's usual deceptively simple style. Recommended for readers from late junior high school age to age ninety and beyond. Dr. Asimov weaves a sketch of the history of our knowledge of the earth and moon into a skillful exposition of our present understanding. A good index plus three appendices giving some facts about the moon, some facts about the earth, and a table of dates make this book an excellent reference work.

Arthur A. Brown, in a review of "The Double Planet," in The Horn Book Magazine, *Vol. XXXVII, No. 2, April, 1961, p. 171.*

SATELLITES IN OUTER SPACE   (1960)

This is an easy-to-read book. It is an easy-to-read science book. It is all right in its subject coverage. It has an index. . . . It puts hard words in blue. It tells what these hard words mean. There is a list of important satellites. It includes space probes, too. It is in the back of the book. The style is not Asimov. The style is like this review. Asimov is a talented writer. He is not needed to do writing like this. Do you like to read books like this? Run, Jack, run!

Theodore C. Hines, in a review of "Satellites in Outer Space," in Junior Libraries, *an appendix to* Library Journal, *Vol. 7, No. 5, January 15, 1961, p. 58.*

This [1964] revised edition of the 1960 original incorporates most of the material of the original and adds a very small amount of new material. . . . The text of the new edition is somewhat more terse than the 1960 edition, to permit the inclusion of some new material and reduce the number of pages from the original 79 pages to the current 61 pages. None of the subject matter is dropped, but occasionally, an explanatory phrase, a reference to an illustration, or a clarifying sentence are dropped. . . . Many of the new developments had been covered in the old book as planned experiments, and the new edition includes them as concluded.

The arguments against the first book are still quite valid as concerns this revised edition. There is very little real explanation. The child is given some facts and figures that can make him seem very knowledgeable, but there is not sufficient material in the book to assist the youngster in really obtaining an understanding of the subject matter. With the editing of the text for the new edition, nothing has been done to improve this, and in spots, elaborations are deleted.

> But the moon is not a magnet. This means that the moon does not have any melted iron inside it. The moon must be solid rock, like the outside part of the earth.
>
> In this way, man-made satellites have told us something important about the inside of the moon.

The above is from the 1960 edition. The 1964 edition prints the same material, but excludes the last sentence and does not offer any substitute. That sentence is one of the few places

where a justification for the expensive space probe program is presented.

The main achievements of this new edition will be that replacements of the earlier edition will be slightly updated. If the other edition is still in good condition, this book will add negligibly to the collection. The book has a certain limited usefulness to the child first showing an interest in the subject. . . . For the child who already has some slight familiarity with the field, the *All About Rockets and Space Flight* [by Harold L. Goodwin] will probably be a much more satisfying book.

Isaac Asimov is capable of, and has given us, truly outstanding science books, such as ***The World of Carbon, The World of Nitrogen, Building Blocks of the Universe*** and others, but the exceedingly limited format of this book does not give his fine talent room to operate.

Robert Cohen, in a review of "Satellites in Outer Space," in Young Readers Review, *Vol. I, No. 6, February, 1965, p. 8.*

Regardless of the age level for which Isaac Asimov writes, his science books are authentic and the vocabulary is suited to the child, without his writing down to them. In this book . . . , accelerated students of grade three and the slower ones of grade six, will find the account of satellites and space probes enlightening and interesting. Index. . . .

Sister Mary Etheldreda, R.S.M., in a review of "Satellites in Outer Space," in Catholic Library World, *Vol. 36, No. 7, March, 1965, p. 475.*

WORDS FROM THE MYTHS   (1961)

Dr. Asimov's complex perceptions and narrative skill are applied to an important subject. The result is a many-sided introduction to philology, present-day science, ethnic history, and the Greek and Roman myths. Chaos and Cosmos lead to gasoline, cosmic rays, and cosmetics. The Titans take us to astronomy, geography, and archaeology. The Minotaur brings us to physiology. All this is lightly done; the introductions are as precise and casual as those of an expert host at a large and lively gathering. A general index and mythological index, both excellent, provide adequate reference. The style is suited to advanced ten-year-olds; the content will provide a myriad "Did you know that . . ." gambits.

Arthur A. Brown, in a review of "Words from the Myths," in The Horn Book Magazine, *Vol. XXXVII, No. 2, April, 1961, p. 164.*

Mr. Asimov has written a clear, simplified matter-of-fact, very readable account of Greek myths . . . , reducing each story to its bare essentials as in a classical dictionary. In each case he shows how proper names and expressions connected with these stories have become part of our language, especially the language of science. Addressed to the illiterate young—the muses are "goddesses of the show business," Heracles the "Paul Bunyan of the Ancient World," Daedalus a "mythological Edison"—this attempts to humanise them through their interest in science. It is a good beginning although literary allusions are largely ignored. Pegasus is a fiery steed, a certain small fish and the great square in the heavens but not the inspiration of poets. Parnassus is not even mentioned, nor, of course the Pierian spring even though Mr. Asimov offers his readers a fair sip of its waters.

"Unusual Books on Science," in Lively Arts and Book Review, *May 14, 1961, p. 32.*

There have been several versions of the classical legends recently, but this is unusual in that it tells the stories in order to show how they have coloured our everyday speech and its imagery. Not a bad idea, in fact, but the treatment is pedestrian in the extreme and is unlikely to arouse interest except from those who would get more satisfaction out of hunting up the information for themselves from a dictionary.

A review of "Words from the Myths," in The Junior Bookshelf, *Vol. 27, No. 3, July, 1963, p. 165.*

REALM OF ALGEBRA   (1961)

In *Realm of Algebra,* Isaac Asimov attempts a sequel to his *Realm of Numbers.* With a more specialized subject, this book must necessarily appeal to a more limited audience. Those who have studied or will study algebra in its proper academic sequence will have little interest, especially since "transposition," a technique now outmoded by the New Mathematics concepts, is the basis for much of the apparent simplification of algebraic "manipulation." Someone to whom algebra might otherwise remain a closed book may find a measure of enlightenment, but it will not be an "Algebra Without Tears."

Fritz Kain, "Math Trio," in The New York Times Book Review, *November 5, 1961, p. 50.*

A remarkably lucid book, in which the material is well-organized and in which new concepts are introduced with clarity and amplified with several examples. There is enough repetition in the writing to make the theories presented easy to understand, but it is not the sort of repetition that dulls. The final chapter discusses some applications of algebraic knowledge, from its use in simple financial transactions or conversions in recipe measurements, to its use by Cavendish in computing the weight of the earth. An index is appended.

Zena Sutherland, in a review of "Realm of Algebra," in Bulletin of the Center for Children's Books, *Vol. XV, No. 11, July-August, 1962, p. 170.*

WORDS IN GENESIS   (1962)

"Whether the Bible is read for love of God or for love of beauty," Isaac Asimov writes in a brief author's note to this valuable book, "no other book has ever been read so much." He then, limiting himself to the book of Genesis in order to keep his work within a reasonable size, proceeds to "trace down some of the words and phrases we use, or come across in our reading, that stem from the Bible or that have been influenced by the Bible." The result is stimulating and informative, a book that can be read in its entirety or dipped into here and there with the aid of its long index.

After an excellent introductory chapter on the accepted versions of the Old Testament in the Jewish canon, the Vulgate of St. Jerome and the modern English Douay Bible used by Roman Catholics, the Authorized Version (King James Bible) and the modern Revised Standard Version used by scholars, the author retells the story of Genesis, pausing to quote and comment on nearly one hundred and fifty individual verses. He uses the King James Version (to our great delight) because these are the words that live in our language, but he conscientiously points out different words and interpretations according to the

Douay, the Revised Standard, or the Jewish Masoretic text. From his first comments on the word God in Genesis 1:1 which range from emphasis on the Jews' negation of a multiplicity of Gods to explanations of the way the word influenced the formation of "gossip," "bigot," "giddy," "goodbye" and "Good Friday," we are led into fascinating bypaths of language, history and religion. We move from Bethlehem to bedlam, from Simon to simony, from Jacob to Jake, from dago to Iago, from sacrifice to sacroiliac. While the derivation and history of words are explained, we are being given fascinating insights into the history of ideas within the Judaeo-Christian tradition, with occasional excursions into barbarian lands. Particular care is taken to present each possible differing tradition from the viewpoint of the Jewish, the Roman Catholic and the Protestant tradition.

An imaginative, informative study which will be used constantly; it is even more helpful than *Words from the Myths.*

Margaret Sherwood Libby, in a review of "Words in Genesis," in Books, *April 22, 1962, p. 9.*

In an easy colloquial style Isaac Asimov uses the Book of Genesis with all of its dramatic episodes to describe the fascinating etymologies of many Biblical words. An old hand at this trade Mr. Asimov knows how to make his selections (he seldom allows an opportunity for the picturesque to escape) and how to spread additional useful information. . . .

There are a few oversights in his etymologies: "Maccabee" is not Greek for "hammerer" but stems from a Semitic root that means "to hammer"; "Sacred" comes from the Latin *sacer,* not *sanctus,* though it is possible that both go back to the same Indo-European root. These, however, do not mar the generally high quality of his discussion.

Mario Pei, in a review of "Words in Genesis," in The New York Times Book Review, *June 3, 1962, p. 18.*

An unusual book, interesting and informative, occasionally humorous; it is, however, not smoothly written and will possibly be used for browsing. It is doubtful that Mr. Asimov's approach could produce any other result: he proceeds through Genesis with erudition, zest, and a detective zeal that leads the reader into fascinating but digressive linguistic tangents. The first part of the book gives excellent background information about writing materials and Biblical compilation, with word-derivations and word-variants. Useful, also, for religious education collections. Appended . . . [is] an extensive index.

Zena Sutherland, in a review of "Words in Genesis," in Bulletin of the Center for Children's Books, *Vol. XV, No. 11, July-August, 1962, p. 170.*

WORDS ON THE MAP   (1962)

Anyone who has had the privilege of hearing Mr. Asimov talk knows his ability to make science come alive and glow for his listeners. Fortunately he writes with the same magic. His latest book is an exhilarating tour of the world—an eye-opener to young readers who up to Asimov time have groaned that geography was nothing but a mass of dry facts—population figures—capitals of—etc. Asimov gives them wings.

A review of "Words on the Map," in Publishers Weekly, *Vol. 182, No. 8, August 20, 1962, p. 89.*

"Places on this earth are named for gods and saints, for kings and presidents, and politicians and warriors, and, often, for complete nonentities. The map is a fascinating storybook and I've tried to trap some of that fascination and put it into this book" (Author's Introduction). Mr. Asimov has done exactly that. The result is the kind of book you may pick up not for reference but to fill a spare moment, only to find yourself hopelessly caught, having to turn just one more page to see what comes next. Two hundred and fifty place names from all over the world are arranged alphabetically, one to each page. Into this small space is packed an amazing amount of historical information explaining how each place came to have the name it bears today. In addition, each name seems to have served Asimov as a springboard for leaps into related facts and stories. For example, the article on Dayton turns into an entertaining discussion of places named for individuals. "Anyone can name a new town after himself if he is doing the founding. With luck, he can then become the owner of an immortal name." (Dayton was a signer of the Declaration of Independence, who was indicted for treason ten years later but never brought to trial.) "Cities can be named for merit, however. A city in northern Australia, founded in 1872, was originally named Palmerston for a British Prime Minister, recently dead. It was renamed Darwin for Charles Robert Darwin, one of the greatest scientists in history. Nevertheless, the number of scientists on the map, compared to generals, politicians, and nonentities, is, alas, negligible." Full of human interest, the information is skillfully assembled to stick in the mind; sight or mention of any of these places will henceforth stimulate meaningful associations.

> *Margaret Warren Brown, in a review of "Words on the Map," in* The Horn Book Magazine, *Vol. XXXVIII, No. 5, October, 1962, p. 491.*

Another of Isaac Asimov's fascinating "word" books has appeared to join *Words of Science, Words from the Myths* and *Words in Genesis*. It is less unified than the other three because words on the map have such diverse origins that in writing little essays on approximately 250 of them (and including six times as many more in incidental comments), Asimov must range over many fields of knowledge. . . . Pick it up anywhere or use the two indexes (one of men, one of places) to find remarks about a particular place. . . . A delightful way to impart information, and a book that is not only inviting to the browser but helpful for reference. Especially pleasing is the very considerable amount of extra information included in each essay.

> *A review of "Words on the Map," in* Books, *Children's Section, November 11, 1962, p. 12.*

THE HUMAN BODY: ITS STRUCTURE AND OPERATION   (1963)

Isaac Asimov has written another worthwhile book. This one describes the evolution and present state of development of the parts of the human body. Asimov has compressed much detailed information into these pages, but the text never becomes obscure or tedious. He gives the basic derivation of most of the technical terms, and explains them in a comprehensible but unpatronizing manner. His sense of humor is evident from time to time, and his ability to construct forceful verbal pictures is demonstrated in every chapter.

> *William K. Beatty, in a review of "The Human Body," in* Library Journal, *Vol. 88, No. 1, January 1, 1963, p. 111.*

Mr. Asimov takes the reader through a structural tour in *The Human Body*. He gives a thorough and carefully detailed study of human anatomy and of the corresponding physiology of our heads, limbs, joints, muscles, lungs, heart, circulatory vessels, blood, intestines, kidneys, skin, and genital organs. The book should be appealing on two counts. First, it is excellently written. . . . Asimov gives an academically and scientifically accurate account. He defines and gives the Greek or Latin derivations of the scientific terminology. Secondly, his book encompasses a topic of extreme interest to the young reader, but seldom covered in his classroom biology text. The author's discussion of our genitals gives a complete yet simple explanation of the organs themselves, their functions, and the hormones which activate them. He includes a brief yet accurate account of such topics as the menstrual cycle, copulation, intercourse, fertilization, pregnancy, and birth. . . . Finally, Asimov makes no reference to the role of the brain or nervous system, which he reserves for another book.

> *Dorothy Kueny, in a review of "The Human Body," in* Best Sellers, *Vol. 22, No. 24, March 15, 1963, p. 472.*

WORDS FROM THE EXODUS   (1963)

The derivations, uses, and changes of meanings of words and phrases in Exodus, Leviticus, Numbers, and Deuteronomy are explored with the author's usual informed enthusiasm. Mr. Asimov incorporates smoothly his selections and the continuity material that ties them together. Occasionally the text goes off on an etymological detective hunt that will intrigue word-lovers; for example, in discussing the Biblical use of the second person pronoun, the use of familiar address in French, German, and English is discussed, with a small excursion into Quaker speech. Entertaining and informative. An index . . . [is] appended.

> *Zena Sutherland, in a review of "Words from the Exodus," in* Bulletin of the Center for Children's Books, *Vol. XVI, No. 10, June, 1963, p. 154.*

Dr. Asimov has a zest for language that cannot be described, only sampled. Packed with information ranging from ancient times to the present, [*Words from the Exodus* is] valuable for reference and for random browsing for sheer pleasure. For example, the verse "Thou shalt not suffer a witch to live" (Exodus 22:18) leads into two delightful pages of information and speculation about witches, witchcraft, and wizards.

> *Margaret Warren Brown, in a review of "Words from the Exodus," in* The Horn Book Magazine, *Vol. XXXIX, No. 4, August, 1963, p. 398.*

THE KITE THAT WON THE REVOLUTION   (1963)

In house-that-Jack-built pattern, it was Benjamin Franklin who won the hearts of the French aristocrats who, against their own long-term interests, provided the money and men who made possible the victory of the American Revolution. And it was Franklin's scientific achievements, symbolized by the famous kite, which opened the doors of the French aristocrats. To find out what contribution to science Franklin's experiments represented, we are taken back to ancient times to begin the history of electricity up to Franklin's time. Having thus established his right to fame, we read his biography, very well told—his inventions, his activities in manifold areas, his long and significant role in American history. The author writes colloquially, and with such zest and wit that readers of any age will be swept along in this unusual combination of science and history.

> *Margaret Warren Brown, in a review of "The Kite That Won the Revolution," in* The Horn Book Magazine, *Vol. XXXIX, No. 5, October, 1963, p. 516.*

The title of this book is as misleading as some of the historical information in it. . . . The world fame [the invention of the lightning rod] brought to Franklin so impressed the French aristocrats, says Mr. Asimov that they put pressure on their government to give aid to the American colonies. "Actually, they were really interested only in helping Franklin, for the aristocrats knew very little about the colonies. They only knew Franklin and his kite—but that was enough for them." Washington is given no credit whatever for helping to bring about the Constitutional Convention in 1787. Many statements are made about events without any explanation of what led up to them. The electoral college is mentioned with no definition of the term. This is a vastly oversimplified and, in spots, erroneous mixture of science and history that will give children no real understanding of either.

> *E. Louise Davis, in a review of "The Kite That Won the Revolution," in* School Library Journal, *an appendix to* Library Journal, *Vol. 10, No. 3, November, 1963, p. 73.*

The title itself is bound to intrigue young readers. It is frankly dangled as bait, but Mr. Asimov justifies it most skillfully. . . .

[This book] is a fascinating combination of scientific and political narrative, keyed to attract the child already interested in one or the other and to lead him into fresh viewpoints in both fields. He will end up amazed at the truly great man he probably knew very little about, and more knowledgeable, too, about scientific research. The presentation is swift and conversational, with never a letdown in suspense.

> *Millicent J. Taylor, "The Men behind the Faces, the People behind the Maps—Sports Shelf: From Longfellow to Leonard Bernstein," in* The Christian Science Monitor, *November 14, 1963, p. 8B.*

THE GREEKS: A GREAT ADVENTURE (1965)

The always fascinating story of the Greeks is covered here from earliest days to modern times, with the main emphasis on classical Greece. In his consideration of the culture, Professor Asimov, predictably, devotes most of his space to science. The unconventionally presented pronunciations of Greek names and the frequent etymologies, one of his specialties, are helpful. Except for a few lapses (King Midas did not have a daughter who turned to gold—not until Hawthorne; Herodotus is not "the earliest Greek writer whose work exists in detail"), the scholarship is sound, and except for occasional colloquialisms, editorializing ("Sparta had nothing to offer the world, except a horrible militarism"), and a predilection for parentheses, the style is pleasant. Its scope alone makes this volume first purchase for all libraries catering to young people, who should, however, be steered to more adequate treatments of, at least, literature and mythology.

> *Ursula Schoenheim, in a review of "The Greeks: A Great Adventure," in* Library Journal, *Vol. 90, No. 13, July, 1965, p. 3129.*

The author has a remarkable ability to breathe life into any subject he chooses to present, and his enthusiasm for all aspects of knowledge usually keeps high the level of interest. In its vitality this book is no exception, nor in its admirable simplicity and clarity. To encompass the great adventure of the Greeks from the Mycenaean Age, more than four thousand years ago, to the 1960s is, however, a formidable task. Reading much of the book at a sitting leaves one with the breathlessness of a race across centuries. Used as a background outline for a study of the Greek civilization, it could be very useful, particularly for the seventh and eighth grades. Every page has much to arouse curiosity, but lacks the details necessary to hold attention. Other books covering less but probing more deeply should be at hand. Of special interest are the explanations of the vestiges of ancient Greek words and names in present-day use. Maps, a good index, and a helpful table of dates add to the book's value. (pp. 398-99)

> *Ruth Hill Viguers, in a review of "The Greeks: A Great Adventure," in* The Horn Book Magazine, *Vol. XLI, No. 4, August, 1965, pp. 398-99.*

Mr. Asimov is the closest thing we have today to the encyclopedists of the Renaissance. (I often have the feeling he must be twins, at least. How one man can acquire, rearrange, and disseminate all the information he has is almost inconceivable!). His latest book deals with the Greeks from Mycenaean times to the present day—a span of about 4,000 years! Of course, in the presentation of such a lengthy period, only "highlights" can be given, but the sense of the sweep of history and the "glory that was Greece" are communicated.

One advantage of this book over the other books about Greece for youngsters is the gathering together in one volume of so much material! The "great adventure" of the title is the adventure of the mind. The Greek beginnings of much of our current way of life are clearly shown. The conquest by Greek culture of much of the Western World, even after the defeat of the Greeks and their loss of military and political power, depended on such a variety of circumstances, people, and events that to explain it so clearly is quite a feat! There is a great deal of information on the "early days" (before the Persian Wars) which is difficult to come by elsewhere, and the later history of the country (after the Golden Age) is also given short shrift elsewhere. This book can be confusing unless it is read slowly and carefully—so many names! so many places! so many plots! so many intrigues! so many battles!

But Mr. Asimov's delightful "asides"—about science, etymology, and legends—provide the richness and extra dimension that we expect in his books. His history is far from neutral. For example "Alcibiades did more to ruin Athens than merely to direct the Spartans into Sicily. His lively intelligence pointed out something to the Spartans that, to anyone but a Spartan, might have needed no pointing out." And again: "At this point, too, disaster loomed for Athens in the shape (of all things) a capable Spartan admiral . . ."

His wit, too, is evident. In speaking of Sappho: and her lost work he says: ". . . however, many of the ancient Greeks considered her the equal of Homer, and their taste can usually be relied on." Or, on Aristotle: "Although the greatest thinker of ancient times, he saw not one inch beyond it." . . .

Mr. Asimov's language is strong, and colloquial—there is no aura of pedantry about this brisk and informative book. The author's experience as a fiction writer and a teacher stands him in good stead; he knows how to capture a reader's attention, and how to hold it. But, of necessity, the book is sketchy. The Persian Wars occupy only about twenty five pages, and the Peloponnesian War about twenty pages. The tangled history of modern Greece (1832 to date) is dismissed in less than ten pages. . . .

> *Phyllis Cohen, in a review of "The Greeks: A Great Adventure," in* Young Readers Review, *Vol. II, No. 1, September, 1965, p. 6.*

AN EASY INTRODUCTION TO THE SLIDE RULE (1965)

Written in the author's well known expansive style, this appears to be an adequate discussion of how a simple slide rule functions, in theory and structure. While it is stated that a grade school arithmetic background is sufficient, anything beyond that will prove helpful, although each new concept (e.g. logarithms) is always fully introduced. There are numerous footnotes which might well have been incorporated in the text. The explanations are difficult to follow without a slide rule in hand.

> *A review of "An Easy Introduction to the Slide Rule," in* Virginia Kirkus' Service, *Vol. XXXIII, No. 20, October 15, 1965, p. 1085.*

The master has done it again. So often people view the engineer's 'slip stick' with great trepidation. For those people and anyone about to approach the slide rule for the first time, this book is a *must*. Even many of those who have acquired some facility in the use of the slide rule will find this a great aid in improving and correcting their technique and in utilizing those other scales that they have never managed to find the time to learn about.

The book assumes no prior knowledge of the slide rule and covers the basic concepts of mechanical analogs. It develops this aspect in some detail using a rule designed only to handle addition and subtraction problems. From this solid base it proceeds to the method of computation by use of the logarithms of numbers, and then shows how the rule provides the quick method of adding and subtracting logarithms. Some considerable space is devoted to the physical arrangement of the slide rule and how the positioning and the design of the various scales are managed to facilitate computation. The book covers the design, handling, and usage of the following standard scales: A, B, C, CF, CI, CIF, D, D(back), DF, DI, K, and L. The concepts of folded and inverse scales are well developed. . . .

The progression of the book is such that whether novice or familiar in the art of using the 'slip stick', you can quickly gather the information you need. It is the type of work that is very useful to the student who is rusty and needs a brush-up.

Even those who do not need the skills of slide rule manipulation will find the early section valuable for an understanding of analog computation.

For anyone who has serious plans for a career in science or engineering, the book will prove most valuable. Dr. Asimov has written another outstanding work explaining a little-understood subject.

> *Robert Cohen, in a review of "An Easy Introduction to the Slide Rule," in* Young Readers Review, *Vol. II, No. 7, March, 1966, p. 2.*

Professor Isaac Asimov is well known in America for his popular scientific writings couched in a personal and rather racy style. . . . His approach is along the usual lines, encouraging the reader to make a simple rule for addition and then, after describing logarithms, showing how it is possible to put the two ideas together, but he does make things sound decidedly easier than most writers do. This, however, is achieved at the expense of relatively slow progress—we only cover as far as simple multiplication, division, powers and roots in 186 pages.

> *Wilfred Ashworth, in a review of "An Easy Introduction to the Slide Rule," in* The School Librarian and School Library Review, *Vol. 15, No. 2, July, 1967, p. 204.*

THE ROMAN REPUBLIC (1966)

This is the record of Rome from its obscure beginnings until the reign of Augustus. . . . Mr. Asimov's greatest competence and fine reputation were not won in history for younger readers. He is a dogged reciter of digested event and incident. The criticisms we applied to his *The Greeks* . . . hold true for this book—two much, too lightly becomes monotonous surface history without the rewards of extra insight which can be gained by reading through the more confined studies for this age level by G. Foster, D. Mills and O. Coolidge.

> *A review of "The Roman Republic," in* Virginia Kirkus' Service, *Vol. XXXIV, No. 10, May 15, 1966, p. 515.*

[The] author of *The Greeks* has produced a magnificent survey of Rome to 27 B.C. which should definitely be first purchase for all libraries catering to young people. With an amazing knack of sizing up the significant, he presents the why as well as the what and how. Generalizations are surprisingly successful; many details are as fresh as they are illuminating. The scholarship is sound; the style is simple but pleasant. The events and the people involved in them are masterfully characterized. The author admittedly concentrates on soldiers and politicians, at the expense of writers, artists, and everyday life, but even so, any reader will be vastly enlightened. There is no bibliography. All will look forward eagerly to the promised sequel on the Roman Empire.

> *Ursula Schoenheim, in a review of "The Roman Republic," in* Library Journal, *Vol. 91, No. 13, July, 1966, p. 3541.*

Long but not dull, erudite but not pedantic, a history that is well organized and written with flowing ease. The text gives an enormous amount of information, yet it has a conversational quality—a quality due in part to the entertaining digressions about such things as the cumbersome Roman calendar or the real estate speculations of Crassus. . . . A table of dates (both the Christian year and the year from the founding of Rome) and an extensive index are appended.

> *Zena Sutherland, in a review of "The Roman Republic," in* Bulletin of the Center for Children's Books, *Vol. 20, No. 9, May, 1967, p. 134.*

THE UNIVERSE: FROM FLAT EARTH TO QUASAR (1966; revised edition as *The Universe: From Flat Earth to Black Holes— and Beyond*, 1980)

Asimov's reputation as a popularizer of science will surely be enhanced by his latest book. He sets out to trace the history of man's quest for the boundary of the universe and in the process presents an accurate and very readable survey of much current astronomical knowledge. . . . Along with his very accessible (and nonmathematical) introductions to the concepts and measurements of astronomy, Asimov provides tables of numerical data, graphs, sketches and photographs (as well as a detailed index) typical of those found in astronomical textbooks. Yet this work has something more, a sense of direction—almost a plot—which lends coherence as well as suspense and excitement to the presentation of astronomy that traditional texts lack. *The Universe* is among the finest introductions available for those of high school age and older with a serious interest in astronomy.

> *A review of ''The Universe: From Flat Earth to Quasar,'' in* Choice, *Vol. 4, No. 2, April, 1967, p. 181.*

As a thrilling and swiftly moving sketch of man's search for understanding of the mysteries of space and time and the incredible dimensions of astronomy, Asimov's book has few equals. He succeeds in conveying to the reader a feeling of the excitement of the scientist as he probes the unknown. But there is little suggestion of the labor and frustration that is the astronomer's lot. There are essentially three parts to the book. The first is devoted to the historical development of our knowledge of the distances and sizes of celestial objects and the scale of the universe. The second considers time with carefully drawn but not very detailed astrophysical explanations of the evolution and life cycles of stars, clusters, and galaxies. The final section takes up those fascinating questions of the origin of the universe, and the modern questions of quasars, ending with a picture of the universe as we see it now. To some readers, the book, replete with dates and names, but frequently sketchy, may have too much of the flavor of a sugar-coated history of astronomy. . . . The index is good. There is no bibliography, but the practice of detailed identification of each contributing scientist may justify the book's use as a reference. Some of the explanations seem inadequate and even misleading. Perhaps the beauty and sweep of the book will best be appreciated by readers with some knowledge of astronomy who want a book that touches lightly on many topics, but rarely lingers over detail.

> *A review of ''The Universe: From Flat Earth to Quasar,'' in* Science Books, *Vol. 3, No. 1, May, 1967, p. 22.*

Asimov has written prolifically on nearly every field of science, and his clarity, wit and captivating style have combined to inspire many millions of young (and not so young) readers. *The Universe,* with all of these fine qualities of writing, covers much of the field of astronomy, from ancient ideas about the cosmos to the frontier of modern research. The book is not merely a descriptive account; Asimov explains the lines of reasoning that have led to our present knowledge—including many false starts and wrong turns that have had to be corrected. Some of the concepts in *The Universe* are quite sophisticated, and here, alas, is the book's only serious problem. No one can know everything, and Asimov has relied heavily on literature describing current work. In a few places, he has misinterpreted the rather subtle ideas (especially in cosmology). But mainly, he has not consistently selected the best current references, and much of the material on stellar evolution and cosmology is 10 to 25 years out-of-date—a shame for a book with a 1980 copyright. These sections (mostly in Chapters 10 through 15) are sometimes misleading, and account for my rating the book less than excellent. I hope that Asimov revises the book with close advice from astronomers in those fields; it is beautifully written

and deserves to be available and read in a form free from serious error. (pp. 13-14)

> *George O. Abell, in a review of ''The Universe: From Flat Earth to Black Holes and Beyond,'' in* Science Books & Films, *Vol. 17, No. 1, September-October, 1981, pp. 13-14.*

THE MOON (1966)

This straightforward, elementary children's book describes gross physical features of the moon, what it would be like to be on the moon, how the moon looks in the sky, and why there are tides and eclipses. It is reasonably accurate, and has the merit of not being descriptive only, but attempts to impart a quantitative understanding of the physical phenomenon. It should awaken an interest in the moon, and perhaps astronomy and physical science in general. The last two pages, suggesting experiments or problems for home or school study, are excellent. Children should be able to follow the ideas presented, but they may provide a challenge for some teachers.

> *A review of ''The Moon,'' in* Science Books, *Vol. 3, No. 2, September, 1967, p. 103.*

A simply written continuous text, a bit repetitive but clear and accurate. . . . There is no index or table of contents; the text is not very full, but it serves nicely as an introduction to the topic for middle grades readers or for slow older readers.

> *Zena Sutherland, in a review of ''The Moon,'' in* Bulletin of the Center for Children's Books, *Vol. 21, No. 2, October, 1967, p. 21.*

THE ROMAN EMPIRE (1967)

The Table of Contents, a tabulation of ruling lines and rulers, is the tip-off: like its predecessor, *The Roman Republic* . . . , this is detailed political history, reign by reign, in this case, with occasional sorties into literature, philosophy and science. Like its predecessor, too, it suffers from galloping factualitis, with one major exception: the extended treatment of Judaism and early Christianity as intertwined with Roman history. Indeed, the very pragmatic explanation of the successes of Christianity—''It seems to have something to please everyone''—may disturb some fundamentalists. The text characterizes each emperor, identifies his associates and opponents, notes his difficulties and achievements, and tries to correct historical error, to connect trends and terminology to the present. As the Empire progressed (?), life expectancy of the rulers became shorter, and ''the business of the Empire (became) the defense of the Empire''; the characters flash by fighting their battles, and depart, leaving little but footnotes behind them. Despite its positive points, most youngsters will find this unrewardingly tedious and would be better served by a more selective approach.

> *A review of ''The Roman Empire,'' in* Kirkus Service, *Vol. XXXV, No. 5, March 1, 1967, p. 281.*

Many of the major catastrophes of the world might never have had a chance to repeat themselves if all histories could be as easily read and understood as Mr. Asimov's. In this sequel to his *Roman Republic,* he brings a reasonable order out of what could be chaos and succeeds in making it seem as though Roman history were being told for the first time. . . .

[He] moves briskly though five centuries of rapid accessions and depositions of emperors, of greatness and creativity, weakness and corruption, of tyrants and assassinations, military rule, civil wars and disorders. He pauses for word derivations (Caligula and Caracalla both got their names from articles of clothing) and for editorial comments, sometimes amusing, always illuminating. . . .

Then the sixth century began, setting the stage for the Middle Ages and, we hope, the next book by Mr. Asimov. (pp. 357-58)

> *Mary S. Congrave, in a review of "The Roman Empire," in* The Horn Book Magazine, *Vol. XLIII, No. 3, June, 1967, pp. 357-58.*

Though recommended to all libraries owning [*The Roman Republic*], this volume is not equally successful, as it shows signs of speed and features rather odd proportions: half the space is devoted to the Severi and their successors. These periods normally are short-changed but do not really deserve all the space they are given here. An unusually large amount of space is also spent on Christianity, including Christian writers, though literature and all other aspects of "civilization" come off very poorly. It is hoped that young readers will feel inspired to pick up other treatments, though, as in the earlier volume, there is no bibliography to help them.

> *Ursula Schoenheim, in a review of "The Roman Empire," in* Library Journal, *Vol. 92, No. 13, July, 1967, p. 2657.*

TO THE ENDS OF THE UNIVERSE (1967)

This discussion of the size, age, composition, and origin of the universe and of man's expanding knowledge of these subjects is written with Asimov's usual skill. The author has the ability to simplify the complicated processes of astronomy so that their underlying principles are comprehensible to the intelligent reader. The book does not give anything new, but it may serve as a stimulus for the interested. The information presented is generally sound but confusing at times, as the author occasionally seems to slide into his points backwards, building up a discarded theory and then suddenly knocking it apart to show the presently accepted picture. Nevertheless, this is an acceptable treatment of an intriguing and rapidly developing branch of astronomy.

> *James S. Pickering, in a review of "To the Ends of the Universe," in* School Library Journal, *an appendix to* Library Journal, *Vol. 14, No. 1, September, 1967, p. 124.*

This fascinating and complete account of the nature of the universe from the earth and solar systems to distant quasars could be one of the better Asimov books for the juvenile audience. Easily more readable and entertaining than Adler's *The Stars* (which is one of the few books comparable in scope and level), it is quite up to date including discoveries until 1965, the more recent being integrated into theories of the universe which appeared in the early 1900's. The junior high audience will find a wealth of information effectively presented.

> *A review of "To the Ends of the Universe," in* Kirkus Service, *Vol. XXXV, No. 19, October 1, 1967, p. 1221.*

Mr. Asimov takes his readers on an exciting, detailed exploration of their universe. . . . [The] author often anticipates the questions of his young readers. And he answers the questions with as many theories as are presently known to science. The . . . author never sacrifices proper terminology for fear of confusing a young audience. Rather, he explains terms as precisely as possible and uses them correctly. The index is brief but adequate. This is a book that challenges young minds to seek more knowledge with the help of modern technology and as such it is an excellent addition to a personal or reference library.

> *Mrs. Bernard Kueny, in a review of "To the Ends of the Universe," in* Best Sellers, *Vol. 27, No. 17, December 1, 1967, p. 359.*

THE EGYPTIANS (1967)

The Egyptians is a most creditable successor to *The Romans* and *The Greeks* which are Dr. Asimov's other excursions into the interpretation of history for young readers. Written in a style which might be termed virile in its directness and lack of ornamentation, the presentation is factual, without digressions. It is only in those blank or hazy areas which dot Egyptian records that we encounter a more inventive spirit from the author. He gives the Hyksos a more definite image than do most historians and his etymology, as exemplified in the case of the word "labyrinth," to which he gives an Egyptian origin, is sometimes unique. The author's scientific approach lends great clarity to his detailed discussions of mummification, of the engineering feats found everywhere, and of Imhotep, the world's first doctor. His often wryly humorous asides on the consistency of human nature through the ages as well as on its inconsistencies will delight mature younger readers.

> *Edith M. Crawford, in a review of "The Egyptians," in* School Library Journal, *an appendix to* Library Journal, *Vol. 14, No. 5, January, 1968, p. 78.*

Dr. Asimov, our favorite encyclopedist, has provided for the Egyptians in the same superlative manner as he has for the Greeks and Romans. . . .

He traces Egyptian history through dynasties and battles from pre-history (sketchy) to the 1960's (sketchy). The concentration is upon the ancient history of the land and people. An immense wealth of information is provided but with Dr. Asimov's inimitable style one does not become oppressed by the mass of information. His clever, witty, and often biting remarks are not only pertinent but make the reader remember the foibles of the men who made the history. . . .

Dr. Asimov's *Egyptians* is lively, entertaining, accurate, and informative. It is a boon for anyone studying the Egyptians, in school or out. It is most fortunate that so many talents are combined in one man and also that he is so prolific a writer.

> *Phyllis Cohen, in a review of "The Egyptians," in* Young Readers Review, *Vol. IV, No. 6, February, 1968, p. 14.*

An extremely well-written history of Egypt. . . . The weakest portion is the short section devoted to Egypt's prehistory. There is no discussion of the Pleistocene occupation of the area; the book begins with the early agricultural settlements in Egypt around 5000 B.C. The discussion of this late prehistoric period is marred by inaccuracy and oversimplification. The author is clearly an historian and out of his element in dealing with prehistoric Egypt. When he turns his attention to the historical period, however, he does an excellent job. . . . There is an excellent index and a chronology of important events and people placed at the end of the book. Unfortunately, there is no bibliography or list of suggested readings. The book is recommended as an enjoyable introduction to the history of Egypt. (pp. 310-11)

> *A review of "The Egyptians," in* Science Books, *Vol. 3, No. 4, March, 1968, pp. 310-11.*

ENVIRONMENTS OUT THERE (1967)

Isaac Asimov's gift for translating scientific gobbledygook into English is evident in this slim but excellent book. He lucidly explains the conditions of surface, temperature, atmosphere, gravity—and all other factors included in the term environment—that, according to current theories, exist on other planets of the solar system. His arguments are rational, his conclusions logical, and any speculations clearly labeled. He gives the best and simplest explanations of the basic possible chemical combinations that have produced, or could produce, complicated living organisms and the environments within which each could exist. His estimate of the great number of possible life-supporting planets is well reasoned and conservative.

> *James S. Pickering, in a review of "Environments Out There," in* School Library Journal, *an appendix to* Library Journal, *Vol. 14, No. 8, April, 1968, p. 122.*

What an entertaining and informative book this is for 10's up! Veteran science-writer Isaac Asimov handles his material with imagination and verve to give an impression of the alien environments of the moon and the other planets. . . . It would be a delightful addition to any interested young reader's bookshelf.

> *Robert C. Cowen, "New Frontiers of Space," in* The Christian Science Monitor, *May 2, 1968, p. B10.*

In his usual, easy flowing, readable style, some new ideas are set forth which are within the realm of feasibility, but which cannot be analyzed conclusively at this time. Some assertions are stated rather positively, though they are still scientifically doubtful or unproven. Dr. Asimov at times loses accuracy in translating some information from a technical to a popular level. The book ends with speculation concerning space travel in the distant future; its optimism about life throughout the universe approaches a viewpoint of science fiction.

> *A review of "Environments Out There," in* Science Books, *Vol. 4, No. 3, December, 1968, p. 192.*

THE NEAR EAST: 10,000 YEARS OF HISTORY (1968)

Section by section, the Sumerians, Akkadians, Amorites, Assyrians, Chaldeans, Persians, Macedonians, Parthians, Sassanids, Arabs (subsuming Hittites, Medes, Seleucids, etc. etc.)—the whole numbing procession from prehistory to the six-day war made coherent if not uniformly readable (which hardly matters since few are likely to read it through). . . . The first half is the more interesting, and not only because it is the more significant. Bringing his Biblical and etymological studies to bear on the origin and dispersion of legend, Dr. Asimov offers arresting insights on mythology as the ancient attempt at science and as history, specifically on the interpretations of the Jews and the Greeks. He sees Hammurabi's Babylon as maligned by Biblical writers, Nebuchadnezzar's Babylon as responsible for the crystallization and preservation of Jewish identity. Another strong strain is technology—the horse swings

the balance of power to the nomad, exploitation of iron and of the siege aids the Assyrians and debases the nature of warfare. Characterization is frequently adroit: arch-villain Genghis Khan, for example, "had a simple world outlook"—scorn for civilization. This is likely to be consulted primarily for peoples, persons and periods: it will serve well to order information and enlarge understanding.

> *A review of "The Near East: 10,000 Years of History," in* Kirkus Service, *Vol. XXXVI, No. 11, June 1, 1968, p. 607.*

[This] digest survey includes competent reconstructions of legendary material to supplement and interpret the known history. Taken as a whole, this is a good, concise account, more complex and advanced than *Other Bible Lands* by Lovejoy, and for a younger audience than Hitti's *The Near East in History*. Teenage readers may experience some difficulty with the many proper names, but each individual and clan is so well identified and placed in time that no serious confusion results.

> *Frances Fleming, in a review of "The Near East: 10,000 Years of History," in* Library Journal, *Vol. 93, No. 12, June 15, 1968, p. 2544.*

Although the subtitle reads "10,000 Years of History," the first 4,000 of these years are glossed over in less than 15 pages. The rest of the book is a rather simplistic outline of historical events in the Near East since the Sumerian invention of writing. The chronologically ordered cultures outlined by Asimov are the Sumerian, Akkadian, Amorite, Assyrian, Chaldean, Persian, Macedonian, Parthian, Sassanid, Arab, Turkish, and European (although a number of scholars would disagree with his terminology). The scope of the book makes for a number of rather tenuous cultural connections and some confusion in the narrative. Religion, for example, is seen as the primary causal factor of culture change in Mesopotamia (there is little or no mention of the possible importance of economic, political, social, or even ecological factors). The writing itself varies a great deal in quality—from fair (it nowhere approaches the excellence of Asimov's science-fiction) to downright shoddy. . . . There are a number of poor grammatical constructions, some glaring redundancies, and an occasional error in fact. There is no bibliography, and the only useful illustrations consist of a series of 12 maps (of varying accuracy) which outline the territorial extent of Mesopotamian peoples during various time periods. There is a short table of important dates appended. The book may be of some use to the general reader as an outline or summary, but it cannot be recommended for anyone with a serious interest in either the history or development of civilizations in the Near East.

> *A review of "The Near East: 10,000 Years of History," in* Science Books, *Vol. 4, No. 3, December, 1968, p. 252.*

THE DARK AGES (1968)

Not the entire Middle Ages but those justly called *dark* and what came before, from the first southward barbarian drift to the nadir of disintegration between 900 and 950—a stunning consolidation of obscure strands that is lit by humanistic and scholarly perspective. It has to be primarily a chronicle of battles, massacres, successions, usurpations, among people who remain only as place-names (an aspect Mr. Asimov as etymologist makes much of); it is also an education. For example, why do they seem to vanish? Because encroaching aristocracies "were without firm roots among the people . . . they could easily be defeated and replaced by another warrior caste . . . the kingdoms are simply the names we give (them) and don't represent the real population at all." The reader is frequently caught up by a significant observation: on the start of the Middle Ages (Gregory's theology), on the extremism of the Visigoths (their late conversion from Arian to Catholic Christianity); on the descent into feudalism (a response to Norse raids, later rationalized as a system). And so on to the turning point, a curious concatenation: the moldboard plow (and the horse collar), the armored knight, the rescue of ancient learning. No other juvenile compares in scope and depth, and few adult books synthesize so simply and clearly. (pp. 1062-63)

> *A review of "The Dark Ages," in* Kirkus Service, *Vol. XXXVI, No. 18, September 15, 1968, pp. 1062-63.*

The sixth of Asimov's survey histories for junior and senior high school students covers 1000 years of European history ending in the year 1000. Emphasis is on political, military and church affairs; legends, some social history, and geographical interpretations are included. Asimov's tracings of the origins of place names, complementing his earlier *Words on the Map* . . . , are especially interesting. An excellent index makes this a good reference tool as well as absorbing general reading. Charts of the Merovingian, Pepin, and Carolingian dynasties are included, as are useful maps and a comprehensive table of dates.

> *Eleanor P. Hawley, in a review of "The Dark Ages,"* in School Library Journal, *an appendix to* Library Journal, *Vol. 15, No. 5, January, 1969, p. 78.*

Asimov's particular genius is in the ability to present an immensely complicated historical chronicle and to make it both interesting and meaningful without slighting major events or sacrificing colorful minutiae or the minor contributing factors that bring the past to life. Here he examines the growing might of the barbarian tribes in the thousand years before the birth of Christ, the thrust and counter-thrust of Rome and the northern tribes, the Roman decline and the pageant of kings and kingdoms in the long centuries during which learning waned and Christianity quietly grew stronger. (p. 38)

> *Zena Sutherland, in a review of "The Dark Ages,"* in Bulletin of the Center for Children's Books, *Vol. 23, No. 3, November, 1969, pp. 37-8.*

WORDS FROM HISTORY   (1968)

I'm sure Isaac Asimov has discovered the secret of living without sleep. There is no other way to figure out where he finds the time to write, edit, compile all the books he creates. I'm equally sure that everyone who is curious about words, especially about their family trees, will be delighted he has discovered the secret of living without sleep, because they wouldn't want to miss the family trees of these words from history.

> *A review of "Words from History," in* Publishers Weekly, *Vol. 194, No. 25, December 6, 1968, p. 40.*

A good dictionary is of more value than this luxury item, which is only for those libraries which can afford the ephemeral. Arranged alphabetically, 250 words chosen for their historical significance are each accompanied by a page of text which gives origin and frequent cross-references to related material— for example: Dixie (See Jim Crow). . . . [The] style is chatty, the tone condescending, and the writing sloppy. The words

chosen—appeasement, ballyhoo, bloomers, cannibal, crusade, dictator, Munich, and so on—comprise an uneven, rag-tag and bobtail assortment of words of varying familiarity and significance. The information given is too slight for reference use with the 12 and up age group for whom the book is intended, and this work is certainly less useful than the author's similar but more specialized books such as *Words from the Exodus* . . . and *Words on the Map.* . . .

> *Margaret N. Coughlan, in a review of "Words from History," in* School Library Journal, *an appendix to* Library Journal, *Vol. 15, No. 6, February, 1969, p. 70.*

One page is devoted to each word, and this means that on some pages there is historical material that serves as background rather than as the origin of the actual words (for example, the fact that an ottoman is called that because the Ottoman Turks had an overstuffed backless seat; the paragraphs that precede this are pure history) but who cares? The material is made fascinating by the easy conversational style, is informative by virtue of the author's encyclopedic knowledge, and is amplified by an index.

> *Zena Sutherland, in a review of "Words from History," in* Bulletin of the Center for Children's Books, *Vol. 23, No. 4, December, 1969, p. 54.*

THE SHAPING OF ENGLAND   (1969)

Peoples and people involved in *The Shaping of England* from the earliest settlement to the signing of Magna Carta: an assiduous recapitulation that suffers, however, from a surfeit of information, a paucity of interpretation. The successive coming of the neolithic Beaker people, the Celts, the Romans, the Angles, Saxons and Jutes, the Danes and finally the Normans, the role of each of their leaders (and to what extent legendary), plus the fortunes of Christianity, Celtic and Roman, comprise the substance of the book; there is virtually no social or economic underpinning and few large themes. The author draws on his considerable knowledge of literature and word origins to good purpose; less germane is some of his encyclopedic scholarship, as when, having disposed of the Vikings in England, he follows Leif Ericsson to America, then pursues other controversies regarding credit for first discovery. Nevertheless the history is sound, the personae are clearly identified, and all that is speculative is labelled as such. There is of course no other juvenile of comparable scope, which should make this a useful source whatever its weakness as sustained reading.

> *A review of "The Shaping of England," in* Kirkus Reviews, *Vol. XXXVII, No. 9, May 1, 1969, p. 516.*

In this loosely written, conversational, sometimes colloquial account, the author describes accurately and extensively the evolution of England, from pre-historic times to 1215. . . . Contributions of scholars, historians, and prominent churchmen are cited, but the book is essentially a political rather than a social history. Asimov has seemingly concentrated on presenting an unbroken chronicle; as a consequence, perhaps, his material is insufficiently edited, and the more important figures discussed don't stand out. But the book is enlivened by Asimov's frequent explanations of the historical derivation of colorful words and phrases. The lack of bibliography and maps is unfortunate, but since there is no American title comparable to this work in scope and detail, the book is a worthwhile purchase and can be supplemented by Quennell's *Everyday Life in Roman and Anglo-Saxon Times* (Putnam, rev. ed. 1960).

> *Sarita M. Worthing, in a review of "The Shaping of England," in* School Library Journal, *an appendix to* Library Journal, *Vol. 16, No. 1, September, 1969, p. 117.*

This is a book bursting at the seams with facts, dates, pithy comments on derivations of names, and the odd bit of information (not always important but usually fascinating) that most histories omit. The author often analyzes a single act (the decision of William the Conqueror to make the English clergy Norman so that there would be less likelihood of the Saxon culture persisting) but does not often interpret historical trends on a large scale. . . . A list of dates, dynastic tables of English and Scottish kings, and an index are appended.

> *Zena Sutherland, in a review of "The Shaping of England," in* Bulletin of the Center for Children's Books, *Vol. 23, No. 5, January, 1970, p. 75.*

TWENTIETH CENTURY DISCOVERY (1969)

Insects and pesticides, the origin of life, the structure of matter, our solar system, and space travel—this hardly encompasses 20th-century discovery. Einstein and relativity get but two sentences; and Bohr, Fleming, and Watson and Crick, to name but a few, are not mentioned. Asimov is fun to read for he has the ability to write science well and to explain things clearly, but even the few topics he did cover cannot be done full justice in this short but entertaining pot boiler. Suitable for the general public or the lower division college student. Recommended only for browsing collections.

> *A review of "Twentieth Century Discovery," in* Choice, *Vol. 6, No. 8, October, 1969, p. 1033.*

A child picking up this book might be put off by the heavy sounding title, or the fact that the book does not immediately launch into the exploration of space, jet engines and hovercraft. This would be a shame because it is an absorbing story of important and fascinating discoveries of the twentieth century. The final chapter deals with space travel but before that we have anything from insecticides to microwaves. Younger boys may get a little tired of reading it but older boys should find not only that it develops their interest in science but also in the world around them.

> *A review of "Twentieth Century Discovery," in* The Junior Bookshelf, *Vol. 34, No. 4, August, 1970, p. 216.*

Asimov does it again. This indefatigable popularizer has here taken several topics which are very much of our century, dealing with the discoveries and problems involved. . . . Information and interpretation are dispensed as skilfully, as reliably and as readably as ever.

> *H. M. Thomas, in a review of "Twentieth-Century Discovery," in* The School Librarian, *Vol. 18, No. 3, September, 1970, p. 340.*

Asimov at his desk. Photo © copyright Jay Kay Klein.

ABC'S OF SPACE (1969)

Asimov's ability to choose significant terms and formulate crisp definitions, plus a glorious color jacket and good, well-disposed photos . . . make this more than a gimmick if something less than a complete glossary. Though limited to two terms per letter, he manages to insert references to many others in his explanations and with the aid of labeled diagrams. There's no attempt to make the subject as simple as ABC: neither, except in its arrangement, does this resemble an alphabet book. It comes off as an unintimidating approach to the theory and practice of space flight, and should rack up considerable mileage.

A review of "ABC's of Space," in Kirkus Reviews, *Vol. XXXVII, No. 20, October 15, 1969, p. 1115.*

An aggressively topical and, because it uses photographs, novel ABC is Isaac Asimov's *ABC's of Space*. . . . Naturally it starts with "A" for Apollo and "a" for astronaut. But by the time we get to "G" for Goldstone "210" (the largest radio signal receiver) and "H" for Hand-Held Maneuvering Unit (for space walks) one wonders why a child who can say H.H.M.U. needs an alphabet at all. But good to see Quark instead of Quilt and Yaw ousting the ubiquitous Yak.

Roger Jellinek, in a review of "ABC's of Space," in The New York Times Book Review, *November 2, 1969, p. 30.*

Asimov has written an interesting glossary. . . . Most of the words can probably be found in a recent edition of any good standard dictionary, but the large print indicates its suitability for young people who probably are not able to use a standard dictionary with ease. Selected and frequently used space terms the reader will have heard on television are illustrated and defined. Under each word are blanks which invite the reader to insert other "space words" beginning with the same initial letter. . . . It is a useful special book for children, one they will like to have at home or be able to borrow from the school or public library.

A review of "ABC's of Space," in Science Books, *Vol. 5, No. 3, December, 1969, p. 274.*

GREAT IDEAS OF SCIENCE: THE MEN AND THE THINKING BEHIND THEM (1969)

This is good Asimov: the right note of enthusiasm pitched in language eminently suited to a high school audience. Carp you may at the Great Ideas or Breakthrough approach to science, there is the didactic point to be made that the broad sweep serves to put all of science in perspective. The familiar are here: Thales, Aristotle, Galileo, Newton, but Asimov's approach is to home in on what these men did to change the direction or philosophical underpinnings of science rather than the results they may have achieved. Thus Thales is hailed as doing away with demons, Pythagoras for the association of laws of nature with numbers, Galileo for the experimental approach. The brief biographical sketches add color, and, in a world in which scientists are too often presented in ideal lights Asimov is to be complimented for occasionally saying nasty things about Great Men when they were indeed nasty: e.g. Count Rumford—traitor, opportunist, spy, you name it as well as innovator in the study of heat. (pp. 1124-25)

A review of "Great Ideas of Science," in Kirkus Reviews, *Vol. XXXVII, No. 20, October 15, 1969, pp. 1124-25.*

As the companion volume to Asimov's earlier **Breakthroughs in Science** . . . , this book is composed of short essays on famous scientists and their accomplishments. . . . Ten years ago a reviewer suggested of **Breakthroughs** that the "general juvenile encyclopedias give far better coverage of the subjects treated" [see excerpt for **Breakthroughs in Science** (1960) dated December 15, 1960]. We feel that the same criticism is valid for **Great Ideas of Science.** Asimov's theme is that "the universe behaves in accordance with certain laws of nature that cannot be altered or changed," but that "it is possible for human reason to work out the nature of the laws governing the universe." He presents this theme in his initial chapter and subsequently discusses how each scientist's contribution has extended human reason. A formal conclusion restating the theme would have been fitting. Asimov's writing is so terse that the knowledgeable student will want more information (there is no bibliography), while other readers need more information for adequate comprehension. . . . The book has a table of contents, an excellent index and frequent cross references within chapters. (p. 12)

A review of "Great Ideas of Science: The Men and the Thinking behind Them," in Science Books, *Vol. 6, No. 1, May, 1970, pp. 11-12.*

Great Ideas of Science is a superbly written general history of science. Asimov includes practically every major scientist, and many minor ones, in an extremely readable and exciting account of the history of physics, mathematics, biology, and chemistry. The central theme, that of the progressive emergence of "great ideas" in science (e.g. atoms, fields, evolution, quanta), is masterfully used as the backbone for the presentation of the historical material. The scientific accuracy is excellent, with complex concepts expressed in an uncommonly simple manner. I would recommend this book highly to every child with even the slightest interest in science.

Shirley Roe, in a review of "Great Ideas of Science," in Appraisal: Children's Science Books, *Vol. 4, No. 3, Fall, 1971, p. 4.*

ABC'S OF THE OCEAN (1970)

This uneven title, similar in format to the author's *ABC's of Space*. . . , tries to cover too much and covers nothing well. Fifty-six terms in oceanography, from A to Z, are defined in large print; these definitions are generally satisfactory as far as they go. Greek and Latin origins are given for some of them, as is pronunciation for the more difficult ones. However, the ABC format is misleading. The vocabulary is much too difficult for beginning readers and would turn off better ones. Some of the terms are capitalized, although there is no grammatical reason for doing so. . . . On balance, this title could serve only as a very general introduction or to stimulate further reading.

Judith Sima, in a review of "ABC's of the Ocean," in School Library Journal, *an appendix to* Library Journal, *Vol. 17, No. 6, February, 1971, p. 54.*

This is an appropriate book for a personal, school or public library. . . . The terms are correctly defined and the explanations are understandable. Blank spaces are provided for terms the reader may wish to write in. This reviewer's only reservation is the choice of several terms; some seem inappropriate or not in common usage especially for a children's book.

A review of "ABC's of the Ocean," in Science Books, *Vol. 7, No. 1, May, 1971, p. 42.*

This is a delightful alphabet book for eight to ten year old oceanographers. . . . Mr. Asimov's oceanography primer is timely, informative, and motivating. The format and facts lend themselves to easy comprehension by the student and do much to foster an awareness of and interest in the future of another developing scientific discipline.

Robert J. Stein, in a review of "ABC's of the Ocean," in Appraisal: Children's Science Books, *Vol. 5, No. 1, Winter, 1972, p. 6.*

WHAT MAKES THE SUN SHINE? (1971)

The questions that this excellent book will raise in the minds of young readers will tax even our better teachers. The book puts the elementary student on the brink of inquiry into cosmology, quantum theory, and chemistry. There are a few places in which the author or editor could have been more careful in choosing words but they are minor distractions. The author considers the formation of the solar system from a gas cloud and the ways in which this might have occurred. The book would be appropriate collateral reading for seventh-grade science students although it is aimed at advanced elementary readers.

A review of "What Makes the Sun Shine?" in Science Books, *Vol. 7, No. 1, May, 1971, p. 122.*

Simple experiments throughout the text on the formation of the solar system complement the step-by-step explanation of what the sun's energy consists of, how it works, and what it does. The glossary/index and . . . [Marc Brown's] illustrations offer further clarification. For the most part this is a well-written book which should satisfy questioners and stimulate further inquiry by young science fans.

Jane Granstrom, in a review of "What Makes the Sun Shine?" in Appraisal: Children's Science Books, *Vol. 5, No. 2, Spring, 1972, p. 3.*

THE BEST NEW THING (1971)

Two children who have lived all their lives on a small world far out in space learn, first from their parents and then from experience on a trip to Earth by spaceship, about such things as gravity, blue sky, and green grass. Presented in a picture-book format this science fiction for the very young is slight, espcially its ending, but the turnabout approach to space and gravity is unique. . . .

A review of "The Best New Thing," in The Booklist, *Vol. 68, No. 5, November 1, 1971, p. 244.*

[**The Best New Thing**] is a truly exceptional book—indicating what can be done with scientific material in children's books. . . .

In addition to the fascinating details of space life, there is the anticipation of a trip to earth—and Asimov's "message" becomes clear. What the children delight in are the simplest pleasures the earth affords—the blueness of the sky, the warmth of the sun, the smell of flowers, the touch of a breeze against the skin, and yes, even the joys of gravity itself. . . . [As] we all cast our eyes longingly toward outer space, Asimov brings

us back to earth, shows us what we'll leave behind and reminds us that it is good.

Barry Ivker, "For Tomorrow's Naturalists," in The Christian Science Monitor, *November 11, 1971, p. B4.*

ABC'S OF THE EARTH (1971)

Another ill-conceived anomaly by the makers of **ABC's of Space** . . . and **ABC's of the Ocean**. . . . For every letter of the alphabet there is an upper case and a lower case word related to geology but not in any way related to the preceding or following entries. Thus Kame and kettle (both made by glaciers) are separated from the more important "G" entry by the H, I and J words, and even "Earthquake" and "Fault" are split by "erosion." The scale of the concepts too is constantly changing: "C" goes from "Cave" to "continent." (And why does Cave get the capital letter?) Each word is followed by a brief definition-description, but though some of the discussions and accompanying diagrams are clarifying (gravity, for one), the selection of entries is arbitrary if not capricious (why xenon, a gas that makes up one ten-millionth of the air, except that it starts with x?), and there are not enough of them to make the book a reliable glossary. . . . Considering that children old enough for the contents don't want an ABC, it's hard to imagine any point to this wholly gratuitous earth catalog.

A review of "ABC's of the Earth," in Kirkus Reviews, *Vol. XXXIX, No. 23, December 1, 1971, p. 1258.*

The text is generally stimulating, somewhat more advanced [than the two-color pictures], and can serve as a springboard for discussion. In places, it may be oversimplified or slightly inaccurate. The alphabetical arrangement's lack of continuity naturally obviates the book's use as a text. It is more suitable for the browsing shelves of an elementary school library.

A review of "ABC's of the Earth," in Science Books, *Vol. 8, No. 1, May, 1972, p. 36.*

Mesas are found where Spanish-speaking people lived, and Xenon comprises less than one ten-millionth of the earth's atmosphere. These and other generally accurate but often trivial and totally unrelated facts about 52 earth-science terms arranged in alphabetical order can only confuse and frustrate any young reader who is looking for either coherent information or a comprehensive glossary. The book's title, conveying as it does the image of both simplicity and thoroughness, presents a sadly erroneous impression.

Ronald J. Kley, in a review of "ABC's of the Earth," in Appraisal: Children's Science Books, *Vol. 5, No. 3, Fall, 1972, p. 6.*

THE LAND OF CANAAN (1971)

By focusing on Canaan from prehistoric times to the final triumph of Rome in 135 A.D., the author has provided the junior-high-school historian with a thought-provoking, readable study, which also demonstrates the need for reexamining the facts of history from various perspectives. Although no bibliography is included, a comprehensive table of dates is appended as well as lists of kings. Pronunciation for unfamiliar names is given in the text rather than in the index. (pp. 60-1)

Mary M. Burns, in a review of "The Land of Canaan," in The Horn Book Magazine, *Vol. XLVIII, No. 1, February, 1972, pp. 60-1.*

That strip of land called the Fertile Crescent (now divided between Syria, Lebanon, Israel, and Jordan) has a long and intricate history, which Asimov presents with his usual ebullient confidence. . . . [The text] includes such a mass of names, dates, and events that the reader may be overwhelmed. But the writing is lucid and cohesive, the information authoritative, and the discussion of Judaism and Christianity especially perceptive. (pp. 80-1)

Zena Sutherland, in a review of "The Land of Canaan," in Saturday Review, *Vol. LV, No. 8, February 19, 1972, pp. 80-1.*

A dull, careless account dealing with the earliest known history of Canaan. . . . The discussions of the Persian and Punic wars provide the book's only interest, and these conflicts are treated in many other books. Asimov presents conjecture as accepted history (what he calls "true facts"!) and fails to document or offer some reference for these kinds of assertions: e.g., "Tyre worshipped the goddess Astarte, with fertility rites that had a strong emotional appeal and with the kind of elaborate mummery that seemed to please women in particular." The observation that ". . . from the time of Ezra onward, Jews were different from the surrounding peoples and deliberately cultivated the difference. This resulted in the growth of religious intolerance, something the world had seen little of until then. The Jew could not make that intolerance effective, of course, sine they were so few in numbers. The view was, however, inherited by Christianity and Islam, and intolerance than became a world tragedy . . ." inaccurately implies that views are inherited and inappropriately lays all the blame on Jews. Asimov's description of Ezra's program for Jewish separateness as "racial purity" and his statement that ". . . the Philistines might expect danger from the Arameans, another group of tribes of the sort endlessly spawned by the fecundity of the inhabitants of the dry Arabian peninsula" are examples of inexcusable prejudice. There is no bibliography, the style is uninteresting and the choice of words often crude ("Hezekiah was penned up in Jerusalem like a rat in a cage."). Van Loon's *The Story of the Bible* (Grosset, 1966) would be more useful for students.

Bernard Poll, in a review of "The Land of Canaan," in School Library Journal, *an appendix to* Library Journal, *Vol. 18, No. 9, May, 1972, p. 83.*

THE STORY OF RUTH (1972)

Isaac Asimov presents the story of Ruth as a plea for brotherhood, written originally as a dissent from Ezra's prohibition of mixed marriages (it contends that King David himself was descended from a non Jew). His admirably clear introduction describes the situation in Jerusalem after the return from Babylonia (when Ruth was written) and the hostility toward Moabites which dates from Balaam's curses on the army of Moses, while painstaking commentary—explaining the custom of levirate marriage, the charitable practice of allowing gleaners to follow the harvest, and the probable motivations of all concerned—alternates with the verses of *Ruth* as translated for the *New English Bible*. Indeed, everything is spelled out in so much detail that the flow of the narrative is lost; this is not, then, a way of meeting the virtues of Ruth for the first time, but a teaching tool which answers all possible questions after the fact.

A review of "The Story of Ruth," in Kirkus Reviews, *Vol. XL, No. 15, August 1, 1972, p. 861.*

The beautiful Biblical story of Ruth and her mother-in-law Naomi is the subject of detailed analysis and interpretation. . . . Liberal quotations from earlier books of the Bible are given to support or enlighten the discussion. A subject that could be confusing and dull is made very readable by the informal, conversational style and the clear logic of the presentation.

Beryl Robinson, in a review of "The Story of Ruth," in The Horn Book Magazine, *Vol. XLVIII, No. 5, October, 1972, p. 477.*

An explanation of the book of "Ruth" which begins by presenting Jewish history as background and stresses Ezra's biblical argument against Christian-Jewish intermarriage. Ruth, a Christian, married a Jew to become one of King David's ancestors, and therefore, since Jewish-Christian relationships were bettered, Ezra concluded that intermarriage is not always harmful. Asimov argues that Ezra was wrong in that Jews have continued to be suspicious and rejecting of outsiders. He moralizes by stating that people should be less narrow-minded and should judge others as individuals. This seems to be a limited interpretation of "Ruth." Readers are not given other explanations; perhaps the social patterns described may be intended to explain ways of acting in those times and inheritance rules. It has also been argued that many Jews did accept strangers and did intermarry. Asimov's writing will disappoint readers and his picture of Ruth comes through as nothing more than a dutiful and subservient woman. A better interpretation of Ruth's story is found in Maud and Miska Petersham's *Ruth* (Macmillan, 1958), even though it is geared to a younger audience. (pp. 113-14)

Bernard Poll, in a review of "The Story of Ruth," in School Library Journal, *an appendix to* Library Journal, *Vol. 19, No. 7, March, 1973, pp. 113-14.*

ABC'S OF ECOLOGY (1972)

This is the fourth of Asimov's ABC books and like the others it suffers from the inaptness of the concept itself. With alphabetical rather than logical order dictating the arrangement, such incongruous pairings as *bark beetle* and *biome, carbon monoxide* and *conservation, game refuge* and *garbage*, are inevitable. So too are such arcane X's as *xerophyle* and *xylophage* following the self-evident *weather* (defined as "the changing conditions of the air. . . . It can be windy, rainy, snowy, foggy, cold or hot.") As for the paragraphs' contents, what is a child to make of the announcement that "A is for *additive*, a material added for improvement. . . . Sometimes additives can harm the body"? Then there is the statement on *detergent*, that "if too much gets into lakes and rivers, it can change the balance of nature," with no hint of how this happens, and three entries later a paragraph on *eutrophication*, with no mention of detergent. The book is printed on recycled paper and we can assume too that it's compiled from scraps of recycled data out of Dr. A's copious files.

A review of "ABC's of Ecology," in Kirkus Reviews, *Vol. XL, No. 17, September 1, 1972, p. 1030.*

Each amplified definition . . . usually [relates] to the effect on man's environment. The brief, clearly phrased explanations do not give a sequential picture, but the bits and pieces form a vivid and effective collage of facts.

> *Zena Sutherland, in a review of "ABC's of Ecology," in* Bulletin of the Center for Children's Books, *Vol. 26, No. 4, December, 1972, p. 53.*

MORE WORDS OF SCIENCE (1972)

In *More Words of Science,* Isaac Asimov exhibits, as he did in his 1959 *Words of Science* (to which this book is a sequel), the same deep attention to the science of words as he does to science. Dr. Asimov's knowledge of his subjects embraces their etymology, lending, in most cases, a simple clarity to even the more complex definitions.

Added to the author's 1500 basic terms in the earlier volume are 250 more entries selected from the live vocabularies of physics, astrophysics, space exploration, chemistry, biochemistry, biology, medicine, genetics and quantum mechanics, plus a number of these fields' specialized subdivisions.

From *ablation* to *zpg*, a full page is devoted to each definition. This page-length treatment permits a scope and style most dictionaries, including children's encyclopedias, do not attempt. Asimov's mode explores both the development of the term he explains and of the idea, process, theory, hardware, organ, cell, behavior or astral body he has selected, defining these subjects' importance to us. Latin and Greek roots for words (often more informative than their modern derivatives) as well as words simply examined as they are, from modern foreign languages, form part of each definition. A full amount of knowledge is packed into each of these small essays. . . .

In all, there is excellent balance struck among the disciplines of biology, anthropology, astronomy, chemistry and physics. Not much, if anything, has suffered neglect. This is an excellent work of modern-day reference, surely—but, more than that, a book that can be read, enjoyably, simply for the sake of reading and learning. I can think of no upper age limit for its perusal.

> *Robert J. Anthony, in a review of "More Words of Science," in* The New York Times Book Review, *September 10, 1972, p. 10.*

More Words of Science takes up where the earlier volume left off and provides the reader with 250 more clearly and interestingly written explanations. Very often, books of this sort are useful only as references; by contrast, *More Words of Science* is so well written that many people will want to read it cover to cover. The book is not a dictionary of science terms. Each word is given a page-long narrative which goes considerably beyond the minimum. Drawn from all fields of science, the terms and their explanatory essays are thoroughly indexed. Cross-references have been avoided, however, in order to do away with the annoyance of flipping from one page to another. *More Words of Science* can be highly recommended to general readers who seek a pleasant and non-threatening introduction to a broad spectrum of words from the language of science.

> *A review of "More Words of Science," in* Science Books, *Vol. 8, No. 3, December, 1972, p. 211.*

HOW DID WE FIND OUT THE EARTH IS ROUND? (1972)

A discussion of the beliefs about the earth that were held in the ancient world, and of the theories proposed by early scientists: the world was flat, was a bowl, was a cyclinder, et cetera. The text concludes with the hypotheses advanced by Philolaus, Aristotle, Eratosthenes, and Ptolemy and with the explorations of Columbus and Magellan. The writing is lucid and the material accurate and well-organized; this hasn't the wit and polish of Asimov's writing for older readers, but it is a good introduction to astronomy in a series that emphasizes the history of scientific discoveries. An index is appended.

> *Zena Sutherland, in a review of "How Did We Find Out the Earth Is Round?" in* Bulletin of the Center for Children's Books, *Vol. 26, No. 9, May, 1973, p. 134.*

This is an excellent little book on the history of man's discovery that the earth is round. . . . It successfully subverts the common myth that everyone believed the earth was flat until Columbus' voyage in 1492 by showing that the round-earth theory was a product of Greek science. The only criticism I have about scientific accuracy concerns the discussion of Aristotle, in which it is maintained that Aristotle's view was that "everything was attracted toward the center of the earth." There is absolutely no force even remotely resembling gravity in Aristotle's physics, for he believed that objects fell to the earth because that was their natural place, not because "they are pulled down toward the center." Apart from this glaring error, the book is well-written and should impart, even to the young reader, a sense of the excitement of scientific reasoning.

> *Shirley Roe, in a review of "How Did We Find Out the Earth Is Round?" in* Appraisal: Children's Science Books, *Vol. 6, No. 3, Fall, 1973, p. 7.*

It takes perseverance to get into the text, which is so much more interesting than it looks. The facts are there and logical explanations for seeming mysteries are presented with imagination. The author poses questions and answers them with science allied to a certain literary style.

> *M. R. Hewitt, in a review of "How Did We Find Out the Earth Is Round?" in* The Junior Bookshelf, *Vol. 41, No. 4, August, 1977, p. 228.*

THE SHAPING OF NORTH AMERICA FROM EARLIEST TIMES TO 1763 (1973)

Isaac Asimov once again demonstrates his breathtaking capacity for cramming in more facts per page than any of the competition. This sweeping survey of the "shaping" of North America by Europeans moves from the voyages of the Vikings (and the likelihood of possible predecessors) to 1763 and includes not only the most famous explorers and lasting colonies but a host of minor voyages, abortive settlements . . . and thumbnail histories of each of the American colonies. . . . Of course, considering the pace, there's not much time to enlarge on any of [the] events or to consider social and cultural developments. Since most collections are well stocked with alternatives to Mr. Asimov's voracious consumption of historical data on this period, *The Shaping of North America* will probably be less serviceable than his previous round-ups on *The Near East, Canaan, England, France,* etc.

A review of "The Shaping of North America," in Kirkus Reviews, *Vol. XLI, No. 3, February 1, 1973, p. 126.*

Asimov does as good a job of making Colonial History exciting, human and interesting as any historian this reviewer has read. By chopping his subject into short sub-chapters, he makes each segment clear and understandable. At the same time, one never loses sight of the whole picture. "Indians" and Blacks are accorded fair treatment, though the main thrust concerns the European colonization. One wishes that Asimov had listed the sources from which he took his superbly chosen anecdotes. Good line cuts, seven maps, a table of dates, and an index all contribute to this fine volume. Highly recommended for all school and public libraries.

Joseph F. Lindenfeld, in a review of "The Shaping of North America," in Children's Book Review Service, *Vol. 1, No. 9, May, 1973, p. 54.*

The wide scope leads to sweeping generalizations, and some of Asimov's statements are controversial. However, the easy-to-read style makes the text accessible to students needing a broad-based introduction to this period, and it may provoke them to further investigation. There is a good index and a detailed chronology but no bibliography.

Johanna Hanson, in a review of "The Shaping of North America: From Earliest Times to 1763," in School Library Journal, *an appendix to* Library Journal, *Vol. 20, No. 1, September, 1973, p. 79.*

HOW DID WE FIND OUT ABOUT ELECTRICITY? (1973)

[Isaac Asimov] takes a historical view of science in *How Did We Find Out About Electricity?* . . . His well-told account concentrates on the knowledge of electricity in the 19th century, mentioning little of the vast burgeoning of our knowledge and use of this resource in our own century. . . .

For the young readers living in a technological world of electromagnetic know-how employed in radar, satellites, rockets, and the release of nuclear energy, the book may seem dated.

However, it does provide good historical background for setting up many simple electro-magnetic experiments—although no guide to such an active learning experience has been included.

Sally Cartwright, "Books to Make Nature Lovers," in The Christian Science Monitor, *May 2, 1973, p. B4.*

This is a very well-written history of man's discovery of electrical and magnetic phenomena. . . . Some discussion occurs at the end of the book on practical uses and inventions, including lightning rods, electromagnets, electric motors, the telegraph, the telephone and the light bulb. However, although the book concludes with the present-day uses of electricity, the science stops with 19th-century theory. The reader may be left thinking that electricity is a fluid that flows from one object to another. Some mention, however brief, should have been made of the 20th-century developments in atomic theory which account for this fluid-like behavior on the basis of the interaction of subatomic particles, primarily electrons. Although it may not have been Mr. Asimov's intent to deal with this aspect of man's knowledge about electricity, the result could be somewhat misleading.

Shirley Roe, in a review of "How did We Find Out about Electricity?" in Appraisal: Children's Science Books, *Vol. 6, No. 3, Fall, 1973, p. 6.*

JUPITER, THE LARGEST PLANET (1973)

A scientist for all seasons and most subjects, Asimov delves into every aspect of what is known about Jupiter, theories of the past, present knowledge, and conjectures about future probes and findings. The text is firmly organized and is written with a lucid informality that is occasionally lightened by a quip. Jupiter is compared to other planets in reference to whiteness, oblateness, speed of rotation, axial tilt, mass, density, orbital speed, etc. The same close scrutiny is applied to the planet's satellites,, and all of the information is summarized in tables, fifty-four of them. There are discussions of the problems yet to be explored, descriptions of what is visible from Jupiter's surface and from its satellites, and theories of Jupiter's formation. A thorough treatment, a good introduction for the layman, and a demonstration of how exciting scientific inquiry can be. A glossary and an index are appended. (pp. 1-2)

Zena Sutherland, in a review of "Jupiter: The Largest Planet," in Bulletin of the Center for Children's Books, *Vol. 27, No. 1, September, 1973, pp. 1-2.*

This is a thorough study of Jupiter for the budding astronomer. The facts about the giant planet are presented in the logical order of historical discovery. . . . What one has in this book is not only a detailed portrait of Jupiter, but also a survey of the entire solar system, a history of planetary astronomy, and an introduction to astronomical method. Only Asimov could fit all that into one book and keep it readable. Some of the explanations do require a strong ability to visualize, but for those who can do it, it will only increase their interest in and appreciation of the subject. Recommended for any young people's or adult's astronomy collection going beyond basic star-gazing guides. The revised edition has been updated to include the most recent findings from the Pioneer probes; most of this information is included in the tables, the text remaining substantially the same. There is a list of charts as well as an index.

Daphne Ann Hamilton, in a review of "Jupiter: The Largest Planet," in Appraisal: Children's Science Books, *Vol. 9, No. 3, Fall, 1976, p. 7.*

Dr. Asimov has updated this book—originally issued in 1973, before the Pioneer data became available—extremely well. Once again, he was caught by the discovery of the fourteenth satellite, but this happens to all of us. I particularly liked the tabular arrangement of data, making it extremely easy to compare factors from different parts of the book. This is not to belittle the verbal descriptions, such as those of the appearance of the sky from various parts of the Jovian system. One hesitates to state that he has caught Dr. Asimov in a mistake, but I think he is wrong on page 163 in saying that eclipses of the sun by other Jovian satellites can never be seen from Callisto. I have no difficulty in visualizing situations in which they *would* be visible, and don't follow his argument; either he is aware of something I am not, or is taking something for granted which is not so. I'll risk my reputation on the latter. (p. 7)

Harry C. Stubbs, in a review of "Jupiter: The Largest Planet," in Appraisal: Children's Science Books, *Vol. 9, No. 3, Fall, 1976, pp. 7-8.*

HOW DID WE FIND OUT ABOUT NUMBERS? **(1973)**

This history of numbers from prehistoric times to the present details how man learned to count more efficiently. Explained are the numerals developed by the Egyptians and Mayans, the disadvantages of the Roman system, the need for a symbol indicating no quantity, and the improvements made by the Indo-Arabic system which is used almost exclusively today. Asimov's treatment is too detailed for young children and is filled with tedious examples which will bore older readers. . . . Children will be better served by Leonard Simon and Jeanne Bendick's *The Day the Number Disappeared* (McGraw, 1963) and Irving and Ruth Adler's *Numbers Old and New* (John Day, 1960).

> *Sandra Weir, in a review of "How Did We Find Out about Numbers?" in* School Library Journal, *an appendix to* Library Journal, *Vol. 20, No. 1, September, 1973, p. 120.*

Each book in [the "How Did We Find Out About"] series emphasizes the process of discovery, but in this particular book there seems to be very little discovery to be described. Yet Asimov has written a clear and accurate history book about numbers. He has provided accurate information on origin of names of numbers; symbols for numbers (Roman and Arabic); and the Hindu origin of zero, vital to today's sophisticated number usage. . . . The book could supplement standard history texts in the elementary school or be a good choice for a book report for language arts classes. Certainly this is a book which should be available in school and public libraries. (pp. 325-26)

> *A review of "How Did We Find Out about Numbers?" in* Science Books, *Vol. IX, No. 4, March, 1974, pp. 325-26.*

This is one of the very many Asimovian divertissements for the nimble minded student. . . . In his usual computer-like style of writing, Mr. Asimov manages to include every related idea or fact along the way and yet make an interesting little ten-finger exercise for a fifth or sixth grade math class. The book is amusing and informative, but not a vital purchase.

> *Heddie Kent, in a review of "How Did We Find Out about Numbers?" in* Appraisal: Children's Science Books, *Vol. 7, No. 2, Spring, 1974, p. 9.*

HOW DID WE FIND OUT ABOUT DINOSAURS? **(1973)**

This is the fourth volume in Asimov's "How Did We Find Out . . ." series which aims at reader participation in the process of discovery, but there is nothing in his lackluster survey of fossil finds and dinosaur features to stimulate any kind of mental activity. The first half of the book, which doesn't mention dinosaurs, skims through some landmarks in natural history from the 1500's on (Gesner—"the first man to draw pictures of fossils," Bonnet's disaster theory to reconcile fossils with the Bible, Linnaeus' system of classification, Darwin's theory of evolution) and might have better been entitled "How We Found Out the Earth Wasn't Created in Six Days." The pages on dinosaurs themselves, after the usual mention of Mary Anning who found the first ichthyosaur and plesiosaur remains, is simply a rundown on the size, names, build and eating habits of a few of the better known species—and as such surely superfluous.

> *A review of "How Did We Find Out about Dinosaurs?" in* Kirkus Reviews, *Vol. XLI, No. 21, November 1, 1973, p. 1203.*

If one is interested in dinosaurs (and certainly there is a lively interest among young children) and in the general subject of evolution, *How Did We Find Out About Dinosaurs?* will be most welcome. This very intriguing study with its considerable number of unanswered questions is clearly outlined in Mr. Asimov's little but busy book. It's nice to have the facts about evolution put tidily in order where one can easily follow them and, better still, remember them. The names of the ancient animals and of the men (and one woman) who found them are spelled phonetically as they are introduced. The process of assigning the various fossil finds to the proper species and genera, ordinarily a confusing thing, is so simply explained that children older than the usual readers of dinosaur books will find it useful.

> *Heddie Kent, in a review of "How Did We Find Out about Dinosaurs?" in* Appraisal: Children's Science Books, *Vol. 7, No. 2, Spring, 1974, p. 9.*

Any large fossil animal is a dinosaur to most children. Asimov's book will not erase this misconception, for his emphasis is on the history of the recognition of fossils as extinct animals. "Dinosaurs" were probably used to capture a larger audience for the book. . . . Asimov's text is clear and highly readable. . . . This is a good introductory story to the history of paleontology, but the reader searching for information on dinosaurs will be disappointed.

> *A review of "How Did We Find Out about Dinosaurs?" in* Science Books, *Vol. X, No. 1, May, 1974, p. 70.*

THE BIRTH OF THE UNITED STATES, 1763-1816 **(1974)**

Chronologically and methodologically this carries on the narrative begun in *The Shaping of North America* . . . by condensing into one volume the political and military highlights of the Revolution, the Constitution, the war in the west, the Federalist-Anti-Federalist struggles, foreign policy and other problems of the new nation. Like other Asimov histories, *The Birth of the United States* is comprehensive, thorough, and immediately suggests itself as a utilitarian one volume text and reference. However, Asimov fastens on only one discernible theme—the country's establishment of its national security through military actions which culminated in the War of 1812. Equally important issues, such as constitutional debates, Hamilton's financial policies, and the Jay Treaty, are adequately summarized but hardly developed. Furthermore virtually no attention is paid to the social conditions under which ordinary citizens lived, only the most famous personalities and anecdotes (Patrick Henry, Nathan Hale, etc.) are scrutinized, and insight and commentary is held to a minimum. Asimov parallels but only incidentally supplements the material found in most high school level American history texts, though his clear and orderly recapitulation will make this a handy alternative to the standard required reading.

> *A review of "The Birth of the United States: 1763-1816," in* Kirkus Reviews, *Vol. XLII, No. 5, March 1, 1974, p. 252.*

A sequel to *The Shaping of North America* is written in the same easy, flowing, and informal style; again Asimov's fresh viewpoint gives vitality to a portion of our history that will be familiar to most readers. The insertion of birth dates after the first mention of almost every figure is slightly distracting but may be useful. . . . [This book] doesn't give the reader the broad picture of trends, movements, and the lives of ordinary citizens that Daniel Boorstin does in *The Landmark History of the American People: From Plymouth to Appomattox* but it's far less dry and just as informative as most history texts. A table of dates and a relative index, both extensive, are appended.

> *Zena Sutherland, in a review of "The Birth of the United States 1763-1816," in* Bulletin of the Center for Children's Books, *Vol. 28, No. 3, November, 1974, p. 37.*

While the book is not burdened with references and details of other research, Dr Asimov does provide a good narrative, eminently readable and soundly based on fact. The paragraphs are short and terse, the spelling American. . . . An excellent book for the non-specialist and sixth-form historian who is beginning a study of the USA.

> *Charles Hannam, in a review of "The Birth of the United States, 1763-1816," in* The School Librarian, *Vol. 23, No. 2, June, 1975, p. 154.*

HOW DID WE FIND OUT ABOUT VITAMINS? (1974; British edition as *How We Found Out about Vitamins*)

A clear, concise account of the discovery of vitamins and their role in nutrition, written in simple declarative prose for children. . . . Asimov presents a story of rational research leading to discovery and definitive knowledge. His doctors and chemists don't follow many wrong leads or leap to conclusions, but he has probably included all that is possible in this short presentation. The author does not avoid difficult, accurate chemical terms, and the book is full of the kind of facts and data that some older elementary children take delight in and will remember for the rest of their lives.

> *George E. Hein, in a review of "How Did We Find Out about Vitamins?" in* Science Books & Films, *Vol. XI, No. 2, September, 1975, p. 96.*

Asimov's easy-to-read account of the discovery of vitamins is brilliantly written. Using an historical approach, the author traces the experiments that led to the discovery of the different vitamins. This exciting presentation is both scientifically and historically accurate. The index should make this book useful to students in the upper elementary grades. (pp. 3-4)

> *Herbert J. Stoltz, in a review of "How Did We Find Out about Vitamins?" in* Appraisal: Children's Science Books, *Vol. 8, No. 3, Fall, 1975, pp. 3-4.*

Intelligent simplifying is the most obvious characteristic of Asimov's *How we found out about Vitamins,* a sustained discussion of the stages by which vitamins were gradually identified and described. The earlier part of the book, offering dates for experiments from the early 1900's and pointing to discoveries about scurvy and pellagra before that date, does perhaps make scientific research seem more instantaneous than it really is, but children around twelve or so should be able to follow the clear account of the atomic structure of vitamins and the reason for the creation of artificial forms. The author takes a cool look at experiments on laboratory animals (and on some American life—prisoners) with no suggestion that this might

be a controversial issue; though the book is clearly meant to be expository rather than polemical, it would be natural for parts of it to lead to discussions of a social kind.

> *Margery Fisher, in a review of "How We Found Out about Vitamins," in* Growing Point, *Vol. 22, No. 3, September, 1983, p. 4125.*

OUR FEDERAL UNION: THE UNITED STATES FROM 1816-1865 (1975)

Electoral politics and the military events of the Civil War are the main threads of Asimov's narrative and he moves briskly through a tortuously complex era. But though Asimov strives for neutrality throughout, his choice of subject matter gives this history an establishment cast—the Seminole War, for example, becomes merely an incident in Spanish-American relations, and the Treaty of Guadalupe Hidalgo is hardly more than a footnote to military victory. And there is certainly little indication here that this was the age of canals and railroads. Cultural history, though it slips in sideways now and then, is barely covered. Asimov does appreciate the ironies of foreign policy—during these years the United States often considered itself the standard bearer for world revolution while Russia defended traditional regimes. And the unfussy outline of presidential policies and the solidification of our two-party tradition (which clarifies the importance of on-issue parties like the Anti-Masons) makes this a useful overview and a good point of departure for more specialized studies.

> *A review of "Our Federal Union: The United States from 1816-1865," in* Kirkus Reviews, *Vol. XLIII, No. 9, May 1, 1975, p. 523.*

The major issues promoting sectionalism and the immediate causes and important campaigns of the Civil War are clearly defined. Unfortunately, the account is cluttered with unnecessary facts (e.g., that Houston is the largest city in the United States to be named for an American), and the author's insists on providing in parenthesis the date and place of birth for every figure introduced. . . . [The] text, accompanied by several maps and a table of dates, will be useful as a factual survey for junior high and slow high school readers.

> *Michael Ann Moskowitz, in a review of "Our Federal Union: The United States from 1816 to 1865," in* School Library Journal, *Vol. 22, No. 6, February, 1976, p. 50.*

THE HEAVENLY HOST (1975)

Christmas future looks even worse than the present in Isaac Asimov's *The Heavenly Host.* . . . Land-grabbing colonizers are ready to overrun Anderson II unless the indigenous solar-powered stones are proven "intelligent" (by human standards, of course). Twelve-year-old Jonathan, visiting with his planetary inspector mother, engineers a stunt that saves the stones from pulverization: he has the Little Rocks hover overhead in Star of Bethlehem formation. Paying lip service to universal peace, this rock-bottom sci fi is disturbing for the extraterrestrial imperialism it touts. (p. 80)

> *Pamela D. Pollack, "Claustrophobia: Closing In On Christmas '75," in* School Library Journal, *Vol. 22, No. 2, October, 1975, pp. 78-81.*

Here's a perfect [book] to treat the already confirmed science fiction reader, or to entice the novice down the sci-fi trail, with an extra bonus in a Christmas finale. . . .

A quick build-up to a gentle Christmas climax leaves a happy feeling. We all rejoice as man has been saved, just in time, from pushing something (or someone) thoughtlessly out of his way. The story is simple and easy to follow, not always true of science fiction. With a little introduction to your readers in grades 3-7, *Heavenly Host* will soar!

> *Mrs. John G. Gray, in a review of "The Heavenly Host," in* Best Sellers, *Vol. 36, No. 1, April, 1976, p. 29.*

[It] is unlikely that this novel, a science fiction Christmas story, will further enhance [Asimov's] reputation. (p. 204)

Asimov's novel is a strangely anachronistic book. . . . The colonists live, think, and form value judgments as if they are unaffected by the tremendous technological innovations which have occurred. Perhaps Asimov is intimating that in spite of all the changes humanity will experience in the future, the species will still be inclined to xenophobia and the urge to manipulate or exterminate whatever stands in the way of its progress. In any case, the import of the novel is unclear. The religious message seems intrusive as the two elements do not meld. (p. 205)

> *Francis J. Molson, "Juvenile Science Fiction, 1975-1976," in* Children's Literature: Annual of the Modern Language Association Seminar on Children's Literature and The Children's Literature Association, *Vol. 6, 1977, pp. 202-10.*

THE ENDS OF THE EARTH: THE POLAR REGIONS OF THE WORLD   (1975)

Asimov, in another quite fascinating work, describes the basic astronomical conditions of Earth's climate and seasons, the physical phenomena of ocean currents, the varied conditions of water on this and other planets, and the action of oceans and of magnetism and similar forces. The ice ages are concisely described, and the newer theories of drifting continents are related to our glacial condition. Several chapters on how the ideas about polar regions were developed and on how those regions were explored are especially well done. . . . An excellent choice for general science collections.

> *R. G. Schipf, in a review of "The Ends of the Earth: The Polar Regions of the World," in* Library Journal, *Vol. 100, No. 17, October 1, 1975, p. 1835.*

A layman's geography and history of the Arctic and Antarctic, the text . . . includes an index, but, unhappily, no bibliography. (p. 320)

Although too extensive to absorb in one reading, this book should provide a good source of background and information about the polar regions both for student and general reader. It should be included in all school and public libraries. (p. 321)

> *Nina Kochmer, in a review of "The Ends of the Earth," in* Best Sellers, *Vol. 35, No. 10, January, 1976, pp. 320-21.*

This volume pretends to treat all polar science and even more; it includes discussions of planetary origins and global tectonics. Asimov considers in turn the reasons for present polar climates,

the history of polar exploration, high-latitude oceanography, the earth's magnetic field, the causes of glaciations, and plate tectonics. In covering this in 350 pages, he must intend the book for the general reader, though this reviewer for one would not recommend it to anybody. The book is an ill-digested accumulation of facts, which attempts to capitalize on fashionable environmental concerns. It appears to have been produced (thrown together) far too rapidly. There is no evidence that any thought was given to unifying the material contained, either conceptually or logistically—many would argue with a definition of the polar regions based on latitude alone. The style is verbose and repetitive; errors and ambiguities of fact appear far too frequently. . . . One wishes that the project had been consigned to the ends of the earth!

> *A review of "The Ends of the Earth: The Polar Regions of the World," in* Choice, *Vol. 12, No. 11, January, 1976, p. 1465.*

HOW DID WE FIND OUT ABOUT ENERGY?   (1975)

The contributions of scientists from Galileo to Fermi are presented in this historical account of how man came to understand thermodynamics and to use various forms of energy. Only brief mention is made of any recent breakthroughs (nuclear fusion, solar heating, etc.). The author glosses over energy shortages, leaving the solution of the problems to scientists to develop new forms of energy and giving no thought to the responsibility of man to conserve what energy there is now. The information given in this book can easily be located in other sources.

> *Carole Ridolfino, in a review of "How Did We Find Out about Energy?" in* School Library Journal, *Vol. 22, No. 4, December, 1975, p. 50.*

How Did We Find Out About Energy? is another book in Asimov's excellent history of science series. . . . My only criticism of Asimov's treatment is that sometimes the necessity of having to explain different energy concepts interferes with the historical presentation, resulting in some minor historical distortions. However, as a good introduction to both the subject of energy and its historical development, this book merits a high rating.

> *Shirley Roe, in a review of "How Did We Find Out about Energy?" in* Appraisal: Children's Science Books, *Vol. 9, No. 2, Spring, 1976, p. 6.*

An examination of the narrative and . . . [David Wool's] few black-and-white illustrations suggests that the book is probably intended for the upper elementary level. Its usefulness is questionable, however, since the areas covered can hardly be dealt with in 64 relatively small pages with large type. The same material is certainly found in much greater depth in textbooks and other tradebooks for this level. The book does make a contribution in terms of its historical approach, but it's hardly more than a potboiler.

> *George G. Mallinson, in a review of "How Did We Find Out about Energy?" in* Science Books & Films, *Vol. XII, No. 2, September, 1976, p. 102.*

HOW DID WE FIND OUT ABOUT COMETS?   (1975)

Readers familiar with other works by Asimov will recognize his unique style of writing, although the level of sophistication is somewhat lower here to accommodate a wider audience. A brief introduction gives a general description of these intriguing celestial objects, and an historical account of early comet sightings and studies sets the stage for an up-to-date discussion of the knowledge that has been accumulated on the subject. Technical data are presented in such a way that the average layperson can gain considerable insight into the nature of these "hairy stars." The book is most appropriate for upper elementary through high school students and constitutes an excellent reference for the classroom. The more able students might, because of the fairly low readability level, find the book to be a bit pedantic; even so, those looking for a good introduction to the nature of comets will find this work an excellent starting point.

> Van E. Neie, in a review of "How Did We Find Out about Comets?" in Science Books & Films, Vol. XI, No. 3, December, 1975, p. 154.

In accordance with Asimov's usual standard, the information is thorough and accurate without being overly technical, and the style clear and simple without being condescending. I found it good reading even though I already knew most of the information. This might do well as a high-interest/low vocabulary astronomy book as well as being a solid addition to the juvenile astronomy section.

> Daphne Ann Hamilton, in a review of "How Did We Find Out about Comets?" in Appraisal: Children's Science Books, Vol. 9, No. 1, Winter, 1976, p. 6.

Asimov is a proven craftsman of popular scientific writing and this book is no exception. The technical content on comets is excellent. . . . The index, although short, was carefully contrived to be useful. This is an easy to read, useful, and accurate book.

> David G. Hoag, in a review of "How Did We Find Out about Comets?" in Appraisal: Children's Science Books, Vol. 9, No. 1, Winter, 1976, p. 6.

THE SOLAR SYSTEM (1975)

The romance of space becomes reality in Isaac Asimov's latest work for young readers, *The Solar System*. Asimov relates postulated theories about the origin of the solar system and smoothly bridges enormous concepts from universe to galaxy to solar system. Gravity and its relationship to the orbits of planets, their satellites, asteroids, and comets are made clear and simple. Although individual planets are not covered extensively, the author provides an excellent overview of the subject. He does award detail to several specific phenomena such as eclipses and meteorites. Briefly explored are the possibilities of life within our solar system, with the conclusion that although some forms of life may exist on Mars, more exciting possibilities lie beyond our solar system on the planets of distant stars. . . . Projects are listed, but not described in detail. However, combined with the text, they may encourage the interested to explore in greater depth the mysteries of space.

> Debbi Robinson, in a review of "The Solar System," in Appraisal: Children's Science Books, Vol. 9, No. 1, Winter, 1976, p. 7.

I know it takes a while to get a book from typewriter to bookstore, but I think that the thirteenth Jovian satellite, discovered in the summer of 1974, might have made it into a small book published in March, 1975. The slip is, I admit, minor. The general descriptions of the planets are good. . . . I don't know whether author or editor is responsible for the picture captions; I know Dr. Asimov knows the difference between carbon dioxide and carbon monoxide, but the caption on p. 23 erroneously gives Venus an atmosphere of the latter. On the next page he suggests that Mercury may have an atmosphere of thin gases—something which Mariner 10's three visits seem to have disproved pretty conclusively, unless the author really wants to call a helium concentration a few times greater than that of interplanetary space an "atmosphere." The suggested activities struck me as very worthwhile.

> Harry C. Stubbs, in a review of "The Solar System," in Appraisal: Children's Science Books, Vol. 9, No. 1, Winter, 1976, p. 7.

HOW DID WE FIND OUT ABOUT ATOMS? (1976)

This is another fine book in Asimov's "How Did We Find Out" history of science series. Here Asimov relates the history of atomism from the Greeks to the early twentieth century, covering Democritus, Boyle, Dalton, Avogadro, Kekule, and several others. The book is, as usual, well written, and the explanations of chemical concepts are clear. Asimov takes his story through the discoveries in the late nineteenth century about the structure of compounds and concludes with a chapter on the "reality" of atoms. . . . The final two paragraphs of the book briefly mention the sub-atomic structure of the atom, concluding that this subject is important enough to warrant a separate book. Let us look forward to a second book on the structure of the atom, which will complete the story begun here in this fine book on a fascinating subject. (pp. 6-7)

> Shirley Roe, in a review of "How Did We Find Out about Atoms?" in Appraisal: Children's Science Books, Vol. 9, No. 3, Fall, 1976, pp. 6-7.

Carefully including phonetic pronunciations of their names, Asimov introduces major figures in the development and acceptance of the atomic theory of matter. The contribution of each is concisely presented without oversimplification, and is related to previous and future developments. Top-quality Asimov—informative and never patronizing.

> Penelope M. Mitchell, in a review of "How Did We Find Out about Atoms?" in School Library Journal, Vol. 23, No. 2, October, 1976, p. 103.

[This is] an excellent introduction to atomic structure. . . . Logically organized and lucidly written, this is a good example both of the science book that is authoritative but not too technical for the layman and of the scientific method.

> Zena Sutherland, in a review of "How Did We Find Out about Atoms?" in Bulletin of the Center for Children's Books, Vol. 30, No. 5, January, 1977, p. 70.

HOW DID WE FIND OUT ABOUT NUCLEAR POWER? (1976)

Asimov tells of the investigations which led to the discovery of the existence of the electron, the nature of the atomic nucleus, and, ultimately, the ability to control nuclear reactions and capture the power from them. Clear, thorough, and accurate, this is an excellent introduction for young people growing up in a world which perforce is becoming more and more energy conscious. (pp. 86-7)

Ovide V. Fortier, in a review of "How Did We Find Out about Nuclear Power?" in School Library Journal, *Vol. 23, No. 5, January, 1977, pp. 86-7.*

This short book covers the history of nuclear energy in sixty-one pages. It moves quickly and presents information in a style that is streamlined and compact but clear.... This book is brief, and the vocabulary is not difficult (pronunciations are given for the scientific words), but its condensed form requires concentrated reading. It is not suited for browsing or for ready reference. It may be useful as an introduction for interested young readers, but supplementary material with more detail is likely to be needed. I personally was dissatisfied with the limited attention given to the problems of nuclear safety, ecology, and arms escalation. However, others may find this to be consistent with the book's overall limitations. (pp. 6-7)

Christine McDonnell, in a review of "How Did We Find Out about Nuclear Power?" in Appraisal: Children's Science Books, *Vol. 10, No. 3, Fall, 1977, pp. 6-7.*

Some books are written to fire the imagination of readers, to charm them into wanting to know more about a subject. Other books provide the factual information one needs to better understand a subject. These also ought to be charming, exciting, and motivating, but all too often they fail in this respect. This book belongs in this latter class. Although the story of the development of our modern concept of the atom is, as the dust jacket says, an "exciting story of how, bit by bit, scientists unravelled the mystery of power wrapped up in the nucleus of the atom," not much of that excitement comes through in this book. Asimov has all of the facts correct and not much of the historical significance is omitted from the story, but the writing style is uninspired and tired. For the student who wants a quick, factual listing of the events in this "exciting story," this book will do the job adequately. But that's about all it will do.

David E. Newton, in a review of "How Did We Find Out about Nuclear Power?" in Appraisal: Children's Science Books, *Vol. 10, No. 3, Fall, 1977, p. 7.*

ALPHA CENTAURI, THE NEAREST STAR (1976)

The book is not exactly misnamed, since Alpha Centauri does keep cropping up in the discussion, but the author has actually produced a terse general astronomy course. He covers the discovery and classification of various kinds of celestial motions and celestial objects; describes some of the historical naming of and cataloging systems for the stars; and discusses the various techniques for measuring stellar distances, temperatures, sizes, and masses. He tabulates many specific facts about the nearer and brighter stars (the two sets don't completely overlap). In describing various types of stars, he tells something about what he believes to be a typical stellar life history and grapples with the question of the planets of other stars. Everything is logically tied together.

I'm afraid I spotted a couple of mistakes. One is minor: Dr. Asimov does admit that the distance to Betelgeuse is very uncertain, but the number he gives combines with the angular diameter on page 135, resulting in about 200 solar diameters, not the 800 of Table 31. More serious is the claim on page 123 that a positive sign on a radial velocity means the star is approaching, and vice versa. This is wrong and not merely a case of getting an arbitrary symbolism backward. Radial velocity is the first derivative of distance against time, and it is positive when distance is increasing. The slip leads to several erroneous statements and tabulations in the next few pages, since the Alpha Centauri system is actually approaching us, not receding. So is Sirius, and so is Barnard's star—whose parallax has increased measurably in the last few decades because of that approach. Alpha's maximum brightness as seen from earth is thirty-five or forty thousand years in the future, not in the past. (pp. 195-96)

Harry C. Stubbs, in a review of "Alpha Centauri, the Nearest Star," in The Horn Book Magazine, *Vol. LIII, No. 2, April, 1977, pp. 195-96.*

The versatile Asimov in a truly excellent book on astronomy explains with his usual craftsmanship the nature of our neighborhood stars. Although some of the concepts he covers are quite complex, he makes them clear even without the help of supporting diagrams. Instead, there are some 39 different tables listing various properties of the near stars: size, brightness, distance, motion, spectral class, etc., are used effectively. He has wisely left out much astronomy of more distant bodies and says nothing about the cepheid variables, quasars, pulsars, and black holes. In so doing he has left a manageable scope which he carries out extraordinarily well to catch the imagination of young and old reader alike.

David G. Hoag, in a review of "Alpha Centauri, the Nearest Star," in Appraisal: Children's Science Books, *Vol. 10, No. 3, Fall, 1977, p. 6.*

It is almost immoral for any man to know so much in such detail about so many things! But Isaac Asimov does! And once again ... he has accurately and perfectly provided for readers a survey of a complete course in astronomy ... as well as a discussion of Alpha Centauri.... There are charts, tables, a glossary, an index—and everything accurately arranged and fascinatingly written.

Virginia A. Tashjian, in a review of "Alpha Centauri, the Nearest Star," in Appraisal: Children's Science Books, *Vol. 10, No. 3, Fall, 1977, p. 6.*

THE GOLDEN DOOR: THE UNITED STATES FROM 1865 TO 1918 (1977)

A follow-up to his **Our Federal Union** ... which carried the history of the U. S. through the costly War Between the States, this surveys the period of immense economic growth and cultural and intellectual transformation between the end of the Civil War and the surrender of Germany to the Allies in 1918. With its emphasis upon elections, political alignments, and presidential administrations, this is basically old-line political history. Asimov repeats a number of myths (e.g., about the impeachment of Andrew Johnson and the presidential election of 1876) and ignores new interpretations of significant forces and events (e.g., the reconsideration of Bryan's role at the 1912 Democratic Convention or the attitudes and policies of Andrew Johnson in 1865-1868). Moreover, the account is often thin, with little attention to the revolutions in transportation, manufacturing, and communication and an almost total lack of reference to original source material. (pp. 119-20)

Ralph Adams Brown, in a review of "The Golden Door: The United States from 1865 to 1918," in School Library Journal, *Vol. 24, No. 2, October, 1977, pp. 119-20.*

As always, [Asimov] crowds his text with people, dates, and events; as always, his erudition, perception, and periodic irruptions of informality in writing style triumph over the weight of the material. . . . A chronology and an index are included. (p. 170)

> *Zena Sutherland, in a review of "The Golden Door: The United States from 1865 to 1918," in* Bulletin of the Center for Children's Books, *Vol. 31, No. 11, July-August, 1978, pp. 169-70.*

Those looking for a survey of American history might well prefer a single volume giving the whole story. Yet the successful science-fiction writer will have a special appeal for the young, and his easy style brings this important period to life.

> *T. L. Jarman, in a review of "The Golden Door: The United States from 1865 to 1918," in* The School Librarian, *Vol. 26, No. 4, December, 1978, p. 378.*

HOW DID WE FIND OUT ABOUT OUTER SPACE? (1977)

This entry in Asimov's series on the history of scientific discovery retraces, in five chapters, man's attempts at flight. The account is well-reasoned and highlights the discovery of the vacuum and the principles of rocketry and space travel. Thumbnail biographical sketches of historic notables (Isaac Newton, Count Von Zeppelin, Werner Von Braun) are included with brief evaluations of their contributions. Discussion of the theories of sci fi writers like Cyrano de Bergerac and a comparison of the Soviet and American space effort add interest to the text. . . . Though this breaks no new ground, Asimov gives just the right amount of detail for young readers' first exploration of the subject.

> *Anne Raymer, in a review of "How Did We Find Out about Outer Space?" in* School Library Journal, *Vol. 24, No. 5, January, 1978, p. 84.*

In five simple chapters the incomparable Asimov fields the question posed in this book's title. . . . The chapters are part of a complete fabric in which many essential threads are woven; still, Asimov displays a fine feel for concept loads. No loose ends are apparent, no details that don't dovetail, no failures of closure. From a book such as this one can come real understanding. Disappointingly, Torricelli's work is described without mention of his teacher, Galileo. The exploration of space really began, after all, once Galileo aimed his telescope at the sky and shattered the Greek spheres. But then, that exploration was and is ground-based astronomy, and the title question is concerned with rocket-based exploration.

> *Nicholas Rosa, in a review of "How Did We Find Out about Outer Space?" in* Science Books & Films, *Vol. XIII, No. 4, March, 1978, p. 220.*

MARS, THE RED PLANET (1977)

The history of our knowledge of Mars from ancient times through the puzzling results of the Viking tests is given along with much information on Earth, Venus, Mercury, and the Moon. Figures on sizes, distances, etc. are summarized in 64 tables, and diagrams and photographs help elucidate the text. There are occasional redundancies and inaccuracies, but this is more up-to-date than Branley's *Mars: Planet Number Four* (Crowell, 1966). . . .

> *Margaret L. Chatham, in a review of "Mars, the Red Planet," in* School Library Journal, *Vol. 24, No. 6, February, 1978, p. 63.*

Isaac Asimov's **Mars** brings us as nearly up to date as a book can be expected to do. . . . Explanations are clear and are frequently supplemented by diagrams. Every science fiction writer who wants to use Mars as a setting, and everyone who wants a clear idea of what the planet is like should have the book on hand. Personally, I find it fun to calculate things like the latitudes from which the Martians can see their moons and the changes in the brightness of these little objects as they travel from horizon to zenith; but some people find it a chore and some can't do it. Dr. Asimov's text and tables will save them the trouble. I picked up only two minor errors. We are told that Mars passes its perihelion on August 28; actually, Mars's perihelion lies in the direction from the sun which Earth occupies on that date. Mars is very seldom there at the time. And mention is made of the twenty-six-inch mirror of Hall's refracting telescope. Refractors have lenses, not mirrors, for objectives. (pp. 188-89)

> *Harry C. Stubbs, in a review of "Mars, the Red Planet," in* The Horn Book Magazine, *Vol. LIV, No. 2, April, 1978, pp. 188-89.*

Here is a thorough treatment of Mars and its satellites. Beginning with observations by the ancients, the text smoothly and satisfyingly follows the historical progression of our expanding understanding of the planet, climaxing with the 1976 landings of the Viking probes. . . . The book probably is not suitable for general reading nor able to capture the imagination of those uninterested in astronomy. . . . Nevertheless, the lucid style and concise glossary make **Mars** comprehensible to the uninitiated and an excellent reference item. It is replete with data and statistics (about Mercury, Venus, Earth and the Moon as well as Mars) which are compiled in 64 tables and readily accessible via a complete index and list of tables. In short, this is a book worth having.

> *Suzanne T. Degnen, in a review of "Mars, the Red Planet," in* Science Books & Films, *Vol. XIV, No. 2, September, 1978, p. 85.*

THE KEY WORD AND OTHER MYSTERIES (1977)

In these five quickie mysteries narrator Larry helps his hard-pressed detective father solve cases by realizing the clues are vocabulary based: in the title story, for instance, the *New York Times* crossword puzzle yields a crucial code-breaking key. . . . The writing is simple, the stories fast developing—Asimov's tidy mental fooling around is agreeably disarming and easy for young readers to enjoy.

> *Denise M. Wilms, in a review of "The Key Word, and Other Mysteries," in* Booklist, *Vol. 74, No. 13, March 1, 1978, p. 1098.*

Isaac Asimov has modelled **The Key Word and Other Mysteries** . . . on the Encyclopedia Brown series (Nelson) but he lacks the vital ingredient of Sobol's tongue-in-cheek humor. The featured young sleuth is Larry, who assists his New York City detective father in fighting crime. The best of the five tales hangs on the dying utterances of a wounded diamond thief. The police are looking for "Sarah Tops" (the man's last words) until Larry figures out that the diamond is hidden in the skeleton of a triceratop dinosaur in the Museum of Natural History. The others are even more far-fetched as Larry helps crack a difficult code, solve a coin robbery, avert a bombing at the Soviet Embassy, and clear a classmate of a cheating charge. Most of the selections have appeared in magazines and that's where they belong. (pp. 83-4)

> *A review of "The Key Word and Other Mysteries,"* in School Library Journal, *Vol. 24, No. 9, May, 1978, pp. 83-4.*

[All of the mysteries] move briskly and efficiently to a satisfying conclusion. The metropolitan setting, the style of writing, and the incidents themselves are more sophisticated in effect than are the popular Encyclopedia Brown stories . . . ; however, the brevity of the selections, the large type, and the copious illustrations [by Rod Burke] may well attract the reluctant older reader. (pp. 272-73)

> *Mary M. Burns, in a review of "The Key Word and Other Mysteries,"* in The Horn Book Magazine, *Vol. LIV, No. 3, June, 1978, pp. 272-73.*

HOW DID WE FIND OUT ABOUT EARTHQUAKES? (1978)

As in his other *How Did We Find Out* books, Asimov begins with the beliefs of primitives and ancients; later come summaries of other theories that "didn't work out" either, plus a synopsis of landmarks in the development and application of the seismograph. As earthquakes can't be considered today without reference to plate tectonics, Asimov starts *that* story with Wegener's continental drift theory, touches on the evidence from the seafloor, and—with a diagram showing where the plates line up today—concludes that most earthquakes take place on the cracks between them. With a stretched-out discussion of whether people should "leave" (evacuate) on the mere possibility of a quake, this is one of the flimsier entries in Asimov's history-oriented series. Readers will come away from Fodor's *Earth in Motion* . . . , about plate tectonics, with a better understanding of earthquakes than they get here; for a fuller all-around discussion of the subject, see Lauber's *Earthquakes* (1972).

> *A review of "How Did We Find Out about Earthquakes?"* in Kirkus Reviews, *Vol XLVI, No. 19, October 1, 1978, p. 1073.*

This is a fine job of organization and description, with about as much depth as is appropriate for the intended readers. The author divides his space reasonably among description, the effects of earthquakes on human beings and their works, theoretical causes, methods of observation and analysis, and what people can do about them (the answer to this is *not* "nothing").

> *Harry C. Stubbs, in a review of "How Did We Find Out about Earthquakes?"* in Appraisal: Children's Science Books, *Vol. 12, No. 2, Spring, 1979, p. 7.*

In this informal but informative discussion of a timely topic, Asimov progresses from historical to present-day ideas about earthquakes and how they occur. . . . The book is lucid, accurate and enjoyable to read, with a great deal of information packed into its 58 pages. I recommend it highly for the novice wishing to learn some basic facts about earthquakes.

> *J. D. Macdougall, in a review of "How Did We Find Out about Earthquakes?"* in Science Books & Films, *Vol. XV, No. 2, September, 1979, p. 100.*

ANIMALS OF THE BIBLE (1978)

Asimov turns his talent on the animals mentioned in the Bible, some of which are extinct or endangered now. He sparks a page-turning hunting expedition as he reveals the books of the Bible where each animal may be found, offering his best guesses as to what a leviathan or behemoth may have been, besides giving the animals' habitats and uses in Biblical times. He hopes the book "will make the Bible mean just a little more" to eight- to 12-year-olds, but this could easily prove a charming reference work for adults.

> *Janet Domowitz, in a review of "Animals of the Bible,"* in The Christian Science Monitor, *October 23, 1978, p. B4.*

Asimov gives some attention to the ancient use of animal symbolism in the Bible, but primarily focuses on the employment and distribution of animals in Biblical times. While his examination of the ambiguities of the English translations of Hebrew animal names will be of most interest to adult readers, children will enjoy Howard Berelson's clear and graceful illustrations of dugongs, hartebeests, aoudads, etc. This attractive and informative book will complement rather than replace two fine earlier treatments of the same material: Ferguson's *Living Animals of the Bible* (Scribners, 1974), with its color portfolio of living animals, is more detailed, while Lathrop's *Animals of the Bible* (Lippincott, 1937), which won the first Caldecott Medal and which uses the Bible alone as its text, remains the most visually splendid treatment.

> *Allene Stuart Phy, in a review of "Animals of the Bible,"* in School Library Journal, *Vol. 25, No. 3, November, 1978, p. 55.*

HOW DID WE FIND OUT ABOUT BLACK HOLES? (1978)

Asimov makes a tidy summation of the research breakthroughs that led to formulating [the presence of black holes]. Explanations of star life and death stages, elementary atomic structure, and key concepts such as Chandrasekhar's limit, escape velocity, and tidal effects are all made in simple, concrete terms. A first-rate starting place for a working definition of an increasingly popular topic.

> *Denise M. Wilms, in a review of "How Did We Find Out about Black Holes?"* in Booklist, *Vol. 75, No. 1, February 1, 1979, p. 862.*

In the latest of his chronological approaches to understanding science, Asimov spares us the observations of the ancients and begins in 1844 when "A German astronomer, Friedrich Wilhelm Bessel, discovered a star he couldn't see." From this first glimmer of a "dark companion" to Sirius up to the sophisticated contributions of Stephen Hawking, Asimov traces a direct, unclouded course through the heady universe of white dwarfs and red giants, supernovae, pulsars, and the rest. Assuming no prior knowledge, he easily assimilates atomic structure and stellar evolution into the same simple, ongoing explanations. More narrowly focused than Berger's *Quasars, Pulsars, and Black Holes in Space* (1977), this lacks the cosmic excitement of Branley's *Black Holes, White Dwarfs, and Superstars* (1976), but by the same token it's less of a trip for the unambitious reader.

> *A review of "How Did We Find Out about Black Holes?"* in Kirkus Reviews, *Vol. XLVII, No. 3, February 1, 1979, p. 127.*

An experienced teacher, Asimov does not arrive at a discussion of the title subject until he has carefully and clearly laid a groundwork for understanding it. . . . Asimov has the ability to write without condescension for the reader with no previous knowledge, and this book is an excellent example of that ability.

> *Zena Sutherland, in a review of "How Did We Find Out about Black Holes?" in* Bulletin of the Center for Children's Books, *Vol. 32, No. 10, June, 1979, p. 169.*

SATURN AND BEYOND (1979)

Another in Asimov's series of astronomy books for junior high, misleadingly titled as always. The first three quarters of the book deal only with the planets known to the ancients, one supposes in order to use a historical approach, but then Asimov talks of the 1977 discovery of Chiron (an asteroid between the orbits of Saturn and Uranus) before admitting that Uranus was discovered in 1781. He spends a great deal of time on the various moons, discussing what one could see from them as well as the usual statistics about size and orbits, which makes the lack of mention of Pluto's newly discovered moon more noticeable. Asimov's *Jupiter: the Largest Planet* . . . is better organized to tell about the outer planets, but is becoming seriously dated as new information piles up, and should be replaced with *Saturn and Beyond*.

> *Margaret L. Chatham, in a review of "Saturn and Beyond," in* School Library Journal, *Vol. 25, No. 9, May, 1979, p. 69.*

The author is very careful to indicate what sort of data are still uncertain, such as the sizes, and hence the densities, of the smaller satellites of the outer planets. He also points out fallacies in various theories of the origin of the system, which are apparent if the supposedly measured values are right; and he doesn't try to push us toward a favored choice of his own. . . . The book is sufficiently up to date to have the information on Pluto's moon, though the author either missed or didn't trust the radar evidence that the particles in Saturn's rings are about snowball size (I'm not sure how far I trust it myself). I caught only one slip; it is true that eclipses of the sun as seen from Titan occur in roughly one quarter of that satellite's revolutions, but Asimov does not indicate that they are not randomly distributed in time. When Saturn is close to its equinox, they occur in every revolution; when it isn't, they don't occur at all. There are numerous useful tables for science-fiction writers, which tell how big and bright the sun looks from various planets and how big and bright the planets look from their various moons. I'm keeping the book; I *can* figure out all these things for myself, but why should I work harder than I have to?

> *Harry C. Stubbs, in a review of "Saturn and Beyond," in* The Horn Book Magazine, *Vol. LV, No. 4, August, 1979, p. 450.*

[A] companion-piece to Dr. Asimov's *Jupiter: the Largest Planet* . . . , this presents the same detailed portrait of its subject as its predecessor did. A vast range of information on Saturn and its satellites (Titan gets a chapter to itself), as well as the famous rings, is set forth in progressive fashion, as scientists discovered it. The keystone of the book is the charts, detailing the characteristics of Saturn (such as size, orbital velocity, albedo, axial tip, equatorial speed, etc.), frequently in com-

parison with the other planets. The same type of information is given for Saturn's moons, in comparison with each other and with other planetary satellites. The text is clear, readable, and interesting, though it lacks some of the smoothness and spark of *Jupiter*. The last third of the book is devoted to "beyond": comets and asteroids . . . , and the three outer planets: Uranus, Neptune, and Pluto. Information about them is presented in the same fashion as in the earlier part on Saturn, though Asimov is careful to emphasize how much of our "information" on the outer planets is uncertain and conjectural due to the great difficulties involved in observing them. The author makes it clear that the solar system is as fascinating far out as it is close in. It will be interesting to see the changes in later editions of the two books as data from the Pioneer and Voyager flights are analyzed and incorporated. In the meantime, this is a fine addition to any astronomy bookshelf as, in addition to its focus, the comparative charts give a good survey of the entire solar system. There are a list of tables, a glossary, and an index.

> *Daphne Ann Hamilton, in a review of "Saturn and Beyond," in* Appraisal: Children's Science Books, *Vol. 13, No. 1, Winter, 1980, p. 10.*

EXTRATERRESTRIAL CIVILIZATIONS (1979)

Although Asimov finds the evidence of UFOs "unacceptable," he believes other technological civilizations do exist because of "the principle of mediocrity"—in a cosmos with billions of possible worlds, our world cannot be utterly atypical. Like a black hole, *Extraterrestrial Civilizations* contracts, moving from a billion trillion possibilities to imaginable probabilities as Asimov shows how the origins of life and the conditions that permit it to evolve limit civilization to 540 planets in our galaxy. The information, ranging from early speculation about space to pulsars and red giants, is impressive and is lucidly presented; but the chain of logic leading to the title's assertion is as unstable as a mile-long game of crack-the-whip. While I respect Asimov's resistance to UFOs, a drunk's sighting of a purple saucer is, finally, as credible as Asimov's argument.

Asimov does wonder "where is everybody" from these civilizations. In the last chapters he discusses the presently insurmountable difficulties of interstellar travel and communication. We are not alone, but we might just as well be. Even so, Asimov ends with a *Battlestar Galactica* vision of the future. A hundred years ago people believed there were holes at the poles. Using Asimov's probabilistic methods, one can believe those holes just haven't been found yet. (pp. 58-9)

> *Thomas LeClair, in a review of "Extraterrestrial Civilizations," in* Saturday Review, *Vol. 6, No. 16, August, 1979, pp. 58-9.*

Asimov turns his talents for clear explanations of complex scientific subjects to the question of the existence of extraterrestrial life. . . . The chemical and physical bases for life are discussed in detail but never beyond the comprehension of high school students. . . . This clearly written discussion of a topic of interest to many young people joins other good books on this subject such as *Who Goes There?* by Edward Edelson . . . and Ian Ridpath's *Messages from the Stars* (Harper, 1978).

> *Mary Jo Campbell, in a review of "Extra-Terrestrial Civilizations," in* School Library Journal, *Vol. 26, No. 1, September, 1979, p. 168.*

There are very few writers who can successfully translate scientific theories into the language of the layman. Asimov is one of them. He has repeatedly attempted to popularize science by simplifying it and injecting it with a good dose of enthusiasm and wit. In this vein, his latest publication is vintage Asimov. Starting with the question, "Are we alone?" he carefully deals with issues raised by scientific thought as well as the more sensational concepts. In the process he manages to convey to the reader enormous amounts of interesting and useful information. At the end, the true value of the book is not its unsurprising conclusions, but the method by which it strives to teach. Asimov has accomplished a great deal in making the average person aware of the parameters of terrestrial and extraterrestrial intelligences.

Valentin R. Livada, in a review of "Extraterrestrial Civilizations," in Kliatt Young Adult Paperback Book Guide, *Vol. XIV, No. 6, September, 1980, p. 63.*

HOW DID WE FIND OUT ABOUT OUR HUMAN ROOTS? (1979)

Simplified catalogue of the major ancestors of modern man and their discoverers.... Discoveries of fossils are roughly in chronological order, so that modern man's closest ancestors are mentioned before more distant ones. There are four main sections on Cro-Magnon Man, Neanderthal Man, Java and Peking Man, and little ape-men (Australopithecines). The information is up-to-date except for the exclusion of recent fossil finds in Ethiopia and northern Kenya. Although the name of the scientist who first found each fossil form is given, little is told of the process of discovery. Controversial conclusions are mentioned, but so briefly that different ideas about the significance of fossil finds cannot really be discussed. Pronunciations are provided but this does not alleviate the density of long and unfamiliar names.

Nancy J. Schmidt, in a review of "Our Human Roots?" in School Library Journal, *Vol. 26, No. 6, February, 1980, p. 51.*

Even though his style is interesting and, in general, perfectly acceptable for the age group intended, many of Asimov's conclusions will seem too simplistic to more advanced students. However, this book is an enjoyable way for beginning students to become familiar with human antiquity.

Alan J. Almquist, in a review of "How Did We Find Out about Our Human Roots?" in Science Books & Films, *Vol. XV, No. 4, March, 1980, p. 208.*

Dr. Asimov presents a simplified, yet scientifically accurate picture of hominid evolution in his latest book.... Through a careful discussion of modern geological and paleontological methods, Asimov explains why methods based on a literal translation of the Bible are unsatisfactory and inaccurate. (Although Asimov's information is scientifically correct, it may offend some religious groups.) ... In his easy-to-follow evolutionary history, Asimov includes the human drama behind the discoveries of skulls and bones. Dubois, von Koenigswald, Dart, Lewis, and Leakey are some of the featured personalities. The text is exciting and fun to read.... The concluding summary of human evolution and [David Wool's] picture chart are especially helpful. In this latest book, Asimov again demonstrates his gift for writing wonderful science books for children.

Martha T. Kane, in a review of "How Did We Find Out about Our Human Roots?" in Appraisal: Chil-

dren's Science Books, *Vol. 13, No. 2, Spring, 1980, p. 9.*

HOW DID WE FIND OUT ABOUT OIL? (1980)

This is a simple, enjoyable introduction to the important topic of petroleum on our society. The author reviews the ways in which oil is formed; some of the early history of the petroleum industry; the uses of oil, past and present; the significance of petroleum in modern society; and the probable future of oil in our world. The last chapter is especially admirable in its willingness to deal with social and political issues surrounding the use of oil. I would have been happier had Asimov paid somewhat more attention to the role of big industry and big government in determining the rate of use of oil, but, all in all, the presentation is complete and well-balanced.

David E. Newton, in a review of "How Did We Find Out about Oil?" in Appraisal: Science Books for Young People, *Vol. 14, No. 1, Winter, 1981, p. 13.*

Asimov presents not only a well-written and thorough discussion of the chemical composition of oil and its historical and contemporary uses, but also a critical and perceptive introduction to the shortage of oil in the U.S. and the politics involved. Alternative energy sources such as hydrogen fusion and solar are also mentioned. Yet one hardly leaves the book as an expert on oil (its components, refining methods, role in industry). There are few subdivisions to synthesize and reinforce information, and the illustrations [by David Wool] are ineffective and frustrating; readers will not be able to imagine the mechanical processes described. These problems weaken an otherwise authoritative text on a demanding and omnipresent subject. Ian Ridpath's *Man & Materials: Oil* (Addison-Wesley, 1975), for the same age level, provides more extensive scientific and technological information and includes many simple instructional diagrams.

Sherri Bush, in a review of "How Did We Find Out about Oil?" in School Library Journal, *Vol. 27, No. 6, February, 1981, p. 62.*

HOW DID WE FIND OUT ABOUT COAL? (1980)

The good doctor has not confined himself entirely to the title material in this book but has come up with a plausible (not provable; most of it took place before written history) account of man's taming of fire and his subsequent development of high-energy technology. He compares the burning of wood and of the various fossil fuels in terms of convenience to humanity and of safety to people and to the environment and goes a reasonable distance into the future of availability as well. The problems and consequences of mining coal are well covered. I would have liked to see in the book a little more real chemistry, but this would probably have been too much for the intended readers. I do think that more should have been made of the fact that there are much more useful things to do with coal than just to burn it; it is a raw material, not merely a fuel. As far as it goes, though, the book is thought-provoking and informative.

Harry C. Stubbs, in a review of "How Did We Find Out about Coal?" in The Horn Book Magazine, *Vol. LVII, No. 2, April, 1981, p. 212.*

The style is the author's usual: lucid, readable, accurate and to the point scientifically, while avoiding the technical and the extraneous. . . . Asimov's book, although slight, is written for an older audience than Adler's *Coal* (Day, 1974) and Chaffin's *Coal: Energy and Crisis* (Harvey, 1974). Like Asimov's book, Kraft's *Coal* (Watts, 1976) is a good stepping stone to more specialized accounts for young students, but for libraries without Kraft's book, Asimov's is a worthy purchase.

> *Connie Tyrrell, in a review of "How Did We Find Out about Coal?" in* School Library Journal, *Vol. 27, No. 10, August, 1981, p. 62.*

Extending beyond the title, the usually versatile Asimov here uses a third of his space on the phenomenon of fire and the use of wood as a fuel. The eleven pages on fire could be better. It uses the term heat and temperature without distinction. It misses the chance to explain that the *rate* of a chemical reaction such as that involved in fire is proportional to temperature. It misses explaining how fire can be extinguished by cooling with water or removing the source of oxygen. The rest of the book and the part on coal is very good except for the little scenarios purporting to represent how coal was discovered and utilized. These are necessarily contrived fiction presented without identification as such and may not be even close to what actually happened at all. (p. 10)

> *David G. Hoag, in a review of "How Did We Find Out about Coal?" in* Appraisal: Science Books for Young People, *Vol. 14, No. 3, Fall, 1981, pp. 10-11.*

VENUS, NEAR NEIGHBOR OF THE SUN (1981)

As he has done in *Saturn* . . . and *Mars* . . . Asimov uses the description of a single astronomical object to relate much basic astronomy in a direct, easily understood manner. The text presents a significant amount of the content of an introductory astronomy and planetary physics course clearly, and without mathematics. The wealth of figures and tables complements and clarifies the descriptions of the relative sizes of the planets when viewed from different distances, the orbital characteristics of planets and satellites, and the appearance of objects as viewed by an observer located on another planet. Most of the astronomical history and observations that constitute the story of Venus have been described before. However, Asimov uses new data, particularly from Pioneer Venus (launched in 1978), to show that astronomy is an alive scientific field, with many theories to be tested and observations to be explained. The ploy of seeing the night sky as a Sumerian astronomer did, and following the development from astronomical observation to theory, works well in leading beginners from their own casual observations of the skies to an understanding of the elementary theories. The book's subtitle is initially confusing; however, the confusion ends when Asimov takes up the description of Mercury, asteroids, and comets—other near neighbors of the sun—in the last four chapters. As a bonus, readers lulled by the regularity of terrestrial phenomena might modify their mundane geocentric world-view; the realization that there are other, comparatively bizarre phenomena (e.g., the playful, hesitant sunrises that can occur on Mercury's surface) may surprise many readers, and start them wondering about the universe. (pp. 876-77)

> *A review of "Venus, Near Neighbor of the Sun," in* Kirkus Reviews, *Vol. XLIX, No. 14, July 15, 1981, pp. 876-77.*

[This book rounds] out Asimov's survey of the solar system undertaken in his *Mars, the Red Planet; Jupiter, the Largest Planet;* and *Saturn and Beyond.* . . . In scope and variety this is most simliar to *Saturn and Beyond,* though I find *Venus* to be more readable and accessible. Again there are numerous charts comparing planetary masses, orbits, atmospheric composition, etc., but (unlike *Saturn,* where one had to stop reading to absorb the charts) the text always remains foremost, providing some fascinating information on astronomical history and speculations concerning Venus and Mercury as well as Asimov's usual clear explanations of such things as synodic periods and Venus's retrograde rotation. In fact, this series of books, taken together, will provide the incipient astronomer with explanations of almost all the principal basic astronomical terms/concepts as well as an excellent picture of scientific method. The rest of us will simply gain more information than we thought of asking about the solar family, our neighbors in space. There is an excellent glossary and an index. (pp. 16-17)

> *Daphne Ann Hamilton, in a review of "Venus, Near Neighbor of the Sun," in* Appraisal: Science Books for Young People, *Vol. 15, No. 1, Winter, 1982, pp. 16-17.*

Unannounced in the title is the fact that almost 40% of this book deals with topics other than Venus, namely Mercury, asteroids and comets. It would have been more honest to have included this information in the title or on the cover. If nothing else, Asimov is thorough, providing us with just about every conceivable bit of information on our planetary neighbors. In fact, one wonders if children are really curious about the apparent diameter of the sun as viewed from Venus (Table 21), the oblateness of the planets (Table 24), and the separation of the planet's orbital foci (Table 37). These are probably of more interest to older students and those with strong interest in planetary astronomy.

But Asimov does write beautifully. Even when he is discussing the most esoteric aspects of his subject, the reader is carried along by his prose. This book is of doubtful interest to the great majority of elementary children, but probably useful at the junior high and older levels.

> *David E. Newton, in a review of "Venus, Near Neighbor of the Sun," in* Appraisal: Science Books for Young People, *Vol. 15, No. 1, Winter, 1982, p. 17.*

HOW DID WE FIND OUT ABOUT SOLAR POWER? (1981)

Isaac Asimov has written an informative account of the development and possible future of solar energy. . . . As in many of his books Asimov is able, although sometimes hurriedly, to impart rather complicated scientific information to the young reader. More diagrams and a glossary would have been useful but an index is included.

> *Althea L. Philips, in a review of "How Did We Find Out about Solar Power?" in* Appraisal: Science Books for Young People, *Vol. 15, No. 1, Winter, 1982, p. 15.*

The history here is fine, the comparison of the advantages and disadvantages of various energy sources well made. The point that just about all the energy available to us is, indirectly, solar in origin is made and substantiated.

The statement about the temperature which a mirror could produce . . . needs some qualification, since this is also a function of the angular size of the mirror measured from the focus;

I realize that this point might be a little heavy for the intended readers, but without it the whole item might better have been omitted—it leads to an erroneous idea which the less critical solar power supporters are apt to use in sales talks. The implication that solar cells were used in space probes sent to Saturn is incorrect; both the Pioneer and Voyager craft used nuclear sources. Past Mars, solar power gets a bit thin.

I particularly liked Dr. Asimov's awareness of the economic aspects of the various energy sources, a matter which many enthusiasts of one source or another tend to overlook. After all, money—in spite of a widespread temptation toward deficit budgeting—is supposed to be some sort of measure of available resources and effort.

> *Harry C. Stubbs, in a review of "How Did We Find Out about Solar Power?" in* Appraisal: Science Books for Young People, *Vol. 15, No. 1, Winter, 1982, p. 15.*

HOW DID WE FIND OUT ABOUT LIFE IN THE DEEP SEA? (1982)

[The prolific Asimov] takes a look at what is under the seas and how it was discovered. Beginning with early scientific thought on the oceans' makeup, Asimov goes on to examine important experiments that led to reevaluation of the life that was found to exist at the lowest depths of the seas. As in the other books of the series, the narrative excels at two essential qualities of nonfiction—it is easily understood and enjoyable to read. The black-and-white illustrations [by David Wool] are only adequate, but it is really Asimov's words that paint the picture.

> *Ilene Cooper, in a review of "How Did We Find Out about Life in the Deep Sea?" in* Booklist, *Vol. 78, No. 18, May 15, 1982, p. 1253.*

In this, the 20th title in his series, Asimov has used his usual format: a handy gathering in one cover of the names, dates, and accomplishments important to the history of a scientific discovery. As usual, he skillfully produces an account, economical in word and uncomplicated in concept. At times, though, facts in this book seem to have been pared unnecessarily: no mention is made of the part the diesel engine played in upgrading the battery-powered submarines of 1886 to the submarines of World Wars I and II; no mention is made of Cyrus Field in connection with the Atlantic cable; no mention is made of Jacques Cousteau, the undersea explorer best-known to children. Even a negative reference would be an educational link. However, those who have the series will want to update it with this addition. Schools where units on oceans are taught will find it useful. . . . [There is] an index.

> *Ruth S. Beebe, in a review of "How Did We Find Out about Life in the Deep Sea?" in* Appraisal: Science Books for Young People, *Vol. 15, No. 3, Fall, 1982, p. 12.*

This book is intended for a juvenile audience, to be read by children or to be read aloud to them. I suggest the latter as the most expedient course because Asimov has a meandering style that conceals an idea in irrelevant information before it comes back to the essentials. It takes experience to follow the trail. Asimov traces man's exploration for life in the ocean depths almost at the anecdotal level. It is not uninteresting, but so much more information might have been conveyed in the same space. He touches on the main oceanographic processes, but

he does this so casually that readers may overlook these facts. Important concepts and irrelevant information are given equal weight. Is it more important to understand the process of heating and cooling in mixing of deep water or to learn that Professor Thomson died five days after his fifty-second birthday? If practice reading or reading aloud is the objective, the question is inappropriate. If an introduction to the least-explored and least-understood region of earth is sought, there are better sources of information.

> *R. J. LeBrasseur, in a review of "How Did We Find Out about Life in the Deep Sea?" in* Science Books & Films, *Vol. 18, No. 2, November-December, 1982, p. 91.*

HOW DID WE FIND OUT ABOUT THE BEGINNING OF LIFE? (1982)

Asimov's writing is always laudable for the way it shows how a body of scientific knowledge is based on the work of many scientists, both those who succeeded in their experiments and those who did not, and for its illustration of the fact that all findings are subject to re-examination. Here, in a clearly written and logically arranged text, he describes the work of those researchers of earlier centuries who demonstrated the error of the theory of spontaneous generation, compares the work of Lamarck and Darwin, and concludes with the statement that scientists are in agreement that species emerged (and are emerging) from other species. The second half of the text discusses the work of contemporary scientists in examining the ways in which, given a source of energy and the proper chemical constituents, it is possible to create new chemical combinations that resemble those of living things. An index is included; phonetic spelling is parenthetically provided for the more difficult words or names.

> *Zena Sutherland, in a review of "How Did We Find Out about the Beginning of Life," in* Bulletin of the Center for Children's Books, *Vol. 36, No. 2, October, 1982, p. 21.*

In a relatively short book, Asimov covers quite a lot of material. . . . The presentation, however, ranges from overly simplistic to overly complex, and a reasonable average never seems to be reached for the grade level intended. . . . [Although] there are some excellent opportunities in the narrative to encourage the reader to conduct some simple experiments—on spontaneous generation and microscopic life, for example—the opportunity is missed. Overall, I think that this book will suffer from not being able to catch and hold the reader's attention.

> *Theodore A. Molskness, in a review of "How Did We Find Out about the Beginning of Life?" in* Science Books & Films, *Vol. 18, No. 3, January-February, 1983, p. 146.*

The author treats each topic with ease and lucidity, and fits them all together for the reader. Like a true scientist, he admits at the end that for all that we have learned, ''. . . scientists are only at the beginning of their attempts to find out how life began.'' . . .

Skillful handling of both the science and the history makes this . . . little book an excellent introduction to this topic. (p. 14)

> *Norman F. Smith, in a review of "How Did We Find Out about the Beginning of Life?" in* Appraisal: Science Books for Young People, *Vol. 16, No. 2, Spring-Summer, 1983, pp. 13-14.*

THE MEASURE OF THE UNIVERSE (1983)

Asimov-watchers know his fascination with measurements. They know, too, that he'll always provide some down-home comparison to make a millimetre meaningful. This volume can be said to represent the apotheosis of Asimov as Ruler of Weights and Measures. He has chosen to celebrate the *Systeme International d'Unites,* known to all metric users as the "SI version." In his compulsive way, Asimov takes the reader up and down assorted ladders of length, area, volume, of mass and density, temperature, time, pressure, and more. He meticulously explains exponential notation at the outset, and goes on to explain the origins of rods, furlongs, acres, and suchlike used in the English system (obsolete, of course, outside England and America). Will this exercise win new friends for litres and metres? (*The* SI spelling.) Will it persuade Congress or the constituency outside science? Probably not. It will serve as a fine reference for schools, however, and might ease the burden of math and science teachers with its inspired examples: "The population of Rumania would also have a total mass of about 1 megatonne"; "A ray of light would, in a decisecond [0.1 second], travel 30 megametres. This is three-fourths of the distance around the Earth at the equator." There is also a hidden agenda: as Asimov pursues the nuances of space or time he can track the age and extent of the universe, the evolution of species, the dimensions of everything from cells to stars; he can explain mass vs. weight, superpressure, superdensities, superconductivity . . . adding an occasional macabre fillip: "5.27 minutes is about the time it takes for a human being to die of asphyxiation." Readers can best savor the full measure of the book, so to speak, in tasty bits and pieces.

> *A review of "The Measure of the Universe," in* Kirkus Reviews, *Vol. LI, No. 7, April 1, 1983, p. 415.*

In their classic film *Powers of Ten,* Charles and Ray Eames give the viewer a sense of the universe's scale by graphically scanning (in just nine minutes) up to the cosmic and down to the atomic level. In this latest demonstration of his all-encompassing erudition and talent for crystalline explanation, Asimov attempts a similar feat in book form, with mixed results. . . . Asimov's hope is that what we can't mentally swallow in one gulp, we can more readily absorb in systematic bites. This can work, but sometimes the sequences become too abstract or arbitrary to give us the better intuitive feel he is striving for, and the endless parade of intriguing facts becomes merely numbing. For all Asimov's expertise, thoroughness and charm, the result might have been more readable with a less rigid format. (pp. 46-7)

> *A review of "The Measure of the Universe," in* Publishers Weekly, *Vol 223, No. 19, May 13, 1983, pp. 46-7.*

Isaac Asimov fans may become bewildered while trying to follow this new book on realms of measurement—not even number addicts will find it light, narrative reading. . . . What may seem to be tedious collections of facts about measurement is not intended to be an artless encyclopedia of numerical trivia— Asimov clearly hopes that determined readers will develop an intuitive feeling for the vast scale of our universe from the submicroscopic to the cosmic—and, in fact, his efforts appear particularly valuable for science teachers, students, science fiction fans, and reference librarians. . . . The various tidbits on the history of our measurement systems are fascinating, and the book is valuable as a single source of the names of very large and very small numbers. The index is also complete and valuable for anyone desiring examples of extremes of scale in various units of measurement. *The Measure of the Universe* will not make it to the best-seller list, but every femtosecond, one of the 4,400,000,000 persons residing on the 520 square megameters of the earth's surface will wish he or she had a copy!

> *Theodore R. Spickler, in a review of "The Measure of the Universe," in* Science Books & Films, *Vol. 20, No. 2, November-December, 1984, p. 80.*

HOW DID WE FIND OUT ABOUT THE UNIVERSE? (1983)

I opened Dr. Asimov's book with some trepidation; with all due respect to his knowledge and skill, I felt that the title implied a scope very hard to compress into so few pages. I knew that as a scientist Asimov would not be delivering the information as gospel but would be justifying the opinions presented; and getting from the sun to the expanding universe takes me a whole school year at two periods a week.

He did it, however, in perfectly ordered and logical stages. From the sun to the other stars, from the Milky Way to the other galaxies, from red-shifted spectra to the Big Bang (or Continuous Creation), Dr. Asimov maintains a coherent line of reasoning bolstered along its full length with observational history. Why we believe what we do, and where we are doubtful about it, are both covered in decently scientific fashion. (p. 481)

> *Harry C. Stubbs, in a review of "How Did We Find Out about the Universe?" in* The Horn Book Magazine, *Vol. LIX, No. 4, August, 1983, pp. 481-82.*

In his twenty second volume of the "How Did We Find Out About" series, Isaac Asimov has again written an informative, easy to read account of the history and development of scientific theories involved in determining the size and nature of the universe. . . . Whether the universe is "open," "closed," or "oscillating" is discussed in Asimov's usual enticing manner. Although definitions and guides to pronounciation are included in the text, I think a general glossary would be a worthwhile addition. . . . An index is included. (pp. 7-8)

> *Althea L. Phillips, in a review of "How Did We Find Out about the Universe?" in* Appraisal: Science Books for Young People, *Vol. 17, No. 1, Winter, 1984, pp. 7-8.*

Dr. Asimov has done a better job of reducing to order the history of our broadening grasp of the universe than I would have thought possible in such a small volume. The key techniques—of measuring with at least some confidence the ever-increasing distances involved—are described clearly enough for the very young, and the decreasing level of reliability in these measures as one moves outward from the Solar system should be clear even to these readers. Isaac expresses the distance to Rigel with more confidence than I would—it is really too far for a good trigonometric parallax, and not typical enough to let one feel complete confidence in its spectroscopically deduced absolute magnitude—but this does not affect the general value of the exposition. . . .

Getting from the size of the Solar system to the expanding universe and the Big Bang in 64 pages is quite a feat.

> *Harry C. Stubbs, in a review of "How Did We Find Out about the Universe?" in* Appraisal: Science Books

for Young People, *Vol. 17, No. 1, Winter, 1984, p. 8.*

HOW DID WE FIND OUT ABOUT GENES?   (1983)

Giving clear synopses of some pioneering scientists in the field of gene and chromosome discoveries, Asimov traces the early history of gene biology. He offers short profiles on the life and works of Mendel (pea plants), De Vries (mutations), Flemming (chromosomes), Morgan (fruit flies) and Muller (X-rays); each made pioneering discoveries that initiated the body of knowledge we now have about gene theory and heredity. Asimov's clarity and interesting conversational tone make this book read like a dialogue between a scientist and a young audience about whom he cares. He wants readers to become involved in his explanations; he neither talks beyond the comprehension of an older elementary age child nor does he simplify condescendingly.

> *Robin Liebert, in a review of "How Did We Find Out about Genes?" in* School Library Journal, *Vol. 30, No. 1, September, 1983, p. 115.*

In general, the topics . . . are presented here in a clear and understandable way. The book's major failing is that the information in it is seriously outdated. The material covered ends with experiments performed in the 1920s; ignored are the revolutionary findings in genetics during the past 30 years. Most importantly, the discovery of the genetic material DNA in the 1950s, which has told scientists much about what genes are and how they work, is not included. This book actually ends up making the subject of genetics seem much more complex and mysterious than it is really is because the more recent discoveries about genes are not covered. . . . In general, this book is acceptable for young readers as an interesting and informative book on the history of genetics, although it should be supplemented by a more modern book. (pp. 296-97)

> *Glen A. Evans, in a review of "How Did We Find Out about Genes?" in* Science Books & Films, *Vol. 19, No. 5, May-June, 1984, pp. 296-97.*

An interesting and well written history of the development of knowledge defining genes and heredity. The best features of this book are the descriptions of the thought processes and experiments done by early investigators. Asimov describes and analyzes the data gained so that the reader feels part of the scientific process. The only faults are a few details which would have made the book clearer, such as a definition of F1 generation used in a number of diagrams and lack of the term mitosis in the text, although it is used in a diagram.

> *Mary M. Allen, in a review of "How Did We Find Out about Genes?" in* Appraisal: Science Books for Young People, *Vol. 17, No. 2, Spring-Summer, 1984, p. 10.*

NORBY, THE MIXED-UP ROBOT   (with Janet Asimov; 1983)

Jeff Wells, the story's futuristic hero, needs a teaching robot to help him pass his Martian Colony Swahili course. The one he can afford looks like a broken-down piece of junk, but Norby (as he's named) has strange and extensive powers including the ability to go into hyperspace. It's fortunate he's so versatile because Jeff, Jeff's older brother Fargo, and Norby all find themselves up against Ing the Ingrate, who wants to take over the solar system. The characterizations are slim, but the Asi-

movs portray a warm relationship between a boy and his robot. Wordiness is a problem here; however robot lovers will probably not be deterred from proceeding with the Star Wars-type adventures.

> *Ilene Cooper, in a review of "Norby, the Mixed-Up Robot," in* Booklist, *Vol. 80, No. 2, September 15, 1983, p. 162.*

Young boys may enjoy the scrapes [Jeff and Norby] experience. . . . Perhaps younger minds can provide explanations for the characters' actions and overlook narrative holes. Creative minds such as this would be better occupied with other challenges than they will find in this book. Recommended only for the younger readers and then, only as being better than television or video games.

> *Susan H. Harper, "Kiddy Robot Series Trivial," in* Fantasy Review, *Vol. 7, No. 7, August, 1984, p. 44.*

NORBY'S OTHER SECRET   (with Janet Asimov; 1984)

It seems that Norby, the robot first seen in *Norby, the Mixed-up Robot* . . . , can travel through time as well as space. Since Norby is unique, his origin and workings are of interest to government and military officials, who plan to dismantle him. He escapes by taking his 14-year-old owner, Jeff, and himself to Jamya, a planet inhabited by friendly dragons. Norby is convinced that his own history is linked with Jamya's, and time travel reveals that he was created by the "Mentors," robots who ruled the planet thousands of years before. His comical errors, some natural and some deliberate, convince the government that Norby is of no use to them; having discovered who he is, he is then free to decide to remain on Earth with Jeff or to return to his now-ancient "father" on Jamya. He chooses to visit Jamya but to stay with Jeff, his friend. Norby's personality and his relationship with Jeff are well developed in this light science fiction story, and his unpredictable escapades supply entertainment and suspense. (pp. 153-54)

> *Anita C. Wilson, in a review of "Norby's Other Secret," in* School Library Journal, *Vol. 31, No. 2, October, 1984, pp. 153-54.*

In an entertaining follow-up to *Norby, the Mixed-Up Robot* . . . , Jeff Wells and his charismatic older brother Fargo help the barrel-shaped robot piece together the history of his scrambled innards. . . . Norby's discovery that he can . . . travel through time is incidental to the plot, although it makes a nice title, and the whole of this fast-paced, futuristic action/adventure yarn is less than the sum of its parts. Fans of light science fiction, however, will enjoy a reunion with the personable Norby, and the Asimovs have bulwarked their story with an array of space-age technological gimcracks that will grab young readers' imaginations. (pp. 439-40)

> *Karen Stang Hanley, in a review of "Norby's Other Secret," in* Booklist, *Vol. 81, No. 6, November 15, 1984, pp. 439-40.*

[Norby's] talents include anti-gravity, hyperdrive, time travel and any other SF/Star Wars cliché you can think of—he's even an R2D2 look-alike.

This is a lively, good humoured, crowded sequel to *Norby the Mixed-up Robot*. It's light-hearted and good fun as the incompetent, unique machine and his partner, Jeff, blunder from one planet to another. . . . Harmless enough material for 9-13s.

> *David Bennett, in a review of "Norby's Other Secret," in* Books for Keeps, *No. 37, March, 1986, p. 17.*

HOW DID WE FIND OUT ABOUT COMPUTERS? (1984)

This is another important addition to Asimov's easy-to-read, non-technical, historically accurate, and informative *How Did We Find Out About . . .?* series. Five short chapters . . . trace the history of computers from abacuses and slide rules; gears and punch cards; binary numbers and switches; tubes and transistors; to chips and microchips. Written in Asimov's characteristic concise, fast-moving narrative style, the well-indexed book is neither intimidating nor condescending. A useful reference for readers aged 10 and up.

> *Betty Herb, in a review of "How Did We Find Out about Computers?" in* School Library Journal, *Vol. 31, No. 3, November, 1984, p. 39.*

This book is a good demonstration of Asimov's skill at providing clear and accurate descriptions of technological advances. He deals with an extremely popular subject—computers—and focuses on a single aspect—their development from abacuses and slide rules through miniaturization to some speculation on their future uses. Careful explanations of the workings of the machine at various stages are found throughout, but they do not impede readers' progress. . . . Cohen's *Simon and Schuster Question and Answer Book: Computers* (Wanderer, 1982) provides broader information but does not progress chronologically in its presentation, nor are the explanations as lucid as Asimov's. Burke's *Microcomputers Can Be Kidstuff* (Hayden, 1984) is written for students of the same age and offers an introduction to direct interaction with the computer through programming along with a very clearly written historical background. Asimov's book will meet a need for material for student reports that is accessible to those in grades four and up, and it will leave them with a good understanding of why various advances like the binary numbering system, the slide rule and microchips were all important.

> *Sarah Berman, in a review of "How Did We Find Out about Computers?" in* School Library Journal, *Vol. 31, No. 3, November, 1984, p. 119.*

Asimov excels at synthesizing complex material into factual yet readable narratives, and his survey of the evolution of computers in just five chapters is no exception. However, he slights two key concepts that children are generally required to master: the distinction between digital and analog measurements is blurry, and there is no explanation of the binary numbering system. Still, this cogent account provides young students with a useful historical perspective that will broaden their understanding of today's computers.

> *Karen Stang Hanley, in a review of "How Did We Find Out about Computers?" in* Booklist, *Vol. 81, No. 9, January 1, 1985, p. 637.*

ASIMOV'S GUIDE TO HALLEY'S COMET: THE AWESOME STORY OF COMETS (1985)

There are many other good Halley's comet titles around these days as we prepare for the Great Return of 1985-86, but As-

imov's fame and undeniable readability recommend this as the one for all public and school collections. Despite occasional condescending asides—explaining that Tycho Brahe and Galileo Galilei are "usually known" by their first names, or attributing the mispronunciation of *Halley* to the popularity of a musical group led by "someone named Bill Haley"—Asimov is a marvelous common-language scientific exegete. It will be a rare reader who doesn't finish this book in a hurry, spurred on by the promise (fulfilled!) of revelations about the possible catastrophes comets might have wreaked in the past and may wreak again.

> *Ray Olsen, in a review of "Asimov's Guide to Halley's Comet," in* Booklist, *Vol. 81, No. 11, February 1, 1985, p. 745.*

Asimov's Guide to Halley's Comet: The Awesome Story of Comets is a straightforward, . . . yet brief account of comets with emphasis on Halley. In his typical easy-to-read style, the author touches on virtually everything from early fears of comets through current debates on the demise of the dinosaurs.

Asimov may be at his best when explaining why space probes (none of them from the United States) are being sent off for the coming encounter. His fans, as well as those desiring a readable, nonmathematical discussion of comets, will not be disappointed. But look elsewhere if you are seeking information on observing P/Halley.

> *George S. Mumford, in a review of "Asimov's Guide to Halley's Comet," in* Sky and Telescope, *Vol. 70, No. 2, August, 1985, p. 131.*

Many of the books that have appeared in anticipation of the 1986 sighting of Halley's comet have contained some of the elements of this guide; no other has all of them or is written with Asimov's distinctive combination of casual, almost conversational style and profoundly detailed knowledge. . . . Information-packed, authoritative, eminently readable. An index is provided.

> *A review of "Asimov's Guide to Halley's Comet," in* Bulletin of the Center for Children's Books, *Vol. 39, No. 2, October, 1985, p. 22.*

NORBY AND THE LOST PRINCESS (with Janet Asimov; 1985)

Norby is a slightly cockeyed robot, and the Lost Princess is the victim of a freak accident that has stranded her on a muddy swamp of a planet, being held prisoner by a gang of musically-inclined beings, trapped in a tree. The rescue party includes Jeff Wells and his older brother, Fargo; Albany Jones, SpaceCop and daughter of the Mayor of Manhattan; Admiral Boris Yobo, who seems to be Asimov's answer to Mr. T; and a small fire-breathing dragon. There are also encounters with a shy female robot and a not-so-shy Queen.

Isaac Asimov is known for his puckish sense of humor. *Norby . . .* is by turns hysterically funny and exasperatingly cute. The plot twists involve space travel, time travel, a singing contest, and several abortive attempts before the princess is finally united with her parents. The Norby . . . series is shaping up to be one that appeals not only to middle-grade youngsters, but also to their older brothers and sisters.

> *Roberta Rogow, in a review of "Norby and the Lost Princess," in* Voice of Youth Advocates, *Vol. 8, No. 3, August, 1985, p. 191.*

[The] plot moves at hyperspacial speeds. The characters all have funny lines, and there is a nice bit of characterization in the princess who has metamorphosed into a talking tree. Needless to say, everyone gets rescued, and there's a surprise about the princess in the breathless conclusion. If this sounds like an episode from the old TV show Lost in Space, it's because both are essentially fantasy with robots and space ships for magic. They work well with an audience that doesn't understand or care what hyperspace means but who want to get on to the next planet. There are never enough of these stories for readers who ask for science fiction but want wish-fulfillment with space props. Sure to be popular in libraries where the "Dragonfall 5" series (Lothrop; o.p.) by Earnshaw circulates.

> *Carolyn Caywood, in a review of "Norby and the Lost Princess," in* School Library Journal, *Vol. 32, No. 1, September, 1985, p. 130.*

HOW DID WE FIND OUT ABOUT THE ATMOSPHERE?   (1985)

Asimov presents a succinct history of scientific speculation and experimentation concerning the earth's atmosphere. Beginning with the ancient Greek philosophers, he explains changes in thought and technology that have led to our present understanding of the subject. In the last chapter he indicates how our atmosphere is unique by comparing it with that of other planets and moons in our Solar System. . . . Asimov answers the question posed in the title in lucid and readable fashion. While this book does not have the popular appeal of others in the series, libraries with a demand for the subject will be well served by this volume.

> *Carolyn Phelan, in a review of "How Did We Find Out about the Atmosphere?" in* Booklist, *Vol. 82, No. 4, October 15, 1985, p. 332.*

Asimov's lucid explanation of the atmosphere will aid comprehension of it among upper elementary and junior high students. . . . Names of scientists and new scientific words are introduced with the phonetic spelling; meanings are given for Greek and Latin roots. . . . Simple vocabulary and sentence structure, as well as the author's ability to explain the subject clearly make this an informative, rewarding book.

> *Mary Wadsworth Sucher, in a review of "How Did We Find Out about the Atmosphere?" in* School Library Journal, *Vol. 32, No. 4, December, 1985, p. 86.*

HOW DID WE FIND OUT ABOUT DNA?   (1985)

Although the book is slim, it is not simple, and readers will probably need some background in chemistry to understand this explanation of DNA, the primary genetic material of living systems. The story begins in 1869 when a young chemist discovered a material called nuclein. This was the first step in learning how genes, made up of DNA, carry inherited characteristics. Asimov guides readers through this complex material but a glossary would have been extremely helpful. . . . [Science] students may find this a useful introduction.

> *Ilene Cooper, in a review of "How Did We Find Out about DNA?" in* Booklist, *Vol. 82, No. 9, January 1, 1986, p. 682.*

Paragraphs are short and sentences are uncomplicated; nevertheless, material concerns molecular biology—double helix, replication, recombinant DNA—concepts which will be difficult for students to really understand in spite of the frequent diagrams used to help explain the text. New scientific words are in italics with the pronunciation in parentheses. . . . Of most interest to high-school science students.

> *Mary Wadsworth Sucher, in a review of "How Did We Find Out about DNA?" in* School Library Journal, *Vol. 32, No. 6, February, 1986, p. 92.*

The writing is admirably clear. . . . Lacking, however, is an introduction that states in simple but comprehensible terms what DNA is and why we need to find out about it. There may well be 10-year-olds with the background in biology and chemistry to find this abbreviated presentation interesting; but as an introduction to the subject for persons not well grounded in cellular biology, the book falls far short. The last chapter mentions Nobel prizes eight times, which underlies the predominant role of DNA research in recent scientific advances, but which perhaps would have been better handled as a separate listing than as a litany. Unless a library wishes to hold every one of Asimov's books in this series, another basic work such as Frankel's *DNA: The Ladder of Life* would better serve readers' needs by presenting a more thorough treatment along with pertinent discussion of the significance of this knowledge.

> *Elsa Marston, in a review of "How Did We Find Out about DNA?" in* Voice of Youth Advocates, *Vol. 9, No. 1, April, 1986, p. 44.*

NORBY AND THE INVADERS   (with Janet Asimov; 1985)

Norby, the petulant robot, returns for his fourth adventure. This time Norby helps to achieve understanding between the dragons of Jamya and anti-technology invaders. The Asimovs glorify the peacemakers but provide such breakneck plots that the message becomes subliminal. Norby, like recent movie robots, is appealing and childlike in his approach to problems, allowing readers to identify with his triumphs. Serious issues of how to enjoy technology without destroying the environment are understandable without being patronizing. Display this with an "If you liked R2D2 . . ." sign.

> *Carolyn Caywood, in a review of "Norby and the Invaders," in* School Library Journal, *Vol. 32, No. 6, February, 1986, p. 79.*

Robotics fans and those who enjoyed Norby's earlier adventures . . . will find this fast-paced plot equally diverting. . . . A funny, lightweight science fiction tale that should work especially well in attracting reluctant readers.

> *Barbara Elleman, in a review of "Norby and the Invaders," in* Booklist, *Vol. 82, No. 13, March 1, 1986, p. 977.*

Margot Benary-Isbert

1889-1979

(Also wrote as Margot Benary) German-born American author of fiction and translator.

Benary-Isbert is remembered for her vivid depiction of post-World War II Germany in realistic stories which are popular with both German and English-speaking children and young people. Focusing on such universal experiences as the securing of a permanent home, keeping a family together, or falling in love for the first time, Benary-Isbert's works reflect her belief in the strength and perennial hopefulness of the young while stressing such themes as courage, initiative, self-reliance, family loyalty, and the healing power of nature. One of the first authors to publish books for German children after the war, she is best known for *The Ark* and *Rowan Farm*, two stories for junior high readers which feature the Lechow family, four spirited children and their mother who rebuild their lives in West Germany after being forced to leave Russian-occupied Pomerania. Benary-Isbert's works include such grim realities as death, defeat, and displacement, but she lightens their seriousness by describing warm personal relationships as well as informative, affectionate portrayals of animals and the out-of-doors. In addition to creating several realistic novels with contemporary settings, she wrote a modern fairy tale based on Old World legends, a quiet novel about a nineteenth-century German family, and a trio of works drawn from her memories of life before the war. Benary-Isbert collaborated closely with her translators when her books were rendered into English; she eventually became her own translator and also translated the works of Julia Cunningham into German.

Critics praise Benary-Isbert for her ability to convey wonder, beauty, and enduring moral values as well as stark reality, and they often assess her family chronicles as outstanding examples of their type. Acclaimed for her lifelike characterizations, fluent storytelling, successful presentation of mature subjects, and objective portrait of Germany, Benary-Isbert is recognized for her compassion, humor, and insight into the minds and hearts of young readers. While some reviewers consider her works sentimental and their pacing slow, most agree that she wrote with rare understanding of both the postwar experience and the concerns of youth.

Benary-Isbert received numerous awards for her books, including the German Order of Merit Officer's Cross for "building bridges among young people of the world."

(See also *Contemporary Literary Criticism*, Vol. 12; *Something about the Author*, Vols. 2, 21 [obituary]; *Contemporary Authors New Revision Series*, Vol. 4; and *Contemporary Authors*, Vols. 5-8, rev. ed., Vols. 89-92 [obituary].)

AUTHOR'S COMMENTARY

[*The following excerpt is taken from a speech Benary-Isbert gave to the Association of Children's Librarians of Northern California in fall, 1956.*]

It is not easy to tell about how my books came to be written, as all creative things have their source in the subconscious.

They rise from we don't know where, like bubbles from a dark pond. All at once there is an idea which slowly gains shape, becomes visible and tangible, grows and demands to be put in form. One word may kindle the spark; a person you meet, a sentence you read; a song you hear on a summer evening from far away; a lonely child you see standing at the street corner of a strange city and crying. Ideas happen to you; they take possession of you, and sometimes it takes years of your life to cope with them.

When I read a short notice in a German paper in the fall of 1948 about a group of young actors who had settled in an old castle in Franconia because they could not pay their rent in town any longer, I knew at once that this was in a way a personal message to me and that I would have to go and see this Castle Theatre. This was not easy, as there was no train to that remote place in the backwoods, no bus, not even a decent road. But my good husband helped me to get there, almost ruining the old tires of our shaky pre-war car on those roads. It was a flaming day of Indian summer, or Nachsommer, as we call it in Germany, when we arrived at the castle, and I immediately fell in love with it. I stayed ten days and they were some of the happiest days of my life. Every morning at ten I sat in my coat in one of the big, high, chilly rooms and attended the rehearsals. Every afternoon I helped load the old truck; we would drive to some village or little town, build up the stage—and then the enchantment of this world of make-believe cast its spell over me once more. I sat on the hard benches of some little village inn and listened to some of the best performances I had ever seen. It was sheer delight living and working with these courageous and enthusiastic young boys and girls, their director and his gentle wife, sharing everything with them. The castle was frightfully cold, the October wind whistling through the halls and staircases, as quite a few windows were still without glass. Food was still very scarce. Luckily I had had sense enough to bring some coffee and tea, powdered milk and sugar from an American gift parcel, and you can hardly imagine what luxuries they were at that time. When I left I had a gorgeous cold, as even our little refugee room in West Germany was more comfortable than this princely castle. They took me to the next railway station with the truck, and when we said good bye, I promised to write a book about the Castle Theatre one day. It was almost three years before I started it, but it was in my mind all the time. We immigrated to this country, and when the ice of the cold winter of '52-'53 was melting on Lake Michigan, I sat in a boarding house in Evanston, in a completely strange town, and drew up the first chapter. It was a long struggle to get the story as I had imagined it. In March '55 I sent the manuscript to Margaret McElderry, the editor of children's books at Harcourt Brace, and this spring *Castle on the Border* has been published. (p. 1)

To be with librarians always makes my tongue itch, because I know it is your job, or better your profession, to handle books, to judge books, and to bring them where they belong: to the reader. Moreover you know all about children and their connection with books. You know the kind of books they like and read, which is, of course, very important for me. For if the books I happen to write fail to appeal to children, nobody on earth can make the youngsters read them, not even you. So here is the first question: how and what must we write to make children read? What can we do to find the way to their hearts and minds—*and* the hearts and minds of adults also. For we must not forget the adult reader when we write for children. Not only because it is the adult who buys children's books! I am convinced that no children's book is any good if fathers and mothers, librarians and teachers, uncles, aunts, and grandparents cannot thoroughly enjoy it also.

If we do not suceed in catching the adults' attention also, we have failed. For every adult remains in part a child, and the few who have not kept the childhood quality of wonder are not worth writing for anyhow. (p. 2)

But after all the important thing is that our *young* readers like what we write. If the adult has kept something from his childhood, so does every child already have the essentials of a grown person hidden in his young soul. One thing he resents is being looked down on. He prefers a book he does not completely understand to one that is below his level. He does not like to feel that the author wants to hand him out a moral, to educate him. He wants nothing more or less than a good story. That sounds simple enough. But what is a good story? Apart from other qualities, I think it is a story in which you feel the enchantment of the storyteller, which in a kind of alchemistic process transfers itself to the reader. Look at an oriental storyteller; remember Scheherezade. Had she not been completely carried away by her own stories, she would not have been able to hold the king's imagination and suspense for one thousand and one nights—and her pretty head on her shoulders as well. Children want stories with adventure, with humor, with human virtues that are not too obvious; stories seriously and at the

same time lightly told; stories about live people with whom they can laugh and cry, not broomsticks dressed up in all kinds of good examples and wise sayings. Of course, children will not tell us all this if we ask them. But don't we all remember our own childhood and what we felt when we had been given one of those books about wonderfully good children, living patterns of virtue, diligence, and good behavior, books which we detested because they bored us to death! We smelled the moral—and turned away.

On the other hand, why did we all love Tom Sawyer, his friend Huck, and the little Swiss girl Heidi? Why do we still love them? Not because they are pale, meek pictures of model children but human beings sparkling with life, a challenge to governesses and aunts and respectable citizens, so vividly real that they have become friends we will never forget.

No, I don't believe in writing educational books. Every good book cannot help having an educational value of its own, but we must be careful to avoid thinking in educational terms when we write. Of course there is a fundamental conception of the characters we are writing about, perhaps the idea of what courage and persistence can do in an adverse world; or the image of a young person who has to learn that nobody has the right to an isolated existence. Or one wants to show the importance of family bonds; loyalty between friends; the need for understanding other people; the close relationship of all life, or as Albert Schweitzer calls it, "the reverence for life"; in short the central idea of a book. It is there of course, because it is in the writer, because it is the way he sees life and people. But I have found that once I am carried away by the spell of a story that insists on being told, once my characters come alive in my mind, I can pretty well let them take care of themselves. In fact they often do it so thoroughly that I gasp when I re-read what I have written. And this exactly is what—for me—makes writing an ever-new, exciting, and glorious adventure, the simple fact that the people in my book start following their own rules, living their own lives, and I am after all only the medium through which they must pass. As soon as that happens, I know that I am on the right track.

There is another rule that I can depend on. If I do not enjoy telling my story, there is something wrong, and I feel pretty sure that nobody will enjoy reading it either. But don't misunderstand me! This joy in writing does not mean that it is not hard work and a fierce struggle from the first page to the last. And when you reach the last page, you turn right back to the first one again and re-write and re-write, perhaps a dozen times, perhaps more, never being content, never coming quite up to the image in your mind. There are doubts, misgivings, the struggle with your own limitations, periods of deep depression and frustration. It may sound crazy, but that is how it is—at least with me.

They tell me that modern children do not read very much. . . . It is true that fifty, or even twenty, years ago, there was more leisure in every realm of life; there were no movies, no radio, no television, and sports were not taken so seriously either. But still I hesitate to acknowledge this all-too-evident reason for not reading. There is always time, when you want to read! (pp. 2-3)

Perhaps reading is made too easy for young people now? They have fine public libraries in almost every community; they have school libraries and bookmobiles; from all sides they are urged to read. They do not have to save pennies from their allowance to be able at last to buy a book they have been longing for.

When I was young there was no urging, beyond the books we read at school. And it was not so easy to get hold of a book either. We usually got a book or two for Christmas and our birthdays, and these had to last over the whole year. They were exchanged among friends, they were cherished and read over and over until we almost knew them by heart. We had long and excited discussions about them. If we could, we sneaked adult books out of our parents' bookcases. This meant secret reading at night with a candle, or on a certain place not originally intended for reading but where at least we were left alone. Reading was considered a reward which you had to earn. "If you bring home good reports this week you may read as much as you like on Sunday," we were told. No wonder we considered reading one of the highlights of life!

I remember living completely in the books I read. One month I would be the strong, silent type, the next a budding young scientist, a lively package of mischief in the third. Once I got hold of a history of saints and there is no telling what could have happened, only that my teachers in school and my governess at home did not recognize the state I was headed for as sainthood. Luckily for the peace of mind of well-meaning grownups, they seldom did guess what I was reading! In fact I read everything printed that came my way. It must have been some time after the saints that I started talking in sentimental, high-sounding phrases of the eighteenth century, and nobody had any idea that I had just made the acquaintance of Werthers Leiden, sobbing my heart out with Goethe's famous young man.

No, they certainly never needed to make me read! (pp. 3-4)

Another obstacle on my way to books was that my father and my teachers agreed that my imagination, far from needing stimulating, was already too lively for their taste.

On our way home from school I told stories to my classmates. These stories were different and in telling them I made a big mistake. I always told them in the first person and as if they were the gospel truth. Probably I believed them myself. Mostly I told about all the animals I had at home, from ponies and dogs to tame tigers and lions and a little alligator or two in my bathtub. There were a lot of adventures with these pets, sometimes funny and sometimes tragic. These stories went on and on without end, and my friends all had their favorites. By and by their enthusiasm lured me into more daring fantasies in which people of our daily life played a part. Once I told how one night I had sneaked into the dormitory of the good nuns of our convent school and found the pious ladies sitting around their dim night light, playing cards and conversing in hearty sailor language such as I had read in *Treasure Island*. But here I had gone too far. I was summoned by our headmistress and was told to stop those regrettable lies right away—or else! I was frightfully embarrassed, because nobody had ever accused me of lying before, and I promised to reform. From now on I told stories only about my own family. My chief hero, and my friends' favorite character of this period, was one paternal ancestor who had been kidnapped by gypsies from his father's castle in Spain when he was a baby, and who went on to lead a most colorful life thereafter. He grew up to be a famous gypsy chief and robber knight, and I don't remember how often he escaped the gallows by the skin of his teeth. They never got him, though, I am glad to say. But even that did not suit the authorities when they heard about it. The headmistress, who was strict but kindhearted and not without a sense of humor, had another talk with me, and at last she suggested that I write my stories down instead of telling them. She prob-

ably guessed that I was to learn that lies written down were not called lies any longer, but fiction!

Henry Stendhal, the famous French writer, said in a letter to his sister: "Our home is such a bleak place. I started reading, and I was happy."

Here is one of the most common reasons for children's reading: the escape from everyday life into the thrill and excitement of a book. It is so easy to enter this other world. We are only separated from it by a book's cover.

Our time is not a time of peace and security, so children need the escape books offer more than ever. How can we show them the way to an indestructible inner peace and a profound security? (p. 5)

Family life, marriage—these are after all the cornerstones of our civilization. It is a good thing to let young readers feel that the sane, sound world of these old values still exists, but at the same time the warmth and security of family life is a thing we must work for. It is not served to us on a silver platter. The best things of life never are. We know that children love stories about happy families, even though they may be poor families struggling with all kinds of hardships, even though they may not have a car, a TV set, and a dishwasher, if only there is the bond of love and understanding, the responsibility of each member for all the others, the *nestwarme*, as old Pestalozzi called it: the warmth of a nest. Family life stands for a lot of things, for mutual help, for consideration of the needs and wishes of others, for discipline, for unselfishness. From the integrity of family life comes a sense of unity with a neighborhood, a country, with mankind.

When a child is of an age to look for ranges beyond his small familiar circle, the time has come for nature books, books about animals, travel to other countries, glorious adventure in olden and modern times, stories about strange peoples and other civilizations, the way our planet is built, the miracle of life development on it, and from there to the dazzling vision of the universe.

But most of all, I think, the young reader needs books about people. About men and women and children of all times and all countries who won in the struggle of life against all odds, because they believed in something, because they had courage and hope, strength and kindness. But do not let us forget to tell them about other people also: about those who succumbed, who did not succeed, but who won in a deeper sense because they learned to resign, to be content, not to pity themselves but to give to others; to accept their fate, and to keep their integrity, even in defeat. (pp. 5-6)

Margot Benary-Isbert, "An Author's Reflections," in Junior Libraries, *an appendix to* Library Journal, *Vol. 3, No. 9, May 15, 1957, pp. 1-6.*

Words are a writer's material, his imperfect tool to transmit ideas, pictures, images. From beginning to end the writer's struggle is for the right word in the right place. It is a lifetime battle, a never-finished one, for there can be no truce between the vision of perfection and the limitations of ability.

To go on in spite of and against these limitations is what Charles Morgan, in the preface to his play, *The Flashing Stream*, called singleness of mind: doing what we have to do with all our heart, all our mind, and all our soul. Morgan tells of an old farm hand ploughing a field. When the squire came by and asked him, "What would you do if you owned my rents?" the man answered, "Something useful," and after thinking, added, "A bit of ploughing." That is singleness of mind.

The peak of dedication, of singleness of mind, is reached by the saint; and every venture into the sphere of creative work, in any field, means following in the footsteps of the saint—at least to a certain degree and at certain periods. It does not matter whether you do a short essay about the eye of a spider, which will perhaps be read by a dozen scholars; or the great novel of the twentieth century, which will be read by millions; or simply—and not so very simply, either—a children's book. In each case you have to be dedicated to your work, to recognize it as what the saint would call a vocation, which necessarily excludes many other things you would like to do. It means renouncement of comforts, of hobbies, of joys; it can mean at times renouncement of your nearest and dearest. If your husband, your wife, your family and friends are able to accept, for a shorter or longer time, as the case may be, that they must leave you alone because you are concerned with your work, and with your work only—you are truly fortunate. If they love you enough to bear with you, the bond will be even stronger when one day you return to their world.

Another thing the writer has in common with the saint is his knowledge of what St. John of the Cross called the Dark Night of the Soul: the periods of inability to do your work, of utter despair, of the deep conviction that you will never write another worthwhile book. This is the crucial test of your existence as a writer. If you give up, you are lost. To struggle with your back to the wall; to hold onto your one weapon against despondency, your pen; to write even if you know that the day's work will end in the fireplace—that is singleness of mind.

Another battle, just as fierce and everlasting as the first, is the battle *against* words, against too many, too worn-out, too cheap words. Our language, all modern languages, have lost their innocence through too much and consequently too indifferent use. They have lost their power, their immediacy. There was a time when language was something sacred, when words were few, and precious, and potent. A word could give life and death; it could bless or curse, exorcise evil spirits, call the protective forces, make the sun rise and the rains come, the crops grow and the animals bear young. Words could lure the fish into the fisherman's net and the wild boar in the path of the hunter's arrow. The reverence for language, for words, has to be part of the writer's quest for truth, for clarity, for the pursuit—never quite accomplished—of the elusive unicorn.

Not long ago I read in the book of a German philosopher, "Every classical art of poetical expression consists in limitation. Compared to what is given, that which is omitted is infinite." Almost at the same time I found another quotation in a book by Freya Stark: "When we write, with the words we *use* we deal with all those which, unspoken, come to the reader's mind. It is not what we actually *say;* it is what we make him think that counts."

What we make him think! And I add, *that* we make him think. To do so, we must rediscover the magical quality of words, must learn again to make words potent and few, as they were in the youth of humanity. We must do what a conjurer does in another way with another medium: make the reader see what is not there; make him create in his own mind what is beyond the words; let him find his own way and not even know that he has been led. This is especially important in writing for children, to counteract the pre-chewed food most television programs offer them; for the growing young mind needs challenge, needs the emptiness that asks to be filled. (pp. 202-03)

It is indeed amazing what places can do and have done to my imagination; how often all at once a process of creativity started when I entered a strange house, walked through a strange city or a landscape I had never seen. Unprepared and unwarned I can get a feeling that this place has been waiting for me and will convey a message that has a very special meaning. It is what the Greeks meant when they said they felt in a certain locality "the God touching them." Such experience has an unrealistic, almost uncanny quality that cannot be described.

My home town, Frankfurt, Germany, is a very old city, saturated with history and so full of stories that you encounter them at every street corner. As a child I was fascinated by the web of crooked, narrow streets around the cathedral and the medieval town hall, called the Römer, in which the German-Roman emperors were elected. Whenever I found an excuse to escape the observant eyes of our succession of unimaginative governesses, I strolled among those old houses, which seemed to emanate tales of human fates, and tried to catch the voices that had long been silent. That must have been the time when I first started to do what disapproving adults called "making up stories."

There was one house that stood in a narrow lane inaccurately called Grosse Eschenheimer Gasse. I passed it often when I went back from school through the inner city instead of through the park, as we were supposed to do. The house had a stately entrance gate, and in my mind I saw footmen in *escarpins* and white wigs, torch lights in hand, directing coaches with glittering ladies and pigtailed gentlemen in them. Goethe's mother was once among the illustrious guests of the Prince of Turn-and-Taxis, who resided here. How I longed to pass through the wrought-iron gate and walk through the wide courtyard and into the magnificent house; how I wished to have lived in the gallant time when ladies wore crinolines and when the palace was the residence of one of the richest princes of the First German Reich. How could I have guessed that as a young girl I would belong to this house, work in it, and love it more every day. Here is how it happened:

I had registered for courses in journalism and German Literature at the University of Frankfurt. At that time a museum of ethnology and anthropology had been established in the old baroque palace in the Grosse Eschenheimer Gasse, of which I had not thought for some time. The man who had been the initiator and was now the director of the museum was a former physician who had worked for the Dutch government in the Malayan colonies and had lived for many years in inner Sumatra with one of the most primitive tribes known at that time. Somehow I had enrolled in one of his courses also and soon got so entangled with his way of teaching and with his alluring subject that I asked him one day where and how I could learn more about it. He advised me to visit the museum, study the collections, and use the small library to my heart's desire. I did; and instead of attending my other courses, I found myself a daily visitor of the house that had been a childhood love: now walking through the once-closed gate, ascending the stairs to the princely rooms with the precious stucco ceilings, and getting acquainted with the collections from strange countries, many of them specimens of Stone Age tribes.

After some time Dr. Hagen asked me to become his secretary. So, against all my intentions, a house and what I had found in it had drawn me into a career I had never planned. I found myself among fetishes and mummies, shrunken heads, tools of witchcraft and poisoned weapons; and I was the only female among a group of the oddest characters I have ever met.

All this held me in a magic circle for more than seven years with never a dull moment; and I might have been held for the rest of my life, had not a young scientist come to prepare himself for an expedition to the Stone Age tribes of New Guinea. Since I was at that time the librarian—probably the most outrageously unqualified librarian in human history—I had to advise this young doctor of philosophy about the use of our library and where he would find the books that were important for his purpose. However, instead of going to New Guinea, the poor fellow had to go into the First World War with the cavalry regiment of which he was a reserve officer. In 1917 he came home on leave, and we were married.

Certainly no other house has ever done quite as much for me as the Frankfurt Turn-and-Taxis palace! Thirty years later, I wrote a book about my slapdash career, *The Maid of All Work,* which one day I intend to rewrite for publication in the United States.

Later the old place of my husband's family in Erfurt had a strong appeal to my imagination. This last home where we were happy and felt secure for many years lives in my books, though I may never visit it again. And there was Rowan Farm, where we found refuge when we fled from Thuringia as the Russians took over, and which became the background for two of my books.

Then there was the case of the Castle on the Border, which cast its spell even before I had seen it. (pp. 205-07)

One day, as I stood in the castle courtyard, almost at once the dim outline of a story began to dawn in my mind. It was not difficult to guess what my heroine would feel standing here for the first time in her life, a young girl with an obsession to become an actress. She would immediately be under the spell of the place, as I was now. Nobody needed to tell her that the little balcony hanging on one of the gray stone walls like a swallow's nest could only be Juliet's balcony; and moved by the enchantment Leni was sure to whisper: ''Good night, good night! As sweet repose and rest come to thy heart as that within my breast.''

Then and there Leni would know that against all odds she would fulfill the dream, would become an actress—just as I knew that I would write a book about this castle and about the young girl of whom I had never thought before.

The power of place was strong in the small German town on the river Lahn, where my father and his four brothers and one sister grew up one hundred years ago, when the Prussians took over the small dukedom of Nassau. My grandfather had been the *Amtmann* there, which at that time was judge and administrator in one person. Twice I started to write a book about that period and about the old courthouse in which the family lived above the offices and courtrooms on the ground floor. But somehow I could not find the right mood, and both times I destroyed the manuscript. Then, in the fall of 1961, I came to this old town with its narrow streets and its thousand-year-old cathedral to sniff around and try to get the scent of the place. I thought I did not know a living soul in the town, and in fact I didn't; but on the second day a chain reaction started. Without doing anything myself, I was handed from one person to the next, and information was poured out to me in the most unexpected way.

When I came home from the trip, I started the book for the third time. It took me another two years to finish it, and now the translator has it. When it comes back to me, I will have to fight the battle of words all over again. For the words of the translator, even with his best intentions, never seem to be *my* words; and I have to transform them back into my own style, often into my own intentions, which have not been completely understood. If you have trained yourself to leave things unsaid, the translator has indeed a hard time putting into words what is only hinted at. I know that I demand the almost impossible; but in the struggle for perfection and for the sake of my own singleness of mind, I deal as ruthlessly with the translator as with myself.

Despite the difficulties in all writing, help sometimes comes to us, undeserved and unrequested—small miracles gratefully accepted. What remains is the never-ending struggle of the writer, of everyone, to achieve not *the* best, for that will remain the ever-elusive goal, but *his* best, as humble as it may be. The furrow well ploughed, the seam properly stitched, the line clearly and truthfully written—let that be enough. (pp. 208-09)

> *Margot Benary-Isbert, "On Words, Singleness of Mind, and the Genius Loci," in* The Horn Book Magazine, *Vol. XL, No. 2, April, 1964, pp. 202-09.*

GENERAL COMMENTARY

JENNIE D. LINDQUIST

When Mrs. Benary's *The Ark* was published in this country last year, it was immediately hailed as an outstanding book for its sympathetic portrayal of the adventures of a family of refugees in Germany after the Second World War. Young people who read it felt that they knew Mother Lechow and all the children, could share their hardships and their fun; could see the old railroad car which they made into a home and called The Ark because of elder daughter Margret's great love for animals and her constant accumulation of ones to be cared for. But the book ended too soon; there was much more children wanted to know about the family, their friends and their animals. Fortunately, Mrs. Benary has written a second book [*Rowan Farm*], quite as good as the first, with Margret as the central character. Once again the people and animals on the Almut Farm come alive. The two books belong together as one of the most satisfying of our family chronicles—warm, lively, full of courage, and a deep understanding that comes from the author's own experiences.

> *Jennie D. Lindquist, in a review of "Rowan Farm," in* The Horn Book Magazine, *Vol. XXX, No. 5, October, 1954, p. 336.*

MAY HILL ARBUTHNOT

Margot Benary-Isbert gives us a vivid picture of Germany as she knew it, a true picture of what happens to farms, cities, families in a war-bombed city. Here is modern reality, grim or terrible or confusing but gallant, too, because in such books as these children find human beings courageously building a better life out of the rubble. (p. 21)

[In *The Ark*] the Lechow family, a mother and four children, are trying to reestablish something approaching a normal life in a bombed-out city. The doctor father may be dead or a prisoner of war. Even so, they waste little time lamenting the past and are grateful to obtain three unheated attic rooms from a reluctant landlady. (p. 502)

The story centers on Margret, who obtains a job as kennel maid to Mrs. Almut, who has brought her farm and famous breed of Great Danes through the war with the minimum care and the maximum grit. Margret loves and nurses the dogs back into condition, serves as midwife to the stock on the farm, and even helps to restore an old railroad car, which becomes "The Ark" to shelter the whole Lechow family.

In *Rowan Farm* . . . the father has returned, new characters are introduced, and Margret suffers the pangs of first love and jealousy. These stories are chiefly focused on the gallant struggles of one family to reëstablish normal life, not only for themselves but for others more lost than they. Both are superlative stories, and through the eyes of these vividly drawn characters young readers see the rubble of bombed-out cities and the wastelands of what were once beautiful farms. They feel the miseries of food deprivations, bitter cold, and, above all, the dislocation of hopes and plans. Yet these stories are filled with minor triumphs—a birthday cake, very dry but miraculously sweet to the last unbelievable crumb, and music, which feeds the spirit and is a glorious link with the past. And every reader will understand Mrs. Lechow's courageous attempts to keep alive the precious traditions of Christmas and will rejoice when, out of cold and deprivation, she succeeds in making not merely a merry Christmas but a blessed one for her family and all those people who have come into the circle of the Lechows' energy and courage.

Mrs. Benary tells us that most of the episodes in these two books are true of someone she knew during the postwar period in Germany. In her youth novel, *Castle on the Border* . . . , which was written in her new home in the United States, she tells a story about a hard-working group of young actors whose lives she shared for a year in postwar Germany. Whether biographical or fictional, these books reflect Mrs. Benary's own overflowing warmth and kindness. (pp. 502-03)

> *May Hill Arbuthnot, "The Adult and the Child's Books: Stories of Family Life," and "Other Times and Places: Margot Benary-Isbert," in her* Children and Books, *third edition, Scott, Foresman and Company, 1964, pp. 20-1, 502-03.*

MARGERY FISHER

During the two years compassed by [*The Ark* and *Rowan Farm*] we see Margret growing into a responsible young woman, with a happy courtship as the natural outcome of her development. There are other characters in the books as strongly drawn as Margret—her sister Andrea, for example, a born mimic with a generous allowance of charm; Mrs Almut herself who (as she says) holds a world championship for defeating bureaucracy; the young schoolmaster Christoph Huhnerbein, seriously disabled in the war, determined to teach his pupils to love and serve their fellow men; Mirri, the old 'bee-witch' who has never recovered from the death of her pacifist son. But because the deepest theme in the books is the healing power of nature and a natural, peaceful way of life, and also because the author's memories of her girlhood are expressed through Margret, it is she who is really the focal point of the action, as she is seen tending dogs, horses and sheep in the wonderful moments of birth, working to the point of exhaustion but fulfilling herself in the satisfying way she has found.

> *Margery Fisher, "Who's Who in Children's Books: Margret Lechow," in her* Who's Who in Children's Books: A Treasury of the Familiar Characters of Childhood, *Holt, Rinehart and Winston, 1975, p. 200.*

DIE ARCHE NOAH [THE ARK] (1948)

In one of the first books for young people to come out of postwar Germany, we meet the Lechow family, refugees from the East Zone. The father is still in a prison camp in Russia, one son is dead, but Frau Lechow and her four children work valiantly to make the best of the two rooms assigned to them in a battered town crowded with other refugees. Margret, almost 14, has the hardest time adapting herself, until she becomes kennelmaid on a farm outside the town. She and her oldest brother live in the Ark, an old railroad car, and gradually the car becomes a home for all the Lechows, as well as for a small lost boy.

The setting is unusual and interesting. But the best part of the book deals with the birth, death and care of the animals on the farm described with knowledge and affection. The story is handled rather amateurishly, with too many characters seen from too many points of view, so that the reader is sometimes confused, and the effect is scattered. Moreover there is constant self-pity and a feeling of a world too small and isolated. Apparently all these people have been living in a political vacuum, where no one of them has ever felt sympathy for the Nazis (who are never mentioned); there is something—to this adult reader, at least—disingenuous about the picture.

> *Marjorie Fischer, "The Refugees," in* The New York Times Book Review, *March 1, 1953, p. 32.*

Mrs. Benary-Isbert is a born storyteller who has been able to create living characters in the midst of the aftermath of war in a defeated country. Whether drawn from life or from the imagination of the author, every one of them takes a natural place in the story. While it is a true picture of life and death among a homeless people, it is lighted by a courage and a warm human sympathy and understanding that leave a glow in the heart of the reader. Whether the old railroad car which is converted into a home on the farm was a reality or of the author's invention, one is fascinated by its possibilities.

> *Anne Carroll Moore, in a review of "Die Arche Noah," in* The Horn Book Magazine, Vol. XXIX, No. 2, April, 1953, p. 102.

[*The Ark* has] a tragic setting, but there is not one really depressing moment in the story. Faith in one another, courage, initiative, humor bring to the saga of the Lechow family unfailing interest and a spirit that is almost gaiety. . . .

This is a book that we have all been waiting for—the story of a family in a foreign country, of a family that had been completely disrupted by war and had won, through their faith in one another, a new security. It is all the more important because the country happens to be postwar Germany. . . . There is no trace of sentimentality in this story but it does "pull at the heart-strings." It is the mother, really, who dominates it, with her courage, her humor, her tolerance, her quiet determination to keep the family together. We leave them reluctantly. We long to know more about them. Boys and girls who read this book will feel as close to Matthias and Joey, Margret and Andrea as though they were next-door neighbors. It is an important book, one that should reach many, many young Americans. (p. 64)

> *Mary Gould Davis, "A Wish Granted," in* The Saturday Review, *New York, Vol. XXXVI, No. 14, April 4, 1953, pp. 64-6.*

How many readers of *Little Women* remember that it was set in a grim post-war period? The poverty of the March family is more evident, but it is the richness of character, incident, and above all, of spirit, which makes their story memorable. The same kind of feeling is left by this German story of a refugee family whose happy life in Pomerania has been overlaid by successive war and post-war calamities. . . .

Mrs. Lechow, like Mrs. March, is a woman of parts, and her four children are lively and intelligent, eager to learn, and able to make a great deal out of next to nothing. Fourteen-year-old Margret is the central figure, but the others are made equally real, and their problems and friends provide a surprisingly comprehensive picture of post-war German life. Margret's main problem is finding her place in the new surroundings which have something to offer each of the other children. When she finds her niche, as kennel-maid on Almut's farm, the author has full scope to show her feeling for animals and the countryside; throughout the book she communicates her pleasure in family life and in the strength and promise of young people, developing and maturing. The people are made vivid, almost visible, especially merry Mrs. Almut, and little Hans Ulrich, who might be about seven but has no past, and not much of a present until the coming of the Lechows. There are several very moving Christmas chapters, and as an added delight, rather than a climax, the safe return of first Mrs. Almut's son and then Dr. Lechow from Russian camps, a return made probable simply because it hasn't been made a necessary pivot of the story. These people can stand on their own feet whatever happens, or wherever they might live—even the hint of coming romance between young Almut and Margret could be ignored by such well-established characters. Altogether, then, a book to grow on, with much wisdom and compassion to offer re-readers in particular. It's good to think that young readers in Germany, England and America may all share the adventures of the Lechows, even as they have long shared the March family, for such contacts can do more than many treaties and pacts and good-will missions.

A review of "The Ark," in The Junior Bookshelf, *Vol. 18, No. 6, December, 1954, p. 295.*

Margot Benary belonged to the liberal tradition of Germany, temporarily eclipsed in the years of Nazi domination. She suffered for this personally during the war, and in the books which she wrote afterwards she showed in fictional terms the dilemma of the liberal in war and its aftermath. Her finest achievement, *The Ark* . . . , is more personal than [Ian Serraillier's] *The Silver Sword*—understandably, for the author was closer than Serraillier to the bitterness and the anguish of political and military strife, and unlike him she had to take refuge in family love.

Essentially *The Ark* is a story not of adventure but of human relationships. (p. 30)

As a generalization, one might say that Europe is not the natural home of the family story. One obvious exception is *The Ark*. Margot Benary's moving novel, if not directly autobiographical, must certainly reflect some of her own experiences after the war. Like Serraillier's *The Silver Sword*, it is about recovery. Its characters, unlike Serraillier's, belong to the defeated race who have to rebuild their lives in the shadow of occupation. The Lechows have a shorter journey to make than Serraillier's Balickis, first to Parsley Street, 'a little lane like something out of a picture book' with houses miraculously surviving from the seventeenth century, and then to Rowan

Farm and the disused railway carriage which becomes their Ark.

The charm of *The Ark* springs from its concern with the realities of love and hunger. Food was a constant preoccupation of the families who clung to life in the harsh years of recovery, and the book is full of the bitterness of hunger and the glorious smell of food. . . . Children's literature is full of feasts, but few are described with such loving concern over each mouthful than the Lechows' Advent party with its four miraculous cakes.

The wonder of *The Ark* is not that it is a good book, for in many ways it falls short of excellence, but that it should have been written at all. It came out of war and defeat and out of the chaos that preceded reconstruction. Of the war there is little in the book; the author and the characters avoid direct reference to it when they can. Dieter, the young musician, recalls briefly his work on the West Wall and remembers: 'At home we never cared much for all the heiling and hurrahing'. After the war there is extreme hardship, humiliation as well as hunger, and the boredom of queueing. Mrs Benary and the Lechows rise above it, largely through a strong sense of family which extends to their motley collection of friends, partly because deprivation and suffering help them to comprehend fundamental truths. Christmas in Parsley Street means more to the children than it had done in happier days. 'The Christmas story was dearer and more familiar to them, perhaps, than it had ever been before to children in all the world's past.'

In its warmth and tenderness *The Ark* comes often to the brink of sentimentality. It never quite topples over. Mrs Benary always harnesses sentiment to reality. Her finest achievement is the character of Margret, who more than the others carries into peacetime the scars of war. There is a remarkable episode in which she fights for the life of the puppies in her charge at Rowan Farm. Somehow the animals become associated in her mind with the dead children she had seen on the refugees' marches. It might be an incongruous and embarrassing moment were the writer's touch less sure. But the reader accepts that 'all the world's suffering had come down at once upon her.' (pp. 180-82)

Marcus Crouch, "High Adventure" and "School— Home—Family," in his The Nesbit Tradition: The Children's Novel in England 1945-1970, *Ernest Benn Limited, 1972, pp. 26-47, 161-84.*

The Ark is a story of how one family managed to survive when their home, possessions, father, and one son were swept away during World War II. As all those chosen by Noah to come into the ark survived, so this story shows that life can be ongoing despite floods and wars, or holocaustal conditions. (p. 108)

The tragic moments of the story are the times when Margret faces the loss of something or someone she loves. The first tragedy is conveyed in retrospect, a device that helps to cushion the sorrow the reader must feel in learning of the loss of Margret's happy home and the death of her twin brother. The sadness is deepest for Margret because she and her twin were very close, and there seems to be no one who can take his place in her life. The trouble is compounded because Margret bears the grief silently within herself. One day she meets an old woman who has lost an only son in the war. Mari has found a way to cope with her sorrow and shares her illumination with the refugee girl. "When what you love best departs, there's a long time afterward when you're never at home anywhere. But wait, the dead come back. They come to life again within us; we have only to have patience and let it happen''. (pp. 108-09)

The old woman tells Margret that some people learn to re-member differently, whereas others must forget. But she says that remembering is the best medicine. And so Mari states the story's theme, which the girl finds to be the means of coping with the problems war has brought into her experience, and her former happiness does have an inner rebirth.

The second tragic moment happens on the farm where Margret is taking care of the livestock. For many sleepless nights and days, she has nursed a family of puppies whom she helped bring into the world. Now they are suffering from distemper and all are near death. One dog with tortured, pleading eyes drags herself to the girl and dies with her head on Margret's lap. The helplessness of having done all one can without avail wells up in Margret, and in her sorrow she remembers the refugee mothers and fathers who carry their dead children on their backs for many miles, clinging to this last presence of a dear one for whom no more can be done. Thus the girl un-derstands and gains compassion for others through her own tragic experience. Going later into the barn, however, she finds that the mare has given birth to a beautiful colt, and deeply stirred, Margret whispers, ''life!'' In her moment of sorrow she has tasted the bitterness of death and now experiences the joy of new birth, feeling something of the reciprocal quality of the two emotions, the latter made richer by the former.

A third moment of tragedy comes with the news of the death of Mrs. Verduz, the woman with whom the family first found refuge. They have all become fond of their hostess, who was very kind and supplied them with many things they could not have found otherwise, and her death seems a great loss. As in the second tragic instance, however, the death of the kind landlady is more than balanced by the homecoming of their father.

At the conclusion of the story, the family has found a new way of life that approximates the old. It is bittersweet because it is touched with the remembrance of people and objects no longer present, but it is a life enriched by suffering, resulting in a more comprehensive compassion for the troubles of humanity. The catharsis conveyed by the story is this clarification the family receives concerning life's ongoingness despite devas-tating conditions.

But the story is always tragedy, although it contains an affirm-ative outlook. There is no substitute for Margret's twin brother. What she finds is that a void created by death can be filled, but that part of the new is made more beautiful by remembrance of the old.

The story's message is emotionally touching and satisfying as well as realistic. There is no need for the construction of a fairy-tale approach to life. Comfort comes from looking deep, rather than turning aside, and, as the old woman told Margret, this kind of remembrance is the best medicine.

The author is able to create moods and atmospheres success-fully. The wind-blown icy night with its desolate streets sym-bolizes cold despair at the outset of the story. The warmth and peace of life on the farm with father, war-scarred but present among them in The Ark, seems symbolic of the peace Margret and her family have found after the suffering of the war years. (pp. 109-10)

> *Carolyn T. Kingston, ''The Tragic Moment: War,'' in her* The Tragic Mode in Children's Literature, *New York: Teachers College Press, 1974, pp. 93-123.*

DER EBERESCHENHOF [ROWAN FARM] (1949)

Rowan Farm carries on the story of the Lechow family begun by Mrs. Benary-Isbert last year in ***The Ark***. The latter volume, it will be recalled, transmitted a sense of excitement and tension in its account of a family experiencing displacement and re-habilitation. This is lacking in ***Rowan Farm;*** but the new book does portray the maturing of the children, the satisfactions of accomplishment, and the feeling of security that comes from problems faced and at least partially solved. . . .

Out of her own experiences Mrs. Benary-Isbert has written with warmth and understanding a worthy sequel to ***The Ark***.

> *Frances Lander Spain, in a review of ''Rowan Farm,'' in* The Saturday Review, *New York, Vol. XXXVII, No. 34, August 21, 1954, p. 35.*

[Margret's story] is the basic thread of a family story that gives many aspects of reconstruction in Germany. It includes inter-esting adults who have felt the war in different ways. It pierces the problems of war guilt as a teenager would feel it. So the book is truly a junior ''novel,'' giving us a rich, full slice of life and the emotions and development of an admirable girl, whose inner life will be recognized as true by girls in any country. . . .

It is a leisurely book, which through its length builds up a deep impression of the hard work on the farm, the beauty of country life, the variety of family problems and the different thinking of varied young people, from serious Margret to the siren from Frankfurt and the famous newspaper girl ''Bomu,'' and the singing ''Cellar Rats.'' There are sufficient throwbacks so that it could be read without reading ***The Ark*** first. Reading both will be a rewarding experience for any girl over twelve; more than any other postwar books for this age, they strike to the heart of problems of our time. Their final effect is one of hope and of beauty, for this writer is deeply imbued with the cycles of nature. There is a notable chapter on the birth of a calf; and in the background there are always the stars.

> *Louise S. Bechtel, in a review of ''Rowan Farm,'' in* New York Herald Tribune Book Review, *August 22, 1954, p. 7.*

Like ***The Ark*** this is an uneven performance. It is frequently sentimental and even a little banal, yet it has little of the Teutonic self-pity which seeped through the earlier book. Its horizons are wider and there are times when the author makes the reader sharply aware of the emotional as well as the physical devastation which follows war.

> *Ellen Lewis Buell, ''The Refugees,'' in* The New York Times Book Review, *October 10, 1954, p. 38.*

Although written as a sequel to ***The Ark,*** this can be treated as an independent story, and is, in some ways even better than the first book. . . . There is warmth and humor in the telling of the ups and downs of the various members of the family, and a depth of characterization and a maturity that will give the book appeal for teenage readers.

> *A review of ''Rowan Farm,'' in* Bulletin of the Chil-dren's Book Center, *Vol. VIII, No. 3, November, 1954, p. 18.*

As is the way of sequels, this book is less perfect than its predecessor, ***The Ark,*** being more loosely constructed, more concerned with the immediate present, and probably attempting too much. It still has much to recommend it and the Lechows' projects and personalities are still worth recording. The story contains much that will please those in search of light entertainment and also contrives to deal with personal and public matters of interest to thoughtful adolescents—and it is the air of contrivance which keeps the book below the level established by *The Ark.* However, there are many good scenes and real, vigorous people, notably the enterprising schoolmaster, a war cripple, who encourages his pupils to build a home for returning veterans in spite of local opposition and red tape. Mrs. Benary respects her readers' right to the truth; she is not afraid to mention death and the existence of difficult problems, and by neither over-emphasizing nor understating, gives a balanced picture of post-war German life. She conveys something of the urgency with which these friendly and responsible young people cut through red-tape and apathy and those conventions which could obtain only when their world was more secure and sheltered. Their reforming zeal is necessary if the more permanent values of sympathy, hope and faith are to be kept alive, and Mrs. Benary is very much on the side of life. Her positive approach, her sanity and understanding, keep this book from floundering in the multiplicity of incident. (pp. 218-19)

> *A review of "Rowan Farm," in* The Junior Bookshelf, *Vol. 19, No. 4, October, 1955, pp. 218-19.*

Rowan Farm is mature . . . , not in the style of its writing, but in its ideas. . . . Without sentiment or wishful-thinking, the children and parents are shown lifting their bruised heads again, the older ones bearing indelible marks, the younger ones relatively unscathed. Margret, the central figure, and her elder brother Matthias are shown adapting themselves to their changed world against a background of country activities which will enthral most children, and it may be that some of their reflections will take root in the young reader who is secure in his own home.

> *A review of "Rowan Farm," in* The School Librarian and School Library Review, *Vol. 8, No. 1, March, 1956, p. 66.*

ANNEGRET UND CARA [BLUE MYSTERY] (1951)

Annegret (of *Shooting Star*) is now back at home with her mother and father in the beautiful old German town where her father has his nursery of prize flowers and plants. Annegret's shyness at school changes to spirited enthusiasm as she raises a pet Great Dane and helps to solve the mystery of the disappearing blue gloxinia. The author's beautiful descriptive style and gentle unfolding of character make this a distinguished story. The adults and children are alive individuals; the mystery is fascinating and logical. The only drawback to the book is in [Enrico Arno's] illustrations. . . . (pp. 133-34)

> *A review of "Blue Mystery," in* Bulletin of the Children's Book Center, *Vol. X, No. 10, July-August, 1957, pp. 133-34.*

The mystery which concerns the theft of a rare gloxinia plant is similar in theme to that of Dorothy Clewes' *The Mystery of the Scarlet Daffodil* (Coward), but, though that is a good story too, this is a much richer book and far more than a mystery. It is distinguished for its warm picture of Annegret's home background filled with kindness, fun, a love of flowers and animals, and a festival spirit that culminates in the celebration of St. Martin's Day at the end of the book.

> *Jennie D. Lindquist, in a review of "Blue Mystery," in* The Horn Book Magazine, *Vol. XXXIII, No. 4, August, 1957, p. 306.*

This book has quality. It is less outstanding than *Castle on the Border* by the same author, yet it is still well above average. . . . [It] is in an almost idyllic setting that the author's understanding of young minds emerges in her portrayal of Annegret, who has a reality of outlook typified in her actions and conversation. Annegret's parents, the cook, the chief assistant Monch are all miniature portraits, placed in their right perspective to Annegret herself together with her child world and all it contains. The style has dignity, quiet humour and poetic feeling, giving a slightly fairy tale effect on a down-to-earth mystery. (pp. 64-5)

> *A review of "Blue Mystery," in* The Junior Bookshelf, *Vol. 22, No. 2, March, 1958, pp. 64-5.*

Margot Benary does not here touch the heart as she did in *The Ark,* but her new novel has sensibility and charm. . . . It is a pleasant story, but the merit of the book lies in its portrayal of human relations and in the quiet gentle charm of its atmosphere. It should give real pleasure to girls approaching their teens.

> *M. S. Crouch, in a review of "Blue Mystery," in* The School Librarian and School Library Review, *Vol. 9, No. 3, December, 1958, p. 234.*

HEILIGENWALD [A TIME TO LOVE] (1953)

There's a seven year span between Annegret Benninger of *The Shooting Star* and fifteen year old Annegret in *A Time to Love.* And in between there was *Blue Mystery.* The appeal in Margot Benary-Isbert's books lies in a sometimes too wholesome blend of reality and sentimentality, but somehow there is a kind of charm of recognition and one meets people known before. Father Benninger is a botanist, a liberal, always on the edge of trouble with the Hitler authorities. It was he who helped Jewish friends escape to England. It was his decision that sent his daughter to Heiligenwald in the Black Forest, the one school which encouraged freedom of thought—and allowed Annegret to have her beloved Great Dane with her. If the author's intent is to convey the likeness of German youngsters to their American counterparts, in this she succeeds. But the unlikenesses—the lack of sophistication, the scarcely resented acceptance of authority, the seemingly deliberate closing the eyes to much of the evil of Naziism—even in the Labor Service camp (quickly glossed over), some of this is hard to accept. On the story line, Margot Benary-Isbert moves right along. Her dialogue (perhaps it is the translation [by Benary-Isbert and Joyce Emerson]) seems too often stilted and unreal. This story ends with Annegret winning distinction as a singer—and with news that Eckhart, whom she loves, has been wounded but will shortly be invalided home . . . Life goes on in Hitler's Germany.

> *A review of "A Time to Love," in* Virginia Kirkus' Service, *Vol. XXX, No. 13, July 1, 1962, p. 571.*

Music and delight in all living things fill the story which seems less like fiction than a true account of a girl's growing years. . . . In spite of the tragic overtones the story is full of fundamental goodness, the beauty and wonder of nature, and the strength of love. The title applies not only to the young lovers but to the times when the need for love was greater than ever. A beautiful book for thoughtful girls who can understand a little the tragedy of the German people under Hitler.

*Ruth Hill Viguers, in a review of "A Time to Love,"
in The Horn Book Magazine, Vol. XXXVIII, No. 5,
October, 1962, p. 486.*

While Annegret's family is consistently anti-Nazi in their attitude, this is not a political novel, since their objection is
passive. The characterization is perceptive, the boarding school
background is lively, the writing has momentum and, in this
book, more variety than in others by this author since some of
the story is told in third person, and some of it is in the form
of the diary and the letters of Annegret. (pp. 37-8)

*Zena Sutherland, in a review of "A Time to Love,"
in Bulletin of the Center for Children's Books, Vol.
XVI, No. 3, November, 1962, pp. 37-8.*

Margot Benary has this time spread her material very thin, and
there is an exclamatory note in the book that seems rather
forced, as though she had lost some of the freshness of interest
in these wartime scenes. Good material, certainly, can be used
again and again, but perhaps this time the re-making has not
been altogether successful, though girls will always enjoy this
author's smooth, readable style, and they will appreciate the
sincere sympathy with which she follows the hazards of war
as they affect the life of her attractive heroine. (pp. 218-19)

*Margery Fisher, in a review of "A Time to Love,"
in Growing Point, Vol. 2, No. 4, October, 1963, pp.
218-19.*

There are things in [*A Time to Love*] that are easily dislikable,
because it has that German mixture of sentimentality, smugness
and earnestness which can grate upon an English mind. But
Mrs. Benary's people are people; they are solid, real characters,
their lives and their hopes and their sorrows matter to the
reader, and the setting of their lives—the country, the town,
house and garden, school friends and animals—all is clear and
concrete. This is what children and young people like, nor do
they despise a certain moral preoccupation. And the setting is
really German, not just a scene yanked abroad for a change. . . .

It is a well-written book and one cannot but be absorbed by
it.

*"Putting Away Childish Things," in The Times Lit-
erary Supplement, No. 3222, November 28, 1963,
p. 974.*

This is that rare object, a teenage novel of literary quality. . . .
The girl herself, obstinate, independent, rather coltish, comes
quickly to life, and the conversations between her and her
friends are colloquial and often amusing, without losing their
German flavour. In the descriptions of the countryside and of
the exquisite agonies of youth, there is real poetry. . . . This
book is particularly to be recommended because it draws the
reader into an understanding of what it was like to be German
and anti-Nazi in the nineteen-thirties.

*R. A. Sisson, in a review of "A Time to Love," in
The School Librarian and School Library Review,
Vol. 12, No. 2, July, 1964, p. 206.*

THE SHOOTING STAR (1954)

[*The Ark*] established this author's name in America. Now,
for younger readers, comes another translation, with a Swiss
Alp setting that manages to recreate the charm of the district
and youthful excitement at being there. Seven year old An-

negret, recovering from a bout of pneumonia, goes with her
mother to Arosa where her apathy quickly turns to enthusiasm. . . . Cheer and atmosphere are carried through to the last
detail of Oscar Liebman's drawings.

*A review of "The Shooting Star," in Virginia Kirkus'
Bookshop Service, Vol. XXII, No. 3, February 1,
1954, p. 61.*

[*The Shooting Star*] is a simple, leisurely, everyday tale, but
is touched with bits of gentle wisdom and made special by the
realism of its picture of Arosa, by the knowledge of the winter
skies, and by the charming bit about Annegret's love for the
little donkey she is certain is the one from Bethlehem.

*Louise S. Bechtel, in a review of "The Shooting
Star," in New York Herald Tribune Book Review,
February 28, 1954, p. 12.*

[Annegret's] discovery of Alpine pleasures, her skiing adventures, her new friendships, constitute a deceptively simple story
with the warmth and unself-conscious goodness which made
Understood Betsy a joy to an earlier generation. The effect
upon Annegret of the beautiful mountain country is conveyed
with rare skill.

*Lavinia R. Davis, "The Happy Exile," in The New
York Times Book Review, February 28, 1954, p.
24.*

[*The Shooting Star*] has neither so many characters nor so much
action as [*The Ark*], but it does have a quiet beauty, a feeling
for the country, and the joy nine-year-old Annegret finds in
discovering the majesty of the mountains. Making friends with
a neighbor boy and with the birds and animals; learning to ski;
a wonderful night when she is allowed to go up into an ob-
servatory to see the stars; and her adventure with a little donkey,
all will interest other little girls of Annegret's age.

*Jennie D. Lindquist, in a review of "The Shooting
Star," in The Horn Book Magazine, Vol. XXX, No.
2, April, 1954, p. 96.*

THE WICKED ENCHANTMENT (1955)

From the realism of her two fine books for teen-age girls about
post-war Germany this distinguished author now turns to fantasy. She offers a modern fairytale full of suspense, fun, excitement, answering children's love of animals, the circus and
magic. She uses an Old World setting and plays with old
German legend, weaving in her memories of old arts of Europe;
the book is both gay and serious, ending in the cathedral on
Easter Eve, where, listening to the ancient bells, we know that
love and courage can overcome superstition and tyranny.

The town of "Vogelsang" is ruled by a new, cruel mayor.
With his coming strange things happen, even to the eleven-
year-old Anemone, whose motherless home is dominated by
an ominous new housekeeper. So Anemone runs away; her
wonderful aunt dresses her as a boy, and together they solve
the mystery of the wicked spell cast on the once happy town.
It is a fairy tale with fascinating fresh turns of plot and a
charming subplot that leads, with the help of a Chinese mar-
ionette show, to the happy end of the aunt's long love affair.
The witch-housekeeper is turned back into the lost statue, the
mayor and his council fly away as an owl and crows, fulfilling
the legend of the wicked owl knight.

With all its wealth of detail the story is clearly told and its very real human relations balance its magic. The pages glow with such colorful imagery that even the distinguished, fanciful drawings [by Enrico Arno] cannot match the words. It is a rare book to stimulate the wits of bright children besides stirring their hearts. It will be savored by families who read aloud and will live long in their minds.

> *Louise S. Bechtel, in a review of "The Wicked Enchantment," in* New York Herald Tribune Book Review, *October 2, 1955, p. 7.*

A delightful semi-mystery, semi-fantasy about a present-day German town with its "crooked streets, a market place, several churches, a few cloisters, and a proud town hall." Central character has something of Pippi's appealing independence; plot is sufficiently absorbing for 8-10-year-olds if the book is read aloud, and the quality of writing, colorful details, and subtlety of humor will be appreciated by the adult reading it aloud.

> *Miriam Snow Mathes, in a review of "The Wicked Enchantment," in* Junior Libraries, *an appendix to* Library Journal, *Vol. 2, No. 3, November 15, 1955, p. 26.*

This fantasy is sharp and bold with a down to earth quality that gives it the appearance of a clear cut black and white etching. The narrative is sometimes a little too rough and coarse, as though it had been ground down, losing in the process its depth and mirrored movements of light and shade. But for much of the time the ingredients of true fantasy are there and while the story resembles many of its kind it is worth individual recommendation. The author gives evidence of a living faith and that faith sheds a light on the story, and a light that reveals a vital truth.

> *A review of "The Wicked Enchantment," in* The Junior Bookshelf, *Vol. 20, No. 4, October, 1956, p. 202.*

Many writers of fantasy have found satisfaction in the idea of a little world, either an invented world or a part of the real world cut off from the rest.

One of these worlds is Vogelsang in Margot Benary's *The Wicked Enchantment.* . . . Vogelsang is a German city. It is not obviously detached from the rest of the world, but through many centuries it has gone its own way, living for the most part contentedly beneath the shadow of the great Gothic cathedral. People from other towns say 'We are all a little touched', but the Vogelsanger madness is of an agreeable kind and the ghosts who haunt the town are mostly 'nice and respectable'. But evil comes to Vogelsang; to be precise, it comes from within the town, from the forgotten vault beneath the cathedral where Earl Owl of Owlhall rests uneasily. (The parallel with Nazi Germany is implicit.) (p. 133)

Margot Benary adopted an appropriately Gothic frame for her story, with an extravagance of style and numerous side-chapels and pinnacles of episode and sub-plot. The book has its share of Teutonic sentimentality too, but the general impression is, like the cathedral, of a unified and harmonious structure. The little world of Vogelsang, in turmoil or at peace, is the true hero of the story. (p. 134)

> *Marcus Crouch, "Magic Casements," in his* The Nesbit Tradition: The Children's Novel in England 1945-1970, *Ernest Benn Limited, 1972, pp. 112-41.*

SCHLOSS AN DER GRENZE [*CASTLE ON THE BORDER*]   (1956)

The Ark and *Rowan Farm* offered girls in their early teens fine realistic reading, with family happiness and romance lighting up days of hardship. They have been greatly enjoyed. Now that these readers are a little older and ready for a more mature novel, Mrs. Benary-Isbert gives them *Castle on the Border*. Here is a wider canvas, deeper insight and a greater variety of mood and characterization. Here are birth, marriage and death, first love, burning ambition and a deepening sense of the responsibility each person has for the lives of others. Here is also a group of young people, living in a beautiful romantic castle, struggling together against handicaps to achieve artistic success, forming almost a family group yet always eager to welcome young friends of any country until the old castle seems a "peace center."

Eighteen-year-old Leni, the central character of this superb story, lost her parents in the war, and has lived alone with her dachshund, Wuschel, while she works as a stenographer by day and studies at night to fulfill her ambition of becoming a great actress. She accepts her aunt and uncle's invitation to live with them in the beautiful half-ruined castle of Winkelberg near the border only to be near her brother Pippo and a troupe of young actors with whom he is connected. At Leni's suggestion the troupe comes to live in the castle and helps make it livable after the war damage. Soon Leni, who had wished to keep aloof from people, free to pursue her ambition, becomes involved in the demands of others. Children, animals and the older people rely on her. She is continually needed to help the village doctor with those who use the castle as a way station for border jumping, and when she is coached in the part of Juliet by the brilliant young actor, Karlheinz, and plays it to his Romeo the reviews astutely notice that "she is a girl who is truly in love for the first time." Receiving a call to a big theater, she wonders if she can accept or should stay in the castle where she is needed, letting the tasks of the world outside wait.

These young people love celebrations; Advent and Christmas at the castle are a delight to read about. They also love to discuss ideas, the interpretation of parts and to discover meanings in lines. There are constant casual references to the plays they are giving and the use of *Romeo and Juliet* and Shaw's *Saint Joan* is masterly. Altogether the book offers rich experiences in living with a story that holds your interest from the beginning to the end.

> *A review of "Castle on the Border," in* New York Herald Tribune Book Review, *May 13, 1956, p. 35.*

This is an unusually rich book for young people, for the author gets so much of life into it. There are Leni and her brother and their friends determined to conquer all obstacles in order to make the Castle Theater Company a success. There are Aunt Frederike and Uncle Hubertus and their courage in beginning life again after escaping from the East Zone, he working on his scientific study of spiders, she making a home of the castle and trying to bring beauty back to its gardens. There are children and animals to lighten the story; and to give it added depth there are the refugees coming over the border and hiding away a night or two in the castle. And there is the effect all this has on Leni and her growth not only as an actress but, more important, as a person. It is a serious book but it has gaiety in it, too; I think it will live a long time.

Jennie D. Lindquist, in a review of "Castle on the Border," in The Horn Book Magazine, *Vol. XXXII, No. 4, August, 1956, p. 273.*

There is much to recommend this superior teen-age novel. Romance, humor and gaiety, the satisfaction in unselfish living, the understanding which can exist between the aged and the young, the joys of a creative life, and a sensitive response to nature are all skilfully interwoven.

Mrs. Benary-Isbert is an author who knows that one faces life with courage and she transfers this truth to young people with the conviction that they will understand.

Norma Rathbun, in a review of "Castle on the Border," in The Saturday Review, *New York, Vol. XXXIX, No. 33, August 18, 1956, p. 37.*

The main interests in the story are the development of Leni from a tight-lipped, old-before-her-time girl, made selfish by suffering, into a generous hearted young woman capable of looking after a bunch of orphaned children as well as being a talented actress; the revival of the old castle made desolate by war and neglect; the maturing and eventual marriage of Leni's gay spark brother; the fortunes of the Castle Theatre Company leading gradually towards more and more success; and the constant drama of the coming and going of unknown refugees who find shelter in the Castle cellars when they cross the border.

It makes a crowded story, full of a variety of interesting people, young and old, gay and tragic. The background of post-war Germany is shown at first as full of gloom and hardships which gradually evaporate as eagerness begins to shine through. The characters all look with enthusiasm towards the future. The many people, and the fact that they are involved with realities, births, deaths, triumphs, ideas, in a real rough and tender world that is not all "holiday adventure," make Margot Benary's book reminiscent of those by Charlotte Yonge. (p. 129)

A review of "Castle on the Border," in The Junior Bookshelf, *Vol. 21, No. 3, July, 1957, pp. 128-29.*

Castle on the Border is as good as, if not better than, its predecessors. . . . Margot Benary's great virtue is that she develops her story through the emotional growth of her characters, without their ever becoming puppets or mere mouthpieces of her strong moral convictions. She enters into their minds and both setting and incidents of the tale are seen through their eyes.

Hugh Shelley, in a review of "Castle on the Border," in The School Librarian and School Library Review, *Vol. 8, No. 5, July, 1957, p. 66.*

THE LONG WAY HOME (1959)

In a way, this story is a love letter to America. It begins in Thuringen—now in Germany's East Zone—when Chris, a sick and nearly dying child, is left on the doorstep of an old schoolmistress, and ends on a ranch in California when he is fourteen years old and has become one of a happy and united American family. The author successfully captures the feelings of the exile who longs for his native country yet makes the new land his own. She sees the United States and its people fresh, through the eyes of a European. The characterization is excellent. The German schoolmistress is especially memorable, and Allan's

love of animals makes him kin to Margret in **The Ark** and **Rowan Farm.**

Aileen O'Brien Murphy, in a review of "The Long Way Home," in Saturday Review, *Vol. XLII, No. 19, May 9, 1959, p. 40.*

Just as Kay Boyle's short stories painted vivid portraits of post-war Germany for adult readers, so have Margot Benary-Isbert's novels traced a similar pattern for teen-agers. . . .

There is a basic honesty in Mrs. Benary-Isbert's writing, refreshing to find in young people's literature. Characterization is fully dimensioned, each personality being clearly defined without glossing or patly resolving weaknesses. And through the travels of a wide-eyed yet mature Christoph Wegener, American youngsters will discover the coast-to-coast wonders of their own land. It's a well-rounded picture. Certainly the most poignant section is the Chicago episode, when the young boy is placed with a kind but busily distracted family in a dingy Loop apartment—quite alone among strangers.

Gracefully the author has also threaded in characters from her other books. In his flight to West Germany, Christoph takes refuge with Leni Winkelberg Furchnit, heroine of **Castle on the Border.** On board ship he meets Matthias and Andrea Lechow, who figured in **The Ark** and **Rowan Farm.** Loyal fans will welcome news of these old friends.

Mary Lee Krupka, "West from Germany," in The New York Times Book Review, *Part II, May 10, 1959, p. 10.*

Too long-winded, over-crowded with people, places, and events, and less deeply felt than the first books, the story of Chris Wegener's experiences is nonetheless a perceptive and often moving one. Readers will be interested not only in Chris's plight but also in a view of themselves and their country as seen through the eyes of a stranger.

Helen E. Kinsey, in a review of "The Long Way Home," in The Booklist and Subscription Books Bulletin, *Vol. 55, No. 20, June 15, 1959, p. 575.*

In her eagerness to be fair to the United States, Mrs. Benary makes too obvious an effort to show the variety of America, the different points of view, cultures, and patterns of life, all of which may be of particular interest to German young people but which detract from her usual skillful writing. However, her perception of people and her insight into their individual problems make the book remarkably real. While this lacks the distinction of her earlier books, it is a moving story and a bridge of understanding between countries.

Ruth Hill Viguers, in a review of "The Long Way Home," in The Horn Book Magazine, *Vol. XXXV, No. 4, August, 1959, p. 290.*

It is easy to be sentimental about refugees without being practical and without really thinking about them as human beings, but Margot Benary concentrates all her craft on the theme of "home" and while refugees of one sort or another besides Christoph become woven into the plot, the basis of the story is always the personal need to belong which affects others than displaced persons but is concentrated in Christoph's eventual arrival and his consciousness of "fitting in." Naturally there is plenty of excitement all along the way: the escape, the voyage, learning to ride, a forest fire and what not, but the basic theme is always there. The wheel comes full circle when Christoph has established for himself the thoughtful pastoral existence which, in Thuringia, made him what he was.

A review of "The Long Way Home," in The Junior Bookshelf, *Vol. 24, No. 4, October, 1960, p. 222.*

'On Saturday evenings he took a bath. That was as definite a thing as the "amen" in Church.' Any story which begins with such forcefulness is worth reading. Margot Benary's previous books have been justly praised in this journal. Her latest is no exception. . . . Told with a keen insight into the different ways of life, the story has a compassion which never descends to sentimentality, while behind every incident there is the authority of a strong standard of moral values. The author never preaches: judgement is made shrewdly implicit. Particularly pleasing was the account of a rock 'n' roll performance. Christoph watches the star's face. 'It began to glow, to look happy and almost childlike, reflecting the rapture of his audience. So that's what he needs, Chris thought. And I am so bad at flattering.' Because Chris, even though old for his years, is a real human being, many twelve- or thirteen-year-old readers will accept that last comment and enjoy it.

Laurence Adkins, in a review of "The Long Way Home," in The School Librarian and School Library Review, *Vol. 10, No. 4, March, 1961, p. 355.*

DANGEROUS SPRING (1961)

In yet another facet of the emerging Germany, Margot Benary-Isbert has failed to paint a convincing picture of the Lorenz family, waiting in anxious anticipation for the conquerors, as victorious American troops approach. Buchenwald was just outside their village, but it is only when Karin is serving as translator that she hears the shocking details—and rejects her Nazi training. Her brother Till, educated in the Hitler Youth, awakens when his friend, Armin, an SS trooper assigned to Buchenwald, wants to escape—and is shot by his "comrades". Despite the fact that Dr. Lorenz, for purposes of safety, had sent his family to live with a German pastor opposed to Nazism, the Lorenz' family and the townspeople are painted as good Germans, though Nazi conditioned, oblivious to the horrors perpetrated, but waiting for their American saviours. A thoughtful reader will wonder whether this is something of a whitewash job, with glaring inconsistencies.

A review of "Dangerous Spring," in Virginia Kirkus' Service, *Vol. XXIX, No. 6, March 15, 1961, p. 265.*

Based on diaries kept by the author and her husband, *Dangerous Spring* is an extraordinary success on two-interdependent levels, fiction and document. The story is well-constructed and minutely controlled. The work of a sensitive, informed, and deeply involved reporter, . . . the documentation strikingly reveals that, behind the solid mass of German national guilt, there were conscientious and distressed individuals. (p. 18)

Mary Louise Hector, "The Americans Came," in The New York Times Book Review, *May 14, 1961, pp. 16, 18.*

This is an absorbing and suspenseful novel. . . . It is a grim, realistic picture of the aftermath of war, lightened by the faith of the young minister Helmut Lobelius and the courage and hope of the girl who loves him, and of all the young people who believe that life can again be good. The varied cast of characters, many of whom are refugees sheltering in Helmut's

home, have surely been drawn from life. Especially appealing are Karin, deeply in love but unaware of the necessary practical qualifications of a minister's wife, and her young brother Till, fanatically devoted to the Hitler Youth Movement to whom the desperate last-ditch activities of the Storm Troopers bring complete disillusionment. A fine book which can do more than a library of factual accounts to make young people see the senselessness of war, and the idealism that can survive in great hearts even through the most devastating experiences.

Ruth Hill Viguers, in a review of "Dangerous Spring," in The Horn Book Magazine, *Vol. XXXVII, No. 3, June, 1961, p. 272.*

[*Dangerous Spring*] is a remarkable book; the most cynical of teenagers, if persuaded to read beyond the first chapters, is likely to recognise its truth and its contemporary relevance. (pp. 293-94)

It is a tough story and Mrs. Benary, although she never dwells on horror, spares not her heroine nor her readers. She blends her tones most brilliantly; here are neither heroes nor villains, blacks nor whites, but here too the reader is in no doubt as to where goodness lies. The portrayal of character, not only that of the charming perplexed heroine, is most skilful, and so is the unobtrusively lovely painting of landscape. The author shows the last spring of war in all its incongruous beauty.

Mrs. Benary has Elfrida Vipont's strength and pervading sense of goodness; her values are more complex, however, and she is harder to read. An occasional uneasiness of expression reminds the reader, too, that this is a translation, a very good one on the whole but slipping now and then into bathos because of a fundamental difference between German and English thought. Such blemishes are few; all in all Mrs. Benary has written another book of high distinction, one which treats of life-size problems with dignity and without condescension. She respects her readers; I have little doubt that they will respect her for this truthful picture of first love in a world falling apart. (p. 294)

A review of "Dangerous Spring," in The Junior Bookshelf, *Vol. 25, No. 5, November, 1961, pp. 293-94.*

[This] is a sincere and moving account of life in Germany as the author herself experienced it at that terrible time, and it has the unmistakable ring of truth. Very far above the average teen-age novel to emanate from America, it could nevertheless be loosely termed a love-story. . . . It is certainly as a love-story that it will be read and judged by the majority of young readers rather than from an initial interest in the setting, and it is doubtful whether as such it will hold their interest entirely as the author has at times used the characters as a vehicle through which to express her own deeply-held convictions. No-one, however, could fail to be moved and impressed by her passionate belief in the immutability of the human spirit, and it is good that a generation to whom the war is only history should have an opportunity of reading something about the cause and effect of the struggle on our enemies, especially those not taken in by Nazi-ism. . . .

It should prove comforting to English and American adolescents to find that, even in such a troubled period of history, the chief concern of young people was to bridge the gap between the generations and they should follow Karin's everyday doings with greater interest because of it.

E. N. Bewick, in a review of "Dangerous Spring," in The School Librarian and School Library Review, *Vol. 11, No. 2, July, 1962, p. 198.*

UNDER A CHANGING MOON (1964)

Paula's year "under a changing moon" brings her first ecstatic love affair, her adjustment to a lively family life after two years in a convent school, and her sober decision about her future. This is a thoughtful novel filled with the quiet formality of an older era. . . . The author, as always, creates a very real background against which the characters stand out unforgettably: slim, quiet Paula, energetic Mama, the gay young lieutenant, and Konrad Overberg.

Charlotte A. Gallant, in a review of "Under a Changing Moon," in School Library Journal, *an appendix to* Library Journal, *Vol. 11, No. 1, September, 1964, p. 128.*

Of plot there is actually none, for no climax is reached and nothing is resolved except the normal problems accompanying changes brought about by the mere passing of time. . . . Leisurely and full of detailed descriptions of the life and customs of a nineteenth-century German village, specifically of the Amtmann's lively and varied household, the novel has a flavor that lasts. Girls who read a great deal should enjoy the chance to enter completely into a life very different from their own, and they are likely to remember the people of the book as friends and relatives.

Ruth Hill Viguers, in a review of "Under a Changing Moon," in The Horn Book Magazine, *Vol. XL, No. 5, October, 1964, p. 504.*

[**Under a Changing Moon**] stands head and shoulders and maybe elbows above most teen-age novels. It really is a novel, and for all ages. Everyone in the book lives, the family as much as the heroine, and her younger brother most of all. The story is set against a background of nature and village life in Germany of 1866 that seems to flow as effortlessly and beautifully as the seasons change.

Evan Commager, "Tailored for Young Ladies," in Book Week—The Washington Post, *November 15, 1964, p. 27.*

The author's skillful re-creation of an era renowned for its formalities and colorful customs, her excellent characterization, and vividly drawn picture of family life in a nineteenth-century German village compensate for the novel's length, slow pace, and lack of a well-defined plot.

A review of "Under a Changing Moon," in The Booklist and Subscription Books Bulletin, *Vol. 61, No. 11, February 1, 1965, p. 525.*

The older girl who enjoys a quiet, slow-moving narrative will return to this book time and again, and still find it richly rewarding. Its accounts of the progression of the seasons and the Church's year, of family relationships, and life in a provincial German town are evocative and moving. But the author is also to be commended for the way she handles moral issues soberly and without embarrassment: few children's writers nowadays can do this.

"Victorian Girls," in The Times Literary Supplement, *No. 3328, December 9, 1965, p. 1145.*

Marcia (Joan) Brown

1918-

American author/illustrator of picture books, reteller, translator, and illustrator.

Renowned for her versatility and artistic skill, Brown is well known as the creator of picture books for preschool through the middle grades which feature widely divergent subject matter and illustration technique. The only illustrator to date to win the Caldecott Medal three times, she is also credited with being among the first to produce single folktales in picture book format. Author of more than twenty self-illustrated books, Brown's varied publications include merry stories based on her observations of childhood in such different settings as the Virgin Islands, New York City, Venice, and Cape Cod; a series of concept books which present a multisensory appreciation of nature through photographs; and an ABC book of two-word phrases. She is best known, however, for her retellings, which range from free translations of Charles Perrault's *Cinderella* and *Puss in Boots* to lesser known European and Asian folktales. Experienced as a storyteller and puppeteer, Brown enlivens her texts with humor and drama. Consistently praised for successfully adapting her illustrations to her material, she portrays her French court tales in delicate pastel watercolors, the medieval legend of *Dick Whittington and His Cat* in linoleum cuts, the ancient fable *Once a Mouse . . .* in woodcut prints, and gay peasant tales such as *Stone Soup* in vigorous line and earthy shades. Her paintings and prints are noted for their movement and use of color and often provide viewers with the motifs associated with various cultures. Brown has also illustrated works by other authors, including several by Hans Christian Andersen. Her illustrations for *Shadow*, a poem by French poet Blaise Cendrars, have met with a mixed reception. These pictures, which depict African natives and symbols as collages, have been called stereotypical and clichéd as well as sophisticated and evocative.

Critics praise Brown for her originality, meticulous research, vivid storytelling, and master craftsmanship in a multitude of media. Several of her books are considered classics and are applauded for the fine art experience they provide for children, their suitability for reading aloud, and as fruitful sources for storytelling. Although some observers lament that her stories do not measure up to her illustrations, reviewers generally commend Brown's ability to depict the long ago with contemporary touches, to recreate authentic settings with lively accurate detail, and to relate directly to her audience.

Besides winning Caldecott Medals for *Cinderella* in 1955, *Once a Mouse . . .* in 1962, and *Shadow* in 1983, Brown has had six of her works designated as Caldecott Honor Books: *Stone Soup* in 1948, *Henry-Fisherman* in 1950, *Dick Whittington and His Cat* in 1951, *Skipper John's Cook* in 1952, *Puss in Boots* in 1953, and *The Steadfast Tin Soldier* in 1954; *All Butterflies: An ABC* was named a *Boston Globe-Horn Book* Honor Book in 1974. Brown was nominated for the Hans Christian Andersen Award in 1966 and 1975, received the University of Southern Mississippi Medallion for Distinguished Service for Children's Literature in 1972, and was awarded the Regina Medal in 1977.

Photograph by Patti Abraham. Courtesy of Marcia Brown.

(See also *Something about the Author*, Vol. 7 and *Contemporary Authors*, Vols. 41-44, rev. ed.)

AUTHOR'S COMMENTARY

[*The following excerpt, originally published in the August, 1955 issue of* The Horn Book Magazine, *is taken from Brown's Caldecott Award acceptance speech for* Cinderella *which she gave at the meeting of the American Library Association on July 5, 1955.*]

From the time when I first wanted to illustrate books, and that was quite early in my life . . . , I was interested in books for younger rather than older children. The greater attractiveness of those I saw in the former group and the often disappointing dullness of those I saw in the latter made me feel that way. I remember a keen resentment that a book was illustrated at all when the pictures were inadequate compared to those pictures that formed in the mind.

A young child shares with the primitive an extraordinary power to identify himself with the people, animals and things of this world, and this power makes him extremely accessible to the magic power of symbol. This same power carried into adult life enables the artist to enter the feelings of his subjects and draw and paint them in such a way that not only do they look as if they felt a certain way, but they also make the spectator feel that same way. Young children have a profound sense of the mysterious, but if the mood of our work is to speak to them, it must relate to other realities they know. The child cannot gape forever at the juggler or shiver endlessly with the tightrope walker. After the circus is over the arc of his own ball in the air will be more beautiful, the sureness of his own foot as he walks the curb will give him pride. He contains his experience.

A picture book really exists only when a child and a book come together, when the stream that formed in the artist's mind and heart flows through the book and into the mind and heart of the child. Before starting to make the book, an artist must be sure the story is worth the time, his time and love spent in illustrating it, and the child's time to be spent in looking at it.

Once the story is chosen, what is its texture? What are the large patterns of action? These might be the very meaning of the story itself.

A picture book is somewhat related in its effect to that of a painting. The whole is greater than any of its parts, but all the parts must relate directly to each other in harmony. The young child might be more receptive to the intuition of the artist than the educated adult, who might be an ignoramus in art, for all his conscious knowledge. But the pictures must be blessed with real intuitive quality for them to speak to him.

The clearest exposition of the creative process I have yet found is Jacques Maritain's *Creative Intuition in Art and Poetry,* in which he tells of inspiration . . . springing from the dark night of the soul in vibrations that he calls "pulsations," "wordless songs," then assuming form as one begins to think of the work in question, and finally being subjected to conscious reason. As an artist develops he gradually becomes aware of the presence of this night, and learns to trust in it; for it is there, not at the surface of his mind, which deals with the problems of existence, but deep in those waters that contain the resources of his spirit and intellect, that his intuition has its birth. That is why, I think, when only vague feelings are beginning to form, an artist should be left alone to let them gradually rise to the surface and take form as visual idea. And that is also why the feeling of others can hardly be incorporated or even listened to at this point if the finished work is to have the integrity which means that it sprang from an artist's own sensibility. His sensibility, of course, has been enriched by his thinking, his seeing, his feeling, his living—all his life up to now, and that is what is drawn on, not the impulses of last week. That might be another reason why the time spent on creating a book in its first form, that is, making the dummy if there is to be a visual plan, can be very short or very long. I have never been impressed by tales of the extraordinary length of time that it took to produce books or paintings. An art student's laborious drawing of a month will not compare with a one-minute impression of a Picasso. All one's life has been spent in preparation for the work at hand. When the greatest amount of inspiration is brought to bear, the least amount of work will bring the idea to realization. Inspiration—no minute in making a work should escape it.

In our modern world beauty is often dismissed in favor of hard labor. People will respect the hours consumed in a project without ever questioning the use of the time spent in the first place.

The artist is overcharged, and works to find a relief, ease for his burden, so that he can take up another as soon as he is

able. At his most relaxed he is often most unhappy; at his most tense, difficult as he might be to live with, he is often experiencing one of his deepest joys, for he is finding his way back into himself. This region is so subjective that he is often hardly aware it existed, but he knows, if he has listened to music, that it exists in others. Rhythms he feels there are old as time and tide, but they are part of the bloodstream of all the morning subway riders. Colors take their meaning from first awareness of light, blue vastness of sea and sky, hot warmth of fire, the sun and his own blood. Sounds, movements, all these rise to the surface to be called into use to speak to the same feelings in another human being. These feelings or this intuition, if it is strong enough in a person, demands to be expressed in work, even if that work is never understood by others. Its strength is such that it will drive an artist to live the life of greatest hardship in order to nourish it, and allow it to have its way with him.

The question of integrity has a direct bearing on one's choice of subject matter for a book. Who knows when an idea can light a match? A sight of children playing in a city street; meeting a stalwart Cape-Codder of three who that day had fallen off a dock when the tide was in and had walked in to shore, as his brother told us, "by hisself"; hearing an old rhyme read or a sly old folk tale; or having one's editor suggest illustrating a tale, the feeling of which, if not the exact images, had persisted in the mind since early childhood; any reason can exist, it seems, for making a picture book. But, and this I believe most strongly, the reasons have to be a part of the person and his feeling before he attempts the book. Contrivance and fad-following impress only those who are unaware of their superficiality. (pp. 21-4)

The whole process of actually getting a picture book ready for the printer usually takes me about five months. It is sometimes difficult to maintain the same high pitch of excitement that was there when the work started, but it must be done. The original idea must always be the aim. In almost all cases, it is the one with vitality and truest feeling toward the text.

Why is it that the paintings of children often have qualities of intensity of expression, beauty of color, and depth of feeling that make us feel that they are works of art? By his desire to say something, to force the meager means, the meager knowledge at his disposal, the child is able to draw what he has to say so vividly that his drawing speaks to us. All during the work on a book, all during his working life, the artist will be forcing *his* means to say what he has to say. The means will always be determined by the subject at hand, and that is why I feel that each book should look different from the others, whether or not the medium used is the same.

The simplicity of a very young child's pleasure in a little street carousel, a tale of a roguish cat that is colored by the sophistication of the Sun King's Court, the longing and immolation of a little tin soldier, the freshness of a lovely young girl's dream as opposed to her stepsisters' delusions of grandeur, and they more waspish than wicked—how could one feel the same about such different books? A technique learned as a formula to apply willy-nilly to any subject often knocks the life out of the subject. The vitality, the quality peculiar to the subject should dictate the method to follow. Is the subject to yield to the manner, or the manner to the subject?

Whatever the means, the only pictures that will arouse interest and love in a child are those created in the same interest and love. Each work, each gesture counts toward giving the fullest value of the feeling. White space, in which the mind rests or fills in its own images, can be as telling as drawing, and will certainly be more effective than empty decoration. Research is done simply to aid in picturing the idea, bringing it into objective being, never for its own sake. Incompletely absorbed research results in costume plates or journalism, not creation. How do the colors speak in this telling, not how many colors are there. One accent rightly placed, whether color, shape or line, can be worth a hundred small forms. One small area can suggest the design of a whole curtain. The mind continues where the pictures end.

A horse is not drawn in a stroke or two because the artist wanted to show his skill. But, feeling strongly, he got the horse down fast, and there it was—in two or three lines. Why add more and get the horse ready for the taxidermist?

We often hear it said of an artist that he or she has developed no personal style yet. One of the most unfortunate pressures put on young artists in this country that sets such a premium on novelty, often while the artist is still in art school, is to develop a distinguishing style to apply to his work.

To me style is the way you walk and talk, what you are as a person. The discerning eye will notice certain traits of personality, certain ways of feeling that will show up in the work. These help to make a person's style, not a technique that is put on like a garment. *Style,* in the larger sense, is something quite different. We live in a world eager for recipe or formula, which, not finding it, hands over its birthright of independent thinking to the self-styled expert who imagines he has it. Any effort to coddle originality is to end by stifling it in self-consciousness. An artist's primary preoccupation is his own *development,* the perfection of himself as an instrument—whether he be singer, dancer, or painter—the better to sing his song. He is faced with all of life, but the mirror he holds up to it can be no bigger than his own mind and heart.

I have never felt that children needed any particular kind of drawing any more than they needed any particular kind of writing. The clarity, vitality of the message, the genuineness of the feeling—that is what is important.

After a book is done, it passes from the artist and has a completely separate and, we hope, strenuously active life of its own in the hands of children. But now it is something apart. Only by putting the feelings that were specifically tied up with it completely out of mind will the artist be free to be ready for something else, to grow by feeling all over again, by trying to look at the new book as if he had never done another. To forget the old solutions, to refuse to copy not only what he has seen but also his own work is one of the greatest problems of an artist, but only by meeting its challenge can he avoid his own clichés.

I have always felt that good drawing is more important than color in a young child's book. Yet color and its symbolism speak very directly to children. Color is often most rich when it means something perhaps too subjective to be put into words, when it is the expression of some life value. Only a hypothetical child brought up in a hypothetical vacuum without the sense of sight, even without that marvelous sight behind the eyelids that little children know in their daydreams, could be impervious to the meanings of color. These meanings are old as life itself. The passion of little children for red has an earthy origin not to be denied. Blue sky, blue sea, green-and-brown earth, red fire—their world radiates from very simple color relationships. By color they can be led into a greater sensual enjoyment

of the visible world, as well as that between the covers of their books.

The choice of a color combination for a picture book will often have been associated with the book from its first imaginings.

Gold of the summer fields, gold of a small boy's thatch of hair, gold of his dream of London, the sunrise when he heard his destiny ring out in Bow Bells, gold of his treasure and of the chain of his office of Lord Mayor—gold was the color for Dick Whittington.

When I was in the Virgin Islands, the unbelievable turquoise water of the Caribbean, the mahogany-skinned people, brilliant white sand, coral-colored houses and bougainvillea, deep green of welcome shadow, chartreuse of leaves filtering sunlight—the colors for *Henry-Fisherman* chose themselves.

The colors for *The Steadfast Tin Soldier* I felt could speak to children on several levels. "Red and blue was their beautiful uniform." ". . . a bright spangle as big as the whole of her face." Red, blue and gold, and black for type became a blue violet that could tell of steadfastness, infinite longing; the red became rose for passion and sacrifice; the gold a minute glitter on the surface; black became charcoal for the somber note of the Troll's warning and the ash in which was found the little tin heart and the burnt black spangle. But how to get all one's colors to speak? In the past few years we have seen more and more books using a crayon-and-line technique, with the drawings reproduced directly from the artist's own color separations by means of a contact method with no camera work. Any process which throws the illustrator back on his own resources is good for him, because if he is not to do the same book over and over, regardless of the subject, he must push what he knows farther and farther in order to encompass the feeling of the new work at hand. By making their own plates, by exploring the variety of effects possible with hand-graphic techniques, illustrators can develop the freedom of fine artists in their printmaking. Color separations are a step, a crucial one, in a long creative process that begins with feeling and should end with feeling. (pp. 24-8)

When I was a child, thinking that I would like one day to illustrate books for children, I always thought of the fairy tales that I loved. It was some years before I felt ready or capable of attempting illustrations for Andersen or Perrault. When an illustrator attempts the interpretation of a folk or fairy tale that already stands as an entity, the problem of adding a new dimension and bringing the whole into harmonious unity is great. Illustration becomes a kind of visual storytelling in the deepest sense of the word. As a storyteller ideally submerges himself in the story until he loses his own identity and becomes a medium for the revelation of the story, the illustrator must likewise submerge himself in the feeling, so that what comes through is an interpretation and intensification of meanings. The big meanings, the big masses, big movements and rhythms must hold the same relationships as in oral telling. Rhythm of speech is echoed in rhythm of line and color. Never must there be a mere recounting of the event. None of these things may be consciously aimed at; yet I feel they are part of the illustrator's feeling as he attempts to make a picture storybook of a fairy tale. The pictures can convey the wonder, terror, peace, mystery, beauty—all he is able to feel or might convey if he were telling the story in words.

The popularity of certain types of subject matter rises and falls, but children remain basically the same, with the same gaiety, eagerness to feel, the same clear-eyed wisdom and wonder in facing the world. Educators and experts on child study, who sometimes seem to have been as supple as straws in the wind, quick to bend to this or that breeze of fad, for a time decided that children no longer needed fairy tales. Not for a moment did the children who came of their own accord to public libraries and were free to choose their own books, desert their heroes, the personification of their dreams. The calls still came for Cinderella, for stories about giants and princesses, for simple people raised to high station because of their own gifts. Some of these stories appeared horrifying to adults, who seemed to lack the balance of the children in these matters. The children looked beyond the horror to the battle between moral forces. The heritage of childhood is the sense of life bequeathed to it by the folk wisdom of the ages. To tell in pictures, to tell in words, to tell in dance—however we may choose—it is a privilege to pass these truths on to children who have a right to the fullest expression we can give them. Neither so self-conscious as a parable nor so contrived as an allegory, fairy tales are revelations of sober everyday fact. They are the abiding dreams and realities of the human soul.

This very day some rogue has by his quick wit opened a new world to his master and helped him win the princess of his heart, to whom he was entitled by sensibilities if not by birth.

Today a staunch soldier, through circumstances not of his own making, goes through terrible trials, but remains steadfast in his devotion to his ideal.

Tonight somewhere Cinderella, through the magic of kindness, has been enchanted into greatest beauty; tonight Cinderella goes to her ball to meet her prince. (pp. 30-1)

> Marcia Brown, "Integrity and Intuition," in her Lotus Seeds: Children, Pictures and Books, *Charles Scribner's Sons, 1986, pp. 19-34.*

[*The following excerpt was originally published in the June, 1967 issue of* The Horn Book Magazine.]

I often think of illustrators as I think of performers of music. Those one can listen to longest are often those most selfless, those who are content to be a medium for the music. They put their own individualities at the service of the music to probe its depths and reveal its spirit, rather than to display the idiosyncrasies of their own personalities. Techniques that hammer can dull the eyes as well as the ears.

Even though I may be the composer, I have come to think of the illustrator more and more as the performer of the spirit of a book. If one lives with a book from its beginning, one may be closer to that spirit. Some spirits speak so loudly their voices are unmistakable. Others are more delicate. No one way can be called the best way to interpret them to a child.

Feelings appropriate to the fine arts, especially painting, are often called forward in speaking about illustration for children. Little children readily look at all kinds and styles of art. They are probably the freest and most imaginative audience in the world. But illustration is illustration, and not painting. It is communication of the idea of a book.

This all sounds obvious and has been said many times before. But every book I illustrate has to be considered in these terms. (pp. 62-3)

Some time ago I was one of probably a great many people who received a questionnaire from the National Council of Teachers of English on the "composing process"—as good a name as any for it—to try to track down what is elusive in the process of making books. The questions were intelligently thought out, as such things go. But I suspect that what is elusive will remain so, since it is a subtle combination of personality, inner drive, and imagination in the author or illustrator himself.

Illustration and writing are often a lonely business, and artists when they get together often compare notes on ways of working. I am often asked why each of my books is apt to look different from the others. Each artist has his own way of working. After a while he works in possibly the only way he can, given his own temperament. I feel about each book very differently. My interest is in the book as a whole, not just in the illustrations. Every detail of a book should, as far as possible, reflect the intention the artist and designer had toward the idea of the book. These intentions need not even be expressible in words, but they should be felt. That quality of the individual book that is strongest—the simple vigor, the delicacy, the mood, the setting—should determine the color, not an arbitrary application of brilliance to whatever the subject.

The atmosphere of a book is extremely important; in older boys' and girls' books it is perhaps more important than depiction of events. A story that is very traditional in feeling can often suffer from illustrations that are stylistically too different in period. When one adapts a modern technique to illustrations for a historical period, one must think of the young child looking, with little knowledge of period. Do the costumes give the feeling of the period if they do not reproduce the details?

Freshness lies in the intensity of expression, not in the novelty of the technique.

In order not to drag the ideas or techniques that I have developed during work on one book into another, I try to take a good piece of time between books, painting or just taking in impressions by travel, in order to clear the way for the next.

Some books are of course related by period, and the same research holds for both; this is true of **Cinderella** and **Puss in Boots.** But the spirit of the two is completely different. The quality in a story itself and in the way it is told determines style. Puss is extravagant, swaggering. The king, a *bon viveur,* enjoys the outrageousness of the cat. **Cinderella,** with the tenderness of the godmother, the dream of the girl, the preposterousness of the sisters, is in a completely different mood.

People speak of some artists who use different techniques as if they had fifty up their sleeves ready to appear, full-blown, when needed. But the life of an artist is one of constant preparation. He almost never feels that he has realized his aim. When a book is finished, he is usually just beginning to feel how it might have been. Stacks of trial drawings and rejects attest to many efforts to find the right way to say what one has to say. One develops the technique necessary to express one's feeling about the particular book in hand. Sometimes this takes several months of drawing into a subject until one is ready to begin the actual illustrations.

People often ask how much time it takes to make a book. Five days, five months, three years—as long as is necessary to get down one's ideas and feelings about the book.

It might be useful for me to tell you of my work on three different books, each of which presented a different problem in illustration and bookmaking. They happen to be mine, and I use them because I know them best.

One is a picture book, one a picture-story book, and one an illustrated book for older children. All three are of folk origin:

From Stone Soup: An Old Tale, *told and pictured by Marcia Brown. Charles Scribner's Sons, 1947.*
Copyright 1947 by Marcia Brown. Copyright renewed © 1975 Marcia Brown. All rights reserved.
Reprinted with the permission of Charles Scribner's Sons.

One is a fable, one of the oldest types of folk tales; one is a synthesis of several European folk tales through a poet's mind; one is a hero legend with chants from a people with an oral culture.

Myths and legends tell a child who he is in the family of man. In a book with ancient, mythic origins, some of the poetic depth of the story should be implied in the illustrations. The child, looking and reading, will understand and recall tomorrow more than he can tell you today.

Once a Mouse is a picture book in which the pictures complete a very brief text and, I hope, add some comment of their own. Since the book is for very young children, the details are only those needed. The woodcut is a favorite medium of mine, one that relates to traditional graphic media and that can be very successfully combined with type on a page.

Though the words of the fable are few, the theme is big. It takes a certain amount of force to cut a wooden plank, and a definite decision. Wood that lived can say something about life in a forest. An artist can make his own color proofs in printers' inks, can mix his colors and give an approximate formula to a printer. Even though the transparent colors on an offset press are different from the thicker ones used at home, this proving can be of enormous help in seeing what one will get.

Each artist has his personal feelings about his way of working, and the finished book is what is to be judged as successful or not, but in my own books I like every color to be cut on a

separate block in order to maintain the optical unity of the medium. A book is like a very small stage. Just as a violent drama on television is sometimes hard to take in one's living room, what is effective in a large print can often break up a comparatively small book page.

The story of *Once a Mouse* moves in an arc from quietness to quietness; from meditation, to concern, to involvement, to anger and action, back to meditation. The colors I chose were the yellow-green of sun through leaves, of earth, the dark green of shadows, and the red that says India to me. Red is used as a force to cut into the other colors when its violence is needed. Excitements are fairly easy to make in illustrations—a chase, a fight, an explosion—and offer immediate release. The quiet power of inner life is much harder to achieve and must be felt more deeply.

Just before I went to Hawaii in 1962, I had reread *The Wild Swans* of Andersen. There are vast images in that story, vast implications and sonorities that can ring in a child's mind far into adult life. It is a story with strong contrasts: dark toads and bright poppies; the forest pool in its shadow and the shimmer of light through the leaves; the darkest part of the forest —no bird was seen, no sunbeam pierced the gloom—"yes, indeed, there was solitude here, the like of which she had never known." And then the free, vast spaces of the sea, the dark waves rearing up to show their white sides.

Between the black cypresses that would be there in an Italian graveyard shines the moon. Over the tumbrel bearing Elisa to her death the eleven swans descend, and the story ends with the miracle of the white flower in a dazzle of light and happiness.

To try to show these contrasts I used a broad lettering pen dragged over rough water-color paper and sumi for the gray washes. I needed the simplest means of achieving dark and light. The rose color for the swans' beaks, for the dawn, for the poppies and the roses I got from rubbing sanguine powder into the plastic contact plate. I was afraid to trust delicate washes either to dropout half tone or hand-clearing. The drawings were frequently vignetted around the type to tie the two more intimately together and to give variety to the movement of the book.

When I was in Hawaii I was so enchanted with the natural beauty of the islands and the charm of the people, I did not even think of looking for material for a book. The Hawaiian folklore I knew was long, involved, and difficult for a Western child. And the wild swans had ensnared me for most of the winter and spring following that first visit.

But just before I left the islands, an elderly lady gave me a historic collection of legends gathered by her husband's uncle, who had grown up on the island of Kaua'i. One story interested me particularly, "The Story of Paka'a and His Son Ku." After the swans were in flight, I decided to return to Hawaii to see if I could get inside the atmosphere enough to do a book for children based on that legend, full of racial memories of the people, also full of courage, of a boy's struggle to find himself, to discover his own place, to leap, at least in thought, beyond the mores of his own culture. The leap beyond the usual, the accepted, is so often what defines the folk hero. His audacity embodies the longings of a people for something beyond—beyond the next promontory, beyond the blue-black water where the sharks dwell, beyond the next island, beyond a restrictive social structure controlled by taboos. The material thrilled me, and I went into it more deeply, reading in Polynesian and Hawaiian myths and anthropological studies, talking to proud people who retained after 150 years of foreign influence some of the old thought patterns and ideals of their fathers.

Dorothy Kahananui, Hawaiian musician and professor of Hawaiian at the University, led me to a full Hawaiian version of the legend, containing the old chants—so significant a part of Hawaiian life—the most important tie of knowledge and feeling of the past to the present and essential to the atmosphere and telling of the story. She agreed to make a literal translation for me, and I worked out my own version from that and from the two other versions that exist in English.

While I was writing the story of Paka'a [*Backbone of the King*], which swings back and forth from the delineation of character to the natural phenomena that form character and provide images of magnificence to describe it, I was naturally thinking of the illustrations. Full color would not only have been out of the question in cost for a long book for older children but would have intruded too insistently on a story that is one of internal struggle and growth as well as external action.

Except for enigmatical pictographs, of great interest to anthropologists but very primitive graphically, and wood and stone images of gods, there was almost no Hawaiian art that seemed effective to me as inspiration for illustrations for a legend for young people with probably a vague picture of a tourist's paradise. I had thought of a carved medium, woodcut or linoleum, one that might hark back to the elegantly simple carvings and also one that could depict the atmosphere in which such legends arose. I finally settled on linoleum, and two points of view evolved in the illustrations that are also in my telling of the story. One is the background of vast natural forces—the winds that were thought to bear the tales; the basalt cliffs that gave an ideal to men's character; the vast spaces of the sea, source of life and food, testing ground of prowess, image of both beauty and poignant and unfulfilled longing. The other is a simple delineation of character, pared down to its essence in the most direct of emotional confrontations. Linoleum, which can be cut or engraved, seemed to be the answer.

The color I chose for the printing was close to that I recall most strongly when I think of Hawaii—the deep green of the clefts in the great palis, where all softness has worn away in wind and rain but where living plants have clad the cliffs in velvet. I chose a deep, warm, almost olive green to harmonize with the warm-toned paper. (pp. 68-74)

I had tried to tell the story with strong, simple words, most of them Anglo-Saxon, words of action, with metaphors taken from Hawaiian life. The pictures would have to reflect the feelings of those words. Big things had to remain big. Action should have meaning, but thought and inner feeling are also action in illustration. I found this illustration for older children a challenge, with a more rigid type page than that of the picture book, with a very different mental approach from the reader.

The title page is symbolic—the steering paddle that meant command; the kahili, the feather standard, that meant royalty and the watchful care of a backbone for his king; the cliff that meant the rock-heart that does not yield or wear away. A windy book from a windy land.

In *The Little Prince*, Saint-Exupéry makes a statement in the context of one human relationship that perhaps we could apply to another: "One is forever responsible for whom one has tamed." Children walk, arms open, to embrace what we give them. To hand on to them the breakdown in communication that is all around us is a very serious thing. Those who work with children should be encouraged to hand on to them their personal involvement with the world. A child needs the stimulus of books that are focused on individuality in personality and character if he is to find his own. A child is individual; a book is individual. Each should be served according to its needs. (pp. 74-5)

> *Marcia Brown, "My Goals as an Illustrator," in her* Lotus Seeds: Children, Pictures, and Books, *Charles Scribner's Sons, 1986, pp. 61-75.*

GENERAL COMMENTARY

ALICE DALGLIESH

[*Author of three Newbery honor books, Dalgliesh was Brown's first editor at Charles Scribner's Sons.*]

[In New York City, Marcia Brown] lived in an apartment on Sullivan Street. From her window she could see the busy life of that largely Italian section—the children playing in the street, on roofs and fire-escapes. Pictures and a story began to come into her mind. *The Little Carousel* began to take definite shape, its central theme the traveling carousel that was such a delight to the city children. It was just after the war, and when soldiers returned, green, red and black Italian streamers were everywhere in that district. *The Little Carousel,* you will notice, uses those Italian colors.

I don't know how much concentrated work went into the making of the dummy of that first book. Experience with Marcia's later work makes me know that many illustrations may have been drawn and discarded. But when it came to me, the dummy had all the freshness of the most spontaneous drawing.... I accepted it—not without thinking it over for a short time, as one does before adding a new artist to the list. But I felt that here was an artist with great originality and many possibilities for future work. I liked the clever, simple use of flat color—so many young artists present their first work in too elaborate technique and color. Authors and artists worry about first books, but so do editors! An editor sending out a book by a new author or artist has all the feelings of a mother sending her child to school for the first time. Such a big group—will the child be noticed? Such a big country, so many books—will this one make its way? *The Little Carousel* made friends immediately.

At that time—still not too long after World War II—we were going a little cautiously with color, and I was pleased that Marcia's next book, *Stone Soup,* was in limited color. Limited color, but such humor and spirit and gaiety of feeling! An old folk tale retold, *Stone Soup* appealed to children everywhere. (pp. 292-93)

By this time she had spent two summers on the island of St. Thomas, then *Henry-Fisherman* arrived in our office. We began to realize that here was an artist who brought something entirely different to each book. Here were the bright colors of the tropics, bold patterns in five flat colors. I look at the pictures now, and those perfectly beautiful end papers with their semi-abstract pattern of palm trees, the charming patterns made by sea and boats and fish throughout the book, and wonder why, why *Henry-Fisherman* did not have quite the general appeal of the other books. Children of the Virgin Islands in the West Indies and Negro children of this country love that appealing little brown boy who wanted so much to be a fisherman. They love him because Marcia really understands Henry and his family. I'd never noticed until this book came out how many reviewers lack words for color. *Henry*'s colors were usually "pink and light blue, yellow and brown." We called them "coral and turquoise, gold and chartreuse and brown"—the commercial firms who make such products as textiles know the value of descriptive color words. And *Henry is* color!

I watched *Dick Whittington* grow, as I've watched a number of books grow, on the big working table in my barn studio in Connecticut, when Marcia was spending a summer there. *Dick Whittington* in its first appearance was in pen line with four colors. The story—first printed in an English chap book—called for a bolder treatment, however. Marcia had been working on wood blocks at The New School for Social Research under Louis Shanker, and linoleum blocks in two colors seemed to be the treatment for this particular story. Cutting a block for each color (and you can't cover up the mistakes of a cutting tool—you have to start all over again) was a long process, but resulted in one of the handsomest books we have published. It reflected Marcia's interest in the Middle Ages, which had begun long before with Howard Pyle's books, and had continued through college, where she studied medieval music and poetry.

The books went on, with *Skipper John's Cook,* made after many summers on Cape Cod, and *Puss in Boots,* who won much acclaim for his swashbuckling airs. *Puss* really began with a puppet that Marcia made, a very gay and gallant little cat with red leather boots and a plumed hat. *The Steadfast Tin Soldier* followed. It seems to me to be one of the best of her books,

with its skillful suggestions of mood and feeling. She had always wanted to illustrate an Andersen story, but hesitated to attempt it until she felt ready for it. The translation to be used was given much thought, too. She selected the one by M. R. James because it is excellent, informal and suited to storytelling.

Then came *Cinderella*—with careful work on the translation and the research that went into the period setting. *Cinderella* has humor and gaiety and magic. It is the *Cinderella* I would, as a fairy-tale-loving little girl, have loved to own and read over and over. (pp. 293-94)

        Alice Dalgliesh, "Marcia Brown and Her Books," in The Horn Book Magazine, *Vol. XXXI, No. 4, August, 1955, pp. 291-95.*

LYND WARD

[No] artist has been more sensitive to the varying requirements of different stories than Marcia Brown, whose work has shown the greatest variety in every crucial element of expression, all consciously directed to making each of her books a completely different experience from the others. (p. 21)

        Lynd Ward, "The Book Artist: Ideas and Techniques," in Illustrators of Children's Books: 1946-1956, *edited by Ruth Hill Viguers, Marcia Dalphin, and Bertha Mahoney Miller, The Horn Book, 1958, pp. 14-35.*

HELEN ADAMS MASTEN

It has been only seven years since Marcia Brown won the Caldecott medal for her *Cinderella.* Comparing the exquisite little *gouache* drawings for *Cinderella* with the strong and rhythmically beautiful woodcuts for *Once a Mouse* ..., one realizes that this artist has come a long way in seven years.

An artist grows by living, by traveling, studying, reading, looking with a seeing eye, drawing and painting everything that comes his way. What he does when he is *not* working on a book often determines not only the nature of his future work but also the quality of it.

A trip to Europe in 1956, which culminated in nearly a year spent in Paris and, later, almost three years living in Venice, opened up a whole new world to an artist whose eyes are quick to take in beauty of form, line, and color. (p. 347)

Everywhere Marcia goes—whether it is Brittany, Denmark, Holland, or Spain—she sketches people, in the parks, on the subways, at the ballet, the circus or the beach. Many days are spent sketching at the zoo: goats, the big cats, birds, scenes through the trees. In her sketchbooks are some of the best drawings she has made. Later, some of these sketches form the basis for paintings in oil. Sometimes they are unintentional preparation for drawings for books.

The Three Billy Goats Gruff sprang onto the pages so fast that the artist's dummy was completed in five days. To create an entire picture book in a few days is only possible when an artist has lived with a story a very long time, when each picture is crystal clear in the mind's eye. *The Three Billy Goats Gruff* was always a favorite story with Marcia and it has proved to be the children's favorite as well.

In a story hour at The New York Public Library, I had the pleasure of using the artist's dummy with the children. There was never any doubt in the minds of the children, from the moment the goats appeared on the Norwegian hillside, that they would get the better of the troll. Little moans of pleasure and anticipation could be heard as I turned the page and they saw the Big Billy Goat Gruff fairly bursting with energy and confidence, sending forth his challenge to the troll. At the end of the story hour every child was clamoring to take home the artist's copy. No other book would satisfy them. For weeks they returned to the Library to ask for *The Three Billy Goats Gruff*, ''the one with all the pictures.'' The drawings for this book are in crayon and ink. Marcia's conception of the troll is based on nature—fog, rocks, earth, and the roots of trees. One sees in the drawings small, rocky islands, some of the hundreds that dot the Norwegian coast. They are the troll after the Big Billy Goat Gruff has disposed of him. (pp. 347-48)

All during the fall and through the winter of 1956 Marcia worked on *The Flying Carpet*. Being one of the more complicated and sophisticated of the Arabian Nights stories, *The Flying Carpet* is seldom included in editions intended for children. After research into translations and versions, the threads of the story were rewoven by Marcia to make a cohesive story, understandable to children. The original drawings for the book have great beauty. Unfortunately, some of this is lost in the printing, because the artist—always eager to experiment with new technical processes—used a combination of gold dust and gum arabic in making color separations. This combination allowed less light to filter through than was intended, with the result that a sky, spangled with stars and filled with beauty, became ominous with black clouds. In spite of the difficulties of printing, it is a beautiful book, greatly enjoyed by older children. (p. 349)

It is a delight to use [*Peter Piper's Alphabet*] in the picture-book hour, the story hour, or with class groups. All one needs to do is to read the witty ''P-Preface,'' found in the first American edition, to send boys and girls off into gales of laughter and pursuit of the riddles in the pictures. The drawings have caught completely the ridiculous nonsense of the verses. Marcia is always quick to see cats, wherever they are, as individuals with marked personalities. Most of her books have a cat somewhere in them. One night while she and I were exploring some alleys in Naples, we saw a cat quivering with anticipation, watching a darkened window high up in a wall. We stopped to watch; and in a few moments a light flashed on. A woman watching with us cried out ''*Ecco!*'' and out of the window came a basket on a long cord, lowered by an unseen hand. The cat raced across the alley, snatched a fish, and ran off with his supper. We stared at each other, delighted. Out of this incident *Felice* was born in Venice. Marcia's studio in Venice is on the same canal where the children swam in *Felice*. All winter long eight or nine stray cats were fed by her in the same way that Gino fed Felice.

From the moment Marcia saw Venice, she, like other artists, fell in love with it. Its decaying architectural beauty, its sparkling waters, tiny *campi,* and mysterious canals are there in *Felice* for children to enjoy and explore, along with the story of the homeless little cat. The original drawings are done in water colors. (pp. 350-51)

In the spring of 1956 Marcia was in Sicily. The fields and hills were covered with daisies and poppies under the ancient, gray-green olive trees, the blossoming fruit trees, and the tall, black cypresses. Everywhere was beauty. Everywhere were big-eyed children and small, worn donkeys. Years before, a Sicilian friend had told Marcia of a childhood experience with a lost donkey. Now the story came alive for her once more as she saw for herself the Sicilian countryside and the village life so vividly described by her friend. The result was *Tamarindo!*,

published in 1960. In the crayon-and-ink drawings the Sicilian landscape blossoms again in a happy story of four little boys and the lost donkey of her friend's childhood. The amusing and delightful pictures reveal many Sicilian ways. One has only to look at the picture of the *men* eating under the arbor to see that the *women* know their place. (p. 351)

On Marcia's return from Europe she drew and painted at the Art Students' League and other studios, sketched often at the Bronx Zoo, and worked on paintings in her own studio overlooking the East River. The paintings were abandoned when she became interested in an old legend from the Sanskrit.

The legend, ''The Hermit and the Mouse,'' she found in a book sent from Italy. Marcia decided to rework the story and cut the pictures in wood. She had made wood carvings as a young student, using only a jackknife, and had cut *Dick Whittington and His Cat* in linoleum. Since, after studying with Louis Schanker, she had made many woodcuts, she came to the book with knowledge and skill. I think, however, she was unaware of the enormous amount of sheer physical labor the book was to exact from her. Since Marcia is a perfectionist, many blocks and prints were discarded. There were nights when she worked until two o'clock, carving, printing, proving the blocks. In July of 1961, after she had seen first proofs, Marcia sailed for Spain, exhausted and drained. Later, she returned to Venice and a studio to paint and draw for a year.

After she had sailed, I found in our wood basket some of the discarded blocks for *Once A Mouse*. . . . Since they seemed far too good and too interesting for kindling, they did not light my fire. *Once A Mouse* . . . has, in some of its pages, a Biblical quality. I have seen pictures of Moses which had less authority than the drawing of the hermit rebuking the tiger. There are fine composition, glowing color, humor, tenderness, and strength in this beautiful book which make it truly worthy of the Caldecott Medal. (p. 352)

Helen Adams Masten, ''From Caldecott to Caldecott,'' in The Horn Book Magazine, *Vol. XXXVIII, No. 4, August, 1962, pp. 347-52.*

NORMAN KENT

Several months ago while browsing through Scribner's bookshop on Fifth Avenue, my eye was attracted to a powerful jacket unmistakably created in color woodcut. Its gay color and broad design held immediate interest, but even before I had a chance to investigate its contents, a sign informed me that this book—*Once A Mouse, A Fable Cut in Wood* by Marcia Brown—had won the Caldecott Medal for 1962.

This experience of discovering a ''new'' illustrator, a circumstance not uncommon for editors and art directors who frequent bookshops, is particularly rewarding when, on subsequent inquiry, they find (as I did) that the artist has a solid record of accomplishment.

From beginning to end, *Once A Mouse* lives up to the visual promise of its striking jacket. Thirty-two pages of minimal text written by the illustrator are enlivened by a series of dramatic color woodcuts, several printed across double spreads. Even the texture of the long-grained plank, as well as every cut or incision of the woodcutter's gouge and knife, has been retained in the offset reproduction. The bold design of the principal figure, the animals, and the landscape backgrounds are all created by simple masses so imaginative in concept that this book, though produced for children, will find an honored place among xylographic items in collections of American graphic art. (p. 26)

[Miss Brown's books] do not follow a pattern, but rather present a variety of techniques ranging from the purely decorative to a fluid pen line and free color patterns. . . . [Subject] matter is equally interesting. Like so many juveniles today, Marcia Brown's books combine her talents as a writer with her special abilities as an illustrator. (pp. 26, 29)

This artist has explored numerous techniques—pen line, linoleum and woodcuts, watercolor, gouache, line and wash, crayon, and various combinations of line and color. For most of her books, Marcia has made color separations—a process that not only effects an economy in the cost of plate making but also adds a special typographic flavor to the character of the illustrations.

I questioned Marcia about her work. "Which comes first after the idea for a particular book has been born—the pictorial conception or the manuscript?" "That is rather difficult to answer," said the artist. "I often conceive a story idea simultaneously with its pictorial possibilities, but for practical purposes, I write my manuscript first and submit it to my publisher with a miniature dummy containing a projected layout plus rough sketches of the projected illustrations. When this is accepted by the editors, I decide on the graphic technique that will best express the spirit of the story, even though this is often dictated to my mind from the start. The making of the final drawings takes place only after the book design has been carefully planned . . . and I know the exact size of the page, where illustrations in color may be printed, and all other manufacturing detail that will have a bearing on the preparation of the art for reproduction." (pp. 29, 31)

In summing up the particular quality in the work of Marcia Brown as an illustrator, the major characteristic is the imaginative content of her pictures, an aura that leaps off the printed page and registers its interpretive message instantly. It transcends style or technique; it speaks especially to children. Marcia is not a self-conscious stylist in the strictest sense of the term. Her illustrations to date vary considerably in manner, but each is an ideal vehicle for the story element. She draws from the heart. (p. 31)

> Norman Kent, "Marcia Brown: Author & Illustrator," in American Artist, Vol. 27, No. 1, January, 1963, pp. 26-31.

DOROTHY M. BRODERICK

One of the best starting points for an analysis of good picture books is to be found in the works of Marcia Brown. Besides being an excellent artist, Miss Brown is willing and able to alter her technique to meet the needs of each book. Since she also writes her own text, the problem of communication between author and artist is nonexistent. Miss Brown as artist knows exactly what Miss Brown the author is trying to convey.

When we look at *Cinderella,* illustrated in pen line and colored crayon, we are immediately captured by the fine lines, the graceful curves and the pastel colors which evoke all the frothy, ephemeral qualities of the fairy tale. *Stone Soup,* on the other hand, is a down-to-earth French folk tale and the black and red wash, the almost square, chunky figures convey the earthy, Gallic humor to perfection. These two books alone, both of French origin, but so different in mood, spirit, and message, demonstrate Miss Brown's capabilities.

But look further. Look at the watercolors used in *Felice* to capture the mystery and beauty of Venice. The double-page spread of the cat fight is a magnificent portrait of "the fur flying"; the double-page spread of Venice at night with the lights, the blackness of the water, the sweep of the canal boats—this is the Venice of our dreams.

Then turn to *Once a Mouse,* in which the woodcuts achieve a fluidity of motion rarely found in that medium. All of the strength of the jungle is on these pages, and the tiger, whether sulking or peacocking it over the other animals, is the essence of the feline—proud, graceful—power oozing from every muscle, self-satisfaction from every whisker. (pp. 98-9)

> Dorothy M. Broderick, "Picture Books," in her An Introduction to Children's Work in Public Libraries, The H. W. Wilson Company, 1965, pp. 95-105.

HELEN W. PAINTER

The storytelling qualities of Miss Brown's books have appealed greatly to children, perhaps because the writer as a former librarian and teller of tales is so well versed in what youngsters like. (p. 841)

Miss Brown's first book was *The Little Carousel* in 1946. . . . Unlike the "too elaborate technique and color" [see excerpt by Alice Dalgliesh dated 1955] of many first books, *The Little Carousel* made simple but skillful use of flat color: green, red, black, and yellow. (p. 843)

The book that followed was *Stone Soup* in 1947, . . . the first of her many accounts of folk tales. Humorous and merry, the old story of Brittany with its pictures in . . . colors of red and black delights children. Wit, dancing, and laughter pervade the book, and the animated expressions on the faces of the French people are some of Miss Brown's best. . . .

After two summers on the island of St. Thomas, Miss Brown next wrote *Henry-Fisherman,* published in 1949. . . . The illustrations, sometimes almost semi-abstract, are vivid and clear. (p. 844)

In 1950 a completely different book appeared, *Dick Whittington and His Cat.* . . . Long before, Howard Pyle's books had kindled Miss Brown's interest in the Middle Ages, and she had studied medieval music and poetry in college. She was familiar with the Old English chapbook version of the tale which she wanted to use. After employing pen line with four colors, she decided that the story called for a stronger medium, and finally linoleum cuts were made. . . . Two colors were used, and the cutting of a block for each color took a long time but "resulted in one of the handsomest books we have published," the editor claimed [see excerpt by Alice Dalgliesh dated 1955]. (pp. 844-45)

Skipper John's Cook came in 1951, . . . one of the author-artist's merriest books. The story grew from Miss Brown's many summers at Cape Cod, where she learned that an eight-year-old boy had once sailed as a cook from Provincetown, Massachusetts.

Puss in Boots followed in 1952, . . . a book of "fresh creative power." Miss Brown had made a puppet of a cat, which suggested the famous story of the swashbuckling French cat who cleverly tricked the king. Truly a work of visual art in soft but exciting colors, it is an opulent and elegant cat whose image appears in the book. The high, coral-shaded boots show off spectacularly against the gray fur, and the sword in paw and the wide-brimmed black hat with its two coral plumes help to create a dashing figure indeed. The fairytale atmosphere caught

From Henry-Fisherman: A Story of the Virgin Islands, *written and illustrated by Marcia Brown. Charles Scribner's Sons, 1949. Copyright 1949 Marcia Brown. Copyright renewed © 1977 Marcia Brown. All rights reserved. Reprinted with the permission of Charles Scribner's Sons.*

in the four colors made the book decidedly unusual in comparison with its predecessors and won extravagant praise for its creator. (pp. 845-46)

Perhaps one of the best of her books is *The Steadfast Tin Soldier,* published in 1953. . . . For some time Marcia Brown had hoped to illustrate a story of Hans Christian Andersen and at last felt ready to try it. Using the M. R. James translation because she thought it ideally suited to storytelling, she worked long over her four-color drawings to suggest emotion and mood. Thus, the Tin Soldier in red and blue is proud and stalwart; the dancer, beautiful and fragile in white as she stands on tiptoe against the rose and lavendar of the lovely paper castle. The exquisite visual interpretation is truly fairylike. (p. 846)

The same kind of research for *Puss in Boots* was used for *Cinderella,* Caldecott Award winner in 1955 and a story also based on a free translation of the Perrault version. While the research into the setting was the same, for the period for both books was identical, the use was different and the point of view different. In the former, some of the shots were from "a cat's point of view" and, therefore, very low, though "not in an exaggerated way from a cat's angle." In *Cinderella* the casein gouache pictures are perhaps more delicate and less dashing, more indicative of enchantment and romance than of

clever trickery. They possess a sketchy and almost mystic quality. (pp. 846-47)

[The story] is a well-loved one, and the magic of prancing horses drawing a golden coach and of a beautiful, fairylike princess waving a lacy fan is illuminated with splashes of rose tint against the blue of the background.

Next, in 1956, came *The Flying Carpet,* one of the stories of the *Arabian Nights* not well known to children. Strong, deep, and dramatic colors, like those of an Oriental rug, are used in this book. . . . (p. 847)

[*The Three Billy Goats Gruff*] (1957) was a special favorite of the author-artist, based upon the Dasent translation of the Asbjørnsen and Moe version. The book appeared so quickly to her that she completed the dummy of it in five days, so clear were the mental pictures of crayon and ink and also the number of the drawings and the intensity within the book. (pp. 847-48)

The next year and a half were a time of "detachment" spent in Europe. Here Miss Brown witnessed a scene which led to *Felice* (1958), a story in which a boy Gino makes a friend of a little striped cat. (p. 848)

Miss Brown loved Venice and put its "decaying architectural beauty, its sparkling waters, tiny *campi,* and mysterious canals" in the book. She used water colors because to her Venice is a water color city, shimmering in its reflections. The printers used her own colors and got almost exact reproduction in the book. The deep vivid blue is especially lovely among the varied color tones.

Sketching continued. More, but different, pictures began to evolve. In 1959 *Peter Piper's Alphabet* was printed. The gay, exaggerated pictures reflect the nonsense of the lines and provide lively answers to the riddles.

The year 1960 saw evidence of much work: the publication of *Une Drôle de Soupe* [a French translation of *Stone Soup* by Hilda Grenier Tagliapietra] and the designing of stage sets and costumes for *The Glass Slipper,* a play of Eleanor Farjeon. Perhaps the chief accomplishment, however, was *Tamarindo!* Some years before, a Sicilian friend had told a true experience with a lost donkey, which formed the basis for the book. Not until Miss Brown was in Sicily in 1956 did she come really to see for herself the village life and the beauty of the countryside. (pp. 848-49)

The crayon and ink drawings of *Tamarindo!* reveal happily the background. One of the most delightful pictures shows the lost donkey with a gleeful expression greeting the startled boy Pepineddu in the cave. (p. 849)

When the Caldecott Award was announced in 1962, another of Marcia Brown's books was the winner: *Once a Mouse....* She had been ready to do a book in a different technique, woodcuts. She had been making color woodblocks, a simple medium though an exhausting one since an artist must do a separate block for each color in a book. She wanted a big subject that would say something to a young child.... (pp. 849-50)

During the fall of 1960 she had been captivated by tigers at the Bronx Zoo, whose likenesses she had been drawing. Therefore, when a friend sent from Venice a collection of animal fables, her subject became immediately apparent. She went directly to a literal translation from the Sanskrit and worked from it. The movement of the story formed almost instantly in her mind. A recent show of Indian work at the New York Museum of Modern Art influenced her choice of colors; she noticed that the people of India used certain ones: a deep, soft green—rather olive-like—, crimson red, and "a very yellowy green that suggested to me light coming through the leaves in the jungle." With color scheme and story idea formed, a special little dummy was done in about an hour to capture roughly the total, the creative idea. Then the actual woodcutting began. Miss Brown says that she made seven blocks for some of the pages before she got one that satisfied the scheme and flow of the book. With tremendous skill and verbal restraint, she developed the brief story. This fable from the Indian Hitopadesa came through with great impact and depth to capture young readers.... (p. 850)

To the observer and student the artist's forceful lines and strong color are exceedingly effective. The long gold stretch of the crow's neck and head show a rapacious quality as a small black mouse scurries from the open beak. The extended flow of line of the hermit's arm from shoulder to pointed finger reaches over the sweep of the defiant tiger's back. The plotting expression of the fierce animal, proud though humiliated, is clearly etched as he lowers chin onto folded paws. Such dramatic pictures are powerful indeed.

Long hours of carving, printing, and proving the blocks for *Once a Mouse* led to physical exhaustion, and in July of 1961 Miss Brown sailed to Spain. Then she went to Venice for a year, painting most of the time....

It was just before a month's trip to Hawaii as guest at a book fair in 1962 that Marcia Brown happened to read "The Wild Swans" by Hans Christian Andersen....

In Hawaii reminders of the story pursued her: the shadow of the plane fell like a bird on great clouds; the sea was ruffled and the white foam was lacy around the cliffs' edges, just as they might appear to the brothers flying. On her return to New York she chose the collection of M. R. James. She felt no desire to rewrite Andersen, as some people do, to make the work appropriate and intelligible for children. (p. 851)

Travel had provided Miss Brown with other background for the book. Living near Hyde Park in London, she had sketched swans there. The birds proved fascinating to draw and later she turned to them, not so much for the movement as for a whole impression of feelings. Since ballet intrigues her, the poses and atmosphere of "The Sleeping Beauty" and "Swan Lake" already had become a part of her. Then, too, she did research to see just how swans alighted, took off, and glided, and just how their wing feathers were used as rudders. The big feathers in the wings can be turned to a 180° angle, she found; the birds can fly 70 miles per hour, and at 5,000 feet. "When you're making a book, all these things go into your feeling about what you're doing," she states. "You never know what you are going to use."

The Wild Swans was intended for older children because of its intense ideas. Its message was one which would depend on drawing and not color, she believed, because it seemed to speak in terms of character. Miss Brown finally chose to use a lettering pen on rough water color paper with wash. The wash permitted the contrast from the white swans to the moody quality of dark forest and gloomy castles. To relieve the gloom so needed for the story content, and also for emotional impact probably, a delicate rose color was used for the beaks of the swans, for the dawn, and for the sunsets.

The most recent book of this contemporary writer-artist appeared in the early summer of 1966. Again we are enthralled by the versatility of Miss Brown. For the first time she has done a longer book, which must be for a child of ten or older. In *Backbone of the King* the writer reveals her absorption with Hawaii and its legends; her great study and research are everywhere evident, perhaps most obviously in the extensive glossary which is indispensable to the reader. Before Miss Brown left Hawaii in 1962 she had been given a collection of native tales. After completing *The Wild Swans* she found herself returning to the islands.... Her year there led to *Backbone of the King,* "not a retelling of the legend. The legend already exists. It's a story that is based on it."

She explains that the Hawaiians, lacking a written language until recent years, had long, complicated stories but accounts full of poetry and a powerful simplicity of telling reminiscent of Anglo-Saxon and Greek fragments. In the first version Miss Brown had been entranced by the boy's wonderful calabash that contained all the winds, but later versions gave chants of power and beauty. Finally she chose a translation by Dorothy M. Kahananui that possessed all the rich elements sought. (pp. 851-52)

The beauty and eloquence of the taut prose and the force and vigor of the olive-green linoleum blocks present an unusual book, to which the reader will return again and again since its power seems to grow. Surely it is a worthy book to take its place in a very distinguished line of fresh, imaginative contributions to children's literature by its originator. . . .

Why does she do books for children? Reminiscing, Miss Brown recalls that at thirteen and reading adult books she took picture books home to study. Somehow she has seemed better fitted to do children's books. . . .

Children must be exposed to good picture books, Miss Brown believes. . . . She urges adults to build some background in art, that they may come to enjoy pictures with their senses and learn to appreciate art as "a communication only in its own terms of line, color and mass." (p. 853)

As a last look at the beliefs of this remarkable woman, let us ask why she turns to folk literature as the subject for so many of her books. Her answer is quick: there is so much *humanity in them*, she says; they are so profoundly true to life. They convey a feeling for ancestors, for trust in self, for truths about people, and for the battle between moral forces. While the tales may not be understood until later, children need them. (p. 855)

> Helen W. Painter, "Marcia Brown: A Study in Versatility," in Elementary English, Vol. XLIII, No. 8, December, 1966, pp. 841-55, 876.

CHARLOTTE S. HUCK AND DORIS YOUNG KUHN

Marcia Brown's sensitivity to the varying requirements of different stories has led her to use different media and styles of illustrating. One feels that she is master of them all. Look at the movement of her wonderful *The Three Billy Goats Gruff* as they come prancing over that bridge in the Norwegian fjord country. Her troll is a muddy, ugly one that you are glad to see crushed to bits! Compare these vigorous crayon and gouache drawings to the fluff and frills of *Cinderella* or to the bold, vigorous concentration of lines and design in the woodcuts for *Once a Mouse*. (p. 121)

[*Once a Mouse*] is a fable from India concerning a hermit who pondered big and little. A mouse was nearly caught by a crow and then a cat. Using magic, the hermit changed the mouse to a cat, and as he was threatened, to a dog, and then a tiger. When the hermit reprimanded the tiger for being so proud, the tiger decided to kill the hermit. Alas! He was changed back to a mouse. The artist uses shadows effectively. For example, the shape of the hills form the shadow of a beak snatching the mouse; the tiger's shadow is shaped like the dog of his previous existence; the jungle pattern is shaped like a tiger leaning toward the final mouse form. (p. 122)

> Charlotte S. Huck and Doris Young Kuhn, "Picture Books," in their Children's Literature in the Elementary School, second edition, Holt, Rinehart and Winston, Inc., 1968, pp. 95-155.

BARBARA BADER

For several years in the Forties Marcia Brown worked at the New York Public Library, in the Central Children's Room and, telling stories, outside (outdoors, often), all the while continuing to study art and ready herself for what she wanted to do, illustrate children's books, young children's books particularly. (p. 313)

[When] her own *Stone Soup* came out she confided to children, "Telling stories to boys and girls all over New York has been

my greatest fun in library work" and "the old tale of the three soldiers" was one that they enjoyed. *Stone Soup* is folklore, venerable but not celebrated, the sort of story librarians culled from collections rather than a Cinderella or Snow White or Three Bears, universally known and passed on. It was from the latter, the traditional nursery literature, that Walter Crane made his toy-books (and the McLoughlins made many of theirs) and an occasional book-beautiful was produced—Helen Sewell's *Cinderella* in 1934, Elizabeth MacKinstry's *Aladdin and the Wonderful Lamp* in 1935. But in the new era fairy tales were old hat or worse, bad medicine, poison, and save for an exceptional *Seven Simeons* creative energies turned elsewhere. In the Forties there did not exist single-volume picturizations of even the most famous of the traditional tales, a void that, like the toy-books before them, Little Golden Books helped to fill.

As a child "thinking that I would like one day to illustrate books for children," Marcia Brown testifies, "I always thought of the fairy tales that I loved"; and in the library she found them persistently popular: "Not for a moment did children who came of their own accord . . . and were free to choose their own books, desert their heroes, the personification of their dreams. The calls still came for Cinderella," but also "for stories about giants and princesses, for simple people raised to high station because of their gifts." That is, for the gamut of folk and fairy tales, which she proceeded to put into picturebooks, in *Stone Soup* into a picturebook that was capable of being read aloud to a group, that could be presented to younger children as effectively as the story itself might be told to older children.

What is special about *Stone Soup*—special to it, almost—is the way the action moves across the pages from left to right, regardless of the relative position of the figures, and how much is accomplished on each occasion with a minimum of words and a single continuous or split picture. . . . The three soldiers are wangling a meal from professedly destitute French peasants: "'And now, if you please, three round, smooth stones.'" Clearly in evidence—one, two, three. "Those were easy enough to find." Yes, the men come carrying them on the run. "The peasants' eyes grew round as they watched the soldiers drop the stones into the pot." The first, under surveillance, is about to go in. So we have, in one spread, the stones requisitioned ("three round, smooth stones"), fetched (they're "easy enough to find") and set cooking; and with the peasants we're wondering what can possibly come of it. (On the verso, "'Any soup needs salt and pepper'" . . . and, "'oh, if there were carrots, it would be much better.'") Not only is much accomplished but nothing is omitted; there is no hiatus, no waiting for words or pictures to catch up. The story is an anecdote, a mere incident, without any obvious pictorial attraction—just an exchange between three passing soldiers and the inhabitants of a village; a good story saved from oblivion and added to the common stock by tight, pungent scripting and nimble nonstop staging.

Marcia Brown had already done an original picturebook the year before, *The Little Carousel* . . .—a book original also in the sense that the story takes place on a real sidewalks-of-New-York street (hers) and features a boy who might well be found there, looking longingly out the window. . . . Done in the red, green and black of the Italian neighborhood, the book has authentic local color, and at a time when picturebooks tended toward archetypes and universals, it is personal and circumstantial. The cure for Anthony's complaint? A roving merry-go-round and a chance to earn a ride by turning the crank for the weary (wise and kind?) proprietor.

Two summers on the island of St. Thomas were behind *Henry-Fisherman,* as unusual then for its realistic portrayal of a black child as *The Little Carousel* was for entering into ordinary urban life. Henry's is the normal yearning to prove himself, which means, in the Caribbean, going to sea . . . ; and barely escaping a shark, prove himself he does. "But a boy like Henry could find many things to do on an island like St. Thomas, while he was waiting to grow up and go to sea." At one opening he's fetching water, balancing a can on his head; at another, searching for coral and shells; further on, helping with the family wash, going to the market place, tending the goats—all temptingly pictured in tropical coral and dark green, turquoise and gold and brown, or simply the coral and deep dark green. But handsomely put together as it is, complete to the neat solid sans serif and the interweaving palm-pattern endpapers, the story is for the most part static, the pictures more suggestive than involving. A pleasure to look at and, with its native lilt, to listen to, it hasn't a commensurate hold on children.

From later travels came other stories colored by a locality; but whether more successful (*Felice* . . .) or less (*Tamarindo!* . . .), they are a poor second to the folk and fairy tale 'singles' and, for that matter, to the illustrations for Philip Sherlock's collection of tales *Anansi, the Spider Man* . . . , product of a stay in Jamaica.

Stone Soup is done in line and wash, *Henry-Fisherman* in flat planes of color, gouache, the next, *Dick Whittington and His Cat,* in linoleum cuts: doing each book differently, in a manner suited to the matter at hand, was to be a hallmark of Marcia Brown's work. The legend of Dick Whittington, the poor orphan scullion deterred from running away by the prophetic ring of the Bow Bells—"Turn again, Whittington,/Lord Mayor of London"—while unbeknownst to him, his cat is making his fortune, is both a personal tale and historic pageantry; and the difficulty is to balance the two. The technique and the use of it give us the rough, vigorous setting; the composition draws our eye beyond the passers-by into the lane where Dick sits huddled . . . ; and the text, telling of his dismay, is also a tale of disenchantment. . . . There's a good deal to the story, and a good deal to the pictures, and not a little humor in both.

With *Dick Whittington* Brown was pioneering to a degree too; the fashion for Olde English stories sedulously half-timbered hadn't yet set in. But Perrault's *Puss in Boots* was one of the favorites of her childhood, much illustrated, that, she attests, "it was some years before I felt ready or capable of attempting." Elsewhere she speaks admiringly of the work of Edy Legrand, his later work in line and wash or pastel, and specifically of *La Nuit de la Saint Sylvain,* published here in 1947 as *The Enchanted Eve.* Printed on paper tinted a dusty rose and blue, the whole page illuminated . . . , it is a big splendorous book harking back to the historical albums of Job but itself a thing of great dash; Marcia Brown refers to it as "one of the most beautiful books I have ever known." In their simpler way her French books particularly, the *Puss in Boots* and *Cinderella,* continue in that illustrious tradition.

She domesticates it, tempers it to the story and the audience. Where Job and Edy Legrand are always imposing and illustrate around the text, Brown illustrates the text itself, scene by scene, now bringing us close to hear Puss's sly command . . . , now carrying the results of his scheme swiftly past us . . . , now—dropping the springy line for pure floating pastel—taking us

with Puss to the object of his scheming, the ogre's great castle. . . . Three openings—and at the fourth the ogre will be dispatched in an explosive arc. That one finds, in place of squared-off blocks of text, text-lines fitted to the design, is the least of the difference; but without such extreme flexibility in type-setting, just then coming to the fore . . . , the overall treatment would be impossible, another example of craft intersecting with art.

Of the technique, Brown observed in 1955: "In the past few years we have seen more and more books using a crayon and line technique, with the drawings reproduced directiy from the artist's own color separations by means of a contact method with no camera work. . . . By making their own plates, by exploring the variety of effects possible with hand-graphic techniques, illustrators can develop the freedom of fine artists in their print-making" [see excerpt in Author's Commentary dated 1955]. It is Charlot's observation turned round, and one has only to look at the mowers, never mind the figure Puss cuts, to appreciate the result. . . . Nor can one fail to notice, throughout, the use of white space "in which the mind rests or fills in its own images."

Despite their common origin, *Cinderella* is quite different, by turns tender and wry where *Puss* is all pomp and swagger. And if it is not to be mere plot, the Cinderella stereotype, the story cannot be similarly condensed or, to the same extent, told in pictures; we need the stepsisters' silly chatter and their taunting as much as we need the spectacle they make of themselves

From Dick Whittington and His Cat, *told and cut in linoleum by Marcia Brown. Charles Scribner's Sons, 1950. Copyright 1950 Marcia Brown. Copyright renewed © 1978 Marcia Brown. All rights reserved. Reprinted with the permission of Charles Scribner's Sons.*

primping for the ball. . . . *Cinderella,* in response, is a picture-story book, its illustrations separate from the text whether or not adjacent, and set into the page rather than bled; the considerable text is framed by white space and so are the pictures, and white space penetrates and binds the two. Line is the other link—quivering threads of line in the pictures and for the text type, a sharp and spirited Bembo. *Cinderella* is colored—chiefly in a rose and blue somewhat reminiscent of Edy Legrand's—but more than anything else it is a book of sparkling and witty drawings.

The Flying Carpet, which followed, takes off again, into vivid varicolored patterns and a bold heavy line . . . and, for the most part, page-filling design. *The Three Billy Goats Gruff,* in turn, is an exuberant tease . . . , pictured big as a billboard and as brash; "Now, I'm coming to gobble you up!" roars the troll at each trip-trapping billy goat gruff, and children in the back row squeal.

Such classics and demi-classics—*The Steadfast Tin Soldier* . . . is another—are the common property of the Western world; but in the course of looking for a particular kind of story—"a big subject, with few words, that would say something to a little child"—Marcia Brown lighted on an Indian fable, "The Hermit and the Mouse," and unwittingly began the combing of other cultures for picturebook material. It would have happened regardless: stories set in the 'emerging' countries were much in demand, folk tales traveled well (they always had), and folklore was felt to be a shortcut to understanding, the attitudes and expectations of a people externalized. That *Once a Mouse* was Marcia Brown's and won the Caldecott . . . simply served to accelerate the process.

"A big subject, with few words, that would say something to a little child"—it almost had to be a fable, and *Once a Mouse* is important to us not because it is Indian in origin but because it is universal in application and, as a picturebook, equally a drama and a work of art. (pp. 314-21)

Cut in wood, which "takes a certain amount of force"—this is Marcia Brown—"and a definite decision," it shows the wood plain ("Wood that lived can say something about life in a forest"). The colors are "the yellow-green of sun through leaves, the dark green of shadows, and the red that says India to me." Whether few or many, the pictorial elements are concentrated, emblematic ("Since the book is for very young children, the details are only those needed"); and the design itself tells much of the story, be it the earth closing in on the mouse or the forest astir, forms blurred, become forces—as cat confronts cat. But the illustration is more than instrumental, it is rich in visual interest and contrast—consider the grove of trees, the stand of grass, the crow and, cutting across, the grain of the wood; in rhythm and movement and, withal, a sense of risk: however much the artist labored over the blocks, one feels them as a leap from mind to hand.

Marcia Brown continues to do books and, from her knowledge of children, of art and of publishing, to write and talk about picturebook illustration with a breadth that lights up the field. Almost alone she has spoken out publicly against the siren song of the cash register. . . . In her own work she has given a new direction to that feeling for past works that is in the best library tradition. "From ancient India . . . a fable cut in wood" for four-year-olds—drawn and told with dignity and dispatch—is in fact no small thing. (p. 322)

Barbara Bader, "Marcia Brown," in her American Picture Books from Noah's Ark to the Beast Within, *Macmillan Publishing Company, 1976, pp. 313-22.*

PATRICIA CIANCIOLO

Marcia Brown is an outstanding example of a contemporary artist who meets the requirements of each story that she illustrates, but manages to do so on her own terms. Each of her picture books is her very own personal creation despite the fact that many of them contain illustrations of well-known folktales. She used vigorous crayon and gouache drawings to illustrate *The Three Billy Goats Gruff,* bold and graceful woodcut designs in *Once a Mouse,* and delicate drawings in pen line and colored crayon for *Cinderella.* In each book, Marcia Brown retains the mood and period of time peculiar to the traditional text, but she makes her own exquisite pictures, using different media and art styles for each story. The story line and the illustrations for each book are undeniably compatible. (p. 29)

Marcia Brown uses a variety of media to create her illustrations, and she uses each medium to the greatest possible advantage. . . . [It] is obvious that a single artist, like Marcia Brown, can be versatile in the media she uses and yet master the technique for each. Marcia Brown has varied the media for her many books, but in each case, she has chosen a medium (means) that will permit her to say what she has to say. (p. 60)

A skillfully contrived picture book illustrated by Marcia Brown with two-color linoleum cuts is *Dick Whittington and His Cat.* Her handling of this medium is vigorous and is nicely integrated with the concise and brief text (prose). The linocut prints in this book are suited to the period and the nature of this old favorite folktale. Much more dramatic are the handsome linocuts that illustrate the Hawaiian legend entitled *Backbone of the King: The Story of Paka'a and His Son Ku.* Once again, Marcia Brown vividly retains the authentic quality of the legend she has illustrated. In *Backbone of the King,* the exact features, the strong lines, and the effective use of color depict the fundamental struggles and powers of the ancient Hawaiians as well as their frailties. (p. 79)

Patricia Cianciolo, "Styles of Art in Children's Books" and "The Artist's Media and Techniques," in her Illustrations in Children's Books, *second edition, Wm. C. Brown Company Publishers, 1976, pp. 28-57, 58-93.*

MAY HILL ARBUTHNOT AND OTHERS

Marcia Brown is one of the most versatile of modern artists. She adapts her style to the mood and content of the story. The sturdy figure of *Dick Whittington* in earthy browns and black is precisely right for that hero. So are the flamboyant pinks for the dashing *Puss in Boots* and the delicately drawn figures in misty pastels for *The Steadfast Tin Soldier* and *Cinderella.* . . . But her book *Once a Mouse* . . . differs from all the others. The artist has used the difficult medium of woodcuts with a posterlike effect that is boldly stylized and wonderfully interpretive of mood and action. The details in these striking pictures will reward a closer look. In rich jungle colors, the story of the rise and fall of an ungrateful mouse is as dramatically told by the pictures as by the text.

May Hill Arbuthnot and Others, "The Artist and Children's Books: 'Once a Mouse',"in Children's Books Too Good to Miss, *seventh edition, University Press Books, 1979, p. 59.*

JANET A. LORANGER

Thirty-seven years ago, Marcia Brown published her first picture book for children: *The Little Carousel.* On June 28, 1983, she received her third Caldecott Medal for *Shadow.* Those years from 1946 to 1983 have encompassed one of the most distinguished careers in American children's books. That her latest book has received such a signal honor and that she is the first illustrator to be awarded the medal three times are evidences of the undiminished vitality and richness of her contribution to the field. It is an uncommon achievement.

The nourishment of such a gift and such an achievement comes from many sources. Marcia grew up in several small towns in upstate New York, one of three daughters in a minister's family. Everyone in the household loved music and reading, and her father also passed along to her, especially, his joy in using his hands. . . . Marcia feels that the most important legacy her parents gave her was a deep pleasure in using her eyes—for *seeing*, rather than merely for looking. Her keen delight in the details of nature and her acute observation of them are evident in all her books—most dramatically, perhaps, in the beautiful photographic nature books *Walk with Your Eyes, Listen to a Shape,* and *Touch Will Tell*. . . . (pp. 423-24)

Marcia's particular interest in folklore and fairy tales is apparent to anyone familiar with her books. Marcia believes strongly that the classic tales give children images and insights that will stay with them all their lives. To each of these stories she has brought her own special vision, her integrity, and a vitality that speaks powerfully and directly to children.

A very important influence in her life and in her books has been the stimulus of travel—that mind- and eye-stretching jolt out of the usual. Marcia has traveled widely in Europe, Great Britain, Russia, East Africa, the Middle East, and the Far East, including China. If she has a "home away from home," it is Italy, the country with which she has felt most profoundly in tune. She lived in Italy, off and on, for four years, spending much of her time painting. *Felice* . . . and *Tamarindo!* . . . are books that grew out of her love for that country and her friendships with Italians. . . . On a speaking trip to Hawaii she was so overwhelmed by the incredible beauty of the islands that she returned to spend many months and to do the research that was the basis for one of her most powerful books, *Backbone of the King*. . . . (pp. 424-25)

Marcia Brown's books have unquestionably stood the test of time. Nearly all of them are still in print—a certain proof of their enduring hold on generations of children. Never has Marcia been interested in passing fashions in children's book illustration. She has worked in many media but not for the sake of variety; rather, she has always let the story and her feeling for it determine the medium and the style. . . . Now, after so many years of creating memorable children's books, Marcia stands in a unique position—one abundantly deserved. (p. 426)

> *Janet A. Loranger, "Marcia Brown," in* The Horn Book Magazine, *Vol. LIX, No. 4, August, 1983, pp. 423-26.*

ZENA SUTHERLAND, MAY HILL ARBUTHNOT AND DIANNE L. MONSON

No generalizations about the work of Marcia Brown are possible, for she varies her style to suit the content of the story she is illustrating. Her illustrations for *Stone Soup* . . . are colorful and earthy, like the rogues who taught the villagers a more generous way of life. *Puss in Boots* . . . is a gorgeous, flamboyant feline, well adapted to the court life into which he catapults his master. Both *The Steadfast Tin Soldier* . . . and *Cinderella* . . . are in misty pinks and blues grayed down to the gentle mood of the tales. The sturdy woodcuts in brown and black for *Dick Whittington and His Cat* . . . are as sub-

stantial as the hero, and in the alphabet book *All Butterflies* . . . the woodcuts are in muted colors. . . . [*Once a Mouse*] is completely different from her earlier work. This fable of pride laid low is in jungle colors, and the stylized woodcut pictures have subtle details of expression or posture that tell the story and repay study. Her third Caldecott Medal was awarded for *Shadow* . . . , an African poem by Blaise Cendrars, a picture book with stunning collage silhouettes. Marcia Brown has written and illustrated some charming stories of her own, and has produced several concept books . . . with stunning photographs, but her major contributions to date are her brilliant interpretations of single folk tales.

> *Zena Sutherland, May Hill Arbuthnot, and Dianne L. Monson, "The Twentieth Century: Marcia Brown," in their* Children and Books, *seventh edition, Scott, Foresman and Company, 1986, p. 149.*

THE LITTLE CAROUSEL   (1946)

This is a book by a new artist, and its title page is a true index to its gaiety and charm. Just above the title there is a tiny red carousel drawn by a dashing white horse. Behind it are the green trees of Washington Square on a spring day, the grey line of the Arch, and, on the horizon, the tall towers of lower Manhattan. For this is a story of a street in Greenwich Village—Sullivan Street. It is pictured on the first page. Anthony lives on Sullivan Street. It is spring and he is mending his kite. But the Street tempts him. He is just a bit bored—until the little carousel arrives. Not tiny now, it is spread across a double page, complete in every detail with Mr. Corelli in the driver's seat wearing a green and black checked shirt. "Five cents for a short ride. Ten cents for a long one!" Anthony rushes out to stand and watch it. The children come running from every direction. They mount the horse, the lion, the elephant, or sit luxuriously on the red-cushioned seat. By and by Mr. Corelli got very tired of turning the crank that made the animals go round and round. "Hey, boy—you there! Would you like to turn the crank and give me a rest?" So Anthony turned the crank. When it was over he solemnly shook hands with Mr. Corelli. "It's the best day I ever had in my whole life," he said.

These delightful pictures are printed in four colors. The red jacket with the little carousel standing out against it makes this a gay book for Christmas and birthday celebrations. We expect to see it in bookstores and in public libraries. We hope to see many copies of it in the hands of the children. (pp. 42-3)

> *Mary Gould Davis, in a review of "The Little Carousel," in* The Saturday Review of Literature, *Vol. XXIX, No. 45, November 9, 1946, pp. 42-3.*

Anyone who has watched the children at play in one of the streets off Washington Square can tell that the artist-author of this book, Marcia Brown, has looked out of her window and caught the very life of the street on a spring afternoon. Even the grownups who appear in the book . . . look just right. The crisp drawings and clear bright colors make a festive picture book for Christmas.

> *Anne Carroll Moore, in a review of "The Little Carousel," in* The Horn Book Magazine, *Vol. XXII, No. 6, November-December, 1946, p. 456.*

Marcia Brown has drawn, in words and gaily colored pictures, the part of New York in which she lives, . . . with a real feeling for the noise and color of the neighborhood. The 5-to-7 year olds will ask for more.

Ruth A. Gordon, in a review of "The Little Carousel," in The New York Times Book Review, *December 15, 1946, p. 27.*

Delightful, childlike picture book. The atmosphere of a city street in summer, the activities of the children from washing doll clothes on the fire escape to flying kites on the roof, and the electrifying effect of the music of the carousel are pictured in bright red and green and a kindly text.

Isabel McLaughlin, in a review of "The Little Carousel," in Library Journal, *Vol. 72, No. 1, January 1, 1947, p. 82.*

STONE SOUP: AN OLD TALE   (1947)

Timeless, like all good folktales, this one has also a timely quality in this hungry post-war world of ours. Children of the picture-book age will like it primarily, though, for the good-humored cunning with which three famished soldiers, on their way home from the wars, coaxed a fine meal out of a reluctant French village. The peasants, seeing them coming, hid all their food, for, they said, "We have little enough for ourselves." The soldiers said, very well, they would make stone soup. It would be delicious, but even better if only they had a carrot, a cabbage, perhaps a bit of beef—and so on, until, curiosity and enthusiasm overcoming frugality, the villagers had provided all the makings of a feast.

Marcia Brown brings out the humor inherent in this old tale with the touch of a skillful storyteller and gives to her bright red double-page pictures a real feeling of a fete.

Ellen Lewis Buell, in a review of "Stone Soup: An Old Tale," in The New York Times Book Review, *November 9, 1947, p. 61.*

Marcia Brown, whose picture book of Greenwich Village, *The Little Carousel,* was so successful last year, has set this folktale in a French village quite a long time ago. The three soldiers who make the miraculous soup wear Napoleonic hats and bright red coats. The streets and houses and courtyards are like those in Brittany and the faces of the people fit perfectly into their background. . . .

This clever picture book with its feeling for the French peasants and their background is printed in brown, black, and a clear red. It has freshness and charm. It is sure to be a favorite with the children and with storytellers.

A review of "Stone Soup: An Old Tale," in The Saturday Review of Literature, *Vol. XXX, No. 46, November 15, 1947, p. 37.*

Bright animated pictures accompany this well-told version of an old story about three hungry and ingenious soldiers just back from the wars. . . . Marcia Brown relates the tale with the storyteller's combination of humor and conviction and her illustrations are in full accord.

Alice M. Jordan, in a review of "Stone Soup," in The Horn Book Magazine, *Vol. XXIV, No. 1, January-February, 1948, p. 32.*

The brown and orange illustrations accompanying this humorous tale of human nature reflect the activity that surrounds the making of the soup. Areas of color and wash, given shape with quick, expressive lines, move the eye across the page and back and forth, creating an air of excitement as the soup is prepared. What could easily become a demeaning portrait of peasant provincialism is skillfully handled by the artist, and the sincerity and gullibility of the peasants result in an advantageous situation for them all.

As in many tales of the oral tradition, the audience is left in the position of recognizing the scam, while the characters in the story remain ingenuously oblivious to the end. Because of this technique, the gullibility of the peasants remains more acceptable to the audience—no harm done. Brown retells this French tale of humor in the tradition of oral literature and allows her audience to share in the fun. (pp. 272-73)

Linda Kauffman Peterson, "The Caldecott Medal and Honor Books, 1938-1981: 'Stone Soup: An Old Tale'," in Newbery and Caldecott Medal and Honor Books *by Linda Kauffman Peterson and Marilyn Leathers Solt, G. K. Hall & Co., 1982, pp. 272-73.*

HENRY-FISHERMAN: A STORY OF THE VIRGIN ISLANDS (1949)

The faraway and the familiar are blended with unusual success in the story of Henry, the brown American boy of St. Thomas in the Virgin Islands. As soon as one opens the book, attractive, stylistic pictures in turquoise, yellow, coral, brown and dark green arouse pleasant anticipation of the story.

Henry is not so very different from boys in the United States. He milks the goat who feeds on guinea grass. He walks to market to buy pineapples and bananas as well as pawpaws and mangoes. He loves to fish. It's a happy day for Henry, who is used to fishing in shallow water with a round net, when he is taken out to fish from his father's boat. The exciting way in which Henry escapes from a big shark helps to finish the story on a note of pride, humor, and satisfaction. Children from 5 to 8 years old and adults who read with them will thoroughly enjoy *Henry—Fisherman.*

Elena Baker, "Caribbean Days," in The New York Times Book Review, *August 7, 1949, p. 22.*

As far as this reviewer knows this is the first picture book about the Virgin Islands that American boys and girls have had. It is printed in full color, and it obviously is the result of close observation and a lively enjoyment of the actual scene. That it is by Marcia Brown, who gave us *The Little Carousel* and *Stone Soup,* insures it a warm welcome. . . . One of the most effective pictures is of Henry deep under the water, unfastening the hook that holds the fish-net with the shadow of a shark hovering over him. One of the gayest is of the harbor with the *Ariadne,* Henry's boat, coming into port. . . . The effect of the drawings and the story of young Henry on this reviewer was to create an almost irresistible longing to take the next boat or plane to the Virgin Islands.

A review of "Henry—Fisherman: A Story of the Virgin Islands," in The Saturday Review of Literature, *Vol. XXXII, No. 38, September 17, 1949, p. 32.*

The artist has captured the sunlit tropical feeling of the Caribbean, and her natural tale of Henry's adventures makes this a distinguished picture-story book for five- and six-year olds.

Frances C. Darling, in a review of "Henry—Fisherman," in The Christian Science Monitor, November 15, 1949, p. 13.

The story of [Henry's] first fishing trip is very slight and probably will not bear many re-readings. The book's chief value lies in the illustrations. These are done with the color and action that children love. The art work in a picture book such as this has a definite contribution to make to the development of a child's aesthetic appreciation that is great enough to offset the slightness of the story.

A review of "Henry—Fisherman: A Story of the Virgin Islands," in Bulletin of the Children's Book Center, Vol. III, No. 1, December, 1949, p. 2.

Native dialect, interspersed throughout the text, lends authenticity to the pages of the story, as do the illustrations, which reflect the primitive and native setting of the tale. Coral, turquoise, brown, dark blue, and yellow create clean, stylized shapes, often abstract in appearance.

On alternating pages, dark blue, white, and red illustrations provide a contrast to the color pages. Shapes appear in solid forms, with little detail needed to explain or interpret the figures. Simplicity of life on the island is recreated in a visual experience that presents a culture and lifestyle in which the sea is the dominant force. Though the text is weak in its climax, man's interaction with nature and this ever-tenuous relationship remains the dominant theme in word and illustration alike.

From Cinderella; or, The Little Glass Slipper, *a free translation from the French of Charles Perrault, with pictures by Marcia Brown. Charles Scribner's Sons, 1954. Copyright 1954 Marcia Brown. Copyright renewed © 1982 Marcia Brown. Reprinted with the permission of Charles Scribner's Sons.*

Linda Kauffman Peterson, "The Caldecott Medal and Honor Books, 1938-1981: 'Henry Fisherman'," in Newbery and Caldecott Medal and Honor Books by Linda Kauffman Peterson and Marilyn Leathers Solt, G. K. Hall & Co., 1982, p. 284.

DICK WHITTINGTON AND HIS CAT   (1950)

[Marcia Brown] here sets the beloved legend of Dick Whittington in a handsome framework. An experienced story-teller, she writes a simple, flavorsome prose, sparked with plenty of conversation to give young children a feeling of reality, of actually knowing the people. Her illustrations—linoleum cuts printed in bold black and yellow ochre—recreate the medieval scene with a vigor and humor reminiscent of early wood-cuts. The result is highly appealing to the eye and to the imagination.

Ellen Lewis Buell, "London Legend," in The New York Times Book Review, August 13, 1950, p. 20.

Handsome linoleum cuts—stylized with a witty flair—enliven the beloved old story of the cat and the bells that called Dick Whittington back to London. Each page is an artistic treat—with half-page tan and black illustrations complementing the text on each page—the robust wise-eyed characters seem to spoof the flat Medieval symmetry, and the line is heavy—to offset the sophisticated conception. Although we prefer a more rhythmic retelling of the old story, the prose is easy and readable.

A review of "Dick Whittington and His Cat," in Virginia Kirkus' Bookshop Service, Vol. XVIII, No. 16, August 15, 1950, p. 464.

Every book by this versatile young artist seems entirely different from the one before it; and each is outstanding in its own way. The linoleum cuts in dull gold and black are exactly right for a sturdy story like **Dick Whittington**, long a favorite with boys and girls. Miss Brown has been a children's librarian and her retelling is good for storyhour.

A review of "Dick Whittington and His Cat," in The Horn Book Magazine, Vol. XXVI, No. 5, September-October, 1950, p. 369.

Marcia Brown's presentation of this famous old tale has the originality and distinction that we have learned to expect from this young artist. . . . One of the most appealing of the pictures is of Dick sleeping while the cat stands guard over him. No one could resist such a faithful and charming pussy! The text is worded from the very oldest versions, as clear and objective as a folktale should be. With its striking dust jacket this book will instantly attract boys and girls of varying ages. (pp. 52-3)

A review of "Dick Whittington and His Cat," in The Saturday Review of Literature, Vol. XXXIII, No. 42, October 21, 1950, pp. 52-3.

Woodcut illustrations and a fairly satisfactory version of the story of Dick Whittington in a picture book that will have more appeal for adults than for children. The monotonous color and heavy, almost forbidding type will be discouraging to beginning readers.

A review of "Dick Whittington and His Cat," in Bulletin of the Children's Book Center, Vol. IV, No. 1, December, 1950, p. 2.

Marcia Brown's linoleum cuts, in black, white, and ochre, produce illustrations of prominently contrasting light and dark patterns. The outlines and textures create movement and vitality in the illustrations, even though there is not much detail present. The stylized and decorative designs capture the setting and mood of the tale, as the patterns of the courtly palace floors and the fabrics of the garments of the wealthy repeat the motifs throughout.

The artist's medium is well suited to the setting of the tale, lends a medieval flair to the proceedings, and demonstrates the importance of choosing a visual means of expressing a text that is compatible and conveys the desired message. (pp. 285-86)

> *Linda Kauffman Peterson, "The Caldecott Medal and Honor Books, 1938-1981: 'Dick Whittington and His Cat'," in* Newbery and Caldecott Medal and Honor Books *by Linda Kauffman Peterson and Marilyn Leathers Solt, G. K. Hall & Co., 1982, pp. 285-86.*

SKIPPER JOHN'S COOK (1951)

[A] delightful sea and salt air picture book about a cocky Provincetown boy who shipped out as a cook for the crew of a bean-weary fishing boat. The crew of the *Liberty Belle* were very tired of eating beans, so when Skipper John advertised for a cook, young Si saw his chance to go to sea. Si's blithe commandeering of the kitchen and the author's rollicking flavorsome illustrations are great fun. In all—a witty, atmospheric story, handsomely decorated in three colors.

> *A review of "Skipper John's Cook," in* Virginia Kirkus' Bookshop Service, *Vol. XIX, No. 19, October 1, 1951, p. 579.*

Marcia Brown's drawings of Si and George, of Skipper John and the crew are so robust and so funny that small boys are going to love them. Her humor lies, too, behind every word of the story. The wharf at Provincetown, the boat in a rough sea, the galley where Si reigned as cook, the deck where the fish were cleaned and packed, the drawing of Si's mother making him a red flannel shirt—all these have such reality that you can smell the fish cooking and feel the motion of the boat. This book will strengthen the rapidly growing reputation of the young author and artist. (p. 54)

> *Mary Gould Davis, in a review of "Skipper John's Cook," in* The Saturday Review of Literature, *Vol. XXXIV, No. 45, November 10, 1951, pp. 51, 54.*

What did Si cook? The answer will make children laugh at about six to eight. They will be pleased with the amusing realism that ends the short tale when Si and the dog George lose their job.

The book is well worth the price for the pictures. . . . [They] show still another style of this talented artist. The variety of design is clever; the realism of the fishermen is well done; Si and his dog are appealing. Strength of line and boldness of spacing across double pages are distinguished. The pictures carry much more than the words, which young readers appreciate, and which lure them back to good art work over again. There even is a whole extra incident on the elegant endpapers. It is one of the best of the fall picture books.

> *A review of "Skipper John's Cook," in* New York Herald Tribune Book Review, *November 11, 1951, p. 12.*

Woven into the tale is a fistful of fishing lore that ought to please all youngsters who have any affection for the open sea.

Marcia Brown has added another delightful book to her list of successes. The colors here are not as varied or as brilliant as in **Henry Fisherman,** but the story is just as original and realistic as her earlier endeavors.

> *Elena Baker, "No Beans Today," in* The New York Times Book Review, *Part II, November 11, 1951, p. 42.*

Marcia Brown is one of the few artists who never repeats herself. One's first reaction to each new picture book of hers is a delighted, "Oh, here's another entirely fresh one!" The intriguing bit of historical information that a young boy of eight once shipped from Provincetown, Massachusetts, as a sea cook set Miss Brown's imagination working with the result that she has created in amusing story and pictures a very much alive young Si who sailed as cook on the *Liberty Belle.*

> *Jennie D. Lindquist and Siri M. Andrews, in a review of "Skipper John's Cook," in* The Horn Book Magazine, *Vol. XXVII, No. 6, December, 1951, p. 402.*

Marcia Brown's red, blue, ochre, black and white illustrations for this 1952 Honor Book seem a bit under par for her talents. The vitality so often present in her work is absent, and the colors do not work effectively enough to pull the book together. The compositions are filled with a variety of textures and techniques that fail to mesh together in any sort of harmony. Unfortunately, the book appears hastily done and does not represent the quality of which Brown is capable. (p. 291)

> *Linda Kauffman Peterson, "The Caldecott Medal and Honor Books, 1938-1981: 'Skipper John's Cook'," in* Newbery and Caldecott Medal and Honor Books *by Linda Kauffman Peterson and Marilyn Leathers Solt, G. K. Hall & Co., 1982, pp. 290-91.*

PUSS IN BOOTS (1952)

A versatile artist, Marcia Brown adapts her illustrative style to her material, ranging freely from crisp, modern patterns as in **Henry—Fisherman** to the manner of early wood engravers as in **Dick Whittington and His Cat.** Now she has given the durable story of **Puss in Boots** a new dress in still another style—seventeenth century in setting but contemporary in technique. The colors, chiefly coral pink, yellow and gray, are brilliantly handled, lush without being in the least vulgar. The effect is one of gaiety and wit. Puss is wily and dashing, according to mood, and the king is as impressive, if not as corpulent, as Louis XIV. The prose, freely translated from Perrault, is flexible, easy-flowing, as lighthearted as the pictures.

> *Ellen Lewis Buell, "Old and New," in* The New York Times Book Review, *October 19, 1952, p. 48.*

Puss in Boots, dressed in the court costume that the King gave him, stands on the cover jacket of this enchanting version of his story. The only word for him is "magnificent." Never has any of his many illustrators made him so alluring. How charming the Princess and the miller's son are as they go hand in hand through the great archway of the ogre's palace! Marcia Brown has dressed them all in the costume of their day, and the color is lovely—rich and soft, without the crudeness of color that one sees in some of the picture books this year. The wording of the story follows rather closely that in Walter De La Mare's *Animal Stories*. It is graceful, clear, and touched with humor. But it is the drawings and their reproduction that make this a memorable picture book. Children who get their first impression of the famous French fairy tale from this artist's work are lucky little people.

> *Mary Gould Davis, in a review of "Puss in Boots,"*
> *in* The Saturday Review, New York, *Vol. XXXV, No.*
> *46, November 15, 1952, p. 47.*

In a year of frequent return to fairy tales, it is fine to have Perrault given a place of honor in a beautiful, gay, very French picture book. Miss Brown has made her own free translation, which is humorous and spirited. She has created such a Master Slyboots as never before has helped to turn a youngest son into a marquis. In his red boots, flying feathers, knowing black eyes, huge switching tail and great black buccaneer's hat, he makes a delightful hero.

The backgrounds hint gaily at old palaces and gold coaches, Louis XIV elegance, the poplars and noble Roman arches of old France. It is done in a floating, free style, quite different from any style yet used by this artist, and as distinguished as all her work. Among the many rich colors wanders her clever pen line, tying the designs into the black of the type.

> *A review of "Puss in Boots," in* New York Herald
> Tribune Book Review, *November 16, 1952, p. 4.*

[*Puss in Boots* is] the gayest and loveliest of picture books. . . .

Not only has Marcia Brown revealed fresh creative power in the freedom of her drawing and the use of color in *Puss in Boots,* . . . the artist's intentions have been completely understood and carried out with such distinction on title page and type page as to render it in my judgment the most distinguished book of the year.

Marcia Brown has had sympathetic treatment and appreciation from her editor from the time of *The Little Carousel.* Alice Dalgliesh has well understood her simplicity of approach to a subject, her direct appeal to children and her capabilities for growth in her art and has given her entire freedom for development on her own terms. Marcia Brown has never repeated herself. Each of her books has integrity, a direct appeal to children born of her own familiar relation to children, and *Puss in Boots* is I think her masterpiece. I like everything about it from her fine, free and unpretentious translation from Perrault to the colorful pages I delight to dwell upon as I turn them again and again. Since I live in a one-room apartment, my choice of books to live with is limited to those of which I never tire. *Puss in Boots* is one of them. (p. 393)

> *Anne Carroll Moore, "The Three Owl's Notebook,"*
> *in* The Horn Book Magazine, *Vol. XXVIII, No. 6,*
> *December, 1952, pp. 393-95.*

Marcia Brown's illustrations for this traditional French tale are lively and full of movement and color. Red, yellow, blue-gray, and green shapes are given definition by her quick, expressive lines that travel across page after page. The compositions are more controlled and cohesive than those of the earlier *Skipper John's Cook* . . . ; the confusion has lessened considerably, though the activity still remains.

Brown's looseness of style is perhaps a reaction to or deviation from the rigid and more controlled medium of linoleum cut, the technique of her 1951 Honor Book, *Dick Whittington and*

His Cat. . . . Whatever her style, Marcia Brown's name remains synonymous with the quality inherent in her interpretations of the folk tales of traditional literature.

> *Linda Kauffman Peterson, "The Caldecott Medal*
> *and Honor Books, 1938-1981: 'Puss in Boots',"* *in*
> Newbery and Caldecott Medal and Honor Books *by*
> *Linda Kauffman Peterson and Marilyn Leathers Solt,*
> *G. K. Hall & Co., 1982, p. 294.*

THE STEADFAST TIN SOLDIER   (1953)

[The Steadfast Tin Soldier *was written by Hans Christian Andersen.*]

A favorite among the tales of Andersen, this story, now in distinguished picture-book format and lightened by Marcia Brown's imaginative illustrations in four colors, has entirely fresh interest. Her drawings, so enticingly spread through the text, bring to life a stalwart soldier and a fragile dancer in white poised on tiptoe against pastel backgrounds of lavender and rose, together with a black troll and real people presented with greater boldness and humor.

> *Virginia Haviland, in a review of "The Steadfast Tin*
> *Soldier," in* The Horn Book Magazine, *Vol. XXIX,*
> *No. 5, October, 1953, p. 347.*

It is probable that a great majority of children come first to Hans Christian Andersen through this story. It is peculiarly fortunate that Marcia Brown should have selected it for her original and imaginative illustrations. She uses the modern translation by M. R. James, and the crisp wording just suits the illustrations. On the title page the Tin Soldier stands straight and stiff on his one leg, and all through the story we are conscious that he never loses his dignity. Miss Brown makes an exquisite figure of the little dancer. The tiny face framed in the dark hair, the lovely outstretched arms, the slim grace of the whole figure are irresistible. No wonder the tin soldier loved her. The last scene, when the current of air from the window carries her straight into his arms while the fire rages about them both, is one of Marcia Brown's finest drawings. This is a book to be treasured, to have and to keep, and to pass on to another generation.

> *Mary Gould Davis, in a review of "The Steadfast*
> *Tin Soldier," in* The Saturday Review, New York,
> *Vol. XXXVI, No. 46, November 14, 1953, p. 60.*

[This is] a beautifully illustrated oversize book for children and for adults. . . . The pictures are dreamy, mysterious, and softly colored in enchanting reds and blues. A lovely presentation of an old heart warming story. Grownups are apt to enjoy this tale more than the children. They can save it for "special readings" and treasure it as an addition to their collection of rare and lovely books.

> *E. D., "The Legend Retold," in* Chicago Sunday
> Tribune Magazine of Books, *November 15, 1953,*
> *p. 22.*

Following her widely admired *Puss in Boots,* Miss Brown dramatizes another long-loved tale in sweeping scenes whose rhythm and color are original and striking. The very French modern style of the previous book here is carried further, with the color spaces of water and sky, the forms of people and toys, all floating on the pages with an eerie, dreamy motion.

The story itself is no more for very small children than is the art work. It makes an unusual gift for a child over ten, or for any older-age person who loves Andersen. . . . What a tribute to Andersen, that this odd, sentimental little story of faithful lovers stays in the mind, and probably becomes a bigger story as one grows older. Miss Brown has tried to give it this timeless, poetic quality. We admire the fine book production, but, the more we look, the less we are sure that this tale needs any pictures at all. As we recall our very young feelings about it, we saw clearly the soldier and the dancer; we knew they were tiny toys, but we enlarged them in our minds to a hero and a heroine of proper size.

> *Louise S. Bechtel, in a review of "The Steadfast Tin Soldier," in* New York Herald Tribune Book Review, *November 15, 1953, p. 14.*

CINDERELLA; OR, THE LITTLE GLASS SLIPPER (1954)

[This] *Cinderella* is a perfect picture book. The text is relaxed and easy, with the simple theme of goodness rewarded running through it like a shining thread. Yet it never becomes cloying or saccharine, for phrases such as "chitter chatter," "puff their ruffles," "the young miss," and "paid them a thousand courtesies" give it a pertness, a kind of sauciness, that refreshes and at the same time reflects its French origin.

Miss Brown has managed in her illustrations also not only to recreate the court of Louis XIV with its velvets and laces, beauty patches and horn-curled coiffures but to give an imaginative interpretation to a fairytale that in its essence knows no barriers of nation or time. Text and pictures are in complete harmony and each well-known moment of magic is satisfyingly illustrated, mostly in French blue and soft rose.

A good picture book of *Cinderella* has long been needed since the Helen Sewell interpretation was allowed to go out of print. That this need should be met so perfectly is a cause of rejoicing by the children and by those who provide them with books at schools, in the public libraries, and at home.

> *Eulalie Steinmetz Ross, in a review of "Cinderella; or, The Little Glass Slipper," in* The Saturday Review, New York, *Vol. XXXVII, No. 46, November 13, 1954, p. 66.*

We do not tire of the work of any artist who has something fresh to say, even though the story may be an old one, as old as *Cinderella* . . . , to which Marcia Brown has given a quality of interpretation in pictures which derive from her own childhood feeling for a story she tells in free translation from the text of Charles Perrault as she would tell it to children. Sensitivity to color and movement give the book a lightness and grace too often lacking in more elaborate and sophisticated illustrations for a favorite story.

> *Anne Carroll Moore, in a review of "Cinderella; or, The Little Glass Slipper," in* The Horn Book Magazine, *Vol. XXX, No. 6, December, 1954, p. 412.*

Once again Miss Brown has used her gifts as a storyteller and an artist to make a beautiful book from a well-loved tale—an excellent choice for a Christmas present for little girls, many of whom count "Cinderella" as their favorite story. These pictures are more delicate in line and coloring—and properly so—than her earlier ones for the adventures of the swashbuckling Puss-in-Boots, but both books have the French feeling that belongs with Perrault.

> *Jennie D. Lindquist, in a review of "Cinderella; or, The Little Glass Slipper," in* The Horn Book Magazine, *Vol. XXX, No. 6, December, 1954, p. 428.*

[Marcia Brown] has provided a setting for *Cinderella* which evokes the splendor of the Sun King's reign minus its fussiness. The pastel tones, the delicate lines are appropriately feminine. Cinderella herself is fragile and wistful and the stepsisters are just homely enough—in a comical way—to be convincing without repelling. The text sticks faithfully to the spirit of the original but Miss Brown turns a phrase here and a paragraph there in a way which bridges the centuries for modern listeners.

> *Ellen Lewis Buell, "In New Dress," in* The New York Times Book Review, *December 19, 1954, p. 11.*

The light, airy drawings of Marcia Brown seem very appropriate to the mood and atmosphere of magic in this fairy tale. Rose, blue, lavender, and gold shapes are defined with quick active lines of black that give the open and loose illustrations some bounds. Brown's style is very synthesized, and though the lines seem spontaneous, they are much more controlled than those in the illustrations for *Skipper John's Cook* . . . and *Puss in Boots*. . . . With fewer lines and extraneous patterns and with a less competitive color scheme, Brown has captured the essence of this fairy story, whose words never become tiresome, reading after reading.

> *Linda Kauffman Peterson, "The Caldecott Medal and Honor Books, 1938-1981: 'Cinderella; or The Little Glass Slipper',," in* Newbery and Caldecott Medal and Honor Books *by Linda Kauffman Peterson and Marilyn Leathers Solt, G. K. Hall & Co., 1982, p. 302.*

[The] soft, delicate curving lines found in Marcia Brown's illustrations in Perrault's *Cinderella* create a mood suggestive of a mythical kingdom that could only exist "once upon a time." These lines are not bold and dark, but only suggest form. The delicate drawings of Cinderella transformed into a beautiful princess by her fairy godmother contain a magical quality. Because they do not show a definite path or form, anything can happen, and no one is disappointed when the pumpkin turns into a coach and the rat into a coachman. Even the architecture has this magical quality. Delicately curved windows, softly flowing draperies, and lightly traced pillars provide the background for a favorite fairy tale. . . .

The fine lines used by Marcia Brown in *Cinderella* are complemented by her choice of colors. Soft pastels—pinks, yellows, blues, and greens—bring a light, shimmering radiance to the fairy tale quality of the pictures. If she had chosen bright, harsh colors, the mood could have been destroyed.

> *Donna E. Norton, "Artists and Their Illustrations: 'Cinderella'," in her* Through the Eyes of a Child: An Introduction to Children's Literature, *Charles E. Merrill Publishing Company, 1983, p. 107.*

THE FLYING CARPET (1956)

One of the 1001 tales from the Arabian Nights—the story of the Princes Husayn, Ali and Ahmad and their quest for the hand of Princess Nur-al Nihar—is retold with a direct simplicity from the Burton translation and illustrated in swirling, glowing eastern line and color by Miss Brown. In her pictures, which show a study of the art of the period and a retention of her own style, she has used the full panoply of colors judiciously. The results might have been heavy; instead they are vivid and should give children a sense of delight as they go to read the rest of the tales.

> *A review of "The Flying Carpet," in* Virginia Kirkus' Service, *Vol. XXIV, No. 22, November 15, 1956, p. 839.*

[*The Flying Carpet*] is a brilliant and colorful picture book with a lavish and oriental splendor. In variety and beauty of composition from page to page, in the sense of movement Miss Brown has gone beyond anything she has created before, even her *Cinderella. The Flying Carpet* is a distinguished addition to Miss Brown's mounting store of good picture books. It is a beautiful volume for any age and especially for the imaginative child who is beginning to read fairy tales.

> *Maria Cimino, in a review of "The Flying Carpet," in* The Saturday Review, *New York, Vol. XXXIX, No. 46, November 17, 1956, p. 48.*

Marcia Brown brings the children and all of us who love beautiful and imaginative illustrations wondrous gifts similar to those the Princes in the story brought their beloved Princess Nur-al Nihar, a magic carpet to fly to India and the marts of the East, a glass to make us see the beauty if it is "our heart's desire" and an apple to quicken us when our perceptions are deadened and dull. This artist is never content to keep to a fixed style and embellish it with minor variations in book after book. Each of her picture-stories differs widely from the rest, the style springing from the subject. . . .

Now in telling this lesser and seldom-told tale from the Arabian Nights she clothes it with the jewel colors of the Moslem world. She has drawn inspiration from ancient, illuminated manuscripts, tapestries, cloisonné, and carpets, yet the results give an effect of enamelled brilliance as original as it is modern. The King is a Sultan of India but in searching for "gifts seldom seen and singular" to win the hand of the Princess, his sons travel to Bishangarh, Persia and Samarcand. The sweetness of the expression on the faces, their verve, and joy in one another, the bewilderingly beautiful riches of the oriental bazaars are all spread out as a rich feast for young eyes. Another beautiful distinguished book from a fine artist.

> *Margaret Sherwood Libby, "Jolly Stories: Gay Pictures," in* New York Herald Tribune Book Review, *November 18, 1956, p. 4.*

The *Arabian Nights* magic carpet story, familiar but not widely available in collections, in a handsome picture-story format ablaze with oriental-rug colors and Eastern motifs. Based on Richard Burton's translation of the much longer story, *Prince Ahmed and Fairy Paribanou*, this presents the Sultan, his three sons and niece, the flying carpet, and the archery contest that determined which prince should marry the princess. It omits the long sequence that follows the finding of the far-flown arrow. The storytelling is rich in words to create images in the listener's mind and the decorative drawings are dramatically alive to hold the eyes of a picture-story group. A distinguished achievement. (pp. 441-42)

> *Virginia Haviland, in a review of "The Flying Carpet," in* The Horn Book Magazine, *Vol. XXXII, No. 6, December, 1956, pp. 441-42.*

A lesser-known tale from the *Arabian nights* . . . retold with directness and charm and illustrated in glowing colors in an

Arabian Nights spirit. Again the author-artist has demonstrated her outstanding storytelling ability and her unusual artistic versatility; unfortunately for children the combination of solid blocks of text printed entirely in capital letters, the vibrant colors, and mottled effect of the pictures make for difficulty in reading.

> *Helen E. Kinsey, in a review of "The Flying Carpet," in* The Booklist and Subscription Books Bulletin, *Vol. 53, No. 8, December 15, 1956, p. 204.*

THE THREE BILLY GOATS GRUFF   (1957)

[The Three Billy Goats Gruff *was written by Peter Christen Asbjörnsen and Jörgen Engebretsen Moe.*]

An old Norwegian nursery tale has been given a new dress in this brilliant and vigorous picture book. (Marcia Brown has used George Dasent's classic translation of the tale.) Here are the three billy goats tripping over the troll's bridge and using all their cunning to do him in. Double-spread pages of vivid drawings in color catch every bit of the humor and excitement in the story, from the quiet beginning to the boisterous end, when the stupid and ugly old troll gets his just desserts. . . . There is little need of reading skill to enjoy this picture book. The story unfolds from the lively end-papers onward, and every picture tells its share of the story as effectively as the delightful words.

From The Flying Carpet, *written and illustrated by Marcia Brown. Charles Scribner's Sons, 1956. Copyright © 1956 Marcia Brown. Copyright renewed © 1984 Marcia Brown. Reprinted with the permission of Charles Scribner's Sons.*

Maria Cimino, in a review of "The Three Billy Goats Gruff," in The Saturday Review, *New York, Vol. XL, No. 19, May 11, 1957, p. 51.*

From the enameled and mosaic brilliance of Persian pictures for **The Flying Carpet** Marcia Brown turns, in her latest picture book, to the sparse greens and prickly silhouettes of the spruce forests of the north. . . . One glance at the Gruff family on the title page and one knows that her pictures are going to be exactly right. They are a sly and knowing trio, quite convincingly able to take care of themselves, trolls or no trolls. The biggest one is a triumph of goat portraiture, magnificently horned, bearded and bony, eyes alert for danger as he chews young green leaves. He'll need all his assurance when he meets the troll—a menacing monster, his head almost filling the page. Every little child will love this book and savor the fierce fight at the bridge with pieces of troll flying all about.

M. S. Libby, in a review of "The Three Billy Goats Gruff," in New York Herald Tribune Book Review, *May 12, 1957, p. 24.*

A totally satisfying book, with vigorous story and wonderful pictures. The troll is properly terrifying, with a nose like a loaf of French bread, great jagged teeth, and enormous bulging eyes. His brownish-bluish skin allows him to blend with the rocks under the bridge and be very dangerous to goats. The goats are just right, from the innocent blue-eyed tiniest Billy to the indomitable Big Billy. . . .

Heloise P. Mailloux, in a review of "The Three Billy Goats Gruff," in The Horn Book Magazine, *Vol. XXXIII, No. 3, June, 1957, p. 211.*

FELICE   (1958)

Venice is the city of canals and gondolas and, according to Marcia Brown, cats. In her beautiful new picture book Miss Brown has given us a simple story about a little striped cat and a small Italian boy. The story and its characters are charming, but the greatest appeal of the book, and its real "hero," is Venice. The color and light of Venice are on every luminous page. The people and buildings float radiantly in shining sky and water. Miss Brown's evident love of Venice and her absorption in its varied scene have had the happiest effect on her work for **Felice** is the best book this author has ever done.

Maria Cimino, in a review of "Felice," in Saturday Review, *Vol. XLI, No. 44, November 1, 1958, p. 42.*

Marcia Brown, a most gifted artist who is always experimenting, always seeking to catch in a fresh way in color and line the mood and setting of a story—medieval London in **Dick Whittington and his Cat**, seventeenth-century France in **Puss and Boots** and **Cinderella,** the northlands in **The Three Billy Goats Gruff**—has done a brilliant, exciting picture book of modern Venice. Here are the velvet skies, the glowing squares, the jostling bustle and jewel-like confusion of this unique city. Dramatic pictures blaze with color, vibrant bright purple blues or deep rose forming a background for golden buildings, shadowy alleys or black gondolas. The tale of a city where "the sky is full of pigeons, the canals full of gondolas and the streets full of cats" is an ever-appealing one for the very young, told with a charming Venetian twist. . . .

Children will love the pictured details, cats hiding in unlikely places, a snarling fight as wild as the struggle of Gruff and the Troll and a cat's eye view of a Venetian *festa.*

Margaret Sherwood Libby, in a review of "Felice," in New York Herald Tribune Book Review, *November 2, 1958, p. 2.*

[Marcia Brown] has conveyed some of the romanticism of [Venice's] canals and gondolas. Her story of the adoption of a stray cat by a gondolier's son, however, will probably not draw much sympathy nor will her somber water colors help.

George A. Woods, in a review of "Felice," in The New York Times Book Review, *Part II, November 2, 1958, p. 52.*

[The story] is warmly told and the richly colored pictures which portray the action of the story against beautifully depicted scenes of Venice are as fresh and distinctive as each of the author-artist's other picture books.

A review of "Felice," in The Booklist and Subscription Books Bulletin, *Vol. 55, No. 6, November 15, 1958, p. 160.*

It is not often that one savors every detail of a book so lingeringly as one does here. The whole is completely Venice, from the first words, "In Venice the sky is full of pigeons, the canals are full of gondolas, and the streets are full of cats." Well-chosen, lively words tell of one nameless, hungry cat and a little boy who needed to be together, while the artist's free lines and richly varied color-tones capture the pulsing shimmer and the depth of shadows that are sun and reflection, lanterns and dark night, water and old stone. A distinguished achievement from one whose work is continuously fresh, who has drawn this picture book from experiences of a recent stay in Venice.

Virginia Haviland, in a review of "Felice," in The Horn Book Magazine, *Vol. XXXIV, No. 6, December, 1958, p. 462.*

PETER PIPER'S ALPHABET: PETER PIPER'S PRACTICAL PRINCIPLES OF PLAIN AND PERFECT PRONUNCIATION (1959)

[Peter Piper's Alphabet, *a collection of popular tongue twisters, was first published in England in 1813.*]

The old tongue twisters that children delighted in almost one hundred and fifty years ago . . . have been given lively setting here. It is no small feat of both imagination and artistic skill to illustrate nonsense, but Marcia Brown has, as usual, proved equal to the challenge. Each rhyme has received individual treatment in brilliant colors and hilarious drawings. . . . [The] characters as Marcia Brown has pictured them should make trying to chant the verses more fun than ever before.

Ruth Hill Viguers, in a review of "Peter Piper's Alphabet," in The Horn Book Magazine, *Vol. XXXV, No. 5, October, 1959, p. 376.*

Marcia Brown has given [the] old rhymes a new setting, with pictures in which characters dressed in the decorous costumes of an earlier day indulge in the zaniest of actions. The result is rather like something that might have happened if Edward Lear had teamed up with Kate Greenaway, and it is very funny.

Ellen Lewis Buell, "A Peck of Pickled Peppers," in The New York Times Book Review, *December 20, 1959, p. 16.*

Each nonsense rhyme follows the Peter Piper pattern: "Andrew Airpump asked his Aunt her Ailment: Did Andrew Airpump ask his Aunt her Ailment? If Andrew Airpump asked his Aunt her Ailment, where was the Ailment of Andrew Airpump's Aunt?" Illustration shows Andrew happily rowing a boat, while a distraught woman clutches herself, very green of face. A delightful book, with gay and colorful pictures drawn with zany and zestful humor. Rare fare.

Zena Sutherland, in a review of "Peter Piper's Alphabet: Peter Piper's Practical Principles of Plain and Perfect Pronunciation," in Bulletin of the Center for Children's Books, *Vol. XIII, No. 5, January, 1960, p. 79.*

TAMARINDO! (1960)

A little Sicilian boy, Pepineddu, is the captain of a troop of soldiers. When his uncle's donkey disappears the boy and his friends take off in search of him. Their day is filled with adventure and misadventure, but a delightful swim leads the happy foursome to the donkey and to fame. The author's illustrations are remarkably expressive, both of the small boy eagerness and innocence of his characters and of the poor but gay country in which they live. A lyrical story which sustains suspense and excitement without sacrificing its characteristic delicacy.

A review of "Tamarindo!" in Virginia Kirkus' Service, *Vol. XXVIII, No. 18, September 15, 1960, p. 815.*

Marcia Brown, who never repeats herself, has been unfolding one treasure after another upon her return from a year and a half in Europe in 1957. This year it is *Tamarindo!* . . . . This joyous picture story book . . . is instinct with the life and color of Sicily. Based on a true story told to Miss Brown some years ago, it took root during her own stay in Sicily and has emerged full blown to delight boys and girls of any age. (pp. 485-86)

Anne Carroll Moore, in a review of "Tamarindo!" in The Horn Book Magazine, *Vol. XXXVI, No. 6, December, 1960, pp. 485-86.*

A pleasant book, with lively illustrations that enhance the story of four very natural little boys who are serious about their make-believe and who are treated with dignity by the adults. Librarians will wish to note that some of the illustrations show the boys swimming au naturel.

Zena Sutherland, in a review of "Tamarindo," in Bulletin of the Center for Children's Books, *Vol. XIV, No. 7, March, 1961, p. 106.*

[Marcia Brown] has written a sparkling and fresh account of a day in the lives of Pepineddu and the rest of his merry band of "soldiers" in *Tamarindo.* . . . As Pepineddu and his friends wander through Sicilian olive and lemon groves, the reader gets a brief glimpse of life in another country. The illustrations are as lively and bright as the rollicking text. This story teaches children that, though cultures may be different, people are essentially the same everywhere. (p. 373)

Constantine Georgiou, "Realism in Children's Literature," in his Children and Their Literature, *Prentice-Hall, Inc., 1969, pp. 359-412.*

ONCE A MOUSE . . . A FABLE CUT IN WOOD (1961)

AUTHOR'S COMMENTARY

[*The following excerpt, originally published in the August, 1962 issue of* The Horn Book Magazine, *is taken from Brown's Caldecott Award acceptance speech which she gave at the meeting of the American Library Association on June 19, 1962.*]

When I was working on **Once a Mouse . . .**, I suspected that it might be my best book to date. (pp. 35-6)

I had wanted a big subject, with few words, that would say something to a little child, and in which I could immerse myself fully. Since I had been making colored wood blocks, I wanted a theme to which colored woodcuts would add another dimension. All fall of 1960 I had been drawing at the Bronx Zoo, magnetized particularly by the tigers in the Lion House and the monkeys. Then a friend sent me a collection of animal fables, published in Italy. Here I found the ancient Indian fable of "The Hermit and the Mouse," and my big subject for little children. The very fiber of wood might say something about a hermit and animals in a jungle. (p. 36)

Painters today have unlimited freedom in the choice of techniques, and an almost fetishistic interest in sensuous materials. But no matter how fascinated an illustrator is by techniques, illustration must still be that—a servant charged with elucidating the idea of the book. It involves a very different mental process from painting and arises from a different level of sensibility. A little child's own art is emblematic, but often falls short of the ideal in his mind. Recognition of species only—man with two legs, dog with four—is not enough to stimulate his awakening sense of personality. The child will have to make his home in the astonishing world of the future that is beginning to erupt about us. How complete is the personality that he takes from us into that future? His books help to make it. (pp. 37-8)

Marcia Brown, "Big and Little," in her Lotus Seeds: Children, Pictures, and Books, *Charles Scribner's Sons, 1986, pp. 35-41.*

There is no doubt that this stands out as one of the most striking books of the year, and one of this versatile artist's best. The old fable from India tells of the evils of pride: through the magic of a hermit a mouse becomes a cat, a dog, a Royal tiger. When at last he turns on his benefactor, he suddenly becomes once more a mouse, retreating into the jungle. For children the pleasure is in the transformations; older children will understand the meaning of the fable.

For adults, some of the interesting features of this book are its color, its pictorial economy, and the method of reproduction, which preserves the effect of the grain of the wood on which the artist cut her woodblocks.

A wide age range is suggested, but at ten the book would still be an art experience.

Alice Dalgliesh, in a review of "Once a Mouse: An Old Fable Cut in Wood," in Saturday Review, *Vol. XLIV, No. 45, November 11, 1961, p. 38.*

Here is a veritable treasure! This "fable cut in wood" is all a picture book should be, a delight for little children to look at and listen to, a simple text that will "plant a seed" in their minds, and a work of art. As we picked it up for the first time we sighed with pleasure. The harmonious and beautiful coloring, the bold clear designs that express plainly the thoughts and actions of the characters and yet form stunning compositions, the type printed to match the deeper tone of green, the end papers and jacket—everything is solicitously worked out by artist, editor and printer to make this a beautiful whole. The text is worth the trouble, for the implications of this fable from the *Hitopadésa* are profound. . . .

Children will love the transformations of the mouse into ever more terrifying animals and the wonderful changes of expression on the tiger's and the hermit's faces as their emotions towards each other change, but best of all perhaps is the way Marcia Brown has shown the ghost of the vanished tiger as it surveys itself again obliged to live in a timid mouse body.

> *Margaret Sherwood Libby, in a review of "Once a Mouse . . . ," in* Books, *November 12, 1961, p. 2.*

As the subject suggests, the illustrations are woodcuts, not in black but in a warmer, more jungly spectrum. They are striking; when a mouse is changed to a tiger, it is a tiger burning bright. But somehow they are not really appealing, at least to this reader, and they may be of more interest to the grade-school child responsive to artistic technique than to the one simply looking for a story book. The fable itself, involving humility and pride, would probably not be lost on anyone.

> *Rod Nordell, "Gentle Pencils," in* The Christian Science Monitor, *November 16, 1961, p. 2B.*

Probably Miss Brown's most handsomely devised and executed book, three-color woodcuts blending Indian and modern designs. Unfortunately, however, the brief, stylishly told tale from ancient India seems to lose its point a bit in picture-book form, and the end comes as a distinct anti-climax, but most children should be fascinated by the masterful way in which the cocky tiger is shown turning back into a mouse, and the moral is worth making even if its meaning isn't clear at first sight. (pp. 33-4)

> *Janice H. Dohm, in a review of "Once a Mouse . . . : A Fable Cut in Wood," in* School Library Journal, *an appendix to* Library Journal, *Vol. 8, No. 4, December, 1961, pp. 33-4.*

[*Once a Mouse* . . . is] an unusually good and valuable book. . . . (p. 51)

[Marcia Brown] achieves the biggest possible effects with the most modest means, with the specific textures of wood, with a few shadings in olive-green and strawberry-red. Her special love belongs to the tiger whose expression always varies, reaching from boastfulness, to anger and to fear. Marcia Brown's hermit has dignity and kindness, but also the severity and relentlessness of an angry god. Modesty in word and picture united with wisdom and humour are the outstanding qualities of this book. (p. 52)

> *A review of "Once a Mouse . . . ," in* Bookbird, *No. 1, (March 15, 1965), pp. 51-2.*

BACKBONE OF THE KING: THE STORY OF PAKA'A AND HIS SON KU (1966)

An invaluable contribution to the heroic literature of our fiftieth state, this is based on *The Hawaiian Story of Paka'a and Kuapaka'a, the Personal Attendants of Keawenuianumi,* collected, assembled, selected, and edited by Moses K. Nakuina with a translation from the Hawaiian by Dorothy M. Kahananui.

This book, with its story for young people and its pictures in green (text in black), is a surprise from Marcia Brown. It has been more than three years in the growing and the making. During the second of her long visits to the Hawaiian islands Miss Brown spent a year painting and doing research for the background of Paka'a. In the powerful book that has resulted, she combines dramatic material and chants with the story of Ku, who helped his exiled father regain his place as "backbone" or personal attendant to the king. Among the fifty-seven linoleum cuts that illustrate the book are several which remind us of the strength of the woodcuts in *Once a Mouse.*

Young people who have somewhat of a struggle with *Beowulf* in school may feel this heroic legend nearer to them. A full glossary helps with the Polynesian names.

> *Alice Dalgliesh, in a review of "Backbone of the King: The Story of Paka'a and His Son Ku," in* Saturday Review, *Vol. XLIX, No. 20, May 14, 1966, p. 42.*

The literary style is distinctive and the scholarship is meticulous. . . . The legend is long; the action rambles and is, in places, repetitious. Most young readers will not have the patience to finish this story despite the fascinating details and basically dramatic plot. The series of traditional chants on the qualities of the winds of Hawaii, as an example, seems interminable. However, storytellers will find the book valuable as a source which could be excerpted or adapted to appeal to a wide age range. There is an extraordinary amount of information included on ancient Hawaiian customs and daily life. The profusion of Hawaiian words which tends to impede the written narrative (and necessitates frequent consultation with the extensive glossary) will add authentic flavor to the spoken narrative of a skillful storyteller. The explanation of Hawaiian pronunciation is clear. Olive-green linoleum block cuts are strong and provide a good visual picture of ancient Hawaiian life.

> *Ann Currah, in a review of "Backbone of the King," in* Library Journal, *Vol. 91, No. 13, July, 1966, p. 3532.*

An extraordinary storytelling cycle could be developed from the book, which will also be a rewarding reading experience for children of ten and over and excellent for reading aloud. The more than fifty woodcuts . . . have strength and feeling in perfect harmony with the Hawaiian atmosphere and the heroic quality of the legend. A distinguished book that will most probably have an important place in literature for children long after most present-day books are forgotten. (p. 429)

> *Ruth Hill Viguers, in a review of "Backbone of the King," in* The Horn Book Magazine, *Vol. XLII, No. 4, August, 1966, pp. 428-29.*

This legend from Hawaii is retold in rhythmic prose, with frequent quotations from ancient chants. It has the song of the winds and the beat of the waves surging through its pages. The

From Once a Mouse . . . A Fable Cut in Wood, *written and illustrated by Marcia Brown. Charles Scribner's Sons, 1961. Copyright © 1961 Marcia Brown. All rights reserved. Reprinted with the permission of Charles Scribner's Sons.*

discursive and leisurely plot, with its wealth of old-time lore, coupled with the lengthy multiple-voweled proper names, may daunt some readers. The main characters appear as a mixture of kindliness and insensitivity, full of *aloha* or love, yet all too often forgetful of debts of gratitude. The block-print illustrations convey the strength and poetry of the story and its setting. (p. 24)

> *Ethna Sheehan, in a review of "Backbone of the King: The Story of Paka'a and His Son Ku," in* The New York Times Book Review, *August 7, 1966, pp. 23-4.*

The many multivoweled Hawaiian names, numerous chants, and a loosely constructed plot may discourage some readers but children who are not so deterred or those to whom the book is read will be richly rewarded by the beautifully written, moving story and the vivid delineation of ancient Hawaiian culture. Harmoniously illustrated with handsome linoleum blocks.

> *A review of "Backbone of the King: The Story of Paka'a and His Son Ku," in* The Booklist and Subscription Books Bulletin, *Vol. 63, No. 3, October 1, 1966, p. 183.*

This is Marcia Brown's first book for older readers. Like her books for the picture book age . . . it is a classic tale and she has done what will probably be the standard re-telling and illustrations for children. This new one belongs next to the hero tales of many lands—next to Howard Pyle's *King Arthur* and *Robin Hood,* Padraic Colum's *Children's Homer,* and *Golden Fleece,* Babette Deutsch's *Heroes of the Kalevala,* and all the other stirring and heroic tales of legendary figures. . . .

There is a haunting beauty in this telling. The chants and descriptions of a vanished culture invest the tale with vitality and clarity. The beauty and complexity of the "simple" life, the ritualistic ways of the court and the commoners, and the beauty of the islands themselves are all vividly presented. Yet the dignity of this retelling is perhaps its strongest point.

The block prints are beautiful and very different from the artist's illustrations for her previous books. They are more robust, yet have the delicacy we think of in connection with *Cinderella* or *Little Carousel.* There is a 15 page glossary-dictionary which is a great help. Happily, the author doesn't interrupt her powerful story to explain Hawaiian words and expressions. Nor does she repeat them in English! Most can be understood because of context, but the exact meaning and pronunciation are relegated to the glossary. This book will not be every boy's cup of tea. Odysseus, Jason, King Arthur, Robin Hood are so well-known and their backgrounds are so familiar that boys can take to them easily. Some few discerning youngsters (and every librarian knows them) will not need a "sales talk," but the majority probably will not be very easy to sell. But this is certainly worth the effort; it should be available for all children, just as other standard epics are.

> *Phyllis Cohen, in a review of "Backbone of the King: The Story of Paka'a and His Son Ku," in* Young Readers Review, *Vol. III, No. 3, November, 1966, p. 4.*

THE NEIGHBORS (1967)

This is a hard review to write. Not because Marcia Brown is a two-time winner of the Caldecott medal . . . but because her work has always been consistently outstanding. Until *The*

Neighbors. While she has retold this old Russian legend of the falling out of animal neighbors with characteristic Marcia Brown verve, she has illustrated it in a slapdash fashion that is not characteristic. No book of hers must be ignored; this one must be called disappointing—by one of her admirers, anyway.

> *A review of ''The Neighbors: A Russian Legend,''
> in* Publishers Weekly, *Vol. 192, No. 12, September
> 18, 1967, p. 67.*

[A] prize-winning artist who doesn't do herself justice is Marcia Brown. *The Neighbors* . . . is her rather pallid retelling of an old Russian tale of the fox outfoxed by a rabbit and a rooster. . . . [The] verses that are interspersed throughout the story are especially weak; the drawings also lack force, just bordering on Saturday morning cartoon kiddie-show style.

> *Eve Merriam, in a review of ''The Neighbors,'' in*
> The New York Times Book Review, *Part II, November 5, 1967, p. 70.*

While not representative of the illustrator's best work the pictures are expressive and seem in harmony with the Russian fable Miss Brown has retold. The large size of the illustrations make the book especially suitable for the picture-book hour.

> *Ruth P. Bull and Mary Simons, in a review of ''The
> Neighbors,'' in* The Booklist and Subscription Books
> Bulletin, *Vol. 64, No. 10, January 15, 1968, p. 590.*

This adaptation of an old Russian tale is devoid of characteristic folk humor and unconvincing in its separation of these animals from their natural roles—especially in that the cock is the most articulate and that the fox, a natural dominant enemy of poultry, accepts his words. The story does not have apparent parable significance, nor is it clearly in the vein of cumulative tales. To illustrate it, Miss Brown has adopted the garishly colored near-cartoon style that has been in vogue lately.

> *Elinor S. Cullen, in a review of ''The Neighbors,''
> in* School Library Journal, *an appendix to* Library
> Journal, *Vol. 14, No. 6, February, 1968, p. 68.*

A picture book in three colours by the distinguished American artist, and written in true folk-tale style. The prose has a rhythmic swing and the repetition which appeals to young children. The illustrations picture amusingly the insolence of the fox . . . , the helplessness of the wronged Hare and the pride of the resplendent Cock who comes to Hare's rescue.

> *A review of ''The Neighbours,'' in* The Junior Bookshelf, *Vol. 32, No. 6, December, 1968, p. 353.*

The simple text and repetitive rhymes will appeal to four- and five-year-olds (if read to them with enthusiasm and good humour). Vigorous ink and wash illustrations capture the spirited tone of the tale. The artist's power lies in her use of line to express action and the moods and endowments of her characters. Colour is applied sparingly to emphasize the energy and controlled pandemonium of the drawings.

This being said, however, one cannot help but wish that a finer example of Marcia Brown's many books could have been the introduction to British children of her undoubtedly distinguished craftsmanship. (pp. 13-14)

> *J. Davies, in a review of ''The Neighbours,'' in*
> Children's Book News, London, *Vol. 4, No. 1, January-February, 1969, pp. 13-14.*

HOW, HIPPO! (1969)

This is Marcia Brown's happiest book; there is laughter waiting for the reader on every page. Loving laughter, at the antics of an endearing young hippo. A hippo *endearing?* Yes, when he belongs to Marcia Brown. Oh, don't waste your time arguing, hurry to look at it. You'll see. You, too, will be surprised by joy.

> *A review of ''How, Hippo!'' in* Publishers Weekly,
> *Vol. 195, No. 14, April 7, 1969, p. 55.*

Beautiful woodcuts in two-page spreads spark a story of survival in the animal world. In contentment or panic, the hippo's characteristic noises are variations on the how sound. ''Mind your hows, Little Hippo. Be sure you roar the right one'' says Little Hippo's mother, prompting her offspring to practice dutifully to be fast enough on the how-draw. But Little Hippo bounces up to the surface one day, away from his mother for the first time, and is almost devoured by a glinty-eyed old crocodile who unceremoniously seizes his tail. Little Hippo hows for all he's worth, however, and in time for Mother Hippo to hear: she promptly dispatches the predator and reminds her son again to always mind his hows until he is big. The blue, green and pink shaded woodcuts, as expert as those the author/illustrator provided for the more heavily detailed *Once a Mouse* . . . , capture the various expressions of the hippo pair and the mean crocodile, and guarantee success for this latest effort by the two time Caldecott Medalist.

> *Elaine T. McDonald, in a review of ''How, Hippo!''
> in* School Library Journal, *an appendix to* Library
> Journal, *Vol. 15, No. 9, May, 1969, p. 73.*

A handsome picture book in which a little hippopotamus . . . learns what can happen when he ventures too far from his mother. The story is uncomplicated and childlike, and the stunning colored woodcuts have strength and heaviness commensurate with the subject. (pp. 1223-24)

> *Ruth P. Bull, in a review of ''How, Hippo!'' in* The
> Booklist and Subscription Books Bulletin, *Vol. 65,
> No. 21, July 1, 1969, pp. 1223-24.*

Of all the major American makers of picture-books Marcia Brown has made perhaps the least impact in this country. At least until now. *How, Hippo!* may change all that. The story . . . is thin. The pictures are brilliant, powerful and strangely beautiful. They are based on woodcuts which give to their forms a remarkable angularity and to their texture subtle variety. They are beautifully economical, with an almost oriental skill in selection. And, if the story is insignificant, the text in which it is told is a model of brevity and rightness. English picture-book writers, who so often have a genius for saying just too much, might study it with profit. (p. 278)

> *A review of ''How, Hippo!'' in* The Junior Bookshelf,
> *Vol. 34, No. 5, October, 1970, pp. 278-79.*

THE BUN: A TALE FROM RUSSIA (1972)

The artist-storyteller has chosen . . . a picture-book folk tale for the very youngest—the well-known Russian version of ''The Johnny Cake.'' (Valery Carrick uses the same source in *Picture Tales from the Russian* [Dufour], but that telling has less felicitous phrasing and detail.) The repetitive chant of the runaway bun is appealing: '' 'I was scraped from the trough, / I was swept from the bin, / I was kneaded with cream, / I was browned in a pan. . . . / And I can run away from you . . . / That I can!''' The amount of text and illustration varies on each page. Brown, gold, and turquoise drawings, some with bright scarlet added for accent, give a superb sense of movement and spirit: The bun dances along from one scene to the next with his grinning face eyeing each new creature that would eat him; the wolf spins in a dizzy motion; the suave fox displays his confidence. (pp. 136-37)

> *Virginia Haviland, in a review of "The Bun: A Tale from Russia," in* The Horn Book Magazine, *Vol. XLVIII, No. 2, April, 1972, pp. 136-37.*

Marcia Brown illustrates this Russian folktale . . . with brightly colored, robust pictures filled with humor, expression, and action. The story is told with an economy of words, ending with a brisk "Snap! That was that!" . . .

> *Barbara Joyce Duree, in a review of "The Bun: A Tale from Russia," in* The Booklist, *Vol. 68, No. 16, April 15, 1972, p. 721.*

A variant of the story of the gingerbread boy, illustrated with vigorous, almost strident pictures. . . . The cumulation and repetition in the bun's song, the lively action in both the illustrations and the story, and the concept of the story are appealing, but neither in the writing nor in the illustrations is this distinguished.

> *Zena Sutherland, in a review of "The Bun: A Tale from Russia," in* Bulletin of the Center for Children's Books, *Vol. 25, No. 10, June, 1972, p. 152.*

In this story, identified only as "a tale from Russia," characters differ slightly from the variations found in such collections as Edna Johnson's *Anthology of Children's Literature* (Houghton, rev. ed., 1970) or the Association for Childhood Education's *Told Under the Green Umbrella: Old Stories for New Children* (Macmillan, 1930): the old woman and her seven children have been replaced by an old man and his wife, and the animals encountered on the journey have also been changed. Pre-schoolers will enjoy the directness of the brief story and the bun's cumulative boasting as he escapes consumption time after time. *The Bun* lacks the plot development and distinguished prose which make Marcia Brown's *Stone Soup* . . . a favorite, but it is an acceptable purchase where lavishly illustrated editions of old stand-bys are in demand.

> *Carol Chatfield, in a review of "The Bun: A Tale from Russia," in* Library Journal, *Vol. 97, No. 12, June 15, 1972, p. 2228.*

As in each of her previous books, Caldecott winner Marcia Brown proves her versatility as an artist, with a new and different use of color and movement to create just the right mood for the tale she is telling.

> *Judith B. Rosenfeld, in a review of "The Bun: A Tale from Russia," in* Childhood Education, *Vol. 49, No. 1 (October, 1972), p. 27.*

ALL BUTTERFLIES: AN ABC (1974)

Marcia Brown's ABC arrangement functions more as a device for ordering her strong, glowing woodcuts than an aid in learning the alphabet. From "All Butterflies" (patterning a serene wood of black trees and dusty blue sky) we turn to a vibrant, energetic "Cat Dance" in red, yellow and black, then to a comically incongruous "Elephants Fly?"—and so on, each double page picture working butterflies into more or less prominent roles. Every turn of the page hits you with a whole new view in a startlingly different key, and one is tempted to describe each one in turn—the sunset mood of "Giraffes High," the dynamic swirls of "Ice-cold Jumpers" (polar bears), the bold posturing and feathery humor and lovely designs that follow. A very first book, and one to grow on.

> *A review of "All Butterflies: An ABC," in* Kirkus Reviews, *Vol. XLII, No. 8, April 15, 1974, p. 418.*

The book is a marvelous example of art and ingenuity. Color pictures are designed to accent Ms. Brown's unusual concept—one letter leading to another. . . . The finale is a page presenting all the letters of the alphabet in upper and lower case. It's a book to be treasured, a genuine classic.

> *A review of "All Butterflies: An ABC," in* Publishers Weekly, *Vol. 205, No. 18, May 6, 1974, p. 69.*

Another ABC book like *Hosie's Alphabet* (Viking), in which the artistry of the illustrations rather than the substance of the text becomes the focus. . . . Not all of the woodcuts are equally successful. Some are marred by uninteresting compositions; some by incongruously heavy lines. But using a form that she long ago mastered, the artist achieves in the best illustrations beautiful modulations of color, delicacy of shape and form, and marvelously varied moods. An unspectacular but lovely creation.

> *Anita Silvey, in a review of "All Butterflies: An ABC," in* The Horn Book Magazine, *Vol. L, No. 3, June, 1974, p. 272.*

Woodcuts in warm, rich colors distinguish this new alphabet book . . . Some word couplings are contrived (e.g., "Umbrella Valentine") and a few will require explanation to small children (e.g., "Ice-cold Jumpers" for polar bears). The concept however, may spur independent readers to compose their own combinations, and younger children will enjoy looking at the animals as well as spotting the incidental appearance on many pages of butterflies of different shapes and designs.

> *Della Thomas, in a review of "All Butterflies: An ABC," in* School Library Journal, *an appendix to* Library Journal, *Vol. 21, No. 1, September, 1974, p. 55.*

Handsome woodcuts in muted colors show creatures of all kinds in realistic or fanciful situations; save for a few pictures in which they would be inappropriate (the Arctic, the ocean depths) butterflies of varied shapes and colors appear on all the pages. . . . Some of the pictures have a grave serenity, others are vigorous or humorous. Moderately useful as an alphabet book, graphically delightful.

> *Zena Sutherland, in a review of "All Butterflies: An ABC," in* Bulletin of the Center for Children's Books, *Vol. 28, No. 2, October, 1974, p. 24.*

In a compression of the one-word one-picture approach, Marcia Brown's *All Butterflies* is created in thirteen frames rather than the usual twenty-six. Using a double spread of fanciful woodcuts as a backdrop for each successive brace of words, she starts with "All Butterflies" and ends with "Your Zoo." But something else is going on—something that we can consider akin to theme. Although no mention is made of the situation, there is *somewhere* one or more butterflies in each frame. I have seen children and college students alike respond with sudden delight at the unexpected discovery of this bonus. (p. 179)

Mary Agnes Taylor, "From Apple to Abstraction in Alphabet Books," in Children's literature in education, *Vol. 9, No. 4 (Winter), 1978, pp. 173-81.*

THE BLUE JACKAL   (1977)

This tale from *The Panchatantra,* a collection of moral fables, tells how the jackal, Fierce-Howl, became king of the animals under false pretenses, and was later dethroned when his true color was discovered. Marcia Brown has eliminated every unnecessary word, strengthening the philosophical, almost mystical impact of the story. The jackal's final statement concludes: "What is my place? My time? My friends? / Expenditure or dividends? / And what am I? and what is my power? / So one must ponder hour by hour." Mehlli Gobhai's version of the story, *The Blue Jackal* (Prentice-Hall, 1968), is more obviously from India with its exotic native costumes and glossary of Indian words. However Brown's bold, crimson, blue, and ochre woodcuts are much more universal and forceful. Superior for reading aloud or for beginning readers.

Dana Whitney Pinizzotto, in a review of "The Blue Jackal," in School Library Journal, *Vol. 23, No. 9, May, 1977, p. 48.*

Brown's spare, poetic text (based on a translation from the Sanskrit by Arthur W. Ryder) gains boisterous vitality when set against her bold, vigorous, four-color cuts that show the terror, absurdity, and loneliness of the situations in which the jackal finds himself. This is superior to the free, embroidered, somewhat condescending retelling by Gobhai. . . . Here, illustrations make comprehensible the difficult questions raised by the tale. . . . This picture book for older children will benefit from introduction by librarians and by teachers. It is excellent source material for units on Indian culture. (pp. 1417-18)

M. J. A., in a review of "The Blue Jackal," in Booklist, *Vol. 73, No. 18, May 15, 1977, pp. 1417-18.*

The text has been modernized, resulting in a more economical and dramatic storytelling style, but the adaptation is intriguing for more important reasons. As in Mehlli Gobhai's retelling *The Blue Jackal* (Prentice), the ending has been altered. In Ryder's translation, when the jackal was found out, he was "torn to bits by a tiger and died"; and in the moralizing tradition of the stories from *The Panchatantra,* a number of verses point out the lessons to be learned from the fickle animal's behavior toward his fellow jackals. Marcia Brown includes one of the verses, whereas none of several familiar retellings— such as the versions in Joseph Gaer's *The Fables of India* (Little) or Margaret Green's *The Big Book of Animal Fables* (Watts)—retain them. The woodcuts in four colors are innovative and exciting: "Wood that lived can say something about life in a forest," wrote the artist, and she proves it in her skillful use of the exacting medium. The pictures do not have the simplicity of her *Once a Mouse* but are filled with complex compositions which lend a sense of vitality to tableaux of animals. Many of the double-page spreads are reminiscent of *All Butterflies.* Her sense of line is tremendously powerful, and highlights of color, such as red around a freshly killed antelope, evoke moods. The juxtaposition of deep colors occasionally results in an effect that is almost muddled, but the artist is nearly always successful in portraying distinctly a considerable

amount of action. . . . [This] new version of the tale [is] a welcome addition to the picture book-folk tale genre. (p. 305)

Sally Holmes Holtze, in a review of "The Blue Jackal," in The Horn Book Magazine, *Vol. LIII, No. 3, June, 1977, pp. 304-05.*

A brilliant adaptor who varies her artistic style to suit the story with which she is working, [Marcia Brown] has created a new book which must certainly be considered another potential [Caldecott] winner. *The Blue Jackal* . . . is a moral fable in the tradition of *Once a Mouse*. . . . It is the story of a hungry Jackal who, trying to escape from a pack of fierce city dogs, jumps into a vat of indigo. When he returns to the forest colored a deep blue, he is mistaken for a king and, until his true identity is discovered, he is treated royally. *The Blue Jackal* is thus a fable of identity, asking such questions as "what is the nature of one's identity?" and "Is one happiest accepting what he is or should he strive for something higher?" Marcia Brown's language captures both the simplicity and profundity of the story's message. It is, as the dust jacket suggests, "a fable for all ages."

The prints Marcia Brown has created to illustrate this tale are vivid and striking. Perhaps, they are too striking and vivid. One of the great achievements of *Once a Mouse* . . . was its ability to use simple combinations of colors to help convey themes and emotions. In *The Blue Jackal,* particularly in the jungle scenes in which the Jackal is treated as a king, too much color seems to be used. Perhaps this is to create an awareness of the falseness of his new splendor, but the result, to me at least, is confusion. Moreover, I'm not completely pleased with the depictions of the jackal himself—too often the poses and facial expressions are exaggeratedly comic.

However, one often tends to be too harsh of the writer-artists he admires; and this may well be the case here. But in spite

From Backbone of the King: The Story of Paka'a and His Son Ku, *written and illustrated by Marcia Brown. Charles Scribner's Sons, 1966. Copyright © 1966 Marcia Brown. All rights reserved. Reprinted by permission of the author.*

of my reservations, I think Marcia Brown's *The Blue Jackal* is a very good book, one well worth buying. (pp. 18-19)

> *Jon Stott, in a review of "The Blue Jackal," in The World of Children's Books, Vol. II, No. 2, Fall, 1977, pp. 18-19.*

Sharp, dramatic woodprints emphasize the movement of the story. Much more colorful and complex than her earlier works, Brown's latest book attests to her growth in design and story-telling. The blue motif is perfect for a tale which asks: "'What is my place? My time? My friends? / Expenditure or dividends?'"

> *Ruth M. Stein, in a review of "The Blue Jackal," in Language Arts, Vol. 55, No. 2, February, 1978, p. 210.*

LISTEN TO A SHAPE; TOUCH WILL TELL; WALK WITH YOUR EYES (1979)

These three titles are Brown's first published books of photographs. They are outstanding concept books with poetic, sensitive texts and strikingly beautiful full-color photographs. *Listen to a Shape* introduces various shapes in nature and the observations that can be made from looking with objectivity. *Touch Will Tell* presents touching as a way of learning and experiencing the world. *Walk With Your Eyes* encourages visual perception and looking beyond the obvious to really *see* the world around. All will provide stimulating discussion and observation for many situations in and out of the classroom. A rare treat indeed!

> *Glenda Broughton, in a review of "Listen to a Shape," "Touch Will Tell," "Walk with Your Eyes," in Children's Book Review Service, Vol. 8, No. 2, October, 1979, p. 14.*

Brown imaginatively trains her camera on everyday nature scenes in three books whose captions evoke sensory images and prod viewers to look, listen, and touch with greater sensitivity. Distinctly composed and sharply focused, the full-color photographs show a spider mending a rain-torn web, a patch of colored leaves whirling in a stream, wind-tossed clouds before a storm, ice-crusted twigs, baby cygnets stretching in the sun, shimmering marsh waters, and a dragonfly resting atop a lily pad. Each image takes on new dimension as the suggestions for careful appraisal result in greater awareness of the environment and oneself. Children sharing these with adults, especially in preparation for a nature walk, will best realize the full potential of this uplifting visual experience.

> *Barbara Elleman, in a review of "Walk with Your Eyes," in Booklist, Vol. 76, No. 3, October 1, 1979, p. 235.*

Already distinguished for her versatility, Brown adds a new medium to her repertory in this concept book [*Listen To A Shape*], illustrated with handsome full-color photographs accompanying a poetic text. The pictures are all of natural objects: the spikes of iris buds in spring, the circle made by dandelion petals, the curved shadow of a straight tree limb, the wind-made ripples on sand or water. "What shape is a cloud? ... What shape is a flame?" the captions ask, or comment "A miracle: Young things have inside them the plan for the shape they will become. So do you!" This can stir a child's imagination, teach observation, and encourage aesthetic appreciation.

> *Zena Sutherland, in a review of "Listen To a Shape," in Bulletin of the Center for Children's Books, Vol. 33, No. 5, January, 1980, p. 90.*

[*Touch Will Tell, Listen to a Shape,* and *Walk With Your Eyes*] are exquisite examples of quality books for young children that are destined to become tomorrow's classics. Without cheap gimmicks, put-downs, poor art work, or inexpressive use of language, these three books encourage children to develop an awareness of the world around them as well as their own ability to perceive their world through the senses. The books' vivid language and new ways of looking at simple things should increase children's creativity, imagination, and vocabulary. The poetic use of language accompanied by beautiful photographs will stimulate children's powers of observation, wonder, and appreciation. Preschoolers as well as children in kindergarten and the first four grades will treasure the experience of reading *Touch Will Tell, Listen to a Shape,* and *Walk With Your Eyes.*

> *Carol Seefeldt, "Marcia Brown Concept Library," in Curriculum Review, Vol. 19, No. 4, September, 1980, p. 328.*

SHADOW (1982)

[Shadow *was written by Blaise Cendrars and translated from the French by Brown.*]

AUTHOR'S COMMENTARY

[*The following excerpt, originally published in the August, 1983 issue of* The Horn Book Magazine, *is taken from Brown's Caldecott Award acceptance speech which she gave at the meeting of the American Library Association on June 28, 1983.*]

A long time ago I found, in Italy, a little book of proverbs collected from various peoples of black Africa. Their pithy pertinence can leaven my words.

Proverb: "It's true that I killed an elephant; however, it's not true that I carried him home on my shoulders."

Have you looked down from a high hill or tower on traffic patterns around a well-engineered intersection? Drivers trust each other; they trust their own ability to drive and react quickly. They trust the reactions of their own machines. There are remarkably few accidents, considering the number of vehicles on the roads. They all seem held, as it were, in orbit by invisible threads of trust.

Proverb: "The tongue is a lion; if you let it run free, it will eat you up."

Illustrators often find themselves in an ironical position. Much of what they say about their work has to be after the fact because they think in images, not in words. Yet if they can't talk, heaven help them!

Proverb: "When you hear a good talker, don't agree with him all at once. What is hiding in the corner has not come out yet."

Many years ago, when I was a storyteller in The New York Public Library, I was fascinated by a little book in the French collection of the Central Children's Room: *Petits Contes Nègres pour les Enfants des Blancs,* published in France in 1929, with semi-abstract and somewhat sophisticated illustrations. Margery Bianco translated that book and published, in 1933, *Little Black Stories for Little White Children* (Payson & Clarke), with handsome woodcut illustrations that suggested African wood carvings. The one piece in the French of Blaise Cendrars that Mrs. Bianco did not translate was "La Féticheuse" or "The Sorceress."

I have been haunted for years by the mysterious atmosphere created by Blaise Cendrars as he evoked Shadow, a spirit coming to life in firelight, wandering in and out of memory, taking part in rituals that gave meaning to life, at times a mirror image of life.

Although the poem had been told more often to adults than to children (hauntingly, by Maria Cimino of The New York Public Library's Central Children's Room), I felt that in the 1980s the prose poem might have meaning for American children. Levels of awareness might be probed that might not have been reached so easily in 1933. We have grown, and we have also suffered a great deal, since 1933. Perhaps we have learned something about ourselves.

A trip to East Africa in 1975 showed me a land of dazzling light that carved bold shapes relentlessly against mysterious shadow, colorful rocks still displaying the scars of the geological upheavals that had formed them, savannahs of golden grasses, and brilliant sunsets before the sudden fall of night. Proud peoples seemed caught between past and present. Magnificent animals were both hunters and prey. The shadow of scavengers hung greedy over the burning land.

One of my strongest impressions was of timelessness, a kind of innocence in which man lived with nature in a way barely imagined by Western man.

My challenge, if I were to make a book of "Shadow," as I had come to call the poem to myself, would be to incorporate the images that had formed in my head from reading the poem with impressions gained from travel in Africa, with records of anthropologists who had very recently tried to record ways of life that are constantly changing and absorbing influences from other societies and, in some cases, are disappearing altogether.

I recognized another challenge: to suggest the element of play with an idea that is implied in the text. I do not think that Cendrars ever imagined himself to be recording a piece of ethnic literature—even though *Shadow* is told in a form suggestive of some kinds of storytelling prevalent in Africa—any more than Picasso's "Les Demoiselles d'Avignon," incorporating impressions of African masks, professed to be a record of those masks. It was a new creation. *Shadow* was in no way to be a documentary performance. Poets, children, and artists often delight in mixing the real and the unreal, intuitively aware that each feeds an understanding of the other. I trusted children to understand many more emotional levels of shadow than the obvious.

Cendrars, and that was not his real name, was in Africa over fifty years ago. He wrote of people living in pastoral and agricultural societies where Nature was beneficent but had to be appeased by ritual for the loss of vital forces taken from the earth. The explosive energy of dance, of song, of storytelling, of all the components of ritualistic ceremonies in which the whole community shared, restored these vital forces, and equilibrium was maintained.

Proverb: "No matter how calm the lake, in it there may be crocodiles."

I was quite aware of the possible nonacceptance of the book on an African subject because I am white. Also, the book, as I had conceived it, would be very expensive to print and pro-

duce properly. I gave my publisher every chance to be released from our agreement. Scribner's decided to trust me and gave me possibly the best printing of all my books, one that united tonalities that had been executed over many months, with a long interruption in between.

Proverb: "If you have tried in vain to fish with the sea low, try to fish at high tide."

I wanted to make the book as vivid as I could, to speak to any child, regardless of color. We all share fear, discovery, loss, and a sense of play.

At one time, I toyed with the idea of photography as a medium for *Shadow*. I would work with images created by a trained dancer. The book would have been very different. I decided to work out my own images. At one time, I had hoped to cut wood blocks for the pictures. Arthritic pain in my hands forbade that. I think of African wood-carvers as sculptors the peers of any in the world, regardless of the original purpose of their carvings—not as works of art in the sense that we enjoy them in museums but as tools of ritual with enormous spiritual and evocative power.

The text was a poem. Black, stark cut-paper figures for people and animals could unify its many episodes and avoid the individualization of character that would limit imagination. I used the deep violet-blue shadows I had seen at dusk in Africa to suggest actual shadows. I cut wood blocks and printed them in white on translucent paper to suggest memories, spirit-images, and ghosts. The round-headed Fang masks suggest that one newborn may be closest to his ancestors. A community consists of the ancestors, the living, and those yet unborn.

When I had completed half the illustrations, I was forced to stop work for a year because of illness. I later worked out the method of blotting to suggest a land scarred by the history locked in its rocks. Fragments of blotted paper were pasted together to build up the landscapes I remembered.

I conceived the book as a kind of day that starts with sunset, moving into night. Probably because of the huge clouds of dust kicked up by running animals, sunsets in Africa can be awesomely brilliant before a brief dusk. The book moves through another day and ends again with the fire that brings Shadow to life.

Since the book was not to be a literal record, I did not wish to limit it to any one group. Clothing in temperatures that can easily hover near 125 degrees Fahrenheit is apt to be minimal, but I also wished to show gesture as probably the most vivid mode of communication among the various members of the human family. Bodily positions were suggested by my own numerous photographs taken in Africa, by recent photographs taken by Leni Riefenstahl of the Kau and Nuba peoples, and those of Michel Huet, who spent years recording dance rituals of many ethnic groups in Africa before they would pass from memory.

Proverb: "A beautiful neck has no need of a pearl necklace."

Translation is not retelling. I decry and fear the growing tendency to think that a translator has the right to change thought, intent, or style. I made my own translation, telling it over and over to myself, keeping in mind the shifting image of a wonderful dancer-storyteller, images darting from her pointed fingers.

When I read *Shadow* to Lee Deadrick, she immediately thought it could speak to children. We were a bit optimistic in thinking that French editors would be more careful of old records than we sometimes are. It took Lee and her staff almost a year of writing back and forth to France before we were able to ascertain ownership of rights and go ahead.

Proverb: "Children sing the song which they hear from their mother and father."

We know, from the child deep within ourselves, that children rarely speak of all they feel. We often violate their privacy and urge them to expose inner feelings that are withered in our scrutiny. I have often trusted children to accept poetic truth when their elders were worried and confused by terminology unfamiliar to them or were too literal of mind. There are levels of response in children we often make no attempt to reach, so anxious are we to cram their small skins full of practical skills and information. We push them out of a time of precious reverie and inner growth at the price of stunted and shallow adult inner life. Worse, we are sometimes guilty of passing on to them fears, hates, all the baggage of our own pain, when there is often no need. One generation of twenty years can change mental climate a good deal.

Proverb: "Today and tomorrow are not the same thing."

The book was to be published as a children's book. Even though I never thought it for very young children, I felt that children would expect to find children in the illustrations. Along with dance, storytelling was often part of a ritual ceremony taking place in an open space in the village, attended by the inhabitants, old and young. I showed an audience of children for the storyteller, who tells his animal tales and passes along to his listeners the lore and wisdom of their society.

Shadow is often paradoxical. Playing with his idea, Cendrars moves back and forth between the shadow seen and known to the child as playmate, an accompaniment to all that lives in light, and shadow unseen, the ancestral past, the spirit that lives after life, after light, after fires are quenched. In no way did I wish to make a literal picture of African life, and indeed what picture book could undertake to show honestly the incredible diversity of a huge continent? Customs of pastoral peoples are not those of the forest, still less those of the cities that have grown so remarkably in the last half century. I would have to range as freely as the poet.

On the title page, a child steps out of her shadow, giving a backward look to the powerful ancestral images of the past. Some of the strongest possible means for instilling awe and reverence for ancestral spirits are the ritual dance masks. They absorb and control an energy released by the death of living creatures and make that energy available as a good, rather than as a surrender to chaos. When making the Bwa mask from Upper Volta, I worked until that mysterious transferal of spirit could take place, the leap from the spirit of the artist into the thing created. The evocation of spirit existing in the husk of an artist's creation is unmistakable when it occurs, the result of concentration and utter submergence of mind into material.

A child awakens in the night, perhaps for the first time startled at the thought, "What if I am not?" and feels the hole of nothingness, the negative of all positive.

In Africa, as Joseph Campbell has written, "Ash is the key to the sacred." Ash, what is left after fire, after growth, after purification, becomes the eyes of Shadow.

A child lifts a stone and uncovers shadow people squirming in the shock of light. A boy child, who had danced so gaily at

noon, is lost. Shadow sits heavy on the heart in the evening, as a child seeks to comfort the grandfather who has lost his hunter son, his warrior son. And the poet sings with his lute to their joy, sings to their grief.

Proverb: "If a village burns, all see the smoke; but if the heart is in flames, no one notices."

Years ago, I told some of Cendrars's stories to children. I knew their power. My first chance to use my book *Shadow* with children came last year before it was published. I showed slides of my pictures and read the poem aloud to a second-grade class in a public school in a nearby town. The children were of many nationalities, many colors—half of them boat people from Laos, Cambodia, and Vietnam. Many had recently lost family members. Some were gifted in art, such as Phovanh Mekmorakoth from Laos, whose picture of a blackbird among little yellow-green orchids hangs on my studio wall; Eddie Pacific, who wrote, "Were we excellent when we read our stories?"; Ruth Ashby, who wrote, "You told us we were casting a shadow on you. You will remember us, won't you?"; and Paul Arbitelle, who wrote, "I'd like to be an artist because it's peace." As I read, shadows flickered over their faces.

Proverb: "Fruits do not shake off by themselves; someone is under the tree."

Vituperations tell a great deal more about those who utter them than about the work attacked. Self-appointed experts are often people who are distinguished—for their ignorance as well as for their arrogance. Their eagerness to take up cudgels for causes they appear barely to understand often seems to be purely careerist in intent. They need not concern us here, and their words had best be forgotten. My concern is for the people who do have an emotional stake in conflicts that confront us, who have suffered real pain and understandably do not wish the children they teach to suffer the same pain. They feel a passionate responsibility to protect children from stigma that is unjust. I would hope that they might also interpret their responsibility as one of leading children away from facile, indignant labels of stereotype into a feeling of pride in a distant background of which we are just beginning to perceive the worth.

Works of art from this background have proudly taken their place all over the world. Were they fashioned by so-called primitive people, these exquisite and powerful objects, with such subtlety and finesse of surface, with the inner power only true works of art possess? I think not. Regardless of whatever fad in art is having its heyday, art history has sifted out those works endowed with spirit, not photographic finish or the product of antlike copying of nature.

Western man, in his arrogance, has left a wake of bruised peoples around the world. The seeking of power demands a putting down to build oneself up.

We are learning that what might have appeared, long ago, to be a meager spiritual and physical diet was far more sound than the endlessly diluted, manipulated fare we sometimes put up with because we think we have no control over it. In the paradox that psychology has taught us to recognize, Western man has envied the wealth of those he chose to label primitive, feared them because their lives were different, and eventually hated them because he had mistreated them.

Proverb: "What the arm cannot do, wisdom can."

We are now in a position of learning wisdom from people we had been taught to think of as primitive. Could children nearer in heritage to those roots be taught pride in them? Many of the rest of us bear in our heritage the shame of what might merit the words *bestial,* even *satanic*—certainly *inhuman.*

Proverb: "A drop of water can be the beginning of a deluge."

Why must we cling to the mental fix that an idea presented to a child be law forever after? Why is one example immediately frozen into an archetype? Or a stereotype? Do we really understand just what that word means? Where do our clichés come from, if not from fact?

Proverb: "A lie can produce flowers, but not fruit."

How are we to enable children to explore different modes of thinking and feeling if we exclude what we, in our literalness, cannot accept? There are those with wounds still open, from hurts some of us can hardly imagine, who are hypersensitive to any wind that seems harsh to barely healing flesh. Their expressions of dismay are honest. I ask them for their trust. (pp. 178-87)

Proverb: "Tasting the fruit, think with gratitude of who planted the tree."

Politicians and their ambitions notwithstanding, the more we learn of the mythologies of the world, the more we learn of the one creature, man. The great themes of his fears, his imaginings, his worship are legion and universal. As Joseph Campbell says in the prologue to his first volume in *The Masks of God* series, *Primitive Mythology* (Viking):

> and though many who bow with closed eyes in the sanctuaries of their own tradition rationally scrutinize and disqualify the sacraments of others, an honest comparison immediately reveals that all have been built from one fund of mythological motifs—variously selected, organized, interpreted, and ritualized, according to local need, but revered by every people on earth.

Come down from the height and watch the cars—Cougars, Sky Hawks, Thunderbirds, Cobras, and Rabbits. We still keep our totemic distinctions. We are still tribal in our allegiances, in our exclusions from our own state of blessedness, and in our mistrust of those we exclude.

We are entering a period forecast hundreds of years ago, one that will probably be cerebral, calculated, terribly competitive for material gain or material survival, depending upon who and where you are. A great deal that is very precious to us may mean next to nothing to this coming generation and those following. But our joy must be in going forward, trusting each other and the children we serve, sharing the common purpose of recognizing the spark of life that can ignite and nourish spirit. Isn't that why we are here? Africa is slowly stepping out of its shadows. Isn't it time that we stepped out of our shadows? (pp. 188-89)

> *Marcia Brown, "Shadows," in her* Lotus Seeds: Children, Pictures, and Books, *Charles Scribner's Sons, 1986, pp. 177-89.*

From an African-inspired French poem, Marcia Brown has created a vibrant picture book that packs a new and unexpected wallop at every turn of the page. The words profile Shadow— a spooky presence, a watcher, a prowler and dancer, a mocking trickster: full of life in the daytime when it "races with the animals at their swiftest," heavy when night falls, blind and groping when the fires go out. Brown picks up each of Shadow's moods and guises: from the first opening, a stunning horizontal symmetry of reflected green land, silhouetted black trees and figures, and bulls-eye sun in a striated orange-red sky—we turn to the deeper reds and blues and dominant, droopy black silhouette of the lush jungle that half-hides Shadow's ghostly presence. Shadow slides up behind the storyteller, blue behind the man's hypnotic black form—or, blind and black itself against blue sky, it crawls eerie and spider-like with reaching oversize hands. It is unobtrusively present behind a crouched hunter in a dazzling, crinkly-textured, gold field— then ascendant in the amusing, "mocking" spread that seems a sort of muted shift on the same chord. The closest comparison is with Brown's *All Butterflies,* except that this is more than a stunning portfolio; throughout, there's a rhythmic relationship among the spreads themselves. A knockout.

> *A review of "Shadow," in* Kirkus Reviews, *Vol. L, No. 10, May 15, 1982, p. 603.*

Marcia Brown's translation of poet Blaise Cendrars' "La Féticheuse," a mood piece that evokes the shamans and storytellers of the African past, is illustrated with collage that may be her best art since *Once a Mouse*. . . . Certainly it is her boldest. The colors flame and the silhouettes of Black dancers and warriors cut sharply into them. Shadow falls in black, in blue, in shades of gray. Tissue paper, dry-brushed acrylics, mottled printing and painting effects as well as smooth washes give texture and glowing life to mountains, sunsets and grasslands. The poem itself is alive and, unlike a lot of tone poems adults admire and children dismiss, this has a spark of mystery to hold a picture-book audience. In these days of high-priced books, it is not so common to see one, like this, worth every penny and then some.

> *Helen Gregory, in a review of "Shadow," in* School Library Journal, *Vol. 28, No. 10, August, 1982, p. 94.*

[Blaise Cendrars, a French poet, novelist, and world traveler], retold African folk tales for children, which were translated by Margery Bianco and published in 1929 as *Little Black Stories* (Payson and Clarke). Not included in that volume, however, was one of the original tales, "La Féticheuse," now the text of a striking picture book by another world traveler—a much-honored illustrator of great integrity and artistry. . . . The artist's work is never predictable or repetitive; her distinction lies partly in the way she suits her technique to the demands of her subject matter. Inspired by the exotic atmosphere and the dramatic possibilities of the text, she has choreographed a sequence of almost theatrical illustrations, placing human and animal figures—and their shadows—against brilliant, contrasting, always changing settings. Resplendent—yet controlled— in color, texture, and form, the work is an impressive, sophisticated example of the art of the picture book.

> *Ethel L. Heins, in a review of "Shadow," in* The Horn Book Magazine, *Vol. LVIII, No. 5, October, 1982, p. 509.*

As in Marcia Brown's other books . . . the illustrations in *Shadow* are splendid. She perfectly captures the pastel steaminess of the savanna, the dark jitteriness of the jungle and the eerie stillness of the faces on ritual masks. Her unusual—and

But it is mute.
It never speaks.
It listens.
It comes sliding right up
behind the storyteller.
Then when the last fire is out
it goes back to the forest.

From Shadow, *translated and illustrated by Marcia Brown from the French of Blaise Cendrars. Charles Scribner's Sons, 1982. Illustrations copyright © 1982 Marcia Brown. All rights reserved. Reprinted with the permission of Charles Scribner's Sons.*

unusually vibrant—palette and bold images evoke an Africa whose mystery is riveting. . . .

Shadow is a prowler that frightens us, spies on us and mocks us, while intending no harm. Unfortunately, though we are given a catalogue of Shadow's traits, tricks, activities and disguises, we do not get a sense of how Shadow gives resonance to the world it inhabits.

Throughout the book are unnecessary and prosaic paraphrases: "It is mute," glossed immediately by "It never speaks." Little more than definitions, they are wasteful and awkward in a text apparently meant to be spare and do nothing to enrich our sense of Shadow. Miss Brown can be a graceful writer, and she should have emphasized this skill.

The voice here is cool, distant and oddly analytical, as though Shadow were a riddle to be solved. That Shadow is paradoxical is, I think, the point of the tale. That which is truly mysterious has a hold on us precisely because it is so, something master storytellers have always exploited. The story of Shadow, as told by the African masters, may well be enchanting, but the way it is handled here leaves the reader frustrated and undernourished.

Marguerite Feitlowitz, in a review of "Shadow," in The New York Times Book Review, *October 3, 1982, p. 30.*

[*Shadow*] presents no authentic cultural clues about African life or spiritual beliefs.

We are told on the jacket that Shadow is an "African experience that is passing into memory," "an eerie image shifting between the beliefs of the present and the spirits of the past." (The book's scenes of "natives" seated in front of "huts" of the past reinforce this idea.) The text personifies Shadow; it prowls at night, it "slides up behind the storyteller." Shadow "is frightening." Here is another book that speaks in clichés that convey a frightening, spooky, magical Africa; an Africa where life and spiritual beliefs are as ephemeral as a Shadow.

A glance through this big, expensively produced book reveals illustrations that have force and rigor; they reflect a skill that makes them powerful persuaders for the uncritical eye. Brown has used a variety of treatments in the application of color; the tones, alternately muted and dramatically vivid, can be said to be attractive. The use of black gives the book an over-all dark quality. That is in itself not "bad." However, in a book about Africa, there is the risk of re-enforcing the idea of Africa as "The Dark Continent."

The African "people" are flat, stylized black cut-outs that overlay the color. Most of the figures are featureless, except for big white eyes. Shades of the minstrel shows and children's picture books before the 60s! Generations of Black people have hated this image with a passion.

In addition, the barely dressed figures, clad in loincloths, carry shields and spears, crouch in savannah grass, leap in dance. Yet no figure reflects the actual grace of an African in dance; no form or gesture from any of the many African traditions of dance can be identified.

The very few female figures are small and play no significant roles. This is an incredible omission, considering that the traditional roles of African women are strong and highly visible, and that women are widely represented in African art. At least the women are thus spared caricature; African men are not. (In this context it seems a blessing that the drum—central to African life—is shown only once and is quite tiny.)

A two-page spread of a dramatic "forest" (not called a jungle but looking like all the "jungles" in a long line of children's books) is empty of living things except for a snake and Shadow. This forest, empty of people, is typical of the book's treatment of African people and how they are shown in relation to their land. Africans are not shown in a positive relationship to (i.e., in command of) their land. Instead they are pictured as having only a tenuous connection to the land. The figures seem to be superimposed on the land or, sometimes, to be leaving the land—and the page itself. Many illustrations evoke death: there are scenes of people at war and burying their dead; buzzards perch in trees. Even the graceful, spritely, colorful lizards of Africa curl up and die on the pages.

The casual use of African spiritual/religious symbols is shocking. For example, Africans apply white color to the face or body during important religious ceremonies to symbolize an important relationship to ancestors. It is a religious practice never fully understood by whites. In this book a "ghost-like" mask streaked white serves as the opening illustration, and streaked white figures and faces appear throughout, divorced from any authentic African tradition. It is insulting and inappropriate.

Masks are another important African symbol. They play a part in African ceremony, ritual and religious/spiritual life and are not "just" works of art. Rooted in centuries of tradition, they are primarily symbols of the belief of a particular people. Brown, however, presents a mask which is grotesque and frightening. She appears to draw—in a limited way—upon some of the elements of masks made by the Fatela and Kongo people. But unlike authentic African masks, hers is quite without discipline, spirituality, order or artistry. Brown's mask serves only to shock, a technique used in a number of her works which have one "scary" illustration: a small boy being chased by a large shark, a little dog who turns quite suddenly into a ferocious tiger, a threatening black cat claiming a fish from a little cat.

No children's book about the European Judeo-Christian experience uses valued spiritual/religious symbols and practices in such a stylized, disrespectful manner. A question occurs: Does an artist have the right to demean or caricature the religious life of another people, particularly in a book for children?

Shadow has won many awards. Given the long struggle to have a varied and authentic selection of books about Africans and people of African descent, *Shadow* does *not* get my vote. (pp. 33-4)

Geraldine Wilson, in a review of "Shadow," in Interracial Books for Children Bulletin, *Vol. 14, Nos. 1 & 2, 1983, pp. 33-4.*

Like many fine works of literature or art *Shadow* evokes ever new understandings, promotes questions, and arouses controversy. What a picture book conveys to readers, its creators can only partially predict. Like any book *Shadow* casts its own shadows, and these both cloud and transfigure whatever the author, artist, publisher, librarians, reviewers, award committees, or critics may say and believe of a book's reality.

Shadows cast by *Shadow* fall on the book's creators, critics, and readers. These shadows take the form of responses that *Shadow* provokes, and it is in responses that a book lives. Some of these shadows seem misshapen and distorted, like those seen when the sun is low on the horizon, when there is insufficient light.

There are troubling shadows. Some have taken the form of critiques decrying the book's potential damaging effect on children. The charge is straightforward: Children reading *Shadow* will receive negative and destructive stereotypes about Africa and black people. Black children will transfer to themselves a primitive and denigrating image. These are shadows of remembered and present pain. Will such shadows lengthen or diminish as the book lives its life? Will there be enough light?

Other shadows are really a reaction to the first ones—other responses coming from many sources which assert unblemished motives, a puzzlement and hurt by the suggestion that *Shadow* could have a tarnishing effect. Great efforts have been made to demonstrate the integrity of the book and of the award. The defense rests on an unlimited confidence in the child, on the belief that children everywhere are free from the distortions of adults, and on the sincere conviction that the book's detractors—whether professional protesters or fellow human beings angry and suffering—are truly unable to see the work for what it is. Again, will these shadows grow shorter or longer? Can there ever be enough light?

Shadow seen under the bright light of noon has almost no shadow. Perhaps this is how children might see the book—without the shadows cast by all the analyzing done by adults. Yet the meaning, not the print and the pictures, is the life of any book; and this meaning is a mysterious mixture of what is on the page with who we are as readers. There must be, however, both shadows and light if there is to be understanding.

This is a book about shadows and about Africa, but who are the Africans? In *Shadow* they appear as a people of the proverb, living in a land of savannas and forests, sharing a natural world with animals and with spirits. Africans here are still uncorrupted by modernism. There is honesty and wisdom in their lives, integrity in their art, imagination in their oral literature. In *Shadow* Africans are seen as storytellers or as children who listen to the lore of their tribe. Is this not indeed a picture of a fast-vanishing Africa?

But how much can be required of one picture book? All facets of an immense and varied continent cannot be explored in one book. What then about Africa should children be encouraged to see? Is it the Africa that has been despoiled? Is it the Africa that has its own integrity? The Africa that is likely to be received by the mind of the child is the one held by the society in which he or she lives.

If one considers the history of relations between Africa and the Western world since the advent of African slavery in the fourteenth century with its ensuing age of colonialism followed by the present era of Africa as a developing continent in crisis, the resulting images are largely of exploitation—unhealthy both for Africa and for the West. Most people would agree that the past five hundred years have been lived to the great comparative disadvantage of Africa and that in the foreseeable future, Africa is likely to remain at the periphery of and behind the developed West, unless a new set of values emerges. This is the context into which most Western children mature. Every child, if Africa is to be taken seriously, is confronted with making a judgment: either that the West has perpetuated evils in Africa for which it must one day atone, or that what has happened in the past was in some way justified. Both perspectives fall short of the ideals toward which we claim to aspire. Both views may also contribute to the continuing pattern of exploitation, however inadvertently.

Can children's picture books of today help bring into reality the ideals of a just society? Can *Shadow* be regarded as part of the building of a more open, healthy, and accurate view of Africa? I think it can if the image that children retain is one of Africans and Americans seen as closely related parts of the same human family. Real shadows give no clue to the color of their owners.

Herein lies a mission for librarians and for others who have the major responsibility to connect books and children. *Shadow* cannot contribute what it could to the one-world we all seek, if it is promoted primarily as an artistic and a literary statement of American appreciation of things African. The book will have greater value if it can be used to help young readers come to know that Africa, and not only Europe, is America's ancestor and a vital partner in our common future. Such an emphasis might also serve to compensate to some degree for the inevitable commercialization in creating children's picture books on Africa—which the sensitive may well perceive as still another exploitation of things African.

Does all this mean that Africa cannot be written about by nonblacks? Certainly not. But it does suggest that the writers, publishers, and other people who give these books life should expect that they will face difficulties as long as Africa is seen as a shadow separate from themselves. For despite their good intentions, until Westerners truly believe—and act as though they believe—that they have much to learn from Africa, and even that they truly desire to be part African, they will remain open to the charge of fostering stereotypic thinking.

Books about Africa for Western children must convey a sense of a common humanity. *Shadow* seen at high noon has this message to offer. But, surely, as the sun rises and sets, the more distorted shadows of evening and morning are inevitable, and *Shadow* will be seen in different lights. Children know that everybody has a shadow and that all shadows are black. Every book lives its own life. *Shadow*'s shadows have called attention to what that life could be, the nurturing of all children's innate sense of one common humanity. (pp. 621-23)

Elizabeth F. Howard, "Shadows and Marcia Brown's 'Shadow'," in The Horn Book Magazine, *Vol. LIX, No. 5, October, 1983, pp. 621-23.*

Robert (Edmund) Cormier

1925-

American author of fiction and short stories.

Cormier is a distinguished writer of controversial, often pessimistic novels which fearlessly explore the relationship between good and evil. Although his nontraditional subjects and uncompromising treatments keep Cormier's books outside the scope of most adolescent fiction, his honesty, sensitivity, and originality place him in the forefront of authors who write for young people. Centering his plots on outside forces that test and often maliciously oppose the individual, Cormier examines such themes as the misuse of power, the consequences of fanatical patriotism, personal and political corruption, and the victimization of the innocent. His protagonists enter or are forced into situations which pit them against potent adversaries, both identified and faceless. Without help or support, these characters come to the realization—as does Adam Farmer in *I Am the Cheese*—that in order to survive they must learn to stand alone. Cormier's novels are not devoid of violence or brutality, and they often end in death, either literal or implied. This strong realism, combined with Cormier's anti-authoritarian philosophy, has caused some of the novels to be questioned as suitable for school libraries. Formerly a newspaper reporter and human interest columnist, Cormier utilizes topical subjects such as terrorism as the background for his works and often writes in quick, short strokes that emphasize dialogue rather than description. Considered a skillful craftsman, he presents his readers with face-paced, gripping narratives and a clear prose style that relies on strong imagery and employs such literary techniques as interior dialogue, multiple narration, and plot twists. Cormier is best known for his first book for a teenage audience, *The Chocolate War*, which is considered a landmark for its frank depiction of unrelenting evil. Prompted by his son's refusal to sell candy for his high school, *The Chocolate War* uses the format of a school story to probe the issues of betrayal, cruelty, and resistance, themes which also occur in Cormier's later works. The popularity and controversy generated by *The Chocolate War* led him to create a sequel, *Beyond the Chocolate War*, which details further machinations by the sinister Archie Costello, Cormier's most fully realized personification of evil. Although the vision in his novels acknowledges the darker side of human nature, Cormier's attitude is one of awareness of evil rather than agreement with it. A more optimistic tone pervades *Eight Plus One*, a collection of short stories centering on family relationships, and *The Bumblebee Flies Anyway*, a novel depicting a group of terminally ill adolescents who assert some control over their destiny.

Acclaimed as an inventive writer who succeeds in involving young readers in his works, Cormier is praised for the excellence of his plot constructions and characterizations, his use of imagery and detail, and the clarity of his prose. While some reviewers denounce his novels as bleak and fatalistic, most appreciate the sincerity of his approach and the sophistication of his artistry. The esteem with which Cormier is held in young adult literature is perhaps best summarized by Charles Michener: "If any author in the field can challenge J. D. Salinger and William Golding, it is Robert Cormier."

Finkle Photography. Courtesy of Robert Cormier.

The Chocolate War won the Lewis Carroll Shelf Award in 1979. In addition to several adult- and child-selected awards, Cormier received the 1983 ALAN Award from the Assembly on Literature for Adolescents, National Council of Teachers of English, for his body of work.

(See also *Contemporary Literary Criticism*, Vols. 12, 30; *Something about the Author*, Vols. 10, 45; *Contemporary Authors New Revision Series*, Vol. 5; and *Contemporary Authors*, Vols. 1-4, rev. ed.)

GENERAL COMMENTARY

STANLEY ELLIN

In two justly admired novels, *The Chocolate War* and *I Am the Cheese*, Robert Cormier has dealt with the betrayal of youth, creating landscapes familiar but unnervingly strange—as in a de Chirico painting—in which one sees a boy in mid-adolescence, exceptionally decent and sensitive, standing alone as invisible forces gather against him.

The betrayals themselves, perpetrated by the elders who were by nature designed to be the boy's strength and support, are breaches of trust that lead to the extinction of trust and the spirit it fires. Parents, teachers, mentors, Mr. Cormier makes plain, can each have their own self-serving need to manipulate the young people in their charge, and when they act on that need the consequences can be deadly.

Presented in narrow focus, never moralizing, written in a lean and graphic prose that creates great tension, the novels provided an experience that this reader cannot shake off. The images and ethical questions they raised are still fresh and troubling; and provided an emotional background for the reading of Mr. Cormier's new book, *After the First Death*.

Here, fixing on the same theme of betrayal, the author widens his focus. A busload of small children on their way to a New England day camp is hijacked by a gang of what we may surmise from the few clues offered is one of the more blood-thirsty adjuncts of the Palestine Liberation Organization. From different points of view we watch the events, minute by minute, until the climax; the pressure mounts steadily until it seems enough to blow the eardrums.

Ben Marchand, in his mid-teens, is our protagonist; his father, Gen. Mark Marchand, is commander of the forces called out against the terrorists. And playing pivotal roles are Miro, an adolescent member of the terrorist gang on his first mission, his test of manhood, and Kate Forrester, the driver of the bus, no more than a schoolgirl herself, and one of Mr. Cormier's more appealing creations.

We move deep into the minds of each of them, but it is Ben whose story this is and whose role gives the book its true meaning. Ben is doubly a victim: first of the event itself, then, even more tragically, of mystifying events behind the event. The adults in whose orbits he moves have their own desperate needs, and no matter what side they are on and no matter how fervently they believe that they act only to create a world fit for their children, it is their children that they sacrifice to the process.

In this small epic of terrorism and counter-terrorism and their consequences, Mr. Cormier pulls no punches. The brutality is all there, the intimations of sexuality in the young, the sour judgments of values by their elders, whose values have been rotted by political cant—all are presented without sermonizing in a marvelously told story. *After the First Death* more than sustains the reputation its author has won with *The Chocolate War* and *I Am the Cheese;* it adds luster to it.

Putting all three books together, one disturbing aspect becomes clear: Their basic theme, no matter how brilliant the variations on it, suggests unrelieved despair. The world of Mr. Cormier's people is a Dantean Inferno without any hint of Purgatorio or Paradiso. This is, of course, an antidote to the mindless Happy Ending school of literature but, like most such medicine, it does leave a bitter taste in the mouth. (pp. 30-1)

> *Stanley Ellin "You Can and Can't Go Home Again: 'After the First Death',"* in The New York Times Book Review, *April 29, 1979, pp. 30-1.*

TONY SCHWARTZ

[*After the First Death* is] a marvelous story, written in crackling prose. . . . It deals thoughtfully with not only the topical issue of terrorism but power and its abuses, loyalty and betrayal, courage and fear. . . .

[If the genre of young adult fiction] has one best-selling heavy-weight writer, an equivalent to Saul Bellow or William Styron, he is Robert Cormier, author of *After the First Death* and two other critically acclaimed young-adult novels whose tough-minded grimness would make most adult readers squirm. But not teen-agers. (p. 87)

It is Cormier's hard-hitting unsentimentality that most sets him apart from other writers in his field, and some critics complain that he goes too far. Several years ago, *Booklist,* an official publication of the American Library Association, felt compelled to run an unprecedented black-bordered review attacking *The Chocolate War* for its violence and downbeat ending [see excerpt dated July 1, 1974 for *The Chocolate War* (1974)]. But Cormier makes no apologies. "As long as what I write is true and believable, why should I have to create happy endings? My books are an antidote to the TV view of life, where even in a suspenseful show you know before the last commercial that Starsky and Hutch will get their man. That's phony realism. Life just isn't like that." (pp. 87-8)

> *Tony Schwartz, "Teen-Agers' Laureate," in* News-week, *Vol. XCIV, No. 3, July 16, 1979, pp. 87-8, 92.*

DAVID REES

[*The Chocolate War*] is, on the surface, a political book. It is about power, power structures, corruption—about how absolute power corrupts absolutely. But, more subtly, beneath the surface, it is about compromise and the choice between hunting with the pack or searching for strength as an individual: about the toughness needed in the struggle to be a successful outsider. Jerry Renault, the central character, is a fascinating and complex creation, considerably more ambiguous than he initially appears to be. One may like him up to a point, and admire his heroic, if futile, refusal to join in the attempts that Brother Leon has organized to raise funds for his school by the sale of the chocolates. There is a strong temptation on the reader's part to identify with him, to agree with his version of events: but it's a temptation that should be resisted. There is much that is not admirable about Jerry Renault. His weakness is an overriding passion to conform to a conventional teenage image of machismo, which is seen mostly in his desire to become an admired member of the football team—looked up to, respected, a boy with a niche in society. He doesn't have any realization that such values are false; that conventional respect from others is no measure of real worth. A similar falseness exists in his attitude to the opposite sex; he wants a relationship with a girl not because it may be more interesting and satisfying than a friendship with another boy, but because

> The one devastating sorrow he carried within him was the fear that he would die before holding a girl's breast in his hand.

He is not the stuff of which heroes are made, and his final compromise is not the gesture of despair that some critics have suggested, but entirely characteristic:

> He had to tell Goober to play ball, to play football, to run, to make the team, to sell the chocolates, to sell whatever they wanted you to sell, to do whatever they wanted you to do. . . . Don't disturb the universe, Goober, no matter what the posters say.

His stand against selling the chocolates is an aberration, quite uncharacteristic of him, and it is interesting that Cormier does not give the reader an adequate explanation for Jerry's decision to opt out in this matter. Goober is much more naturally an outsider type than Jerry, and though his appearance in the book is disappointingly fleeting, Cormier would have manufactured a much less worthwhile novel if he had made Goober the central character for it would have become a rather conventional struggle between good and evil.

The Chocolate War is not an entirely satisfactory book. Goober is not the only person left undeveloped; the author shows us the thinking processes of too many of his characters, and he flits more rapidly than he should from one to another; the writing is at times too purple, especially in the scenes of physical violence. One wonders if the author may be enjoying these scenes a little, and, I feel, he may also share Jerry's belief in a false idea of masculine value. . . . The evil characters, Archie and Brother Leon, are so one-dimensionally villainous that they are no more than caricatures. They present a considerable threat to the reader's ability to believe in the reality of what he is being told. But the central theme—to conform or not to conform—is handled with great skill, and the book's message is more subtle than it seems: Cormier is not saying that the might of evil institutions inevitably corrupts good people, but that the desire to be accepted is a major weakness which can easily be exploited by the wicked. *The Chocolate War* is a very popular book with teenagers in England as well as in America, and on the whole deservedly so.

There is little obvious compromise in *I Am the Cheese,* for political power and corruption are not illustrated in this book through the world of school life, but by the power of the government itself, and Cormier's message here is much more bleak: that the stand of one or two individuals against the whole apparatus of government is hopeless. Adam, the central character, is someone we might find in many novels for young adults, a teenager who is struggling to find—on many levels—who he is and what his place in the world should be. We see his first meaningful love affair and we explore the complexities of his feelings for his parents; but what makes Adam's situation different from that of the hero in almost all teenage fiction is that the reader knows, at the end of the book, that he is going to die; either he will be "terminated" as his parents were, or the treatment he is receiving in a psychiatric hospital will "obliterate" him. Complaints by critics that the hopelessness of *I Am the Cheese* is inappropriate to a story for young people are not justifiable in my opinion; there is no good reason why a teenage novel should not express total despair: the young do not have to be protected in this way. And there are parts of this novel which, by any standards, are far from hopeless—Adam's relationship with his father, for example, is a rare thing in today's fiction for the young: there is love, care, thoughtfulness, and admiration on both sides. Indeed it is a model of what such relationships should be, despite the evidence presented in too many novels.

The writing is excellent throughout; none of the faults that mar *The Chocolate War* are to be seen in *I Am the Cheese.* The prose has a very positive sound to it; an appealing music in its cadences; an appropriateness in its images:

> So they drove and his father recited some fragments of Thomas Wolfe, about October and the tumbling leaves of bitter red, or yellow leaves like living light, and Adam was sad again, thinking of his father as a writer and how his life had changed, how it had become necessary for him to give up all that and become another person altogether, how all of them had become other persons, his father, his mother, and himself. Paul Delmonte, poor lost Paul Delmonte.

In such a passage as this is the kind of compromise that is not obvious, because it lies beneath the surface of the narrative: Adam sadly accepting that the fugitive existence to which he and his parents have been reduced is inevitable. *I Am the Cheese* is a much better book than *The Chocolate War;* the explanations revealed at the end are quite shattering, and the author's skill in concealing them until this point is immense. The structure, in fact, is very satisfying throughout. Technical expertise and the quality of the writing are of equal merit. It's a pity that it is not as widely read as *The Chocolate War,* but the reason is easy to see: it's much more difficult, requiring a quite different order of intelligence in the reader.

After the First Death has the same skills as *I Am the Cheese;* tension, conveyed fear, ability to write a narrative so exciting that the reader is gripped completely, but it is not a book that breaks new ground or that extends Cormier's range. It is undoubtedly very good, probably the best of the spate of novels about terrorism and hi-jacking that have appeared in recent years. . . . Where it scores higher than similar stories do is in the exploration of the weaknesses of the victims—the General's willingness to put country before family even when he knows it will destroy his son's self-respect; Kate Forrester's realization that her only weapon in the struggle is to use her sexual attractiveness; Ben's inability to come to terms with both his own supposed cowardice and the fact that his father has cold-bloodedly exploited that cowardice as a pawn in the bargaining game with the hi-jackers. Once again, the young—Kate, Ben, and the sixteen-year-old terrorist, Miro—are forced to compromise. Some of them, Cormier suggests, can survive with their integrity intact: Kate does so (though minutes later she is killed) and the new aspects of himself that Miro discovers are rapidly suppressed, so strong is the power of his upbringing. Yet Ben goes under, irrevocably maimed, and in him lies the real tragedy of the story: compromise totally destroys him.

Cormier, in this novel, questions some fundamental beliefs—the commonplace views of patriotism, of cowardice and courage, of the expectations of both parties in father-son relationships. (Miro's relationship with Artkin exactly parallels that of Ben and his father, and all four are seen to be guilty of false assumptions about the nature of such relationships—assumptions that are the products of conditioning and prove inadequate when put to the test.) Very interesting, too, is his suggestion that although innocence in itself is good and valuable, it is a severely limited concept—dangerous and even outrageous. . . . (pp. 156-60)

How good a novelist is Cormier? His work is greeted with almost hysterical praise by reviewers. He is compared with Bellow, Styron, Salinger, Golding; it's almost as if critics had never before seen real talent in authors of young adult novels. The comparisons do not hold up, of course. Consider his work and that of Saul Bellow and Cormier is seen at once to have obvious limitations, particularly in the narrowness of his chosen area, for the situations in his books are always extreme: no one is ever observed in the middle of the processes of ordinary living. The relationships he writes about are also limited, indeed repetitive—father and son, manipulator and pawn. Kate is the only female character in the three books who is explored in depth. The themes of *After the First Death* are much the same as *I Am the Cheese* and *The Chocolate War*—the corruptness of authoritarian institutions and people; the violence and destruction they engender. The most disappointing characteristic of *After the First Death* is that, though remarkably well done, it appears to be going over the same ground again.

Nor is there a feeling in his work . . . of the immense variety and richness of human experience, for while the dramas and tragedies he writes of are, to say the least, unusual, they are certainly not those that the vast majority of people will experience in the course of a lifetime. Good, yes: he *is* a very good writer: but it is far too soon to reach for superlatives of praise. (p. 161)

David Rees, ''The Sadness of Compromise: Robert Cormier and Jill Chaney,'' in his The Marble in the Water: Essays on Contemporary Writers of Fiction for Children and Young Adults, *The Horn Book, Inc., 1980, pp. 155-72.*

ANNE SCOTT MacLEOD

Robert Cormier is a conspicuous oddity in his chosen field. Writing for the adolescent reader, he has departed from standard models and broken some of the most fundamental taboos of that vocation. Each of his hard-edged novels for the young goes considerably beyond the standard limits of ''contemporary realism'' to describe a world of painful harshness, where choices are few and consequences desperate. Moreover, his novels are unequivocally downbeat; [*The Chocolate War, I Am the Cheese,* and *After the First Death*] violate the unwritten rule that fiction for the young, however sternly realistic the narrative material, must offer some portion of hope, must end at least with some affirmative message. Affirmation is hard to find in Cormier's work, and conventional hopefulness is quite irrelevant to it.

But while these sharp breaks with accepted practice have been much noted by reviewers, and have furnished Cormier's reputation for bleakness, curiously little notice has been taken of another, and, to my mind, equally interesting departure from the norm in his novels. Quite aside from his attitudes and conclusions, Cormier is a maverick in the field of adolescent literature because he is writing what are, at bottom, political novels. George Orwell once claimed that there is no such thing as a ''genuinely nonpolitical literature,'' but the dictum seems to me inapplicable to most writing for young adults. A consistent feature of almost the whole body of adolescent literature is its isolation from the political and societal, its nearly total preoccupation with personality. The typical adolescent novel is wrapped tightly around the individual and the personal; questions of psychological development and personal morality dominate the genre. In fact, most authors of adolescent literature seem to take for their model adolescents themselves, with their paramount interest in self, individual morality, interior change, and personality.

Cormier, on the other hand, is far more interested in the systems by which a society operates than he is in individuals. His novels center on the interplay between individuals and their context, between the needs and demands of the system and the needs and rights of individuals—in other words, on the political context in which his characters, like all of us, must live. He is, obviously, concerned with moral questions, but the morality involved is of a wholly different order from the purely personal moral concerns of most teen novels.

Cormier's political cast of mind explains the relative unimportance of characterization in his work. Inner character is less to him than situation. In *Chocolate War,* for example, the wellsprings of Archie's evil are never adequately explained, and Jerry's motivation for his lonely rebellion, while plausible enough, is not dwelt upon at any great length. Certainly it is not the centerpiece of the narrative, as it would be in most teen novels. Adam, of *I Am the Cheese,* is more a victim than

a protagonist. If we care about what happens to him, it is not because of any crucial internal decision he must make, but precisely because he is the helpless victim of processes he cannot affect, let alone control, and because we recognize the circumstances of his tragedy as part of the world we actually live in. In *After the First Death,* characterization is again—as several critics have complained—clearly secondary to the situation set out in the novel, and to Cormier's view of the commitments and choices that have brought about that situation.

The book that has drawn the most critical attention is *Chocolate War,* possibly because it was the first, perhaps because its statement of defeat is explicit and made by the protagonist, or maybe simply because it is hard to recognize until the end just how shatteringly this novel differs from others of its genre. It looks, after all, like a school story, about school boys, and can be read just that way—in which case the unhappy comment by several reviewers about its negativism is understandable. But of course *Chocolate War* has another life outside its familiar form: it is a metaphor, a parable of political evil and a small manual on the sources and uses of political power.

The evil in *Chocolate War* is initiated by individuals, but not contained in them. Archie and Brother Leon are manipulators: Archie manipulates the Vigils, Brother Leon manipulates his students; together, during the chocolate sale, they manipulate the whole school. Yet neither could work his will without the cooperation of others. The acquiescence of the community is essential to their power, as the classroom scene makes clear. In an episode that is a virtual cliche in school stories, Brother Leon singles out a student for torment, accusing him of cheating, mocking and humiliating him, while the rest of the class laughs uncomfortably. If this were all, the scene would simply establish (without much originality) that Brother Leon is the kind of teacher who abuses the power of his position for some private satisfaction. But Cormier's interest here is not really Brother Leon, still less the reasons for his abuse of position. What he wants to demonstrate is the source of the power, which is, of course, the students themselves. The harassment goes on exactly as long as the class lets it; when at last one student speaks up in mild protest, the spell breaks. And it is Brother Leon himself who points the moral, asking contemptuously why no one had objected sooner, suggesting the parallel with Nazi Germany.

Still, the message of the novel as a whole is neither so simple nor so hopeful as the episode might imply. If it were, then Jerry's lone dissent would succeed, would break the combined power of Archie and Brother Leon—and would place the novel squarely in the long American tradition of the triumphant lonely hero tale. Instead, there is that final scene which laid the cornerstone of Cormier's reputation for bleakness: Jerry carried away on a stretcher, his face too battered to allow him to speak the message he wants to convey to Goober:

> . . . to play ball, to play football, to have fun,
> to make the team, to sell chocolates . . . to do
> whatever they [want] you to do. . . .

The lone dissent has not only failed, it is repudiated. The American Adam is brought low; Huck Finn turns Jim over to the slave-catchers, Gary Cooper lies in his own blood in the street at high noon—no wonder the reviewers gasped. In one brief, bitter paragraph, Cormier has abandoned an enduring American myth to confront his teenaged readers with life as it more often is—with the dangers of dissent, the ferocity of systems as they protect themselves, the power of the pressure to conform.

In his second novel, *I Am the Cheese,* Cormier dispenses with metaphor. This stark tale comments directly on the real world of government, organized crime, large-scale bureaucracy, the apparatus of control, secrecy, betrayal, and all the other commonplaces of contemporary political life. Its message is, if possible, even less ambiguous than *Chocolate War*'s. The most optimistic reader will find it hard to locate an exit as the story moves to a conclusion. Adam is doomed, as his parents were; he will be "obliterated" one way or another because he is a threat to one or possibly to both of the systems with which his life is entangled. There is certainly some ambiguity about the role played in this tragedy by Mr. Grey, supposedly the family's government protector. Might he have been instead their betrayer? Which side did he really work for? As the narrative rolls coldly on, it occurs to the reader that it hardly matters. And this is clearly Cormier's point. The two systems are equally impersonal, and equally dangerous to the human being caught between them. What matters to the organization—*either* organization—is its own survival, not Adam's.

I Am the Cheese is the most Kafka-esque of Cormier's three novels. The narrative technique, combined with a nearly overwhelming sense of loneliness, helplessness, and hopelessness give the novel a surreal quality. When his parents are murdered, Adam is left in a world empty of human figures; he has only memories of those few he has loved and lost. It is as though he were alone in a computer room where every machine is programmed to cancel him out; he is like a mouse in a maze, searching for an opening, unaware that every exit has been blocked. The language of the "psychiatrist's" reports, bleached of emotional accuracy, underlies the impersonal, bureaucratic character of Adam's cold enemies. And when Adam's trip to Vermont is revealed for what it is, a bicycle ride within the fenced grounds of the institution where he is confined, the sense of nightmare recalls Kafka's terrifying world.

After the First Death both reiterates and extends concepts found in the earlier books. The plot is built around an episode of political terrorism—the ultimate weapon of an outnumbered dissident group—directed against the technically superior, equally purposeful security apparatus of the established government. In the course of the story, Cormier explores the outer limits of patriotism and the inner perception of fanaticism. Here, as in the first two novels, Cormier shows privileged position and privileged information used to manipulate the weak and the unwary. Here, as in *I Am the Cheese,* the discussion of political evil is cast in fiercely contemporary terms, and the shadow of statism stretches long over the narrative.

One episode brings into sharp focus concepts central to this novel and also, I think, to Cormier's general outlook. The scene takes place between Miro, the young terrorist, and Kate, the girl who is to become Miro's "first death." The tentative human relationship created between them when Kate encourages Miro to talk about his past dissolves abruptly when Kate recognizes the depth and the terrible simplicity of Miro's dedication to his political purpose. For the sake of a country he has never seen, and never really expects to see, Miro has made himself into an instrument of guerrilla warfare. Save for his mentor, Artkin, he has no connection with the actual world of human life, nor does he expect any. He envisions no future for himself, takes no interest in his own qualities except as they make him an efficient weapon in a struggle whose political terms he cannot possibly know. He has no feeling for the

innocent victims, past or potential, of the undeclared "war" he wages; indeed, he cannot even understand what it is Kate expects him to feel for them. In short, as Kate realizes with shock, he is "a monster." Not only monstrous, Miro is innocent as well:

> The greatest horror of all was that he did not know he was a monster. He had looked at her with innocent eyes as he told her of killing people. She'd always thought of innocence as something good, something to cherish. People mourned the death of innocence . . . But innocence, she saw now, could also be evil. Monstrous. . . .

The attitude toward innocence explicitly expressed in this passage seems to me to underlie all three of Cormier's books and goes far to explain his break with prevailing standards for adolescent novels. Like Kate, most literature for the young has assumed that innocence, particularly in the young, is desirable, and that its loss is a regrettable, if inevitable, part of the transition from childhood to adult life. The celebration of innocence is a romantic attitude, of course, and one that has been losing ground, even in children's literature, for many decades. But Cormier is forcing the pace considerably in his work and it is political, rather than personal innocence that he is talking about. He is saying that political innocence is a dangerous quality, that it can be a kind of collaboration with evil, that innocence is often acquiescence through moral neutrality in the abuse of power by the powerful, and in the sacrifice of the individual to the political organization.

In his novel, Miro's awful innocence has a parallel in the other "monster" of the story, Ben's father, General Marchand. Like the terrorists, the General has dedicated his life to the service of his country; like Artkin, he has extended his own commitment to his son's life, which becomes forfeit to the State's needs. General Marchand has had his son observed, recorded, and cataloged throughout his developing years, so that he is able to predict Ben's behavior under any circumstances. As the dangerous game begun by the terrorists comes to a climax, the General uses that accumulated knowledge of Ben's strengths and weaknesses—uses Ben, in fact, as a pawn to win the game, and so destroys him.

One may reject the basic assumption behind this phase of the story—that it is possible to reduce a human being to an entirely predictable quantity—but I think that this is not really Cormier's main point. The point here, with the General, as with Miro, is the consequences of a surrender of moral will to the abstract concept of patriotism which General Marchand describes as "sweet and pure and unquestioning." . . . The point is the General's willingness first to subject a human being to secret scrutiny and then to use him as though he were but one more instrument in the governmental arsenal. The fact that the human being so used is the General's son underscores the monstrousness of the action; that the General suffers doubt and remorse afterward emphasizes the political, as opposed to the purely personal, aspects of the father's choices. He does what he does, not because he hates his son, or is indifferent to him, nor because of some destructive psychological flaw in his own personality, but because he, as much as Artkin or Miro, has given himself wholly—"innocently"—to the service of the State.

The parallels are clear throughout. The detached professionalism of the terrorists is not different from the General's; Marchand himself acknowledges that "they are professionals just as I am a professional." . . . The coldness with which Artkin murders a child or tortures a boy is neither more nor less monstrous than Marchand's choice of Ben for the mission on the bridge, or his calculated anticipation and use of Ben's break under torture: "Expediency is the rule." . . . The violence initiated by the terrorists is matched by the equally violent response of the government, and the children are the victims of both. "Perhaps," says Artkin, "they [Americans] cherish their children more than their agencies." But they do not. No wonder Artkin and the General "recognized each other." . . . (pp. 74-9)

Here again, the questions raised are not primarily concerned with personal morality. When is it that such men as Artkin and Miro and Marchand becomes monsters? It is not when they murder or lie or torture, but earlier, at the point where they make the initial choice to surrender their moral will to the State. They disavow their humanity in the same moment that they seal their innocence by choosing never to question nor even to contemplate questioning. Cormier makes it abundantly clear that, in the political context they have accepted, the General's decisions and Artkin's are not only logical, they are correct. It is humanly that the choices are monstrous. Ben's suicide, Raymond's murder, and Kate's death are Cormier's comment on the human cost of political abstraction; in the end, he tells us, the price is often paid by those who have been given no choice in the matter.

Cormier's teen novels are not "great books"; I doubt that they will outlast their topical relevance. But they are important books just the same. Cormier writes of things few books for the young acknowledge at all. He has evoked a political world in which evil is neither an individual phenomenon nor a personality fault explainable by individual psychology, but a collaborative act between individuals and political systems which begins when the individual gives over to the system the moral responsiblity that is part of being human. He suggests that innocence can be a moral defect, that evil is . . . banal, and, above all, that political bureaucracies are often—perhaps always—a potential danger to individual freedom because they are fundamentally committed to their own perpetuation, which is always threatened by individual dissent.

These are aspects of contemporary reality not often set out in literature for the young, as the reactions of many reviewers attest. Yet the young are not immune to political reality. Far from it, they are its chief inheritors. Though it may be true—it undoubtedly *is* true—that adolescents are primarily interested in themselves, it does not follow that adults who write for the adolescent readers must share this narrow preoccupation. All of us, including the young, live in a political as well as a personal world. We are not safer for ignoring it.

Surely, if message there is in Cormier's work, this is the most insistent. I cannot discover that he wants to tell his readers that by recognizing their dangers they can escape them, and I do not think his books can be reduced to a positive statement about the protective virtue of political understanding. "Know your world and you will be safe" is far too bald and optimistic. Put negatively, the proposition may come a little closer; "what you fail to understand about your world can destroy you, either literally or as a human being." Certainly these novels suggest that no one will escape who does not know where the threat lies, how the annihilating process works.

Neither the issues Cormier poses nor the answers he implies belong to the same moral world as the themes of adjustment, acceptance, and understanding that undergird most adolescent fiction. Instead, his work opens again the complex questions of the function of literature and of whether that function varies with the age of the intended reader. Cormier's three adolescent novels answer for him. . . . (pp. 79-80)

Anne Scott MacLeod "Robert Cormier and the Adolescent Novel," in Children's literature in education, *Vol. 12, No. 2 (Summer), 1981, pp. 74-81.*

REBECCA LUKENS

Chronicling the quest of Holden Caulfield for people and experience that could verify his most optimistic wishes [in *The Catcher in the Rye* (1951)], Salinger shows the growing disappointment as Holden finds many of his idols standing upon feet of clay. And yet Salinger's hero, although he writes from a sanitarium, becomes a realist. Many of his idols have fallen, and his quest for perfection has left him with only ten-year-old Phoebe, whose innocence is still inviolate. But Holden will work himself out of his depression; by novel's end he is rising from it. His self-told story shows that within himself are the seeds of good. If there are others like him—and his millions of readers over thirty years prove that to be true—the world cannot be all bad.

Robert Cormier, on the other hand, begins from quite another premise. The world is rotten; the honest people flee; those who remain are corrupt; the government is ineffectual but controlling; organized violence is ubiquitous. There is no hope. Between 1951 and 1974 the world-view in popular literature flipped; it has gone from realistic *bildungsroman* showing youth's awakening awareness of evil, as Young Goodman Brown and Redburn discovered it, to another world view: The pervasive forces of the unseen and the sinister are in control. Hope is gone; despair remains. (p. 38)

Brutality opens Cormier's novel [*The Chocolate War*], and it crescendoes to unbelievable heights in the final beating. It envelops adult and adolescent; it shows no one with strength sufficient to withstand evil.

The source of the novel's conflict is, or seems to be, Jerry's wish to hold out against The Vigils, to disturb the universe by resisting evil. The real protagonist in the novel, however, is not Jerry but the villain Archie. By skillful use of omniscient point of view, Cormier makes us see Archie's compulsion to keep himself on top. To forestall his own defeat and to retain control of The Vigils and thus of the school, Archie must concoct one more, and one more vicious scheme. Archie must create the terror-producing plans, plans that use his club members for evil, then turn back upon them so that no one can win—save Archie. (p. 39)

In payment for his obstinate refusal to sell chocolates, Jerry suffers. In scrimmage, when he makes his assigned tackle and gets Carter, he suffers a blinding blow to the kidneys. To the macho society of Trinity School, the ultimate disgrace is to be called a fairy, and this Jerry suffers, too. At Archie's charge, Emile enlists the neighborhood children, a ruthless gang of evil tots; wanting to kill him, to blind him, they pile into Jerry, kicking him in the groin. Children, too, are corrupt and ruthless; they join the attack as hired assassins. Archie's Vigils will not suffer disobedience or defiance. They make silent phone calls to Jerry all night long. They call out to him, evening phantoms on the street. They destroy and clean out Jerry's locker so that he does not exist. Ignored by students and faculty alike, he is nothing, no one.

The violence and brutality of the chocolate raffle and the rigged fight conclude the bitter novel. What The Vigils have done to the school and to Jerry, "they would do to the world when they left Trinity.". . . Greed and cruelty—the chance to win a hundred dollars and to see a bloody fight—control everyone. "That's why it works . . . because we're all bastards," . . . explains Archie. Finally even Jerry, the last holdout against evil, strikes out furiously and illegally in the ring at Emile in a "beautiful" blow. He is invaded by a "new sickness . . . of knowing what he had become, another animal, not disturbing the universe, but damaging it. He had allowed Archie to do this to him.". . . (pp. 39-40)

If *The Chocolate War* had not ended with Jerry's defeat but with the banishment of Brother Leon or The Vigils, or with an uprising that set things at least into a neutral or holding pattern, it would not end in despair. Instead, in the final pages of the novel Jerry wishes he could tell Goober "Don't try to disturb the universe. You can't." Brother Leon, who to serve himself manipulates kids and other priests, remains in power. There is no hope. Despair wins.

In 1977 Cormier added to this tale of terror a second novel, *I Am the Cheese*. . . . In a complexity of three interwoven levels, Cormier weaves a story of a boy's psychological search for his father with his search into his memories of the past. The novel revolves and circles in Adam's continuous and frustrating struggle to remember, mingled with fear of remembering. His search for his dead father cannot end; the novel opens and closes with the same paragraph: "I am riding the bicycle and I am on Route 31 . . . on my way to Rutterburg, Vermont . . . the wind like a snake slithering up my sleeves . . . But I keep pedaling, I keep pedaling." The circular movement of the novel is like "The Farmer in the Dell," the child's continuous and circular game. Throughout the story Adam, his father, and his mother sing the song, calling it the Farmer family's own song. The last verse is not sung until the final pages when psychologically damaged Adam, orphaned by the violent gangland murder of both his father and his mother, sings the last lines: "The cheese stands alone. . . . I am the cheese."

Early in the fantasy of Adam's search for his father, he hears that "it's a terrible world out there. Murder and assassinations.". . . Such fears are only the beginning; they are followed by paranoiac fear of someone's stealing his bike, of homosexual overtures, of careening cars, of his mother's Never Knows, of a bomb on the accelerator, of strange voices that answer Amy Hertz's telephone. Endless fears. Throughout Adam's fantasies and memories run recollections of Amy's mindless mischief as cheerfully unmotivated as the violence of the young thugs and as unpredictable as Mr. Grey's comings, goings, and plans. Not until the final pages do we know that suspicious Mr. Grey is a legitimate government agent whose real task is to relocate prime witnesses.

The enigma of the novel is how much does Adam Farmer, once Paul Delmonte, know about his past, and more importantly, who needs to find out—Adam or the government. Adam's father, an investigative reporter, has uncovered important evidence of corruption and been given a new identity; the family has been relocated and lives in fear of discovery. Adam learns his parents' secret and must become a stranger to his school world. The normal reticence and isolation of adolescence are exacerbated by fear and puzzlement, then by distrust of Mr. Grey, and by absolute terror of attacking dogs and predatory young loafers. As the story moves back and forth between Adam's bicycle ride through his fantasy and his dia-

logue with the psychiatrist, we are exposed to the actual events of his life in immediate narrative. At the novel's end we discover that Adam is not being psychologically healed after all. The interrogation which seems at times humane and therapeutic is merely politically expedient.

The reader's puzzlement carries the novel along; our fears are never allayed. Adam Farmer/Paul Delmonte will never be able to live free of the annual interrogation, or to move outside the sanitarium walls. The disturbed adolescent who loves Amy Hertz and wants to love her forever is the same dependent child who clutches his stuffed animal, Poley the Pig. The government is vigilant; should Adam remember all and so be healed, he becomes dangerous. In the clinical records we see that Grey, Adam, his father and his mother are all merely numbers. No matter how healthy he might become, Adam will never be able to untangle himself from the maze of regulation and red tape. In his fantasy Adam continues his search for his father and keeps pedaling, keeps pedaling. In reality, he is only a series of digits in a government file.

The effect upon the reader is not merely fear, but often sheer terror—terror not only of cars and dogs and secret agents and theft and homosexual invitation, but of the endlessly connected underworld and of uncontrollable impulses to speak the forbidden or to discover what must be left undiscovered. Again Cormier has written skillfully, with plausible happenings and shocking attacks on the reader's sensibilities. The effect once again is that life is filled with sinister elements—government-related at that. There is no hope for the honest citizen in today's society. The forces of evil prevail, and despair is the winner.

Cormier's third novel, *After the First Death* . . . , is another skillfully written narrative. This time Cormier poses two father and son combinations against each other, one ostensibly the good guys and the other the bad guys. As this tale unfolds, commitment to patriotism results in the suicide of the good-guy son and the assassination of the bad-guy father. Our sympathies lie with the American general and his victim son, and yet the sacrifice of that son to the good of the state is no more admirable than the comparable sacrifice made by father and son on the other side of the conflict. Subtly, with all his artistry in building plot and portraying character in a brilliant style, Cormier once again gives us a sinister world. This time it is not the microcosm of a school dominated by evil in *The Chocolate War*, or of a wider American world controlled by the mobs in *I Am the Cheese*, but the international macrocosm of terrorism motivated by patriotism. (pp. 39-40, 42)

Within the novel are several significant statements about values and motives, and questions about commitment and sacrifice. For example, suspicious Artkin hearing that General Marchand will send his own son on the dangerous assignment of emissary to the bus controlled by the terrorists, asks "Who knows about Americans? Perhaps they cherish their children more than their agencies?". . . Who knows? Perhaps. Not so. On the wireless Artkin and his counterpart General Marchand speak of the General's generous offer of his son. Artkin says, "Either you are a great patriot or a great fool." Ben's father thinks that Artkin knows

> exactly what I was. What I am. Just as I knew exactly what he was and to what lengths he would go. We knew each other across the chasm; we had recognized each other across the ravine, although we had never met. . . .

The two fathers are the same breed. Again, reminiscing about World War II, Ben's father speaks silently to Ben.

> We were poorly trained in those days, Ben, but trained superbly in one thing: patriotism. There are all kinds of patriotism; ours was pure and sweet and unquestioning. We were the good guys. Today there is patriotism, of course. . . . But this generation looks at itself in a mirror as it performs its duties. And wonders: Who are the good guys? Is it possible we are the bad guys? They should never ask that question, Ben, or even contemplate it. . . .

General Marchand advocates blind obedience to patriotic duty; it kills his son. Similar blind obedience to patriotic duty motivates Artkin as he trains his boy to torture and to murder.

We have always had tales of terror. For generations American adolescents have thrilled and chilled to Poe's gruesome and yet fanciful tales of men and women laughing diabolically at their systems for perpetrating a living death. Poe's characters, however, are mad, insane; readers marvel at Poe's ingenuity. George Orwell in *1984* creates another tale of terror, this time of a political stranglehold on people's lives. But in the allegorical style of the novel, this is a totalitarian state with language and institutions unlike our own. By using an unemotional narrator who reports happenings in a country different from our own, where an abstraction called Big Brother represents institutional surveillance, Orwell creates distance and objectivity. As for adolescent protagonists, William Golding's *Lord of the Flies* has Ralph who opposes Jack, reason and humanity opposing impulse and violence. Although oblivious to any comment on original sin, readers are struck by their own capacities to relate to both Ralph and Jack and are thus frightened at the potential for savagery they detect in themselves. But the fantasy island setting in a remote time permits readers at least to hope that in the here-and-now *they* would not behave with savagery.

Poe, Orwell, and Golding permit us to discover and to contemplate the evil sides of society and ourselves, to search within for the source and the placement of our sympathies, and to hope that we can withstand. Cormier, on the other hand, takes another view. He does not deal with the existential *angst* of humankind—the eternal issue. The immediacy of Cormier's situations, the feeling of "today," the skillfully portrayed reality of the particular evils in the "now," produce terror in the reader. Like Salinger, Cormier disillusions the adolescent reader, but unlike Salinger who offers discovery, Cormier offers only despair. (p. 42)

> *Rebecca Lukens, "From Salinger to Cormier: Disillusionment to Despair in Thirty Years," in* The ALAN Review, *Vol. 9, No. 1, Fall, 1981, pp. 38-40, 42.*

ROGER SUTTON

Cormier has, to my mind, unreasonably become a symbol for all that is good and bad in adolescent literature. His books are certainly not typical of the New Realism, for two reasons. They have unhappy endings and, as Anne MacLeod has noted [see excerpt dated 1981], his books do not concern "the individual and the personal," do not concern themselves for the most part with "psychological development and personal morality," a major preoccupation of typical realistic novels for teens. Yet, Betsy Hearne cited *The Chocolate War* . . . as indicative of a "trend of didactic negativity," Donelson and

Nilsen call the same novel a "touchstone example of the problem novel," and Rebecca Lukens, using Cormier as her example, claims that "the world-view in popular literature has flipped," to a view in which "the pervasive forces of the unseen and the sinister are in control" [see excerpt dated 1981].

Cormier's three novels for adolescents all tell compellingly of a universe where the good guys lose. But under the grim, no-win surface lies a very conventional, respectable morality: wrong may triumph over right, but the reader is certainly shown which is which.

Jerry, in *The Chocolate War,* refuses to sell candy for the parochial school fund drive. He is the only student who won't, and in the end he is brutally beaten in a rigged fight witnessed by the entire school. Jerry, the good guy, loses. He goes down fighting, though, and his defeat only shows more clearly the difference between him and the bad guys, who can triumph only through the use of physical force. This is a very simple book: Readers know who to root for all the way. What if, though, Jerry gave in and became the best chocolate salesman of them all? This kind of ironic sophistication, while commonplace in fiction for adults, is absent from Cormier's work and from adolescent literature in general.

When adolescent novels do trade in tragedy, they do so in a very safe way, encouraging readers to identify with an innocent protagonist. All of Cormier's protagonists are virtuous and brave and all of them—even the terrorist Miro in *After the First Death* . . .—are trying to do the right thing. They are not victims of their own mistakes or tragic flaws so much as they are victims of an evil beyond their control. (pp. 34-5)

> *Roger Sutton, "The Critical Myth: Realistic YA Novels," in* School Library Journal, *Vol. 29, No. 3, November, 1982, pp. 33-5.*

JOHN ROWE TOWNSEND

It is true and obvious that in real life the good guys don't always win, and it can be strongly argued that fiction for young people should not present an unduly rosy view of the world. But it is equally arguable that young people should not be given to understand that the world is worse than it really is. To pile on the violence and corruption is sensationalism. Cormier indeed seems to me to go to extremes. Although in all three books [*The Chocolate War, I Am the Cheese* and *After the First Death*] the father/son relationship is of great importance, in *After the First Death* it is actually Ben's father who destroys him, by sending him as a messenger to the terrorists in possession of misleading information which (his father calculates) he will give to them when tortured. This strains belief to breaking-point. (p. 340)

> *John Rowe Townsend, "Since 1973 (i): Older Fiction," in his* Written for Children: An Outline of English-Language Children's Literature, *second revised edition, J. B. Lippincott, 1983, pp. 329-40.*

W. GEIGER ELLIS

"Oh yes, Cormier really writes well, but I couldn't use *The Chocolate War* (or substitute another Cormier title) with my students. It is just too depressing. There would be some parents who would complain about his dark view of life. I really don't think it is good for kids to concentrate on such a negative portrayal of humanity."

This kind of reaction to Robert Cormier's novels is widespread. I regard such reactions with more than a little suspicion that the holders of this view lack a sound critical understanding of

Cormier's work, and they lack faith in individual young people. This second shortcoming becomes ironic when the first fault is overcome. (p. 10)

If you have not yet read [*The Bumblebee Flies Anyway*], I can assure you that this novel is consistent with Cormier's other work by focusing on the struggle between individuals and an institution. Institutions are dehumanizing, but humans do not succumb easily—or necessarily. While the larger theme is unchanged, he has forced us to think in yet another area, for the battle we see in *Bumblebee* involves the medical establishment. Yet it would be a disservice to suggest that this novel is an expose of the world of medicos. Like its predecessors, it explores the boundaries of human spirit together with the possibilities within these boundaries.

In noting these things about this recent novel, I am, of course, commenting on the other three novels as well. Consistently the central theme has been the struggle between individuals and institutions. In *The Chocolate War* the institution is a combination of church and the educational establishment; in *I Am the Cheese* it is a combination of government and a psycho-medical institution; in *After the First Death* it is a military/political combination; and *The Bumblebee Flies Anyway* presents the medical establishment as it dabbles chemically and psychologically with individuals.

In each instance the institution holds overall control of the arena within which the characters move. It sets the boundaries, both physical and psychological, and most of the people are behaving in acceptable patterns—acceptable to the institutions because the patterns do not disturb the universe. But Cormier, again in each instance, focuses our attention on individuals. In doing so, he causes us to see, through these individuals, that the boundaries and the controls need not be accepted passively. They can be challenged; indeed, they *must* be challenged.

Jerry clearly bucks the system by making decisions for himself so that he can gain control of his life. Adam is constantly trying to gain such control. In his mind he is courageously travelling beyond the constraining boundaries of his institution, and in reality he is fighting to grasp the reality that he glimpses. Kate relentlessly schemes against her captors and takes actions whenever possible. Barney Snow undertakes a surreptitious project that carries him across the imposed boundaries.

So here are these characters, this body of work, set in the existing milieu of adolescent literature in which realisticizing had been the dominant mode. [According to Lois Duncan, not] one of Cormier's characters is concerned with "alcoholism, drug use (except where imposed by institutions), premarital sex, childbirth, physical handicaps, social and racial problems, divorce, mental illness (except where imposed by institutions), and homosexuality." . . . His focus has not been on menstruation, rape or prostitution.

Cormier's characters stepped boldly and independently into the world of adolescent literature where most characters finally got their first bra, reached a decision about having intercourse, chose to have an abortion or a baby, kicked a drug habit or adjusted to a single-parent home. While surely Jerry, Adam, Kate and Barney will sometime in their lives have to confront similar concerns, it took the good sense of their creator to have a larger view and see the much greater problems that young people face.

Cormier clearly has been out of step with the mainstream of adolescent literature, as out of step as his protagonists are with their environments. It is by hearing a different drummer that a person may become an individual. (pp. 11-12)

While different in important ways from his contemporaries, in one respect, a most important one, Robert Cormier is a part of the movement of adolescent literature, for he not only contributes to the expanding number of fine books, but he is a leader in their creation. . . . Cormier's books explore the boundaries of literary expression for his audience rather than safely following the pack. . . .

[Cormier] has given us carefully-crafted, inspiring novels that give readers a feel for the struggle between . . . two forces, the individual and dehumanizing institutions, which are ostensibly good but have an insidious nature. School, church, hospital, government—surely these are people-serving, individual-enhancing institutions. Look more closely, as Cormier guides us, for unsettling views are waiting. (p. 12)

These negative portrayals of established institutions are bound to be unpopular in some circles and will make some individuals uncomfortable, especially when they themselves are a part of and subject to such institutions. Specifically, many teachers feel that they dare not disturb the universe, and as Cormier has made perfectly clear, there is danger in doing so.

It is no more difficult to understand why a teacher would choose not to assign a Cormier novel to a class than it is to understand why Jerry Renault would choose to go along with the crowd. As Lois Duncan pointed out, "To achieve success in life you play by the established rules." Make no mistake about it, "established rules" mean the rules of the established institutions. But the question remains for the thoughtful individual: What kind of success do I want? And that is certainly a worthy question for young people to consider.

It may be pointed out that the evil is not conquered in Cormier's novels. His heroes are more tragic than not. It may be suggested that their flaw is an unwillingness to "play by the established rules." They share this trait with Phineas in *A Separate Peace*, who was too pure, too individualistic to survive, rather than being like Gene who was willing to make accommodations. I can say only that had Cormier's protagonists annihilated their institutional adversaries, the novels would have been absurd.

The fact is that the evil has not been overcome. It is still with us and must be fought with all the wit and courage that individuals can summon, just as happens in the novels. Rather than saying that the struggle is hopeless, it might be better to say that it is formidable. Besides, adolescents have an innate sense of immortality, and they perennially carry the seeds of the idealism which is the lifeblood of humanity. No one is better suited for recognizing and taking up the challenge.

I hope that idealism is not only tolerated but encouraged in our schools. Idealism is not for the young alone nor is it predestined for defeat. . . . [A] Nobel Prize winner, the Hindu poet Tagore said, "We do not raise our hands to the void for things beyond hope." In the works of Robert Cormier, I see a writer of hope, not despair.

Is Robert Cormier a pessimist? Hardly so. Nearly fifty years ago, Bernard DeVoto said of Mark Twain, "Pessimism is only the name that men of weak nerves give to wisdom." Cormier is a writer of hope who may heighten the awareness of those who are subject to the forces he depicts and inspire his readers with ennobling portrayals of human beings as individuals. (pp. 52-3)

W. Geiger Ellis, "Cormier and the Pessimistic View," in The ALAN Review, Vol. 12, No. 2, Winter, 1985, pp. 10-12, 52-3.

BOOKS FOR KEEPS

Tough, outspoken writing for young readers today no longer causes any particular controversy, yet the novels of Robert Cormier continue to be banned from various American schools and over here [in England] still cause strong argument. It's not so much the detail in his books; it's their overall atmosphere of decay and disillusion that offends many adults, although adolescent readers have no problems getting through the books—it's rare to find a Cormier novel half-read. To have achieved this reputation with only five books for young readers in ten years is no mean achievement. . . . (p. 14)

For some adults, teachers and librarians especially, Cormier's novels are . . . so determinedly dark themselves it's possible they could occasionally help dash just those idealistic hopes in the young necessary for a better future. But while this might be said about his earlier novels, the later ones do show small but important changes in tone. In *The Chocolate War,* for example, the defeated hero's final message is never try to do your own thing; instead, 'Play ball . . . don't disturb the universe.' In its sequel, written eleven years later, the same hero now refuses to give in and even though badly beaten up, as before, preserves his moral ascendancy. *The Bumblebee Flies Anyway* also shows that even the most desperately handicapped children can still cooperate to achieve something positive in their lives, despite horrendous opposition.

In all this, however, Cormier remains a sombre writer, offering all sorts of painful messages to his audience. Adults who wish to protect children from these must consider very carefully what their own motivation is here, since merely to keep children's literature as a repository of cosy, sentimental set pieces is to serve no-one's interests. As it is, children already know something of the darker side of life if only from the evidence of their own playground squabbles or the sudden hatreds that can flare up at home. Cormier can hardly be faulted for raising such matters in his novels, and by putting them on occasions into a political context can help children to realise that governments too can sometimes behave like school bullies. Politics in children's literature is still something comparatively new, unless one counts previous lack of political discussion as itself a political act, preaching unthinking acquiescence to the status quo. But after reading a Cormier novel children can not only see some of their own realities reflected, albeit in a somewhat one-sided way. They might also be stimulated to ask hard questions about the society in which they live. Cormier hopes they will and the evidence in letters to him from readers suggest they do. Whether they get straight answers is another matter, but hardly something that can be laid at Cormier's door. (p. 15)

"Authorgraph No. 34: Robert Cormier," in Books for Keeps, No. 34, September, 1985, pp. 14-15.

PATRICIA J. CAMPBELL

What exactly is it that Robert Cormier is trying to say? Many reviewers, speakers, and essayists have had a try at analyzing it. . . . The most common description of his worldview, and one that Cormier himself has used, is "the plight of the individual versus the system." (p. 30)

[Most critics base their] conclusions on only three of Cormier's eight published novels. It is true that the system is the enemy in *The Chocolate War, I Am the Cheese,* and *After the First Death.* The political evil increases in power and scope with each book, from the authoritarian excesses of a parochial school to the authoritarian excesses of the world military conspiracy. But when we include Cormier's other novels in the question "Who is the enemy?" a different pattern emerges from the answers.

Isolating the central fixed point, the immovable factor, the solid wall against which the action crashes, is the key to understanding the fiction of Robert Cormier. It is tempting but not quite accurate to think of this force as "the enemy." In *A Little Raw on Monday Mornings* it is pregnancy against which good Catholic Gracie struggles. In *Take Me Where the Good Times Are* it is old age, and in both *Now and at the Hour* and *The Bumblebee Flies Anyway* it is death. But most revealingly, in the unpublished novel *In the Midst of Winter,* the force is God Himself, the Holy Spirit that pursues the agnostic with implacable love until he finally surrenders.

The "enemy," then, is not necessarily evil. The unifying characteristic in all these manifestations of the concept can be neatly pinned down with the word "implacable." Unalterable, inflexible, inexorable—that which cannot be appealed to. What fascinates Cormier, the eternal question that draws him back again and again, is "How can we confront the utterly Implacable and still remain human?" His emotion centers on the individual made powerless, cut off from all recourse. Thus Cormier's plots often turn on the symbolic regaining of power through one supremely irrational but self-determined gesture. (pp. 31-2)

[*The Chocolate War*] works superbly as a tragic yarn, an exciting piece of storytelling. Many young adults, especially younger readers, will simply want to enjoy it at this level, and Cormier himself would be the first to say that there is nothing wrong with that. A work of literature should be first of all a good story. But a work of literature also has resonance, richness, a broader intent than just the fate of the characters. For the reader who wants to dig a bit beneath the surface, there is a wealth of hidden meaning and emotion in *The Chocolate War.* How does Cormier achieve this atmosphere of dark, brooding inevitability? What are the overarching themes from which the events of the plot are hung? And, most of all, just what is the crucial thing that he is trying to tell us?

A look at Cormier's style in this book will show first of all the driving, staccato rhythms. The sentences are short and punchy, and the chapters are often no more than two pages. He uses dialogue to move the action quickly forward and to establish character and situation in brief, broad strokes. His technique is essentially cinematic; if he wants to make a psychological or philosophical point he does so visually with a symbolic event or an interchange between characters, rather than reflecting in a verbal aside. Tension is built by an escalating chain of events, each a little drama of its own. (p. 36)

The point of view snaps back and forth from boy to boy in succeeding chapters, a more focused use of the technique called "omniscient observer." First we see Archie through Obie's eyes, then we are inside Jerry's head, then we watch Leon and The Goober squirm under Archie's gaze, then we are looking up at him from Emile's dwarfish mind, then we watch Brother Leon's classroom performance through Jerry's quiet presence, and so on. The variety of perspectives develops our understanding of the characters and reveals the complex interweaving of motivations and dependencies. The shift is unobtrusive but can be easily detected by a close look at the text. Less subtly, there are occasional tags that clue the reader to a change in voice: Brian Cochran and Obie, for instance, are inclined to think, "For crying out loud!" while Archie, among others, is addicted to the ironic use of the word *beautiful*. Cormier is too fine a writer, of course, to descend to imitation slang in order to indicate that this is a teenager speaking. (pp. 36-7)

Much has been made of Cormier's imagery, and many essays and articles have been written on his metaphors and similes, his allusions and personifications. Sometimes it seems that Cormier is merely exercising his virtuosity for the reader: "his voice curled into a question mark," or "he poured himself liquid through the sunrise streets." But most of the time his metaphors are precisely calculated to carry the weight of the emotion he is projecting. Carter, about to tackle Jerry, looks "like some monstrous reptile in his helmet." Leon, thwarted, has "a smile like the kind an undertaker fixes on the face of a corpse." Jerry, happy, scuffles through "crazy cornflake leaves" but, sad, sees autumn leaves flutter down "like doomed and crippled birds." Jerry's father, preparing their loveless dinner, slides a casserole "into the oven like a letter into a mailbox." Sometimes the imagery is vividly unpleasant, as some reviewers have complained, but it is always appropriate to the intensity of the thing that Cormier is trying to say. There is a whole bouquet of bad smells in *The Chocolate War*, starting with Brother Leon's rancid bacon breath. The evening comes on as "the sun bleeding low in the sky and spurting its veins." Sweat moves like small moist bugs on Jerry's forehead. The vanquished Rollo's vomiting sounds like a toilet flushing.

Literary and biblical allusions, too, enrich the alert reader's experience of the novel. Shakespeare, the Bible, and the poetry of T. S. Eliot are the most obvious sources. (pp. 37-8)

Many of these allusions are not isolated flourishes, but fit together into larger structures of meaning. As one example, the Christian symbolism in *The Chocolate War* is an indication of the importance of the book's theme to Cormier. Before tracing that imagery, however, it is essential to clarify that the school itself is not part of this symbolism. It is a gross misunderstanding of the theme of the book to interpret it as an attack on parochial schools or the Catholic Church. If that had been Cormier's intention, it should be quite clear from his biography that he would have drawn on his childhood memories to picture a school where nuns, not brothers, presided. No, the fact that Trinity is a Catholic school is as irrelevant to the meaning of the story as that fact is irrelevant to the characters. But Cormier does use Christian symbolism to show the cosmic implications of the events he is relating. When Jerry refuses to sell the chocolates, the language suggests the Book of Revelation. "Cities fell. Earth opened. Planets tilted. Stars plummeted." In the first chapter, the goal posts remind Obie of empty crucifixes, and in the last chapter, after Jerry's martyrdom, they again remind him of—what? In his graceless state, he can't remember. When Jerry is challenged to action by the hippie, the man looks at him from across a Volkswagen so that Jerry sees only the disembodied head. The image is John the Baptist, he who was beheaded by Herod after he cried in the wilderness to announce the coming of Christ. Archie's name has myriad meanings from its root of "arch": "principal or chief," "cleverly sly and alert," "most fully embodying the qualities of its kind"; but most significantly, the reference is to the Archangel, he who fell from Heaven to be the Fallen Angel, or Lucifer himself. The Vigils, although Cormier admits only to a connotation of "vigilantes," resonate with religious meaning. The candles placed before the altar in supplication are vigil candles, and a vigil is a watch on the night preceding a religious holiday. The members of the gang stand before Archie, who basks in their admiration like a religious statue before a bank of candles. But most important, the understanding of the ultimate opposing forces of good and evil in *The Chocolate War* is a deeply Christian, or perhaps even a deeply Catholic, vision.

How does the theme of this book fit into Cormier's fascination for the nature of human confrontation with the Implacable? Each of the three villains is vulnerable, and if they cannot quite be placated, they can at least be manipulated. They are quick to see each other's weaknesses, and quick to take advantage of them for more secure positions of power. Leon has put himself in a shaky place by his overreaching ambition, and Archie sees him "riddled with cracks and crevices—running scared—open to invasion." Archie fears Leon's power over him as his teacher, and his domination of the Vigils is dependent on thinking up ever more imaginative assignments. And then there is the black box—a nemesis over which he has no control. Emile's weakness is his stupidity; he is easily conned by Archie into believing in the imaginary photograph. So none of the three is an implacable, unconquerable force; all are subject to fears and weaknesses.

Why then does Jerry's lone refusal seem so very doomed from the beginning? Why does the contest seem so unequal; why does the action move so inevitably toward tragedy? The answer lies in the nature of what it is he is saying "no" to. What he is opposing is not Brother Leon, not Archie, not Emile, but the monstrous force that moves them, of which they are but imperfect human agents. The Goober gives it a name. . . . The word is *Evil*.

The unholy trinity of Trinity are studies in the human forms of evil. Brother Leon, who as a priest is supposedly an agent of the Divine, has sold his soul for power, even down to his exultation in the small nasty tyrannies of the classroom. . . . The image that gradually accumulates around Leon is that of a hideous, colorless insect, a poisonous insect, crawling damp from its hiding place under a rock. Or perhaps he has emerged from even deeper underground, as Jerry suspects when he sees "a glimpse into the hell that was burning inside the teacher."

Archie is far subtler and will ultimately, when he is an adult, be more dangerous, because he is not in bondage to ambition. . . . For him, the pleasure is in building intricate evil structures for their own sake. . . . Yet, Archie, too, is in hell, the hell of understanding only the dark side of human nature. "People are two things," he tells Carter. "Greedy and cruel." From this knowledge comes his strength, his ability to make anybody do anything. But it is bottomless emptiness. "Life is shit," he says without emotion.

Emile is the purest embodiment of evil. In him we see the horror of evil's essential quality: silliness. Emile loves to "reach" people. He giggles when he leaves a mess in the public toilet, when he gives an already-tackled football player a secret extra jab, when he loudly accuses a shy kid of farting on a crowded bus. Essentially evil is pointless. Purpose and structure belong to goodness; evil can only turn back on itself in chaos. Archie and Leon have clothed their evil with intelligence and worldly power, but Emile's surrender to darkness is revealed in all its terrible nakedness. The others recognize his nonhumanity quite clearly. "An animal," they call him. (pp. 38-41)

Cormier deliberately gives us no hint of the origins of their devotion to darkness. . . . To understand is to forgive, and to forgive real evil is to make alliance with it. To render these characters psychologically understandable would be to humanize them, to undermine their stature as instruments of darkness, and therefore to erase the theme of opposition to the Implacable.

For those who would turn their eyes away from the ultimate and prefer a smaller and more comfortable theme, Cormier has thoughtfully provided an alternative. It is possible to view [*The Chocolate War*] as an examination of tyranny. The pattern overlaps, but is not identical. Seen this way, the trinity has a different cast. There are three structures of misused power: the school, as headed by Brother Leon; the athletic department, as headed by the coach; and the mob, as headed by Archie. Each has a passive assistant to tyranny, characters who have decent impulses but are ineffectual because they lack the courage to act. Obie is Archie's reluctant stooge; Carter agrees with the coach's approval of violence; and Brother Jacques despises Leon but condones his actions by not opposing. Shadowy outlines of the Government, the Military, and the Church might appear in this interpretation.

The question ultimately turns back, no matter whether tyranny or absolute evil is the enemy, to "How can we resist?" If evil had inherent power, there would be no answer. But Leon, Archie, and Emile all find their power source in their victim's own weaknesses. . . . [Archie] has realized that "the world was made up of two kinds of people—those who were victims and those who victimized." But the moment Jerry, of his own volition, refuses to sell the chocolates, he steps outside this cynical definition. In that is the source of hope. (pp. 42-3)

[It] is Brother Leon himself who has taught Jerry that not to resist is to assist.

Jerry is the *only one* who has learned that lesson, and this is what makes his destruction inevitable. Evil is implacable and merciless to a lone hero, in spite of the folk myth to the contrary. But could it have turned out differently? What if the marble had been black? Or Jerry's first blow had knocked Emile out? But these would have been arbitrary tamperings by the author. Ironically, the key to the real triumph of good comes again from Brother Leon. If others had joined Jerry. . . . There are a number of places in the story where this might have happened. The Goober, of course, is often on the verge of acting on his friendship for Jerry, but in the end, like Hamlet, he only thinks, and doesn't act until too late. For a moment he even hopes that it will all end in a stalemate. The Goober speaks for all the others in wanting to avoid confrontation at any cost. Obie might have acted on his disgust for Archie: "I owe you one for that!" he thinks when pushed too far. In the end he settles only for hoping that fate will punish Archie with a black marble. Carter, too, might have used his simple strength to end it.

Any of these isolated actions might have started the group movement that would have saved Jerry and defeated Leon and the Vigils. Even without such a spur the school comes close to following Jerry's example at the midpoint in the sale. But the motivation is negative—they are tired of selling—and selfishly individual—"let each one do his own thing." Without a conscious joining together for the good of all, they can easily be maneuvered separately back into doing the Vigils' will.

So here at last is Cormier's meaning. As one critic has written, "Jerry's defeat is unimportant. What is important is that he made the choice and that he stood firm for his convictions." Only by making that gesture can we hold on to our humanity, even when defeat is inevitable. But there is more—when the agents of evil are other human beings, perhaps good can win if enough people have the courage to take a stand together. Evil alliances are built with uneasy mutual distrust, but only goodness can join humans with the self-transcending strength of sympathy and love. (pp. 43-4)

Adam [in *I Am the Cheese*] is to some extent based on Cormier himself as a boy. Not only his fears and phobias and migraines, but his personality and ambitions recall Cormier at fourteen. He is shy and book-loving, and home is a warm, safe retreat from a hostile world where wise guys lie in wait at every corner. (p. 67)

Between creator and creation there is an ironic contrast in one respect. "I'm not built for subterfuge and deception," says Adam. It is this quality that makes him a too-perfect subject for interrogation. Because he is so guileless, they—who are so complex in evil that they cannot comprehend simple honesty—persist in thinking he must be hiding something. Again and again he willingly turns the pockets of his mind inside out for them, but they still suspect he has something up his sleeve. It occurs to him to hold back, but he always ends by telling all.

His resistance has been channeled in other directions. The fantasy bike ride is Adam's gesture of defiance in the face of the Implacable. This explains the fierce intensity of his determination to make the journey "for my father," and the inevitability he feels in the beginning about his decision to go— "I knew I would go the way you know a stone will drop to the ground if you release it from your hand." Like Jerry, his gesture is stubborn and half-aware, not the grand, controlled action of a hero. "I am a coward, really," he admits, but in the refrain "I keep pedaling" there is persistant courage. Adam must repeatedly overcome obstacles and break through his fears, but each time he does he can soar for a moment and he finds new hope and strength.

As in dreams real emotions are translated into fantasy people and events, so as the bike ride progresses Adam's hidden awareness of the menace all around him begins to come to the forefront of his mind and take on personification, shape, and form as Whipper and the wise guys, as Fat Arthur and Junior Varney, as snarling dogs and the terrible ferocious vomit-pink car with the grinning grille. Meanwhile in the interrogations he is bringing to consciousness memories that bleed their terror into his secret life of the mind so that he is less and less able to sustain the fantasy. As he approaches the final truth, his newly discovered knowledge of the amount of time that has passed intrudes into the dream in a collision of logics. When he gets to the motel where he and his parents spent a safe night "last summer" he finds it "feels as if it has been neglected for years and years." The effect is eerily disorienting. One last time he tries to call Amy, but the gruff man on the phone and his own mind tell him she is gone; he is no longer able to delude himself with hopes of her comfort or with the defiant illusion of escape. He wants to wake up—"I would give anything to be folded into bed, the pills working their magic, soothing me"—and in a moment he does. The dream begins to smear and waver like the woman's face through the wet windshield. Everything slows down; sounds are distorted, like a movie in a disintegrating projector. The darkness gathers him. Yet still—on a first reading—still we believe this is reality.

Like Amy, Cormier "always withholds information about the Numbers until the last possible moment, stretching out the drama." Even here at the end, there is one last tiny gleam of false hope. We think Adam has arrived in Rutterburg at last. Then he turns the corner and sees the hospital, and as he greets one by one the people from his fantasy the shattering truth crashes down. For the first time he sings the *last* verse of "The Farmer in the Dell." The cheese stands alone, and he is the cheese. (pp. 68-9)

In the third chapter the old man at the gas station has asked Adam, "Do you know who the bad guys are?" He doesn't, and neither do we. What is so overwhelming here is not just that evil is powerful, but that the good guys and the bad guys turn out to be—probably—indistinguishable. It is not a matter of good against evil, but of the cheese standing alone against everything, his whole world revealed at last as evil. Where now is Cormier's imperative for collective good? There is nobody left to come to his rescue. This is not a metaphor. . . . We could all be the cheese. (p. 70)

While the construction of *After the First Death* is not as intricate as the circular triple levels of *I Am the Cheese,* it is still a fairly complex structure with built-in puzzles and trapdoors. There are two main narrative streams: the first-person ruminations that are presumably the voice of Ben and later the general, and the events on the bus told in the third person from the alternating perspective of Miro and Kate (and—very briefly—Raymond and one other child).

The first level takes place two weeks before Christmas at (maybe) Castleton Academy, in Pompey, New Hampshire, where Ben has been sent after the summer of the Bus and the Bridge, and (at first reading) seems to last for the space of one afternoon, while Ben types the journal and later his father reads it and waits for him. In the course of these sections the story of the hijacking proceeds in their memory at the same pace as it is being told in the main narrative.

The second level, or Kate-Miro narrative, takes up three times as many pages as the Ben-general sections, and is the main device for telling the story. It takes place near Fort Delta and just outside Hallowell, Massachusetts. We know Monument is somewhere close off-stage because the bridge spans Moosock River—a waterway that Adam and Jerry know as Moosock Creek. The action lasts for twenty-four hours—from one morning until the next, with the exception of the introductory scene in which Artkin befuddles a waitress in a café for Miro's benefit. The season is summer, the summer before the time of the Ben-general sections. (pp. 74-5)

Perhaps the most difficult element in the book, and one that remains somewhat enigmatic even after close study, is the identity of the voice in the primary narrative, the sections that take place at Castleton Academy. There are two possible interpretations. The first is that Ben sat in his room at the school typing to fill the time before his father was to arrive for a first visit since the hijacking. The general came, was uneasy, and left for a few minutes to recover his composure. Ben typed his feelings about this, then went out to leap off Brimmler's Bridge to his death. His father came back, found the pages, guessed what had happened, and tried to stop Ben but was too late. The shock and guilt unhinged his mind, and in the last section he is in a mental hospital going over and over his need for

forgiveness, which compels him to re-create Ben in his own mind and even to give up his identity to him.

A second interpretation, and one that can be substantiated with much internal evidence, is that *all* of these ruminations are the voice of General Marchand, and that we never actually hear Ben. The typing is done by the father in his false identity as the son, and the place is not Castleton Academy but a mental hospital. The general imagines his old school because it is a place where he was happy and where he can easily picture himself as the same age as his son. There are multiple clues to this interpretation. Most obvious is the mother's "Freudian" slip when she calls "Ben" by his father's name—"Mark." (But this clue loses credence a page later when she calls him back from drifting away mentally: "'Ben,' she said, her voice like the snapping of a tree branch.") When Ben/Mark quotes a teacher's description of the father, the mother points out, "You realize you were describing yourself, don't you?" Ben/Mark does describe himself, but as "a skeleton rattling my bones, a ghost laughing hollow up the sleeves of my shroud, a scarecrow whose straw is soaked with blood." He refers often to being invisible, or to a feeling that someone is listening, looking over his shoulder. At the typewriter he says, "I am a fake, here" and "I am trying to deceive myself not anyone else." The son, seeing his father approaching, finds with terror that his face is a blank, and after the visit types, "It's hard to believe he was really here." About his own death and burial, "Ben" says: "Once in the ground, in the military cemetery at Fort Delta. And again inside of you. Buried me deep inside of you." And toward the end he says, "Put yourself in my place. Or put myself in your place."

It is plain that this is the version that Cormier intends us to accept, even though it is far more difficult and far less satisfying. It is clever and yet somehow not convincing; it feels as if the clues have been scattered in among the lines like so many crumbs for gullible pigeons and English teachers. And there is even a third possibility: could this be entirely Ben's voice, a Ben deluded by his guilt and shame into believing that he can become his forgiving father? A father who has perhaps ended his own guilt by jumping off Brimmler's Bridge? In any one of the three interpretations we miss the perfect click of recognition as the piece fits exactly into place—a click that we learned to love in *I Am the Cheese.*

Other structural devices enrich the deeper meaning of the novel. As in *Wuthering Heights,* each of the main characters can be seen as a reflection of one of the others, a pairing that brings out similarities and contrasts. Miro recognizes this relationship on his first sight of Ben, "the boy who was almost a mirror to himself." They are two sons, two innocents. Artkin and the general are a pair: both fanatical patriots and both fathers willing to sacrifice their sons. There are two boys rejected by girls: Miro by Kate and Ben/Mark by Nettie. There are even two bridges.

Another kind of doubling is the paradoxes that give impact to the themes: murder as virtue, betrayal as service, the traitor as patriot, and above all, innocence as evil. Even the link between Miro and Kate is paradoxical: two young people, sexually attracted to each other and potential lovers but also potential murderer and victim. (pp. 75-7)

After the First Death gives Cormier a chance to show off his powers as a stylist. The book is written in two distinct flavors, which are most strikingly contrasted at the point where the reader first encounters the difference, the switch from part 1 to part 2. Ben's narration has been wavering, limping, truncated paragraphs jumping suddenly from one subject to another. With the introduction of Miro's point of view in part 2 the style changes abruptly and becomes strong and taut and purposeful. There are some brilliant set pieces. Artkin's baiting the waitress is a subtle delight in a book otherwise devoid of joyful moments. In the long paragraph that ends part 8, in which Kate tries to deny to herself that Raymond has been shot, the words skitter frantically like squirrels in a maze with no exit. Artkin's dance of death as he whirls the body of the murdered child above his head like a priest of evil offering a hideous sacrament is an unforgettable evocation of the Black Mass.

The title itself is also part of Cormier's riddling technique. The quotation, "After the first death, there is no other," is drawn from a Dylan Thomas poem called "A Refusal to Mourn the Death by Fire of a Child in London." It applies in one way or another to all the main characters; each has a "first death," but then also a second. For Miro, of course, his intended "first death" is Kate, his sacrificial victim. But it is Artkin's death that turns out instead to be his first, and Kate's his second. Kate has had a pseudodeath from choking long before her real death at Miro's hand. Ben has been "buried" twice, once at Fort Delta after his suicide and once in his father's mind. Both Artkin and the general have died morally and emotionally in their commitment to fanaticism and both die later because of their sons, although the general's "death" is not literal. (p. 77)

Four interlocking themes are explored in *After the First Death:* betrayal of trust, identity masked or disguised, innocence as evil, and patriotism as fanaticism. (p. 81)

The theme of hidden and disclosed identity is a recurring preoccupation with Cormier. He returns again and again to play with the idea—in *I Am the Cheese*, in *Bumblebee*, in the unpublished **"Rumple Country,"** and in *After the First Death.* Here the symbol is the mask—the knitted ski hoods that Artkin and Miro don to hide their faces, but that paradoxically reveal their evil by showing only the cruel eyes and mouths. (p. 82)

Kate too has disguises. Her public self is the blonde, ever-smiling cheerleader, but behind that shiny identity that she presents so carefully to the world she senses other unexplored selves. . . .

The general also hides his identity, by merging with his dead son. In addition, like Artkin and Miro, he has a false name that represents his patriotic self: General Rufus Briggs. . . .

This toying with the idea of hidden identity and names leads up to the central theme of *After the First Death.* "The monstrous," says Cormier, "is so often disguised as innocence". Although all the characters are "innocent" in one sense or another, it is Miro who most clearly illustrates the idea of innocence as evil. At first Kate sees him as simple, like an animal—"a dog straining at a leash." Only gradually does she uncover the extent of his corruption. (p. 83)

Artkin and the general are innocent in the sense of "not guilty"— in their own eyes. Both feel that their side is supremely right and the others are always wrong, and anything done in the name of that right is justifiable. In this surrender of moral judgment they have also surrendered their humanity. Once the total commitment to the cause is made, all other choices vanish. (p. 84)

The general is neither more nor less evil than Artkin; each is capable of anything in the name of patriotism. There are no limits—killing a child, sacrificing a son—they are a pair. . . .

In a way Artkin is an exaggerated reflection of the general, just as Emile is a caricature of Archie in *The Chocolate War.* Artkin's fanaticism is a warning, the logical end result of such a total commitment. The general is for us the more dangerously seductive figure because to some degree we agree with his cause and are in danger of justifying his actions. He moves, after all, through the landscape of American patriotism—Lexington, Concord—and it is our own country he thinks he is defending. (p. 85)

The four dark young adult novels—*The Chocolate War, I Am the Cheese, After the First Death,* and *Beyond the Chocolate War*—form a tetralogy of political statement and are undoubtedly Cormier's mature masterpieces. The brilliant and complex structure, the intricate wordplay and subtlety of thought, and above all the power and conviction of theme are unequaled by anything of his that came before or has yet come after. (p. 87)

Until the publication of *The Chocolate War* Cormier continued to write short stories although, as he himself recognized, he is not at his best in the form. The retrospective collection that appeared in book form in 1980 under the unimaginative title *Eight Plus One* is a fairly typical selection of his later stories. (p. 89)

In the long view, the real value of *Eight Plus One* is in the light it sheds on Cormier's later work. (p. 90)

Well-crafted and touching as some of these stories are, the final critical judgment has to be that Cormier's pleasant works, characters, and scenes are not memorable. Only in darkness does he show his real power. (p. 91)

[The] one moment of exaltation and hope as the Bumblebee sails out into space [in *The Bumblebee Flies Anyway*] was the goal toward which Cormier worked for several years. The novel was troublesome. "The thing is," he says, "I had the concept. I wanted to have that soaring ending. . . . I didn't know if I could pull it off". . . . There is no doubt he has pulled it off. That one chapter is magnificent, unforgettable. But the rest of the novel shows the effects of the not entirely victorious struggle that went into its making. (pp. 101-02)

The complex and demanding project almost defeated him. It was five years in the writing. He put it aside in despair for nine or ten months, and then began over again from page one, finally coming to grips with the problems in the manuscript. Basically, the difficulty revolved—and still does—around the character of Cassie. . . .

[It] is understandable that Barney would be completely entranced with Cassie, even if she is not really as "compelling and vibrant" as he thinks. After all, except for a few dim memories of spin-the-bottle at parties, she is the only girl he has ever seen because his past is only five weeks long. But her psychosomatic link with Mazzo *is* puzzling. Aside from the fact of being twins (*nonidentical* twins), they seem to have neither more nor less closeness than the average friendly brother and sister. There is nothing to explain The Thing, nor does Cormier appear to try. It doesn't seem to work as a metaphor, either—it is just pasted onto the story, and because Cassie is basically unlikable, there is only a mild, abstract suspense in wondering if she will be drawn in to Mazzo's death.

Perhaps an explanation was to be found in earlier versions of *Bumblebee*, in which Cassie played a much larger role. (p. 103)

An additional problem with *Bumblebee* is the *blankness* of the outer and inner setting: the sterile hospital and Barney's amnesiac mind. By its very nature there can be none of the sweat, noise, collisions, the *events* of, say, *The Chocolate War*. In the Complex everything is silent, bare, colorless, like the empty, drab gray and dull white corridors. The only sounds are the distant humming of machines; all human noises are hushed. . . . Barney's memory is equally blank, no allusions, anecdotes, connections from the past to anything he sees or feels. Even his senses of taste and smell are gone, and his emotions are deliberately muted and suppressed. This sterility gives the narrative a peculiar flatness of surface. The story moves along on silent rubber-tired wheels like a gurney carrying a patient to surgery. It feels to the reader as if nothing happens at all until the flight of the Bumblebee—which is one reason that moment stands out with such impact. (pp. 104-05)

Five of Cormier's seven other novels take place in institutions, and in them a steady progression toward equating the Institution with the state of existence itself can be seen: the comical and benevolent old-folks home, the parochial school, the diabolical mental hospital with no escape, the Mafia/government, the international military conspiracy. In *Bumblebee* Cormier has achieved his goal. The Institution is all. Only Mazzo has a link with the world outside, and he won't answer the phone. This connection, which he might use to reach out for comfort and love, is to him only a way to punish. When Billy tries to find human contact over the phone, he finds that it is too late. From inside the Complex they are all Wrong Numbers.

There are hopeful symbols, too, in this book, which has been called Cormier's most affirmative. On their first excursion to the junkyard, Barney sees a lilac bush growing against the fence, "the purple clusters so heavy they made the branches droop," but it reminds him only that he can no longer smell their fragrance. . . . The blooming bush is the only thing soft and alive in the hard stone and metal of the Complex and the junkyard, growing stubbornly in almost no soil. (pp. 106-07)

Cormier has used the symbol of the lilacs in *Bumblebee* . . . to affirm the renewal of life and the hope of victory over death. Barney, after his love for Cassie has restored his sense of smell and taste and his appetite for life, returns to the junkyard. This time he sees the lilac bush with new eyes and smells the fragrance. . . . He tries to pray, but that knowledge has been almost obliterated with the rest of his memory. . . . A moment later he climbs the fence and sees the MG once more. A glimmer grows in his mind: ". . . he let the vision burst full flower. He saw for the first time the flight of the Bumblebee. . . ."

Through the symbolism of the lilacs, Barney gropes for the faith in an afterlife that has been erased from his mind. Only fragments of the structure of belief remain—a snatch of a prayer, a brief memory of religious instruction from a nun. . . . Barney suddenly remembers that he has been Catholic, but the candles, the wafer, the altar no longer have meaning for him. He finds that he has clothed his faith with the words "tempo, rhythm," the screen that the Handyman has instilled in his mind to comfort his fear of death. But the outer shape doesn't matter—it is still prayer, it is still faith. (pp. 108-09)

"Free choice, the Handyman said, you have free choice here. A laugh, of course," thinks Barney. Yet, outside the terrible, implacable fact of impending death, they do have free choice, and the other characters have used it. Billy the Kidney and Allie Roon have chosen to come to the Complex so that their deaths might help others, and although they are embarrassed to talk about it, the commitment does give each of them some spiritual comfort. . . . Barney, too, has made the choice, but he doesn't know it. The decision to commit himself to the Complex happened in the immediate past that has been erased from his mind. So Barney must find elsewhere that humanizing gesture against the Implacable that is so central in Cormier's cosmos.

Before he can act he must find out who he is. Or perhaps the other way around, as the existentialists would have it. Through action we make our own meaning for our existence. Cassie's first words to Barney are, "I know who you are." But *he* doesn't. Just before the terrifying experiment in which his identity is to be entirely obliterated, he writes down what he knows about himself: his name, his age, his weight, his height. That is all. . . . He is given the drug, and awakes in a room that is the classic existential place between worlds: bare, hard chairs lined up against the walls, coffee table with magazines, flat calendar art on the wall—a waiting room for hell. "He was alone, cast adrift, lost, unrelated to anything." A face appears on a television screen and asks him, in the fairy-tale manner, the obligatory three questions. They take the form of word associations. "Snow," "car"—before the third question can be asked, Barney in a panic finds it for himself. *Who am I?* and then *What am I?* He can find no answer. Here, in the existential dilemma, Cormier's preoccupation with identity is laid bare.

But all the while through his labor on the Bumblebee Barney has been finding the answer without being aware he was seeking it. (pp. 110-11)

When he is finally, undeniably confronted with the fact of his mortality, the Bumblebee, which began as an attempt to transform his nightmare of the rainy car, is itself transformed. Now it becomes a defiant affirmation, "a shared vision of freedom and rebirth." When Barney first gazes down from the skylight in the attic he sees only the junkyard, rows of bleak tenements, an old cemetery "with tombstones like small teeth scattered on a rug." But when he stands with Mazzo and Billy on the threshold of the flight, the view, like his soul, is transfigured— "the sweep of sky spinning with stars, the moon radiating silver, turning the sloping roof into a glittering ski slide, the lights of Monument center glowing in the distance, staining the sky with gold." At the last minute he realizes that suicide is irreconcilable with an act of faith. The Bumblebee soars, and in this supremely irrational gesture is ultimate hope. (p. 111)

[*Beyond the Chocolate War*] is a work that in close analysis reveals itself as complex and dense, but on first reading has the spare and compelling clarity of great storytelling. The plot is an intricate delight of glittering illusions, magic tricks and surprises, yet paradoxically it moves with the utter simplicity and inevitability of absolute truth. The reader has no trouble at all keeping track of the more than a dozen major characters. The pacing is breathlessly irresistible. Unanswered questions and unresolved tensions layer from scene to scene as the characters collide in a rich choreography of shifting expectations, allegiances, and perceptions. (pp. 112-13)

It is the paradox of surprise and inevitability that is the chief pleasure of the book. In spite of all the unexpected jolts that lie around each corner of the plot, the overwhelming experience for the reader is a sense of rightness. We know these characters, and this is just what they *would* do, just what *would* happen.

eyes were drawn immediately XXXXXXX to the stage and the reason

for the curious attitude of the students. Center stage, in a

spotlight, standing alone wXXXXXXXXXXX on an otherwise empty

stage was the XXXXXX guillotine. Ugly, dangerous, its blade

gleaming in the XXXXXX harshness of the spotlight's glare,

XXXXXXXXXXXXXXXXXXXXXXXX a nightmare object suddenly thrust into

reality. XXXXXXX Or, maybe, Ray Bannister thought, it's me,

dramatizing, exaggerating. But as he looked around the auditorium

at the other students, leaning toward or tilting toward each other

in puzzled whispering attitudes, he realized the full impact of

the guillotine on XXXXXX their sensibilities. He thought of

Obie. He also thought, My God, what's happening here?

What was happening there was exactly

Revised typescript page for Beyond the Chocolate War. *Courtesy of Robert Cormier.*

We knew it all the time—except we didn't, until Cormier told us. (p. 113)

"Ray Bannister started to build the guillotine the day Jerry Renault returned to Monument." A lapel-grabber of an opening, and one that sets up appropriately sinister expectations. (pp. 113-14)

The important thing to remember about *this* guillotine is that it is an illusion. It cuts, and it doesn't cut. Cormier plays with our uncertainty about its nature and thus sets us up for the whole bag of magic tricks that he will perform in *Beyond the Chocolate War*. (p. 114)

[The] first chapter is written in a rather flat narrative (as contrasted with the vivid scene on the football field that opens *The Chocolate War*). The effect is like a prologue, a statement before the real action begins that establishes the unanswered question of the guillotine. That done, Cormier the conjurer sweeps aside the curtain, and here we are back at Trinity, plunged with a shock of glad recognition into the familiar scene of a Vigils meeting. (p. 115)

In *Beyond the Chocolate War*, Cormier has come into his full strength as a brilliant storyteller, and there is no need for that play with metaphors and allusions for the sheer joy of virtuosity that characterized the style of *The Chocolate War*. But there are many arresting phrases that strike home a meaning like

Carter's gavel, "a hammer driving a nail through wood into flesh." Jerry and his father occupy their apartment "the way mannequins inhabit rooms of furniture in a department store." (p. 121)

There are brief references from the Cormier symbology that have become almost obligatory: a menacing dog, a whiff of lilac, a forbidding nun. Names often reveal hidden meanings to the Cormier reader who is willing to dig a bit. (p. 122)

Cormier the magician has always entertained his readers with secrets and games, illusions and surprises. In *Beyond the Chocolate War* his bag of magic tricks yields one astonishment after another. Ray Bannister calls misdirection "the magician's most powerful tool," and, as he explains it, "a magician guided the audience to see what the magician wanted them to see, made them think they were seeing one thing while another surprise awaited them." Cormier is a master of this technique. Caroni's oblique references to "the Letter" misdirect us to think of it as a missive like Carter's note to Leon, until it is revealed as a test grade. The realistic tone of the scene in which Leon opens a package lulls us, so that we are astounded when it blows his head off, and jarred again when at the end of the paragraph we realize that it is Caroni's fantasy and we have been fooled. Other illusions of death abound: Leon shot by a sniper, Obie's dream of the guillotine, Ray as a killer in the false newspaper clipping, the near-misses of Caroni's first suicide, Leon pricked by his knife—and Obie's murder attempt.

But the illusion of the black marble is Cormier's most amazing and complex effect. . . . [We] are as startled as Archie is when he draws the black marble from the box that Obie has so carefully rigged to expose his sleight-of-hand. Cormier has misdirected us, and much later we are surprised even again, when Archie tells Obie that he deliberately took the black marble, to find out what would happen, how far Obie would go. But why then was he startled? Mysteries still remain after the trick is completed.

All through both books we have longed for Archie to get the black marble. But when he finally does, Cormier plays one last masterpiece of a trick. He cheats us of the sweetness of retribution by manipulating our sympathies. The delicious first sight of Archie as The Fool is not as delicious as we thought it was going to be. As he is led (the great Archie—led!) across the parking lot, head held high in spite of the "Kick Me" sign on his back, suddenly we very much do *not* want to see him humiliated. When he sits quietly on the platform of the Water Game, "neat and spotless in his chino pants and white jersey," he has dignity, grace, even nobility. The crowd is silent and hangs back. When Obie tries to bribe a boy to throw the ball at the target that will drop Archie, soaked and struggling, into the pool, he protests, "I'm not dunking any Archie Costello." Neither are we. When the hawker dismisses him ("I'd go broke with you there all day long . . .") and he leaps gracefully to the ground, we feel like cheering. It is no surprise when nobody is willing to *kick* any Archie Costello either.

But what about the guillotine? It must fall, but if we didn't want Archie dunked we certainly don't want him beheaded. As he kneels so coolly to be "executed," he has become a heroic figure, and it is Obie who is despicable. The tension at this point is almost unbearable. Cormier has built it to the shrieking point with one emotional scene quickly following another. The audience is in the palm of his hand. The blade descends—but before it reaches its target we are plunged into the midst of Caroni's suicide. Only when his body hits the ground with the "hollow, thudding sound" we expected from the guillotine, only then is the tension released.

The illusion is ended. In the next line Archie marvels "You wanted to kill me, Obie," and we know we have been misdirected again. Archie, of course, did not know that he was about to lose his head. What seemed to be dignity and bravery was only casual acceptance of a silly magic show. The trappings of an execution have made us believe in Archie as the heroic condemned criminal. Now suddenly he is the old Archie and our loathing is firmly back in place as he demolishes Obie by praising him for attempting murder. (pp. 122-24)

Archie has had it all his way for four years, and now as he leaves Trinity he sets one last scheme in motion that will bring the school down around Brother Leon's ears for good. . . . The plan is diabolical in its simplicity: [Archie] saddles Bunting with Emile Janza as right-hand man, and then offers Emile a number of suggestions about how things might be run next year. Bunting bites the bait gladly—violence is something he understands.

So the book ends as it started—in deepening darkness. Or does it? There *is* hope for next year if you know where to look for it. Henry Malloran with his knack for well-timed action is president; levelheaded Ray Bannister will still be around; Jerry and The Goober may be back with new strength. And doesn't Brother Leon know very well how to squelch the kind of dis-turbance Bunting and Janza have in mind? Things may work out for Trinity, with Archie gone.

Yes, but remember—Archie has now been unloosed on the world. (pp. 124-25)

Patricia J. Campbell, in her Presenting Robert Cormier, *Twayne Publishers, 1985, 151 p.*

DEANNA ZITTERKOPF

Cormier's knowledge of young people and his refusal to underrate them is evident in his fiction. His unhappy endings would not be so distressing if he had not created multi-dimensional characters who are so likeable—and so vulnerable. The boys, like Jerry Renault and Barney Snow, are bright, sensitive kids who want to fit in but who lack the physique to be football stars, the charisma to be leaders or the polish to impress girls. The girls, most notably Cassie Mazzofono and Kate Forrester, initially appear stronger than their male counterparts. They are pretty, popular and poised. But their appearance is a facade that masks inner doubts about who they are and their ability to cope with life.

At the same time, these seemingly fragile adolescents possess considerable resources. All are caring, compassionate and capable of great courage. Cormier as author may or may not be cynical, but his heroes and heroines are not. Rather than crumbling before school tyrants, disease or terrorists, they fight back, reaching out for life, love and hope. When the adult world fails them—and except for deceased parents, there's scarcely a sympathetic adult in the novels—the children encourage and comfort each other. Ultimately, however, these young people are pushed beyond their capabilities by forces much stronger than they. Being imperfect, they make mistakes. Some survive. Most don't. But throughout their ordeals they live and act by a set of humanistic principles which prevent a defeat of the spirit. Jerry Renault is brutally beaten, but he decides to return to Trinity rather than retreating to Canada. Barney Snow refuses to die until he has given Mazzo a last ride in the bumblebee. And Kate Forrester receives her fatal bullet because she instinctively offers solace to her captor. Admittedly, the ends these young people meet are undeserved and terrible, but their refusal to compromise their values is admirable, reassuring, and ultimately, positive. (p. 43)

Deanna Zitterkopf, "Robert Cormier," in Children's Literature Association Quarterly, *Vol. 11, No. 1, Spring, 1986, pp. 42-3.*

THE CHOCOLATE WAR (1974)

AUTHOR'S COMMENTARY

[The following excerpt is from an interview by Geraldine DeLuca and Roni Natov.]

[Geraldine DeLuca]: Why did you start to write for adolescents?

[Robert Cormier]: Well, I didn't start writing specifically for adolescents. I was surrounded by my kids and their friends who were teenagers, and I realized that they were really leading a life that was more exciting than mine. I was going to work every day and coming back home, but for them the emotional pendulum was swinging back and forth all the time. They were getting invited to the prom, falling in love—you know those things—and even though the experiences might have been transient, they were really lacerating for them. So I began to write short stories about young people. They appeared in magazines, not as young adults' stories, but in *Redbook, Saturday Evening Post, McCall's,* and they were usually about a relationship between a father and a daughter or a father and a son. So the next step seemed to be to do a novel.

I didn't look for it, but what happened was, my son was a freshman in this jock boys' Catholic high school and he came home with chocolates to sell. He wanted to play football and he's an average student so he knew he had to do a lot of homework and then suddenly he also had to sell these chocolates. It reminded me of the Depression when all of us sold everything in a Catholic school—chocolates, candy, greeting cards, chances—and I thought, "How far have we come in a generation?" He's going to a Catholic prep school, we're paying tuition, and he's still selling chocolates. So we kidded around about it in the evening, you know, like families do over the dinner table. And suddenly I said, "You know, Peter, there are options available. You don't have to sell the chocolates. One option is that we can buy them—there were twenty-five boxes at a dollar apiece and I was hoping he wouldn't say 'Yeah, Fine'—or you can not sell them." And he decided he wouldn't sell them. We figured as a family we'd take a stand.

So I wrote a letter to his headmaster to say that he wasn't doing this frivolously, that we had thought about it, that it was a free society and that his option was not to sell the chocolates. So the next day he had to bring the chocolates back. I said, "Well, you won't go on the bus with two bags. I'll take you to school." And as I let him go up the walk with the two bags I thought, "God, what am I letting him in for?" Because he was a freshman, and it was only the end of September in this very active school. I felt kind of guilty about it. And that's where the emotions came from to allow me to write about it, because I do write from the emotions. So, what happened is, he gave the letter to the headmaster, who read it and said "Fine, Peter," and nothing happened. The kids later kidded him a little bit, the way kids do, but the emotions started growing in me.

Then I started to explore the situation, you know the old crutches that we all have: "What if?" What if the headmaster hadn't been that understanding? And then, what if the chocolate sale was very important to the school? And then, what if he had peer pressure?" So I started writing about this situation, and frankly, the boy at that point was Peter, my son, and the school was his school. So I just wrote, because I write every day—it's part of the fabric of my life. When I got about a third into what became *The Chocolate War,* my agent [Marilyn Marlow] asked me, "What have you been doing lately, I haven't heard from you?" and I said, "I don't know, Marilyn, I'm writing this crazy thing about kids selling chocolate in high school and I'm not sure what I've got." So I sent her what I had and she called back and said, "You know, this sounds like a young adult novel." This was the first time I really thought of it as a young adult novel or thought of a young adult novel as something that people really read. I knew vaguely that writers wrote books for children, but I didn't know about the young adult market. I didn't know about Paul Zindel. But she sort of scared me when she said that. I thought, "Oh, my God, do I have to go back and simplify and take things out?" I didn't even know what kind of language was in it. But she said, "Bob, don't worry about it. Just write as you were writing before, and let me determine the market." (pp. 109-11)

[Roni Natov]: There's so much energy in this book. I keep feeling that it must come from something that did happen or

that you were afraid would happen. The story is very intense and I think that's what makes it feel authentic. It doesn't feel like the typical young adult novel, sort of trumped up to air issues or to solve problems.

[Robert Cormier]: I was exploring. I should go back to what I said about the emotions. I've always been an emotional writer, which has been both good and bad for my career. It's been bad for my career because I've been led into unpopular themes. If I sat down and just wanted to construct something I thought would sell, things might have been easier. (pp. 111-12)

[Robert Cormier]: I don't mean to pretend that I'm not writing for publication. I want to be published, and I have enough of an ego to want the feedback. But that has never been primary to me.

So when I came to *The Chocolate War* I was exploring these emotions and situations rather than worrying about the market or "examining the theme of the individual against society," even though I'd always been interested in that. When people read it, they impose these ideas on it. Critics say, "This is a novel about the individual against society." And I say, "That's right, it is." But I didn't say, "I'm going to sit down and explore this." There are patterns in my work. Like the old man running away, I realized, looking back, that there has always been a pattern. In a very small way, I am sometimes a rebel myself without anybody knowing it.

[Geraldine DeLuca]: Do you think that the odds against the individual surviving are as great as your books suggest?

[Robert Cormier]: Well, yes. I don't think that there are always happy endings, but you can get satisfaction out of experiences even though you fail. Like *The Old Man and the Sea.* The sharks tore the marlin apart, so he failed in one sense. Yet, it was a great story of fulfillment. I know people feel my books are depressing and I suppose *The Chocolate War* is depressing because, at the end, Jerry is apparently defeated and I couldn't help that. When I began writing it, I just wanted to set the situation up and then the characters became real to me. In every story, once an author has established the people and the situations, there's an air of inevitability about it that can't be tampered with. You know, one day while I was sitting at home, I got a phone call from Marilyn who had heard from the second editor. He had said, "Fine, it's great." If I would change the ending, they would buy the book. Now I had no way of knowing that Pantheon would eventually buy the book as is and that it would sell. And here was this editor saying, "Its great. However, we don't think young people will accept it." Well, first of all, that raised my hackles.

[Roni Natov]: It's like, SELL THE CHOCOLATES!

[Robert Cormier]: That's right. He was doing the same thing. And yet it was very tempting to say, "Well, let me see about it." But I knew that in my mind the curve of the story was to build and then go down. And I had this crazy image in my mind of trying to fix up the ending to make it go up—"zip"—which seemed untrue, but it was tempting.

Now when Pantheon accepted it, Fabio [Coen], my editor, suggested a change that was very effective. In the first version of the fight, Jerry was annihilated immediately, because I didn't think I could sustain the raffle idea, and thought I'd better get rid of the fight quickly. But Fabio said, "I think for reader response and for balance you should think about prolonging the fight to let Jerry get in a little more." He said, as all good editors say, "Think about it." So I thought about it and said, yes, I could see where it was an abbreviated fight. I had built it up and then it was over like that. Artistically I felt it could go longer and I tried it. So Jerry did get in a couple of licks and yet the inevitability of the story imposed itself, because when he did, he realized he was lowering himself to Janza's level. So again, the truth of the book was sustained. I believe in this sense of inevitability. And when I'm bothered by a book that I read that doesn't ring true, I wonder whether the author, playing God, didn't tamper somewhere, by not following the natural outcome.

[Geraldine DeLuca]: That's interesting. I remember this book being discussed once at a children's literature conference where one of the women kept insisting that it was just like *Hamlet*. And you do make references to Shakespeare, so I was wondering if you have a sense of inevitability being tragic, of the options becoming narrower and narrower for Jerry.

[Robert Cormier]: No, it's funny. Lou Willet Stanek, who did the Dell teacher's guide for both *The Chocolate War* and *I am the Cheese*, made all these Shakespearean references, comparing *The Chocolate War* to *Hamlet*. She likened the conversation between Archie and Obie to that between Rosencrantz and Guildenstern. So I was pleased. I thought, what a comparison! But I wasn't conscious of it when I was writing. I was conscious, of course, of using Eliot's line from "Prufrock": "Do I dare disturb the universe?" Which is essentially a middle-aged man's question, because that's what Prufrock was. And yet, you can disturb the universe on all levels.

[Roni Natov]: I also felt that Jerry was identifying and worrying about identifying with his father there. His father was so bleak, so defeated, and he was wondering, "Is there any other way? Do I dare do something else?"

[Robert Cormier]: Yes, there were circumstances that dictated his rebellion, more than he realized. There's the scene early in the book with the hippie who comes across the street and says, "Go back to your closed little world," and his father's world *was* closed. There was a time, I remember, when I was that age, that I'd go out after supper and the place I wanted to be was out of the house, seeing what was going on downtown on the street corner. And I'd see my father taking a nap after supper, after working all day, and I'd think, "My goodness, is this all he has to live for?" Now, of course, I take naps after supper. And when my own son is going out I think, "Thank God, the search is over for me." I don't have to search those streets for love and so forth. So this generation repeats. If I have total recall of anything, it's of my emotions when I was young. . . . [And] apparently it comes out in the books, because kids write me marvelous letters. So apparently, I do have that recall. And I don't worry too much about trends or styles. I figure that if the emotions are right, the response will be there. It seems to have worked so far.

[Roni Natov]: I'm interested in the connection between power and guilt, and shame and fear in your work. They seem to be all tied up in *The Chocolate War*. Archie's power comes from understanding, in some very intense way, that other people are ashamed of things. He could know that through his own feelings—he knows about shame, he knows about guilt, and he knows what to do about it. Were you conscious of the different things that people, that teenagers, hide, and that this huge figure, Archie, is trying to uncover and use? Like the incident of Janza in the bathroom?

[Robert Cormier]: I've been aware of people like this all my life. There are people who can intimidate other people very

easily and I've always been interested in why they can do it. I think it's because most people want peace. (pp. 113-16)

I knew, when I started the book, that eventually there had to be a confrontation between the good guys and the bad guys, between Jerry and Archie. And I didn't know then who would win and who would lose, I just knew there had to be a showdown. I introduced this fellow named Emile Janza in order to show Archie in a different light. You know, not to show him from the point of view of someone he'd been intimidating, but to show him through the eyes of a guy who was almost at his level, but not that sharp. So that's all Janza was. But he kept popping up, I found him very convenient, and suddenly I found him growing. And part of the joy of writing, at least the way I do it, is that suddenly I had this full-blown character on my hands, and it made me realize that Archie would never risk a confrontation with anyone. He would have Janza do it. And this is what I mean about setting your characters in motion. If I had insisted, as an author, that I had wanted Archie in that ring with Jerry, I don't think it would have rung true because Archie wouldn't have done it. But I didn't know that at the beginning of the story. Of course, there is danger in this too. You can be carried away by people who throw your book off, and sometimes you have to go back and cut. Amy, for example, almost ran away with *I am the Cheese* because I fell madly in love with her, and then I just had to eliminate her.

[Roni Natov]: She's appealing, I can see it.

[Robert Cormier]: Yes, she really captured me. I went on and on about her and then I just had to throw those pages away because she didn't belong.

So there are people who use power in a very small way because they know that most of us want to go along and just live our lives. I have met people like that.

[Geraldine DeLuca]: They don't have any satisfaction within themselves and the only way they can get any is to provoke hostility in others. Archie's like that. The only thing that seems to give him any pleasure is manipulating others, making them feel as wretched as he feels. It's the same thing with Brother Leon. He's such an unhappy character.

[Robert Cormier]: Yes, their own unhappiness comes back. And yet I feel that they're not prototypes; I hope they're just individuals. However, there are Brother Leons in schools everywhere.

[Roni Natov]: He felt totally insidious. He's a very dangerous person because he is an adult. More dangerous than Archie.

[Geraldine DeLuca]: And he's not dealing with other adults, he's dealing with kids, who are more vulnerable.

[Robert Cormier]: Yes. There is that scene in the classroom where he manipulates Gregory Bailey. And yet that scene is also about the guilt of all of us. You know, the biggest sins in the world are not so much the sins of commission, as the sins of omission. I think about how many times I've stood in mixed company while somebody told a real dirty joke, and I didn't say anything, didn't say, "Look, why did you tell that?" That's the sort of guilt I wanted to show—how we all collaborate in these situations. I started out writing that chapter to show how terrible Brother Leon was and then in the writing I suddenly realized, "My God, the class is as guilty at this moment as he is."

[Geraldine DeLuca]: Except that they're very vulnerable.

[Robert Cormier]: Except that they're very vulnerable, yes. And they are intimidated by it. Again, intimidation can reduce people to do things they don't want to do. Or to do things collectively that they wouldn't do alone. So if you're going to fight this kind of thing, you've got to be collectively good. Most people have missed this. The fact is there was only one good person in the book.

[Geraldine DeLuca]: There's Goober and there's Brother Jacques.

[Robert Cormier]: But they're weak, ineffectual. If they were collective, if they banded as the evildoers did, they would have had some power.

[Geraldine DeLuca]: Were you aware of how bleak a vision you were presenting? Did you feel that this school was in some way a microcosm?

[Robert Cormier]: No. As I went along I was aware that I was exploring things. And it occurred to me at one point that this high school was really a metaphor, that I could just as well be writing about someone in business who refused to conform, . . . where everybody had to wear a tie all the time and one guy decided not to. And I realized that that's why I didn't think of it as a young adult novel. I thought it was more than just a book for young people. I was hoping that even though most of the characters were youngsters, older people would get shocks of recognition and say, "Yes, I remember how it was."

[Roni Natov]: How it *is*.

[Robert Cormier]: How it is. And how it was for them when they were young.

[Geraldine DeLuca]: You have those scenes where kids band together and taunt other kids, which you see more openly among adolescents and children than you do among adults— it's much more subtle among adults.

[Robert Cormier]: Yes. You know, what astounded me was that some people got upset and said they couldn't accept that kids would do this. But really, children are the cruelest of all, because they haven't entered society yet and realized that if you want to make a living you've got to get along. Some schools have refused to have *The Chocolate War* because they feel it's a bad portrait of youth. I don't know what their motivations are, but. . . .

[Roni Natov]: It's not a very positive portrait of the Catholic school.

[Robert Cormier]: It isn't. And there has been controversy about that, but I have had very little complaint from Catholics.

[Geraldine DeLuca]: Are you a Catholic?

[Robert Cormier]: Yes, I'm a Catholic, and I went to those kinds of schools. But I was writing about a specific situation here. I had a horrible time in parochial school and I also had a great time, you know? When an advance review came out, it said the book would be very controversial, especially among Catholics. But I spoke at the Catholic Library Association in St. Louis a couple of months ago and we had a very good time. A couple of people there did tell me, though, that they are librarians in Catholic schools and they don't have it on the shelves. However, in the school my son went to, the book has achieved a sort of legendary status. (pp. 116-20)

You know, the funny thing about writing is that it is such a private act and it becomes such a public thing. When I was writing, I was just trying to find a specific truth. I was once asked at a seminar, "Why did you make it Catholic? You said it could happen in any school; there are Brother Leons in public schools, in private schools and in parochial schools, so why did you make it Catholic?" And I said, "Well, you've got to be specific."

[Roni Natov]: You've got to make it *something*.

[Robert Cormier]: You've got to make it something. You know, if I just made it a bland school somewhere, then the next thing to say would be, well I'd better not make this kid French. I'd better not make this one Italian. I'd better not make this one Irish. And you end up with homogenized milk. So once I made the decision to make it a Catholic school, I hoped readers would see that it's universal, that these people exist everywhere.

[Roni Natov]: I feel like it had something to do with it's being a boy's school, though. There's something frenetic going on there.

[Robert Cormier]: Yes. There's something about a boy's school. As I said, my son was going to this school and it was a jock school and it was—frenetic is a beautiful word for it. The chocolate sale there is a real annual thing in the town and people sort of know it's coming. But I never heard a word of criticism about the book from the school. In fact my son helped me. I had him check out the teenage slang. He'd say things like, "They don't say 'broads' anymore, Dad, they say 'chicks.'" Things like that. But anyway, when the book was done and he was still there, I told him that if it would embarrass him I wouldn't send it in. Because I was always writing other things. I said I'd wait until he was out of the place. But he said, "Dad, it wouldn't bother me at all." In fact, he's that kind of kid. (pp. 120-21)

[Geraldine DeLuca]: It's interesting, though, that the characters in your books don't have support from their parents the way your son has. The parents are dead or in some way rendered impotent. And they're very separate from their children.

[Robert Cormier]: Yes. Well, you know, about the only father who appeared in *The Chocolate War* was Jerry's father and he was indifferent because of his grief about his wife's death. I did that purposely. I have a private belief—and like all beliefs it's not total—but I have the feeling we should judge people more often on what they do rather than excusing them for coming from unhappy homes. I think the essential individual, the true thing that a person is, probably does not have a lot to do with where he comes from. I may be wrong. I've argued a lot about this and I'm always willing to concede. I don't mean to say that people who come from a very hard background don't have it hard. What I mean is that there is a spirit of a person, you know? So I purposely left out all families—there are no other mothers and fathers around—because I wanted the boys to be judged on what they did, not "why did Archie do that?"

[Roni Natov]: Yes, I noticed there was no attempt to psychoanalyze Archie.

[Robert Cormier]: People can't say Archie did this because he was a deprived child or he was a victim of child abuse. I wanted him judged solely on his actions. So that's why Jerry's father was the only one. And he was more or less ineffective because of his own sorrow. He wasn't that vital a character anyway, or he wouldn't have been that devastated.

[Geraldine DeLuca]: People do notice though that Jerry doesn't have that support, that his father is not aware that he is getting beat up, that he's unhappy, that people are calling him and threatening him. If some adult figure had been there to say something, the outcome might have been different. (p. 121)

[Geraldine DeLuca]: Your books are beautifully written. Adolescent novels tend not to be very well written and these really stand out, *The Chocolate War* particularly.

[Robert Cormier]: Well, thank you. I love to hear that, naturally.

[Roni Natov]: Oh, we'll say more. The dialogue is wonderful in *The Chocolate War,* very inventive. Each character has a clear voice.

[Robert Cormier]: I love to hear that because I'm a frustrated script writer, screen writer, I think. I love writing dialogue.

[Roni Natov]: I can see it, because the books are dramas. They're not novels of sensibility. The characters collide, things happen, they are constantly talking to each other. Even when they're talking in their heads, they're talking out whole scenarios.

[Robert Cormier]: Yes, I write cinematically but try to keep that forward thrust. I want to keep the reader turning those pages. I'm conscious of the reader. And I try to write the way I would like to read a book, so I create incident and conflicts. Rather than waiting for one big climax, I try to create a lot of little conflicts between people. Part of that comes from my short story training where you have to get quick climaxes in a short space of time, rather than waiting until the middle of the book for a great one. I try to create a series of explosions as I go along.

[Geraldine DeLuca]: The opening line of *The Chocolate War* is explosive: "They murdered him."

[Robert Cormier]: Yes. I had a call from some kids down in South Carolina. They were at school and their teacher gave them permission to call me. They were calling from a corridor apparently—I could hear them talking—and they were having a big argument. Half the class said that Jerry died at the end, because I had said at the beginning that they murdered him and they took it literally. And the other half said he didn't, so they asked, "What do you think?" And I said, "Well, in my own mind, he's still alive," so one kid says, "Great! Now will you tell this other guy here so he'll hear you?" So I said, "Well, I'll do better than that. Give me your address." So I wrote to them. It's terrific to get this kind of feedback, to have kids care enough to have a big argument. It must have delighted the teacher, and it's a delight for me to think that they're taking what is probably a very downbeat book, which has caused controversy, and getting something out of it. You know, it's better than arguing about what Starsky and Hutch did last night? (pp. 121-22)

> *Geraldine DeLuca with Roni Natov, in an interview with Robert Cormier, in* The Lion and the Unicorn, *Vol. 2, No. 2, Fall, 1978, pp. 109-35.*

In the early sixties it was discovered that realistic children's books don't have to be whitewashed. We have yet to discover that they don't need to be blackwashed. Robert Cormier's *The chocolate war,* for instance, is a book that looks with adult bitterness at the inherent evil of human nature and the way young people can be dehumanized into power-hungry and bloodthirsty adults.

The author drives his point home over and over with a jackhammer style that leaves no pause for the characters to develop into real human beings of mixed emotion and action even to the extent that the characters in *Lord of the flies* do. Cormier is good at building and playing on dread. With a powerfully stacked plot and see-through characters he manipulates readers into believing how rotten things are by loading the dice while pretending to play fair. See these regular old dice? Whammo, you lose.

Do adult critics like the book because they agree with the message, because they've been slugged by some morbidly fascinating action, or because they've actually been convinced by a teenage character with the consciously effective live genius of a full-fledged Hitler? Here the characters are the message, and the characters are unbelievable. The book may make some interesting classroom discussion, but as a piece of realistic writing, I don't buy it.

> *Betsy Hearne, "Whammo, You Lose," in* The Booklist, *Vol. 70, No. 21, July 1, 1974, p. 1199.*

The big book of this YA autumn is clearly—and justifiably—Robert Cormier's *The Chocolate War.* . . . Too many young adult novels only promise an outspoken revelation of the relevant. *The Chocolate War* delivers the goods.

The goods in the story are 20,000 boxes of chocolates that a depraved teaching brother means for the students of a tottering parochial school to sell. Sweet charity is the mask for Brother Leon's sharp and shady fund-raising. Since nothing is petty to the institutionalized, the chocolate sale consumes the school.

The plot paces to a cataclysmic conclusion. The young will understand the outcome. They won't like it, but they'll understand.

The Chocolate War is surely the most uncompromising novel ever directed to the "12 and up reader"—and very likely the most necessary. It depicts the mass psychology behind the looming menace of the gangs that have never been more omnipotent than now. In his money-making venture, Brother Leon enlists the aid of Trinity School's invisible empire, a club of middle-class thugs who deal in mental—and ultimately physical—torture.

Significantly, we never learn the family backgrounds of the gang leaders. The author, who is free of the fatal susceptibilities of a guidance counselor, judges them unforgivingly on the evidence of their corruption. The measure of Brother Leon's own depravity is plumbed when he explains away the gang's excesses: "Oh, once in a while they get carried away but it's good to see all that energy and zeal and enthusiasm."

Archie Costello is the Machiavelli who runs the gang, called "The Vigils." Its members are drawn from the Central Casting of adolescence. Carter—the jock who serves as figurehead leader. Obie—the silent questioner who nevertheless complies. At the fringes of the pliant hangers-on is Janza. Archie practices sexual blackmail on him to do the gang's most obvious dirty work. The reader can never drift far from Archie, whose casual look masks an egomaniac's reptilian fury. Archie is the perfected product of the permissive society, and a promise for the future.

The Vigils' victim—and the reader's surrogate—is Jerry Renault. He is a boy who says no to the gang's demands repeatedly, and finally once too often. The values of our time being what they are, we are probably only at the beginning of a Literature of the Victim. Jerry is a notable example, for he is no quiet recipient of his fate. He resists to his limits. And anyone looking for a pat triumph of the individual had better avert his eyes.

In his *New York Times* review, Theodore Weesner recommends *The Chocolate War* as "an ideal study for the high school classroom." It's ideal too for a teacher-training program. And anyone banning this book for its locker-room-realistic language is committing a crime against the young. (p. 492)

Richard Peck, "Delivering the Goods," in American Libraries, *Vol. 5, No. 9, October, 1974, pp. 492-94.*

This is a thoroughly nasty book about a thoroughly nasty American private school. The characters have that dedication to corruption which seems to flourish in small closed societies presided over by an evil mind. . . . (pp. 194-95)

This may be a brilliantly written tour de force but despite the publisher's claim it is no more a children's book than is *The Exorcist*. The forces of good and evil are better balanced in *The Lord of the Flies* and the cruelty of *Portrait of the Artist as a Young Man* is compensated by the presence of a lyricism of awakening adolescence. *The Chocolate War* depicts a life without hope in which boys prey upon each other like prohibition gangsters, masturbate in the lavatory and drool over girlie magazines. It presents in one neat package all the most repellent aspects of the American way of life. Here in embryo are the forces of commercialism, of corruption, of sadism and the triumph of the beast. If you are an adult and an American it may shock you out of your complacency but English children will at the best be confused and at the worst enjoy it as a sadistic spectacle.

There is no place on the shelves of a children's library for such a delight in the destruction of innocence. (p. 195)

D. A. Young, in a review of "The Chocolate War," in The Junior Bookshelf, *Vol. 39, No. 3, June, 1975, pp. 194-95.*

Recently we have seen a trend in literature for young people that some call realism, but in fact it is not realistic at all. Realism is an honest attempt to picture people and events as they really are. To portray things from the brutal or dark side only, as is being done in current literature, is no more realistic than presenting only those sweet and idealistic stories of an earlier age.

As an example, *The Chocolate War*. . . is described as a realistic junior novel, and it meets some of the requirements for realism. Cormier has written honestly, I believe, what he thinks could happen at a private boys' school in the 1970s when one student decides to flout the system. Such honesty is basic to realism. He has also structured the novel masterfully; each incident builds up independently of the others, yet each contributes strength to the structure of the story, all with careful understatement. Cormier knows his craft; he has written a compelling novel.

But it is not realistic. In it there are no adults worth emulating; Jerry is the only decent kid, and he is victimized by his peers, with the cooperation of school officials. Only the ugly is presented through the novel's language, actions, and imagery; goodness and honor are never rewarded. Love and concern for other people is ignored, and hopelessness pervades the entire story. The presentation of people and events shows only the evil, the ugly, and the sordid. It is not appropriate for young people because it presents a distorted view of reality and because it lacks hope.

Of the adults in *The Chocolate War* Brother Leon is the very portrayal of evil, the malevolent force who controls the school, since the headmaster is conveniently out of the way, ill and in the hospital (almost the cliché of the dead mother in young people's stories, including this one). The other teachers? Brother Eugene, done in by the destruction of his classroom, falls apart just as surely as the classroom furniture did. Brother Jacques at first seems honorable, but because he is weak, he remains subservient to Brother Leon.

The other adults? Jerry's father, torn by grief over the death of his wife, is separated from Jerry except for whatever contact is necessary in their living together. Their separation had been a physical one the previous summer when Jerry lived with cousins following his mother's death; we know we can expect little more from Mr. Renault. The other parents in the book are stereotypes, praising their children for trivial accomplishments, ignoring them most of the time. All are vapid and depressing.

And the kids. Archie is Brother Leon's counterpart among the boys; it is his cunning that makes him a leader. Jerry is the only honorable boy, the only boy with the guts to be a non-comformist, to stand up to the bullies who rule the school. We think at first that Goober will be honorable and an ally in this brutal war, but he is not; rather he is one of those people who want to "shrivel into invisibility" rather than make trouble, or face trouble.

The other kids run the gamut from those who do anything to conform to rules set up by the bullies, to the bullies themselves, who intimidate, humiliate, and harass the weaker boys. All are shaped by the society at Trinity High; all are trapped by a cruel, ugly, sadistic system.

The language in the novel is ugly as well. It has become popular to "tell it like it is," and for some writers this means including the crude slang we know kids use. So Cormier uses much of it, but generally it is appropriate to its context and will probably not disturb the book's readers; kids can handle four-letter words with greater ease than my generation can. However, I don't think it is necessary for a writer for young adults to feed back to them their own slang any more than it is necessary for a writer for five-year-olds to include the bathroom language he or she knows five-year-olds use and find titillating.

The actions of the characters are almost without exception ugly, exemplifying only the most sordid side of their natures. Our senses are assaulted by kids cringing, sniveling, humiliating each other, stealing, and bullying. There are frequent references to masturbation and vomiting. Jerry, in particular, vomits a lot, an ugly picture but one that is perhaps in keeping with the one-sided view the book presents. The adults' actions are not as sordid, but they are as depressing. They nag, drink, sleep, watch television; they are trapped in dull jobs; they do dull things. None are involved in anything worthwhile with their children. People, we are told by Archie, "are two things: greedy and cruel." Cormier's people certainly are.

Most of the imagery is deliberately ugly. The word "beautiful" is used repeatedly by Archie, but only in sarcasm. "Beautiful" describes his intimidation of another student or the chaos he has created. We are assailed with images of the unpleasant odors of vomit, sweat, pee, and Leon's breath. Leon's smile is "like the kind an undertaker fixes on the face of a corpse." Sweat, for Jerry, moves "like small moist bugs on his forehead." Nature imagery is especially unpleasant as the sunset becomes the "sun bleeding low in the sky and spurting its veins," and the autumn leaves fluttering to the ground are "like doomed and crippled birds."

The Chocolate War has been compared to *A Separate Peace* and *Lord of the Flies,* which is expected. All deal with boys forming their own societal group complete with rules, taboos, value systems, and leaders—like any society.

But in *A Separate Peace* there are some sympathetic adults, adults to trust and to emulate. There is genuine, healthy rapport among the boys on the playing field. The book does not include tasteless language, and ugly incidents are limited to those essential to the story line. Finally, there are forgiveness and love to offset an otherwise harsh story.

Lord of the Flies tells an ugly story with cynical harshness, and it includes many ugly incidents and much ugly imagery, but it is set in a real jungle, on an island, with the boys completely cut off from adult intervention. *The Chocolate War* takes place in a large New England city, and involves more than eight hundred adults directly concerned with the society of boys. It goes beyond *Lord of the Flies* in that it suggests that adults are no more willing or capable of controlling their environment than are youngsters. It insinuates that it is possible that this many parents and teachers would be totally unconcerned about their own children or their students. It states not only that civilization can break down on an isolated island among a group of British school boys, but that it has broken down also for a large and diverse group of adults in a major American city.

This distorted view of humanity, this strange sense of what makes civilization work is hammered home by the conclusion of the story. Hints are given throughout that justice will finally triumph. Through foreshadowing we are led to believe that Jerry is going to win his battle, but this is just a trick of the author's.

We learn early in the story that Archie, as the "Assigner" of the Vigils . . . , is kept in line by a box of marbles. He has pushed his luck for three years; he has never once drawn the black marble that would force him to carry out the assignments he gives to others. It is suggested in the story that "the law of averages may catch up to him; his luck may be running out." Another hint comes in the classroom when Brother Leon baits a weak student unmercifully until a voice from the back of the room interrupts with "Aw, let the kid alone," and we are led to believe that others, particularly if they can remain anonymous, *will* speak out for justice.

Later when Obie learns that Archie has taken Brother Jacques into his confidence, tricking the boys so that their reaction to the word *environment* was used against them instead of to bait the teacher, Obie is furious at Archie. He walks off thinking, "I owe you for that." We expect Obie to take some kind of action that will prevent Archie from remaining the school leader.

Still another hint of the eventual triumph of goodness comes after Jerry appears before the Vigils for the second time and Archie "asks" him to sell the chocolates. Obie can scarcely believe the word *asks*: "as if Archie was trying to bargain with the kid, *asking,* for crying out loud. I've got you, Archie, you

bastard," Obie thinks. He "had never known such sweet victory. The goddam freshman was going to screw Archie up, at last." This is the final clue we need to believe that Jerry eventually will win.

But he does not win. He is brutally beaten and carried away broken and unconscious. The reader feels tricked. This completes Cormier's destruction of all that is good and honorable and becomes the most disturbing element in the book. Jerry, like us, is let down with a sickening thud.

So I struggle with *The Chocolate War.* I do not believe writers should be dictated to by librarians, by parents, by me, about what they should write. Yet I am disturbed by this book because, in spite of being brilliantly structured and skillfully written, it presents a distorted view of reality and a feeling of absolute hopelessness that is unhealthy. We know from the work of Abraham Maslow that people need a firmly based, high evaluation of themselves for their own self-respect and for the respect of others. We know they need positive experiences as well to mature wisely and well. There are no positive experiences in this book. We know also from the work of Curt Richter and Martin Seligman that we can teach hopelessness to our young if they are taught that no matter how hard they struggle they cannot win. This story teaches that hopelessness.

It is as inaccurate to present only the sordid and call it realistic as it has been in the past to present only the idealistic. It is probably even more damaging. *The Chocolate War* endorses and supports the thesis that one is better off not struggling for what is right because one cannot win and thus is, in effect, an object lesson in futility. (pp. 214-17)

> *Norma Bagnall, "Realism: How Realistic Is It? A Look at 'The Chocolate War'," in* Top of the News, *Vol. 36, No. 2, Winter, 1980, pp. 214-17.*

Norma Bagnall describes *The Chocolate War* as a hopeless novel about the forced sale of candy in a boys' parochial high school [see excerpt dated winter, 1980]. She considers it an unrealistic picture of adolescent life and unsuitable reading material for teenagers. We think her description is inaccurate and her criticism unwarranted.

Cormier's novel is only superficially about the fund-raising activities at a Catholic institution; its greater concerns are with the nature and functioning of tyranny. While it demonstrates the inability of a decent individual to survive unaided in a corrupt and oppressive society, it does not imply that such defeat is inevitable. To see the book as something "which could happen at a private boys' school in the 1970s when one student decides to flout the system" is to confuse setting with substance and plot device with purpose.

Cormier persistently uses figurative language as one device to remind the reader that the meaning of the book is not limited to the confines of the story line or the campus of Trinity High. After Archie decides that Jerry Renault's first assignment will be to refuse to sell chocolates, Obie notices that "the shadows of the goal posts definitely resembled a network of crosses, empty crucifixes." This reference to the central symbol of Christianity should certainly suggest that more is at issue than merely the selling of chocolates. When Jerry, defying the Vigils, announces he still will not accept the candy, the effect is cataclysmic: "Cities fell. Earth opened. Planets tilted. Stars plummeted." The author has clearly moved the action from the campus to the cosmos.

The metaphorical quality of the three power structures within the school is spelled out specifically and hinted at obliquely. The most obvious symbol is the athletic department, which provides for the testing of individuals, including each one's willingness and ability to withstand physical abuse. The football field is an arena where violence is ritualized, sanctioned, and even demanded. After the brutal fight in which Jerry is physically beaten and psychologically destroyed, he warns his friend to "play ball." This metaphor, taken from sports, is not restricted to the game but encapsulates the lesson Jerry has so painfully learned: he had better cooperate with the power structure or he will be crushed.

The school itself is a microcosm of society. In one of the most telling and ironic scenes in the story, the metaphorical implications of life at Trinity are baldly stated. Brother Leon accuses an "A" student, George Bailey, of cheating, humiliating him in front of his embarrassed but unprotesting classmates. Suddenly turning from his victim, he castigates the other students for not coming to the boy's defense. He likens them to the citizens of Germany who allowed the rise of Nazism, not through their support of Hitler, but through their inertia. His comparison is tragically prophetic.

Cormier further draws the reader outside the perimeters of a particular school by his frequent use of literary and biblical allusions. References to Hamlet, Shylock, J. Alfred Prufrock, Saint Peter, Moses, and John the Baptist invite comparisons and underscore the persisting and timeless relevance of events.

The most significant object in the story is the poster in Jerry's locker that asks: Do I Dare Disturb the Universe? When Cormier introduces it he describes it in detail, suggesting through Jerry's uncertainty that the caption may be subject to various interpretations. The question does not remain idle, tucked away in Jerry's locker, but is raised repeatedly when anyone—Jerry, his father, his classmates, his teachers—either challenges or bows to the demands of the establishment. Jerry ponders, expands, and twists the quote, and as his definition of the universe grows and changes, he realizes he is not just a single individual but a part of an interlocking social order. Following Jerry's ruminations, readers gain similar insight into the book's intent and theme. Cormier is clearly not writing about this existential question solely within the context of an isolated secondary school, but as it is applicable to the larger world.

Bagnall's criticism that *The Chocolate War* is not realistic is equally insupportable. She claims Cormier's work is distorted because "only the ugly is presented . . . goodness and honor are never rewarded."

Northrop Frye claims that "the world of literature is a world where there is no reality except that of the human imagination. . . . There are two halves to literary experience. Imagination gives us both a better and a worse world than the one we usually live with, and demands that we keep looking steadily at them both." If Cormier chooses to concentrate on the "worse world," he is exercising a literary privilege claimed by many major writers since Sophocles. Although this is not the only side of reality, it is certainly a significant one and remains a persisting concern of authors because it is a persisting component of human behavior.

It may be desirable for a library collection to encompass the full spectrum of human imagination, but such a comprehensive range cannot be reasonably required of every individual work. Condemning Cormier for ignoring the sunnier aspects of human behavior is as inappropriate as castigating Cresswell for avoiding serious matters in *The Bagthorpe Saga*.

Literary realism is not journalistic reporting. . . . [Novelists] choose particular elements of the world—distill, concentrate, and juxtapose them in such a manner as to illuminate a particular facet of the human condition. This, it seems to us, is exactly what Robert Cormier accomplishes in his junior novels, remaining well within the tradition of literary realism.

In *The Chocolate War* he has chosen to focus on tyranny and evil—not as vague abstractions, but given flesh and substance in the persons of Brother Leon and Archie. Bagnall disapproves of Cormier's concentration on that which is displeasing and concludes that the book is inappropriate for youngsters because its language, actions, and imagery are ugly. The unpleasant should not be confused with the unsuitable. Cormier's responsibility to his craft requires him to present characters and images, not as one would like them to be, but as they must be in order to make the novel and its message credible. Consequently, the language and images are disturbing, but then, so is tyranny. To mask evil with delicate similes would only diminish its potency, and to introduce a noble adult to save the day would truly be unrealistic.

Bagnall contends "*The Chocolate War* endorses and supports the thesis that one is better off not struggling for what is right because one cannot win and thus is, in effect, an object lesson in futility." Such a reading makes sense only if Jerry's destruction is inevitable. The reason Jerry was not saved was because he stood alone. But he need not have been alone, as Cormier states clearly and with consummate irony through the words of Brother Leon when he falsely accuses Bailey of cheating. The boys at Trinity could have come to Jerry's defense, if they had not lacked courage. Mr. Renault could have saved his son if he had not been so self-absorbed. The brothers could have checked Leon's ambitions if they had had the will. No one did. Jerry paid a terrible price for everyone else's inadequacies.

Robert Cormier does not leave his readers without hope, but he does deliver a warning: they may not plead innocence, ignorance, or prior commitments when the threat of tyranny confronts them. He does not imply that resistance is easy, but he insists it is mandatory. (pp. 283-85)

> *Betty Carter and Karen Harris, "Realism in Adolescent Fiction: In Defense of 'The Chocolate War',"*
> in Top of the News, *Vol. 36, No. 3, Spring, 1980, pp. 283-85.*

The action [in *The Chocolate War*] is set in a private school of Catholic foundation in the States, and it is its American flavour which first strikes an English reader. This is partly its literary convention and diction—a grating, staccato mixture of Salinger's *The Catcher in the Rye* and its much less accomplished, more deliberately gruesome and unreflective successors in the graduate schools of creative writing for teenagers. But also, and more pervasively, its American quality comes out in the conventional determination to tear away all the conventions of writing for children. The hero is not victorious, he is broken and humiliated; the repressive Mafiosi who run the school have clenched their fists even more tightly upon their power; the story is remorselessly tense, and only loosens the tensions momentarily in order to tighten it more frighteningly in a new corner—a sort of *Marathon Man* for children. The hero is entirely a victim, but the more entirely a latter-day victim in that his victimization stands for nothing redemptive or succouring to others in his community. He is entirely solitary, and his defeat is only debilitating.

But to judge in this way is to invite misunderstandings. My criticism is not simply a consequence of disliking and fearing the author's world-picture; it is obviously possible that the heroic resistance of individuals to evil and cruelty may be futile.... What is deeply wrong with *The Chocolate War,* ... is its grossness and indelicacy in telling its child-readers that heroism is, strictly, such a dead end. Trapped by prose and convention within the hero's skull, the author can find no way to qualify the helpless narrowness of his vision, and give the reader some detachment from and purchase on the hero's plight. This wouldn't matter if the only moral were to advise children not to let their parents send them to such a school. But Cormier sounds like yet another dispirited radical of the 1968 generation, of Miami and the siege of Chicago. The radical moral taken to heart after a term and a half on the steps of Nixon's Pentagon was that *all* structures of authority and institutions were deadly, and all would, in their super-ruthless and efficient way, break the spirit of the individual. (pp. 276-77)

The gang, with the connivance of the priests—the collusion of formal and informal Old Corruptions—. . . beat [Jerry] up horribly and break his spirit as well as his body. It is at such moments . . . that the prose moves with the greatest conviction. It runs its fingernail along the line of the nerve, and the reader wriggles with the routine sympathetic thrill of at once feeling and inflicting pain:

> His stomach caved in as Janza's fist sank into the flesh. He clutched at his stomach protectively and his face absorbed two stunning blows—his left eye felt smashed, the pupil crushed. His body sang with pain. . . .

Hero-victim and reader are left with the pain, and the clichés of concussion. The crude lesson is threefold: that all institutions systematize violence; that violence upholds power without reason; that individuals cannot hope to change these facts. These are the sentimentalities of disenchantment, understandable enough when you are faced with the 'realism' of Kissinger's and Nixon's blockade of Vietnam. But they are constantly rebutted in history and they leave no room for the necessary violence without which decency and civilization will not survive.

The Chocolate War is a children's novel. Inasmuch as this is so, the thrill and relish with which it plays on the raw edge of its readers' nerves seems not to spring from the old having-it-both-ways of the realistic thriller.... The sex-and-violence thriller—to accept that association—notoriously gained a spurious moral credit by being on the side of right while permitting the reader to enjoy all the sadistic satisfactions of inflicting pain and enjoying cruel power. There may be a touch of this in Cormier's novel, but . . . the more likely responses on the part of a child aged, say, twelve are horror and incomprehension. Even the toughest egg of the second year expects more justice from life than this, and insofar as the prose is effective in creating the thrill of pain, the novel has something of the realism of a movie like *Marathon Man* with its torture scenes in a dentist's chair, or Boorman's *Deliverance* with its discomfortingly immediate wounding and dreadful deaths. The writing is never far from the clichés of echo-chamber and beating-up by sound waves, of course, but its vividness makes its strongest effects very hard to negotiate, to know what to do with. The differences in moral climate could be best brought out if one were to compare in tone, reticence, and decorum the description in *War and Peace* of Pierre's narrow escape from execution after capture at Borodino, and the shockingly unfeeling explicitness with which a crude war novel like Mailer's *The Naked and the Dead* details arbitrary murder, mutilation, and callousness.

This is more than fixing a fight between the giant Tolstoy and the modern pygmy. It is also a matter of social convention and literary decorum, particularly since the audience at hand are children. The *intention* of *The Chocolate War* seems to be to force the child directly up against the pain of pain, the facts of cruelty and oppression, by way of showing him that the adults have always told lies about the world's being a fine and benign place, the guardians of the social order being friendly and just, the nature of action being unambiguous and generous. 'Here, kid, this is how it really is.' Time they lost their innocence.

Now adults have often lied, as it is the point of *Huckleberry Finn* to show us. It has already been suggested that some idealizing of what really happens is necessary, not in order to fool children, but in order to show them an image of finer forms of life. We tell children of a more nearly excellent world . . . not in order to anaesthetize them but as a prompt to the future. Or so the best novelists do. Their business . . . is to come to the life they write about with a keen, reciprocal, and animating sense of the finest life they can imagine.

The Chocolate War, and many lesser novels, fails that test. Luxuriating in their radical realism, the authors make an evil of necessity, and leave no means of criticizing on behalf of a better life the oppressions, power systems, and their violences, which the novelists seek to expose. The group of writers in question intend to pull the mask of benignity from society's cruel face, or to show that experience is bitter and painful. (pp. 278-80)

Children, of course, like a dose of the terrors at times—well-controlled times, with a warm fire and all the lights on all the way upstairs to bed. But as we have already noted, the choice to take a deliberate dose probably needs to be nicely balanced against the incredibility of the tale. If ghost or horror stories and films press too hard against the limits of the conventions, then the imaginative experience begins to get out of hand and 'become too real.'

It is not however such studied risk-taking which we are talking about; the author-teachers in hand seek to break the convention, precisely because it doesn't permit them to tell children about the many political menaces and atrocities of the real world, and allows children far too much well-lit room to escape into, on the way to bed or into adolescent life. My objection to *The Chocolate War* and some of its peers is that this determination leads the author-teacher into three related errors all evident in their prose and structure: first, a grossness and indecorum which forces brutal events too abruptly on the reader; second, a raw thrillingness about the prose which makes the authors' attitudes to power very ambiguous—the ambiguity of many modern films like *A Clockwork Orange* . . . ; third, the narrative convention which traps us inside the hero's skull and denies us the means of freeing ourselves from and criticizing his plight. The strictures stand; so does the charge that children must know political wrong for what it is. (pp. 280-81)

*Fred Inglis, "Love and Death in Children's Novels,"
in his* The Promise of Happiness: Value and Meaning

in Children's Fiction, *Cambridge University Press, 1981, pp. 271-91.*

I AM THE CHEESE (1977)

We have as the hero of this book a 14-year-old boy. Perhaps that makes *I Am the Cheese* a juvenile. This boy is biking from Massachusetts to Vermont to see his father in the hospital, and is bringing him a gift. On the way he has adventures.

That is one part of the book. The other, running concurrently, is a series of interviews with a psychiatrist. Obviously this is a disturbed boy. The psychiatrist is trying to dig into his subconscious to release stubbornly held memories.

Little by little, things come out. The boy discovers that his parents are not what they seem. Indeed, he himself is not what he seems. The family is on the run—but from what? There is a mysterious gray man. Who is he? There are phone calls the parents try to hide from their child.

So Cormier has written a novel of psychological suspense. He is a fine technician and this is an absorbing, even a brilliant job. The book is assembled in mosaic fashion: a tiny chip here, a chip there, and suddenly the outline of a face dimly begins to take shape. Everything is related to something else; everything builds and builds to a fearsome climax. At the end the boy discovers that he is indeed the cheese—the bait around which the rats gather. Little can he do about it, except react the way God and Freud have provided. The ending is grim indeed.

It is not that *I Am the Cheese* is in any way sensational, sadistic or anything like that. Cormier merely has the knack of making horror out of the ordinary, as the masters of suspense writing know how to do. The story moves along quietly enough. The bicycling adventures of the boy are the kind of adventures anybody today could experience. Where the tension enters is in the mind of the boy, who (as it turns out) is faced with a situation with which no child should have to cope.

The book is written in a highly sophisticated style, and the plotting and literary workmanship will delight the connoisseur. But, one wonders, will the style and, indeed, some of the actual content be above the heads of most teen-agers? It may be, however, that kids are more sophisticated today and that nothing much comes as a surprise to them.

> Newgate Callendar, *"Boy on the Couch," in* The New York Times Book Review, *May 1, 1977, p. 26.*

Robert Cormier's first novel, **The Chocolate War,** gave a terrifying picture of the psychological and physical cruelties perpetrated on a young boy who refused to submit to authoritarian pressures. His latest book *I am the Cheese* is no less harrowing but perhaps more effective in its overall impact. Official brutality is no longer personified in easily recognisable archetypes; it is transformed into society's collective unconcern for the individual human being. . . .

[The] story evolves into a psychological thriller whose climax is as uncompromising as that in **The Chocolate War.**

The complex portrait of Adam is a masterly creation. His role as a human cipher is revealed in sterile, coded messages, psychiatric transcripts and subtle shifts in the narrative voice. To those entrusted with his care he appears to have no more importance than a little black box to be decoded for the information locked in his mind. Yet Adam is a juvenile everyman,

cut off from any blood ties, whose eventual discovery of his past will do nothing to enhance his future. A sensitive and moving novel from an author who shows nothing but respect for the youthful audience he writes about.

> Patrick Verriour, *in a review of "I Am the Cheese," in* The World of Children's Books, *Vol. II, No. 2, Fall, 1977, p. 58.*

Until recently one mark of the novel for young adults that distinguished it from some adult novels was that the narrative mode was straightforward. Alan Garner was probably the pioneer in breaking this barrier; now *I Am the Cheese,* as if it were a *nouvelle vague* text, alternates a first-person present tense account of an alarming cycle ride across New England with a series of tape-recorded interviews between a boy, whom one may assume is the same as the cyclist, and someone who may be a psychiatrist; sometimes the boy's memories, in the third person, interrupt this colloquy.

Through this complex, and indeed irritating, pattern of narration, a grim story of fear, repression and betrayal establishes itself; the ending, in which one is almost simultaneously confronted with the extent of the boy's insanity and the deadly truth at its root, is entirely bleak: another way in which this novel makes no concessions to tender sensibilities. What worries me about this book, which admittedly grips intensely once one has come to terms with its manner, is that it could possibly do real harm to a disturbed adolescent, since it communicates all too effectively the paranoid fear that a psychiatric questioner may be an enemy—and then shows that it is true.

> Audrey Laski, *"No Laughing Matter," in* The Times Educational Supplement, *No. 3258, November 18, 1977, p. 34.*

For his new novel, Robert Cormier has returned to the theme which dominated his outstanding earlier book, **The Chocolate War:** that of innocence and morality destroyed by the ruthless ambition of the masters of a corrupt society. In **The Chocolate War,** this society was a private school, and the victim a boy who alone stood out against corruption. Now, in *I am the Cheese,* Robert Cormier has extended this dark theme. The hero is an unwilling, uncomprehending and truly innocent victim of a greater, more hideous conspiracy; the corrupt society is our own, and the innocent victim must be completely destroyed in order to sustain it.

At first sight, the narrative construction of the novel seems difficult and pretentious. . . . As the novel nears its end, the point and meaning of the book's construction become plain, and the narrative strands combine in a climax of depressing violence and a conclusion of almost intolerable despair. . . .

I am the Cheese is, first and foremost, a novel of suspense through which the reader is lured by the excitement and tension of the story. But the book is more than just a good thriller: Robert Cormier has written a chilling study of a mind on the verge of disintegration, and presented us with a view of our society that is too dire to contemplate. Robert Cormier does not hesitate to challenge and disturb his readers and, although *I am the Cheese* is no book for the emotionally squeamish, it deserves to be widely read. Beside it, most books for the young seem as insubstantial as candyfloss.

> Lance Salway, *"Death and Destruction," in* The Times Literary Supplement, *No. 3949, December 2, 1977, p. 1415.*

Don't ever begin *I Am the Cheese* at 3:30 in the afternoon when you have an appointment at 5:00. You will look at your watch every fifteen minutes and mutter, ''I can be a little late. I can be a little late.'' And you'll gobble up more pages, knowing you can't finish, fighting the urge to read six lines ahead of yourself. Because Cormier is Svengali *redivivus*. He leads you on, and you say, ''Oh, I see,'' when of course you don't really see at all. And you find you're right. And you're wrong. Both at once. (p. 25)

From the very start, there is something askew. Why is this boy pedaling, exhaustedly, the seventy miles to Rutterburg, Vermont? And it's never just ''Rutterburg'' but always ''Rutterburg, Vermont,'' like ''Perceval Wemys Madison, The Vicarage. . . .'' Then, out of nowhere, chapters are interspersed in which ''A'' is talking on tape to ''T,'' who seems to be a psychiatrist. And he well might be. But ''T's'' diction seems at times just the slightest bit stilted. Understandable, of course, but why does he always conclude the tape with, ''We'll suspend now,''—not ''stop'' or ''Let's call it a day,'' but ''suspend''? And then finally, so late, after you know you know, the word ''terminate.''

Part of it is those pernicious end-of-chapter sentences, like the ones in *The Exorcist* (''There were no disturbances. That night.'') which make the next chapter no longer a matter of free choice. What's more, from the first page, the book is pitted with question marks—why is the boy's father in the hospital? why are the dates on the tapes deleted? what possible relation have the tape-chapters to the bicycling-chapters? why does the boy have two birth certificates?—and a question mark is an inverted hook.

The two plots run parallel, converge, throw clue-hooks into one another. They build, become impending, until you know ''it'' is coming. And yet, right up to the end, you find yourself saying, ''What's going *on*????'' Then the final chapter takes the whole thing, twists it round, shakes it up, and punches you right in the solar plexus. To put it in no way facetiously, this novel is like *I Never Promised You a Rose Garden* written in collaboration by Ian Fleming and Franz Kafka.

The inter-cutting of the plots is masterful: just as the tape is about to uncover another climax, there is the marvelously infuriating cut back to the boy on the bike. But it is not just the manipulative plotting that makes your heart race as if you were pedaling yourself. It is the fact that, right from the start, young Adam Farmer has hold of your heart. (pp. 25-6)

You *care* about a kid who tells you, right off, as he's pedaling along, ''I pass by a house with a white picket fence and I spot a little kid who's standing on the sidewalk and he watches me go by and I wave to him because he looks lonesome and he waves back.'' He is claustrophobic even on baseball fields; he can't stand rooms without windows, even restrooms; mysteriously, he has dumped some kind of pills out just before beginning his frightening little odyssey in search of his father; he is scared. But he's going. He has pluck. Not Tom Swift pluck. Real pluck; coward's pluck.

This is not a ''kids' book''; it doesn't insult with over-simplifications as most of television does. (p. 26)

In this dis-spirited age of adolescent computers and Playboys, it is a joy to meet Cormier's young people. No matter what comes, they are—to the end—spirited. They show that, under all the pitiful facades, adolescents, too, are vitally human beings.

I just received an advance copy of the cover for the paperback edition of *I Am the Cheese*. My fear was that the people who pick the back cover blurbs would call this book ''the new *Catcher in the Rye*.'' It's the original *I Am the Cheese*. It stands alone. (pp. 27-8)

William J. O'Malley, S. J., in a review of ''I Am the Cheese,'' in Media & Methods, *Vol. 14, No. 9, May-June, 1978, pp. 24-8.*

''But,'' thinks Adam Farmer at a key point in *I Am the Cheese*, ''this is absurd.'' Adam is right. In Robert Cormier's novel, this apparently ordinary boy discovers that his ordinary life was mere fabrication, and the truth beneath the lies is an improbable stew of secret documents, spies, murders, and assumed identities. But most readers are too caught up in the novel to think about how improbable it is. *I Am the Cheese* is like the ''Numbers'' it describes—the practical jokes Adam's friend Amy Hertz invents to persuade innocent bystanders that something improbable really did happen. Cormier tells us ''Amy Hertz was beautiful to watch when she was doing a Number. The process had to be carried out seriously, with no hint of mischief''. . . . Cormier carries out his own number just as seriously, just as beautifully.

Cormier tells us that Amy ''always withheld information about the Numbers until the last possible moment, stretching out the drama''. . . . He does that himself in the novel. The reviews quoted on the back cover of the paperback edition speak of how ''gripping'' it is, of how ''the suspense builds relentlessly,'' of how ''everything builds and builds to a fearsome climax'' [see excerpt dated May 1, 1977]. Generally, suspense arises from uncertainty about what will happen next in an orderly chain of events; but while readers of *I Am the Cheese* experience uncertainty about what *fact* they will discover next, the facts are all about past events. Our attention is focused not on what happens next, but rather, on what has happened already; in that way, *I Am the Cheese* is more like a mystery novel than a suspense thriller. Cormier makes much use of the world ''clue'' throughout, and *I Am the Cheese* demands of its readers the detached, investigative attitude engendered by the sort of mystery novels that contain clues. . . . I became a logical, detached detective.

But despite my detachment, I still felt anxiety. I wanted to know what was happening, not just to satisfy my intellectual puzzlement about an intricate mystery, but also because I felt genuinely disoriented and confused, genuinely involved in that uncertainty we call suspense. The genius of the novel is that it is both logical puzzle and exciting thriller, that it engenders detachment and involvement at the same time.

Cormier achieves that paradoxical combination by focusing our attention on the past—making us think about what might have happened, as mysteries do—while at the same time keeping us ignorant of the present that mysterious past led to. Most mystery novels begin by showing us things as they are *now*: the dead body in the library, a telephone found in the freezer. The detective reads back from those present circumstances to determine how they came to be. But in *I Am the Cheese*, we don't know what Adam's present circumstances are; figuring out what they are comes to be a part of our concern. We must both try to solve the mystery and be unsure about what the effects of it are—or if, indeed, there were any effects at all. Since we do not know what effects the mysterious past we are trying to understand led to, we act less with the cool certainty of mystery novel detectives than with the anxiety of confused people asked to think logically about incomplete information.

That sounds uncomfortable—and it is. Cormier cleverly makes us accept and enjoy our confusion by providing *one* genuine past, a set of events that happened and are now over, and what appear to be *two* different presents that the past led to. The story of Adam's bicycle trip to Rutterburg is in the present tense; but so are the sections labelled as tapes. Since we know that two such dissimilar sets of events cannot both be equally present, we must ask which precedes the other. It is possible that something happened in the past that led to Adam's confused state of mind as he embarks on the bicycle trip, and that something then happened on the bicycle trip that led to his apparent therapy as it appears on the tapes. But it is also possible that something happened in the past that led to the therapy, and that it is a partially recovered Adam who sets off to visit his father *after* his sessions with Brint. With our attention focused on sorting such things out, looking for clues and making guesses, we accept our uncertainty about present circumstances as part of the pleasure of the mystery.

Just as important, we let Cormier do his Number; for of course, the real truth is right before our eyes. The two presents are both equally present, just as they appear in the novel. That Adam is both undergoing his sessions with Brint and riding his bicycle to Vermont at the same time is the one possibility we don't consider; Cormier cannot allow us to consider it, for it depends on our knowledge that the bike trip is a fantasy, knowledge that is the key to the entire mystery. He deflects our attention from the literal truth of the novel, the impeccably chronological ordering of events that seem to have no chronology, by making them seem to have no chronology.

How Cormier manipulates readers into believing the wrong things and ignoring the right ones is fascinating to explore; and I believe that *why* he does it is the key to the meaning of the novel. But such an exploration is not easy. The Number only works once, for each reader on a first reading. A second reading, with knowledge both of what happened in the past and of what is happening in the present, is a different experience. Now the novel seems filled with clues, with obvious evidence of what seemed incomprehensible before, and with huge ironies. Even on the first page, Adam claims to be heading for a hospital on a hill that reminds us of his actual circumstances, which we will learn only much later; and he refers to "a Thomas Wolfe October" that offers second-time readers a poignant foreshadowing of his parents' death in an October his father described the same way. Such ironies occur throughout; in one of the earlier tape sequences, Adam even spills the beans about the bike trip, for those who know about the bike trip already, when he thinks, "If I can step outside myself like this, maybe I can go to other places. . . . (pp. 95-7)

But as in most literature, the real significance of *I Am the Cheese* is less the truth that eventually emerges from it than the way in which it emerges; what is interesting about the bike trip is less the truth it hides than the fact that it is hidden, and the way Cormier hides it. For that reason an attempt to recreate a first reading of the novel in order to show how it conceals and reveals its truths is not just desirable, but necessary. What follows is my attempt at such a recreation.

The first section of the novel implies many mysteries. A nameless person is on a bike trip: who is he? He is going to visit his father in a hospital: why is his father in hospital? He is bringing his father a gift: what is it? Novelists usually make

us ask such questions at the beginnings of novels, in order to arouse our interest. But they usually quickly answer them, and then focus our attention on new developments. In *I Am the Cheese,* only the first question is answered quickly, and the answer turns out to be wrong: Adam Farmer is not really Adam Farmer. In keeping us in the dark about some apparently important information, Cormier extends throughout most of *I Am the Cheese* the disorientation we usually stop feeling a short way into other novels.

In addition to those unsolved mysteries, the first section contains two details that attract attention. The person speaking tells us he is "afraid of a thousand things, a million". . . , and says he has decided not to take some pills: "I wanted to do this raw, without crutches, without aid, alone". . . . These comments plant the suspicion that the speaker is mentally disturbed. Then we come to the first tape sequence, which can easily be read as an interview between a therapist and a patient. The interviewer's insistence on going back to early memories, the interviewee's conviction that "the medicine was always playing tricks on him". . . , his reference to "the doctor," all confirm the suspicions engendered by the first chapter: this person must be under psychiatric care. In fact, I assumed that the interviewee and the bike rider were the same person only because they seem to share emotional difficulties. Consequently, as I heard of the boy's past, I looked for clues to his illness. I had been made to think in the comfortably superior way that psychoanalysts think of their patients, allowed both to feel sympathy for this suffering creature and to explore the events of his life with cool detachment. I knew there was a mystery to solve here; but Cormier manipulated me into playing, not Hercule Poirot, but Sigmund Freud.

Consequently, I took for granted that the boy's frequently expressed fears were paranoid, a distortion of reality rather than a just response to it. I accepted the doctor's apparently reasonable explanations of Adam's suspicions, and thought Adam had a point when he asked himself, "Was he really manufacturing mysteries to satisfy his literary longings, finding mysteries where they did not in fact exist?". . . Given Adam's apparent illness, these reminders that less dramatic explanations are possible deflect attention from the truth.

Furthermore, having been asked to think as a psychoanalyst would, I found it hard to doubt that Brint was a psychoanalyst. I trusted Brint because Adam did *not* trust him, and I had been made to think of Adam as untrustworthy. Adam himself confirms that: "he was wary again, on guard, distrustful. Yet he had no reason to distrust Brint". . . . (pp. 97-8)

Above all, the suspicions Cormier created about Adam's sanity distracted me from questioning the biggest lie in the novel. It did not occur to me that Adam might not be, as he said he was, riding to Rutterburg. The details of this trip are weirdly unreal; but I put that down to Adam's confused state of mind. I took for granted that this was a reality he was distorting, not one he was inventing. Upon reading, I find it hard to see why I wasn't more suspicious—particularly about Adam's conversation with an old man near the beginning of his trip, who seems to be as paranoid as Adam himself. But I didn't have the evidence to realize the ironic truth in the old man's statement that "it's a terrible world out there . . . you don't even know who to trust anymore". . . . Trusting that the old man was indeed at a gas station, I put his distrust down to the conservatism of age.

In the first third of the novel, then, Cormier convinced me of the truth of three falsehoods. I believed that the "doctor" was a doctor, that Adam was actually Adam and the Farmers actually the nice, normal Farmers, and that Adam was in fact on a bike trip. While Adam himself doubts the truth of all three, Cormier has manipulated me into distrusting Adam. Cormier has made me accept fantasies as truth, and assume that truth is mere delusion. He has done a Number on me.

What Brint tells Adam about the phone conversation he overhears between his mother and his aunt is true also for those who read the book: ''and so, for the first time, you had actual and direct evidence that there was something wrong, that something was askew''. . . . But while I changed my interpretation of the situation at this point, I still didn't get it right. I still thought Adam was mentally disturbed—possibly because of some genuinely disturbing information he had learned about his family; and Cormier helped me to believe that by giving Adam some particularly intense moments of apparent paranoia: ''I hate this place. The people here hate me, too. . . . They know I'm not like them''. . . . But I did begin to wonder about Brint. Cormier now makes Brint's interest in psychologically insignificant information more obvious; but I noticed that, as I hadn't earlier in the novel, because of my disorientation after I shared Adam's discovery of his secret aunt. Up to that point, I'd thought I understood the sort of book I was reading. I was wrong. The mystery was not merely psychological. And if it wasn't, then why should a psychologist be involved in it? Adam says, ''There was nothing to be suspicious about, until I became suspicious of everything''. . . . I felt the same way as I read about him, and realized I had been no better than Adam himself at penetrating deceptions, at distinguishing justified suspicion from foolish paranoia or real mysteries from psychological fancies.

But even after I became suspicious of Brint—in fact, even after I learned the truth about Adam's past, I still had no doubts about the bike trip. In fact, and in spite of many clues, I came to understand the nature of Adam's delusion only as he did so himself. My attention had been focused elsewhere: on sorting out the time sequences, on the enormity of the truth about Adam's family, on my growing suspicions of Brint. Even as I read the chapters describing the bike trip, my growing knowledge of the past led me to focus my attention more on what suitably horrible episode might have led to Adam's father being in that hospital than on the inconsistencies of the trip itself. So I was surprised to learn the truth, just as I was surprised earlier to learn the truth about Adam's family. Cormier so controlled my response to the novel that he played the exact same trick on me twice, without my suspecting the second was indeed a trick even after I learned about the first.

While my recreated first reading shows what a master craftsman Cormier is, it doesn't necessarily justify his trickery. The question remains: does Cormier's clever deception of his readers accomplish anything in addition to demanding involvement in what is, after all, an outrageously improbable plot?

I think it does. In *The Implied Reader*, Wolfgang Iser suggests that in good fiction, ''the reader must be made to feel himself the . . . meaning of the novel. To do this he must actively participate in bringing out the meaning, and this participation is an essential precondition for communication between the author and the reader.'' Cormier's Number in *I Am the Cheese* forces exactly that sort of participation. By tricking readers into believing lies and then revealing the truth they hide, Cormier makes *us* undergo the same experience Adam does. Both Adam and those who read about him believe that he is an ordinary member of an ordinary family, and overprone to fool-

ish suspicions; that Brint is a therapist and that Adam is his mentally disturbed patient; and that Adam is on a bike trip to visit his father in a hospital. Adam's discoveries are more horrifying, and the disorientation that results from them more intense, because Cormier provides readers that same faith in untruths that Adam has, the same discoveries, and the same awesome sense of having trusted too much.

In fact, and also like Adam, learning that our first interpretations were wrong leads us to doubt our ability to interpret. . . . In *I Am the Cheese,* if we started out thinking like Freud and diagnosing Adam as a paranoid, the novel clearly teaches us to distrust the comforting logic of psychoanalytic thinking. Because our first conceptions were so wrong and so foolishly trusting, we are made to understand the justice of the sort of thinking we might otherwise dismiss as paranoia. In fact, it teaches us to think like paranoids, to replace our common sense faith in the abiding security of normalcy with the deep cynicism th.. ..ar acceptance of Adam's horrifying experience implies. In other words, it teaches us that paranoia is not paranoia at all, but wisdom. Because we have acted as Adam's father was advised to act by his editor, because we have tried ''to go beyond the superficial aspects of stories, to find the meanings below the surface, to root out what might be hidden or not apparent to the casual reader''. . . , and because our logical investigation has brought us knowledge of a world as illogical and as corrupt as the one Adam's father learned of in *his* investigations, we have no choice but to find the cynicism convincing and thoroughly unsettling. In Iser's terms, *I Am the Cheese* forces us to participate in its meaning.

In his earlier novel, *The Chocolate War,* Cormier used a more probable set of events to express much the same cynicism about the inability of individuals to protect themselves from the corruptions of the powerful. Yet the attitudes that are so involving in *I Am the Cheese* seem merely paranoid in *The Chocolate War,* merely adolescent and self-indulgent—except, perhaps, to those adolescent and self-indulgent enough to share them already. In fact, *The Chocolate War* reads like countless other unremittingly naturalistic, unremittingly negative novels, designed to please adolescent readers by pretending that the corrupt world they describe is actually the real one. Despite their naturalistic settings, such novels are fantasies, pleasingly paranoid in their insistence that the world is not only corrupt, but out to get nice, innocent, young people just like *you*. For those adolescents who need to shield themselves from their growing knowledge of their personal involvement in the human condition and of the subtle confusions of good and evil in themselves and others, such fantasies are undoubtedly satisfying; for the rest of us, they seem a little silly.

In *The Chocolate War,* Archie thinks that ''the world was made up of two kinds of people—those who were victims and those who were victimized''. . . . In *I Am the Cheese,* Adam constantly sees himself as a victim, and assumes that everyone is out to victimize him. The fact that *The Chocolate War* supports Archie's crude vision makes it seem hysterical. But Adam is right. He *is* the only ''normal'' person in a crazy world. His life *is* a mess, and it is not his fault. Those in authority *are* corrupt, *are* power hungry, and *are* out to get him. In fact, and unlike *The Chocolate War, I Am the Cheese* turns the conventions of adolescent fiction inside out. What characters in such novels usually merely imagine about their lives (albeit with the support of their novelists) turns out to be literally true in *I Am the Cheese;* and meanwhile, what is literally true of the lives of characters in other novels turns out to be merely what Adam has imagined. The characters in those other novels live ordinary lives, but see them in terms of melodrama; Adam lives a melodramatic life, but poignantly imagines himself to be ordinary, an ordinary member of an ordinary family who is taking an ordinary bike trip.

Adam himself speaks of his life as "living through a Number that's the biggest one of all". . . . Letting Adam do so is Cormier's biggest Number. Adam's world is so clearly unlike our own that we do not confuse it with our own; free from accusing the novel of pretending to be realistic, we can see it for the fantasy that it is, and both find it powerfully convincing and appreciate its metaphoric thrust. Anne Scott MacLeod suggests that in *I Am the Cheese,* "Cormier dispenses with metaphor. This stark tale comments directly on the real world of government, organized crime, large-scale bureaucracy, the apparatus of control, secrecy, betrayal, and all the other commonplaces of contemporary political life" [see excerpt dated 1981 in General Commentary]. But while the comment is direct, it is so exaggerated that it comes to stand for something both larger and more personal than politics. Adam Farmer is a far more poignant image of individual powerlessness than the self-pitying draft-dodgers of *The Chocolate War.*

Furthermore, the distance between Adam's plight and our own lives ought to make us realize how comparatively illegitimate our own self-pity might be. In *After the First Death,* . . . Cormier tells us that the young terrorist Micro "felt contempt for all these American boys and girls who led their selfish, unthinking lives and thought they were so smart and brave until situations developed that showed their true worth". . . . Meanwhile, Miro himself is literally what many American boys and girls seem to enjoy imagining themselves to be: alien, orphaned, "innocent," a brave idealist doomed in his fight against the corruptions of those in power—or so he thinks, for the normal American girl Kate quite rightly concludes that innocence like Miro's "could also be evil. Monstrous . . .". . . . The contrast between the alienated terrorist and selfish, normal boys and girls is interesting because it makes obvious what *I Am the Cheese* more subtly implies: that we should be grateful for the distance between the lurid melodrama we love to imagine and the usually unexciting world we actually live in. By making readers share Adam Farmer's horrifying discovery that the secure, normal world he thought he lived in hides illogic and evil, *I Am the Cheese* brilliantly encourages our acceptance of the ambiguous boredom and glory of normal life. (pp. 98-103)

> *Perry Nodelman, "Robert Cormier Does a Number," in* Children's literature in education, *Vol. 14, No. 2 (Summer), 1983, pp. 94-103.*

AFTER THE FIRST DEATH (1979)

Young adults are exploring the outer reaches of their powers and responsibilities. They are re-evaluating preconceptions and myths. They are the most original and daring of thinkers, constantly re-examining everything they have grown up with. For them in particular, Robert Cormier's latest young adult novel, *After the First Death,* must ring false indeed.

The action in the book concerns terrorism. Refugee "freedom fighters" seize a busload of young children. They have three demands: the release of political prisoners in the US, a cash ransom, and the dismantling of a top-secret US Army installation. The plot is further complicated when the head of the army operation chooses his 15-year-old son to act as intermediary. Three young adults of different perspective are brought together by the incident—Kate Forrester, the bus driver; Miro Shantas, a 16-year-old terrorist; and Ben Marchand, the army general's son.

The plot is compelling and the language, as in Cormier's other young adult novels, is crystalline and precise. The book jacket promises the reader a look at such fundamental problems as the limits to patriotism. But the novel does not make use of the situation's rich potential. The characters and events are jumbled together pointlessly like pebbles in a jar.

There is an absence of both thought and commitment in all the protagonists. Miro Shantas seeks the return of his homeland not out of emotional yearning or deep political conviction, but rather because that is what he has been trained to do. Ben Marchand has only a cloudy awareness of the agency his father heads and of the terrorists' purpose. Kate Forrester, who shows the most independence of thought and action, is embroiled in the drama through a fluke. She acts out of self-preservation and is constantly measuring herself against a vague idea of heroism.

The main characters are indeed humanized, which Cormier achieves mainly by referring to various bodily functions and carnal desires. But the higher realms of personality are never broached. Neither individuality nor ideals have any part in their behavior, and in fact, seem not to exist.

Perhaps as a necessary result of Cormier's perspective, there are no surprises in the book, with the exception of a twist in the last chapter which introduces the chilling idea that madness is the only indeterminate element in human behavior.

Certainly the possibility of human predictability should be explored; but such a weighty issue deserves a thoughtful treatment which suggests some explanation. Cormier merely states a simplistic idea: the past decides the present.

> *Lorraine Hirsch, "Novel of Terrorism with a PG Rating," in* The Christian Science Monitor, *June 1, 1979, p. 22.*

A demanding novel, both frightening and profound. . . .

Cormier takes his reader on an agonizing journey into the very soul of human consciousness—a journey which is apt to leave readers feeling dishevelled, awkward and strangely vulnerable. . . . On one level the book is about the nature of individual and collective identity. On another, it is about the victimization of innocence. On still another, it is about the life and fate of Marchand, a modern-day Abraham, who sacrifices his son to patriotism and fatherland. Cormier has us ask, who is this Abraham and who is his son? What are their true names, and what is the true name of patriotism and fatherland? Who are we? Who am I? . . .

With uncompromising intensity, the author shatters the individual and collective myths of our times and demands a deeper level of truth-telling. His story is raw, and it has intriguing dualities and ambiguities. He is a remarkable craftsman. His shifts in point of view and the interior dialogues and monologues prod us to see each character as a reflection of the others and to see ourselves reflected in them all. Cormier's vision is most closely realized in Kate Forrester, who in the span of twenty-four hours rises to a call of epic proportions. In her the author reveals the heroic possibilities of the unsung American teenager. For Cormier, life calls for an internal quest, like Kate's, a peeling away of disguises until essential truths emerge. Although he knows that truth will always be limited by human frailty, truth is the ideal for which he struggles. And it is the nature of the Eden and the nature of the journey that he would have us examine. (pp. 426-27)

> Barbara F. Harrison, in a review of "After the First Death," in The Horn Book Magazine, Vol. LV, No. 4, August, 1979, pp. 426-27.

Here is a story which is topical, desperately relevant, demanding on the intellect and the emotions, highly controversial. I would not say that it is wholly successful, but it is better to score a near miss at this enterprise than to succeed in a conventional namby-pamby undertaking. . . .

The story is told through the eyes of four major actors: a young terrorist, the driver, the American general, and his teenage son. This device, which gives variety to a narrative which deals necessarily with inaction rather than action, also leads to some confusion and intolerable demands on the reader. One has to switch too often and to share out one's sympathies too widely and therefore too thinly. It is made no easier by the writer's ability to think himself into the heart and brain of each of these characters. Brilliant as a tour-de-force, the book may not win the wide audience it deserves.

Some adult readers may be worried both by the theme and its inbuilt brutality and by the need to sympathise with the terrorists as well as their victims. In the event all are losers, and those who wish a children's novel to have clear-cut issues and the triumph of right over wrong must be distressed. It is, after all, not a children's book, but a powerful disturbing novel in which some young readers will be able to share.

> M. Crouch, in a review of "After the First Death," in The Junior Bookshelf, Vol. 43, No. 4, August, 1979, p. 216.

[The] novels of Robert Cormier have consistently transcended the limitations of the genre. He has avoided the thin characterizations and glib language that are so familiar to us perhaps because he is faithful to his own vision, writing more truly for himself than many other writers for this audience. He is unafraid to bring a story to its aesthetically inevitable conclusion, and his lucid prose style, which is easily accessible to adolescents, seems natural rather than contrived to catch the interests of that audience.

His newest work, *After the First Death*, continues the exploration of issues presented in his first two novels for adolescents. His preoccupation with the child as victim and with mind control will be familiar to his readers. In *The Chocolate War*, an untrained adolescent's cool observations of people's vulnerabilities allow him to exploit and control them. In *I Am the Cheese*, the manipulators are the forces of government, empowered to change and ultimately destroy lives in the name of national security. This newest work combines both forms of control. Cormier explores both the very personalized form of brutality and intimidation employed by international terrorists and the behind-the-scenes government manipulations that may engender and result from such terrorism. (pp. 139-40)

Cormier makes the link between personal relationships and the machinations and power struggles of government by balancing the father-son relationships of Artkin and Miro, and Ben and the general against the larger events of the novel, showing how each father ultimately sacrifices his son for his cause. (p. 140)

Cormier does not ask us to sympathize or forgive. In fact, he seems to have a special interest in the unforgivable. He is fascinated by the pathology. But, in this novel more than his earlier works, he explores the circumstances that nurture characters who stir our hatred and fear. He also forces us to consider the extent to which we are all manipulated by powers we seldom think about—powers invested in people like the well-meaning but misguided General Marchand, for example. (p. 141)

[The] form of narration is somewhat experimental. The book opens with Ben's journal and, after fifteen pages, shifts to Miro's perspective. Events from that point on are narrated in the third person, but through the alternating eyes of Kate and Miro, with brief returns to Ben and to the dialogue. The parts are skillfully juxtaposed, and it is with the discovery of each character's point of view and personality that the issues of the story emerge, with Cormier demonstrating how well-meaning people go about destroying each other in futile attempts to control their world.

Though the political concerns are adequately explored, Cormier's primary focus is on the individuals. He develops them, elicits sympathy for them, and then as often as not destroys them. One minor example involves one of the children on the bus. He draws a brief sketch of the boy, gives us a touching detail about him—he is anxious about being late because he has often heard himself referred to as a "late baby"—and then we see him led off the bus and shot. The effect is horrifying, but we can see the honesty of Cormier's method. He seems to be saying they are all individuals with histories, feelings, families, and it is only by forgetting this, by becoming numbed by rhetoric or by too much brutality in one's past, that human beings become capable of destroying so casually. So while one could argue that Cormier is too pessimistic a writer for adolescents, the book stands finally not as a cynical but a loving work. Cormier's portraits are deeply compassionate. Kate, who was braver than she ever thought she could be; Miro who killed her in a moment of pain because he couldn't stand to hear what she revealed to him about himself; and Ben who killed himself to stifle his sense of shame—all three are innocents who tried to live up to some impossible ideal fostered upon them by dangerously misguided adults. (pp. 143-44)

> Geraldine DeLuca, "Taking True Risks: Controversial Issues in New Young Adult Novels," in The Lion and the Unicorn, Vol. 3, No. 2, Winter, 1979-80, pp. 125-48.

What is the truth about Robert Cormier, the controversial writer whose artistic power is universally acknowledged, yet whose vision of the world seems schizophrenically split: "savage" in his novels, "gentle and warm" in his short stories? . . . It may be possible . . . to resolve some of the confusions and contradictions surrounding the world view in Cormier's work by closely scrutinizing his own statements about himself as an artist: by looking closely at, first, his romantic view of the writing process, his insistence upon truthfulness to his artistic vision, and then by investigating his use of the technique of irony to achieve his most dramatic effects. His most recent novel, *After the First Death*, will be used as a case in point to demonstrate how his ironic technique "works."

Cormier's own comments on his writing process clearly characterize him as a romantic artist. His inspiration begins always, he tells us, with an "emotion," and he proceeds to get its "impact" down on paper. The sequence of creation is invariably the same: the emotion he desires to create gives rise to character; character suggests plot. The goal is always to communicate the emotion he wants the reader to feel: "'I sacrifice everything to that.'" This requirement explains his use of "'any word, any unpretty image, to communicate that emotion.'" Clarity, precision of effect, is what he aims for.

This romantic approach to the creative process strongly suggests Wordsworth's "emotion recollected in tranquillity" and also conjures up recollections of Edgar Allan Poe's concept of the genesis of a "tale":

> A skillful literary artist . . . having conceived, with deliberate care, a certain unique or single effect to be wrought out, he then invents such incidents—he then combines such events as may best aid him in establishing this preconceived effect.

Everything, Poe continues, must work towards "the one pre-established design." Cormier's pre-established design, the emotional effect, relates to his predilection for adolescent protagonists, for as he has observed, their emotional lives are more intense and vivid, "'far more exciting, more excruciating, more intriguing than mine,'" and the vivid intensity of their experiences awakens within him "'memories of my own.'"

The invention of the emotion itself may be spurred by incidents so seemingly insignificant that none but the gifted novelist would give them a second thought: when his son, a freshman trying out for the football team, came home "'with two shopping bags of chocolates to sell,'" Cormier's imagination asked "'What if . . . ,'" evoking the sinister possibilities inherent in this everyday event, and "'a novel was born.'"

Cormier is also a romantic in his view of art as a process of discovery. "'. . . one of the joys of sitting down at the typewriter is finding out what's going to happen.'" He sees his whole writing career as "a process of growth and learning," and he immensely enjoys the "dialogue" he carries on with his young readers.

Cormier is moreover a writer committed to expressing his vision of life as a quest for truth. He has spoken of the need for any story or novel to be "written honestly and without regard for a specific audience" (thus his refusal to delete the ambiguous and the puzzling and the evil from his novelistic world, for to do so would be to "'write down'" to his readers). The "shocks of recognition" he wishes to elicit depend upon holding fast to his own perceptions of truth. He will not compromise for the sake of happy endings. . . . Despite criticism of his novels on the basis of "violence" and the use of the "downbeat ending," Cormier persists in truthfulness to his artistic intuitions, and young readers find his cheerless novelistic world credible: "'I still get letters from kids saying that what I wrote about in *The Chocolate War* is mild compared with what's going on in their school.'" Credibility is witnessed by the reaction of eighth graders in a small Massachusetts town when a few parents objected to *The Chocolate War;* the students insisted that the book "'rang true'" for them. Even more significantly, they showed their true comprehension of the ironic nature of *The Chocolate War* by refusing to emulate the tactics of the vicious characters in the book. When one student urged that "'Everyone in this class should sign the petition'" in support of the novel, another stood up to say: "'Wait. If we insist that everybody sign this petition, then we'd be doing what happens in *The Chocolate War.* Let's not pressure anybody to sign.'"

Young readers not only accept the moral complexities and the evils Cormier portrays in his novels as truthfully mirroring their world, they are also intrigued; they question; they rise to the challenge of the ironic mode in which he writes: they search

for further answers. Like the consummate artist he is, Cormier refuses, however, to provide those final, definitive answers. He asks simply, "'Why should the writer have to provide all the answers?'"

In this question, I believe, lies the key to the "ironist" nature of Cormier as a writer. Literature in the ironic mode has "missing pieces": ironic literature presents us with an incomplete world, leaving out something essential, which the reader must supply. In this lies the special power of ironic art, for it demands greater reader participation and heightens reader response because the reader must ask, "What is missing from the universe of this novel or story?" The ironic artist deliberately focuses on a partial, incomplete presentation of reality—perhaps choosing, as Cormier repeatedly does in his novels—to depict a world lacking in love and joy and hope, the world of "unrelieved despair," the "Dantean Inferno without any hint of Purgatorio or Paradiso" [see excerpt dated April 29, 1979 in General Commentary]. This explains why he presents to us, again and again, the theme of the betrayal of trust (the most hideous sin, remember, in Dante's catalogue of sins in the *Inferno*). *After the First Death,* for example, presents a young person betrayed by his elders, "who were by nature designed to be the boy's strength and support." The reader can react only with revulsion for such evil, and so desolate a vision, calls up a counter-vision of a possible better world—the world that lies within human will and choice to realize. Cormier does not suggest that the betrayals are inevitable; on the contrary, with the exception of Ben, who is as we shall see a special case, he leaves abundant room to suppose that his corrupt characters had it within their power to have chosen good rather than evil.

A careful examination of the way in which Cormier depicts the evil of betrayal of trust in *After the First Death* will clarify his ironic technique and its relationship to the reader's response. There are in the novel three central incidents of betrayal, each different. There is Ben Marchand's betrayal of the (supposed) time of the attack of the government forces upon the terrorists holding the hostages. To put this failure of Ben into perspective, it is important to remember that he fits the definition of the hero of fiction in the ironic mode, for he is a vulnerable child, "not sufficient to have stood" against the terrorists' tactics, and he is also "in a lower state of freedom than the audience." The hero of tragic irony does not necessarily have any tragic *hamartia* and hence cannot be seen as shaping his own tragic destiny. Such a hero is a victim, a *pharmakos* or scapegoat, who is "innocent," yet "guilty in the sense that he is a member of a guilty society. . . ." Since Ben is chosen as a victim by his father, however, this definition does not fit precisely, and it remains to be seen how significant his father's betrayal of him becomes to the ironic effect of the work.

The reader witnesses the moment of Ben's failure through Miro's eyes, when Ben breaks under the torture of "the fingers." Miro sees in the boy's eyes "the look of the betrayer," a look "beyond terror or horror or pain. A look of such anguish, such regret . . . a doom that went beyond the fingers, beyond even death. A look that left the boy hollow, empty." This emptiness foreshadows the similar emptiness that results later from Miro's betrayal, as he believes, of the leader of the terrorists, Artkin, his surrogate—or possibly actual (the reader can never be certain)—father. When Kate, in an attempt to salvage her own life, tries to convince Miro of the possibility that Artkin was his father, the attempt backfires. Miro's torment at the thought that he has betrayed the man who *may* be his biological father is graphically portrayed: "... there was a worm crawling in his heart, a worm that said he had been responsible for Artkin's death.".... In his hurt and rage over his own guilt, Miro kills Kate, and not long after, he kills again—a chance victim, a passing motorist, whose clothes and car he then appropriates. Unlike Ben, who is finally driven to self-murder, Miro survives physically the knowledge of his capacity for betrayal, but he does so at the sacrifice of his humanness. He resolves never to feel emotion again: "He would keep himself empty, like before." ... That is, before he felt Kate touch his arm on the bus, and before she made him believe Artkin was his father—the two moments in the novel when he displays human emotion. Miro's "suicide" is a suicide of his emotional nature; his "survival" is terrible, in that he lives on as an automaton programmed to kill for the sake of his cause.

It is Kate who puts Miro into perspective with her insight into his "monstrous" innocence. Earlier in the novel, she asks him if he does not feel anything for the mother and child he had killed when he had taken part in a terrorist attack on a post office. His response is to stare at her blankly. She realizes,

> ... the greatest horror of all was that he didn't know he was a monster. He had looked at her with innocent eyes as he told her of killing people. She'd always thought of innocence as something good, something to cherish. People mourned the death of innocence.... But innocence, she saw now, could also be evil. Monstrous.
>
> (pp. 50-3)

Ben's father, General Marchand, is Cormier's most complex portrait of betrayal. The general betrays his son when he negates his identity as his son and makes him into a pawn for the sake of patriotism. This act torments the general as he reflects upon it later: "At the moment you left my office, you had ceased to exist in the minds of those at Inner Delta as my son." ... "I had to forget you were my son." ... Artkin's reaction to Marchand's offer of his son as a messenger underscores the irony of the act; "'Either,'" says Artkin, "'you are a great patriot or a great fool.'" The general's reply, "'Perhaps both,'" is prophetic....

The internal conflict of General Marchand pits the demands of his patriotism against the demands of fatherhood. Early in the book, the general is characterized as the kind of patriot who refuses to allow self-doubt or self-questioning to interfere with the performance of duty. The perniciousness of this sort of patriotism is evident in the general's reflections on the difference between the patriotism of the soldiers of World War II and that of the young today:

> There are all kinds of patriotism; ours was pure and sweet and unquestioning. We were the good guys. Today, there is still patriotism, of course. But this generation is questioning. This generation looks at itself in a mirror as it performs its duties. And wonders: who are the good guys? Is it possible we are the bad guys? They should never ask that question, Ben, or even contemplate it....
>
> (p. 53)

By revealing the general's *hamartia*—his inability to doubt himself, to question the morality of his patriotism—Cormier

skillfully prepares the ground for the central irony of the novel, his decision to squelch the intuitive feeling that could have saved him from the error of sacrificing Ben. Much too late he has his "recognition": at the moment he saw Ben's eyes go to his notepad and read the time of the attack—0930—the general should have "'called it off, removed you as messenger, cancelled the arrangements, picked up the telephone and told Washington I had changed my mind.'" ...

The general's crucial decision to go against his human feeling for his son, to depersonalize him for the sake of patriotic duty, raises the problem of credibility. What could possibly move a man to offer his own son as a scapegoat? Even more horrifyingly, he does so knowing his son would betray his country. It is Ben's knowledge of this dimension of his father's betrayal that drives him to suicide: "'To find out that I had not only betrayed my country but had been expected to do it. To find out that I was expected to act as a coward, unable to take a little pain'".... (p. 54)

In Part II, in a dialogue that takes place in the mind of the demented general after his son's suicide, Ben asks his father, "'Is a country worth that much, Dad?'" ... Cormier has been careful, however, to show us the complexity of the general's dilemma and to demonstrate his ability to rationalize his choice. Pondering his own acceptance of the plan to use scapegoats, if the attempt at rescue should result in sacrificing more children than were saved, Marchand thinks, "This is the greatest patriotism: to accept disgrace for the sake of your country. The traitor as patriot." ... Ben, being incapable of this kind of rationalization, cannot accept this sort of "inverted patriotism" as authentic and, hence, cannot go on living.

The two most admirable characters, Ben and Kate, are sacrificial victims; both die, Ben by suicide, Kate at the hands of Miro. Their deaths are the more ironic and terrible because, within the world of the novel, their sacrifices seem to have no redeeming value. Cormier's point, however, is not that heroism has no value; rather, he encourages us to ask, what is wrong with this novelistic world (and by extension, with the actual world it partially reflects)?

The answer to this question lies in the truth that emerges from closer scrutiny of the reason why General Marchand makes the mistake he does. He has, first of all, allowed himself to become depersonalized. Ben perceives the problem: "His is the kind of profession that not only disguises the man but consumes him as well. And his family, too." ... The general has devoted himself to the false absolute of patriotism at any cost (the parallel with Miro is obvious), and the consequences are unthinkably catastrophic. He has put loyalty to an abstraction (patriotic duty) ahead of fidelity to a concrete, individual human being, and the treachery is compounded by kinship. By showing the reader so vividly the consequences of the general's wrong choices, Cormier creates the emotion he intends: revulsion for the evil of worshipping a false absolute. The reader has little choice but to be filled with loathing for the false god of blind patriotism, and Cormier does us the greatest service an artist can render—to show us evil in its full ugliness (and in its full complexity, for by his own mistaken lights the general tries to do right). By bringing the reader to the recognition of the evil of the false absolute, Cormier helps to exorcise it, for to recognize evil as evil is the first step towards the free choice of good.

Those who are bedevilled by their own desperate needs and passions, as Stanley Ellin observes, "... no matter what side they are on and no matter how fervently they believe that they act only to create a world fit for their children . . . will sacrifice their children to the process" [see excerpt dated April 29, 1979 in General Commentary]. The power of Cormier's ironic art has been well expressed by Barbara F. Harrison: "With uncompromising intensity, the author shatters the individual and collective myths of our times and demands a deeper level of truth-telling" [see excerpt dated August, 1979 for *After the First Death*].

Martin Buber has spoken eloquently of the dangers of false ideals and false absolutes to our world today:

> False absolutes rule over the soul, which is no longer able to put them to flight through the image of the true. Everywhere, over the whole surface of the human world—in the East and in the West, from the left and from the right, they pierce unhindered through the level of the ethical and demand of you 'the sacrifice.' . . . And [honest men] really and truly believe that brother-murder will prepare the way for brotherhood. . . .

There is no escape from this kind of idolatry, Buber believes, unless and until we can summon up a "new conscience" that can help us demolish illusion, toppling the false absolutes and revealing them in their treacherousness.

Robert Cormier is to be thanked for his unflinching artistic presentation of evil, for by it we may rediscover the vision of the good. Only then shall we have a chance to escape becoming hostages to a world ruled by terrorists, monstrous innocents like Miro. Only then shall the morally sensitive, full human person, like Kate, have a true chance for survival. Kate wonders early in the book about the possibility that "hope comes out of hopelessness and that the opposite of things carry the seeds of birth—love out of hate, good out of evil. . . . Didn't flowers grow out of the dirt?" . . . Her ponderings give us the perfect metaphor for Cormier's technique as a romantic ironist, a writer whose vision of "dirt" generates, paradoxically, a conviction of the need to reaffirm the reality of the flower. (pp. 54-5)

> *Millicent Lenz, "A Romantic Ironist's Vision of Evil: Robert Cormier's 'After the First Death'," in* Proceedings of the Eighth Annual Conference of the Children's Literature Association, *Vol. 8, March, 1981, pp. 50-6.*

I wish to share with you insights that I have acquired as a result of total absorption into the world of the realistic young adult novels written by Robert Cormier.

I will explore the obvious relationship of the archetypal theme of adolescent initiation to the adolescent reader as presented in Cormier's *After the First Death*. . . . (p. 19)

Cormier, in hard-hitting, succinct prose and in realistic dialogue, captures the reader firmly, forcing affective responses of fear, hate, love, pity and anger as the characters unfold on the page. This affective response is, of course, not unique to Cormier in the genre of young adult fiction; however, the associative response that follows, that response that is evaluative rather than merely participatory, finds a depth in *After the First Death* that I have not experienced in most other young adult novels.

Cormier's characters intrigue, indeed captivate to the extent that reading *After the First Death* leaves the reader with com-

plex, analytical questions. Thinking about the "what" leads the reader to the "how" and the "why" of the matter and so on to the symbolic level, that level on which we discover the significance of the fictional life as it relates to real life.

After the First Death is a problem novel in which the protagonists are in conflict with society. It deals with themes of alienation and despair, but there are sub-themes that bear close scrutiny, such as relationships, responsibility, loyalty and betrayal, courage and fear, as well as adolescent initiation. The author's style, tragic mode, tone, point of view, setting, characterization and dialogue are of such quality that they lend themselves well to close examination.

After the First Death tells the story of a terrorist hi-jacking of a bus loaded with young children. It is about demands that threaten the secrecy of a government project. Ultimately, it is about three teenagers, Ben, Miro and Kate, whose lives are irrevocably changed by events beyond their control.

The theme of adolescent initiation exists and can be traced through the lives of the three teenagers. For my purposes, I will use the term adolescent initiation synonymously with the adolescent's search for self: "Who am I?", "Where am I going?", "What will I do with my life?" This search for self implies a transition from childhood to adulthood that is marked by growth toward acceptance of the spoken and unspoken rules of society. (pp. 19, 37)

The characteristics of the actual process of initiation in Cormier's *After the First Death* strongly resemble the characteristics of the quest theme as observed in traditional novels of adventure-romance. The quest here is a quest for self-identity rather than the quest of fantasy. It is a quest for the knowledge and experience that mark the closing of the gap between childhood and adulthood. . . . The necessary mentor guides the novice through the dangers of "becoming", and the traditional sacrifice is made. The quest of adventure-romance ends happily in success. Cormier's novel ends in failure and in an aura of pessimism. The initiate is unable to successfully confront the realities of adulthood and society. He is alienated. He has more foibles than strengths, and he is changed in the course of the novel both in his discoveries about life and in his relationships to others. He must make adjustments to those discoveries and live with the consequences of his decisions or be doomed. He must come to grips with his capabilities and limitations or be self-convicted and condemned.

In *After the First Death*, we meet a teenage terrorist known as Miro Shantas. He has not yet been accepted into the brotherhood of the cult. Miro's quest is for manhood and his "initiation" will be the killing of Kate Forrester, the bus driver in charge on the day of the terrorist hijacking. She is to be his "first death" and his ticket of admittance into the world of men that comprise the "freedom fighters". Miro's mentor is Artkin who guides him through this transition with orders that consistently keep him headed in the direction of manhood, even though Miro vacillates between childhood and adulthood with anxiety, sexual confusion and loneliness which are typical of the transition phase of adolescent initiation. Miro's sacrifice is himself. He gives himself to Artkin. Artkin keeps Miro in a state of innocence of evil that belies confirmation into the real world. The black ski mask that Miro wears is symbolic of his initiation process. "Without the mask, he was Miro Shantos, the boy. With the mask, he is Miro Shantas, freedom fighter. He often wondered which person he really was." . . . The mask gives Miro a sense of power and authority that he equates with manhood. The philosophy of life that Miro comes to embrace is best said as it is written. "Do not seek to own anything, do not try to make anything belong to you, do not look for pleasure in anything. It will be taken from you sooner or later just as you must take from other people." . . .

Ben Marchand, fourteen-year-old son of an army general, is the protagonist in *After the First Death*. Ben's quest is for adulthood and for survival itself. The ordeal of crisis that he endures is not the torture at the hands of the terrorist hijackers, but the betrayal by his father who uses Ben as a pawn to protect the safety of the secret project which is under his command. It is this betrayal at the hands of the man who is his mentor that literally alienates Ben from successful incorporation and, indeed, destroys him. Ben is doomed and his suicide merely seals that doom. (p. 37)

In the archetypal pattern of initiation, three phases have been identified: separation, transition and incorporation. Cormier's male characters are alienated rather than incorporated because of the image of Self they discover. Their very innocence is their destruction.

The female character in the novel is Kate Forrester. Cormier has developed a character in the "round", and the reader shares Kate's emotions as they range from disbelief, revulsion, terror and outrage to strength and courage. Kate, too, is caught between childhood and adulthood. She also is separated and experiences loneliness, doubts and sexual confusion. "All the Kate Forresters. Were other people like that, she wondered, not simply one person but a lot of them mixed together? Did the real person finally emerge? But suppose that real person turned out to be someone terrible? Or someone who never found love? Isn't that what life was supposed to be—a search for love?" . . . Kate's initiation differs from that of Miro Shantas and Ben Marchand in that she must pass through the transition phase alone. She has no mentor, so she is forced into independence. She must rely on "that unknown quantity: herself." . . . Kate is left to use her own capabilities and face her limitations in coping with the situation. "She had to summon a Kate Forrester she'd never known before: the brave Kate Forrester." . . . Cormier has poignantly painted hope in Kate Forrester in contrast to the hopelessness evident in the male characters. "She caught her breath, pondering a new thought: the possibility that hope comes out of hopelessness and that the opposite of things carry the seeds of birth—love out of hate, good out of evil. Didn't flowers grow out of dirt?" . . . It is this hope that we find expressed at the end of the story when Kate tries once more to reason with Miro Shantas and thereby save her life. "How about all the things you could do in this world? Don't you want love? What's wrong with a little love? Instead of death and fighting and that war you're always talking about?" . . . The reader is left with the certainty that had Kate Forrester lived, she would have successfully stepped into the adult role, and s/he will understand that even in her death, she triumphed.

Cormier has woven his tale so well that even the bus in which Kate and Miro live the ordeal becomes symbolic of the journey into adulthood. "The bus climbed steadily, lumbering, like some huge beast being driven against its will. She hoped the bus would collapse, like a beast, and die there on the road. She wondered what would happen if the bus stopped and didn't go on." . . . This feeling about the bus is a reflection of the feeling the novice experiences when faced with his isolation. Escape from the dilemmas of life presents itself as an answer and as a relief.

I believe that Cormier's *After the First Death* would be a worthy book for in-class reading in a unit on human values in the senior high classroom. A human values study is in itself nothing new in the classroom, but I feel that we have presented a somewhat distorted view of life in our society, heretofore, by regaling students with success stories that have invariable happy endings. We shy away from failure when students themselves are experiencing this failure along the path to adulthood. I want to show my students both sides of our world. This will help students who are confused by and struggling with human values and relationships, and who are searching to find themselves. It is in dealing with personal values and social significances that Cormier provides the very transition characteristic that is the heart of young adult literature. By using *After the First Death* in the classroom, we can provide vicarious experiences in which the demands of society conflict with individual values. (pp. 37-8)

Cormier's *After the First Death* is a worthy novel for use in helping students clarify their values and assess their attitudes as they move through the process of adolescent initiation. (p. 38)

> *Amelia M. Bell, "Adolescent Initiation in Cormier's 'After the First Death'," in* The ALAN Review, *Vol. 12, No. 2, Winter, 1985, pp. 19, 37-8.*

EIGHT PLUS ONE: STORIES (1980)

Written between 1965 and 1975, Cormier's stories do capture the agony and ecstasy of adolescence—but primarily from an adult viewpoint. A father observes his son's romances with a cynical, vaguely envious commentary ("**Another of Mike's Girls**"). In "**Mine on Thursdays**," a divorced father escorts his daughter to an amusement park only to realize he can never be as close to her as he wishes. At a farewell party for a daughter leaving for college, a father catches a glimpse of the child who was once his but whom he must now relinquish ("**A Bad Time for Fathers**"). A young man comes to the same realization about his father—that he has his own identity away from his family—in "**Guess What? I Almost Kissed My Father Goodnight.**" In the final story, "**Bunny Berigan—Wasn't He a Musician or Something,**" which the author agrees does not fit thematically, a middle-aged man must cope with his best friend's divorce and much younger girlfriend. The author's introduction to each of the nine tales traces the germination of an idea and its integration into fiction. This guided tour is ideal for an English class. But as independent reading, the stories, though well-crafted and occasionally poignant, seem dated and bland. The female characters, in particular, are poorly developed and none of the tales are as dramatic as Cormier's brilliant and imaginative novels.

> *Cyrisse Jaffee, in a review of "Eight Plus One: Stories," in* School Library Journal, *Vol. 27, No. 1, September, 1980, p. 81.*

The Cormier writing here has substituted warmth, gentle wit, and quiet reflection for the harsh relentlessness of his teenage novels. . . . [These] slice-of-life vignettes, most of them previously published as adult stories, demonstrate Cormier's accessibility to young adult readers. Three stories are set during the Depression, the remainder during relatively modern times. Neither slick nor sentimentalized, they are occasionally awkward, but affecting, outgrowths of personal experiences that triggered emotional responses from the author. Each investigates human relationships—largely those between fathers and children. The most significant departure (and of least interest to teens) is the closing piece, in which a middle-aged man reflects on the changes in the life of his best friend. All are written in first person—but while the narrators vary from small boys and teenagers to fathers, Cormier's presence can be strongly felt. In separate story prefaces (rather jarring at first, these perhaps should have followed the stories) he reveals even more of himself and passes along personal insights into his writing craft. Although this will have a rather special teen appeal, for the most part it's a strong collection—one bridging the gap between teen-centered and more sophisticated adult short stories—that probes the emotions of adults and young people with equal sensitivity.

> *Stephanie Zvirin, in a review of "Eight Plus One: Stories," in* Booklist, *Vol. 77, No. 2, September 15, 1980, p. 110.*

This book is a clear reminder that there are still fathers who love their children and boys who love their fathers and brothers intensely.

The best story in the collection is the tragic **"My First Negro"** which describes a young white boy's summer-long play with a poverty-struck black boy who had just moved out to Fitchburg from Boston. Through a series of boyish pranks, the black family is ironically run out of town, terrified at the surprise raid that was no raid at all. This case of misunderstanding captures beautifully adolescent confusion and guilt. (p. 300)

Other stories revolving about boys collecting baseball cards, growing a first moustache, and teenage puppy love touch the serious and ponderous moments that teenagers could relate to immediately. Indeed any reader could become attached to this wholesome world of fond family memories of loving parents and children.

8 Plus 1 adds one of the brighter fictional records of family life in the last two hopeless decades. Teenagers as well as their parents will love it. (p. 301)

> *Jeanne Kinney, in a review of "8 Plus 1," in* Best Sellers, *Vol. 40, No. 8, November, 1980, pp. 300-01.*

The focus throughout [*Eight Plus One*], as the author describes it, is "family relationships, fathers and mothers, daughters and sons . . . growing up [and] the knowledge, often bittersweet, that the passing years bring." (p. 55)

Here and there in the book cheerfulness breaks in. There's a piece about a younger brother who helps an older brother by selling a favorite toy to finance the purchase of a corsage for elder brother's date. And once or twice a class or race problem surfaces, providing other distraction from pervasive paternal gloom. But only brief distraction. The fathers in *Eight Plus One* are kind, understanding about acne, fond of books and gin, but they are, to a man, overwhelmed by a sense of the tears of things, and utterly without capacity for relishing their kids' physical and intellectual growth.

Equally troubling, Mr. Cormier, their creator, also seems overwhelmed by the mystery of his own processes of creation. He prefaces each story with a lengthy rumination on "my development as a writer," on the time and place of composition, sometimes even about his physical condition as he tapped the typewriter. ("On this particular Sunday, I was under assault by a migraine headache: a riveting pain in that vulnerable spot above my left eyebrow in partnership with nausea sweeping my stomach.") If the writing itself bore a stamp of distinction, this sort of chatter might be tolerable, but in fact the writing

is uniformly banal. This is a book in which minds race, brakes squeal, conversation languishes, dismissals are blithe, memories are seared, successes are roaring, barks are worse than bites and knowledge is, to repeat, bittersweet—a book, in short, with an exceptionally high cliché density. (pp. 55, 65)

[*Eight Plus One* is] an ill-written, cliché-infested book awash in self-pity, and I can't think of a "young adult" anywhere upon whom I'd be willing to inflict it. It is a very bad book. (p. 65)

> *Benjamin DeMott, "Understanding Fathers," in* The New York Times Book Review, *November 9, 1980, pp. 55, 65.*

While the book should interest many young adult Cormier fans, it seems even more suitable for an adult audience, not because of the difficulty or sophistication of the writing but because of the subject matter; most of the stories are written from an adult's viewpoint. . . . [While] they are not as trenchant or exciting as the author's *The Chocolate War* and *I Am the Cheese,* they are adroitly crafted, perceptive, and often poignant vignettes about the complexities of human relationships. (pp. 67-8)

> *Zena Sutherland, in a review of "Eight Plus One: Stories," in* Bulletin of the Center for Children's Books, *Vol. 34, No. 4, December, 1980, pp. 67-8.*

THE BUMBLEBEE FLIES ANYWAY   (1983)

In a story that is as trenchant as it is poignant, Cormier shows the courage and desperation of adolescents who know that their deaths are imminent. Barney, sixteen, is the only patient who is in the experimental hospital who is not in the group of the doomed but is there as a control; all of them are there voluntarily, some to contribute to research and some, like Mazzo, hoping for a quick death. In love with Mazzo's twin sister, Cassie, who turns to Barney for help because her brother refuses to see anyone in his family, Barney thinks of a plan that will give Mazzo the quick, daring death he wants; secretly he reconstructs a life-size model of a car from the dump next door, pulls the plug on Mazzo's life-support system, and helps him to the roof where the car waits to be pushed off for one last glorious flight. The story, which has an element of twin telepathy, involves questions of medical ethics and freedom of choice, and ends with Barney, who in the course of his treatments and his conversation with his doctor, has learned that he too is going to die, remembering with persistent joy, despite his gray fog of pain, the beauty of the flight, his last achievement. This is, although it is tragic, a stunning book: Cormier creates convincingly the hospital world of the terminally ill, the pathos of Barney's love for Cassie and his struggles with the hallucinations induced by the treatments that are designed to block his knowledge and help him forget his true condition. It moves, with relentless inevitability, like an ancient Greek tragedy, with the compassion of the staff a contrapuntal note, to the requiem of hopeless despair that, for each patient, still holds some passion for an affirmative act of life. (pp. 3-4)

> *Zena Sutherland, in a review of "The Bumblebee Flies Anyway," in* Bulletin of the Center for Children's Books, *Vol. 37, No. 1, September, 1983, pp. 3-4.*

The major weakness in characterization is the portrayal of Cassie, who is convincing as Barney's love idol, but less so as her twin's empathetic alter ego. Barney is the most viable and memorable character; the others—his peers and the hospital staff—become real from his perspective. Subtle foreshadowing and well-crafted metaphors and similes enable readers to mentally visualize setting, action, and characters; and there is a rhythm to Cormier's writing that compels reader reaction much the way a musical score underlines emotion in films. The story's climactic blockbuster is marred only slightly by a double denouement—one weak, the other fitting. The depressing situation aside, the overall effect is one of a reaffirmation of the humanity of humankind that contrasts with the images projected by *The Chocolate War, I Am the Cheese,* and *After the First Death.* (p. 38)

> *Sally Estes, in a review of "The Bumblebee Flies Anyway," in* Booklist, *Vol. 80, No. 1, September 1, 1983, pp. 37-8.*

[The] air of ambiguity and vaguely totalitarian menace, a common thread in Cormier's fiction, sometimes seems a little contrived and arbitrary here, but it is far from inappropriate to a patient-inmate's view of hospital life. And if that final triumphant push of the car, with Mazzo dying on the roof in Barney's arms . . . , is a little clichéd, it is not sentimentally rendered at it might be in other hands. All in all the novel hasn't the consuming, focused tension of previous Cormier YAs, but that is not to deny its crisp, sure craftsmanship, suggestive applications, and holding power.

> *A review of "The Bumblebee Flies Anyway," in* Kirkus Reviews, *Juvenile Issue, Vol. LI, Nos. 13-17, September 1, 1983, p. J-172.*

In yet another intense, confined world characteristic of his novels, the author probes medical ethics. . . . A master of taut, twisting plots and clear prose, the inventive writer creates sufficient mystery, deception, and irony to rival the force of *I Am the Cheese*. . . . But because the narrative events are less ambiguous, the feelings less subtle, and the symbolism more obvious, the reader's discoveries are diminished. Although the Madonna-like Cassie and her parallel story are less convincing and some secondary characters are clichés, Barney and the others do come alive. And their ability to triumph in some measure over the depersonalizing situation represents a marked change from the author's previous work. (pp. 715-16)

> *Nancy C. Hammond, in a review of "The Bumblebee Flies Anyway," in* The Horn Book Magazine, *Vol. LIX, No. 6, December, 1983, pp. 715-16.*

In this novel, the twin themes of masochism and paranoia, never very far away from any of Robert Cormier's writings, this time run out of control. . . .

It's just possible that Dostoevsky could have made something of this, but certainly not Mr Cormier. By the time the novel has ended, any intended serious purpose has long been swamped by tendentious philosophizing and a shameless pulling of authorial strings into order to achieve an instant pulverizing effect. The prose style itself, for example, often goes in for the cheap and slick, so that at one moment Barney's "eyes leaped in their sockets, threatening crazily to spill out onto his lap". While not exactly the literary equivalent of a video nasty, *The Bumblebee Flies Anyway* remains a repulsive work, mixing self-pity and self-loathing in roughly equal proportions.

> *Nicholas Tucker, "Sickness," in* The Times Educational Supplement, *No. 3524, January 13, 1984, p. 42.*

With the publication of *The Bumblebee Flies Anyway,* Cormier not only begins a new phase of his writing, he also provides teachers of American and contemporary literature with a superb young adult novel which exemplifies much of the best of our literary tradition. (p. 43)

The final revelation, fo. both characters and readers, shares in its literary vision one of those transcending moments we have come to expect in our better literature. Like Santiago's fish and Issac's bear, Barney's Bumblebee becomes a kind of totem, a sacred object through which he is able to transcend his faltering flesh. Like Hemingway's *The Old Man and the Sea* and Faulkner's "The Bear", Cormier's *The Bumblebee Flies Anyway* continues the tradition of the central paradox of both Christianity and transcendentalism: to triumph one must renounce one's own desires and obey a Higher Law.

As Issac in "The Bear" had renounced the mechanical objects of this world so that he could meet the bear on its terms and "see the two of them, himself and the bear, shadowy in the limbo from which time emerged, becoming time; the old bear absolved of mortality and him partaking, sharing a little of it, enough of it" . . . , so Barney

> . . . saw a flicker of understanding in those eyes and realized Mazzo was seeing what Barney could see, sharing the vision with him; the marvelous flight of the Bumblebee, out into the night, soaring off the roof, a small soaring maybe but enough to set them free, joining the stars and the moon and the planets . . .

In Faulknerian fashion, Barney, like Isaac, is able to keep his transcending experience alive through "retrospection and recollection and exactitude" ("The Bear" . . .):

> . . . and that's when he saw the Bumblebee again, breaking through the grayness and the loneliness, glowing and glistening as it moved off the roof and across the sky, out into the stars and the planets and beyond, always beautiful, always flying, always his. . . .

In similar manner, Cormier's main character not only continues the transcendental tradition, he also exemplifies the mystical/religious levels of a Hawthorne, a Hemingway. The pervasive aura of the Christian tradition of renunciation of the self to open the way to something greater lies just beneath the surface of this novel as it does in *The Scarlet Letter* and *The Old Man and the Sea.* Santiago prays: ". . . Blessed Virgin, pray for the death of this fish. Wonderful though he is". . . . "In the Name of the Tempo and the Rhythm" . . . , chants Barney Snow. Although Barney, victimized by our modern times, uses the jargon of today's psychology, the formula is that of Christian faith. Thus Cormier, like Hawthorne and Hemingway and many other writers, shares in a Trinitarian vision of the universe.

For teachers of literature searching for contemporary adolescent novels that are not only appealing to students but continue and expand the traditions of American literature, Robert Cormier's *The Bumblebee Flies Anyway* is a good choice. This novel rises, in theme, scope and craft, so far above the regular fare, that there is little doubt that it more than stands comparison with John Knowles's *A Separate Peace* and William Golding's *Lord of the Flies.* Moreover, it stands the test of John Gardner's belief that ". . . true art is moral; it seeks to hold off, at least for a while, the twilight of the gods and us . . . Art is essentially serious and beneficial, a game played against chaos and death against entropy''.... Robert Cormier's *The Bumblebee Flies Anyway* is a serious game; we ought not to deprive students of the opportunity to play it. (p. 44)

> Betty Ann Fargnoli, ''Of Fish and Bears and Bumblebees: The Craft of Robert Cormier,'' *in* The ALAN Review, Vol. 12, No. 2, Winter, 1985, pp. 43-4.

BEYOND THE CHOCOLATE WAR (1985)

AUTHOR'S COMMENTARY

[The following excerpt is from an interview by Anita Silvey.]

[Anita Silvey]: Why did you write a sequel to *The Chocolate War* . . . ? What motivated you to do it?

[Robert Cormier]: Actually I resisted a sequel. I don't particularly like sequels—mostly because they are usually disappointing. But I go into the schools and get a lot of mail from kids, and kids kept saying, ''What happened to Archie? And what happened to Jerry?'' These questions kept the book alive, eternally fresh, in my mind. Because I'd be challenged by kids about what happened in the third chapter with Tubs Casper, it would force me to read and reread the book. I got to a point where I had just finished a novel, and so I began to wonder what did happen to these people, particularly to Tubs Casper. He was the key. He had a very minor role in *The Chocolate War.* He was a device. I wanted to show how the sale was going—so I demonstrated it by showing one kid not selling the chocolates, another kid who was an eager salesman, and then Tubs, who was keeping the money because he wanted to buy a bracelet for a girl. Inevitably, when I go into a school, students will ask me about Tubs Casper, and they're angry about him. Kids are so great; they're very honest about everything. They scold you if they don't like something. So they'd say, ''Why did you do that to Tubs Casper?'' I kept thinking about Tubs. In the first stages of *Beyond the Chocolate War* I wrote a little about Tubs before realizing that I would go into a formal sequel.

Then, I really got interested about what might have happened to these kids. I sketched a couple of scenes with Tubs Casper showing what might have happened to him and Rita which don't appear in the book. There was one scene between Tubs and Rita that I still love that had to come out. Yet, for me it was necessary to write it at the time, even though it didn't advance the plot at all.

But when I realized that I did have something going, I began to formally structure it as much as I could. I knew I needed a new voice for the reader who isn't familiar with Trinity. It's an old ploy. So Obie explains what happened to the newcomer Ray Bannister. Here again, I work in serendipity. I set myself challenges. That first line of the novel, ''Ray Bannister started to build the guillotine the day Jerry Renault returned to Monument,'' is the biggest challenge of all because I introduce Ray Bannister and I introduce the guillotine. I knew, by all the laws, that the guillotine had to fall. That's the fun of writing—to set up a situation like that and have it hanging there. (pp. 145-46)

[Anita Silvey]: The first sentence in *The Chocolate War* is ''They murdered him.'' Did you have that in mind at the beginning or did it come later?

[Robert Cormier]: One thing I like to do is plunge into my novels. That line in *The Chocolate War* seemed like a good lapel grabber. In my books I go immediately for action and set scenes later. I have the image of grabbing someone by the lapels and saying, ''Listen.'' I wrote that first chapter of *The Chocolate War* probably thirty-five times because that first chapter contains all the dramatic foreshadowing, all the similes and metaphors—such as ''sweat like bugs on his forehead.'' Sometimes kids tell me that they started reading *The Chocolate War,* and then it got very violent. I tell them that they were warned in that first chapter. I didn't pull a switch on page ninety-eight where things get nasty. ''They murdered him'' is like a big shadow hovering over the novel.

[Anita Silvey]: The first book was written as a ''what if'' response to the fact that your son refused to participate in a school chocolate sale. *Beyond the Chocolate War* was written in response to many questions from children. Are you more aware of a child-audience now than you were ten years ago?

[Robert Cormier]: I still don't write thinking that I'm creating for children. But it would be dishonest for me to say that I don't know they are there, that I don't know that they will be reading the book. I wrote the book because of them, so actually it was an answer to all of their questions. I was aware of them in the questions that they had posed to me. When people say they write for themselves, that's probably what they do. I will admit that I don't write for myself; I write to be read. I've got the reader in my mind all the time. That's another part of the whole process.

I had my own private catalyst in the book. Whenever I reread *The Chocolate War,* or discussed it, I always thought that Obie was the most neglected character in the book, probably the most poignant, and the one that I sympathized with. Kids ask me questions like, ''Which character do you like best?'' They're always surprised when I don't tell them Jerry. I sometimes half shock them and tell them Archie. He is a terrific character; I really love him dearly. Obie was a tragic kid who went through his entire high school career and had nothing to show for it, and he was aware of that. I knew Tubs didn't have the stature of a major figure to carry out a revenge motive so I figured that for any dramatic movement Obie seemed the perfect vehicle. While writing *The Chocolate War* I had contemplated bringing in romance. What if Obie did have a girl? He was so devoted to Archie, and suddenly his loyalties would be divided.

Then this wonderful thing happened when I sat at the typewriter. I started writing about Obie being in love, and suddenly this girl Laurie Gundardson came onto the page. I can't track where she came from. She started to ask about the Vigils, and Obie suspected she knew about his role. Not only did his feeling for Laurie alienate him a bit from Archie, but he saw himself in her eyes as a stooge, and that began the big change in him.

Writing, even though it's hard work, is really a joy when you get these characters to come alive. It's hard to trace where they come from. I can't say that I am sitting here one night at nine o'clock and that a character occurs to me. The magic for me happens at the typewriter.

[Anita Silvey]: David Caroni comes back in a very poignant way; is that because you asked ''what if'' or because children asked you about him?

[Robert Cormier]: Children never asked me about David Caroni, but he appealed to me as a sensitive character who was left undeveloped in the first book. He is a tragic character in the sequel because of that "what if" question I posed about him. What if he became devastated by something that would seem almost trivial to other people? We often think that tragedies happen because of great earthquakes in people's lives. I think they sometimes occur because of small things that become obsessive to a particular person. So I went ahead on that assumption in dealing with David Caroni. As I wrote about him, it seemed to ring true. (pp. 146-48)

That first scene with David, the aborted suicide, was written in one session. . . . I hardly touched it afterward. . . . (p. 148)

Actually I was going to have him commit suicide in the scene. That's the way things were going: "Look thy last on all things lovely." He got into the bathtub, and then I thought—he doesn't. Suddenly, the entire Caroni aspect changed. I had no idea that eventually he would be connected with Brother Leon in a climactic scene at the end. By not killing himself at that moment he brought in Leon. "Why should he go alone, leaving Leon behind, sparing him?" Again, serendipity. I started out writing a suicide scene, and instead I set up a later development. There are always options. If it hadn't worked out, I could always go back and say, "No, he will die." So I just said, "I'll pick that thread up later." I let it sit for a couple of weeks and went on with other things. When, for the sense of pacing, the time came for David Caroni to come back again, I carried him further. That's the joy of writing—letting things happen.

[Anita Silvey]: What happens to Archie in *Beyond the Chocolate War*?

[Robert Cormier]: I knew that Archie would have to get the black marble, because kids had bothered me so much about his always getting the white one. . . . I had to work out some way in which Archie isn't a miracle man; he's human. So again I thought, what if he does get the black marble, what will happen? I kept talking to [my wife] Connie about this. At one point I said, "You know, Archie is really going to get it in this book. I can feel it because once he gets the black marble (I'd set up the Fair Day and the Fool) he's really going to be humiliated." Then, as I started to write that segment, he got the marble, but nobody dared to do anything to him. So he surprised me. Very early when he was training Bunting to be the Assigner, it bothered me that I'd created Bunting to be the Assigner, because he is so unlike Archie. Then it occurred to me that Archie has a motive for picking a kid like Bunting. Archie doesn't want someone there who would outdo him. He really isn't going to tell Bunting his secrets about how to manipulate people. I said, "I'll solve that later when I come to it." I have always planted these little time bombs in my books. Sometimes they don't work though, and I go back and remove them.

Another serendipity figure is Emile Janza, whom I introduced in the first book as a thug to show Archie from another viewpoint. He kept popping up. In *Beyond the Chocolate War* I realized how he could be manipulated by Archie, even after Archie's gone. I had no idea that I'd be writing that particular final scene for the book. In fact, I was a little disappointed as I neared the end. Obie and Archie have that great scene where Archie says, "You could have said no all along. I'm your other side; I'm your evil side." I ended it when Archie says, "Good-bye," which he has never done. I figured, that's good-bye to the readers. They'll never hear from him again. I knew my last scene would be Bunting sitting there contemplating the following year. But then I sat down to write, and I said, "Well, why not bring in Emile Janza?" Then these marvelous things

happened. Even though Archie's gone, he is still there because of his influence. He's going to ruin the school, maybe. The boy Henry Malioran suddenly comes out of nowhere with a tomato, possibly a sign of good things to come.

[Anita Silvey]: And there's been some transformation of Jerry?

[Robert Cormier]: I suppose the natural thing would have been to bring Jerry back to Trinity and have him confront Archie again. But I didn't want to do that. It would be like rewriting *The Chocolate War*. I wanted to keep him away from Trinity and yet have him involved with a Trinity character. Graham Greene, my favorite novelist, said that in every book he writes one character always gives him trouble, a character that you worry about. . . . In *The Chocolate War* it was Jerry. I was trying not to make him sound like my son, so I wasn't writing naturally. To me he was stubborn and refused to come to life; I worked so hard on him. In *Beyond the Chocolate War* he was the problem from the very beginning. In the first version I had him more psychologically defective than he is in the actual book. I had him mute for a good time. In that version because of the language problem in Canada, he wasn't speaking, and suddenly he realized that he couldn't talk anymore. So when he came back to the States, he wasn't able to communicate at all during Goober's first visit. In fact, because he wasn't able to talk, he let out a terrible scream of frustration that sent the Goober out of his home in horror. I wrote several scenes in which he was trying to talk and was talking haltingly. It just wasn't working for me; it just didn't ring true. I did an awful lot of writing. Here Jerry was again, giving me problems.

A novel must work as a story because no one's going to get to the other themes if you don't entertain the reader. But I like to have another layer of meaning, although you can read the book on one level and not bother with that other layer. I wanted Jerry to be the opposite of evil, to begin to have an aspiration to something greater than what's going on at Trinity. That's why I had him thinking about the church in Canada, aspiring to return. Just a hint that he could do that. He'll probably go back to Trinity and go through a Purgatory but be triumphant in the end even though he looks as if he's defeated. I was very tentative about writing those scenes, and I really had to work hard on them. I didn't want a fourteen-year-old kid to sound like a Christ figure. He still had to sound like a kid. That's why I made him groping, not quite sure what he wanted to do. But he still has a quest, a mission. I wanted something to balance Archie's evil. Jerry would transcend all of this evil. He may become a contemplative; in a way I tried to hint at that in the first scenes when he was praying in Canada, repairing his mind and body and soul. I didn't want Jerry to become part of the revenge plot because that would have been out of character. I gave more thought and more rewriting to Jerry Renault in this book than I did to any other character.

Cassie in *The Bumblebee Flies Anyway* . . . caused me no end of grief. She ran away with the book for awhile, and I wrote page after page of her life. She ended up not being a particularly likable person until I changed her. So in almost every book there's a person who is a problem or who doesn't behave.

[Anita Silvey]: So essentially you become attracted to a character; you start to work; and then a scene evolves?

[Robert Cormier]: When I see things that I've started that don't work out, that I've abandoned, I find that it's because I wasn't that emotionally involved with the characters—they didn't come alive. Always, it's the emotion that gets me going, and then immediately I create a character. In *Beyond the Chocolate War* the characters were already there, and I had to get emotionally involved with them again. That's why I didn't choose to bring back some characters; I brought back David Caroni rather than Brian Cochran because Brian didn't particularly move me.

[Anita Silvey]: Then it's a combination of character and emotion? Because what the reader feels in the chapter about David Caroni is that wave of despair, that life is indeed worthless.

[Robert Cormier]: And David is still carrying on this act of being normal. So often you read about suicides, and people say, "He acted the way he always did. Oh, he probably was a little distracted." What has always struck me is a line from a Stevie Smith poem that some day I may write a novel about: "I was much further out than you thought and not waving but drowning." That happens all the time. So you get a kid like David Caroni who was devastated; and yet he carried on these planes of existence; he was still a brother and student and son. When you get emotionally involved with a character like that, you really have this sense of doom hanging over him, and you hate to see what's going to happen. I could see what was happening to Kate in *After the First Death* . . . ; inevitably she'd make that fatal error that all amateurs do. She was braver than I thought she ever would be when I started the novel. When I got to that scene where she and Miro were nestled together, and I knew it just had to end that way, it affected me too. There's that strange thing about characters; you become very attached to them. Even to the villains. (pp. 148-54)

[Anita Silvey]: How do you achieve the incredible pacing and tension in *Beyond the Chocolate War?*

[Robert Cormier]: The rewriting is always crucial to what I do; whenever I do a scene, I always tell myself that this isn't final and that I can do it again, better. The pacing is probably from experience. I've always liked gradual disclosure. I keep thinking of my rubber-band theory. You have a rubber band that you keep pulling and pulling and pulling, and just at the moment of snapping you release it and start another chapter and start pulling again.

The editing was crucial in this book, and Dinah Stevenson was so important in that process. The book was much longer than I wanted it to be, simply because in the first version I wanted the people to go their way. I thought it would be easier to cut than to add. So I sent in this large manuscript, and I was beginning to lose my perspective. Dinah wrote me this letter that was glowing about the book but also so insightful about what I might do to cut the manuscript. She gave me major suggestions that affected the book, particularly the climax. I had disclosed pretty early what Obie had in mind for the guillotine, and I'd told the reader what I was going to do. She spotted that flaw right away and said we should let the reader find out for him or herself. That change made a big difference. She knew exactly what I wanted to do and really came through with insights that I needed. (p. 154)

[Anita Silvey]: The philosophy of your books is very often brought back to you, sometimes negatively. What do you think you are saying to the reader in terms not only of character and emotion but also of content? What are the most important statements in your books?

[Robert Cormier]: In *Beyond the Chocolate War* it's that choice is always possible. I've always been aware of moments in life when I had a clear choice. I was more explicit in *Beyond the Chocolate War* about the themes. I spelled out a lot of things in it that were only implicit in the other book. Obie could have

said "No" all along. The power of the leader comes from those who allow themselves to be led. There's a scene in *The Chocolate War* in which Brother Leon falsely accuses Gregory Bailey of cheating, and nobody comes to his rescue. I made a Nazi Germany comparison. The same kind of idea is expressed in *Beyond the Chocolate War:* Terrible things happen because we allow them to happen.

Frankly, I was astonished at the reception of *The Chocolate War* when people started talking about its downbeat philosophy. I thought, what's that got to do with me? You know I have family, friends. I'm an optimist. A writer is separate from his work. Looking back on the body of my work I suppose there is a certain theme running through it. When I wrote *The Chocolate War*, however, I didn't realize I was going to write *I Am the Cheese*. So it's not as if I sat down in the seventies and eighties to write these novels exploring these things. It's not a philosophy that I have tried to tow from book to book, though I hope there are serious things in the books.

I am frightened by today's world, terrified by it. I think that comes out in the books. I'm afraid of big things. Some of these schools have three thousand kids, and even the size of the schools frightens me. Big government frightens me; so does big defense. I think that those fears come out in *I Am the Cheese*. The terrorists who call themselves freedom fighters commit indiscriminate bombings. How could anybody do that in today's world? In *After the First Death* I was trying to answer that question for myself: that it could only be done out of a total innocence, a monstrous innocence, which is what Miro was. My philosophy is not that set and determined—it varies from book to book. (p. 155)

Anita Silvey, in an interview with Robert Cormier, Part I, in The Horn Book Magazine, *Vol. LXI, No. 2, March-April, 1985, pp. 145-55.*

Wow! It was worth waiting a decade for this sequel! Usually I am disappointed by books with characters I have met before because they steal my imagination. But, not Robert Cormier's finely tuned *Beyond the Chocolate War*. In fact, I think it is even better than *The Chocolate War*. Never have I read a book that is more carefully-crafted. A book in which the writer's craft does not get in the way of the reader becoming a part of the action, a participant in the disturbing plot.

Though many of the characters we have come to know in *The Chocolate War* appear again on the pages of the sequel, we meet them anew. For, like the author, they have matured. Archie, still the arch-villain, helps his stooges and the readers understand that a villain needs not only victims, but followers who are willing participants in the evil. "Oh, I'm an easy scapegoat, Obie. For you and everybody else at Trinity. Always have been. But you had free choice, buddy. Just like Brother Andrew always says in Religion. Free choice, Obie, and you did the choosing . . ."

Jerry Renault has returned to Monument, beaten and bruised, but not defeated by his refusal to involve himself in the chocolate sale and his nearly fatal fight with Emile Janza, the bully controlled by Archie's bidding. Jerry proves by his bravery and willingness to take Janza's punches unreturned, that "Janza's the loser . . . He'll be a loser all his life. He beat me up but he couldn't beat me . . ."

Other characters are part of this sequel: Brother Leon who has become the headmaster, Brother Eugene whose presence is felt though never realized, the Goober who always believes he is letting Jerry down, and David Caroni who out of fear of failing allows himself to succumb to Leon's threats and inform on Jerry Renault. All of these characters become three-dimensional in this stunning sequel.

A new character, Ray Bannister, and his involvement in a world of magic tricks that is not always what it seems, is introduced in the first chapter. His magic tricks allow Obie to plot the downfall of Archie, and allow Cormier to examine his theme. Things are not always what they seem; people are not always how they appear; evil does not only come from evil.

Beyond the Chocolate War is a captivating book, not only for young readers, but for all readers. Surely this book will win Cormier the prizes that have eluded him. Readers will remain glued to the pages for many decades. Teachers will experience the joy of teaching a modern classic. Censors will complain of its honesty, though they won't call it that. And, the world of young adult literature and all the readers of the book will be influenced by its power.

Charlie Reed, in a review of "Beyond the Chocolate War," in The ALAN Review, *Vol. 12, No. 2, Winter, 1985, p. 8.*

Cormier has not compromised **The Chocolate War** in a long-awaited sequel that is as grim if not grimmer as it completes the school year begun in the first book. The same insidious unrelieved tension pervades from the first sentence, "Ray Bannister started to build the guillotine the day Jerry Renault returned to Monument," to the last ironic chapter, which forebodes the next school year. . . . The fact that Cormier's writing has matured since publication of **The Chocolate War** in 1974 shows up in the difference in literary style between the two books. At least twice, though, he employs a self-conscious but effective literary device designed to stun the reader momentarily, and it's almost as if he is manipulating his readers while similar manipulation goes on within the story. However, this novel is more complex in construction, style, theme, and characterization than its predecessor—indeed, the portrayal of Archie, in particular, is much more finely honed and convincing. Another disturbing look at the darker side of human nature and the misuse of power that is sure to provoke discussion. (pp. 1048, 1050)

Sally Estes, in a review of "Beyond the Chocolate War," in Booklist, *Vol. 81, No. 14, March 15, 1985, pp. 1048, 1050.*

[In this sequel to **The Chocolate War**], Cormier continues his exploration into good and evil, focusing attention on insidious Archie, the snake in the garden. The pacing is relentless here, as violence, psychological torture and Archie's adroit manipulation infects the entire school (universe?). However, where events in **The Chocolate War** seemed demonically propelled and tragically inevitable, in the sequel the tragedy is piled on, accumulating rather than culminating. Metaphor is heavy handed, and chapter endings are like portentous cliffhangers in a metaphysical soap opera: "A bird cried piercingly, as if wounded. The soil that his father had turned over in preparation for planting the garden lay in turmoil, like a new grave." Individually, many scenes are vividly horrific, but as a whole this is less compelling as fiction than it is as a commentary on **The Chocolate War**—Cormier here intensifies and explicates what was powerfully implicit in the first book. While the sequel can be read independently, readers new to Trinity may be puzzled by what is essentially a string of thematic reverberations.

Roger Sutton, in a review of "Beyond the Chocolate War," in School Library Journal, *Vol. 31, No. 8, April, 1985, p. 96.*

[**The Chocolate War**] was a milestone in the writing of fiction for young adults, for it translated the attitudes, concerns, and relationships peculiar to the microcosmic world of the private high school into symbols of a far larger universe—yet remained quintessentially a story about and for adolescents. When a book achieves such status, the evaluation of its sequel poses special problems. Often the second book, which in any other context would be superior, seems weaker in comparison with its predecessor; less frequently, the second becomes a logical extension of the first, rounding out the theme and bringing events to an aesthetically satisfying conclusion. **Beyond the Chocolate War** belongs in this latter category: first, because it fleshes out the pivotal characters into more complex personalities; and secondly, because it probes the effects of violence and the abuse of power on the victimizers as well as on the victims. "Power tends to corrupt and absolute power corrupts absolutely," the aphorism attributed to Lord Acton, is made concrete, ugly, and immediate—not in the weary world of politics but in the shelter of school and playground. But the sequel is not simply a continuation, for it introduces Ray Bannister, newcomer to Monument, who not only provides a new point of view as the bystander to whom events of the previous autumn must be explained but who also serves as the unwitting agent for the final confrontation between the manipulative, amoral Archie Costello and Obie, once one of his loyal satraps. Nearly four months have elapsed since the chocolate sale which precipitated Brother Leon into power as headmaster and established Archie, his mirror image, as the unofficial power among the students. On the surface the school is calm; in reality, tension—not resolution—supports the fragile façade. That revolution lies just beneath the surface is foreshadowed in the first gripping sentence, "Ray Bannister started to build the guillotine the day Jerry Renault returned to Monument." These two seemingly disparate events set in motion a chain of circumstances which move inexorably to their final, dramatic convergence as Obie, less blind than formerly to Archie's ploys, seeks to eradicate what he considers to be the source of all the school's problems. He does not succeed; but the attempt forces him to confront what few wish to acknowledge—that evil exists because it is tolerated. Curiously, but not surprisingly, it is Archie—cold, calculating, Mephistophelian Archie—who articulates the theological principle which is at once the glory and the price of being human: "'You had free choice buddy. . . . free choice . . . and you did the choosing.'" And it is this principle, implicit in **The Chocolate War,** which is developed as the major thematic motif in the sequel, for each of the characters has the opportunity to find a solution to the problem, and each makes a choice appropriate to his personality: Carter, subterfuge; David Caroni, self-annihilation; Goober, retreat; Brother Leon, accommodation; Emile Janza, intimidation; Obie, vengeance. Only Jerry Renault elects to continue the battle, a choice which postulates change and offers hope, for in the larger world outside Trinity these are the choices made daily—and adolescents who adopt the fatalistic attitude that they are powerless need somehow to learn that despair often becomes a self-fulfilling prophecy. It is generally acknowledged that a profound theme is one of the elements separating genuine literature from simple entertainment; conversely, a dominant theme can overwhelm other considerations, transforming story into sermon. **Beyond the Chocolate War** is remarkable for maintaining the balance between plot and philosophy characteristic of the most memorable novels. Quite simply, the work is one of Cormier's finest books to date: combining the sense of immediacy that a good newsman can convey with the psychological insight of a mature writer. Nowhere is this combination better evidenced than in the descriptions of Obie's first experience with love; suggestion instead of explicit documentation somehow touches the heart rather than titillates the senses. And it is this ability to suggest and ultimately to provoke response which raises Cormier's novels above the mass. Consequently, his are among the few books written for young adults which, in all probability, will still be discussed in the twenty-first century. (pp. 451-53)

> *Mary M. Burns, in a review of "Beyond the Chocolate War," in* The Horn Book Magazine, *Vol. LXI, No. 4, July-August, 1985, pp. 451-53.*

Robert Cormier believes the life of man to be nasty, brutish and long. The years at school, in particular, encompass enough alienation and brutishness to fill several lifetimes. Fitful rays of remorse and compassion occasionally lighten the darkness, but Trinity High remains a thoroughly nasty place and the pupils are every bit as beastly as they were in *The Chocolate War*. . . . Hell has always been fascinating, however, and once again Cormier has managed to make a strong and compelling novel out of the baser aspects of human nature. . . .

The secret of Cormier's success does not lie in his much praised realism. Though they talk and outwardly act like real boys, these monsters are grotesques, and credibility must surely be strained when a respectable school of 400 boys produces a torturer, a blackmailer, a suicide, a religious maniac, and a sadist. These are not the products of a mere observer of mores, but of a real writer who has a tale to tell and knows how to tell it. The events within the story are skilfully manoeuvred, and the timing controlled. People sweat a lot in this novel, and so does the reader, for the atmosphere of menace is quite suffocating.

Plot-weaving and atmospherics are the regular stock-in-trade of any good storyteller: where Cormier really excels is in his juxtaposition of the horrific and the ordinary; of the sinister and the explicable. The black box is a good example. As Assigner of the Vigils, Archie always submits himself to the black box which contains five white marbles and one black. If he picks the black marble, Archie must perform the assignment himself. In all his years as Assigner Archie has never picked the black marble—a result, Obie discovers, of sleight of hand. It is a mark of Cormier's subtlety that Archie does not always cheat, but occasionally allows himself the thrill of a real gamble. Similarly, in Brother Leon's final hypocritical speech to the boy hearing Brother Leon talking away his own guilt, the reader is simultaneously aware of a boy surreptitiously eating out of his lunchbox. The boy only half listens to the speech while delving into his box and musing on its contents. When Brother Leon finishes his speech by accusing the boys of responsibility for the suicide, Henry's fingers find a tomato. Almost unconsciously, he throws it with unerring aim straight at Brother Leon's forehead.

This is the kind of reality that interests the author: the flashpoint at which violence can suddenly erupt, and as suddenly turn

tragedy into farce. And Cormier aptly sets that flashpoint in late adolescence, the stage in life when the emotions are nearest to the surface and the restraints (of parents, work, money, and society) least effective. It is also an exciting time. For all its nihilism, Cormier has captured that raw energy which characterizes the verge of adulthood.

> *Sarah Hayes, "One Black Marble," in* The Times Literary Supplement, *No. 4313, November 29, 1985, p. 1358.*

Robert Cormier has kept us waiting ten years for a sequel to his *Chocolate War*. To be honest I would have been prepared to wait longer.

This is not to say that he is anything other than a writer of outstanding powers, master of a brutal and brittle style which crackles and spits out of the page like sticks on a fire, and ruthless in the completeness of his picture of a world. But surely I am not alone in finding that world totally repulsive and, thank goodness, far distant from reality, at least in this part of the globe.

Trinity High, like all schools, is a microcosm. Here are acted out the rackets, the feuds, the pursuit of power to be found on another scale in the adult world. The titular head of Trinity is Brother Leon—it is a Catholic school but one would have to look hard to find any evidence of spirituality—but power in reality rests with Archie Costello. . . . Archie is a strange character. He seems to get no satisfaction out of his position. He uses it for mostly quite futile ends, setting in motion activities which, apart from bringing a degree of humiliation and discomfort to those involved, apparently have no object other than a demonstration of Archie's pre-eminence. No one has seen Archie do any school work. He likes nothing and nobody, not even—one suspects—Archie himself. Cold, untouchable, even his sexual exploits appear to be more for prestige than pleasure. Like a spider Archie stretches his net over Trinity High, entangling not only all the boys from smallest to strongest but also Brother Leon and the rest of the staff. Archie calls the tunes, and pretty unmelodious they mostly are.

Mr. Cormier uses a large canvas, and there are a host of portraits, none of them particularly attractive but all crisply drawn. If only the reader could care about any of them, victims or victimizers. So, while admiring unreservedly the writer's skill, his mastery of every detail of the complicated plot, the building of climaxes, this reader at least passed from repulsion to indifference. A plague on all their houses!

Archie leaves school before the last chapter, but, *in absentio*, he still has the last word. He has chosen as his successor an ambitious weakling and saddled him with, as chief of staff, a sadistic Godfather-in-the-making. Archie has ensured that Trinity will look back to his reign as a golden age. Meanwhile there are opportunities for his talents in the larger world. As the pathetic and Christlike Jerry says: 'How many Archie Costellos there are in the world. Out there. Everywhere. Waiting.' It is not a pretty thought, but then this is not a pretty book.

> *M. Crouch, in a review of "Beyond the Chocolate War," in* The Junior Bookshelf, *Vol. 49, No. 6, December, 1985, p. 274.*

Jane (Mary Pearson) Gardam

1928-

English author of fiction.

Acknowledged as one of England's most outstanding contemporary authors for children and young adults, Gardam writes compact, sophisticated, and exuberant books which reveal her understanding of the difficulties in passing from childhood to maturity. She is well known for her economical use of words and skillful integration of contrasting styles within well-paced narratives; her books, which are set in the periods both before and after the Second World War, reflect her deep affection for the northeastern coast of England. Particularly adept at juxtaposing tragedy with comedy, Gardam demonstrates both tenderness and honesty in plots which focus on characters learning to discriminate between reality and appearance. Her novels often center on sensitive, individualistic heroines who find themselves in collision with middle-class norms and adult anticipations. These young women, who represent a variety of ages, backgrounds, and personalities, occasionally look to literary figures for inspiration: Athene Price in *The Summer after the Funeral*, for example, fancies herself as the reincarnation of Emily Brontë, and Marigold Green (nicknamed "Bilgewater" in the book of the same name) often refers to James Joyce and Thomas Hardy. Gardam has also written three books for younger children—*Bridget and William, Horse*, and *Kit*—which are recognized both for their success as literature and suitability for their audience.

Critics praise Gardam as a writer whose works have helped to reduce the distinction between literature for children and literature for adults; several of her books, notably *A Few Fair Days, A Long Way from Verona, Bilgewater*, and *The Hollow Land*, are considered classics. Reviewers also admire Gardam's ability to recreate setting and the changing moods of growing up. While some observers agree that she tends to become too literary, most acclaim her combination of humor and pathos, originality, perceptiveness, and command of language and form.

Gardam has won several awards for her books including the Whitbread Literary Award in 1981 for *The Hollow Land. The Summer after the Funeral* was a *Boston Globe-Horn Book* Honor Book in 1974.

(See also *Something about the Author*, Vols. 28, 39; *Contemporary Authors New Revision Series*, Vols. 2, 18; *Contemporary Authors*, Vols. 49-52; and *Dictionary of Literary Biography*, Vol. 14; *British Novelists since 1960*.)

AUTHOR'S COMMENTARY

One of the greatest surprises when you begin to write fiction in middle age is the questions you get asked. You can cope with the wide-eyed stares and frank disbelief. In fact, they are rather pleasant. What you cannot cope with is the questioning—utterly astounding, unanswerable questioning from people you have known or thought you have known these twenty years.

'How do you think of your plots?', for instance. (Well, answer me that!)

Photograph by Mark Gerson

'How do you think up the people? Is it yourself?' is another. The most usual.

Yet another—and I have taken to answering 'yes' to this one though I'm really not sure about it at all—is, 'Oh, are they for *children*?'

'Yes'.

'Oh, I *see*.'

Mrs Hookaneye is comforted by this very much. Any old nut can write for children. She has thought of writing for children herself. What do I think of . . .? And a long list of other writers for children follows, for Mrs Hookaneye has several children or grandchildren of her own, and spends money on good books for them. And oh dear! I don't know how other writers of books for the young feel: I only know, heaven help me, that I read very few children's books and that, with about three blazing exceptions, a serious impediment in my speech occurs when I am asked to talk about them.

A pause, then back to question two. 'Oh, the first little girl *was* you, wasn't she? The one in your first book. She does so remind me of you,' say Mrs Hookaneye, Mrs Pollywog, my mother's friend. 'It is you, isn't it?'

Only in so far as every hero is oneself. Only in so far as no hero in fiction can really be oneself. Autobiography is dangerous stuff. I can never see how anyone has the audacity to write autobiography until he has been famous a while. Even then it's usually better not to. No, dear Mrs Hookaneye, Mrs Toodles—not myself. I was never so fearless and strong, never so lucid and loving. I tied my little brother to a chair when he was two and went off to the pictures. I spent my days in endless fret at the impression I was making on people, drained by misery because everybody hated me. Don't you remember, Mrs H? You've known me since the pram.

'I knew from the first page, dear, that Lucy was you. And what a lovely picture of the town.'

And here I beam and embrace her and adore her: for yes, please, it is meant to be an attempt at the town and the landscape where I was brought up, in the North Riding by the sea which I loved and I love and I will love for ever. That is true. I can stand any amount of discussion about that. The trouble is that nobody but the other people in the town really wants to join in. You can't be too careful with regional passions. Unless you're a genius, watch out and remember Mary Webb. Joe Bloggs's childhood looked as good as yours and mine to Joe Bloggs, and the same sun came creeping in at morn at his little window.

'*Just* like the town,' continues Mrs Hookaneye, 'but I don't quite remember all those people, Jane. A little poetic licence there, perhaps?'

'Well, yes,' says I.

For of course they weren't there. They just wandered in, some of them. Some were there. My beloved aunts were there, and the sea-coal woman on the beach (I think), and my father and the maid. But some wandered in from somewhere outside. They are all rather mixed up in my mind now, the real ones and the rest.

Where do characters come from anyway? What a question! It is such private territory, such an undergrowth. All one knows, without a mighty search, is that they are there—the characters—urgent to get out, and that there is no point in writing fiction otherwise: unless one is very short of money, and then one might do better to take other and more lucrative employment.

I wrote my books, dear Mrs H, because I so badly wanted to write them. I think I would probably have died if I hadn't written *A Few Fair Days.* But do you understand what I'm talking about, Mrs Hook? Mrs Bobtail? Mrs Splendiferous?

And do you understand—before you start thundering out tales yourselves—and I tell you, it plays havoc with the ironing—do you understand that I was most unusually lucky in my publisher, who accepted my first book even after I had committed the insanity of telephoning her unintroduced to inform her that my first MS was on its way? . . . She accepted the book and said was I thinking of another? I said I might now have written my book. She said no, and was right.

For in the first book there was a sort of seed of a second. I wanted to examine somebody growing up in the landscape I had described which was then partly removed from her by a war, and I had touched on this in the last page or two of my first book.

I wrote a few new chapters of this new book. They were no good, so I did them again. Then what I was doing got hold of me, and I could think of nothing else. The girl in the new book

possessed me. When I'd finished with her—and what a small step on I'd got! How little I knew of her and what she would become and when; or if there is any when, or becoming—or real understanding!—; when I'd finished with her, I felt quite lost.

She was as different from me, that girl in *A Long Way from Verona,* as any child could be. I was a mouse, at that age, sometimes a mouse and sometimes a clown. The point about Jessica Vye is that her dizziness is meant to amount at moments almost to genius. No genius about me. I was considered pretty dim at school until I was sixteen and met a Lance-Corporal in the Army Education Corps who wrote poetry and decided I should go to Cambridge.

But again.

And again.

'I think that you are writing about *yourself,* Jane,' says Mrs Hookaneye.

So I set out quite deliberately to sort out another girl—one who could not possibly be thought to be me. She had raised her stately head in *A Long Way from Verona*—called by another name and just drifting in for a minute. She was beautiful, clever and good, and I had been a bit interested by her. I felt that being beautiful, clever and good should not be held against her. I wanted to get at her, somehow—find out how she'd be if her lovely happy background in a marvellous Georgian Rectory near Wilton Woods, where I used to go to tea when I was about nine (I met her there once, though her teeth stuck out a bit)—how she'd be if she lost it all.

So off I went, very slowly this time, with Athene Price. I got a bit too taken up with her ugly sister on the way, I think, who rather threatened to take charge of the book; but I liked old Athene, too, in the end, and it was painful when I destroyed her. For destroyed she is, of course, poor duck. Gone, gone like fifteen wild Decembers—or fifteen rainy Augusts, anyway. Gone, my dear American psychiatric critic who went for me so vigorously. 'Gardam,' he says, 'suggests that Athene is no more than a "high-spirited animal".' Oh dear me, no sir. It is much worse even than that.

What have I learned in three books? Not much. Mostly about my limitations. A little about form, perhaps—a few experiments. I think that it may be in form and structure that the twentieth century so-called 'children's book' might in time be in advance of the rest. The novel at present, apart from the 'children's novel', seems to me to be often literally as well as figuratively in rather poor shape.

I have learned to wait for reviews and read them quietly without physical sickness, though still with unease. I haven't learned much yet about living with what I'm writing. I haven't learned yet how to cope with Mrs H. How not to be lonely for talk of books. The illustrator of my first book, Peggy Fortnum, said to me, 'Don't ever talk about your work to outsiders. Let it be like a secret sin.' But I can't decide whether this is right or not. I rise from my desk every day at three thirty-five to collect my youngest child from school, and stand looking rather battered at the school gate. It would be wonderful to start talking about what is really in one's head instead of which day is the concert and do you want a pair of size twelve football boots. To talk about work again as one did at college.

But, of course, one can't. One doesn't. One chatters on and goes home and, yes, well I'm sorry: I did forget to buy the blasted crumpets. One wonders whether it's worth stumbling on with two ramshackle lives at once. But really in one's heart one knows that it is stupendous luck and happiness to be able to work at all at what makes one most content. (pp. 77-80)

Jane Gardam "Mrs. Hookaneye and I," in The Thorny Paradise: Writers on Writing for Children, edited by Edward Blishen, Kestrel Books, 1975, pp. 77-80.

I am rather ill at ease when I am asked to discuss how I have tried to break new ground or apply new techniques in the writing of children's books; the truth is that I have not done anything of the sort. When I sat down and considered how to explain what it is I have been trying to do, it became harder and harder to say. Each book I have written I have desperately wanted to write. Whether or not they had anything to do with children has never occurred to me. . . .

I have not the faintest idea where I am going, whom I am writing for, or why I am compelled to write fiction at all. (p. 489)

Once upon a time I did try to write a children's book—a book children would really love. I wrote it in the early sixties in the public library at Wimbledon after dropping my eldest children at their nursery school. I wrote painlessly for two hours a day with a smile upon my face. There are two kinds of people convinced that it is easy to write for children: mothers of five-to seven-year-old children and established authors of so-called adult fiction, who need money fast and think it's a pushover. Both are mistaken.

I was mistaken. My book was called *The Astonishing Vicarage* and I wrote away among all the other Wimbledon mothers writing books with roughly the same titles. . . . When I had finished—it was a book about boarding-school children, tunnels, butterfly collections, and clergymen—I confidently sent it off to a distinguished publishing house where I had a friend, and expected to hear from her immediately.

But time passed and grew heavy, and it was several weeks before an embarrassed voice on the telephone asked if she could talk to me about *The Astonishing Vicarage.*

"Talk now," said I. Long pause.

"Well, it's difficult."

"You don't like it?"

"It's not that exactly," she said, "but I wonder if you realize that the curate is a homosexual?"

"No," I said. "No. Not really." I hadn't. Or if I had, maybe I had thought it didn't matter. "Leonardo da Vinci," I said. I was really very disturbed.

"But he's not Leonardo da Vinci," she said. "He's a curate. Anyway children don't want to know. It's not what matters." I agreed with this. "The book is funny," she said, "but it is very strange."

So I burnt it up, thank goodness, for it was quite hideously bad, not analyzing at that moment the line—if there is one—between the novel and the tale for the young, which has always, anyway, been a very wavering one. I did not even dwell on the interest to children of curates below the waist. I felt that such things were beyond me. As reviews of distinguished children's books began to take my eye—the sixties were certainly the time, says Maurice Sendak, when England and America were leading the world in children's literature, in narrative,

and in lovely illustration—I began to see that I was a woman with too simple a mind to compete. Perhaps, I thought, I had better try something easy, about which the critics were less clever and sometimes kind, something a bit more widely educated, like the experimental novel or the postmodernist novel. I rather liked the thought of the postmodernist breakthrough: the kind of novel now called sur-fiction or meta-fiction. I write so slowly when I am not in the Wimbledon Public Library that by the time I have finished such a book it might not be as advanced as all that. It might even have become dated and make some money—rampant with homosexual curates in whom the children of the eighties could take innocent delight.

I would cut out the tunnels, though, and the butterflies. In fact, I would cut out a lot of things. There is a comforting school of thought or development or prediction in modern fiction which advocates that more and more should be cut out, refined, reduced, released into anarchy—and even form itself eventually abandoned. (pp. 490-91)

As I spent so much time before I had my children doing post-graduate work on the eighteenth century and its classicism, it might be a lovely rest to consider formlessness. A void. Like Book One of *Paradise Lost.* I was never modest. Well, of course, I did nothing of the sort. If writing a book for children was beyond me, considering a void was harder still. I returned not to the eighteenth century but to an almost bookless life—shepherd's pie by day and sewing name tapes by night and only the old comforters to read to the children of an evening, like *Biggles* and *Tin-Tin* and Beatrix Potter and Laura Ingalls Wilder and Richmal Crompton's *William.* It was a harrowing time, ending after some years when it occurred to me to write a book which sprang from a single image of a child very young, under five, alone on a long beach, and to try to recreate the mystery of this time, the temporary freedom from fear and anxiety and the need for people which occurs now and then in very early childhood.

John Fowles says that "[c]haracters [in fiction] . . . are like children . . . they need constant caressing, concern, listening to, watching, admiring." I don't agree with this entirely. Both characters in fiction and children often need to be left alone to grow. Children ought not to be in need of consolation all the time, of fantasy, of myth, of being stroked like queen bees. In fact, I think it's bad for them. Enid Blyton, a prime example of this consolation, is a long way from the truth, though she's a lovely read for a lazy day when you're about seven. For children are usually very strong. (pp. 491-92)

So I tried to describe childhood in very bare words and clear colors, and whether I thought I was writing poetry or painting, I don't know. The exercise was impossible: trying to recreate moments of absolute peace that one is lucky if one remembers at all as soon as one is out of the pram—moments which appear afterward to be on the edge of dream. I didn't bring the experiment off at all, but I liked trying. It felt like real work, and when the book was published as a children's book, the critics said that I had entered the field of children's literature. And when I wrote a novel about an older child and found that I was now called a children's writer, I was very pleased. The field was interesting, and I certainly didn't make for the gate. Once last year I stepped outside to write a book about Jamaica which would not interest any child unless he were very peculiar—it wouldn't, as Robert Louis Stevenson said, "fetch the kids." But even though, perhaps because, the critics said that they were pleased that I had moved to something serious, I found myself back in the field again writing another book about a child. This one, I am delighted to say, was published complete with a schoolmaster who gave bunches of flowers to little boys and an ogrelike headmaster's wife who ran off with the captain of the school. Nobody turned a hair, least of all the children who are used to all that, being near to it.

But nobody fancies the idea of "being cut in two like a wasp in the marmalade," and I do see that there are tiresome dangers in being thought to write for children only, unless you are very good, indeed. A genius like Carroll. Some of the best writers do state ferociously that they write for children only: William Mayne, "because it is the only sensible thing to do"; Alan Garner, because "it imposes a literary discipline . . . a compulsion to find a language that will bring all the complexity of the reality children share with adults within the verbal and conceptual compass of the young." P. L. Travers, not new but still going very strong with that—to me—rather unalluring witch Mary Poppins, says she writes for children because she respects their eyesight. They find visible "the ill-defined area between the possible and the impossible, fantasy and unreality . . . the gap between the first and last strokes of midnight at the end of one year and the beginning of another that is soldered over for adults." She says, "I think about myth. It is like talking to the cosmos." But she agrees—and so of course must the others—that no book which children like, even if the author says it is written for children only, is much good if it is liked by children only. C. S. Lewis said long ago that books enjoyed only by children are by definition bad books.

Why one writes fiction at all, of course, one never knows or does well not to try to say. Novelists are usually and mercifully quiet about it. Among children's writers—who are, as I'm trying to indicate, on the whole a waspish lot since they have the unfortunate image of being thought rather sweet by people who don't know any—among children's writers one remembers Carroll saying that he sent Alice off down the rabbit hole without the faintest idea of what was going to happen to her . . . ; and Swift, one remembers, speaking of the first glorious dawn over Lilliput, says, "Nothing to it. You think of big men and little men and you're away." And of R. L. S., who wrote *Treasure Island* because one wet day a boy was messing with chalks at a table and Stevenson sat down alongside and drew a map. (pp. 491-94)

.   .   .   .   .

For myself I came upon children's literature through my Auntie Nellie, a rich woman who lived in nursing homes and who presented my brother and me, when I was seven and he was three, with china mugs from which we drank milk at teatime. I was an undersized child, and so for some years my mug was at eye level every day. I spent much time regarding it. The handle was the frightful tail of a fawn-colored caterpillar, curling down and round the mug in low relief, ending at the back in a patient face and a harness of clean cobwebs. On its back all kinds of parcels were being heaped by the familiar flat synthetic elves wearing bluebell hats and the expressions of health visitors. Written beneath the cartoon were the words "Something attempted, something done, Has earned a night's repose"—a sentiment which has perhaps been the reason for my dread of finishing anything and a habit of wandering the house at night. Across the table my brother's mug had as a handle a glorious, fat red robin with a glaring black eye and for a legend, by some fine accident, the words "A Robin Red breast in a Cage/ Puts all Heaven in a Rage." From that moment, not knowing of his existence, I felt Blake to be a superlative children's poet, and I have never changed my mind.

But apart from the mugs, the literature on offer was very watery marmalade, indeed. I think that I was unfortunate in that neither of my parents seemed to have read anything as children, and there were no thumbed or even unthumbed copies of Mrs. Molesworth, E. Nesbit, or Frances Hodgson Burnett about the house. Worse, there were no Brothers Grimm, no Hans Andersen, no Andrew Lang. In 1936 my Auntie Nellie produced a book of songs by A. A. Milne—bears and honey jars, a nannie in flowing dress and huge apron that seemed archaic, a golden-haired little boy, much loved and rich, who wandered in summery spinneys in Sussex (we lived on Teesside), hung thoughtfully over bridges, and sweetly said his prayers. He had heartbreaking dents in the backs of his knees. I reacted violently. . . . A vile, Iago-like child, I hated Christopher Robin because "He hath a daily beauty in his life / That makes me ugly." I looked elsewhere.

And oh, so few places to look. It seems extraordinary that our house was a schoolmaster's house, but there were only three bookshelves. My father taught mathematics and physics, and I don't think had ever read a novel. My mother was an Anglo-Catholic, and all her books seemed to be by Dean Inge. There was no book shop in the town, no public library, no library at my kindergarten or at the junior part of the high school to which I went when I was eleven. In the senior school there was the county library cupboard, locked with a padlock, which contained forty books, changed at monthly intervals and unlocked for an hour on alternate Wednesdays. I went back to my old school three years ago to present the prizes there—I had written a book about it, a book which I had thought modestly (like Dickens) might cause the establishment to be closed. But no. I was invited back and shown a library of such splendor that I was humbled and ashamed and decided that the bi-Wednesday cupboard must have been a myth. And it certainly seems a myth that through this cupboard—like Alice grabbing at the pot of marmalade as she fell—I achieved a place to read English literature at a university and, several happy years afterward, in the reading room of the British Museum.

A good part of the year, however, was spent during my father's long holidays at his father's farm in West Cumberland, and here there were no books at all except the family Bible. It had a big metal clasp, and when you opened it, a waft of must blew out. The pages had fawn-colored blobs on them and cauliflower- and cumulus-shaped fungi, but I read the Old Testament through. The New Testament I avoided, perhaps because there were so many pictures of Jesus on the bedroom walls at home—Jesus robed like Christopher Robin's nannie, emasculated like an elf—for all I know even accompanied by an elf. (pp. 672-73)

The farm dining room where I had the luck to find the Old Testament was a very grand room in which I never remember eating a meal and could be quite alone. The table was covered with a furry carpet. There were mirrors and lustres and embroidered texts and the best china in a cabinet. Out of the window beyond the geraniums on the sill was Skiddaw Mountain, and across the room was a huge old court cupboard with 1691—the year of *The Secret Commonwealth*—carved on it, a cupboard so big that, we were always told, the new eighteenth-century farmhouse had been built round it. As a child I used to climb in through one of its lower doors and along inside and out the other end, as if crawling down a tunnel. Tunnels, tunnels! Have no fear—my progress down the cupboard did not land me in marmalade; nor did I come out at the other end finding that there had been a time-slip and everybody was in mob caps or periwigs; nor did the back of the cupboard fall out and I find myself in a land of lions who were really God and witches who were much less seductive than Satan. Nor did it lead me to the new, liberated children's fiction in which the young do more advanced things in cupboards than their parents were allowed even to read about forty years ago at the dingier end of the dingier book shops in the Charing Cross Road.

No. I crawled one summer day through the dining room cupboard at the farm where for a long time there had been a moldy old heap of paper, and I pulled a book out of the middle of it. It was a thin, cheap-looking book, its cardboard back bent up at the corners and the pages freckled and stuck together. It was called *Northanger Abbey,* and I carried it about the farm and fields a good bit afterward. I should like to say that I read it; but I don't believe I did read much. I suppose I was a bit young for it if I was still crawling about in cupboards. But I do remember feeling something particular about it. The name seemed beautiful. I was very taken with the way the sentences went. My grandmother quickly took it from me anyway. She did not like to see time wasted out of doors reading. (pp. 674-75)

It would be fun to pretend that I let it be known to my agent, when years and years afterward I began to write fiction, that I had had a Lake District childhood—an enormous advantage to a writer of children's books. The North West has been an ancient place for stories which children enjoy. Most of the stories certainly are about people on very short visits. Sir Gawain in search of the Green Knight somewhere round the Trough of Bowland was glad to be home. Beowulf and his not particularly merry men, off after Grendel and his mother in what sounds very like Wastwater, were much relieved to get back to base and start the party; and the ubiquitous Arthur seems to have been content to choose the North only for his mausoleum under Richmond Castle, though his father Pendragon, the cannibal of Castlethwaite, was resident and no weekender in the very heart of things at Mallerstang; a gallop would have got him to Beatrix Potter by lunchtime and to Arthur Ransome for evening cocoa. They are a testy, sometimes ferocious collection (not King Arthur) and stern with the young.

"When I was a little girl I was satisfied with about six books. I think children nowadays have too many," said Beatrix Potter. Arthur Ransome seems not to have liked children at all, though he wrote of the most blissful happiness of his own Lake District holidays as a boy, when he was in the Middle East and in middle age, operating so surprisingly as a secret service agent.

My time in the Lake District was not a bit like that—no boats, no camps, no giants or knights in armor. We were all expected to work and get the harvest in. There were still—noticeable even to a child—the remains of the awful poverty of the twenties when farmers in West Cumberland were hungry. Life was still frugal. Farm servants were still called hinds, even in the forties, the women hired-girls, often too poor to marry. Illegitimate children were usual and accepted and on arrival were brought round from farm to farm by their grandmothers and given shillings like other new babies. There was most tremendous hard drinking. Language, especially in the fields, was rich and funny and foul—strong stuff for a schoolmaster's daughter whose mother read Dean Inge. I have been eternally grateful for it. There had been this murder—and other things. A neighboring farmer in his cups used to hunt his sons with a gun round a spinney where there was neither Pooh nor Eeyore. In winter, as in Laurie Lee's Gloucestershire at precisely this time, "in winter incest flourished where the roads were bad."

A long way from *Swallows and Amazons* (Lippincott). In fact, in whispering distance, sometimes, of *Cold Comfort Farm* (Penguin).

But not such a great way from Beatrix Potter. Even before the days of Auntie Nellie's milk mug I had met her—literally met her because my mother, discovering *Squirrel Nutkin* (Warne) in a shop in York when she was on a Mother's Union outing, deserted Dean Inge at last and proceeded to Sawrey, which was not far from our farm. I remember a little, bent, sideways-glancing person looking at me over a gate, and a sense of toughness and purposefulness of a high order. I was being led along by a hand—my mother's—and high above me was my mother's face, pink with pleasure at seeing the bunny lady. (pp. 675-76)

I doted and I dote upon Beatrix Potter especially when she is murky—the terrible house of Mr. Tod, the awful wet dark Lake District afternoon leaden through the windows, the slate, the dripping trees, the fearful smell of decay, the awful teeth of the badger lying on the bed with the dreadful gallows bucket above him. Years later in a lecture to do with Old Norse at the University I awoke to hear the lecturer likening the atmosphere of *Beowulf* to Mr. Tod's cottage. Among current writers both William Mayne and Alan Garner, who live in the emptier places of the North and don't only visit for their summer holidays, evoke this atmosphere—sometimes equally powerfully.

I wonder if it could now happen that a child—in what was called an educated home, at the best school in the district, taught by women with good degrees, whose only talent was telling stories—could have read so few books? . . . The new availability of books; the excellence of most children's libraries; and the people believing in and promoting them, forming groups to urge children's imaginations on would have had children like me as their prime target. I think, however—though I'm not saying that it would have been any loss except to my own happiness—that such a barrage of kindness might have stopped me writing anything myself. Children's books are now so good, so scholarly, so special, I think children may now react sometimes as I did to Christopher Robin and turn to Richmal Crompton's *William*. They still can, because there are new editions and it's on the television of a Sunday afternoon. William is as deathless in his own way as Billy Bones; he has the weird formality that children have; he is earnest, logical, dirty, maddening, and harebrained. He is not entirely without interest in "the roots of existence," but he will never be "captured by the forces of evil." If he goes through the back of a cupboard, it is because he has broken it.

He is also—which some of the new didactic writers forget about children—hilariously funny. Children like to see themselves as funny. The best sound in the world is a child by himself laughing out loud at a book. I see the solemn faces of children sometimes brooding over *The Lord of the Rings* or *Red Shift* (Macmillan), and I feel rather sorry for them. Children need a lot of nonsense. They even need a lot of time to be without books at all. I think if I were a child now I would have disregarded all the delectable literature spread out for me and me alone, and on Puffin Club days I'd have been the child who stayed at home rolled up in bed with some rubbishy comics, which, thank goodness, like *William* are still about. (pp. 677-78)

Perhaps all this fiction of the golden age of the children's books would have slowed me up and left me stuck in the marmalade forever. The great pity of the new children's fiction is that it is cut off from the rest of fiction at least until it is about thirty years old—it has special reviewers, special sections in the literary journals as well as in the book shops and the libraries. On television book programs, if it's children's books night, you will see that the chairmen of the panels have a special sort of face, like uncles at birthday parties waiting for the home-going balloons and the restorative gin and tonic. Writers of children's books sometimes understandably deal with this by a rather dotty arrogance, refusing to read any other literature themselves, relentlessly reviewing only each other—"incest flourishes where the roads are bad"—becoming at last pathetic people, ever feebler, and finally, deep in the marmalade, unable even to twitch.

I like to think such few books as I have done have nothing to do with new directions in children's literature; but then I suppose no writer of fiction ever admits a precise debt, unless . . . it is in one of their books they don't like. . . . I like, for example, some of what P. L. Travers says about children's eyesight; but I could never talk to the cosmos. Quite beyond me. Similarly, for all my awe of Alan Garner, I could never do the homework of getting my characters to unlock the power of the past. And I can't at present even write about violence. Sex in my books has to be tentative, suggested, and not gymnastic; politics I can't cope with at all. I have never, I hope, written a word meant to ennoble or to educate. I write only to entertain. And although I almost worship [Sylvia Townsend Warner's] *Kingdoms of Elfin* as I almost worship Swift, I don't suppose I shall ever write about tearing monkeys in half. "One writes what one can, not what one should," says Iris Murdoch.

I can only write very tame tales, mostly about the tragicomedy of being young. I sometimes even sing of vicars' daughters. If people read my books, and particularly if they sometimes laugh at them, I could not ask for any more. (pp. 678-79)

> *Jane Gardam, "On Writing for Children: Some Wasps in the Marmalade, Part I" and "On Writing for Children: Some Wasps in the Marmalade, Part II," in* The Horn Book Magazine, *Vol. LV, Nos. 5 and 6, October and December, 1978, pp. 489-96; 672-79.*

GENERAL COMMENTARY

COLIN MILLS

Jane Gardam seems particularly effective at portraying the 'inner life' of communities in stories such as *Bridget and William*, in *Horse* and in *The hollow land*. Even the texture of the conversations in her books shows the ways in which the old and the young, the traditional and the new, can learn from each other and co-exist. (p. 312)

> *Colin Mills, " 'But I'm the Reader, Not the Book': Some Trends in Junior Fiction," in* The School Librarian, *Vol. 32, No. 4, December, 1984, pp. 310-16.*

A FEW FAIR DAYS (1971)

This is a delightful book with much to please young readers and their parents. The former will identify with Lucy, the central figures of the episodes which involve a variety of simple incidents from stolen afternoons on the beach to the excitement of a ship in the sand, all given special interest by the enthusiasm with which Lucy experiences them. Many parents will appreciate the evocation of the pre-war period.

Yet the book is not nostalgic; it has the urgency and the air of living for the moment of Lucy herself, achieved in part by the writer's eye for vivid detail and economical style. Lucy's relatives, including many aunts, are effectively brought to life. Along with times of misery or fear there are moments of delightful humour and times too of utter, simple happiness in which the reader shares.

> *Judith Aldridge, in a review of "A Few Fair Days," in* Children's Book Review, *Vol. I, No. 5, October, 1971, p. 160.*

Jane Gardam has made aunts the very centre of *A few fair days*. The autobiographical aspect of this enchanting book has given it a positive edge of detail but there is none of the rambling disorganisation of some reminiscences. Supremely well-planned, crisply and deftly written, this is a book of exceptional literary value. Most of its unforgettable scenes take place in North Yorkshire in the years between the wars, with an interlude in Cumberland. Everywhere aunts provide the pattern of the book, its layers of present, immediate past, remote past. One day in a storm a ship is driven on to the sand and Lucy goes to see it, 'standing up quite straight like a decoration on a Christmas cake'. When she rushes off to tell great-aunts Fanny and Bea, Aunt Fanny makes the simmering child sit down and takes her back more than a century to the time when a 'ship in the grass' driven on the sandhills in a storm, was blown free by a great wind and Great Aunt Sarah and her brother Alfred found beside it an old man, 'dry and thin as the ship's timbers', who had been on the *Victory*. "Nelson were a cock sparrow," he tells them. "There's a Frenchie up a rigging sees a glitter far off and he aims his gun and down goes Nelson—but you see he *would go dressing up*." This reaching back into the past is the prerogative of aunts: a particular kind of straightening-out also belongs to them, an unreplaceable bridge between the generations.

I haven't space to enumerate all the delights of this book. One outstanding virtue is its selectiveness; the author has a piquant style and uses words confidently and with notable economy. Again, she keeps a masterly balance between an adult's sense of the ridiculous and a child's observation of oddity. The young who can read the book can be right in it all with young Lucy as small child and schoolgirl and at the same time they can glimpse the status, attitudes and enjoyment of life of the aunts. Cherish this book. (pp. 1798-99)

> *Margery Fisher, in a review of "A Few Fair Days," in* Growing Point, *Vol. 10, No. 4, October, 1971, pp. 1798-99.*

For tenderness and humour nothing can touch a shortish book on pre-war childhood—*A Few Fair Days* by Jane Gardam. . . . It has nine incidents about a child's life in North Yorkshire and Cumberland, each with a nicely-rounded plot and including a discussion by three little girls on lines by Shelley, a meeting with a witch when the heroine is developing measles, a cake which the children poison with seaweed, and the dyeing of a grandmother's hair bright green with a shampoo bought from a tinker. The incidents are unusual; the style poetic and gay. A charming book—for adults as well as older children.

> *Gwendolen Freeman, in a review of "A Few Fair Days," in* History Today, *Vol. XXI, No. 12, December, 1971, p. 887.*

There is originality in the mode of telling these stories, difference in the episodes narrated, variety in the scenes of these apparently autobiographical tales, imagination and humour in the presentation but something quite inconsequential about all of them. However this book of tales of a pre-war childhood does not really come off. In fact, each story so much fails to impress that it is likely to be forgotten before one reads the next but one! The reason to a degree is that it is not selective enough and does not make and keep the main events sufficiently clear. . . . It is the kind of book about which opinions could differ. Dare one say that an "old-fashioned" child could like it? One verdict, though, is that it is a bold experiment but one which does not quite succeed.

> *H. Budge, in a review of "A Few Fair Days," in* The Junior Bookshelf, *Vol. 35, No. 6, December, 1971, p. 397.*

If there ever was a time when the very nicest people wouldn't dream of using paper napkins, when ladies never slumped or went out without their gloves, and when people were generally kind, then these "few fair days" have been admirably captured by the author. Using a spare prose laced with humor, she has deftly sketched, in nine finely drawn vignettes, the childhood of a little girl named Lucy. . . . [Lucy] is very much alive—imaginative and energetic. With her best friend Mary Fell and her little brother Jake, Lucy explores the wide world of Yorkshire by the North Sea. Adults move on the periphery of this world, contributing love and structure to it; but the perspective of the book is the perspective of childhood. An earlier and quieter book than the award-winning *A Long Way from Verona,* it may not appeal as much to American readers. But, it is no less polished and has high moments of gentle humor as in the episode "Mr. Crossley's Wig." This is a book that should be shared and read aloud. (pp. 47-8)

> *Sheryl B. Andrews, in a review of "A Few Fair Days," in* The Horn Book Magazine, *Vol. XLIX, No. 1, February, 1973, pp. 47-8.*

This was Jane Gardam's first book for children and one is tempted by hindsight to say that the short stories gathered together in it foreshadowed the success of her witty satirical novels for teenagers, *A Long Way from Verona* and *The Summer after the Funeral.* Beautifully written, with the economy and shrewd observation of character now known to be Gardam hallmarks, the stories about little Lucy and her extraordinary friends and eccentric elderly relations are literature for the 7-year-old—a rarity.

> *Elaine Moss, in a review of "A Few Fair Days," in her* Children's Books of the Year: 1974, *Hamish Hamilton, 1975, p. 118.*

A LONG WAY FROM VERONA (1971)

Precocious Jessica Vye is marked (or, if you will, scarred) for life by a well-known author's verdict that she is "a writer beyond all possible doubt." Jessica's account of school days in war time England reflects a rather solipsistic, though far from negligible, sensibility, and, for a time, all her experiences feed into premature disillusionment—aristocratic Christian (who reminded her of Rupert Brooke) goes to pieces in a moment of danger, a teacher counsels her to be ashamed of her writing, a reading of *Jude the Obscure* imbues her with a pervading pessimism. Still, much of Jessica's truthtelling must be taken on faith; we never read the poem over which she suffers such creative agonies, nor (with the exception of her understanding teacher Miss Philemon) do the other characters have any in-

dependent vitality. Her sharp perceptions are thus somewhat limited by their insulation from experience, but Jessica's introspection will speak to others like her.

> *A review of "A Long Way from Verona," in* Kirkus Reviews, *Vol. XL, No. 5, March 1, 1972, p. 266.*

Jane Gardam's book is a masterpiece beyond all possible doubt. I was reminded of Joyce Cary's *The Horse's Mouth* by the plunging pace, by Jessica's constant collisions with authorities less impassioned and keen-witted than herself, and by the author's joy in describing settings which bound into full color before one's eyes.

Jessica is comic, earnest, mean, splendid, clairvoyant, charming, and a genius. She is a mind thinking; her excessive sensitivity is always alive and quivering.

> *Jane Langton, "Grand Girls All," in* Book World— Chicago Tribune, *May 7, 1972, p. 5.*

One inclines naturally to identify Jessica with Jane Gardam: the book has the nubbiness of memoir and, in the conventional sense, no plot. But no plot does not mean no progression. Equally critical—what sustains *A Long Way From Verona* as the novel it would be—is the fact that Jessica's narrative is less confession than revelation. We don't need steady Florence Bone's "Calm down . . . We like you all right" to know that she is not the outcast she presents us with. ("I am fond of putting prepositions at the ends of sentences, as in fact was Shakespeare.") And long before her father's remark that Cissie Comberbach looks "utterly wretched" catches Jessica up, making her wonder if she really does know what's in people's minds, it is apparent that what she attributes to others, the disgust and dismay, are her own dark thoughts.

That is to say, Jessica's telling, her first-person (help!) narrative, is not a device or a dodge, it is itself the story. Just as the subject isn't for once alienation or angst or antithis-Establishmentarianism, the jacket blurb notwithstanding. The book is Jane Gardam's, and this, her first novel, makes her immediately an author to watch for, but the story is Jessica's in all its glorious passage from self-intoxication to tentative self-searching. Read her.

> *Barbara Bader, "The Nubbiness of Memoir and No Plot," in* The New York Times Book Review, *Part II, May 7, 1972, p. 28.*

Thirteen-year-old Jessica's lively account of her year as a student at the High School in Cleveland Spa, England during World War II is sparked by perceptive comments about people and events and deliciously funny dialogue. Jessica is a believable and endearing combination of maturity and childishness. The other characters—eccentric teachers; a legless slum dweller; a violently revolutionary school boy; her exuberant father; and her flyaway mother—are convincingly portrayed. The English background and vocabulary (how many American teen-agers know what "smalls" are?) will put off some, but mature readers will appreciate the style and wit of Jane Gardam, who proves in her first novel that she also is a "writer beyond all possible doubt."

> *Sister Avila, in a review of "A Long Way from Verona," in* Library Journal, *Vol. 97, No. 12, June 15, 1972, p. 2243.*

In *A Long Way from Verona* Jessica and three friends meet a dotty old lady in a dreadful tea-room:

'I know them all,' said the woman across the room, staring ahead of her through the archway at the quiet, drizzly road. She stubbed out her cigarette in the éclair and pushed her plate away. 'Now I don't suppose you girls even know who Henry James was?'

'The Old Pretender,' I said. It was polite to have a go.

'That's her,' said Florence. Cissie collapsed. So did I as a matter of fact, but Mrs Hopkins didn't appear to notice.

'He was a Man. He was more than a Man, he was a Mind. He was a great and civilized Mind. He loved England. He understood England. He even lived in England.'

'Well we all live in England,' I said.

'Shrup,' said Florence, 'I think he must have been an American.'

'The Old Pretender was a Scotsman.'

'The Old Pretender was *not* the same as Henry James,' said Florence.

'Why wasn't he?' I said, getting angry.

'He was Henry James to all the world,' said Mrs Hopkins. 'But he was Harry to me.'

'Oh, Henry Fifth,' I said. 'God for Harry.' It was something my father was always saying.

'WHAT did you say?' For the first time Mrs Hopkins seemed to see us. 'You, child, what did you say?'

'I said "God for Harry",' I said uncomfortably, and then I added, 'England and St George.' I shouldn't have.

'My dear child!' she cried, 'my dear child! That's what I thought you said. My *dear* child!' and she came tweedle-deeing over the room and kissed me! There was a terrible old smell about her like chests of drawers, and I shuddered and pressed back and nearly sent the busylizzie going for the second time. 'Well, would you believe it!' she said.

'"God for Harry, England and St George". My dear children, might I just shake you by the hand? I'm going to write this down. Every word. I'm going to send it to the papers. I'm going to send it to Winston. Now would you mind if I were just to ask you your ages?'

'Around twelve,' said Florence, watchfully.

'And thirteen,' said Helen.

'My dears! Oh, my dears, how lovely. On the threshold. Four little Juliets. Younger than she are married mothers made! My dears, I want to repay you. Repay you just for being what you are. Little English Juliets. Lovers of dear old England. Now, I'm going to tell Winston about all this.' She spotted Helen's roll of music under the table. 'And what's this, you play music, too—what's this? Chopin? No! This has been a wonderful afternoon. Oh I do wish I could thank you *dear* children for it in some way.'

She shook hands all round and went off. We heard her saying 'Chopin, Grace,' to the counter lady, 'Chopin! He may have been Chopin to all the world but he was . . .'

'Quick,' said Florence, 'get her tea.'

We divided sandwiches, éclair, bread, butter, jam, sugar lumps. In less than two minutes there were none of them to be seen. . . .

There is great love and a strong smell of death in the book. This passage is entirely typical of what Jane Gardam can do. She can recreate the rambling, directionless lines of such conversation with the fidelity of Harold Pinter and the much more satisfactory humour of Alan Galton, and at the same time give the scene its historical location, in a beleaguered, incoherently patriotic England in which healthy schoolgirls living out of ration-books are inevitably hungry. Since Jessica is a striking and exceptional girl, though believable and natural for all that, we are not trapped but freed by living in her consciousness. She is spontaneously funny—'a terrible old smell about her like chests of drawers'—and the novelist creates brief spaces in the narrative for her own contribution to a novel with a strong sense of the interdependence of comedy and tragedy, and a style capable of insisting that both may include laughter. Jessica's adenoidal brother; her only just overdrawn clergyman-father, exuberant, generous, huge, funny; the crushingly upper-class trio Claire, Sophie, and Magdalene whom naturally Jessica loathes on the spot: all sort perfectly in their admirably comic way with the scene in which a random bomb blows up the street in downtown Middlesbrough, and almost kills the heroine and her newfound social-conscience-stricken Romeo:

When I opened my eyes I was right down the street by myself lying on the pavement and looking at a broken china alsatian. There was glass everywhere. I felt about and found I was near the doorstep of one of the houses. The door had blown inwards and there was someone lying still in the passage just inside. 'Where's Christian?' I thought—I think I said it. 'Oh goodness! Where's Christian?' The dark bundle in the passage got up and began crawling towards me. It wasn't Christian but the man who had been coughing. We looked at each other on our hands and knees about a foot from the ground for what seemed a very long time. Then the man turned his head away and began to cough again, very horribly, until he was tired of it. He sat back on his haunches and leaned back against the wall just inside the door. 'Aye-oop!' he said.

I blinked. 'Aye-oop now. We'd best go inside and see what's tooken moother.'

'What?'

'Aye-oop now. That's a daisy. 'Ere we are. Now then.' He was heaving me up and pushing me along the passage as he spoke and into a front room where a man was cowering in a corner with his back to the room like a shell and the most enormous woman I had ever seen was bulging back in a battered arm-chair. She had no legs and she was roaring with laughter.

I began to shake. For the first time since I had opened my eyes after the bomb—it must have been a bomb. That terrible avalanche, that dreadful wind—for the first time I began to be afraid. 'She has no legs. She has no legs,' I heard myself saying. I saw the little old man shaking his head back across the room, and back on to his chair. 'No legs. No legs.'

They must have been blown off. I found myself looking round the room for the legs.

'Eh, Ernie lad, bring 'er. Bring 'er 'ere,' said the woman. 'Now then! Now then! Thast all right. Hush then. Hush lass, thast all right.'

(No legs. No legs.)

'I cannot come to thee,' said the great woman. 'I cannot come. I's no legs. Never for years. Not sin a bairn. There lass, there. Git kettle on now, Ern lad. Hush lass, hush. She's afeared . . .'.

The terrific life of people, of *the* people, goes on, but there is a death, as Jessica's father shrewdly and sympathetically sees. Jessica sees its shadow in some inconsequential and unstated way, when her stunning new Rupert Brookeish boyfriend goes vaguely home to mother after the air-raid and abandons her, and she emerges from colossal concussion and its aftermath of despair into an unforeseen and surging renewal of her love for life. The book returns great moral force to that grand cliché. Its wartime setting is without nostalgia, but provides a way of speaking of love and death which subordinates both to the necessity of life. (pp. 288-91)

> Fred Inglis, "Love and Death in Children's Novels," in his The Promise of Happiness: Value and Meaning in Children's Fiction, *Cambridge University Press, 1981, pp. 271-91. [The excerpts of Jane Gardam's work used here were originally published in her* A Long Way to Verona, The Macmillan Company, 1971].

[Mature] British writers seem to have found from their own childhoods a voice and source for stories that ring with conviction. The same conviction does not follow from the realistic novels with contemporary setting which so dominate the American publishing scene.

Perhaps a close look at some examples will demonstrate ways in which this is true. Take, for instance, three widely circulated stories of girls just entering their teens, the American novels *Are You There, God? It's Me, Margaret* by Judy Blume and *Nobody Has to Be a Kid Forever* by Hila Coleman and the British *A Long Way from Verona* by Jane Gardam. All of these are written in the first person in the ostensible voice of the twelve-or-thirteen-year-old protagonist. . . . Although the American books have "now" concerns—Margaret is preoccupied with menstruation, and Sarah's mother, in *Nobody,* leaves home to find a more fulfilling life in Greenwich Village—none of the three has a particularly sensational central problem. All three are mainly about the conflicts and problems with self and family faced by a girl at this end of childhood. But Jessica's problems in *A Long Way from Verona* keep me continually interested while Margaret's and Sarah's do not.

One reason is that the characters in *Verona* are alive and vividly drawn people out of real life, remembered or imagined from a wide acquaintance with individuals, not invented from preconceived ideas for the occasion. The characters of the mothers in both *Margaret* and *Nobody* are mainly flat and undeveloped. Although we are told that Margaret's mother is from a Protestant background and that she paints still lifes, she is never really described and is chiefly characterized by her daughter's observations of her everyday habits, intended to be amusing but not very individual:

> I found my mother with her rear end sticking out of a bottom kitchen cabinet. She was arranging her pots and pans.
>
> (pp. 73-4)

This could be any woman, observed when she thinks no one is watching her, not an individual mother we come to know in the story. Sarah's mother is more unusual but less believable, the stereotype liberated-woman-as-hippy:

> I didn't even recognize her walking down the street—she looked like one of those crazy ladies you see on the street, not like anyone's mother. She was wearing jeans, a crazy, raggedy coat with fringes, a floppy hat, and high-heeled boots. She didn't have on any makeup, and she looked a hundred years old. I thought, oh, God, if this is her *real* self, she's flipped. I think she thought she looked young and with it.

Jessica's mother is far more complicated, struggling with her changed status from being wife of a schoolmaster, with a servant and leisure, to harried wife of a poor vicar:

> My mother's very new to the job too and finds it much harder than father. She was marvelous at being a schoolmaster's wife, going to Founder's Day in a hat and helping with the Old Boys' dinner and drinking coffee with the other wives in nice, plain, good-taste sitting-rooms and giving little supper parties. . . . She had a lot of free time, and had her hair done. She wasn't bad looking then.
>
> She's got a bit red in the face now and rather wild, slamming and crashing about and her clothes are vile. It does no good telling her and to tell the truth I try not to think about what she looks like with her hair all frizzed all over her head and her red hands. When she gets angry she seems to grow knobs all over her face.

Margaret's mother is purely functional; she drives her husband to the hospital when he cuts his hand in the mower, understandingly shops for a bra with her embarrassed daughter, and cooks a fancy meal when her estranged parents come to visit. Sarah's mother, after her break from the family, is seen mostly as homesick and hoping to rejoin her husband without giving up all her new-found independence. But Jessica's mother is a more developed character, torn between exasperation and love for her daughter, between admiration, even envy, for the boarding-school status of the Fanshaw-Smyths and contempt for their pretentions.

Or, consider the teachers, minor characters of some importance in all three books. Sarah, starting a new school, has just acquired a boy friend named Roger and a new teacher, Mr. Travers:

> Mr. T. is kind of old, he's got a white mustache and a brownish small beard, but he says funny things and sometimes very nice ones. Roger told me to keep the copy of Keat's poems, and he wrote in it "To Sarah, who might have inspired 'La Belle Dame Sans Merci'." . . . Mr. T. picked up my book and saw the inscription. He didn't laugh, he only said, "I would have let it go with 'La Belle Dame'." And now he sometimes says, "And how is La Belle Dame today?" No one's ever called me a beautiful lady before.

Margaret also has a new teacher, a young man in his first teaching position:

> When he turned away from the blackboard he cleared his throat. "That's me," he said, pointing to the name on the board. Then he cleared his throat two more times. "I'm your new teacher." . . . He put his hands behind his back and kind of rocked back and forth on his feet. He cleared his throat so I knew he was going to say something.

The teachers in *Verona* show much more individuality, from the "papery-pale" headmistress, Miss LeBouche, and the art mistress, Miss Crake, who is "a huge-boned, bleak sort of woman," to Miss Dobbs:

> She is a fine looking woman, Miss Dobbs, with a noble sort of figure and a great deal of golden hair. Some of it is on her chin. On the hockey field she cries "Up the FIIIIIIELD, Forward," and she looks just like a Viking.

and brilliant, eccentric Miss Philemon, who is introduced first by the sound of her elderly footsteps:

> Then I heard . . . the feet return, flip-flap, flip-flap, flip-flap, flip. I looked out of the folds of the shoe-bags and saw a grey-haired, very small woman with her petticoat coming down. Her face had a very wide smile on it and her head swung up and down. She was wearing a navy blue felt hat with a curiously uneven brim and carrying a huge, battered suitcase which, as she stood there, burst open and spilled exercise books all over the floor.

Although one might argue that examples from other American books would compare more favorably, there seems to be a fundamental difference in a large proportion of the current realistic fiction from the two countries, exhibited strongly in these three books, a difference in tone. How is the reader supposed to feel about the characters and the action? In Margaret, the pre-teen audience, I am sure, is supposed to identify with the main character and her problems, relieved by an occasional chuckle, for instance when the boys overhear the girls at their exercises: "I must, I must, I must increase my bust." Adults, however, who read the book (and the author herself, apparently) can only laugh *at* Margaret, not with her. The same is true for Sarah of *Nobody*. There are few if any laughs for the child reader, and the adult who is not too bored to finish can only smile wearily at the main character's intense conniving to straighten out her parents' problems and her worrying over

whether she should let Roger kiss her. These are youngsters observed by adults, then put into books as adults assume they must be feeling, faced with today's situations. Jessica Vye, however, is a girl living a generation ago. As such, she is not only ourselves at twelve, but ourselves now since our twelve-year-old selves are still a part of each of us in our more mature years. We can at the same time identify with her and laugh both with and at her as we can both at and with our younger selves.

The resolutions to the three books reflect most clearly the difference in the authors' attitudes toward their protagonists. Margaret's original confusion about whether she should be Protestant or Jewish and her subsequent rejection of God is resolved, strangely enough, by the onset of her monthly periods. Either of her problems—religious ambiguity or fear that she will not develop normally—could be major concerns for a girl of her age, but their connection for the sake of humor is condescending and trivializes both of them. Sarah's problem of her parents' separation is resolved in a less realistic way when they reunite, largely as a result of Sarah's manipulating, and the family moves to Cape Cod, where her father will paint and her mother has a job. The ease with which they solve their problems makes the situations seem inconsequential, and, again, the tone is condescending.

In *Verona* the resolution is more complex, working on several levels at once. Jessica's dissatisfaction with herself and her life has settled into a deep depression brought on, she tells us, by the reading of *Jude the Obscure*. This most pessimistic of Hardy's novels is enough to create a black mood, certainly, but we discover, from what Jessica does *not* tell us, that her depression is caused by a series of genuinely disturbing incidents: her encounter with an Italian prisoner in the sea-wood, the bombing in Dunedin Street, and, most importantly, the death of Miss Philemon when the school is bombed. It is significant that she never says directly that she worries about the prisoner or about the two children killed in Dunedin Street, though we know this because she determinedly *keeps* herself from thinking about these incidents. She never even says directly that Miss Philemon has been killed; in fact, it is possible to read the book the first time without realizing that this has happened. On the surface, her depression seems to be lifted when her poem wins the prize and is printed in the *Times*. On a deeper level, however, her problems are resolved only when she finally faces the three incidents directly. She writes out her concern about the prisoner in the poem she titles "The Maniac." In the final chapter she uses her prize money to buy an enormous painting and wrestles it on and off the train repeatedly in a futile effort to take it to the people who befriended her in Dunedin Street only to learn—and finally face the fact—that the street is destroyed and the remaining houses evacuated. In the same hilarious odyssey with the unwieldy picture—an artwork she has purchased in imitation of Miss Philemon (though she doesn't tell us this, either)—she lugs it to the site of Miss Philemon's house and, at last, forces herself to look at the house and admit it is a ruin.

The very complexity of the resolution in this book shows a respect for the depth of Jessica's feelings that only a mature writer can produce and a mature reader fully grasp. This does not presuppose an older reader; I believe a sensitive twelve-year-old will appreciate the difference in tone between these novels. (pp. 74-7)

> *Agnes Perkins, "Romantic, Fantastic and Realistic Stories for Children: What Books Should Be Sent to*

Coventry?'' in Children and Their Literature: A Readings Book, *edited by Jill P. May, ChLA Publications, 1983, pp. 71-8.*

THE SUMMER AFTER THE FUNERAL (1973)

The latest of Jane Gardam's English heroines are two sisters, twelve and sixteen respectively, left to fend for themselves after the death of their elderly clergyman father and their mother's distracted departure in search of a new home and livelihood. Nearsighted, homely Beams endures her summer stay as the guest of a boisterous, sports-fixated family with a sense of humor, and her report on her childhood failures with school and reading suggests that she has already begun to suspect what brother Seb later confirms—that dear Father's devotion to his daughters' spiritual development may have left them a bit freakish. But while we'd like to spend more of the summer with Beams, her older sister Athene's hyperemotionality and tendency towards hysterical gestures wears on our nerves. Athene flees from a cold welcome at her aunt's summer cottage, flees again from the cabin of a shabby gentleman who takes her in (believing that she may have been raped in her sleep) and runs away a third time from a crush on a distracted, sweetly drab teacher who happens to be acting as holiday caretaker of her brother's deserted school while her aunt, the matron, has gone on vacation. Athene's physical and emotional dislocation is treated elliptically and empathically, with a sure blend of charged sensitivity and comforting middle class English certainties that allows Gardam to build a whole personality around Athene's identification with Emily Bronte. But the conclusion, which brings the scattered family together just at the moment of Athene's greatest crisis, is overly fussy, and scarcely less annoying is the suggestion that Athene's problems can be dismissed as one would overlook the actions of a high-spirited animal, as ultimately a sign of class—''Breakdown my eye, . . . She'll be grand. She'll be grand directly'' opines one of the inexplicably present bystanders. And that is apparently that. Athene does show promise of turning into something grand, and though the signs may be a little too obscure for some adolescent readers to divine, Gardam's high spirited epiphanies will reward the more adventurous.

> *A review of ''The Summer after the Funeral,'' in* Kirkus Reviews, *Vol. XLI, No. 21, November 1, 1973, p. 1211.*

Jane Gardam's second novel, set ''some years back when middle-class English females were called artless, breezy names that went well with tennis'', is riotously funny, alive with visual imagery (''her stockings lay in two sad pinkish heaps at her feet, like dead roses'') and shot through with social comment of devastating accuracy. Its pattern, like that of an Iris Murdoch satire, is as intricate and delicate as that of a mazurka. . . .

Nothing in Jane Gardam's brilliantly compact, mocking and witty novel is unplanned. The characters, young and old, are observed with unwavering directness, their emotional hang-ups and outlets quietly understated so that the adolescent reader can take or leave the undertones. The lightness of touch, the resistance to overplaying the comedy in the farcical set-pieces, is truly admirable: to enjoy the full impact of this marvelously entertaining book one cannot afford to skip a single word.

> *''Who Is Athene?'' in* The Times Literary Supplement, *No. 3742, November 23, 1973, p. 1429.*

With this book, Jane Gardam confirms her reputation as a talented and original author. Here she handles a potentially difficult and disturbing theme with sureness and wit, yet without belittling her subject. The book is profound and humorous, distressing at times and ultimately delightful. . . .

The gallery of characters includes some splendid eccentrics, as well as an obese aunt who lives in flabby, stifling luxury and a pallid hypochondriac victimised by her lesbian friend. There are additionally some truthful vignettes of many aspects of human nature. The incidents are sharply recorded with an eye for their humour, or poignancy, or bizarre quality.

This is a brilliant and moving book which deserves to be read and reread.

> *Judith Aldridge, in a review of ''The Summer after the Funeral,'' in* Children's Book Review, *Vol. III, No. 6, December, 1973, p. 178.*

Reminiscent of Jane Austen's superb evocation of English manners, the story is witty, brilliant, and sophisticated. It will appeal to a more mature audience than did *A Long Way From Verona,* partly because of the subtlety of characterization but principally because of its structure, which blends letters and journals entries into a basically third-person narrative. For the right reader, it is a rare literary experience. (p. 56)

> *Mary M. Burns, in a review of ''The Summer after the Funeral,'' in* The Horn Book Magazine, *Vol. L, No. 1, February, 1974, pp. 55-6.*

Jane Gardam arrived on the literary scene recently with two books published almost simultaneously: *A Few Fair Days,* for slightly younger children, and *A Long Way From Verona,* set during World War II. Both were eminently readable, witty, perceptive, vivid and consequently highly praised—justifiably I think.

Well, Mrs. Gardam marches on. Her new book, if more polished, lacks *Verona*'s fierceness and rather interesting edginess. But it is beguilingly well-written and quite as funny. . . .

Mrs. Gardam once again is very good on young grief, desperation, elation, first love—American teen-agers should identify also; very good on settings (for instance the hotel where the window blinds are ''half drawn down, the acorn string just not touching the big polished plant below it in its spinach-green pot''), very good on subsidiary characters, mostly English spinsters, auntlike if not actually aunts. There are some darker Freudian undertones such as Athene and her brother's disquiet at being fathered by so old a man—hints, too, at adult wretchedness. But generally the tone is discreet, contained.

It seems to me that both books, but this one especially, move towards a very particular genre of English adult fiction in which female writers describe the vicissitudes of strong-charactered, sensitive, middle-class heroines amid a gallery of middle-class eccentricity; a genre ranging from writers as distinguished as Elizabeth Taylor at one end to light-weight novels like *I Capture the Castle* at the other. Jane Gardam can write as well as the best of them, but generally I'd put her at the lighter end. A definite if muted element of wish-fulfillment is one reason her books are so readable. This is not to belittle them; nor to accuse her of sentimentality. Jessica Vye in *A Long Way From Verona* convinces us she would win the poetry competition (someone has to, after all). Athene meets her Heathcliff but only briefly, and though she will again we are left to guess the details.

But turning the convention upside down, superlatively well, and being exact and strong and truthful within it, makes it no less a convention and so, ultimately, safe. The families in her books may be poor, may live in or visit houses which smell of cabbage or even poverty with unspeakable mould growing in their larders, but fundamentally they are safe too—the bell may toll very close, but we know it will never, actually, toll for them.

Penelope Farmer, "Hard-Working Moggy and Beautiful Alice: 'The Summer after the Funeral'," in The New York Times Book Review, February 17, 1974, p. 8.

The Summer after the funeral explores a theme through some of the most electrifyingly real individuals we are likely to meet in fiction. . . . Jane Gardam draws Athene and the rest of the characters stroke by exquisite stroke, using talk and gesture, letters and soliloquy, action and stillness, to reveal them to us. There is Aunt Posie, rich, fat, regarding her difficult guest with "a watery, distant look"; it is natural to her to seek to console Athene with creature comforts—"Have another scone. Let's ask for more jam . . . Shall we have two dishes more do you think?" Here is the self-contained schoolmaster who for a brief space serves as a Mr. Rochester for the disorganised girl, commenting on the people boarding the "usual Brontë bus" to go to Haworth—"They come from London, Americans, and back for supper. From Rome, Tibet, Afghanistan. Hurrah for the three weird sisters". In small, comic, sharp touches like this, Jane Gardam gives us clues—never conclusions—about the people she has observed with such a piercing eye. (pp. 2333-34)

Margery Fisher, in a review of "The Summer after the Funeral," in Growing Point, Vol. 12, No. 8, March, 1974, pp. 2333-34.

BILGEWATER (1976)

Individual [is] the voice in ***Bilgewater,*** the voice of orange-haired, self-aware Marigold Green who, in spite of an unusual upbringing with an elderly, reclusive father in a boys' boarding-school, finds herself just like any other girl when it comes to small-eyed but handsome Jack Rose:

> Christianity is supposed to be all about love but it's utterly useless when you're in love. There's not a blind thing you can do about being in love it seems to me except sit it out. Jesus said love one another. He said the only commandments that matter are to love God and each other. He didn't say that loving, especially each other, tears you to pieces. Might have been better if he had said *Don't* love one another. Just try and get along with each other and if you feel love coming on go for a long brisk walk. . . .

A long stumbling walk on a dark wet night is only one of several awkward situations through which Marigold (called with the dotty logic of nicknames Bilgewater) talks herself during the years in which she learns to do without the protection of her father and the dramatically sensible Paula and to do without the illusion that the object of love is necessarily worth loving. As a first-person book ***Bilgewater*** has less of the author's voice in it than the others reviewed here [Paul Zindel's *Pardon me you're stepping on my eyeball,*! Antonio Forest's

The Attic Term, Benjamin Lee's *It can't be helped,* and Christine Nöstlinger's *Girl missing*] or, rather, she has identified herself completely with Bilgie, who is in any case looking back at her young self from a mature standpoint and so can supply her own ironic comments on the past. Jane Gardam writes with a strong, sharp immediacy. She is unrivalled in the way she can establish a state of being. The day of happiness is Durham, the disastrous weekend at No. 16 Ironstoneside West, are experiences we cannot help sharing with the heroine, so emphatic are the contours and colours of the places concerned, so exact the movements and gesture of the characters, so droll and sad the wit and humour, so spontaneous and inevitable the heroine's reactions. This is tragi-comedy of a very high order.

The social aberrations which Jane Gardam introduced into her story (like the unpleasant elopement of the Headmaster's middle-aged wife with Jack Rose and the lubricious snooping of porcine Mrs. Deering) seem almost like fantastic embroidery beside the tough reality of Bilgie's perplexities. (pp. 3043-44)

Margery Fisher, in a review of "Bilgewater," in Growing Point, Vol. 15, No. 7, January, 1977, pp. 3043-44.

The elements which compose the narrative imagination of Jane Gardam's novels cannot be plucked out of the compound texture of her writing to be discussed in the mode of reviewing which tells either 'what happens next' or, in any simple way, 'how the author does it'. One must report in a form of multi-consciousness how the story of the later schooldays of Marigold ('Bilgewater') Green progresses (like chess) towards the certainty of maths examinations, while her adolescent anguish about herself and speculations about the way of the world weave in and out of a series of comic surprises about people she thought she knew well. The strange harlequinade of living in a boys' school turns into the menace of growing up.

The author's obvious pleasure in the powers of the growing minds of her characters, the heroic-comic scenes nailed to the bedrock of a northeastern coast town with a pier, and the brilliant narration that carries other narratives, combine to make this a remarkable literary experience.

Margaret Meek, in a review of "Bilgewater," in The School Librarian, Vol. 25, No. 1, March, 1977, p. 60.

Here is a major novel of our times (even if much of the action is in the past), a beautiful study of a girl growing up, an examination of adolescent psychology and adolescent mores, above all a finely controlled story growing out of the clash of characters and the influence of environment. . . .

A clever and unobstrusive device keeps this story of far-off youthful days in a contemporary frame. The story has its richly funny moments, moments too of pathos and pain. The author probes delicately the most sensitive nerves of her characters, finding weakness at the heart of strength, and resilience where a less sensitive writer might suspect only flabbiness. The writing is exquisite, full of sharp and relevant phrases. Mrs. Gathering, the terrible wife of the headmaster, whose ultimate fate is one of the many surprises in the story, is, in Bilge's eyes: "like someone you've vaguely heard about in a rather bad book." Then there is the visit to Durham, near the end of the story, when they do very ordinary things which are "important and beautiful and namelessly good"—an experience "one is the better for having had even when the brain grows soft and slow and can't remember whether it has just locked the door or was just about to do so.''

One could go on indefinitely, recollecting the delights of this wise, moving and altogether delightful book. Enough now to commend it to sensitive girls growing up in a bewildering world, and to their parents, and to anyone who wants a novel to be creative, amusing, and a guide to experience.

> *M. Crouch, in a review of "Bilgewater," in* The Junior Bookshelf, *Vol. 41, No. 2, April, 1977, p. 110.*

The reminiscence starts off as slow and uneventful as [Bilgewater's] life at the school. . . . But it builds into an almost surrealistic confluence of encounters, involving the same boys, with Bilge at seventeen climbing in and out of windows, buses, and beds in a panicky but ambivalent attempt to escape uncomfortable contacts. The same sort of distraction, dislocation, and impetuous flight marked *The Summer After the Funeral* . . . , but compared to *Summer* . . .'s Athene, rueful, ironic Bilge takes herself—well, not less seriously perhaps but with something of an outsider's perspective. ("Beware of self-pity," the housekeeper's motto, could be hers as well.) At once detached and painfully self-preoccupied, Bilgewater has a sharp inner eye that is equally cool and observant whether it is turned inward or out onto the variously flawed and dotty Britishers of her constricted world.

> *A review of "Bilgewater," in* Kirkus Reviews, *Vol. XLV, No. 15, August 1, 1977, p. 789.*

In the prologue to this extraordinary novel, a candidate for Cambridge silently cries to the adult interviewers: "Have you ever run mad for love? Considered suicide? Cried in the cinema? Clung to somebody in a bed?" It is this suppressed intensity that has characterized all of Gardam's novels about adolescence—an intensity embodied this time in "orange-haired, short-sighted . . . thick-set, hopeless" Bilgewater. . . . Like Jessica in *A Long Way from Verona* . . . and Athene in *The Summer After the Funeral* . . . , Bilgewater is a young woman of character, sensitivity, and individuality. Even the novel's minor characters are finely drawn and memorable; the style combines humor with compassion, romanticism with honesty.

> *Linda Silver, in a review of "Bilgewater," in* School Library Journal, *Vol. 24, No. 3, November, 1977, p. 70.*

Is this a children's book, a teenage novel? Not, one would have thought, unless *Romeo and Juliet* is a teenage play. True, it is about adolescence—like *Catcher in the Rye* with comedy the dominant tone instead of angst. *Catcher in the Rye* was published on the adult list, but then that's some time ago. The way the world is going, adults stand to lose a lot of fun, for they would surely appreciate Jane Gardam's special quality as readily and thoroughly as young readers. . . .

Jane Gardam is a humorist, and a stylist. The language—dry, clear and sparkling—would belie the first-person voice of the callow heroine, were it not that though naive, she is brilliant, the sort of person who really might, in later life become . . . but one must not give the plot away. A part of the humor lies in choosing very eccentric and extraordinary people to write about. Really there can be few girls so odd, and oddly circumstanced, as Bilgewater; but a transformation is worked on all this oddity by Jane Gardam's clear daylight vision. Bilgewater does not *seem* old, but totally understandable and lovable;

instead we perceive that *anybody's* life is strange and extraordinary, that life itself is crazily particular, arbitrary, full of comic accident and peculiarity.

Will this kind of social comedy survive an Atlantic crossing? That's hard for a British reviewer to judge. The United States, as far as I have heard, has no schools like St. Wilfred's. So here's a test: Bilgewater goes to stay with the parents of the glamourous Jack Rose believing them to be doctors, but when she gets there she finds they are dentists; her disillusionment has begun! British snobberies can be very delicate and perplexing; much of Jane Gardam's sharp bright comedy depends on distinctions as fine as this.

Delightful as it is, this book is not faultless. The plot does run rather wild in places, and though many a girl has like Bilgewater gone off with neither of the two she was involved with, but with a hitherto unregarded third party, the reader might have liked to know more about him earlier, might like to know what he looked like. It's disconcerting when a well-loved heroine departs with a shadowy figure, leaving two brilliantly envisaged characters behind her.

> *Jill Paton Walsh, "The Belles of St. Wilfred's," in* Book World—The Washington Post, *January 8, 1978, p. E6.*

BRIDGET AND WILLIAM (1981)

Jane Gardam's normally effusive style is sharply restrained in *Bridget and William*. Limitations of space require strict discipline and words are pared down into hard smooth images. This is a variation of *I wanted a pony* set on the Yorkshire Moors; a quiet blend of empathy and no-nonsense humour lifts the tale above the more standard fare for all its standard storyline.

> *Peter Fanning, "Tin Can Treasure," in* The Times Educational Supplement, *No. 3376, March 6, 1981, p. 29.*

Jane Gardam has a more complex theme and a longer story [than Bernard Ashley's *Dinner Ladies Don't Count*] making more demands on the reader and offering more by way of reward. Bridget gets a fat pony, rather against father's wishes, and in a spell of bad weather proves that there is much to be said for tough hill-bred ponies. There is matter here for a full-length novel, but Miss Gardam tailors it beautifully to its mini-role: beautiful writing, not too easy, and an authentic picture of home and country.

> *M. Crouch, in a review of "Bridget and William," in* The Junior Bookshelf, *Vol. 45, No. 3, June, 1981, p. 111.*

I was delighted when this book by one of my favourite authors arrived; then sorry to see that it was for a younger age group than her other books. I read it at once, giggled happily through much of it, and nearly cried at the end, which came too fast for me. The length is reasonable for young readers though, and I think they will appreciate the down-to-earth style: "'Hey, give over,' said Bridget and the pony gave over. Right from the beginning it did most things Bridget said. It didn't do everything Todd said though, or anything Bridget's father said.''' . . . Well worth having in any school library and one I shall keep for myself. (pp. 132-33)

> *Rodie Sudbery, in a review of "Bridget and William," in* The School Librarian, *Vol. 29, No. 2, June, 1981, pp. 132-33.*

There may seem little hope of finding any new way with the ubiquitous pony-story, but Jane Gardam has found her way, in *Bridget and William,* in the fine economy and selectiveness of her prose and the individuality of her characters. . . . A plot used scores, perhaps hundreds of times, but given sparkling new life here just by words that provoke and startle and inform. The pony, 'rough as heather, black as a tarn and round as a partridge', establishes himself as a personality as he battles with the snow. 'After the first gate he gave his tail a wave and went merrily on' but after the fourth gate, facing 'a nice smooth sweep of snow like the slope of a tent-side', he 'shook his head and made the motor-bike noise'. In the same quick, allusive way Jane Gardam sets the family pattern, pointing to Bridget's love and respect for her father, her mother's gaiety complementing his matter-of-fact eye on life. . . . [The] quality of this short book will certainly point [beginner readers] in the direction of simple but real literary pleasure.

> *Margery Fisher, in a review of "Bridget and William," in* Growing Point, *Vol. 20, No. 2, July, 1981, p. 3910.*

[This is] an English story that is not unusual in plot . . . but is delightful because of the deceptive simplicity and the flavor of the style, the vivid evocation of setting, and the satisfying warmth of family relationships. This has little of the humor that has distinguished Gardam's books for older readers, but it is written in a style far more appropriate for the primary grades audience for which animal stories and those about achievement . . . appeal. For American readers some terms may be puzzling, but in most cases the context makes words clear enough.

> *Zena Sutherland, in a review of "Bridget and William," in* Bulletin of the Center for Children's Books, *Vol. 35, No. 2, October, 1981, p. 29.*

[In the world of children's books] 1981 wasn't all depression. . . . [Near] the beginning of the year [there was] the small perfection of Jane Gardam's *Bridget and William,* which I would have given the Whitbread to, even over her *Hollow Land.* It takes more than just talent to write specifically for 7-8 year olds and produce, in a few thousand words, a beautifully shaped story that is both literary and entirely accessible to an inexperienced audience. (p. 55)

> *Nancy Chambers in a letter to Lance Salway, in* Signal, *No. 37, January, 1982, pp. 52-5.*

THE HOLLOW LAND (1981)

[Jane Gardam's] setting is the Cumbrian fells: "hollow" not in the sense of being opposed to hilly, as in the Yeats poem, but because of the disused mine workings which lie beneath the ground. It is a place of distinct character, with becks, tarns and quarries at every turn. In the opening episode the narrator (eight-year-old Bell Teesdale) remembers the derelict farmhouses scattered all along the dales—"too old or too far out or that bit too high for farmers now". Abandoned to weather and birds and sheep—until holidaymakers, tired of the Lake District, think of buying or leasing the little stone dwellings.

Light Trees is the farmhouse the Bateman family rents. Batemans and Teesdales nearly fail to get along at first, before Bell and young Harry Bateman take a hand (these two meet and quickly become friends for life). Friction—the result of a misunderstanding—is smoothed over and an alliance established

between the two families. Summer after summer the London Batemans come; and often in the winter as well. The place is rich in anecdotes and alarms; something is always going on, and everything is relished to the utmost. This goes for weather and seasons too. . . . Burning or sodden or snowbound, the countryside is full of enchantments.

A ring of old green turf marks a Celtic settlement; secret water runs inside the hills where gorse and wild thyme grow in profusion. The supernatural is evoked with feeling and also with a spark of humour. "Used to be vampires up yonder", Bell declares; outlandish stories and legends abound in the fruitful uplands. . . . Every action and every custom is charged with significance.

With this book, Jane Gardam has reverted to the "linked stories" framework of her earlier *Black Faces, White Faces* (for adults only). In each episode a satisfactory advance in neighbourliness is achieved or a disaster averted. . . .

The children's story traditionally ends on a bright note, as these stories do; nothing else in Jane Gardam's approach is conventional. She makes the most, as always, of the subtle and the untoward. Her work has always created problems of classification: when she writes about children, it is in a way that does not exclude an adult readership. *The Hollow Land* is typical in this respect: there is not a limited, trite or chatty observation in it. It creates an overwhelming impression of vigour and freshness. The aids to picturesque living it enumerates—the lovely red-and-white patchwork quilts, the old oak settles and grandfather clocks—all contribute to the sense of order and continuity which is part of the countryside's charm. . . .

Jane Gardam's writing is as exact, as condensed and striking as ever. Underlying the engaging plots of these stories—plenty of frolics and fun—is a single theme: attachment to a special locality.

> *Patricia Craig, "A Country of Customs," in* The Times Literary Supplement, *No. 4094, September 18, 1981, p. 1065.*

Jane Gardam's is an OK name in the world of children's fiction. *The Hollow Land* has been acclaimed and has just won a Whitbread award. I feel uncomfortable in offering a dissenting opinion. But it has to be done. If this book were the work of an unknown writer I would think it highly promising, though imperfect. Coming with the credentials it actually has, it's a slight disappointment. . . .

Geographically and emotionally, the book comes close to territory occupied by William Mayne in *A Grass Rope* and, especially, *Ravensgill.* Stylistically, too, there are some resemblances, including touches of Maynelike whimsy. Yet Mrs. Gardam has her individual flavour. She has a pleasantly quirky mind and a fine comic gift. Though there is nothing here that quite matches her gloriously funny set-pieces in *Bilgewater* or *The Summer After the Funeral,* there are some nice chapters: for instance the one about Granny Crack, who has taken to her bed but comes down when there's nobody about.

Two episodes have more dramatic action: the trapping of a couple of boys underground and the appearance of a distant relative from South America claiming the reversion of the farmstead and wanting to pull it down and mine under it. But these are dealt with perfunctorily, almost as if the author were ashamed of introducing such commonplace children's-book ingredients. Like many other books, this one strikes me as being "for" children only in the sense that it doesn't contain anything which is obviously *not* for children.

Disappointment sets in because it is all, I think, rather sketchy and casual. Sometimes a speaking likeness is caught with enviable accuracy, other times it is surprisingly missed. Some characters, notably the farming family, are full of life and vigour; others are uninteresting or, like the "Household Word" (a telly lady) stereotyped. There's some carelessness about ages and relationships and, more important, a failure to shape and sharpen. *The Hollow Land* reads to me like a draft of a potentially excellent book that still needs working on.

> *John Rowe Townsend, "Fell Country," in* The Times Educational Supplement, *No. 3412, November 20, 1981, p. 34.*

I knew that Jane Gardam was one of the brightest hopes among the younger writers, but I never imagined that she had in her such a book as this. In *The Hollow Land* she has uncovered a seam of the purest ore, authentic gold in every syllable.

The book is well named. It is not Bell or Harry or even old Grandad Hewitson who is the hero, but the land itself. . . .

A book for children? Nonsense! This is a book for readers, for people—of whatever age—who enjoy a good tale finely told, who respect integrity and love the land. Without sentimentality, and with almost no words of description, Jane Gardam reveals her deep love of this country and her understanding of the nature of its people. It is a very good, quiet book which yields up its meaning more fully at each re-reading. Like the Hollow Land itself, it has enduring qualities.

> *M. Crouch, in a review of "The Hollow Land," in* The Junior Bookshelf, *Vol. 45, No. 6, December, 1981, p. 249.*

For longer than I care to remember I have been looking for books that make quite clear to children what reading and literature are all about. It has become even more important now to find them for the pre-teens, when stories are still a means of living your life forwards and the slump of adolescent ambiguities hasn't yet taken over. The search yields too few unmistakable paradigms of excellence. Mayne, Garner, Boston, Pearce are safely there; but this book is outstanding, by any standards. All the strengths were clearly visible in Mrs Gardam's earlier novels (especially in *A few fair days*): the humour, dialogue, behind-the-child's-head sighting of adults. But these stories about people who live on the Cumbrian Fells by right of inheritance and those who come for holidays, turn the pastoral tradition of children's literature into something searching. Comic situations, characters of all ages and sensibilities enfold a deep richness of writing that needs examples and many more lines than these to demonstrate the wiry subtlety, the colloquial ease and narrative astuteness of the prose. This is the best book I have read this year, and streets ahead of the author's *The Sidmouth letters,* a collection for adults which I hoped to read with sixth-formers. I'll read these instead. (pp. 343-44)

> *Margaret Meek, in a review of "The Hollow Land," in* The School Librarian, *Vol. 29, No. 4, December, 1981, pp. 343-44.*

This is not at all like Jane Gardam's other books, but it is just as polished and entertaining. The people are warm and real, but it is the sense of the land and the rural community that plays the stronger part. . . . This is a series of stories, but they are so closely linked that there is no sense of separation; the

writing style is smooth and flowing, with a judicious use of local dialect. The characters are strongly developed, and the shifting viewpoint (sometimes first person, sometimes third) gives a good coverage of the several generations who participate in Bell's and Harry's lifelong friendship. Because of the structure, this is an excellent book for reading aloud in installments to a group.

> *Zena Sutherland, in a review of "The Hollow Land," in* Bulletin of the Center for Children's Books, *Vol. 35, No. 9, May, 1982, p. 168.*

The collection of nine narratives attains the scope of a novel, for the pervasive sense of place—specifically Westmoreland—and the strongly individualistic characters are always imminent. . . . The enduring friendship between Bell Teesdale . . . and Harry Bateman . . . rounds out the story, which surprisingly—and daringly for its down-to-earth realism—ends in 1999. Although adults are always present, especially Bell's grandfather, one has a feeling that the book is essentially about the naturalization of Harry Bateman, who quickly and not always with his mother's approval falls into using the local dialect. . . . Aware of the influence of the Celts, the Romans, and the Danes on the land west of Yorkshire, the author is especially sensitive to the topography, the weather, and the other natural phenomena that molded the people of the Cumbrian fells; and in richly textured prose she subtly incorporates glints of humor and understatement—the hallmarks of local life and character. (pp. 297-98)

> *Paul Heins, in a review of "The Hollow Land," in* The Horn Book Magazine, *Vol. LVIII, No. 3, June, 1982, pp. 297-98.*

HORSE (1982)

[This] addition to the Blackbird series will be welcomed by six-year-old readers. The author is well-known for her work for older readers and her skill is no less apparent in *Horse*.

A great white horse cut in the green hillside is threatened and saved from destruction. Susan and the villagers who are involved in the affair are brought to life by vivid writing yet the sentences are all short and the vocabulary simple although the author is quite prepared to use words which are interesting and necessary even if beyond the average six-year-old reader. A delightful story.

> *D. A. Young, in a review of "Horse," in* The Junior Bookshelf, *Vol. 46, No. 3, June, 1982, p. 97.*

Like Mayne's short books (*The Last Bus,* for instance), *Horse* stands out for its impeccable sense of form and for the selection of small, apt details through which people and place take shape in the reader's mind. The refurbishing of the overgrown chalk horse on the hillside, just in time to stop forestry planting, is seen through the eyes of a small girl for whom Horse is such a part of life that she has never noticed its slow deterioration. Through Susan we watch the village, listen to the dry authoritative humour of centenarian Mr. Grandly, admire the decisive actions of his grand-daughter, realise the close-knit community of pub, school and cottages. A gem of its kind.

> *Margery Fisher, in a review of "Horse," in* Growing Point, *Vol. 21, No. 2, July, 1982, p. 3933.*

Jane Gardam's short books are a joy; I get to the end and read them again straight away. The humour and the pathos are both so well handled that in the last chapter, like Susan, I was unsure whether to laugh or cry. Within a very brief compass the important characters are vividly conveyed—Susan and her parents, old Mr Grandly, his son young Mr Grandly (aged 75), and his flyabout granddaughter, and in particular the redoubtable Mrs Pail, who single-handedly runs the village school. Every word is important. . . . I don't want to reveal any of the story in case I spoil for anyone the enchanting experience of reading it.

> *Rodie Sudbery, in a review of "Horse," in* The School Librarian, *Vol. 30, No. 4, December, 1982, p. 334.*

KIT (1983)

Kit is in an altogether different class [than Ruskin Bond's *Tigers Forever*]. Here a novelist of outstanding talent and greater promise cuts her craft down to size with no apparent loss of spontaneity or creativity. The little girl and her farming family and their animals are evoked vividly in just a few phrases, and the story has relevance, suspense and vitality. . . . Aspiring writers might take this little book as their textbook, learning from it not only how to tell a tale briskly and well but how to conjure up a vivid character in half a dozen words of dialogue. Lovely stuff! (pp. 64-5)

> *M. Crouch, in a review of "Kit," in* The Junior Bookshelf, *Vol. 48, No. 2, April, 1984, pp. 64-5.*

The Kit is the crybaby of the family. With an isolated farm to run, her parents haven't got patience with a dislike of black beetles or a fear of rats. It all gets too much for The Kit when her father is laid up with a broken leg, but she wins through in the end. Jane Gardam has really understood the needs of her intended readership, and has combined the freshness and originality of her language with a good plot and vigorous pace to make a satisfying story. The characterization is strong: the roaring father and The Kit's dislike of the mucky side of farming while admiring the grandeur of the bull are memorably described.

> *Mary Steele, "Fiction 6 to 9: 'Kit'," in* The Signal Review of Children's Books 2: A Selective Guide to Picture Books, Fiction, Plays, Poetry, Information Books Published during 1983, *edited by Nancy Chambers, The Thimble Press, 1984, p. 19.*

Ann Jonas

1932-

American author/illustrator of picture books.

Considered an ingenious and skillful creator of picture books, Jonas is recognized for her simple yet sophisticated artistry and understanding of the child's mind. Her books generally explore basic concerns of the preschooler and impart reassuring messages in economical texts. Wife of the award-winning author/illustrator Donald Crews, with whom she worked for many years as a graphic designer, Jonas composes watercolor paintings characterized by clean lines, bright colors, unusual perspective, and a playful use of scale. Her illustrations, which produce the semblance of simplicity, actually incorporate subtle, complex techniques. This is experienced most dramatically in the topsy-turvy *Round Trip*, in which black-and-white silhouettes combined with a brief text invite readers to travel from the country to the city, turn the book upside down, and discover inverse images on the return home. Jonas's best-known work, *Round Trip*, is seen as both a successful experiment in visual perception and a model of graphic design.

Critics praise Jonas for her psychological insight into the needs of young children and her ability to stimulate their imaginations with eye-catching patterns and uncluttered detail. Observers also find her use of contrasting colors and shapes effective and her texts and double-page spreads well harmonized. Regarded as an original and thoughtful artist, Jonas is perceived by most reviewers as an author whose tales of comfort, fancy, and fun hold wide appeal.

Jonas has won several national and regional awards for her works including a *Boston Globe-Horn Book* Honor Book award in 1986 for *The Trek*.

(See also *Something about the Author*, Vol. 42.)

Photograph by Donald Crews

WHEN YOU WERE A BABY (1982)

The first illustration, showing the top of a crib with a baby's feet flying up in the air, reads, "When you were a baby, you couldn't do very much." The first clause of this simple statement is artfully repeated and followed by a list of comfortably familiar toddlers' activities: piling blocks, splashing in puddles, drinking from a glass, making sand castles. "But now you can!" is the soothing message, as uncluttered and clear as the 7 ½" x 8 ¼" double-page spreads. The objects of a small child's world are sometimes painted with the simplicity of Harlow Rockwell's art in *My Nursery School* (Greenwillow, 1976) and sometimes display more complex details, as in pictures of grass, a quilt, or a doll's dress. Jonas' pleasing illustrations, with their generous use of secondary colors and her flair for lively perspective, enhance the text's loving encouragement of a child's capabilities.

Sally Holmes Holtze, in a review of "When You Were a Baby," in School Library Journal, *Vol. 28, No. 5, January, 1982, p. 66.*

With no whole child seen—with only simple forms, flat, mellow colorings, and exceptional use of patterns—there is a con-

stant sense of activity: "you couldn't teach your doll to sit in a chair," almost an anecdote in-a-nutshell, is accompanied by an endearingly floppy rag doll who's never going to really sit up. As a very early book, it reverberates—and so one is hardly too surprised to learn that Ann Jonas is the wife of Donald Crews.

A review of "When You Were a Baby," in Kirkus Reviews, *Vol. L, No. 4, February 15, 1982, p. 201.*

With simple sentences and sturdy, bright pictures, this book reminds preschoolers what it was like when they were "little." Sharply focused objects and subtle blends of muted and vivid colors attract immediate attention. Not only will the clean lines of the large-scale drawings appeal, but also the memory of the things the child couldn't do then (e.g., drink from a glass). The final injunction, "But now you can," offers a solid sense of accomplishment to young listeners.

Ilene Cooper, in a review of "When You Were a Baby," in Booklist, *Vol. 78, No. 13, March 1, 1982, p. 898.*

This deceptively simple book helps to feed the young child's ego. . . . The graphic illustrations perfectly convey the thought patterns in the text and both extend and amplify what is said. Highly recommended. . . .

James A. Norsworthy, Jr., in a review of "When You Were a Baby," in Catholic Library World, Vol. 54, No. 4, November, 1982, p. 181.

Illustrations depict a baby's legs wiggling in a crib, and the same legs at the end wearing shoes with laces. . . . The legs are brown legs, and we see no additional parts of the body. This playful treatment of scale—objects partially visible or moving on and off the page—adds interest to the precise, poster style. The narrative concept calls for a clear, calculated technique, and some warmth is added by means of color and textural differentiation. There is a quiet charm in the illustrations, with one opaque color shape building against another and with an interplay between hard and soft edges on different objects.

Donnarae MacCann and Olga Richard, in a review of "When You Were a Baby," in Wilson Library Bulletin, Vol. 57, No. 4, December, 1982, p. 365.

TWO BEAR CUBS (1982)

An ultra-simple picture book, in flat solid colors, this opens with some pleasantly rounded family groupings: one shows the two cubs play-wrestling, with the mother bear a large protective shape behind them. Then, a lighter color is introduced, a more quickening curve, and a new creature—a strutting, high-tailed skunk. The cubs go off after the skunk; then the skunk turns and chases them. "But where are they? And where is their mother?" They find a honey tree and are chased by angry bees. "Where is their mother?" They try but fail to catch a fish. "Where can their mother be?" Finally, "There she is!" And, as Jonas' audience will have noticed, she's been there all along, watching them from behind a tree or a bush or tall grass. It's an old-fashioned picture-book ploy, not transcended here, but enacted with warmth and assurance.

A review of "Two Bear Cubs," in Kirkus Reviews, Vol. L, No. 12, June 15, 1982, p. 675.

The illustrations done in vibrant colors could alone relate the adventures of two wandering bear cubs; but a minimal text in boldface type tells how the youngsters become separated from their mother. . . . The simplified shapes and flat areas of color in the illustrations create crisp, almost abstract, patterns and enhance the puzzle aspect of the cleanly designed picture book.

Kate M. Flanagan, in a review of "Two Bear Cubs," in The Horn Book Magazine, Vol. LVIII, No. 5, October, 1982, p. 511.

The simple text is nicely matched by the clear blocks of green and brown in the drawings, accented with but not confined by fluid black lines. Text and illustrations form a well-integrated whole for young readers, complicated only by the adult preoccupation with the dilemma of independence vs. protection— the question being whether the average preschooler would interpret Mama bear's reticence as a benignly comforting encouragement to independence or as a mean trick at the expense of the worried youngsters. (pp. 141-42)

Kristi L. Thomas, in a review of "Two Bear Cubs," in School Library Journal, Vol. 29, No. 2, October, 1982, pp. 141-42.

The illustrations in Jonas's story demonstrate her unerring sense of how to use boldly contrasting colors and uncluttered shapes for maximum effect. Tots will love following two baby bears through an exciting time while parents read the simple text,

the few words necessary to explain what the pictures, by themselves, tell. (pp. 59-60)

A review of "Two Bear Cubs," in Publishers Weekly, Vol. 222, No. 22, November 26, 1982, pp. 59-60.

ROUND TRIP (1983)

More than her **When You Were a Baby** and **Two Bear Cubs** . . . , the emphatic black-and-white silhouettes and basic concept of **Round Trip** bear considerable resemblance to the picture books of Jonas' husband Donald Crews—but Jonas, in one of the smartest of the turnabout tricks, stands the visual journey on its head by reversing ground and figure on the return trip. Going through from the beginning, with black trees and houses outlined against the white sky, "We started out as soon as it was light. Our neighborhood was quiet, the houses dark." Continuing through black streets, fields, water (below a bridge), and other scenes, we end up in an urban grid of buildings: "We watched as the sun set. Time to turn around"—whereupon, as we reverse the book for the return, the same scene becomes night: "The sky was dark. Lights came on all over the city." Proceeding back, we look up at a tall building we've just looked down from, dine in a restaurant that we'd visited as a movie theatre, and watch as a subway train becomes a garage, lights in black skyscrapers become stars above white skyscrapers, bridge underpinnings become telephone poles, highways turn into searchlights and winding roads to lightning—until, "Home again," the white road leading up to the house in early morning is now smoke issuing from the chimney at night. Even without trying you may catch some of the reversals in advance, but not enough to spoil the look-again transformation. Show-stopping sleight of pen.

A review of "Round Trip," in Kirkus Reviews, Vol. LI, No. 3, February 1, 1983, p. 118.

[Jonas] tops her previous works with this visual stunner, a trip from the country into the city, then back again. The format is wonderfully inventive . . . with the black-and-white pictures taking on new meanings through Jonas's masterful use of contrast. A farm passed on the way in, with silos and plowed fields, becomes a factory belching stacks of smoke; waves on the ocean are transformed into flocks of birds fluttering above trees. . . . [The] book's graphics are sure to delight and fascinate youngsters of all ages, as well as demonstrate that there can be more than one way of seeing a picture.

A review of "Round Trip," in Publishers Weekly, Vol. 223, No. 10, March 11, 1983, p. 86.

Although one or two pictures too easily suggest their upside-down images and the device is occasionally strained, the author-artist displays a fine sense of graphic design and balance, and pictorial beauty is never sacrificed for mere cleverness.

Ethel R. Twichell, in a review of "Round Trip," in The Horn Book Magazine, Vol. LIX, No. 4, August, 1983, p. 432.

Older readers will remember Oho!, Rex Whistler's brilliant collection of reversible drawings. Ann Jonas is no Whistler, but she is a very clever designer and her book is a tour de force. . . . The drawings are in monochrome with masses of matt black . . . against which the dead white shows to powerful effect. Words are used with the utmost economy so that nothing distracts from these remarkable designs. Young children are

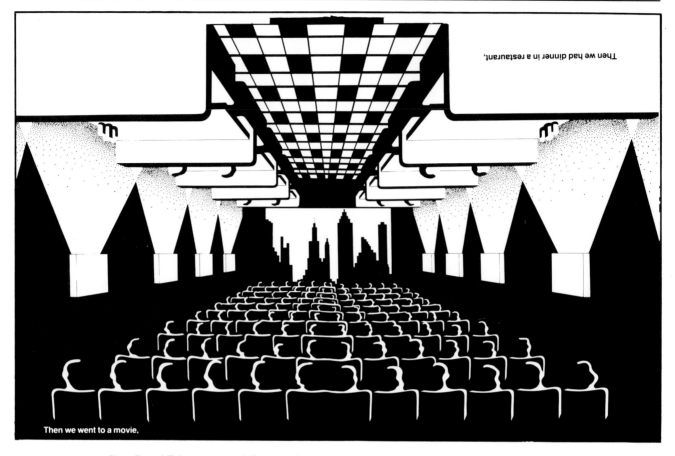

From Round Trip, *written and illustrated by Ann Jonas. Greenwillow Books, 1983. Copyright © 1983 by Ann Jonas. All rights reserved. By permission of Greenwillow Books (A Division of William Morrow & Company, Inc.).*

likely to be fascinated by the book, but its true public, I believe, will lie in the art colleges where its lessons of simplicity and economy will not be lost.

> *M. Crouch, in a review of "Round Trip," in* The Junior Bookshelf, *Vol. 47, No. 4, August, 1983, p. 154.*

The illustrations, done in black and white, make fascinating use of positive and negative space. . . . Though the story line is thin and rambling, it is the visual experience that counts, and for the most part, it works beautifully. However, some visual effects are not as successful as others—particularly the one of a subway right side up that becomes a parking structure upside down. Regional motifs such as the expressway, a tunnel under the river and a subway may not be readily identifiable by all readers. Among the most creative and visually pleasing is the picture of a bridge tnat becomes a line of telephone poles along a country road and one that shows the city skyline with windows lit in the skyscrapers. Turning the book upside down changes the windows to a starlit sky.

> *Reva S. Kern, in a review of "Round Trip," in* School Library Journal, *Vol. 29, No. 10, August, 1983, p. 52.*

Well chosen words provide a brief narrative that begins, "We started out as soon as it was light," and finishes in the dark, "Home again." The pictures are stark and dramatic. This is

most effective when a tall building seen from above reverses handsomely to become a tall building seen from below. If, however, blacks and whites are not perfectly balanced (black buildings silhouetted against a white sky, for instance), the transformation from positive to negative is unconvincing. And on some pages details refuse to alter when the page is reversed. A train heading across a grain-field still reads as a train when the field converts into a rainy sky.

Miss Jonas has set herself a series of challenging graphic problems that may confuse the very young. Those older children who are not put off by the simplicity of the text should have the patience needed to tackle the games these pictures play.

> *Karla Kuskin, in a review of "Round Trip," in* The New York Times Book Review, *August 21, 1983, p. 26.*

HOLES AND PEEKS (1984)

A young child of unspecified gender asserts that she or he doesn't like holes, as the pages show holes in pajamas, a stuffed toy, an empty tub and a toilet. ("They scare me.") The child does like to make places to peek through with a towel or rolled paper, though. Then the child observes that cloth can be patched, the tub plugged and the toilet made welcoming with a child's seat and a little stool. It's all absolutely matter-of-fact in its presentation, and indirect in its message. Both text and illustrations are from the small child's perspective, yet rendered with a sophistication that is impressive. The whole book takes place in a white-tiled bathroom, and the high-tech quality of all those rectangles makes a crisp contrast to the warm colors of fabrics and brown skin. Each of the illustrations fill the double page from edge to edge. The child, and the parents who are shown only from the waist down, are outlined with a fine black line, but many other objects are not—a focusing device that is softening, subtle and effective. This is a charming, reassuring book. (pp. 145-46)

> *Mary B. Nickerson, in a review of "Holes and Peeks,"*
> *in* School Library Journal, *Vol. 30, No. 7, March,*
> *1984, pp. 145-46.*

Jonas, whose last book **Round Trip** . . . was a masterpiece in black and white, returns here to her more familiar color work. The solid pictures with their full-bodied colors and interesting perspectives will suit preschoolers, and the issues raised will both comfort and intrigue.

> *Ilene Cooper, in a review of "Holes and Peeks," in*
> Booklist, *Vol. 80, No. 13, March 1, 1984, p. 992.*

Behind the apparent simplicity of the text is a sensitive and thoughtful consideration of holes as they appear to youngsters. Children really do fear toilet bowls and bathtub drains!

The book is graphically powerful. The illustrations form an intricate grid pattern of interconnecting lines which reflect the bathroom's stark white floor and wall tiles.

The child in this book reminds us that we frequently live with things we don't always focus on. What else are children aware of that grown-ups are not? (pp. 525-26)

> *Ronald A. Jobe, in a review of "Holes and Peeks,"*
> *in* Language Arts, *Vol. 61, No. 5, September, 1984,*
> *pp. 525-26.*

This clever picture-book proclaims its American origin on every page. Ann Jonas is psychologist as well as artist. For the small child holes are frightening, peeks are reassuring. This simple message is conveyed in fifty or so words, printed in bold sans-serif type, and in a series of pictures whose bathroom setting emphasizes the somewhat clinical nature of the whole. It is all very clever in its naivety, but somehow I don't see it having much to do with the British child, for whom fear of plugholes and W. C. pans may seem as irrelevant as this immaculate tiled-overall bathroom.

> *M. Crouch, in a review of "Holes and Peeks," in*
> The Junior Bookshelf, *Vol. 48, No. 5, October, 1984,*
> *p. 203.*

THE QUILT (1984)

The intricate illustrations in Jonas's new book can be described only in superlatives. Backed by a length of golden-yellow calico imprinted with small red flowers, a quilt fashioned from squares in a variety of colors is the prize shown to readers by a dear little girl. Her father and mother have just finished making it for her, she says, sewing together bits of "my old things." Before she snuggles into bed with her adored rag dog Sally, the young miss muses that the quilt looks like a town. In her dream, she scours a carnival grounds, a dark forest, the banks of a lake and other eerie places as she searches for lost Sally. An artist's feat of imagination creates these landscapes from each square in the quilt, scenes that diminish into individual realities in the morning. The girl awakens to find Sally

safe beside her. This is a rare work, but a bit disconcerting because of the jolting switch between the story's two parts. First the child talks confidently about her gift from parents she clearly knows cherish her. That premise doesn't set readers up for the nightmare, especially since the quilt pieces are part of her own familiar world. The book is, nevertheless, a landmark in children's literature.

> *A review of "The Quilt," in* Publishers Weekly, *Vol.*
> *226, No. 7, August 17, 1984, p. 59.*

Jonas begins her story with an idea that is as warm and cozy as the quilt of the title, but the pleasant reassurance and sense of security that children are led to expect turns, without warning, into sheer nightmare. . . . The quilt that Mother made is warm and warming, but the story and illustrations in **The Quilt** are ice cold. What starts from a widely recognized artifact for comfort is reworked into a discomfiting dream shared. (pp. 110-11)

> *Trev Jones, in a review of "The Quilt," in* School
> Library Journal, *Vol. 31, No. 3, November, 1984,*
> *pp. 110-11.*

Totally engaging, from the first glimpse of the little girl, in sleepers—"I have a new quilt"—peering out from under a billowing patchwork of patterned squares. There's a definite, '80s lifelikeness too: "It's to go on my grown-up bed''; "My mother and father made it for me. They used some of my old things." And what happens is almost preordained: holding her stuffed dog Sally, thinking "It almost looks like a little town . . . ," the girl drifts off to sleep and drops the dog, as the quilt comes alive. . . . With the calico pattern of the quilt's lining for the endpapers, and a delicately brown child with a soft cap of crinkly hair: a natural fancy appealingly presented.

> *A review of "The Quilt," in* Kirkus Reviews, *Ju-*
> *venile Issue, Vol. LII, Nos. 18-21, November 1, 1984,*
> *p. J-90.*

The Quilt would make a good basis for a soulful, beautifully animated film for children. The book is intricately constructed around a new quilt sewn by a young girl's parents and made of multifarious swatches from every fabric that has been worn or slept in over several years. . . .

As the swatches of fabric literally *absorb* us into highly magnified and detailed life situations, the reader is struck by the tasteful plausibility of these images, which reflect the way past, sleep, and new life are all inscrutably intertwined. Overridingly, however, the book is about *newness*: The past doesn't simply rewind and play back; it is a carnival or a mood or a natural setting from which new experiences are entered into.

If, indeed, the book conveys this simple affirmation of the nature of past and present, it only does so by virtue of an honest capturing of the way life actually happens. Even from a visual standpoint, the way colors and images are extended from swatches to dreamscapes is brilliantly natural, letting the beginning and experienced reader alike easily affirm. "Yes, that's the way it is." It's a book that captures and articulates a simple truth, and makes us feel *affectionate* toward it.

> *Darian J. Scott, "Children's Books Alive with Vision*
> *and Verve," in* The Christian Science Monitor, *Jan-*
> *uary 4, 1985, p. B5.*

Ann Jonas is surely among the cleverest of the younger picture-book makers in the U.S.A. She uses the simplest of ideas and from that starting-point probes deep into the heart of the child's imagination. . . . The drawing, in its strong stylized way, is very beautiful, the basic understanding profound. A finely economical text is printed in bold sans-serif type, easy and tempting to read. And yet. . . . I wonder if the very small children for whom this exquisite creation is designed really like something so subtle, so elusive.

M. Crouch, in a review of "The Quilt," in The Junior Bookshelf, *Vol. 49, No. 3, June, 1985, p. 121.*

[*The Quilt*] is a remarkable piece of illustration as well as a good early reading book. . . . The intricate pleasure of matching the quilt's patches with the features of the dream land lasts right through this book, which is partly about pattern itself—fascinating, comforting, and occasionally threatening. The treatment of the dark and of night fears is helpful and reassuring.

Myra Barrs "Domestic Dramas," in The Times Educational Supplement, *No. 3605, August 2, 1985, p. 21.*

THE TREK (1985)

Jonas's books appear regularly on lists of the best every year. But to convey the impact of her latest, one needs the old-time vaudevillian's crow, "You ain't seen nothin' yet!" The story is whispered by a wary little girl on her way home from school through a "jungle." Holding her breath, she slips past cam-

ouflaged creatures: a vulture, an alligator, a python, a mean-eyed elephant herd and other wildlings. Halfway, the narrator meets a friend who helps her cross a desert, a river and a mountain all teeming with menace, before the "trek" ends at the safe "trading post." Jonas's marvelous color pictures make the safari intensely real. She transforms a gnarled tree into chattering monkeys, trash bags into warthogs and numerous other ordinary sights into convincingly disguised animals. One ingenious example is a fruit stand when a halved watermelon becomes the gaping mouth of the "hippo" formed by the row behind the round, red, split melon. The book is a virtually guaranteed award winner.

A review of "The Trek," in Publishers Weekly, *Vol. 228, No. 9, August 30, 1985, p. 422.*

Jonas artful watercolor transformations of familiar objects create camouflage creatures everywhere, immediately engaging children in this game of discovery. "My mother doesn't walk me to school anymore," the story begins, as Jonas presents, with clarity of form, a daughter kissing her mother good-bye at her front door. Immediately children will get the physical sense of standing on a threshold, adventure beckoning. Reality melds into dream as *The Trek* offers an alternative world, ripe with creative possibilities. Taking its colors from nature, *The Trek* exudes light and warmth. Each picture invites the eye to enter into a jungle world whose boundaries are defined and controlled by the little girl. Best about this book is that as Jonas changes stone chimneys into giraffes, garbage bags into rhinos, creeping ivy into creeping lizards, she inspires children to keep

She doesn't even see
what's right outside our door!

From The Trek, *written and illustrated by Ann Jonas. Greenwillow Books, 1985. Copyright © 1985 by Ann Jonas. All rights reserved. By permission of Greenwillow Books (A Division of William Morrow & Company, Inc.).*

looking beyond her pages, showing what visual metamorphoses are possible to those with fresh, seeking eyes.

Susan Powers, in a review of "The Trek," in School Library Journal, *Vol. 32, No. 3, November, 1985, p. 73.*

Jonas has ingeniously insinuated a menagerie throughout the pages of otherwise innocuous city and park scenes. Readers will enjoy her wizardry and delight in discerning the sometimes subtly hidden creatures. The paintings have a light touch: Jonas creates her shapes without line work and uses rich-looking pastels.

Denise M. Wilms, in a review of "The Trek," in Booklist, *Vol. 82, No. 6, November 15, 1985, p. 496.*

The paintings encompass a range of muted colors reminiscent of the hues of an African game park. Jonas has ingeniously camouflaged both familiar and little-known animals such as a peacock, wart hog, and koala. Used as a learning tool, the book should invite discussion of the various species and their natural habitats, while at the same time offer a visual hide-and-seek adventure to spark the imagination.

A review of "The Trek," in Kirkus Reviews, *Vol. LIII, No. 22, November 15, 1985, p. 1264.*

Daydreaming is a private canvas on which we can all paint. The fantasies we sketch can get us into deep trouble or lift us even into the realm of genius.

Ann Jonas has done several acclaimed picture books including *The Quilt. The Trek*—the story of a young girl's daydream on her way to school—has a promising start: "My mother doesn't walk me to school anymore," the narrator begins sweetly. "But she doesn't know we live on the edge of a jungle."

So our young heroine, who looks to be a first grader, wends her way to school through small-town streets and is eventually joined by a girlfriend. Their route is absolutely littered with gorillas, tigers, zebras, monkeys and elephants mostly disguised as trees and bushes. The most successfully camouflaged animal is a hippopotamus with his big, open, red mouth which is really the inside of a nice ripe watermelon sitting on a vegetable stand.

But the trek past the watering hole (a small pond), through the desert (a mound of sand), across the river (a laundromat's hose), is unfortunately static. The watercolor illustrations are done from a uniform perspective, all middle range and flat, and the pacing of the story and pictures is somehow predictable. Nothing looms, no mood darkens, the density of the forest is not counterpointed by the vast bright desert.

Perhaps the approach is just too benign; the problem is that jungles are not gentle places. If we are to take a perilous walk through the untamed, things must leap out at us, chase us, hide, pounce, slither and groan on the pages. If the text states that we are scared, that our amazing skill saves us day after day, then the graphics must reflect this fear. We must hurry with anticipation, wiggle with worry, throb with expectation and rejoice in our eventual safety.

The Trek is a gift from one daydreamer to another. The exciting quality of real adventure is what it lacks.

Barbara Bottner, in a review of "The Trek," in The New York Times Book Review, *March 16, 1986, p. 30.*

We already know Ann Jonas as an artist who finds beauty and wonder in everyday things. In *The Trek* a little girl is now old enough to go to school on her own.... It is a deliciously terrifying trek, but she makes it up the mountain to the haven of school. Ann Jonas' rather stiff watercolours are just the right medium for this unusual and cleverly executed adventure story. For unobservant parents the artist provides a set of naturalistic pictures of the animals as an appendix. This is a book which will not yield up all its secrets at a single reading.

M. Crouch, in a review of "The Trek," in The Junior Bookshelf, *Vol. 50, No. 4, August, 1986, p. 140.*

NOW WE CAN GO (1986)

A small child refuses to leave on a trip until all favorite toys have been meticulously sorted from the toy box into a traveling bag. The box on the left of each spread empties as the bag on the right fills up. Various toys and a book . . . go one by one from box to bag. Then the child is ready. To the youngster hearing this book aloud, the movement of the toy may be too subtle and the illustration too flat to show the acts of taking out and putting in. To the older reader, the spreads may seem redundant or dull. Jonas's previous books have impressed and delighted readers with their illusory worlds and imaginative illustrations; expectations for her new works always run high. Perhaps that's why this book is a little disappointing.

A review of "Now We Can Go," in Publishers Weekly, *Vol. 229, No. 17, April 25, 1986, p. 77.*

Each of Ann Jonas' books captivates the preschool reader, and this latest publication is sure to be one that young children will identify with. Little ones will naturally gravitate towards this story of a child packing up treasures for a trip. The large, colorful illustrations complement the simple text perfectly. (pp. 106-07)

Elizabeth W. Proto, in a review of "Now We Can Go," in Children's Book Review Service, *Vol. 14, No. 10, May, 1986, pp. 106-07.*

Jonas has again combined a simplistic and on-target story line with colorful, non-sexist illustrations to create a prime example of what a book for very young children can and should be.... This lesson in object identification is reassuring and appealing; the illustrations, executed in vivid colors and with simple lines, combined with the easy text, mark this book as a good choice for both story times and for beginning readers. (pp. 77-8)

Xenda Casavant, in a review of "Now We Can Go," in School Library Journal, *Vol. 32, No. 9, May, 1986, pp. 77-8.*

Given Ann Jonas's flair for discovering new dimensions in familiar experiences and original use of the figure ground, this picture book catalogue for the very young is as intriguing as it is comprehensible. The opening sequence, a perfectly ordinary event, gives the audience a side view of a large blue toy box toward which a determined child, clutching a red tote bag, is running while exclaiming, "Wait a minute! I'm not ready." Then the perspective shifts from a side to a top view: on the left, the blue box with an assortment of toys; on the right, the empty tote, ready and waiting. One by one each toy is transferred until, on the last page, we see the youngster lugging off all the treasures while simultaneously proclaiming, "Now we can go!" The ritual is certainly standard procedure in any household with young children. Consequently, the concept is both logical and appealing as a unifying motif for the illustrations. A fine black line, used in conjunction with colored dyes, defines each object with precision and clarity. The colors are bright without being garish; the perspective such that the relative position of each toy in the box or bag is easily discernible. This approach adds still another dimension—predicting which object will be selected next. Tucked discreetly among them, incidentally, is a copy of *Now We Can Go.* The endpapers deserve special mention: designed in a pleasing wallpaperlike pattern, they are decorated with miniature versions of the toy box's contents, thus encouraging the toddler to look again and again for favorite items. Exactly right for preschoolers who, like Adam and Eve, enjoy naming things, the book is a fine choice for home use as well as for institutions serving the young child.

> *Mary M. Burns, in a review of "Now We Can Go,"*
> *in The Horn Book Magazine, Vol. LXII, No. 3, May-*
> *June, 1986, p. 319.*

WHERE CAN IT BE? (1986)

A search is underway as a small girl discovers that something beloved is missing; readers will be instantly curious about the identity of the lost object. She knows she brought it home, but a trip to the closet reveals "Just my clothes." A look in the cupboard is just as futile, and her cat keeps showing up—first under the bedcovers and then under a table-cloth. Mounting desperation inspires her to open the refrigerator, but what does she find? "Just cold food." She wonders if she left it at Deborah's house. The doorbell rings, and Deborah is there, with the lost *blanket*. Split pages act as flaps, providing readers with a glimpse of the growth marks on the cupboard door, the chance to point out familiar items in the fridge, and the ability to relive that reassuring ending again and again. Jonas's paintings tie the reader into the action with her richly detailed and textured settings.

> *A review of "Where Can It Be?" in Publishers Weekly,*
> *Vol. 230, No. 13, September 26, 1986, p. 79.*

Cleverly designed half-page doors open to reveal the contents of the closet, the refrigerator, etc., that the little girl sees as she searches for the lost object. Jonas' use of geometrically patterned wallpaper against the clean, bright colors and the whites of the cupboards and refrigerator make the action clear and crisp. Things such as the little girl's toys, clothes, pets, or the food in the refrigerator are rendered in loving detail with watercolor and colored pencil. A beautifully designed story of loss and recovery for a slightly older audience than for John Burningham's *The Blanket* (Crowell, 1975).

> *Susan Hepler, in a review of "Where Can It Be?"*
> *in School Library Journal, Vol. 33, No. 2, October,*
> *1986, p. 162.*

The familiar dilemma of searching through the house for a misplaced object is the simple theme of this guessing game, which utilizes a half page in each double-page spread to expedite the search. Very similar in concept and content to Bruno Munari's *Jimmy Has Lost His Cap, Where Can It Be?* (World), this smaller volume lacks the cleverness of construction and humorous juxtapositions characteristics of Munari's work but provides a warm and satisfying look through a conventional, pretty house. . . . Only when the closet door is opened on page five and there are dresses and pink bunny slippers is the gender of the protagonist established. . . . Jonas's characteristic warmth in use of color and attention to homey detail invite repeated viewing after the brief puzzle is solved. The endpapers differ on the front and back; for they are the wallpaper in the various rooms through which we have moved. Large, heavy print, making the simple text very manageable for young readers, has the same clean look and attractive placement as the other components in this carefully constructed and appealing book. (pp. 735-36)

> *Margaret A. Bush, in a review of "Where Can It*
> *Be?" in The Horn Book Magazine, Vol. LXII, No.*
> *6, November-December, 1986, pp. 735-36.*

Christine Nöstlinger

1936-

Austrian author of fiction.

One of Austria's best-known children's writers, Nöstlinger is internationally recognized for the perceptive social commentary and humor of her fantasies for primary-school and middle-grade readers and her realistic novels for young adults. The author of over fifty books in German, more than ten of which have been translated by Anthea Bell, Nöstlinger writes witty urban tales of magical mayhem, friendship and loyalty, and domestic strife from the child's viewpoint. Nöstlinger's fantasies often feature zany characters and a reversal of roles; in *Konrad*, for example, a factory-made boy programmed as a perfect child is taught to misbehave in order to stay with the free-spirited woman to whom he was sent. Although Nöstlinger is noted for presenting an honest depiction of contemporary life from an Austrian perspective, she focuses on such universal problems as juvenile delinquency and sexual promiscuity in her books for older readers. Throughout her works, Nöstlinger expresses nonconformist sentiments on such subjects as war, authority, and women's liberation, while displaying a warm understanding of children and stressing the child's need to contribute to family harmony.

Critics applaud Nöstlinger for deftly combining serious themes with imaginative light comedy. In addition, they admire her shrewd appraisal of human nature, nondidactic approach, and buoyant, polished style. Although a few observers point to the uneven pace of her works, many reviewers compliment Nöstlinger on the variety and appeal of her characters and her skill in portraying them.

Nöstlinger has won several European awards including the Deutscher Jugendliteraturpreis in 1973 for *The Cucumber King*. She received the Hans Christian Andersen Award in 1984 for her body of work.

(See also *Something about the Author*, Vol. 37 and *Contemporary Authors*, Vol. 115.)

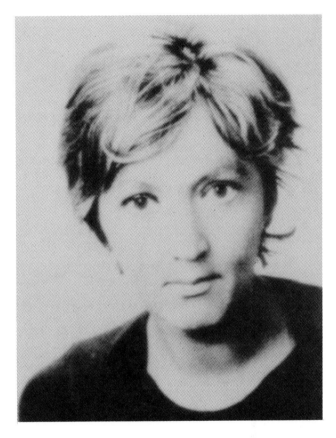

AUTHOR'S COMMENTARY

[The following excerpt is from a sketch originally written in November, 1983.]

I grew up in a working-class district of Vienna, where I was considered a "posh" child, because my mother ran a nursery school and my grandfather had a shop. In the area where I lived, these were very exalted positions. My father was unemployed at the time of my birth, and during my childhood was marching on the return trip to Moscow. Photographs prove that he was a very handsome man. It is my own story that he was the dearest, cleverest and most magnificent possible of human beings, and I shall probably stick to it until my dying day, since I have been offered plenty of evidence that this was not entirely the case, and have rejected it indignantly.

Like all daughters, I always had a rather difficult relationship with my mother. The answer I give to the frequently asked question of whether I had a "happy" childhood is sometimes a radiant "yes" and sometimes a sad "no". Both are true. All childhood is very happy and very unhappy.

I began writing because I was not a good artist. I illustrated a picture book and wrote my own text for it. The book was published; the text won more approval than the pictures. As I was very keen on approval at the time, I took to writing, had some success, and became so fascinated by it that I kept writing away, as busy and productive as a bee.

Sometimes, when I stop to think of what I actually have produced, I get a rather uneasy feeling. I tell myself that over fifty books, over twenty television plays, countless radio programmes, and newspaper articles by the cubic metre are simply too much for sixteen or seventeen years of one's writing life. I feel rather like a one-man literary factory.

I do not intend to describe here the particular problems of writing for children, when one cannot formulate ideas out of one's own consciousness, but must be constantly adapting oneself to readers of whom one knows nothing, at whom one can only guess. That would be a mammoth undertaking. I would just like to admit that I am always wangling things. I have certain notions of what children like to read, and certain notions of what children ought to read. Then I have the urgent need to get certain things written out of my mind and brain. And I also have a firm conviction that children like to laugh when

179

they read. I usually mix these four ingredients together to make my books. Sometimes, however, I break out of this self-imposed cage of mine and write a children's book just to please myself. These books get a few more favourable reviews from the critics, but are not so well received by my readers. So then I draw my horns in again, and my next book follows my usual recipe for success, treading the narrow line between triviality and literature.

All this, I suppose, sounds rather deflating, and has nothing to do with the transmission of values, concepts of the good, the true and the beautiful, the offering of help in life's troubles, the raising of deep questions, and all the other things children's writers like to cite as justification for their writing. Maybe—but for the moment anyway, it seems to me reasonably honest. It could be, however, that in a year's time I shall see myself and my "message" quite differently. (p. 51)

Christine Nöstlinger, "Autobiographical Note," translated by Anthea Bell, in The Junior Bookshelf, *Vol. 48, No. 2, April, 1984, pp. 50-1.*

Very little in the world is as it should be. Almost everything in the world is as it should not be.

Life is good for only a few people. For most people, life is bad. And where adults are badly off, children are even worse off.

There is more need just now to shout out loud, to fight, to team up with others, to change things, than to pick up a book and read it. But in order to change the world, you must know all about it. You must be able to tell right from wrong and not be taken in by lies. People lie in words and in sentences. When words and sentences are written down, it is easier to check if they are right or wrong than when you only hear them.

It is certainly not true—as many people say—that television makes you stupid and that books make you clever. But in most countries television belongs to the people who are in power, and these people want the world to stay as it is. Many books want this too. But there are also plenty of books which tell you what is really happening in the world and why it is happening.

Books can help you find out what to shout aloud, what to fight for, with whom to team up, and where you can begin to change things. They can help you in a way that no one else can.

Christine Nöstlinger, "Message to All Children for International Children's Book Day 1985," in Bookbird, *No. 4 (December 15, 1984), p. 4.*

When I started writing children's books over 16 years ago, I didn't know much about children but I was full of enthusiasm. It was a very good period—at least in Central Europe—for someone with my outlook. We could be optimistic, because change seemed possible. Just a year or two of work, commitment, cunning, struggle and toughness (so I told myself) and we'll be halfway towards a world in good order—by which I meant an appealing socialist disorder, far removed from true Socialism.

If you think and believe as I thought and believed then, there is good reason—if you want to write at all—to write for children, who are regarded as less dull, stuffy, stupid and rigid than adults. They are considered fairer, franker, more honest and more creative, so that there is less resistance to overcome before they understand what you are saying.

My children's book recipe at that time was quite simple: since children live in an environment which offers them no encouragement to develop Utopias for themselves, we have to take them by the arm and show them how beautiful, cheerful, just and humane this world could be. Rightly done, this will make children long for that better world, and their longing will make them willing to think about what must be got rid of and what must be initiated in order to produce the world they long for.

It is often difficult in retrospect to say how and when illusions fade and resignation sets in. All I know is that for me it was a slow, laborious process. But I retain a painful memory of some of the shocks which hastened the decline of illusions and the onset of resignation: the invasion of Prague by the USSR and the murder of Allende in Chile were just two of those agonizing events. And if anyone should ask what this has to do with the writing of children's books, I would say: for me, a great deal.

Among many other things, literature for children must give them courage and hope, and whether this can be done by a writer from whom courage and hope are slowly slipping away is doubtful. For me, at least, it was so doubtful that I gave up the unequal struggle. Or, in medical terms, I stopped trying to effect a cure and went into the sticking-plaster business. The craft of the sticker-on of plasters is not to be despised! There is a lot to be said for consolation plasters, for instance, and cold plasters against the prevailing chill in human relationships can be a help. A bit of explanation about connections, because you live better when you know more; and a bit of prodding to make you kick out, because you feel better if you don't always lie down and take it; and a bit of encouragement to love one another, because it helps you to get through the knowing and the kicking—they are all part of the sticking-plaster business.

I was quite content with that for years, and I assume my readers were, too. But in recent years I have had to question this activity as well. To put it in the jargon that earns me applause from my readers and disapproval from conservative critics, "the dung is steaming so hard" that I no longer know where to apply the plasters. There are two things that produce writer's cramp: the state of the world in general, and the electronic media in particular.

Even when you have given up the whole idea of trying to change society by writing, and are only helping, comforting, explaining and entertaining, to make children feel better in the social environment they inhabit, you have to ask yourself: What is important? Where is help most urgently needed? Should we still be thinking of marks in class, first love, rows with parents, playgrounds, pocket money, desire for adventure, dreams and freaking out? Or should we be thinking about Pershings and SS-20's, resources and the Third World? Or about the extinction of species and the survival of mankind? Or about the third World War, acid rain and lead pollution? Are children more distressed today because they have too little pocket money, or because 44,622 children are dying every day? Do they want an explanation as to why Mum is getting divorced from Dad, or why there is an armaments race and a balance of terror? Do they need support in their differences with teachers, or support for a children's demonstration against a power station with no filters?

I have never been quite sure what children can deal with on their own and where they need help. I am even less sure now. In Austria, for instance, there is an area where the children are suffering from pseudo-croup; they cough all the time, they have bronchitis, have to take antibiotics and use inhalants in order not to be destroyed by the polluted air. Of course, these children also read books in which little men with propellers on their tummies create mischievous chaos, and books in which a child suffers because he gets a "Poor" in Latin. But I confess that I am not happy with the thought that one of these children may put down his inhaler and pick up one of my books. "That child needs a different book altogether!" I tell myself. But what kind of book, I don't know. What kind of books should be read by children in countries where things are far, far worse than in mine—in Chile, for instance, or in Iran, in Irak, in South Africa, in Afghanistan, in Chad, or wherever war, poverty, exploitation and oppression prevail—I do not even dare to contemplate. It is not for me to say I want these children to have books. It's not that I don't think the hungry, the exploited, the oppressed and the fighters need books—on the contrary. It's just that I don't think people like me should make any judgment in this area. I have not yet been able to sort out—for myself—whether the little bit of surplus money we have collected for these countries would be better used to buy food, medicine and clothing and to build schools and homes, or to buy weapons. In the past I was for weapons! Now I am against them, not because I am a pacifist, but because it is obvious that those who are in power and who exploit and oppress always have better weapons and more of them. So "Children's Books as a Contribution to Development Aid", or "Children's Books as a Contribution to the Liberation Struggle" are not topics on which I have anything to say.

Apart from these great insolubles, however, the writer of children's books is also under pressure from competition by TV and video, and one gradually begins to wonder if "competition" is the right expression after all, and whether words have not long been vanquished by images.

Formerly a children's writer had a public simply because children were often bored, and spent the time when they could not think of anything else to do in reading. Nowadays, although children are more bored than ever—where I live, at least—they watch television in order not to be aware of their boredom. At the same time, they forget how to read—or don't learn to read properly in the first place—because it is easier to consume pictures than to work through a text; and people, including young people, are all for doing the easiest thing. The author who feels capable of seducing children from the screen by virtue of his stories and his language has yet to be invented.

I conclude from this—however reluctantly—that the children's book market is shrinking and will be quite small in a few years' time. The percentage of children who read will then be no greater than the percentage of adults who read. As with the parents, so with the children: only the "genuine readers" will be left.

If I had a sunny nature, I might say: "OK, it's not that bad." At least there would be a chance of creating a real "children's literature", because nowadays the children who prefer "rubbish" sit in front of the TV, and the author no longer has to bother about trying to tell his stories so that they too will enjoy them, but can write for a small—and refined—bunch of young thinkers with sensitive souls.

Children's literature would then be what adult literature already is: inaccessible to the majority, an élite offering for élite children. There is no doubt as to the countries and classes from which these élite children would come. They would come from the highest levels of the industrialised countries, because all the recipes for seducing children from TV ultimately amount to offering the children a fine and fair existence which is "childworthy". If anyone can ever do this, now or in the future, it will only be someone who lives in a geographically, politically, economically and consciously neutral zone, which enables him to defy the "directives of his culture", to ignore the Zeitgeist and to keep the "tradition of humanity" awake.

So there is now less chance than ever of increasing equality of opportunity through reading.

Whether this process is, as many people believe, inexorable, I do not know. What I do know is that it can be stopped only if everything in the world changes for the better.

And it is obvious to me that scarcely anything can change for the better as long as the dominant economic and social systems remain as they are. The longer man is prevented from leading a life which is worthy of him, the less chance children's books will have of achieving anything for and in children.

Those who are determined not to let themselves be got down have a principle which runs something like this: "Even if we have no hope, we must go on working as if there were hope."

This can of course also be taken as a working basis for writing children's books. But one should at least know the direction from which the hope we haven't got might come. There is certainly not much time left in which to think it over in our case. (pp. 8-11)

Christine Nöstlinger, "Acceptance Speech for the 1984 Andersen Writer's Medal," in Bookbird, *No. 4 (December 15, 1984), pp. 8-11.*

GENERAL COMMENTARY

THE ECONOMIST

It is not hard to see why Christine Nöstlinger has been picking up prizes in her native Germany. *Girl Missing* might so easily have been yet another run-of-the-mill novel for adolescents which concentrated on "real" life to the exclusion of reality. Too many writers have foundered with such stories, overburdened by an excess cargo of divorce, teenage pregnancy, generation gaps and adult incomprehension. Christine Nöstlinger has a rare gift of writing unselfconsciously for adolescents and about adolescents: to portray their own overwhelming self-centredness without falling into that trap herself. The adults are not cardboard enemies.

Ilse's mother is still the villainess of the piece, sure enough: the main cause of her elder daughter's inability to cope with broken and remade family life. But her villainy is the result of ordinary human deficiencies of character, not of middle-aged complacency; she is, as a result, something more than a punchball for teenage frustration.

In *Conrad*, Miss Nöstlinger shows that she can write as well for middle childhood. . . . Conrad is factory-made, programmed to behave just as a mother would wish, and becomes wildly over-anxious when not allowed to be "good". Any child would find this story funny, because Miss Nöstlinger does not make the mistake of poking adult fun at technology. This is not to say that the humour is crude or heavy-handed; rather, that she does not use the story as a vehicle for jokes about an adult world miles above children's heads. (pp. 90-1)

"Mothers and Machines," in The Economist, *Vol. 261, No. 6956, December 25, 1976, pp. 90-1.*

ANTHEA BELL

Can there be something conducive to humour about the letter N? I'm almost tempted to think so, since two of the children's writers I most admire and enjoy have surnames with that initial, and though there is the better part of a century between them, they also share a strong and decidedly similar sense of humour.

When I first read a book by the Austrian writer Christine Nöstlinger (*The Cucumber King . . .*), I was immediately enchanted. I felt the same way when I had finished translating it, and working on a book in the close detail necessary for translation is an acid test, comparable to reading out loud. (p. 49)

I also knew, when I had translated **The Cucumber King,** that the English writer of whom Frau Nöstlinger most reminded me was E. Nesbit. Some ten years and nearly a dozen Nöstlinger translations later, I still see a likeness, entirely modern as the Austrian writer is in her style and her choice of subject matter.

In Christine Nöstlinger's books for younger children, such as **The Cucumber King** and **Conrad,** the similarity lies in the neat mingling of comedy and fantasy. In her books in general, it is in the ability to write from the child's own point of view, with a child's fresh, shrewd observation of life's follies. Like E. Nesbit, Frau Nöstlinger unobtrusively, and therefore successfully, includes serious matters of contemporary social concern in her stories. Both writers present the reader with fully rounded and credible—indeed, memorable—fictional families. But the most striking likeness is simply that they are both funny, and know the importance of not being earnest.

As I have indicated, Christine Nöstlinger's books for the younger age-range can generally be described as comic fantasy. If one absolutely must classify, then I suppose that her books for older children, such as **Marrying Off Mother, Luke and Angela, But Jasper Came Instead,** would fall into the Teenage Problem Novel category, though fortunately (since the heart tends to sink at the thought of the Teenage Problem Novel) you would never notice it because of the comedy. It is not just surface comedy either, but runs deep to the heart of her stories. (pp. 49-50)

Humour, then, is the keynote of Christine Nöstlinger's work. . . . (p. 50)

Anthea Bell, "Christine Nöstlinger," *in* The Junior
                    Bookshelf, Vol. 48, No. 2, April, 1984, pp. 49-50.

PATRICIA CRAMPTON

Christine Nöstlinger's earliest and still much loved books **Die Kinder aus dem Kinderkeller** [*The Disappearing Cellar: A Tale told by Pia Maria Tiralla, a Viennese Nanny*] and **Die feuerrote Friederike** [*Fiery Frederica*] . . . immediately found critical acclaim for their characteristic humour and fantasy, combined with social criticism—all three elements which are to be found again and again in the ever-lengthening list of her work. In 1972 she received the Award for Special Achievement in the Field of Juvenile Literature for **Wir pfeifen auf den Gurkenkönig** (*Cucumber King*), in which it is the children who see through the pretensions of the basically ill-intentioned Cucumber King.

This book, with an even stronger, universal message about the abuse of power and a skilful exploitation of absurdity, was successful in many non-German-speaking countries; but above all it underlined Nöstlinger's committment to children. To her, this has never meant protecting children from reality—on the contrary: she has discovered the way to reveal and illuminate reality by means of fantasy. The amazing **Rosalinde** [*Rosalinde*

Has Thoughts in Her Head], **Luki-live** [*Luke and Angela*], who tries to find his identity by becoming a punk, awful English Jasper in **Das Austauschkind** [*But Jasper Came Instead*] are treated by Nöstlinger with an affectionate respect which we, as adult readers, can share as readily as the young readers, whose sympathy Nöstlinger's non-heroes and heroes and heroines capture from the start. Other outstanding works include the somewhat controversial **Lieber Herr Teufel;** the more autobiographical **Maikäfer flieg!** [*Fly Away Home*], a truly anti-war book just because it is never didactic; **Ilse Janda, 14** [*Girl Missing*]; **Rosa Riedl, Schutzgespenst** [*Rosa Riedl, Guardian Ghost*]; **Gretchen Sackmeier; Konrad, oder das Kind aus der Konservenbüchs** [*Conrad: The Hilarious Adventures of a Factory-Made Child*]; and **Hugo—das Kind in den besten Jahren.**

The awards she has received for her work are many. But above all, to open a new book by Nöstlinger and to read half-a-dozen sentences is to recognize that one is in the presence of a great writer. (pp. 5-6)

Patricia Crampton, "Christine Nöstlinger," *in*
                    Bookbird, No. 2, (June 15, 1984), pp. 5-6.

PAT THOMSON

Christine Nostlinger seems less well-known in this country [England] than she deserves to be. Her books have been honoured in German-speaking countries and internationally, and there is certainly no barrier for British readers in the translation, as Anthea Bell works on the books with the kind of skill which could have you believing that they were written in English to start with. Anyone looking for fresh books with a modern, humorous, urban atmosphere should take a closer look at this author.

The books for younger children, about 7-11, usually contain a fantasy element. **Mr Bat's Great Invention** is the most conventionally magical. Robert allows his Granny to try Mr Bat's rejuvenation process and finds himself responsible for an infant Granny.

"Hey, what did Robert give you to pretend to be his Granny?"

Looking crosser than ever, Granny put out her tongue and went: "YAAAH!"

In **Lollipop,** the magic may or may not be what it seems. Lollipop is the nickname of a boy who by staring through a well-licked lollipop makes others obey him. This becomes his aid to coping with the demands of junior life. Here, Christine Nostlinger is exploring the feelings of a younger age range in a way usually reserved for older children. She does it seriously but with a light touch. On one occasion, for example, the technique backfires on Lollipop. In an effort to persuade his sister that only girls should help with the housework, he practises his compelling stare in the mirror! By the end of the story, he no longer needs this special prop. He can depend on himself.

The Cucumber King is overtly critical of parents. The father is dominated by conventional concerns so when a strange cucumber-like figure emerges from the cellar, it only has to claim that it is a King, ejected from his kingdom by rebellious subjects, for the reactionary father to rush to its defence. The rest of the family loathe it and its nasty ways and make common cause with the downtrodden subjects, so when they defeat the Cucumber King so, in a way, is the father defeated. This author makes no special allowance for adults. Their motives and self-deceptions are exposed as rigorously as the children's. Her most unusual book is **Conrad,** the story of a factory-made child delivered to the wrong address. The fun lies in the reversal of roles, for Conrad is beautifully programmed to be the perfect child, while Mrs Bartolotti is unconventional and extremely easy-going. The crisis comes when a very disagreeable couple arrive to claim their property, and to save himself, Conrad has to behave like an ordinary boy. As the damp patch on the ceiling spreads, the light fittings sway, and Conrad arrives head first down the banisters, the would-be parents hastily renounce all claims and Conrad and Mrs Bartolotti are left to live affectionately together.

In all these books, Christine Nostlinger speaks very directly to the reader, involving them in an immediate way. She is anti-authoritarian, writing largely from the child's point of view, but without abdicating adult responsibility. The characters always recognise ultimately that they, too, must contribute to family harmony whatever the parental shortcomings. She acknowledges the pressures of being a father and is often interesting on the role of mothers. They fight to retain their personalities in much the same way as the children do.

In her novels for older readers, two of them make intriguing references to England. Luke, in *Luke and Angela,* returns from an English summer school with a new, liberated personality which gradually alienates him from Angela, till then his most faithful friend. There is some high comedy, as when Luke patiently, honestly and sincerely explains to the Latin mistress why he is wearing his brother's cast-off pyjamas and cannot now obey ordinary, stultifying rules. She does not appreciate his sincerity or appearance. At the same time, the book raises the questions about friendship, faithfulness and stability, all serious matters to Luke and Angela and to others like them. *But Jasper Came Instead* involves a family's reactions to an objectionable English exchange student. Anyone who has been involved in such an exchange will cherish the account of the drive back from the airport, Dad valiantly making conversation in English.

'"This is the big oil refinery. This is the Zentralfreidhof. All the dead people of Vienna are lying here!" Jasper didn't bother to look out of the window in search of all the dead Viennese people living in the cemetery.'

Jasper, in fact, is a great shock to Waldy's formal parents. It takes Billie, the elder sister, to see through Jasper's behaviour, discovering his painful insecurity and offering him support and friendship. Realising that Jasper's problems are so much greater than any of their petty frictions brings the whole family together in a better understanding.

One other book, for mature juniors or teenagers, makes compelling reading for adults, too. It is *Fly Away Home,* based on Christine Nostlinger's own experiences in Vienna towards the end of the war. The Nazis retreat and the Russians move in. Christel and her family survive the confusion and disorder which follows. Perhaps when someone has grown up during this period, they see only too clearly that adults are not always right, that conformity is not always the proper goal, and that loving concern for each other matters more than anything else.

These are all contemporary books in urban settings which could be labelled 'problem' novels, but they are saved from being heavy, oppressive documents by the author's humour, inventive moments and imaginative situations. She has said that she sees four elements in writing for children: their love of humour, what they like to read, what they ought to read, and what she feels compelled to write. She tries to combine these factors while being honest about contemporary life. In doing this, she has succeeded in working out serious themes through fun and

an element of fantasy, looking at parents, brothers, sisters and friends and managing to say something serious but funny about all of it.

        Pat Thomson "Christine Nostlinger," in Books for
        Keeps, No. 28, September, 1984, p. 26.

PATRICIA CRAMPTON

In addition to artistic excellence, the criteria applied by the [1984 Hans Christian Andersen Award] jury were based on simple and important concepts: the writer's or artist's permanent contribution to the genre, his or her originality, range, consistency, development as an artist; his ability to extend the emotional experience of the reader, his social commitment, the moral quality of the work; its implicit compatibility with the aims of IBBY [International Board on Books for Young People]. (p. 6)

Every one of the criteria we applied is fulfilled by our writer-winner, Christine Nöstlinger. Christine Nöstlinger's range covers all young readers, from 6 to 16: for the youngest, **Mr Bat and his Great Invention, Fiery Frederica, The Cucumber King** and half a dozen more give us Nöstlinger's humour and her almost ever-present fantasy—that inestimable bonus in a socially committed writer—but they also point a clear moral: no one should be made to suffer just because she is different; no one should believe that their position, as parent or teacher or official, gives them the right to wield undisputed authority over others, including and especially children. Christine Nöstlinger is on the side of the children, first, last and all the way. (pp. 6-7)

For older readers, **Luki-live** is a richly comic book, about Luke, who visits England and returns as a punk. . . . But in his clashes with school and parents and his friends' efforts to keep up, lessons emerge about friendship, consistency and loyalty which concern all children—and indeed all of us, as do the trials of the Austrian family who take in the dreadful Jasper in an exchange scheme in **Das Austauschkind.** Their gradual appreciation of Jasper's problems builds one of the most satisfying two-way bridges I have come across in children's literature. Christine Nöstlinger, as the mother of two girls, also exhibits a tender and teasing understanding for parents—more now, perhaps, than in the past—I was doubtful, years ago, about **Ilse Janda, 14,** but as she herself says, she has changed, and she intends to go on changing. Now, *that* I do understand. When you are no longer capable of change, you might as well stop living. In the past her zest for the right—and the rights of children, in particular—was sometimes vented at the expense of compassion, seeming to deny the very individuality she so passionately defends. The high literary quality, the polished handling of narrative and dialogue, were already there; now, there is a maturity which has rounded out her wit and which enables her social comment to be carried elegantly on the wings of her fantasy. Above all, her sympathy now encompasses all her characters, while her themes enrich the reader emotionally and extend his or her understanding, both inwards and outwards. I was going to say "the young reader", but no, that is quite wrong. Parents and teachers, please read **Conrad,** read **Luki-live,** and learn, and *laugh!* (pp. 7-8)

        Patricia Crampton, "There Is Always a Bridge," in
        Bookbird, No. 4, (December 15, 1984), pp. 4-8.

ANTHEA BELL

A good book, which is also a funny book, but has a level of serious intent beneath the laughter: the novels of Christine

Nöstlinger fulfil this translator's ideal of mine to a very high degree.... [Her] characters display that healthy irreverence which attracts children, while the reader is aware of firm values beneath the fun. The irreverence is much to the fore in her fantasies for younger children, where topsy-turvydom holds sway: a grandmother is magically reduced to little-girl status in **Mr. Bat's Great Invention** (**Mr. Bats Meisterstück**), the impossibly virtuous factory-made child Konrad, in the story of which he is the eponymous central figure, has to be taught naughtiness in order that there may be a happy ending. In Frau Nöstlinger's novels of everyday life for older children and young people, there is what may appear to be comic irreverence too, although it often turns out to be shrewd observation on the part of her young heroes and heroines as they turn a penetrating eye on adult folly.

For the parents in Frau Nöstlinger's novels are the characters who tend to be conformist, while their offspring have clearer perceptions, and often better sense. I think of the horror of the young narrator's father in **But Jasper Came Instead** (**Das Austauschkind**), on hearing that his son would like to spend part of the summer alone with a pile of books in the summerhouse on his grandmother's allotment; Erwin the narrator himself is just expressing that desire for a little solitude which comes over most of us at times, but he is not behaving, in his father's opinion, as a healthy boy ought to behave. These young people of Frau Nöstlinger's creation are all individuals and all different. I am particularly fond of her sensitive young heroine in **Luki-Live** (**Luke and Angela** in English), facing the inevitability of adulthood with the fastidiousness of the near-anorexic girl, but able to help her childhood friend Luke through his own adolescent troubles. It is good to see the theme of the problems of adolescence, so recurrent in the teenage novel, treated with acute and *humorous* observation, and accommodating social comment on the way. This particular title has a strand of discussion of the women's movement running through it, but—as with Nöstlinger's social comment in general—there is nothing didactically obtrusive about its presence. It's brought in through the medium of humour. (pp. 11-12)

Anthea Bell "Translating Humour for Children," in
Bookbird, *No. 2 (June 15, 1985), pp. 8-13.*

MR. BATS MEISTERSTÜCK; ODER, DIE TOTAL VERJÜNGTE OMA [MR. BAT'S GREAT INVENTION]   (1971)

Magical events in *Mr Bat's Great Invention* have some amusing rough edges. A rejuvenation spell gets out of hand, a time-machine dumps its occupants in the wrong century and throughout the book magic is mischievous rather than airy-fairy.

The story is set in present-day Vienna and it unfolds at a cracking pace. Robert, the leading character, is a small boy whose relationship with his chivvying parents and elder sister is affectionate but abrasive. He enjoys visiting his grandmother because she is as solid and comforting as the delicious yeast dumplings that she cooks for him.

Granny, however, suffers from creaking legs and swollen ankles so she takes a rejuvenating potion. This has been provided by Mr Bat and, in the tradition of fictional inventors, he is not only eccentric but somewhat inept. His potion of course has dramatic results; there is a ghastly transformation from solid, homely Gran to lisping-six-year-old and "Little Gwanny" turns out to be a handful. Her erratic behaviour produces problems for Robert, and entertainment for the reader. So too does the

process of putting things back to normal with Mr Bat's time-machine going into action.

Zany magic is central to Christine Nostlinger's plot and in keeping with the story's exuberant tone....

Mary Cadogan, "Misguided Magic," in The Times
Literary Supplement, *No. 3979, July 7, 1978, p. 764.*

Granny has become sufficiently uninhibited to strip off the cumbersome clothes designed for a large old lady, and she cannot pronounce the letter r, but otherwise she retains her mature mind. It seems a pity that the author does not extract more fun out of this, preferring to concentrate on the complications in Robert's life, both generally and those produced by the new situation.

The lighthearted style of the story and short punchy sentences in which it is told are suitably complimented by the sturdy caricatures shown in the illustrations [by F. J. Tripp]....

R. Baines, in a review of "Mr. Bat's Great Invention," in The Junior Bookshelf, *Vol. 42, No. 4, August, 1978, p. 192.*

WIR PFEIFEN AUF DEN GURKENKÖNIG [THE CUCUMBER KING: A STORY WITH A BEGINNING, A MIDDLE, AND AN END, IN WHICH WOLFGANG HOGELMANN TELLS THE WHOLE TRUTH]   (1972)

Taken straight or drawn obliquely, family tensions are among the most useful quarries for material for writers of children's stories. Flexibility and variety are there for the taking; almost any tone of voice can be made appropriate. Christine Nöstlinger has chosen to see a short period in the life of the urban Hogelmanns in terms of fantasy. Wolfgang, who is twelve, is well chosen for the role of narrator. He is young enough to take a fairly insouciant view of the machinations of the Cucumber King, even when he is most annoyed with the strange squashy monarch; he is neither preoccupied like his love-lorn older sister Martina nor puzzled like little Nik.

In fact it is largely the schoolboy solidity of his words that lull the reader into accepting the wildly improbable element in the story; when you have read something as composed and ordinary as this:

> We had spaghetti for dinner. When we have spaghetti Mum usually gets annoyed and says we eat like pigs, because we don't wind the strings of spaghetti round our forks, we slurp them up from the plate instead. But that's the whole fun of eating spaghetti.

you are likely to be in a mood to believe in the personage "about eighteen inches tall" who appears in the kitchen, looking not unlike a pumpkin or a large fat cucumber but with "a golden crown, with red jewels in between its points", white cotton gloves and red varnish on its toenails. Malicious, exacting and conceited, the Cucumber King splits the family. Father respectfully finds sprouted potatoes for him (surely recognising, if unconsciously, his own secret image of himself as head of the family) and Nik finds him an entrancing new toy; to Grandfather he is odious, to Mum sinister, while Martina and Wolfi soon discover that if his subjects in the bottom cellar have indeed exiled him (as he explains when he asks for political asylum), it is for the good reason that he has tyrannically opposed their right to education and freedom of thought.

In fact, the Cucumber King is a symbol, of wide and of domestic issues. He appears at a moment when the family needs to express its secret rebellions. It is no accident that among the objects the curious little horror steals to use for blackmail there are several bills that Mum would prefer to keep secret from her frugal husband; it is no accident that Wolfi finds himself wondering when he stopped having fun playing with his father and began to suffer criticism of his personal habits, that Martina feels able to burst out:

> We can only watch things that Dad likes on television! We can only eat things that Dad likes! We can only wear things that Dad likes! We can't even laugh except when Dad likes!

This is "teenage rebellion" but also a clear young view of the adult world. Handled lightly and with a masterly use of circumstantial detail, the book is still serious and full of sound sense. Perhaps it does belong, in a general way, in the category of anti-establishment literature which has been prominent in Germany now for some years. If so, it belongs only by virtue of the attitudes expressed in it. This is no exaggerated political manifesto but a neat, amusing piece of fiction in which the author has steered a course between nonsense and sense with serene confidence. (pp. 2655-56)

> *Margery Fisher, in a review of "The Cucumber King,"* in Growing Point, *Vol. 14, No. 2, July, 1975, pp. 2655-56.*

[This] fantasy is soberly told by twelve-year-old Wolfi (Wolfgang) in a smooth style and at a good, if occasionally uneven, pace. . . . Everyone in the family detests the Cucumber King except little Nik, not old enough to see through the petulance, and Dad, who (unconvincingly) is greedy and believes that the King can get him a promotion and a raise. And that's the weakness of the book: the motivation for the fantasy and the gullibility that precipitates conflict and action seem superimposed; it is not the fantasy that fails to merge with reality, but the contrivance of the situation that is at fault.

> *A review of "The Cucumber King,"* in Bulletin of the Center for Children's Books, *Vol. 39, No. 7, March, 1986, p. 134.*

EIN MANN FÜR MAMA [MARRYING OFF MOTHER] (1972)

Sue's parents separate after one argument too many; this is hardly a likely scenario for a funny, warm, thought-provoking novel for middle graders, but Nöstlinger presents it with the same understanding of kids' concerns that she displayed for older readers in **Luke and Angela**. . . . Sue, an outspoken 12 year old who has a penchant for entering houses through windows, detests the household of neurotic maternal aunts where she must live with her mother and older sister J. She schemes to marry her mother off (to a neighbor, or a teacher), and her hilarious methods eventually land her in a child psychologist's office. As Sue single-mindedly and dramatically pursues her goal, wiser J works behind the scenes to guide the stubborn parents into a reconciliation. Sue accepts this successful maneuver first with astonishment and then with congratulation, "without a trace of envy." Both adults and children are, in turn, loving, immature, selfish and forgiving. Nöstlinger's great skill at characterization and her fine observation of people results in a healing, humorous story.

> *Sally Holmes Holtze, in a review of "Marrying Off Mother,"* in School Library Journal, *Vol. 29, No. 4, December, 1982, p. 73.*

[First published in 1972], this has neither the fluent style nor the perspicacity of Nöstlinger's later books. It's light and amusing, however, and if the characters are exaggerated they are also vivid: Sue's tyrannical grandmother and her slightly batty great-aunt Alice.

> *Zena Sutherland, in a review of "Marrying Off Mother,"* in Bulletin of the Center for Children's Books, *Vol. 36, No. 6, February, 1983, p. 114.*

Nöstlinger presents an interesting array of characters who are unique yet univeral and a situation that is not bounded by its Viennese setting. Except for Sue's naiveté (she is certainly less precocious than sixth-graders found in American stories), readers will easily identify with her. The reconciliation between Sue's parents provides an upbeat ending.

> *Ilene Cooper, in a review of "Marrying Off Mother,"* in Booklist, *Vol. 79, No. 13, March 1, 1983, p. 909.*

Those looking for a happy ending in a separation story will find one, for a change, in Sue Kaufman's adventures. . . . Although the book is set in Vienna, the foreign flavor is minimal. . . . An amusing, preposterous book in the way of Mary Rodgers's *Freaky Friday* (Harper). (pp. 166-67)

> *Ethel R. Twichell, in a review of "Marrying Off Mother,"* in The Horn Book Magazine, *Vol. LIX, No. 2, April, 1983, pp. 166-67.*

MAIKÄFER FLIEG!: MEIN VATER, DAS KRIEGSENDE, COHN UND ICH [FLY AWAY HOME] (1973)

From the opening scene of the bombing raid over Vienna this first-person narrative moves, with a fast realism devoid of self-pity, through the last days of World War II, when young Christel watches the Nazi military regime replaced by Russian combat forces. Lucky to be together and not starving, Christel's family still experiences the hardships and harrowing brushes with death common to the times. Yet Christel's factual acceptance of her situation, her developing bravado and determination, and her adeptness in finding friends—whatever the color of their uniform—make this a fine characterization as well as a gripping survival story in a setting rendered vivid by common but carefully chosen details. The resulting filmlike clarity convinces the reader of Nöstlinger's positive statement about human beings in the inhuman situation of war.

> *A review of "Fly Away Home,"* in The Booklist, *Vol. 72, No. 1, September 1, 1975, p. 44.*

Christine Nöstlinger has constructed a blithely comic, sub-acid piece of fiction from her own wartime experiences. . . . It is a brilliant reconstruction of the time from a child's point of view, in which incident by incident, character by character, a picture of the past is built up that has nothing to do either with thriller-melodrama or political propaganda.

> *Margery Fisher, in a review of "Fly Away Home,"* in Growing Point, *Vol. 15, No. 2, July, 1976, p. 2906.*

The variety of characters and incidents is rich and each has its own place in the story of experience. What could have been a farrago of reminiscences is made, by the author's skill and judgement, into a satisfying whole. At the same time, she never loses the eight-year-old's perspective. The reader is constantly aware that the story is being told by two selves—the child of 1945 and the adult of 1973—held in fine balance. . . . For eleven-year-olds and any age above, this book should prove both enjoyable and rewarding.

> *M. H. Miller, in a review of "Fly Away Home," in* Children's Book Review, *Vol. VI, October, 1976, p. 20.*

The sufferings and privations, the violence and loss of moral standards in wartime are not minimised. . . .

Christel herself is not an attractive character. She acts foolishly with no thought of the consequences for her family. She admires the wrong people, she scorns her parents—in fact she is a typical rebellious adolescent.

Not a cheerful book nor a pleasant one, but an honest portrayal of the reactions of a group of human beings to war and to the struggle for existence.

> *E. Colwell, in a review of "Fly Away Home," in* The Junior Bookshelf, *Vol. 40, No. 5, October, 1976, p. 282.*

Using a first-person narrator Christine Nöstlinger has turned the events and details of her life in Vienna in 1945 into a kaleidoscope of a story with shifting patterns and colours, and vivid concrete impressions as befits an eight-year-old heroine more inclined to action than to judgment. . . . The end is a story ending: the motley crew in the villa, a kind of primitive commune by this time, move on to the next stage of European history. The ebullience of the heroine is the pattern in the fictive texture that guarantees continuance and survival. For those who have read accounts of the Second World War only from the English side, this book is a humane corrective.

> *Margaret Meek, "Taming Past Terrors," in* The Times Literary Supplement, *No. 3915, March 25, 1977, p. 358.*

In clear and often witty prose the author takes us back to her childhood in Vienna at the end of the Second World War. (p. 64)

Christel is a convincing and lovable urchin who has no fear, even when the Russians arrive, because she knows she has done nothing wrong. (p. 65)

The Russians are not so tame when drunk and this danger, combined with Christel's often foolhardy escapades, breed the continued tension which makes this novel hard to put down. Her relationship with the Russians' cook Cohn is finely, often comically drawn. He's a gentle, smelly gnome of a man who speaks good German and jollily admits to being a 'great coward'. (pp. 65-6)

The two innocents, Christel and Cohn, provide a compassionate centre to this book, rich in social detail, which does not gloss over suffering but remains joyous and suitable for any older child, boy or girl. (p. 66)

> *Sally Emerson, in a review of "Fly Away Home," in* Books and Bookmen, *Vol. 22, No. 9, June, 1977, pp. 64-6.*

ILSE JANDA, 14 [GIRL MISSING: A NOVEL] (1974)

A blunt exposure of an unhappy situation from a more truly childlike viewpoint than usual: the 12-year-old narrator, instead of making something out to be worse than it is, stumbles along as best she can through something really miserable. Her candidly youthful expectations and surprised disappointment make the reader feel the pain of living with a mother who has no real capacity for loving her children—or anyone outside of herself. Characteriscally, Erika is telling her sister's story, but it is also her own; 14-year-old Ilse has run away from home with a playboy after escaping her reality for years through lies. With Herculean stick-to-itiveness, Erika manages to find out where Ilse is, but the ending is no solution: Erika has been implanted with a helpless fear for the future of her sister, herself, her young stepbrother and stepsister (who carries the self-centered seed of her mother and Ilse), her beleaguered stepfather, perhaps even her distant, remarried father and three grandmothers (one of whom is caring)—the whole unstable yet abrasively bound "family." Nöstlinger's characterization is just as good, the writing style starker than in *Fly Away Home* . . . , where we saw warmth in spite of war. Here a time of plenty camouflages bitter struggles among people who hurt each other on a daily peacetime basis. (pp. 324-25)

> *Betsy Hearne, in a review of "Girl Missing: A Novel,"* in Booklist, *Vol. 73, No. 4, October 15, 1976, pp. 324-25.*

Though Erika's idealism and gullibility provide some comic relief, strong characterization and tense dialogue make this a harsh and upsetting novel—and it is one that does not have a happy ending. Unfortunately, some American readers may be put off by the stiff English translation which distorts the well-drawn Austrian atmosphere with British slang.

> *Julia B. Fuerst, in a review of "Girl Missing," in* School Library Journal, *Vol. 23, No. 3, November, 1976. p. 72.*

Girl Missing by Christine Nöstlinger and *It can't be helped* by Benjamin Lee belong to what is probably the biggest "growth area" in children's fiction: adolescent problems and problem adolescents. . . . *Girl Missing* is about a fourteen-year-old who runs away from home with a much older man; in *It can't be helped* Max's father dies on the second page, and his mother goes mad shortly after her husband's funeral. Neither book seems to make a successful story out of the material. Christine Nöstlinger's novel reads like a well-documented social worker's case-book, even though the narrative is told in the first person by the runaway girl's younger sister, and despite the dreary family background (divorce and not-too-successful remarriage of the mother) being fairly convincing. One can imagine it being seized on by certain teachers for the kind of sociological work that is too often done in schools under the disguise of the English lesson, but it is difficult to imagine many teenagers reading it for themselves with a great deal of pleasure. . . . [Tracing] the missing Ilse is made all too easy by her sister's discovery of a boy at school who knows her every movement because he is madly in love with her. . . .

Sexual naivety, sexual experimentation, death of close relatives, extremist politics, children running away from home, mad mothers, divorced parents, selfish parents, old-fashioned and conservative parents: all may be perfectly proper themes for teenage fiction, though not in just two short books. And how does it feel to be young and faced with such problems; how do the young succeed or fail in these situations? Neither of these novels presents real flesh-and-blood people, feeling and thinking, and coping credibly.

> *David Rees, "Growing Pains," in* The Times Literary Supplement, *No. 3900, December 10, 1976, p. 1549.*

This is an uncompromising book, written in a plain, cool, under-stated prose appropriate to Erika.

In the deadly quiet of this young, uncertain yet matter-of-fact voice, an unhappy situation is explored—not solved, for the Austrian author has showed herself in all her novels to be a realist, looking at people without fear or favour and keeping nothing back from her readers. If one can judge from almost weekly news-stories in local papers, Ilse's situation at fourteen is likely enough. Christine Nöstlinger has used it not to preach or warn or lay down rules of conduct but to shape a story round a particular family, a story which will affect each reader in proportion to the emotional understanding it provokes.

> *Margery Fisher, in a review of "Girl Missing," in* Growing Point, *Vol. 15, No. 7, January, 1977, p. 3044.*

In *Girl Missing*, Christine Nostlinger has created a taut, emotional book with excellent insights into the psychological impact upon two sisters of being shuttled about between relatives after their parents' divorce. . . . This story could be unbearably depressing if it were not so skillfully handled. The deft insertion of humorous touches relieves the tension at exactly the right moments. This is an excellent book for the mature reader.

> *Barbara Ann Kyle, in a review of "Girl Missing," in* The Babbling Bookworm, *Vol. 5, No. 4, May, 1977, p. 3.*

KONRAD: ODER, DAS KIND AUS DER KONSERVENBÜCHS [CONRAD: THE FACTORY-MADE BOY] (1975; U. S. edition as Konrad)

Conrad is a fantasy about a boy who comes to a woman 'in her prime' by post and who is raised to normal size by the use of a sachet of nutrient solution. The boy has been conditioned to behave with perfect manners, and much of the story comes from the need to have him retrained to normal behaviour. Many children might find this interesting and amusing, but before the end the idea palls. The cover refers to 'the hilarious adventures of a factory-made child', but this is an exaggeration. The book is a translation from German, which might explain why the pace of the story seems so slow.

> *John Owen, in a review of "Conrad," in* The School Librarian, *Vol. 25, No. 2, June, 1977, p. 159.*

The children in the story act more like kindergarteners than third graders, but the battle for Konrad against the forces of conformity represented by his original programmers is zany. Amusing on several levels, this will be most enjoyed by children for its slapstick portrayal of Konrad's behavior modification from goody-goody to regular kid. (p. 61)

> *Matilda Kornfeld, in a review of "Konrad," in* School Library Journal, *Vol. 24, No. 3, November, 1977, pp. 60-1.*

Canned children? The notion is offbeat and Nostlinger fashions it into a curious story that takes some potshots at propriety as it builds to its comedic finale. . . . The satire proves agreeable

more for its sense of family relationships than for its messages; the slapstick ending is predictable, but the previously generated warmth, heightened by Konrad's danger, is what stands out at the end.

> *Denise M. Wilms, in a review of "Konrad," in* Booklist, *Vol. 74, No. 5, November 1, 1977, p. 482.*

The conception of a manufactured child captures the reader's imagination, but the story succeeds largely because of the skillful satire on the relations between children and their parents and teachers. Although the translation is smooth, children would probably feel more comfortable if Konrad's friend Kitty were not called his girl friend.

> *Charlotte W. Draper, in a review of "Konrad," in* The Horn Book Magazine, *Vol. LIII, No. 6, December, 1977, p. 665.*

In a deft blend of fantasy and realism, an eminent Austrian author tells the story of a factory-made child of seven who is delivered by mistake to a scatter-brained but delightful woman. . . . It's daftness made believable, it's great fun, and the translator has done a very nice job of conveying the author's blithe style.

> *Zena Sutherland, in a review of "Konrad," in* Bulletin of the Center for Children's Books, *Vol. 31, No. 6, February, 1978, p. 98.*

STUDENPLAN: ROMAN [FOUR DAYS IN THE LIFE OF LISA] (1975)

The interaction of school with home is dominant in *Four days in the life of Lisa,* a book whose candour and toughness is refreshing as a counter to the often over-purposive, over-intense tone of American teenage fiction. A schoolgirl of fourteen, Lisa feels herself too old for her peers and has attached herself as a kind of mascot to a group of older boys and girls at her school. She sits in on their coffee-bar sessions where conversation ranges from the school magazine to gossip about sexual encounters. In this heady atmosphere Lisa tries to attract the attention of handsome, unreliable Wolf and values very lightly the offers of friendship from the more honest and intelligent Stefan. Time, common sense and observation are just as instructive to her as lessons in Latin and Maths, or the shrewd, offhand advice of her sensible mother. Christine Nöstlinger has built up a composite picture of an Austrian town and of the people—teachers, neighbours, boys sophisticated or studious, girls confident or confused—who in one way or another influence Lisa's behaviour and her thoughts during four wintry and eventful days. There is a piquant flavour in this shrewd, uncompromising domestic chronicle.

> *Margery Fisher, in a review of "Four Days in the Life of Lisa," in* Growing Point, *Vol. 16, No. 3, September, 1977, p. 3168.*

Unpleasant though it is, the book reflects a kind of truth. Newspapers also frequently tell us of a younger generation interested only in sex and aggravation. Lisa herself is self-absorbed and unappealing, but credible. But I am a mother and a teacher, and detest this book's insistence that all females in these categories are overweight, under-sympathetic and sexual ignoramuses.

R. Baines, in a review of "Four Days in the Life of Lisa," in The Junior Bookshelf, Vol. 42, No. 1, February, 1978, p. 46.

LOLLIPOP: KINDERROMAN [*LOLLIPOP*]   (1977)

[*Lollipop*] is about a boy who calls himself Lollipop. He manages to manipulate people by looking at them through a thin, well-licked lollipop which has thus become transparent. This lollipop-power helps him out of a variety of awkward situations most of which involve his family and a friend, Otto, who keeps a shop nearby. The characterization is excellent and the dialogue rings true but parts of the narrative are wordy and laboured and tend to slow down the stories.

Pamela Oldfield, "Through a Lollipop Brightly," in The Times Educational Supplement, No. 3441, June 11, 1982, p. 44.

It is difficult to see why a book such as this has been worth the trouble of translating from the German. It is a lack-lustre story of a boy in a one-parent family, living in an apartment, who has discovered (before the story opens) that if he licks a green lollipop to a very thin state he can make people do what he wants. There is no explanation for this and sometimes it gets him out of hot water in morally questionable circumstances, for example when he steals money from his grandmother's purse. A strange story, with little appeal, . . . aimed at eight- to ten-year-olds. Surely there must be better stories to translate for British children to read.

Janet Fisher, in a review of "Lollipop," in The School Librarian, Vol. 30, No. 3, September, 1982, p. 236.

Christine Nostlinger's best-known book *Conrad the Factory-made Boy* is certainly a fast mover within the library stock and I shall be very happy to add a copy of *Lollipop*. The style is reminiscent of Astrid Lindgren—matter of fact, brisk. As with Astrid Lindgren's heroes and heroines, Lollipop's escapades bring to life the seemingly unimportant but very real frustrations of childhood. How he hates his name (Victor Emmanuel), longs for a proper friend, fights with his sister!

Each chapter is a story in itself so for younger children it is a satisfying book to tackle in short spurts. For the same reason it is an excellent book to have on the classroom shelf for reading aloud.

Cathy Lister, in a review of "Lollipop," in Books for Keeps, No. 24, January, 1984, p. 8.

LUKI-LIVE [*LUKE AND ANGELA*]   (1978)

Luke and Angela takes us into the world of the prosperous Austrian middle classes, and very entertainingly too. I have to report that Austrian kids are into personality development, self-analysis, women's liberation, and male knitting as a political act. Angela's best friend Luke (they are both 14) decides to become more interesting. He begins with some endearing eccentricities of dress and a policy of total honesty highly disconcerting to teachers.

All this is most successful, but he escalates through Stakhanovite, French kissing, guerrilla classroom tactics, and a grown-up girl friend to alarming debts and a nervous breakdown. All this—you have to believe me—is done in a way that is not only convincing, but also very funny and very touching, par-

ticularly as narrated by Angela, who manages to be a nice and clever girl without a touch of the Biddies. . . . I can't wait to read more books by Christine Nostlinger.

Andrew Davies, "Sweet Sixteen and Never . . . ?" in The Times Educational Supplement, No. 3319, January 18, 1980, p. 39.

This is a story which involves the reader. The author in her many books faces life as it is through her characters, young people and adults as well. To compare her books with those of Judy Blume is to realise how different the approach can be to the same problems.

[This is] a thoughtful book.

E. Colwell, in a review of "Luke and Angela," in The Junior Bookshelf, Vol. 44, No. 4, August, 1980, p. 197.

[This is a] touching and trenchant story by a major Austrian writer, convincingly told. . . . A touching story, lightened with affectionate humor and strengthened by its universal appeal, is effectively constructed and written with polish and perception. (pp. 177-78)

Zena Sutherland, in a review of "Luke and Angela," in Bulletin of the Center for Children's Books, Vol. 34, No. 9, May, 1981, pp. 177-78.

If we are not sure at story's end if either Luke and Angela's or her parents' relationship survives, the novel is still satisfying, since the characters and situations throughout are honest. . . . A good choice for better readers. (p. 77)

Robert Unsworth, in a review of "Luke and Angela," in School Library Journal, Vol. 27, No. 9, May, 1981, pp. 76-7.

Despite the fact that Angela is mostly just brooding over the behavior of others, her own personality and developmental glitches come across—her habit, for example, of taking "refuge in illness" when unhappy. In another plus for the story, Angela recovers and takes control. First, she confronts her parents with her worries about them, and, later, she goes to Luke's aid and comfort when he is most despondent. Nostlinger's setting is consciously contemporary—mothers into women's lib and so on—but unlike most American juveniles with similar material and universally shallow, stereotypical characters, this has sparks of wit and a cast of parents and children alike who are intelligent, if sometimes befuddled, human beings. (p. 806)

A review of "Luke and Angela," in Kirkus Reviews, Vol. XLIX, No. 13, July 1, 1981, pp. 805-06.

DER DENKER GREIFT EIN [*BRAINBOX SORTS IT OUT*]   (1981)

Christine Nöstlinger is [a] writer who looks straight at life and in *Brainbox sorts it out* she offers one kind of truth to her readers in a tale of petty pilfering at school that has more implications than at first appear. Skilfully she establishes a number of boys and girls and develops her theme through their interactions. Many of the pupils of Class 3D have problems. Lizzie is trying to assert herself against an over-possessive, anxious mother: Daniel, known as Brainbox for obvious reasons, has not seen his father for many years: and Wolfi Hahn, disliked and shunned by his school-fellows, has his own very real troubles which he tries to forget in association with a fat, vicious boy, living rough, who leads him into crime. Brainbox does find out who is stealing in the school, by logical deduction and by his personal knowledge of the people concerned; but when the truth is known it is Brainbox who has learned most, as he begins to understand why the crimes were committed in the first place. Into a fast-moving, direct tale, with a firm background of school and home, the author has unobtrusively woven a wisdom and warmth of understanding which could set many young readers thinking. (pp. 4463-64)

> *Margery Fisher, in a review of "Brainbox Sorts It Out," in* Growing Point, *Vol. 24, No. 2, July, 1985, pp. 4463-64.*

Christine Nöstlinger writes in a somewhat old-fashioned style, heading her chapters with summaries of their contents. Her story seems slight but in fact raises some issues which are significant and worthy of consideration, and presents problems child readers will recognise.

> *R. Baines, in a review of "Brainbox Sorts It Out," in* The Junior Bookshelf, *Vol. 49, No. 5, October, 1985, p. 232.*

Discovering the real thief involves clever detective work as well as compassion, with the emphasis more on why any child steals rather than who dunnit, when and how. All this is conveyed with an admirably light touch and no hint at preaching. That the story is set in Germany hardly matters; native readers may blink at boy pupils offering their arms to female ones and jumping to their feet when teachers enter the classroom, but actual characters are recognizable enough.

> *Nicholas Tucker, "Betwixt and Between," in* The Times Educational Supplement, *No. 3633, February 14, 1986, p. 14.*

DAS AUSTAUSCHKIND [BUT JASPER CAME INSTEAD] (1982)

What's missing from *But Jasper Came Instead* is the studio audience's reaction—the spiralling laughter and the dying falls that signify "Oh No! Things can't get worse—can they?" and "What *will* they get up to next . . .?" For this is Situation Comedy writ large, and writ in translation at that. Not that the translation is stilted—Anthea Bell is too skilled a hand for that; but in its relentless hilarity, this Austrian novel is closer to Paul Zindel and Judy Blume than Robert Leeson and Gene Kemp.

It's larger than life fare to be consumed at smarter than life pace, and young readers (or classroom listeners) attuned to the regular rhythms of the gags and crises of TV comedy would almost certainly oblige with laughter and incredulity in the right places. We're in Vienna, with the Family Mittermeier. Herr und Frau M are even more rigidly appalling and uncom-

prehending towards their children than most parents in teenage novels; Mother is so determined that son should score better grades in English that she leaps at the chance of entertaining a Brit. exchangee. *TES* parent-teachers may well feel that problematic exchanges are no fit matter for comedy; certainly, Jasper (a last-minute substitute for a brother with a broken leg) surpasses known precedents. On first acquaintance, he is something of a cross between a Man. United warrior on foreign service and a Trappist monk.

So the horrendous adventures begin. Beneath it all, however, as the veteran teenlit reader will have foreseen, Jasper is lonely, unloved and self-conscious. All of the Mittermeiers learn from his visitation; about themselves and about each other. An adult reader might find the plot rather predictable, but the novel rarely threatens to take itself over seriously and young readers will probably be caught up in the whirling fun.

> *Geoff Fox, "Larger than Life," in* The Times Educational Supplement, *No. 3492, June 3, 1983, p. 43.*

Fresh, colloquial language carries the serious points that Christine Nöstlinger makes in *But Jasper came instead* about the confused role-playing of the 'teens. All the familiar clichés are here; the anticipated dumb insolence, untidy appearance, violent moods, wayward fancies are all noted in Jasper, a 'fat, sandy-haired, freckled boy'. . . . The Austrian boy's view of the holiday weeks, with all the embarrassments and conflicts caused by the unwanted guest, remains central to the story, but the first-person narrative is stretched a little now and then so that we get to know the other characters well enough to accept the total picture of family life and the bitter-sweet dénouement. (pp. 4100-01)

> *Margery Fisher, in a review of "But Jasper Came Instead," in* Growing Point, *Vol. 22, No. 2, July, 1983, pp. 4100-01.*

Is there statistical evidence to confirm my impression that we get fewer translations from the Continent than we used? This clever and amusing novel from Austria has a rarity value to add to its undoubted merits. (p. 35)

[The story] is told by Ewald, and the cadences of an articulate young teenager are captured most successfully. Although caught up in the action Ewald maintains a certain detachment and his relaxed irony is one of the many charms of a highly readable book. For English readers there is an added bonus in the picture of Austrian life, especially a home life which has its many points of comparison and which is yet quite different from its English counterpart. (p. 36)

> *M. Crouch, in a review of "But Jasper Came Instead," in* The Junior Bookshelf, *Vol. 48, No. 1, February, 1984, pp. 35-6.*

Bill Peet

1915-

(Born William Bartlett Peed) American author/illustrator of picture books.

The creator of droll picture book fantasies which have regaled preschool and primary school children for over twenty-five years, Peet is recognized for his concise writing style, clever verse, and individualistic illustrations of animals and anthropomorphic machines. Repeatedly likened to Dr. Seuss, he is considered a consummate professional whose works evoke both mirth and empathy. Peet creates Aesopian fables in rollicking verse and lively prose which he augments with alliteration, internal rhyme, wordplay, and nonsense names. His humorous tales frequently feature an unlikely hero who faces an acute personal problem like cowardice or rejection and triumphs over it. Some of Peet's stories convey serious social messages: *Farewell to Shady Glade,* for example, addresses environmental conservation while *The Wump World* presents young readers with an antipollution theme. Adept with pen and ink, colored pencil, crayon, and watercolor, Peet often creates two-page spreads which he fills with vigorous movement and amusing detail. Formerly an artist and screenwriter for Walt Disney Studios, he distinguishes his easily recognizable characters by comically exaggerating their natural traits and drawing them with particularly expressive eyes, mouths, and body stances.

Critics frequently praise Peet for the unity and balance of his pictures and texts, the inventiveness of his storylines, the twists he gives to traditional plots, and the strength of his illustrations. Although reviewers point out that his verses do not always scan well and that he is occasionally uninspired and overly moralistic, Peet's whimsical imagination, storytelling skill, engaging art, and entertaining language play have secured him a wide and faithful following among picture book enthusiasts.

Peet has won several regional and child-selected awards.

(See also *Something about the Author,* Vols. 2, 41 and *Contemporary Authors,* Vols. 17-20, rev. ed.)

AUTHOR'S COMMENTARY

I was born on January 29, 1915, in Grandview, Indiana, a very small town on the banks of the Ohio River. My only vague memory of Grandview is the two pigs we raised in a pen in our back yard, one dull white, and the other rusty red. When I was three my family decided to move to the city of Indianapolis. . . .

Looking back on those early days in Indianapolis I realize that it was as good a place as any for a boy to spend his childhood. Until I was twelve we lived near the edge of the city no more than a half-hour hike from the open countryside, with its small rivers and creeks that went winding through the rolling hills and wooded ravines. On Saturdays and all during the summer my two brothers and I along with the neighborhood boys would organize safaris to explore this region.

One of the most memorable experiences of early childhood was a trip to my grandfather's farm in southern Indiana. It was

the first train trip for me and my two brothers, something of a treat in itself. Not that it was at all eventful. The old two-car train clickety-clacked along through a hilly landscape of barns and haystacks dotted with horses, cows, and pigs. Past small towns, over rivers and creeks, and through forests. Since I was so very fond of the farm country it was a great pleasure to see it all pass by in rapid review, and so very conveniently. A fine show to the very last scene, which was the railway station in the historic old town of Vincennes. There we were met by our grandfather in his dusty old touring car and we were off again, bouncing along for the last thirty-five miles on rambling dirt roads that were forever doubling back and forth all over the county.

Grandfather's rustic old farm was far more exciting and spectacular than the countryside around Indianapolis, for the land that was not planted in corn and wheat was a thriving wilderness with steep-walled gullies of slate and limestone carved out by the twisting creeks, and the whole place was teeming with wildlife.

Hawks and buzzards sailed above the treetops, rabbits scampered everywhere, and six-foot blacksnakes slithered through the fields. The dark woods swarmed with squirrels, chipmunks, weasels, opossums, and raccoons. There were foxes too, but I caught only a very brief glimpse of one—a flash of red streaking along a picket fence—and in seconds he disappeared into the brush.

Animals have always been of special interest to me and I often regretted that Indianapolis had no zoo. My first visit to a zoo was on a trip to Cincinnati. I wanted to make the most of it, so I spent all the money I had saved from selling newspapers to buy film for a small box camera, hoping to get a picture of every animal there. Fortunately our day at the zoo was sunny and bright, just right for picture taking, and I went clicking merrily away through the whole afternoon, never suspecting that the shutter wasn't working and not a single one of the pictures would turn out. But not all was lost, for I learned a bit of a lesson from that deceitful little camera which made all the proper clicking sounds without taking a picture. On future trips to the zoo I was armed with a sketch pad and pencil; then if the pictures didn't turn out I had only myself to blame.

Drawing had been my main hobby from the time I was old enough to wield a crayon, and since my mother was a hand-writing teacher there was always plenty of paper about the house. This hobby was especially handy in the wintertime after the first snows had turned to sleet and slush and the sledding and the snowball wars had become impossible. I drew just about anything that came to mind, all sorts of animals (including dragons), trains, fire engines, racing cars, airplanes, gladiators, pioneers fighting Indians, World War I battles, Revolutionary War battles, football games, prizefights, or what have you.

There was an art class in grammar school, but that wasn't enough, and my drawing soon crept into the other classes. I always kept a small tablet in my desk and at every chance I would sneak a drawing into it. Quite often I'd be surprised by the teacher standing over me and my tablet would be confiscated. However, on one occasion it was different. This particular teacher snatched my tablet away just as the others had done and marched to the front of the room with it. Then turning to the class she said, "I want you to see what William has been doing!" Then with an amused smile the teacher turned the pages for all to see. After returning the tablet she encouraged me with, "I hope you will do something with your drawing someday." I *did* have hopes of doing something with it, for in those days my secret ambition was to be an illustrator of animal stories. Yet, it was hard to believe that drawing could ever be practical as a career. It was too much fun and therefore it seemed wrong.

Then at some point during high school it occurred to me that drawing was something I couldn't possibly give up, and some-how it must be turned into a profession. And upon graduation, to clinch matters, I was awarded a scholarship to the John Herron Art Institute there in Indianapolis where I studied drawing, painting, and design for the next three years. Outside of school in my spare time and during vacations I continued to sketch and paint. The subject matter of these pictures was usually the farm, the circus, the slums and shanty towns along the railroad, zoo animals, and a variety of quaint old characters.

A number of these pictures received prizes, which was greatly encouraging, but after leaving school I realized I would have to do something else. I had met Margaret in art school and we were planning to be married as soon as I could figure out a way to make a living. What I needed was a steady job, and I found one at a greeting card company in Ohio. But I soon discovered it was not the job for me when I was told that

rendering delicate roses and tulips for sympathy cards was my assignment for the summer.

When I learned that there were opportunities for artists in the movie industry out in California, I headed west. There I became a sketch artist, laying out screen stories with a continuity of drawings, and as soon as the job began to show promise, Margaret and I were married.

We have two sons, Bill and Steve, and when they were very small I would make up a bedtime story for them almost every night. With so much storytelling practice I began to think in terms of writing and as the years passed contributed more and more ideas to the motion picture stories. Finally I became a screenwriter, still illustrating the continuity. After all, I couldn't possibly give up the drawing habit. As a hobby I began to experiment with ideas for children's books. Once the first one was published it became more than a hobby, it grew into a second career. And just in time too. By then my bedtime story audience had grown up, Bill was in college, and Steve was in art school. Now my wife Margaret is my best audience and her interest and encouragement have been most important to the books.

So my early ambition to illustrate animal stories was finally realized, and a little bit more, since I had never considered writing one. This way I can write about things I like to draw, which makes it more fun than work. And I still carry a small tablet around with me and sneak a drawing into it now and then.

Bill Peet, "Bill Peet," a promotional piece published by Houghton Mifflin, 1983.

GENERAL COMMENTARY

S. L. BLANDFORD

Bill Peet's picture-story books are in the tradition of the American tall tale. Kermit is an old crab living under the rocks, whose greediness leads him to near catastrophe. He is saved by a boy, and his efforts to repay him are spectacular and effective. The author has chosen the rhyming couplet to tell the story and this restricts his expression, but the lithographic illustrations are delightful. Seashore and undersea are the carefully observed settings for the drama of Kermit's battles with a hound, a shark, and lugubrious looking fishes, and for his encounters with the boy. In *Farewell to Shady Glade* six rabbits, two possums, one skunk, five green frogs, one bull frog and a raccoon are driven out of their home by the encroaching city. The raccoon has a solution, and they all jump on a train and ride across country in search of a new home. The text is more successful than that of Kermit, as the author has not limited himself to the rhyming couplet. In both books the pictures convey great humour achieved through the portrayal of the animals. By just heightening their natural physical characteristics Bill Peet shows us individuals: the range of expressions he gives Kermit without sacrificing his essential crablike nature is remarkable. Six-year-olds up will find these books great fun.

S. L. Blandford, in a review of "Farewell to Shady Glade" and "Kermit the Hermit," in Children's Book News, *London, Vol. 3, No. 1, January-February, 1968, p. 10.*

BARBARA BADER

While others invented different plots for a stock character, Bill Peet invented different characters for a stock plot. . . . To meet

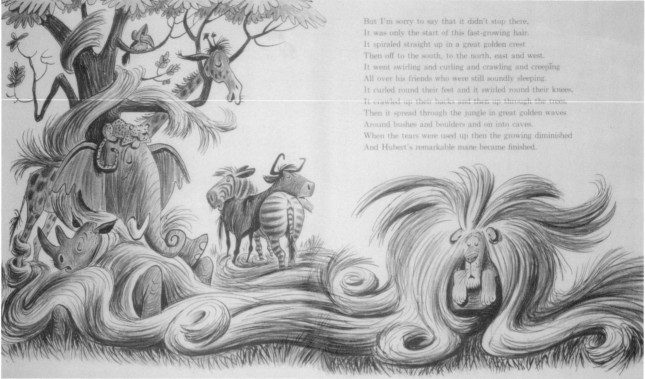

But I'm sorry to say that it didn't stop there,
It was only the start of this fast-growing hair.
It spiraled straight up in a great golden crest
Then off to the south, to the north, east and west.
It went swirling and curling and crawling and creeping
All over his friends who were still soundly sleeping.
It curled round their feet and it swirled round their knees,
It crawled up their backs and then up through the trees.
Then it spread through the jungle in great golden waves
Around bushes and boulders and on into caves.
When the tears were used up then the growing diminished
And Hubert's remarkable mane became finished.

From Hubert's Hair-Raising Adventure, *written and illustrated by Bill Peet. Houghton Mifflin, 1959. Copyright © 1959 by William B. Peet. All rights reserved. Reprinted by permission of Houghton Mifflin Company.*

Chester the Wordly Pig, Huge Harold the overgrown rabbit, Ella the egotistical elephant, Kermit the Hermit crab is to know them always: each is a personality.

"Until a character becomes a personality, it cannot be believed." Not a novel observation but particularly apt coming from the old maestro Walt Disney, Peet's long-time employer. Built into it is the distinction between a character with a gimmick and a repertoire of gags, and the one with a rounded, independent reality. (p. 209)

Peet's books are different, most of them. He is the most humane of cartoonists. His heroes are sometimes blamelessly odd, sometimes ornery, but always victims; whether we are born with big ears or get swelled heads, we suffer. There is first hope, then disaster, then discovery of some peculiar advantage in being different. (Not, be it noted, miracle surgery or renunciation.) The funniness starts with the incongruity of a pig balancing on its nose or a crab of a crab—but the incongruity is not itself made fun of: we don't laugh at Chester for wanting to be an acrobat, we laugh at the figure he cuts . . . , nor at Kermit for making a face, but at the face he makes. . . .

Buford is a runt of a mountain sheep all of whose growth goes into his horns until he's hopeless, and helpless, as a mountain climber. . . . He might be another Dumbo, but where Dumbo is taunted for tripping over his big ears . . . "The rest of the sheep were greatly alarmed by Buford's close call. From then on they pitched in to help." (In Disneyland cruelty evokes pity; in Peet country misfortune elicits sympathy.) Buford, of course, refuses to be a burden and heads for the lowlands and the security of flat ground.

Enter Peet the master of spatial composition, the peer of McCloskey in this respect. The particular landscape is always part of the action, and exploited for dramatic effect. Buford, standing on a ledge "gazing into the valley far below," is a tiny figure against a sky rimmed with mountains that descend to a boundless plain; safely down, the sun too going down, he trots through a straggly pine forest, respite but not shelter, leaving behind among the last rocks the ravens and buzzards that, black silhouettes against the crimson sky, signify danger averted. One has to read the scene.

The scene may take in real people doing real things, like the man who comes to fix the windmill. . . . All is placid, the cattle go about their bovine business, but Buford, recognizing a new danger, conceals himself. Here the exaggerated flatness and the dispersal of the cattle throw into relief the intentness of the man and the woefulness of Buford in hiding, a detail that is prime Peet. However large the scene, the leading character is always distinct, always individuated; played against the broad sun-lit rump of the steer, Buford, standing in its shadow, has the poignance of the shut-out who has only to make his presence known to become prey.

How Buford overcomes his handicap is typical of Peet's ingenuity . . . , just as each of the stories demonstrates his inventiveness. (p. 210)

Barbara Bader, "The Storytellers," in her American Picture Books from Noah's Ark to the Beast Within, *Macmillan Publishing Company, 1976, pp. 199-210.*

JIM TRELEASE

Bill Peet has been writing stories and drawing pictures for children for more than half a century. He spent most of the first 27 years of that time working anonymously in the Walt Disney studios, sketching out (and eventually writing) screenplays. Since then, as author and illustrator of children's books that have sold more than one million copies, he has brushed aside the curtain of anonymity.

He was one of hundreds of artists whom Walt Disney recruited in the Depression years, a crew that served as the backbone for many of the Disney company's golden years—*Fantasia, The Sleeping Beauty, Alice in Wonderland, Peter Pan* and *101 Dalmatians*. "As far as I was concerned, Disney was only going to be temporary, a way out of the dead end job I had in a greeting card company," Mr. Peet says. "But I ended up staying."

But eventually the lack of applause began to wear on him. "I was always illustrating or writing screenplays of other people's stories," while a growing fund of his own stories collected dust in a bottom drawer. Moreover, the audience feedback so important to the creative process was always directed toward the front office. The creative department didn't receive fan mail. "Walt had an intuitive ability to see the better side of creative work but he rarely allowed anyone to think he was doing well. He thought he could get more out of you by keeping you in doubt."

In 1954 Mr. Peet, while still at Disney, made his first attempt to carve out an identity of his own with a picture book called *The Luckiest One of All*. It was roundly rejected by every publisher he tried. "I was pretty discouraged at the time but I never threw the story away and eventually, in 1982, it became my 27th book."

Encouraged by the positive response of his two sons to his bedtime stories, Mr. Peet continued to sketch out his own ideas and characters away from the animation studios until Houghton Mifflin took a chance with *Hubert's Hair-Raising Adventure* in 1959. Four books and five years later he left the Disney studios for his own, one that rests over the garage of his hilltop home in Studio City on the southern rim of California's San Fernando Valley.

At a time when the average picture book stays in print less than five years, Mr. Peet's show a remarkable staying power: All of his are in print—two-thirds in paperback as well.... And while he has never won or even been a runner-up for any of the major children's book awards, children in four states have chosen him as their "favorite author" in annual state polls and his stories have been translated into six languages.

His colored pencil and ink work, to say nothing of his story lines, do not rival in sophistication that of Maurice Sendak (although both acknowledge the Disney influence in their work), his palette does not approach the richness of Ezra Jack Keats's, and his plots lack the dramatic punch of William Steig's. Yet Mr. Peet succeeds. The key is his consistency: His stories and art are consistently good. His characters are less eccentric and have a dollop more warmth than Dr. Seuss' and like Dr. Seuss, Mr. Peet often writes with a message in mind, using animal characters in a fable-like but not didactic fashion.

"I think it's a misconception that children have to be in children's books," he says. Fantasy plays a more formidable role in childhood, he believes, and points to his fanciful animals as supporting that element. But each of his fantasies is firmly rooted in reality as the characters wrestle with life's imponderables: arrogance (*Big Bad Bruce*); conceit (*Ella*); courage (*Cowardly Clyde*); hope (*The Caboose Who Got Loose*); self-

ishness (*The Ant and the Elephant*); and loyalty (*Jennifer and Josephine*).

His characters are often flawed by personal problems that require introspection, courage and persistence to overcome: *Hubert's Hair-Raising Adventure* deals with a lion who has lost his mane, *Merle the High Flying Squirrel* with a city squirrel afraid of his own shadow, *Buford the Little Bighorn* with a young sheep whose horns have grown so large he has to give up mountain climbing, *Encore for Eleanor* with an aging circus elephant forced into retirement. In Mr. Peet's books the battle is not between the good guys and the bad guys but with ourselves. While his plots may be light, he never writes down to his audience. His style is rich in figurative language and, again as with Dr. Seuss, many of his tales are in rhyming verse.

Although Mr. Peet is apt to draw his story line as easily from today's headlines (*The Wump World* deals with pollution) as from the pages of history (*Cowardly Clyde* deals with knighthood), his basic ingredients are always close to home. Reflecting his own Depression childhood (his parents were separated, the family moved 13 times before he finished high school, and he ran away often), Mr. Peet's characters are frequently on the move: migrating pigeons (*Fly Homer Fly*), traveling circuses (*Ella*), runaway dogs (*The Whingdingdilly*), and outmoded steam engines (*Smokey*). All of them wander in search of themselves, seeking answers to the questions that haunt all children: Who am I? Why am I?

Notable for their humanity, the characters reflect the rich sense of humor and imagination that served Mr. Peet so well during his Disney years: circus lions with "cage fright"; crocodile tears used as an antidote for a lion's baldness; a spotted pig whose spots, fortunately, resemble the map of the world; and a timid dragon who occasionally rents out his head for the king's trophy wall.

Farewell to Shady Glade, published in 1966, is a sensitive indictment of urban sprawl. In it, Mr. Peet traces the emigration of a hardy but fearful band of meadow animals as they flee the giant earth movers that have invaded the meadow. Four years later but well before the cries over toxic waste and acid rain, he wrote *The Wump World,* an allegorical world of green pastures that is suddenly overrun by visitors from outer space (Pollutians from the planet Pollutus) in search of a new world. Both books stemmed from Mr. Peet's dismay when, returning to Indiana to show his sons the creeks and meadows of his youth, he found only asphalt and concrete.

> Jim Trelease, "Disney Animator to Durable Author," in The New York Times Book Review, *March 11, 1984, p. 23.*

HUBERT'S HAIR-RAISING ADVENTURE (1959)

A bright, bouncy animal story such as this, with amusing illustrations and a plot full of surprises, is bound to win favor among young children. Blissfully free of moral, this is the tale of a proud and arrogant lion, whose much-prized mane goes up in smoke. His jungle friends proceed to dream up a cure for his baldness.... And when Hubert's hair begins to grow and grow, and envelop all of his waiting companions, they call in a cooperative baboon who gives him a haircut so stylish and unusual that he becomes prouder than ever before. The story is told in slightly Seuss-ish verse, and is filled with delightful touches. The hyena promises not to laugh, the crocodile preaches

"You can't have your friends and eat them all too." And the four-color drawings of the animals are wonderfully zany.

> *Alberta Eiseman, "Lion without a Mane," in* The New York Times Book Review, *September 30, 1959, p. 52.*

"Hubert the Lion was haughty and vain and especially proud of his elegant mane." So begins a riotously funny picture-book tale which, though not so preposterous as the Dr. Seuss yarns, will be a strong contender for Seuss audiences. . . . [The story] is recounted in rollicking rhyming verse and laughable four-color drawings.

> *Helen E. Kinsey, in a review of "Hubert's Hair-Raising Adventure," in* The Booklist and Subscription Books Bulletin, *Vol. 56, No. 4, October 15, 1959, p. 126.*

On the last page of this picture book a lion sits and smiles, his face framed in a square mane. Because of the incongruity, there is a touch of real humor here that is lacking in the rest of the book. . . . Though Bill Peet's lines trip along gaily, his book demonstrates that the genuinely comical is not produced by letting fantasy run riot; nor does the slapstick caricaturing of familiar animals necessarily make them funny. The overall quality of this picture book is closer to that of a nightmare than a comedy.

> *A review of "Hubert's Hair-Raising Adventure," in* Saturday Review, *Vol. XLII, No. 45, November 7, 1959, p. 54.*

Hubert's Hair-Raising Adventure is brilliantly drawn and very funny in a not-quite-nice way. Hubert is a lion who has the misfortune to lose his mane. After taking advice of jungle friends he succeeds only too well with a hair-restorer. Beatrix Potter used the same idea very gently and in exquisite taste in the beginning of *The Fairy Caravan*. There is nothing gentle or tasteful in Mr. Peet's robust line or swaggering verse. Lively and amusing as he is, Mr. Peet has been outclassed by his compatriot Dr. Seuss whom he resembles somewhat in style.

> *"Deep Roots of the Picture-Book," in* The Times Literary Supplement, *No. 3065, November 25, 1960, p. V.*

[Bill Peet's] talent as a writer is evident in all his children's books, but *Hubert* shows a quality of imagination that is rare. Like Dr. Seuss, Bill Peet illustrates in cartoon fashion, but the drawings are more complex than those of Dr. Seuss and are more expressive of characterization. He achieves a visual exaggeration that suitably emphasizes the ridiculous. Also like Dr. Seuss, he is a perfectionist when it comes to the rhythms and rhymes of a text in verse. (p. 98)

The ridiculous heights this story reaches would take too long to describe, but the humor is of the rowdy kind and highly pictorial. (pp. 98-9)

Besides the ingenious idea of having a vain lion burn off his mane, this text has many little sidelights on human character and behavior. The cast includes not only the conceited Hubert, but also a gossip, a long-suffering friend, a pure rogue of a crocodile, and a whole group of animal acquaintances who are always ready with advice but never willing to do anything.

Descriptions are exceptionally vivid, but they never bog down the action. We learn just enough about each character to be sympathetic or, as with the crocodile, appropriately horrified. . . .

Bill Peet insists upon logic in every development of the plot, enabling the listener to thoroughly believe in the climax, one of the most boisterous slapstick scenes in all of picture-book literature. (p. 99)

> *Donnarae MacCann and Olga Richard, "Outstanding Narrative Writers: Bill Peet (1915-)," in their* The Child's First Books: A Critical Study of Pictures and Texts, *The H. W. Wilson Company, 1973, pp. 98-9.*

HUGE HAROLD (1961)

The rhyming couplets which describe [Harold's] career flow with easy nonsense, accompanied by four-color lithograph-effect drawings of swift action and humorous detail. The Dr. Seuss audience has good variety here for their diet of absurdities.

> *Virginia Haviland, in a review of "Huge Harold," in* The Horn Book Magazine, *Vol. XXXVII, No. 2, April, 1961, p. 154.*

Instead of choosing a tiny, fluffy little creature, Bill Peet has made things hard for himself. His rabbit is enormous, larger than economy size, overlapping a human being's bed. Yet somehow he manages to be helpless and irresistibly endearing too—and as lively and comic as the artist's absurd verse, which tells the 4-8's how huge Harold found a happy home and his enormous niche in life.

> *A review of "Huge Harold," in* The Christian Science Monitor, *April 20, 1961, p. 7.*

The inherent absurdity of a buffalo-sized rabbit is emphasized . . . in a series of large pictures showing Huge Harold's predicament when he became a giant rabbit. He is a hideous creature, shaggy-haired and lop-eared, with an expression of permanent disgust on his blunt face. No wonder every creature chases him, foxes and children, and farmers with guns. The only surprise is that he finds a farmer kind enough to care for him and harness him to his buggy to compete at the race-track. . . . There is practically no need for words for this picture-scenario for a cartoon movie, but Mr. Peet has provided a lengthy narrative in verse to explain each moment of Harold's desperate flight and final success. It will probably produce giggles as *Hubert's Hair-Raising Adventure* did but Harold's place seems to be in an ephemeral comic, not a handsome and expensive picture book.

> *Margaret Sherwood Libby, in a review of "Huge Harold," in* New York Herald Tribune, *September 17, 1961, p. 11.*

Here is the current American mode of illustration, the almost cartooned people, the Bugs-Bunny face of the hero, the hillbilly treatment. If you can take this kind of humour (and probably most children can), there is a lot of fun in this extravaganza. . . . The story is told in rough-cut verse that goes with a swing and suits the pictures very well.

> *Margery Fisher, in a review of "Huge Harold," in* Growing Point, *Vol. 3, No. 2, July, 1964, p. 345.*

From Chester the Worldly Pig, *written and illustrated by Bill Peet. Houghton Mifflin, 1965. Copyright*
© *1965 by William B. Peet. All rights reserved. Reprinted by permission of Houghton Mifflin Company.*

SMOKEY (1962)

Undoubtedly there are too many stories of obsolete little trains who run away to save their lives and to seek adventure. But Mr. Peet's version is told in such excellent, free-swinging verse, and illustrated with such vigorous and funny pictures that it outranks most of its predecessors. Besides, there are many fresh twists of the old plot, such as an Indian chase, and the happy accident which so twisted Smokey's smokestack that his smoke rings come out as letters and numerals. This development was seized upon by the quick-witted Miss Adelaide Fry to use in her schoolteaching. As in *Huge Harold,* Mr. Peet uses many colors in an individual, effective way.

> *Margaret Warren Brown, in a review of "Smokey,"*
> *in* The Horn Book Magazine, *Vol. XXXVIII, No. 2,*
> *April, 1962, p. 168.*

A fresh, ingenious approach to the old theme. . . . As in this author's two previous books, this is pure fun. Written in simple verse and illustrated with bold, expressive, colorful pictures, it is certain to become a favorite of our youngest readers.

> *Inger Boye, in a review of "Smokey," in* Library
> Journal, *Vol. 87, No. 12, June 15, 1962, p. 2408.*

Domestic and endearing humour in the adventures of a small shunting engine with main line ambitions . . . Peet's semi-grotesque style of drawing suits the potentially human expressions of locomotives very well.

> *Margery Fisher, in a review of "Smokey," in* Grow-
> ing Point, *Vol. 5, No. 6, December, 1966, p. 823.*

RANDY'S DANDY LIONS (1964)

Randy's lions suffer from cage fright and cannot perform their magnificent tricks before the circus audiences. But after one night under the cruel whip of a new lion-tamer, nothing can frighten them again. Randy puts them through their paces before the audience with no trouble at all. The pictures of the lions are just as entertaining as the bouncy, rhyming story. The lions' ridiculous facial expressions are priceless. Sure to please small children.

> *R. Geraldine Hall, in a review of "Randy's Dandy*
> *Lions," in* School Library Journal, *an appendix to*
> Library Journal, *Vol. 11, No. 1, September, 1964,*
> *p. 110.*

What can a circus do with five cowardly lions whom the spotlight gives a bad fit of cage fright? Here is show-biz melodrama, to be sure. Mr. Peet may seem a bit vague about the remedy—even for 6-10's—but he shows no signs of butterfly stomach himself, and his knockabout rhymes, by sheer self-confidence, seem to carry along the lions, and the story.

> *"Reversed Huck Finn," in* The Christian Science Monitor, *December 24, 1964, p. 5.*

CHESTER THE WORLDLY PIG   (1965)

Chester is the neatest trick in illustrations in a long time. It's right there for all the world to see all the way through the book, but not until the end is Chester's secret given away. Younger, sharper eyes may spot what Chester's got that will make him a sideshow attraction and if they don't, they'll still have the pleasure of being pleasantly fooled. Before Chester comes into his own, his story is a funny exciting rundown on the perils of circus ambitions. Like *Ella* and *Randy's Dandy Lions,* and all the other amusing and color-filled Peet favorites, Chester is going to be a laugh aloud choice.

> *A review of "Chester the Worldly Pig," in* Virginia Kirkus' Service, *Vol. XXXIII, No. 3, February 1, 1965, p. 106.*

An over-extended plot and a climax too dependent on punning humor, which may not reach the story's audience, are somewhat compensated for by the author's funny pictures of pig perils and of circus life as seen before in *Ella* and *Randy's Dandy Lions.*

> *Elva Harmon, in a review of "Chester: The Worldly Pig," in* School Library Journal, *an appendix to Library Journal, Vol. 11, No. 9, May, 1965, p. 96.*

[*Chester the Worldly Pig*] is like an animated cartoon, and the illustrations in ink and colored crayon are banal. After many adventures trying to escape the usual pork and bacon destiny of all pigs, Chester grows big enough to become a sideshow curiosity, with a natural conformation of the map of the world on his back but by this time one really doesn't care. (p. 5)

> *Barbara Novak O'Doherty, "The World of Tangerine Cats and Cabbage Moons," in* The New York Times Book Review, *May 9, 1965, pp. 4-5.*

Mr. Peet has gone from his customary facile rhymes to a colorful prose for this exaggeration about an enterprising pig. . . . Children need nonsense, and they will find it in Chester's frustrated efforts to be a true circus performer, followed by discovery of his surprising side-show value. Dashing colored drawings follow the wild turns of adventure, provide rustic background detail, and give personality to Chester. . . . (pp. 269-70)

> *Virginia Haviland, in a review of "Chester the Worldly Pig," in* The Horn Book Magazine, *Vol. XLI, No. 3, June, 1965, pp. 269-70.*

Whether the happy ending completely convinces in the face of what is a rather depressing theme must rest with the individual. Whatever the verdict, the opportunity to enjoy another example of this author/artist's work should not be missed. Bill Peet's stories are lively and interesting, full of humour, good sense and humanity. His effortless-looking crayon illustrations tell the story quite independently of any text. Furthermore, they never anticipate the plot. Seldom can a book be said to appeal to the age group four-to-eight and mean it in the truest sense

of appealing to the youngest four and the oldest eight (in matters of reading experience). This does.

> *J. Jackson, in a review of "Chester the Worldly Pig," in* Children's Book News, *London, Vol. 3, No. 5, September-October, 1968, p. 245.*

KERMIT THE HERMIT   (1965)

Kermit the Hermit was a greedy, grabby crab. One afternoon his curmudgeonly ways brought him to the very edge of the grave. He had nipped an old hound's sensitive snout and that sensible beast tried to bury him on the spot. A shabby little boy effected his release. Like so many others who have sinned the while and then looked death in the jaws, Kermit became a reformed crab. Clasping his claws in anxiety he tried to think of a way to repay the boy. Chance, dangerous ocean floor journeys, mighty effort and a pal of a pelican with a leak in his beak allow Kermit to play out his role of crustacean Scrooge to reward the boy and his family with a fortune in pieces of eight. The illustrations are touched with inspired lunacy (as is the rhyme) and the color is arresting. This is Peet's best since *Chester,* which was his best since *Randy's Dandy Lions,* which was his best since *Ella,* etc., etc., etc.

> *A review of "Kermit the Hermit," in* Virginia Kirkus' Service, *Vol. XXXIII, No. 13, July 1, 1965, p. 622.*

The rhymes are crisp and commonsensical, and the art, making excellent use of realistic detail, heightens the drama. *Kermit,* too, is happily free of false sentiment: we have no final panel of boy and crab walking off together in the sunset, hand in claw. My only complaint is that for all its forward (and occasionally crabwise) movement, the story is half again as long as it should have been. (p. 16)

> *Richard Kluger, "Hi-Jinks, and Low," in* Book Week—The Sunday Herald Tribune, *October 31, 1965, pp. 6, 12, 16.*

The rhyming story of a miserly and crabbed old crab is highly amusing and inventive. But it is what Bill Peet can do with pictures of a sad crab and a canny pelican which will bring glee and giggles to the lips of his small fry readers. And big fry readers, too.

> *Guernsey Le Pelley, "These Small Tyrants of Taste," in* The Christian Science Monitor, *November 4, 1965, p. B2.*

Four-foot couplets drive the fantasy forward with a swing; the semi-caricature style suits sea-creatures better than it has suited the raccoons and bunnies which Bill Peet more usually chooses as characters for his fantasies.

> *Margery Fisher, in a review of "Kermit the Hermit," in* Growing Point, *Vol. 6, No. 6, December, 1967, p. 1034.*

FAREWELL TO SHADY GLADE   (1966)

You seldom see much critical contemporary social commentary in a book for the youngest story audience. It is very difficult to do without winding up as finger-shaking priggish. Bill Peet's often demonstrated sense of nonsense . . . would naturally save him from such a stance. His subject is quite serious and will be an issue that tomorrow's voters will help decide if we are to survive. Dedicated to Rachel Carson, the simple story follows the forced departure of Shady Glade's population: "half a dozen rabbits, a pair of possums, a single skunk, five green frogs, one bull frog and an old raccoon." Their glade is laid waste by mindless machines sent out to expand the city's boundaries; their trees are torn up and their creek is stopped. A handy railroad bridge allows them to hop a passenger train which carries them so fast through the countryside they can't get off. The stops are all in cities where the streams are polluted by industry. Their luck holds and an emergency stop allows them to descend to an unspoiled spot like Shady Glade. The fun is all in the pictures, wonderfully colored as usual. The message and question about preservation will linger.

A review of "Farewell to Shady Glade," in Virginia Kirkus' Service, *Vol. XXXIV, No. 3, February 1, 1966, p. 106.*

In most children's books, animals succeed in outsmarting humans. The 16 animals of Shady Glade know when they are licked and, instead of attempting to fight the steam shovels and tractors which are razing their territory, they escape to a new and safer home. The text here is simple and not particularly distinctive; however the gay, colorful illustrations add charm to the book and make it stand out. Kindergarteners will enjoy the story, and older children will absorb the message about conservation.

Johanna Hurwitz, in a review of "Farewell to Shady Glade," in School Library Journal, *an appendix to* Library Journal, *Vol. 13, No. 7, March, 1966, p. 226.*

[In *Farewell to Shady Glade*], text and illustration are so happy an amalgam that we are no longer aware of any dividing line between the two. It's not really that we can't imagine the story illustrated by someone else but that story and pictures have blended so perfectly that somehow there is no meaningful separation. *Farewell to Shady Glade* relates the plight of 16 irresistibly drawn animals—two possums, six rabbits, five green frogs, one bullheaded bull frog, a skunk and a patriarchal raccoon—who are routed out of their happy home by man's remorseless machinery of progress. They escape, via a lovingly-depicted sycamore, onto the top of a speeding streamliner and, after a poignant odyssey, arrive at a new glade almost exactly like the first. The happy raccoon, thereupon, pronounces: "In fact, everything is perfectly right." It is. Mr. Peet's illustrations never echo narrative but complement and add nuance to it. His drawings make an eloquent case for conservation, though the notion is never hinted at in the text. The book is, in fact, dedicated to Rachel Carson and we can hope, with Mr. Peet, that the generation which reads his book—may its numbers be legion—"will carry on her all-important work toward preserving what is left of our natural world." (p. 16)

Selma G. Lanes, "Fun on All Fours," in Book Week—The Washington Post, *April 3, 1966, pp. 9, 16.*

A special recommendation should be given to a remarkable book called *Farewell to Shady Glade*. . . . It deals whimsically with conservation problems already upon us, and one can only say, may Shady Glade live forever. Bill Peet's special kind of humor is something which should be discovered and not told about.

"More trouble," grumbled the bullfrog.
   "No trouble at all," chortled the raccoon pointing to a twisting sycamore limb just a few feet above the roof of the streamliner — "Last stop everybody! All off! End of the line!" — and the sleepy-eyed passengers from Shady Glade went trooping down the treelimb. Somewhere below in the darkness they huddled together to finish their night's sleep.

From Farewell to Shady Glade, *written and illustrated by Bill Peet. Houghton Mifflin, 1966. Copyright © 1966 by William Peet. All rights reserved. Reprinted by permission of Houghton Mifflin Company.*

Guernsey Le Pelley, "Magic Is What Lies All Around Us," in The Christian Science Monitor, May 5, 1966, p. B2.

Bill Peet, who's usually wildly whimsical, is serious this time. He's concerned about preserving the natural beauty of the country's glens and glades . . . How [16 woodland creatures] hop a train and travel past polluted streams, junk yards and fenced-in fields looking for a new home makes a satisfying story. Mr. Peet's droll, animated illustrations done in bright colors speed the tale along. At the same time they accent its unobtrusive conservation theme. Children will get the message.

Margaret F. O'Connell, in a review of "Farewell to Shady Glade," in The New York Times Book Review, August 7, 1966, p. 24.

A pleasant read-aloud book . . . ; not as farcical as Mr. Peet's books have been in the near past, but with humorous touches in the writing and in the lively illustrations. . . . The ending is somewhat of an anticlimax; indeed, the slight story line seems only to serve as a frame for the cheerful dialogue, cozy friendship, and the mild but clear message of conservation. (pp. 16-17)

Zena Sutherland, in a review of "Farewell to Shady Glade," in Bulletin of the Center for Children's Books, Vol. 20, No. 1, September, 1966, pp. 16-17.

CAPYBOPPY (1966)

The title is one of Bill Peet's catchiest, but the story, a family documentary rather than comic fantasy is more easily passed over than his others. . . . Capyboppy was the Peet family's own capybara (which "is the largest existing rodent and looks something like a giant guinea pig"). He was brought into the family by the elder Peet son, and while affectionate, his less desirable antics ran the gamut from mowing down the family lawn and furniture (the animals grow to 200 lbs.) to converting the swimming pool to a swamp. When he nipped a neighbor on the head . . . , the Peets finally had to give Capy up to the local zoo. The illustrations are in black and white, which emphasizes the book's quality as on the spot record. They do bring out all the silliest features of the text—like the astounded cats, or the family vision of a boa (the alternative to Capy) reclining on the sofa—and like all the other Peet animals, Capy and friends are very personable. The book is definitely preferable to owning a capybara yourself, and a pleasant but not outstanding interlude for Peet fans. (pp. 1098-99)

A review of "Capyboppy," in Virginia Kirkus' Service, Vol. XXXIV, No. 21, October 15, 1966, pp. 1098-99.

A straightforward, very amusing story of an unusual pet. . . . Mr. Peet's illustrations or his factual account make a picture book that is just as funny as his other books. Since the format is smaller than the usual picture book, there is the hope that it will not look "too young" for older children, for, as a humorous true story, it can delight many readers well over the picture-book ages.

Ruth Hill Viguers, in a review of "Capyboppy," in The Horn Book Magazine, Vol. XLII, No. 6, December, 1966, p. 729.

Bill Peet's earlier books have delighted children with preposterous animals that seemed completely credible. This time he

writes the true story of a completely incredible animal, a capybara. . . . How [the Peet] family adjusts to the engaging but demanding star boarder which eventually reaches the dimensions of a hog makes a hilarious story. The black-and-white illustrations are as lively and descriptive as only Mr. Peet can make them.

Wilma Mater, in a review of "Capyboppy," in Childhood Education, Vol. 44, No. 1 (September, 1967), p. 48.

BUFORD THE LITTLE BIGHORN (1967)

Bill Peet, that peerless brewer of Instant Laughter, has topped himself again: *Buford the Little Bighorn* is the funniest animal character he has ever created. I know, I'm a moral coward. I don't dare look in our Houghton Mifflin file to confirm my hunch that I write those same words about every new Peet book. But what else *is* there to write about a book by a man whose imagination is wild enough to think up a little sheep with horns long enough to make him the only bighorn with a built-in rocking chair; by a man whose pen turns the little sheep into the most beguiling example of "What Happened?" you'll ever see on any ski slope? Oh, *Buford* is a very funny book!

A review of "Buford, the Little Bighorn," in Publishers Weekly, Vol. 191, No. 9, February 27, 1967, p. 103.

Buford's insecure expression and strange anatomy, the angry cows, the grinning hunters, the gay skiers, all caught in hilarious pictures—Buford could be the new Rudolph (and Bill Peet couldn't be better).

A review of "Buford the Little Bighorn," in Kirkus Service, Vol. XXXV, No. 5, March 1, 1967, p. 265.

[We] could all use a little laugh—which is supplied by Bill Peet's *Buford The Little Bighorn*. . . . We really shouldn't laugh at Buford's problems; this mountain ram has horn trouble. They've grown so long and curved he looks like he's carrying a rocking chair. What's more, he's now easy game for hunters. But Buford keeps his head, using horns and hoofs in surprising fashion. Mr. Peet has been a dependable laugh-provider over the years with his genial, extravagant animal stories illustrated in a serio-comic style. He doesn't fail us here.

George A. Woods, in a review of "Buford the Little Bighorn," in The New York Times Book Review, Part II, May 7, 1967, p. 53.

Bill Peet has a way with animals. Lions, pigs, rodents, you name 'em; Mr. Peet has brought them amusingly into the human family. And so he has done with Buford. . . . Buford's expressions as he tries to solve the problem of his unmanageable horns are a delight to behold.

Robert Ostermann, "Through a Misty Land to a Lock for 'Golden Key'," in The National Observer, October 9, 1967, p. 22.

[Buford's] courage, gaiety, wit and determination are as endearing as his physiognomy is ludicrous. I read Buford's adventures to a group of forty children, ages six and seven, who howled with laughter, and unusually for this type of book, it was the text rather than the pictures which provoked the greatest mirth.

Mrs. G. Maunder, in a review of "Buford the Little Bighorn," in Children's Book News, London, *Vol. 3, No. 4, July-August, 1968, p. 187.*

JENNIFER AND JOSEPHINE (1967)

Bill Peet can't miss with this one—a book that combines the stories of an ancient car and a scrawny cat is irresistible. Both start out their literary life as strays. Both, thanks to Bill Peet's humor and ingenuity, find a home and T.L.C. It's redundant to say, "Don't ever miss a Bill Peet," but just on the chance you've been in Mesopotamia on a dig for the last ten years, we'll do the decent thing and repeat—"Don't ever miss a Bill Peet."

A review of "Jennifer and Josephine," in Publishers Weekly, *Vol. 192, No. 10, September 4, 1967, p. 57.*

Josephine, a scrawny stray cat, discovered Jennifer, an old touring car, in a junkyard and raised a litter of kittens on her back seat. When the car was sold Josephine went along, and thereby hangs the tale. Told in colorful prose by the author-illustrator, each bend in the road leads to a new adventure. Dashing colored drawings of the comical twosome, cat and car, add to the enjoyment. A warmhearted amusing addition to Bill Peet's earlier books.

Carolyn A. Hough, in a review of "Jennifer and Josephine," in School Library Journal, *an appendix to* Library Journal, *Vol. 14, No. 5, January, 1968, p. 64.*

I would . . . offer *Jennifer and Josephine* to a small boy, for here is a story with an underlying point that has feeling in it and is completely part of the story. . . . I dislike Bill Peet's way of caricaturing animals but his interpretation of human vagaries in this story, and his unobtrusive humanising of the car, make a highly diverting book. (pp. 1529-30)

Margery Fisher, in a review of "Jennifer and Josephine," in Growing Point, *Vol. 9, No. 1, May, 1970, pp. 1529-30.*

Peet's story about the junkyard car Jennifer and the cat Josephine has been a favorite of children since 1967 and an example of why all the author-illustrator's books are so warmly welcomed. . . . A switch . . . brings a gratifying end to the tale which is copiously illustrated in dashing colors by a master.

A review of "Jennifer and Josephine," in Publishers Weekly, *Vol. 218, No. 9, August 29, 1980, p. 366.*

FLY HOMER FLY (1969)

[In *Fly Homer Fly*] Bill Peet's pictures are so excitingly illustrative of what is going on, his words almost aren't needed. But still, with both words and illustrations, it is a happy but suspenseful story of a country pigeon trying to be with it in the city.

Guernsey Le Pelley, "Mod Make-Believe," in The Christian Science Monitor, *November 6, 1969, p. B3.*

Nobody, but nobody, can draw a bird cocking a leery eye as can Bill Peet, and in a bouncy, breezy book that contrasts urban and rural life styles (pigeon-wise) he has ample oppor-tunity to do so. . . . The writing is fresh and funny, the dialogue has some bite to it, and the puns are not too liberally distributed.

Zena Sutherland, in a review of "Fly Homer Fly," in Saturday Review, *Vol. LII, No. 45, November 8, 1969, p. 64.*

The odds are stacked a little heavily on the side of the country, but maybe that's the way a pigeon sees it. The story, however, is fast-paced, suspenseful and just plain good fun. Homer, looking nonplussed and chuckly through all, dominates the illustrations, which offer a neat combination of realism and humor, although the details—cars and clothing and buildings—sometimes seem a little dated.

Mary Ellen Ballou, in a review of "Fly Homer Fly," in The New York Times Book Review, *November 23, 1969, p. 42.*

Children who liked Bill Peet's previous books . . . will enjoy this one, too. . . . Peet misses the boat by having his animal characters behave too much like humans, and the story is carried primarily by the colorful, better than average crayon drawings. But while the book provides challenging reading material for grades 2 and 3, its flaws prevent its being a first choice.

Muriel Kolb, in a review of "Fly Homer Fly," in School Library Journal, *an appendix to* Library Journal, *Vol. 16, No. 6, February, 1970, p. 74.*

Looking back on the long line of picture story books created by Bill Peet, many of them very successful, one finds a single common denominator. Each story involves a lovable character, whether realistic or imaginary, who appeals to children in the seven to ten age group, for they all have one predominant quality—they are characters the children would like to be, or be with, to share in their stories and adventures. Homer, the farm pigeon, is typical of Peet's creative ability to present an animal character in a modern setting with whom children will identify. . . . Some of Bill Peet's American slang expressions and phrases will be sure to attract criticism and can be irritating, but this apart, Bill Peet's latest title with its eventful story and his usual excellent coloured crayon illustration will be read with great enjoyment.

Edward Hudson, in a review of "Fly Homer Fly," in Children's Book Review, *Vol. IV, No. 2, Summer, 1974, p. 56.*

THE WHINGDINGDILLY (1970)

Mr. Peet has consistently, year after year, created wonderfully funny and endearing picture stories for the young. He's still consistent in 1970, with his newest character, Scamp, who is tired of being a dog. Just wait until you see what he, with the help of a wacky witch, turns into—wait until you see what happens to him. No, don't wait. Go buy *The Whingdingdilly* and find out. (pp. 90-1)

A review of "The Whingdingdilly," in Publishers Weekly, *Vol. 197, No. 5, February 2, 1970, pp. 90-1.*

[Here] we have a dog who wants to be a horse. This is in the *Whingdingdilly*. . . . Bill Peet does well with his story and can do no wrong with his pictures. They let you see right through the page out onto the faraway roads and into the woods . . . and even into the heart of the dog Scamp who, wanting to be

From Buford the Little Bighorn, *written and illustrated by Bill Peet. Houghton Mifflin, 1967. Copyright © 1967 by William Peet. All rights reserved. Reprinted by permission of Houghton Mifflin Company.*

a horse, has some ridiculous adventures as a Whingdingdilly. Adults and children ought to see eye-to-eye on this one.

Guernsey Le Pelley, "Some People Who Want What They Haven't Got," in The Christian Science Monitor, *May 7, 1970, p. B2.*

The author-illustrator has lost none of his flair for entertainment in his story of Orvie Jarvis's old dog Scamp, who has moped about in a dark mood for weeks.... Zildy, the little witch, knows how to alter his condition; with magic incantations she turns him into a "Whingdingdilly"—exactly in Dr. Seuss style. Except for this episode in rhyme, the story rolls along in easy prose with a giddy, swinging abandon.

Virginia Haviland, in a review of "The Whingding-dilly," in The Horn Book Magazine, *Vol. XLVI, No. 3, June, 1970, p. 291.*

[A] lot of picture-books are ugly, deliberately ugly, these days. There's a spate of grotesque monsters. The whingdingdilly in Bill Peet's book stands out as being as disagreeable to name as to look at—it's got a camel's hump, an elephant's legs, zebra stripes, a giraffe's neck and bits of rhinoceros and reindeer. It's what a discontented dog gets turned into by a witch— and one understands the dog's relief when he finds himself a frowsy mongrel again.... Coarse and upsetting fantasy ... whose use I don't believe in.

Derwent May, "Nuns' Tale," in The Listener, *Vol. 86, No. 2224, November 11, 1971, p. 665.*

This is a very satisfactory book because the fantastic springs so naturally from the solid earth of an American farm. It is also completely successful in playing the very funny pictures against the accompaniment of a rather sad text, like the two hands on a piano.... This is one of this artist's most successful works, and if the pictures are still somewhat cartoonish, they lack the crudity of those in earlier books and are bright, clear and full of humour.

C. Martin, in a review of "The Whingdingdilly," in The Junior Bookshelf, *Vol. 36, No. 1, February, 1972, p. 27.*

THE WUMP WORLD (1970)

How nice it must be to be Bill Peet. To create a picture book secure in the happy knowledge that you will bring laughter to all the lucky children who will see your book! How nice it must be to have Bill Peet's talent: a talent that enables him to create new breeds of animals who are never grotesque, always endearing. And a talent that makes him one of the flying Wallandas, for he is able to keep his equilibrium as he carries a tale with a message (the message in *The Wump World* is the danger of our world going down the drain because of pollution) without once pattering into preaching. That, my friends, is tightrope walking!

A review of "The Wump World," in Publishers Weekly, *Vol. 198, No. 5, August 3, 1970, p. 60.*

The telling is adequate and the color crayon drawings are a delight in this Space Age idyll of pastures and pollution.... Peet peters out at the end of his forced allegory, with the non-climactic, vague: "... in time the green growth would wind its way up through the rubble. But the Wump World would never be quite the same." Also, readers may question certain glossed-over details: e.g., the mechanisms of the interplanetary travel; the precise time sequences; etc. But they will be captivated by the very energetic, humorous drawings which carry the book. The Wumps are extremely endearing, lovable-looking animals. The Pollutians, while human in form, are distinctly pig-faced. Their clothing is old-fashioned; their buildings, cars, planes, etc. sleek and futuristic in design. Particularly amusing is the jodphurs-sporting, becaped Pollutian leader, whose hat resembles a smokestack and who looks like an old-time movie director or a World War I martinet. The Pollutians' machines and spacecraft have voracious human expressions; their comically symbolic flag bears vertical stripes in the form of smokestacks and horizontal ones which evoke streams of smoke. On balance, this reproachful little view of the short-sightedness of "civilizers" and the harm they do to the natural world and innocent creatures is sufficiently humorous and lively to guarantee it an appreciative young reading, listening, and—especially—viewing audience.

> *Diane G. Stavn, in a review of "The Wump World,"*
> *in* School Library Journal, *an appendix to* Library
> Journal, *Vol. 17, No. 1, September, 1970, p. 95.*

An undisguised lament for our declining environment. To the placid pastoral planet of the fuzzy, moose-jowled little Wumps comes a fleet of fire-spitting monsters, discharging the Pollutians who plant their flag, loose their chewing, flattening, hoisting machines, and set building next to building, overpass next to underpass . . . while the Wumps, gone underground, tremble. Comes the day when smoke chokes the sky and even the World Chief is gagging, the Pollutians search out and em-

From The Caboose Who Got Loose, *written and illustrated by Bill Peet. Houghton Mifflin, 1971. Copyright © 1971 by Bill Peet. All rights reserved. Reprinted by permission of Houghton Mifflin Company.*

bark for a new and better world, leaving to the Wumps the dead buildings, the heaps of wreckage and rubble . . . and one grassy meadow, "all that was left of their lovely world" . . . Disenchantment coupled with virtual elimination of the comical makes it a queasy juvenile and can a Pollutian identify with a Wump when we are so obviously what he warns us against?

> *A review of "The Wump World," in* Kirkus Reviews,
> *Vol. XXXVIII, No. 17, September 1, 1970, p. 945.*

This delightful book was prepared as a cartoon of environmental pollution . . . The problems illustrated are realistic. The book is worthwhile for all to read beginning in elementary school. Even adults will enjoy it, for its message is more explicit than that of some adult treatises.

> *A review of "The Wump World," in* Science Books,
> *Vol. 6, No. 3, December, 1970, p. 227.*

Consciousness of people's impact on the environment has at last become an important topic of study and of action. There's a great range in the materials about ecology. Bill Peet's *The Wump World* . . . is a blatant "hard sell" fiction book in which fanciful creatures must figure out what to do when they're invaded by polluters. Didactic though it is, the book can be easily dramatized—one class used it effectively for a puppet play—and can have impact when you want a source for motivating interest in the subject. (pp. 381-82)

> *Sam Leaton Sebesta and William J. Iverson, "Non-*
> *fiction in the Curriculum," in their* Literature for
> Thursday's Child, *Science Research Associates, Inc.,*
> *1975, pp. 354-411.*

HOW DROOFUS THE DRAGON LOST HIS HEAD (1971)

Dinosaurs are scary. Dragons are, too, but even the most ferocious have a quality no dinosaur has ever claimed: they have charm. What or who could be more beguiling than Bill Peet's dragon with his underslung jaw? And when he celebrates his conversion from villain to hero by opening up his steam shovel of a mouth to laugh, all the world will laugh with him. That's Droofus for you. And that's Bill Peet, bless him.

> *A review of "How Droofus the Dragon Lost His*
> *Head," in* Publishers Weekly, *Vol. 199, No. 18, May*
> *3, 1971, p. 56.*

[Droofus is] Bill Peet's fantastically sympathetic dragonet. The gangly adolescent (who in flight resembles a primitive version of the SST) spends most of his time trying to find useful things to do, and hide from the King's men at the same time. The reader will never tire of watching our hero's attempts at peaceful coexistence—Droofus learning to like eating grass rather than grasshoppers, Droofus posing as a somewhat unconventional scarecrow, or plowing a farmer's field and sawing wood with his sharp, spiky tail.

And Bill Peet's jolly drawings are simply superb.

> *Jennifer Smith, "Dragons: 'I Seen 'em Myself!'" in*
> The Christian Science Monitor, *May 6, 1971, p. B5.*

How the cooperative dragon managed to accommodate the king without harm to himself is the source of a very entertaining tale—neat, compact, and thoroughly satisfying. The bright, full-color illustrations are in the author-illustrator's customary style and show an amiable, pink-winged dragon dominating almost every scene. (p. 280)

Beryl Robinson, in a review of "How Droofus the Dragon Lost His Head," in The Horn Book Magazine, *Vol. XLVII, No. 3, June, 1971, pp. 279-80.*

The air has been thick with the beating of dragon wings for a long time now and the least one expects from another dragon book is some measure of originality. This one doesn't really make it, either in the ungainly, semi-colloquial style of the story, or the sketchy cartoony pictures.

Ruth Marris, in a review of "How Droofus the Dragon Lost His Head," in The Spectator, *Vol. 229, No. 7533, November 11, 1972, p. 764.*

THE CABOOSE WHO GOT LOOSE (1971)

Bill Peet couldn't create a character without charm if he tried. Thank heavens he doesn't try, but rolls right along contributing charmers to children. Katy, the red caboose, who wants to stop riding the rails and settle down, could out-charm Helen Hayes. Katy ends up living in a tree and giving children still another Bill Peet to love.

A review of "The Caboose Who Got Loose," in Publishers Weekly, *Vol. 200, No. 6, August 9, 1971, p. 47.*

Peet is travelling a well-worn route here, and Katie's ultimate destination—a tree-top niche where she settles after becoming uncoupled and sliding backwards over the ledge—hardly seems worth the trip. It's all conveyed in unrelieved singsong that jerks and joggles along like the tired old train.

A review of "The Caboose Who Got Lost," in Kirkus Reviews, *Vol. XXXIX, No. 17, September 1, 1971, p. 937.*

[Katy Caboose's] problems are solved in a highly satisfying manner.

It's possible some of today's children may wonder what a steam engine is, or what use is a caboose, but Bill Peet rides full throttle with a happy story and his beautiful incredible crayon pictures.

Guernsey Le Pelley, in a review of "The Caboose Who Got Loose," in The Christian Science Monitor, *November 11, 1971, p. B3.*

Peet's colorful crayon drawings are humorous but the rhymed text is only fair, and there's little to interest the intended picture book audience in either Katy's plight or its resolution since most kids don't equate isolated peace and quiet with happiness.

Barbara S. Miller, in a review of "The Caboose Who Got Loose," in School Library Journal, *an appendix to* Library Journal, *Vol. 18, No. 4, December, 1971, p. 54.*

THE SPOOKY TAIL OF PREWITT PEACOCK (1972)

The diction has about as much verve as the tired pun in the title and Prewitt ends up all too predictably "proud" (with the other peacocks "behind him 100 per cent"). Peet's visualizations of the misfit Prewitt (whose tail resembles a bushy eyebrowed witch doctor's mask) and the gummy old tiger he scares right out of the bush are somehow restful in their soft, crayony color and absolute literal-mindedness—and they have the dubious virtue of making no demands on the imagination.

A review of "The Spooky Tale of Prewitt the Peacock," in Kirkus Reviews, *Vol. XLI, No. 3, February 1, 1973, p. 111.*

The daffy drawings (including surely the least ferocious tiger that has ever leaped from behind a bush) compensate for a routine story line.

Children especially liked the pictures showing Prewitt's dream of giving up his tail: in this dream an elephant without a trunk, a giraffe without a neck, then a camel without a hump parade by. . . . On the other hand, missing altogether is any illustration of the climactic confrontation when the tiger finally lays eyes on the spooky tail. All we see is the tiger running away.

Prewitt's literary ancestor is Rudolph the Red-nosed Reindeer: both are poor creatures, set apart from their fellows by a physical oddity, but both ultimately save the day and Go Down in History.

David K. Willis, "More Fun Than Playing," in The Christian Science Monitor, *May 2, 1973, p. B3.*

A conventional but pleasant tale of a peacock named Prewitt, who discovered that even the most maligned feature can turn into the most admired asset. . . . No one really loves a hangdog peacock; but the toothless tiger Travis is very appealing. There is sufficient movement in both story and illustrations to sustain interest. (pp. 260-61)

Sheryl B. Andrews, in a review of "The Spooky Tail of Prewitt Peacock," in The Horn Book Magazine, *Vol. XLIX, No. 3, June, 1973, pp. 260-61.*

Bill Peet is always engaging, very funny and never dull. Prewitt the peacock is in the tradition of the ugly duckling and all other "under-dogs". . . . Of course, it all comes right in the end as all good fairy stories must.

A gem of a book that is ideal for reading aloud to five and six year olds, and one that would enhance any classroom bookshelves.

J. Russell, in a review of "The Spooky Tail of Prewitt Peacock," in The Junior Bookshelf, *Vol. 43, No. 4, August, 1979, p. 198.*

MERLE THE HIGH FLYING SQUIRREL (1974)

Peet's latest yarn concerns a timid city squirrel named Merle, lured by park bench tales about the beautiful big trees out West—"standin' there for thousands of years just storin' up quiet." Merle decides to follow the telephone lines West, and just as he has concluded that he'll never get out of the city he is carried off on the tail of a kite he has tried to untangle from the wires, sailing and whirling through all kinds of landscape and weather until he lands at his initial destination, on top of a giant redwood. Peet's artless crayon pictures of Merle's sweeping flight to the clear Western forest through factory smoke and rainstorm and whirlwind will carry his substantial following through this mere wisp of a story.

A review of "Merle the Flying Squirrel," in Kirkus Reviews, *Vol. XLII, No. 5, March 1, 1974, p. 240.*

The plot is frail but the pictures are colorful and vigorous, with the contrast between urban pollution and clean, fresh countryside giving variety—and also giving Peet an opportunity to reiterate the anti-pollution message found in other of his books.

Zena Sutherland, in a review of "Merle the High Flying Squirrel," in Bulletin of the Center for Children's Books, *Vol. 28, No. 1, September, 1974, p. 15.*

A dull story about a timid city squirrel who sets out for the West. . . . The thin plot is slow moving and, though Peet's familiar crayon pictures give **Merle** . . . a boost, they can't keep this lackluster effort aloft.

Carol Chatfield, in a review of "Merle the High Flying Squirrel," in School Library Journal, *an appendix to* Library Journal, *Vol. 21, No. 1, September, 1974, p. 67.*

CYRUS THE UNSINKABLE SEA SERPENT (1975)

Challenged to go out and wreck a ship, sea serpent Cyrus decides to protect one instead when he hears an old man putting a curse on a vessel full of poor people bound for a new land across the sea. Cyrus puffs the Primrose out of the doldrums, sees her through a squall by making a life preserver of his body, smashes a threatening pirate ship, and finally tows his charge to shore when she loses her sails in a battle. Whereupon the landed passengers wave and cheer from atop a huge rock and Cyrus, "very tired for some reason or other," goes off to rest for a month on a Caribbean island. Cyrus won't make history but Peet's crayoned storms, smashed hulls and volleys keep this moving at a comfortable clip while the general amiability makes it easy to drift along in Cyrus' wake.

A review of "Cyrus the Unsinkable Sea Serpent," in Kirkus Reviews, *Vol. XLIII, No. 5, March 1, 1975, p. 237.*

Bill Peet's books are not for people who don't like do-gooders. Chivalry is not dead in his world—despite occasional lapses—and knights errant are as likely to be dragons as anything else. . . .

A fine storyteller and artist, Bill Peet is here at his best. And Cyrus is a joy to watch, whether engaged in superhuman deeds or floating, pooped, on the crest of the waves.

Jennifer Farley Smith, "A Dragon Who Wanted to Be Noticed," in The Christian Science Monitor, *May 7, 1975, p. B4.*

If you like your picture story books to be rather more traditional then there is no better choice than this latest story from an author/illustrator who has been delighting children for generations. . . . Fun to read aloud with big pictures on every page illustrating every detail.

A review of "Cyrus the Unsinkable Sea Serpent," in Books for Your Children, *Vol. 13, No. 1, Winter, 1977, p. 12.*

THE GNATS OF KNOTTY PINE (1975)

The Gnats of Knotty Pine is a sharp, uncompromising story against hunting, so it probably won't be a big seller in homes with a moosehead over the mantel or antler hatracks in the hall. It is full of those audacious, loving caricatures of animals which Bill Peet does so well in free, crayon style.

The story almost has a plot. The animals are worried about the start of hunting season when the Gnats come in and save the day. Not only are the hunters completely defeated but not one single Gnat got swatted! These may have been very noble Gnats, but they're not on my endangered species list.

Guernsey Le Pelley, "Gnats Swarm to the Rescue in Knotty Pine Tale," in The Christian Science Monitor, *November 5, 1975, p. B8.*

Although lacking the rollicking humor and rhyme of many of his former books, this will have Peet fans chuckling over the hunters' rush for safety and the V formation signaling victory on the part of the gnats. Bright full-color crayon illustrations in the artist's familiar style will add to picturebook collections where his work is popular.

Barbara Elleman, in a review of "The Gnats of Knotty Pine," in The Booklist *Vol. 72, No. 6, November 15, 1975, p. 457.*

Peet clearly regards hunting as killing for fun and doesn't hesitate to propagandize. . . . The message is too blatant—even for those who share Peet's view—and Margolis' *Homer the Hunter* (Macmillan, 1972) and Duvoisin's *The Happy Hunter* (Lothrop, 1961) tell the same tale more amusingly.

Alice Ehlert, in a review of "The Gnats of Knotty Pine," in School Library Journal, *Vol. 22, No. 5, January, 1976, p. 39.*

An ingenious story of how a group of gnats unite to drive off the hunters from the hill called Knotty Pine. The robust theme, lively illustrations and entertaining story can serve as enrichment or as a source of group discussion around the concept of working together as has proven successful in such stories as Lionni's *Swimmy* and Aesop's *The Lion and the Rat*. Highly recommended for Bill Peet fans and other students grades K-4.

James A. Norsworthy, Jr., in a review of "The Gnats of Knotty Pine," in Catholic Library World, *Vol. 47, No. 7, February, 1976, p. 310.*

[**The Gnats of Knotty Pine**] shows that "when a billion gnats get their heads together it adds up to one big brain." Like a horde of Tom Thumbs they demonstrate that small is beautiful by driving the huntsmen out of the forest and back to their cars (registration number: OGRE). There's a cartoon quality about these crayon figures (possums, bears and jack rabbits sitting in rows on a log), as in the humour: "this is no time for small talk, gnats." But there's nothing hip or sentimental about the wrong end of the barrel of a gun.

Peter Fanning, "Down to Earth," in The Times Educational Supplement, *No. 3282, June 2, 1978, p. 21.*

BIG BAD BRUCE (1977)

Big Bad Bruce, who finds cheap thrills rolling boulders at small animals, is shrunk from bear- to chipmunk-size after annoying a small witch. The now-huge rabbits and quails of Forevergreen Forest have their revenge on the former bully before he's rescued by Roxy the witch. "She soon grew fond of the tiny bear," so she adopts him and keeps him tiny. Though we're set up for a repentant Bruce, "little bears have short memories," and the last page finds him happily rolling pebbles at insects in a flower-forest. While decidedly a moral tale, it's subtly done; the message comes across, not by punishing the bully, but through a sympathetic look at his victims. Peet's workmanlike illustration is part of the calculated appeal.

A review of "Big Bad Bruce," in Kirkus Reviews, *Vol. XLV, No. 4, February 15, 1977, p. 163.*

The best elements of a Saturday-morning cartoon show are delivered in this picture-book story which will satisfy young readers and listeners as well as the adults who share it with them. The language of the text is almost musical, with lots of words used for the sheer pleasure or appropriateness of their sounds.... The illustrations are colorful and amusing. Sure to be enjoyed by slightly older readers for its humor and language, this is also a winner for story-telling. (pp. 115-16)

Lauren L. Wohl, in a review of "Big Bad Bruce," in Children's Book Review Service, *Vol. 5, No. 12, Spring, 1977, pp. 115-16.*

The scrabbly illustrations are vigorous and colorful, and the story has vitality, but the ending seems weak—not because it lacks a punitive, didactic note (children may enjoy Bruce's incorrigible mischievousness) but because it is anticlimactic structurally.

Zena Sutherland, in a review of "Big Bad Bruce," in Bulletin of the Center for Children's Books, *Vol. 30, No. 10, June, 1977, p. 163.*

In **Big Bad Bruce** the "human" conflict involves a high-spirited grizzly who makes a sport of frightening small animals by shoving rocks down hills. A witch's spell ultimately shrinks him to chipmunk size, and he is rescued only after the former victims have had their revenge. This rigorous justice, Bruce's new diminutive stature, and the playful inclusion of magic and incantation will appeal to children. But the plot's chief surprise is that Bad Bruce ends up as insensitive to his new neighbors (beetles and grasshoppers) as he was to his old ones. Bruce is not the typical reformed character of fiction, but a credible and humorously depicted community nuisance.

Bill Peet's illustrations are vigorous and aggressive animations. His technique of line-over-color varies from object to object, serving to enhance movement and textural diversity. Most important, the drawings express great energy.

Donnarae MacCann and Olga Richard, in a review of "Big Bad Bruce," in Wilson Library Bulletin, *Vol. 52, No. 2, October, 1977, p. 179.*

Anybody who has read and enjoyed a Bill Peet picture book before will not be disappointed with this one. At the same time as telling a story, with a proper plot, and drawing delightful illustrations, a moral is told in such an unobtrusive fashion that children will only be aware of what an enjoyable story it is.

G. L. Hughes, in a review of "Big Bad Bruce," in The Junior Bookshelf, *Vol. 44, No. 2, April, 1980, p. 63.*

ELI (1978)

Who but Bill Peet would cast a flock of vultures as a decrepit old lion's best friends? Lion Eli, reduced to eating leftovers, is plagued by the vultures' squawking presence—until, roused by an especially ear-splitting scream, he discovers that the poor bird is screaming for help, and he drives off the jackal attacking her. Now, to his disgust, the worshipful vultures follow him everywhere. "In some way," they tell him, "we old birds might prove useful to you some day." No sooner said than a band of spear-carrying Zoobangas enter on the seedy lion's

From How Droofus the Dragon Lost His Head, *written and illustrated by Bill Peet. Houghton Mifflin, 1971. Copyright © 1971 by William B. Peet. All rights reserved. Reprinted by permission of Houghton Mifflin Company.*

trail—and the vultures, persuading him to play dead, take up their customary corpse-side watch. Everybody likes to see hunters foiled, see losers win, see a promise kept, see baddies do good or uglies look good—which is, collectively, why Peet's latest doesn't have to be his best (they aren't always) to win friends and please lots of people. What's lacking is the single compelling image that makes a book like **Buford the Little Bighorn** memorable.

A review of "Eli," in Kirkus Reviews, *Vol. XLVI, No. 7, April 1, 1978, p. 368.*

Bill Peet has done it again with **Eli**.... In lilting prose, the strange relationship of a lion with a band of vultures unfolds to the delight of all. Third-graders who listened to it chuckled over "Tumbaba" and "Kumbumbazango" and loved it as much as Peet's other works. Though I personally prefer his stories in verse, Peet's witty turn of phrase and his zany illustrations guarantee that this will not sit on the shelf.

Janice P. Patterson, in a review of "Eli," in Children's Book Review Service, *Vol. 6, No. 11, June, 1978, p. 105.*

Peet's animal portraits are as expressive as ever. Frequent use of the vernacular may grate on adult ears, but the language is generally vigorous: "In one frantic leap and with a wild swing of a paw, Eli caught the jackal with a clout to the snout." Alliteration and internal rhyme, twists of phrase—"every cat for himself"—and nonsensical names, such as "tumbaba tree" and "gumbazunka swamp" spark a rather predictable text. His depiction, however, of the marauding Zoobanga tribe, complete with loincloth, headdress, and spear, edges close to a stereotype.

Charlotte W. Draper, in a review of "Eli," in The Horn Book Magazine, *Vol. LIV, No. 3, June, 1978, p. 267.*

For the sake of humor, most of us willingly give special license to cartoonists and the conventions of caricature. But the fatuity of Peet's imaginary Africans is a painful and familiar type of ridicule; his drawings represent a shorthand that reiterates cultural bias.

Olga Richard and Donnarae MacCann, in a review of "Eli," in Wilson Library Bulletin, *Vol. 53, No. 10, June, 1979, p. 710.*

The same contrast [as in John Dyke's *Pigwig and the Pirates*] between a rather stilted text and energetic pictures is found in Bill Peet's *Eli*. . . . The story is set in a comic strip kind of African country. . . . When the Zoobanga hunters leave over the horizon they are comic strip natives too. It is a pity that this kind of crudity is resorted to, and that Bill Peet's funny quick pictures in nice crayony colours serve such a tired text.

Myra Barrs, "Anomie in Dreamland," in The Times Educational Supplement, *No. 3336, May 23, 1980, p. 29.*

COWARDLY CLYDE   (1979)

A mundane picture book tale of a Knight, Sir Galavant, and his cowardly horse, Clyde, who go to do battle with a local ogre. Clyde runs scared, then recovers his courage sufficiently to save the day (and the Knight). Moderately humorous full-color pictures help to carry the action along. But out of the many children's books Bill Peet has on the market, this is not one of his noteworthy attempts.

Hara L. Seltzer, in a review of "Cowardly Clyde," in School Library Journal, *Vol. 25, No. 7, March, 1979, p. 128.*

Peet's approximately 25 comedies have all been warmly received by readers who revel in the author-illustrator's originality and eccentric point of view. His latest offers plenty of what can be called horse laughs in the absurd adventures of Sir Galavant and his charger, Clyde. . . . The end is unexpectedly gratifying. The story's attractions include racy cartoons in bold colors.

A review of "Cowardly Clyde," in Publishers Weekly, *Vol. 215, No. 16, April 16, 1979, p. 75.*

The new book, an adventure story told in picture and text, is one of Peet's best creations. With a play on names, the brave Sir Galavant and his cowardly steed Clyde are introduced. . . . The exploit is entertainingly described with the exaggerations of a tall tale and with such mouth-filling words as "whuffling and gruffling" and "'huffling snuffling.'" The text and the full-color drawings perfectly complement each other in the hyperbolic drama. (pp. 294-95)

Virginia Haviland, in a review of "Cowardly Clyde," in The Horn Book Magazine, *Vol. LV, No. 3, June, 1979, pp. 294-95.*

The tale is nonsensical, but the combination of swashbuckling knight and anti-hero Clyde, and the action that ends in victory,

should appeal to the read-aloud audience. The writing is brisk and casual; the illustrations are colorful and vigorous.

Zena Sutherland, in a review of "Cowardly Clyde," in Bulletin of the Center for Children's Books, *Vol. 32, No. 11, July-August, 1979, p. 198.*

ENCORE FOR ELEANOR   (1981)

Too old to perform her tricks any longer, Eleanor the Elephant is retired from the circus and sent to the zoo. There she languishes, missing the excitement, applause, costumes, and star rating of the center ring. One day, however, Eleanor finishes a sketch begun by a young girl and quickly finds herself top attraction as resident artist at the zoo. Peet's line work comes to life with crayon color spreads that are large enough to be used in group presentations, simply yet carefully executed, and typical of the artist's direct appeal. Humor is injected through facial and body expressions of both the people and the animals; and the circus and zoo auras are vividly captured, making this not only a prerequisite for field trips but also a story that will elicit empathy for a "discarded" character. (pp. 966-67)

Barbara Elleman, in a review of "Encore for Eleanor," in Booklist, *Vol. 77, No. 13, March 1, 1981, pp. 966-67.*

Bill Peet continues to charm his audience with his watercolor illustrations, which complement the story. Those who are used to Peet's comic, often slapstick style of writing may be disappointed with *Eleanor,* for this is a sensitive story that very quietly delivers a message. This book will be well received and read in both large and small groups. It will have a little extra impact if its theme is discussed with the reader.

Fellis L. Jordan, in a review of "Encore for Eleanor," in Children's Book Review Service, *Vol. 9, No. 11, June, 1981, p. 94.*

Stilt-walking elephant Eleanor, retired from the circus, becomes a star again at the zoo—by (gulp) drawing pictures. It's not one of Peet's livelier or likelier inventions—once he's gotten poor Eleanor out of the circus . . . and into a cozy pen in the zoo . . . , the story just peters out in the sort of solution that anyone might have come up with: a teenage girl comes to draw the animals, then throws down her charcoal in disgust when her rhinoceros-subject moves; Eleanor, who's been watching, picks up the charcoal and—presto!—starts drawing her old circus comrades. . . . As usual, the pictures make the cunning most of Eleanor's changing states of mind (or, see just her derriere when she's feeling like "an overgrown wrinkled ugly big bloop of a thing" in the zoo). There are still some good lines, then, and some good pictures, for the (understandably) avid Peet following.

A review of "Encore for Eleanor," in Kirkus Reviews, *Vol. XLIX, No. 14, July 15, 1981, p. 871.*

Following the pattern of a typical Peet tale, Eleanor's dejection yielded to elation when in a triumph of self-discovery she found fulfillment in an exhilarating new career. Turning to pachyderm geriatrics, the author-artist proves that he has lost neither his spontaneity nor his skill; Eleanor is as appealing and expressively drawn as are his other celebrated characters.

Ethel L. Heins, in a review of "Encore for Eleanor," in The Horn Book Magazine, *Vol. LVII, No. 4, August, 1981, p. 416.*

[Bill Peet] is a master of economy. The text and pictures are beautifully balanced in *Encore for Eleanor*. . . . A nice story, told with the right seriousness of tone and with plenty of variety in the presentation.

> *M. Crouch, in a review of "Encore for Eleanor," in* The Junior Bookshelf, *Vol. 47, No. 2, April, 1983, p. 69.*

THE LUCKIEST ONE OF ALL (1982)

A great favorite of young readers, for very good reasons, Peet is at his most inventive and astonishing best in his new book, illustrated by jazzy, skillful, colorful pictures. In verses that sing in perfect cadence, we hear from a boy who wishes he were a bird. . . . But a harassed thrush declares her work is never-ending and that she would love to be a lazy old fish . . . who envies a turtle, who would be happy as a frog pining to be a lion. A truck would rather be a train; a train wishes it were a plane and so it goes until a cat, bored with the cushy life, confesses, "To be a small boy would really be great, / A lively young sprite of age seven or eight."

> *A review of "The Luckiest One of All," in* Publishers Weekly, *Vol. 221, No. 3, January 15, 1982, p. 98.*

Peet's rhymed text flows fairly smoothly as he catalogs the complaints of [the] various entities and makes his low-key point about the merits of wanting what the other guy's got. Kids will have fun trying to guess what each speaker, given his or her druthers, would choose to be—and deciding who really is "the luckiest one of all." The full-color pictures that dominate the pages are pure Peet—the faces he's worked naturally into the inanimate speakers, adding a particularly clever touch.

> *Nancy Palmer, in a review of "The Luckiest One of All," in* School Library Journal, *Vol. 28, No. 7, March, 1982, p. 137.*

Message and medium become partners in a carefully crafted, joyous interpretation of the familiar observation that the grass is always greener on the other side of the fence. Told in rhyming couplets, the story is developed as an extended fable. . . . The rhymes are unforced; the rhythm infectious. Particularly notable is Bill Peet's gift for personifying objects through the integration of details into a series of marvelously expressive faces. Thus, on closer examination a craggy mountain side appears to be a disgruntled, white-haired hermit; a barn, a straw-haired countryman longing for excitement; and a street lamp, a down-at-the-heels denizen of the city whose "'brightness is wasted in the glitter and glare / Of a hundred street signs flashing on everywhere.'" The book exuberantly proves that humor can be elegant as well as entertaining.

> *Mary M. Burns, in a review of "The Luckiest One of All," in* The Horn Book Magazine, *Vol. LVIII, No. 3, June, 1982, p. 281.*

[*The Luckiest One of All* is] illustrated by crayoned line drawings that have a free, rakish line and humor. . . . This is a one-gag extension, but it has a concept that may appeal to children, and the verses, while their scansion is at times a bit shaky, do have rhythm.

> *Zena Sutherland, in a review of "The Luckiest One of All," in* Bulletin of the Center for Children's Books, *Vol. 35, No. 11, July-August, 1982, p. 212.*

Bill Peet is [in the American picture-book] tradition. Indeed one might say that he helped to create it, for he has been around for a long time. . . . Each wish [in the text of *The Luckiest One of All*] is accompanied by a strong, colourful and amusing drawing, executed with virtuosity and high spirits. Here is the true professional at work, assured, confident in his powers.

> *M. Crouch, in a review of "The Luckiest One of All," in* The Junior Bookshelf, *Vol. 48, No. 1, February, 1984, p. 14.*

NO SUCH THINGS (1983)

The highly individual books by Peet have made him beloved by children of all ages. His latest is like a three-ring circus, with color cartoons of "no such things" displayed in zingy, laugh-out-loud situations and described in verses that beg to be chanted and shared with pals. . . . [Some] baddies that never were are the pie-faced Pazeeks, spiky-tailed Tizzy, great Gullagaloops, etc., all a joy for little kids and a cinch to banish fears of imaginary monsters.

> *A review of "No Such Things," in* Publishers Weekly, *Vol. 223, No. 19, May 13, 1983, p. 56.*

Peet introduces a hilarious array of characters reminiscent of those who inhabit Dr. Seuss' books. . . . The descriptions of all [the] outlandish creatures are elaborated in likable verse, and the energetic full-color pictures are guaranteed to tickle individual or collective funny bones.

> *Ilene Cooper, in a review of "No Such Things," in* Booklist, *Vol. 79, No. 19, June 1, 1983, p. 1278.*

Fifteen creatures the likes of which Darwin never dreamed of display their peculiarities on the pages of a picture book that in humor and imagination rivals the work of Dr. Seuss. . . . And if you don't believe that the beasts described in the verses could exist, the vigorous, full-color drawings just might change your mind.

> *Kate M. Flanagan, in a review of "No Such Things," in* The Horn Book Magazine, *Vol. LIX, No. 4, August, 1983, p. 434.*

Wildly extravagant creatures in Seuss style (silly names, outlandish anatomical features) are the subject of double-page spreads with descriptive verse. The pictures are amusing, the verse is often metrically faulty; for example, "The Juggarums have a most impolite way / of overpowering their high-flying, lacy-winged prey / They use their strong breath, one potent *ker-puff* / to stun dragonflies if they fly close enough." The concepts of the nonsensical beasts are more impressive than the text; the pictures should appeal because of their animation and their expressions.

> *Zena Sutherland, in a review of "No Such Things," in* Bulletin of the Center for Children's Books, *Vol. 37, No. 4, December, 1983, p. 75.*

PAMELA CAMEL (1984)

Once more, Peet's color cartoons and funny, moving story demonstrate his genius for creating a picture book with more pith than the average. Kids will giggle while they sympathize with denigrated Pamela Camel, despised as the one no-talent animal at the circus that owns her. Enough already of sneers and insults. Pamela runs away. Sheltering from a storm in a

From Big Bad Bruce, *written and illustrated by Bill Peet. Houghton Mifflin, 1977. Copyright © 1977 by William B. Peet. All rights reserved. Reprinted by permission of Houghton Mifflin Company.*

rustic hut, she can't forget the break in a rail track she has noticed and the danger it can cause. Trembling with fright, Pamela nevertheless quits her hideaway and plants herself on the track where a train is racing toward her. It's nice to learn that courage is rewarded and what the future holds for the "stupid, ugly, ill-tempered camel."

A review of "Pamela Camel," in Publishers Weekly, *Vol. 225, No. 4, January 27, 1984, p. 75.*

Peet brings home his message about everyone having a sense of worth in a gentle, humorous way. As always, children will be attracted to the bright colors, sense of action and drama, and expressive faces characteristic of this highly popular author/artist's work.

Barbara Elleman, in a review of "Pamela Camel," in Booklist, *Vol. 80, No. 15, April 1, 1984, p. 1120.*

Economically narrated and embellished with meticulously executed, colorfully expressive drawings, Pamela's story is a joyous exaltation of the humble, presented as good old-fashioned melodrama. Although unabashedly romantic, it is not maudlin but succeeds in eliciting appropriate responses because the comic quality infusing every page acts as a controlling force as well as a leavening agent. Blithe-spirited, bright, and best of all, a toast to the ornery and the ordinary who can—given a chance—become super-special. (p. 322)

Mary M. Burns, in a review of "Pamela Camel," in The Horn Book Magazine, *Vol. LX, No. 3, June, 1984, pp. 321-22.*

It's all a bit pat, and Pamela's side trip to a deserted barn is pointless. The illustrations—typical scratchy Peet cartoons—rely on exaggerated mugging to make their effect and add little to the luckluster text.

Kristi Thomas Beavin, in a review of "Pamela Camel," in School Library Journal, *Vol. 30, No. 10, August, 1984, p. 64.*

Back, once again, in Bill Peet's perky bright interpretation, is a misunderstood and unrecognized hero, a near casualty, and a wonderfully satisfying ending. The easy style is a sensation of sound, lilting word choices, short humorous phrases and vibrant action words. The text is great fun to read aloud . . . even to oneself! (p. 423)

Ronald A. Jobe, in a review of "Pamela Camel," in Language Arts, *Vol. 62, No. 4, April, 1985, pp. 422-23.*

THE KWEEKS OF KOOKATUMDEE (1985)

While the competition strains for zaniness, Peet manages (in his less topical entries, at least) to pull off one after another genuine nonsense fable. The kweeks of the jungle island of Kookatumdee are big-beaked, small-winged birds forced, by their peculiar anatomy, into utter dependence on the ploppolop fruits that fall from the island's single tree. The problem of dividing the limited, erratic food supply is aggravated when one kweek, troublemaker Jed, seizes more than his share. Jed grows fat, while the others shrivel; a spunky little kweek named Quentin leads an attack; and, pursued by the irate Jed, he finds himself "at the edge of a bluff, with nowhere to go" . . . and flies!! "Now come on everyone! Flap your wings and just try it! / We're all light as a feather from our starvation diet." Leaving heavy Jed behind, they find another island, with plenty of ploppolops for all—but no inducement to overeat: they "enjoyed flying too much for that." Maybe that last line is a gentle nudge, maybe not: the whole moves along on sympathetic projection, life-and-death challenges, and high hilarity.

> *A review of "The Kweeks of Kookatumdee," in* Kirkus Reviews, *Juvenile Issue, Vol. LIII, Nos. 1-5, March 1, 1985, p. J-9.*

Peet's legions of fans can't get enough of his inimitable rhymes and wacky creatures, usually wrestling with problems they conquer heroically, after a few hilarious and ineffectual jousts with fate. Such is the story of the flightless birds on the island of Kookatumdee. . . . [The] story's ending is a real treat. Colorful pictures add mirth to the swift verses. (pp. 81-2)

> *A review of "The Kweeks of Kookatumdee," in* Publishers Weekly, *Vol. 227, No. 16, April 19, 1985, pp. 81-2.*

Humorous cartoon-like colored pencil illustrations combine well with the rhyming text. As in past books, Peet uses some original words, such as *Tumbuzzaroo* and *Kookatumdee*. Yet this book is not as imaginative as his previous books. The message is heavy-handed and often the meter and rhyme are forced. *The Kweeks* . . . will probably not win any new followers for the author, but readers who are already Peet fans will welcome this addition.

> *Dona Weisman, in a review of "The Kweeks of Kookatumdee," in* School Library Journal, *Vol. 31, No. 9, May, 1985, p. 81.*

ZELLA, ZACK, AND ZODIAC (1986)

With wit and wisdom, Peet delivers gentle morals using animals to demonstrate human foibles. And what wonderful, whimsical animals they are. The author's 31st book proves the adage, "One good turn deserves another." A zebra named Zella adopts and cares for a baby ostrich, who has hatched all alone. When Zella gives birth to a rather awkward baby, the now-grown ostrich saves the zebra colt from a lion and protects him until he is on his own. The story is told in verse, perfect for reading aloud. Peet takes Aesop one step further: he doubles the fun of his delightful stories with mirthful full-color illustrations. Whether he's drawing a perplexed ostrich chick, a baby zebra with hooves too big, or a foiled lion, Peet once again adds much laughter to his tale.

> *A review of "Zella, Zack, and Zodiac," in* Publishers Weekly, *Vol. 229, No. 17, April 25, 1986, p. 72.*

[*Zella, Zack, and Zodiac* is reminiscent] of Dr. Seuss' *Horton Hatches the Egg* (Random, 1940). . . . Written in Peet's usual nonsensical and poetic fashion, this story appears to be wordy and preposterous at times yet comical in its own endearing way. Colored crayon and pencil drawings accompany the text, increasing the humor of the tale. The uncluttered illustrations, showing animals and wide expanses of sky and grass, make the story especially suitable for reading aloud to primary grade listeners.

> *Rita Soltan, in a review of "Zella, Zack, and Zodiac," in* School Library Journal, *Vol. 32, No. 9, May, 1986, p. 83.*

Not Peet's neatest effort, this does have the narrative rhyme appeal and ready action of all his work but also features several too many syllables in several too many lines, along with a fairly disjointed plot. . . . Although adult readers will have their mouths full getting around all those words, children will no doubt respond to Peet's sure sense of the ridiculous, as in a double-page spread featuring the black-and-white ostrich rising righteously above the level of the black-and-white striped herd.

> *A review of "Zella, Zack, and Zodiac," in* Bulletin of the Center for Children's Books, *Vol. 39, No. 10, June, 1986, p. 194.*

Ann (Lane) Petry

1908-

Black American author of nonfiction and fiction.

Petry is best known for her objective and carefully researched presentation of black slavery in two biographies for a junior-high audience. Prompted by her dismay with textbook stereotypes of slaves as passive, content, and obedient, she wrote *Harriet Tubman, Conductor on the Underground Railroad,* **which spotlights the celebrated black woman who helped more than three hundred slaves reach freedom, and** *Tituba of Salem Village,* **which focuses on a young girl's trial as a witch in 1692. These well-crafted character studies reflect Petry's enthusiasm for the richness of black American history, provide insight into the nature of bigotry and oppression, and give a positive message of hope and pride to her readers. In her adult novels and short stories, Petry also explores racial themes. She has written two additional books for children:** *The Drugstore Cat,* **a picture book about a cat who learns to control her anger and use it wisely, and** *Legends of the Saints,* **a collection of short biographies for middle grade readers which focuses on victims of religious persecution.**

Critics praise Petry's skillful narration, perceptive characterizations, and ability to sustain suspense. Though her reputation as a children's author centers on two biographies, the controlled prose and calm poignancy with which she invests the sturdy personalities and dramatic events of these works has brought Petry respect and recognition.

(See also *Contemporary Literary Criticism,* **Vols. l, 7, 18;** *Something about the Author,* **Vol. 5;** *Contemporary Authors New Revision Series,* **Vol. 4; and** *Contemporary Authors,* **Vols. 5-8, rev. ed.)**

Courtesy of Ann Petry

AUTHOR'S COMMENTARY

[The following excerpt is from an edited version of a talk Petry gave at the New York Public Library on November 16, 1964.]

All too often our world fits Herodotus' description of a Greek market as "a place set apart for people to go and cheat each other on oath." That aspect of the world is revealed in newspapers, on the radio, on television.

The world of children's books obviously offers another set of values, for it is a world diametrically opposed to the Greek market place—and it is something more.

The same Herodotus who described the market place was, according to Edith Hamilton, the first person to give Greece the idea that an expression in prose could have the worth of a line of poetry. The expression in prose of a poetic idea is the something-more always to be found in the best books for children, books that seem to have been written by people who had a touch of honey on the lips. If you are willing to accept the Greek idea that a true poet's lips are touched with honey, then many of the people who write children's books are poets. (p. 147)

Certainly I have tried to add [to my own books] the something-more for which I have expressed admiration. My only comment is to say sadly that a writer's reach always exceeds his grasp.

I don't know that I have ever questioned my own intentions, and the degree to which I have carried them out, quite as seriously as I did just a few weeks ago. I had been at the library in the small town where I live. As I was about to leave, a little girl came in to return a book of mine, a book I wrote about Harriet Tubman. She was carrying it hugged close to her chest. She laid it down on the table, and the librarian said to her, "You know, this is Mrs. Petry, the author of the book you are returning."

I must confess that I was dismayed, because though I have received letters from children and from adults who had read my books, and though I have had children tell me they enjoyed something I had written, I had never had a face-to-face encounter with a young reader who was actually holding one of my books. The child looked at me, and I looked at her—she didn't say anything and neither did I. I didn't know what to say. Neither did she. Finally she reached out and touched my arm, ever so gently, and then drew her hand back as though she were embarrassed. I copied her gesture, touching her gently on the arm, because I felt it would serve to indicate that I approved her gesture.

Then I left the library, but I left it thinking to myself: What have I said to this child in this book? What was I saying in the other books I have written for children and for young people? What am I really saying to them? Of course, I have been saying, Let's take a look at slavery. I said it in *Harriet Tubman* and again in *Tituba of Salem Village.*

But what else was I saying? Over and over again, I have said: These are people. Look at them, listen to them; watch Harriet Tubman in the nineteenth century, a heroic woman, a rescuer of other slaves. Look at Tituba in the seventeenth century, a slave involved in the witchcraft trials in Salem Village. Look at them and remember them. Remember for what a long, long time black people have been in this country, have been a part of America: a sturdy, indestructible, wonderful part of America, woven into its heart and into its soul.

What else was there in these books for the child who had touched my arm? Why did she touch my arm?

Perhaps, I thought, because there is something more in the books than the excitement that lies naturally, innately in the stories themselves. These women were slaves. I hoped that I had made them come alive, turned them into real people. I tried to make history speak across the centuries in the voices of people—young, old, good, evil, beautiful, ugly.

There is, however, something more than that. For there is a common ground on which all the people involved in the world of children's books—authors, illustrators, editors, publishers, librarians, teachers, critics, and reviewers—there is a common ground on which we meet, or perhaps I should say a belief that we share with that little girl in the library in Old Saybrook.

The shared belief? The common ground? What is it? It is the very antithesis of Herodotus' description of a Greek market as a place where men go to cheat each other on oath. This belief is, I think, summed up by Archibald MacLeish in that magnificent book, *The Dialogues of Archibald MacLeish and Mark Van Doren,* edited by Warren V. Bush:

> I know for myself if I were put through the orange squeezer and squeezed to the point where the pips began to squeak . . . (and he repeats this) I do think if I were squeezed down to the point where the pips began to emit high, shrill sounds, I would have to say, that what I surely do believe in is the unspeakable, infinite, immeasurable, spiritual capacity of that thing called a man; a capacity which expresses itself in so many ways, but expresses itself nowhere more perfectly than in the capacity for friendship, which is really a capacity for love.

(pp. 150-51)

Ann Petry, "The Common Ground," in The Horn Book Magazine, *Vol. XLI, No. 2, April, 1965, pp. 147-51.*

THE DRUGSTORE CAT (1949)

Buzzie, that round, fat, smoke-colored kitten, will surely endear himself to every 7- to 10-year-old who doesn't positively hate cats. They will like him especially because he was—like you and me—not at all perfect. His temper was as short as his little Manx tail, and he almost lost his job at the drugstore because of that. He had quite a struggle lengthening his temper, but Mr. Smith, who was very old and therefore could under-

stand cat talk, helped him. And Peter, who was very young and could also understand Buzzie, was a good friend too. How Buzzie lost his temper at the right time for once and thus saved the drugstore and his job brings to a climax a beguiling story which catches the essence of kitten nature.

Ellen Lewis Buell, "A Tempery Cat," in The New York Times Book Review, *November 6, 1949, p. 24.*

Buzzie is one of the most real and enchanting kittens to come purring into a story. . . . In delightful short chapters we hear how he "lengthened" his temper and earned the right to stay [at the drugstore].

The style is fresh, sensitive and witty. . . . Together [the text and Susanne Suba's pictures] make one of the happiest new picture-stories for boys and girls of about six to ten. It will leave them thinking that perhaps they are just a bit too old to talk with cats and make them very curious as to which of their relatives really can do so, but they will probably be able to work out the question as Buzzie did and try to lengthen their tempers, too.

Louise S. Bechtel, "Adventures with Animals," in New York Herald Tribune Book Review, *November 13, 1949, p. 16.*

HARRIET TUBMAN, CONDUCTOR ON THE UNDERGROUND RAILROAD (1955; British edition as *The Girl Called Moses: The Story of Harriet Tubman*)

There's a quality of writing in this biography of the famous woman who led many of her race to freedom that distinguishes the book from the two other standard juvenile biographies,— Hildegarde Swift's *Railroad to Freedom* and Dorothy Sterling's *Freedom Train.* . . . Good as they are, the emphasis is more on the adventure. Ann Petry, well known through her poetry and adult novels on racial themes, has muted the stresses of event, in Harriet Tubman's hovel plantation childhood and underground railroad activities, and with objective control shared her interpretation of the currents of revolt, the physical and emotional hazards, the resentments harbored against the "free" Negro, John Tubman, who became her husband, the failure to achieve the recognition she deserved in the aftermath of Reconstruction. The very quality of calm statement gives the book a poignant and sensitive reality.

A review of "Harriet Tubman," in Virginia Kirkus' Service, *Vol. XXIII, No. 11, June 1, 1955, p. 366.*

Although her book is intended primarily for young people, Ann Petry, writing with sympathy and fidelity, has made Harriet Tubman live for present-day readers of any age, who pick up this biography and come under its power.

The story is deeply moving. . . . At the end of each chapter are a few italicized paragraphs which tell of the march of events taking place at the same time in different parts of the United States, all of which contributed to the drama of Harriet Tubman's activities. The author's broad perspective enables her readers to see the pattern of a single career with all the events that fitted into it. . . .

[Harriet Tubman's] story is a segment of history which has tremendous significance for today's readers.

Elizabeth Yates, "To Freedom by the Underground," in The Christian Science Monitor, *August 25, 1955, p. 13.*

Ann Petry tells [Harriet Tubman's story] with insight, style and a fine narrative skill. This is a longer, more introspective study than was Dorothy Sterling's *Freedom Train* (published in 1954) but in its own fashion, just as dramatic. The personal drama is heightened by the brief historical summaries counterpointing the outstanding events in Harriet's life, thus giving us a perspective upon the period and upon the growth of the Abolition movement.

Ellen Lewis Buell, "The Deliverer," in The New York Times Book Review, *October 16, 1955, p. 34.*

The biography of Harriet Tubman, told with restraint and dignity. The book is more a character study than an adventure story, although the events of Harriet Tubman's early life and of her exploits in leading her people to freedom are not minimized. There is a perceptive insight into her reactions to the events of her childhood; to the unhappy ending of her marriage; and to the effort of settling down to a peaceful, uneventful life after the Civil War that brings her vividly to life as a real person. In quality of writing the book compares favorably with good adult biographies and its emphasis on the character and personality of Harriet Tubman is not duplicated in any other juvenile biography of her.

A review of "Harriet Tubman: Conductor on the Underground Railroad," in Bulletin of the Children's Book Center, *Vol. IX, No. 3, November, 1955, p. 40.*

With great simplicity and unusual skill, the author portrays a courageous and resourceful woman who was called Moses by her friends.... The book is a combination of fine writing, careful research, and economy of description that is both quiet and evocative. Other biographies on Harriet Tubman seem meagre by comparison....

Esther Walls Pappy, in a review of "Harriet Tubman: Conductor on the Underground Railroad," in The Saturday Review, *New York, Vol. XXXVIII, No. 46, November 12, 1955, p. 75.*

Ann Petry has written a first-rate biography.... Petry's eloquent prose creates a vivid picture of a slaveholding society, of the operation of the Underground Railroad, and of this remarkable woman. The first chapters set the scene; then the events of Harriet Tubman's life, narrated without exaggeration, build suspense and power. The last few pages are inevitably anticlimactic, for they describe the last, somewhat ordinary years of Tubman's life, but this merely sets off the amazing accomplishments of her earlier years. (pp. 101-02)

Margaret Mary Kimmel and Elizabeth Segel, "What to Read? 'Harriet Tubman, Conductor on the Underground Railroad',' in their For Reading Out Loud! A Guide to Sharing Books with Children, *A Dell Trade Paperback, 1983, pp. 101-02.*

TITUBA OF SALEM VILLAGE (1964)

First of all Tituba is Tituba, a warm, vital human being with whom we identify, and about whom we care. Secondly, she is a colored woman, and a slave. But it would be a mistake to think that Miss Petry's book is simply a well-written his-torical novel about racial problems presented at a time when these problems are in the forefront of all our minds. *Tituba* is a novel of character and suspense; and because it deals with universal issues, it transcends the moment.

In Salem Village in 1692 wolves lurked in the forest, and so did Indians with war paint and a wild and primitive religion. The so-called Christianity of the settlers was based on fear, and it became easier for them to believe in the devil and in evil than in God and in good. Ann Petry tells the story of those days in beautifully controlled prose, catching us up in the feeling of terror and doom which culminates in the famous witch trials. The reader will be carried along by the sheer excitement of the story, and it is a tribute to Ann Petry's artistry that at the end of the book we are left with a feeling of hope, and of the ultimate triumph of good over evil.

Madeleine L'Engle, in a review of "Tituba of Salem Village," in The New York Times Book Review, *November 1, 1964, p. 8.*

One of the strongest books of the year, and the best one about witchcraft that has yet been written for young people. The story centers around a Negro slave from Barbados. The first chapter is memorable: Tituba and her husband John are sold by their mistress, and so forced to leave the warm sunny island to go with a Puritan minister to Boston....

After the arrival at Boston fate takes Tituba and her husband, with the minister and his family, to Salem. The steps that lead to the accusation of witchcraft against Tituba and others are built up skilfully and inexorably; the author is never carried away by emotion but is always in full control of her narrative. The reader, however, watches with a feeling of impotence as hysteria builds up among the young girls and the adults of Salem. Then the trials, fully documented, begin. Tituba is one of those from whom a confession is extorted, but she later retracts it. At the end, a note reassures us about her ultimate fate; by this time we have become completely identified with her—we *must* know.

Alice Dalgliesh, in a review of "Tituba of Salem Village," in Saturday Review, *Vol. XLVII, No. 45, November 7, 1964, p. 55.*

Tituba has appeared in literature before—in Marion Starkey's *The Devil in Massachusetts* and Arthur Miller's *Crucible*—but never has she emerged in such simplicity and beauty of spirit. Her story becomes a masterful construction of innocence betrayed by mounting malevolence.... For adults and teen-agers this biography promises gripping enthrallment. Most children will lack the frame of reference to comprehend all the components of sinfulness (such as fortunetelling with cards) and the ingredients of witchery—prescience, possession, hypnotism, incantation, and fetishism—which are here unlabeled, unexplained, but nonetheless here. The author never intervenes to explain but leaves the reader watching frantically just outside the demented time and place that was Salem Village, and just inside Tituba as she wonders if perhaps she *is* a witch.

Jane Manthorne, in a review of "Tituba of Salem Village," in The Horn Book Magazine, *Vol. XLI, No. 1, February, 1965, p. 65.*

Based on the story of the Salem witch trials in 1692, this book should give 12-16's a vivid picture of those harsh, uneasy times. Ann Petry makes Tituba ... an entirely believable character. She uses her goodness and equanimity to show up the hatred that can be generated by hysterical fear. Tituba's simple Christianity is contrasted with the rigid Puritanism then prevalent. Inevitably good triumphs over evil as this moving tale shows clearly that it must.

> *Patience M. Daltry, "The Cold That Came In with the Spy," in* The Christian Science Monitor, *February 25, 1965, p. 7.*

Mrs. Petry has recreated the hysteria of the Salem Witch Trials of 1692, in an absorbing tale distinguished by its historical accuracy, readable style and brilliant characterization of an accused witch—the slave Tituba. It is a worthy successor to the author's excellent young adult title, **Harriet Tubman: Conductor on the Underground Railroad.** . . . *Tituba of Salem Village* is exciting for youngsters in grades six through nine. (p. 23)

The author's careful historical research will add immeasurably to young people's understanding of both the Puritan outlook and Negro history in the Bay Colony. (p. 25)

> *John Gillespie and Diana Lembo, "Building a World View: 'Tituba of Salem Village'," in their* Juniorplots: A Book Talk Manual for Teachers and Librarians, *R. R. Bowker Company, 1967, pp. 23-6.*

This brilliant novel . . . tells of the bigotry that pursued an innocent Negro, Tituba, until she suspected herself guilty of the incredible charge of witchcraft. The timely implications cannot be mistaken. Tituba is drawn with great simplicity, and she emerges as a person of profound spiritual beauty. This fictionalized biography . . . gives important insights into the workings of the bigoted mind and the tragedy of molested innocence.

> *Constantine Georgiou, "History in Children's Literature: 'Tituba of Salem Village'," in his* Children and Their Literature, *Prentice-Hall, Inc., 1969, p. 341.*

LEGENDS OF THE SAINTS (1970)

To say that these ten placid tales are ecumenical is not to deny their reverence but to indicate that what is 'worshipped' is human integrity rather than Christianity per se. Each graceful distillation . . . encapsules the certain kind of greatness of a traditional 'hero,' if you will, about whom people want to

know: St. George's conquest of the dragon, converting a city to the faith; St. Nicholas' gift of anonymous aid "so that I will never expect anything in return"; the beatification of Offerus, a ferryman, into Christopher, or "one who has carried Christ"; the honoring of Martin de Porres, a black man apprenticed to a barber-surgeon, as the Angel of Lima for his powers of miraculous cure. There are those—St. Joan, St. Thomas More— whose denouements were tragic, but if their rewards of punishment seem unconventional Mrs. Petry's laconic last lines blunt the morbid or maudlin edges.

> *A review of "Legends of the Saints," in* Kirkus Reviews, *Vol. XXXVIII, No. 20, October 15, 1970, p. 1157.*

[*Legends of the Saints*] seems fine for younger children, less for Anne Rockwell's drawings than for the ten crisp tales, well suited to ages 7 to 10. Except for Christopher, who is a legend in himself, the saints are real and the stories about them just a bit tall.

> *Oona Sullivan, in a review of "Legends of the Saints," in* The New York Times Book Review, *November 29, 1970, p. 38.*

The author relates the bare bones of each saint's story, highlighting marvels and miracles but conveying the firm personal faith and conviction of each man and woman. Still the text is disappointingly flat, lacking in excitement, although it records astonishing events.

> *Diane Farrell, in a review of "Legends of the Saints," in* The Horn Book Magazine, *Vol. XLVI, No. 6, December, 1970, p. 611.*

Ten Catholic saints are given a chapter each in this slender book, their stories simply told in a manner appropriate to the interests and capabilities of young children. . . . Incidents chosen are significant (the wolf of Gubbio) and characteristic of the saints. One is a little sorry to learn that St. George's dragon was ultimately sacrificed after allowing himself to be led about on a blue satin ribbon. Since many are martyred saints, it is interesting to note that the demise of each is briefly and cheerfully mentioned.

> *Marianne Hough, in a review of "Legends of the Saints," in* School Library Journal, *an appendix to* Library Journal, *Vol. 17, No. 5, January, 1971, p. 44.*

Ellen Raskin

1928-1984

American author/illustrator of fiction and picture books and illustrator.

Raskin is recognized for the original, zany ingenuity of her picture books for primary-school readers and puzzle mysteries for middle graders. Noted for intricate problem-solving plots, fantastic characters, and unexpected but satisfying resolutions, Raskin's lively stories are verbally and visually complex. Abounding in absurd situations, ludicrous names, incongruous protagonists, and inventive wordplay, they still maintain their credibility. Raskin is best known for *The Westing Game*, a murder mystery in which sixteen heirs (and suspects) compete to find Mr. Westing's murderer and win a gigantic inheritance. In this work, she provides her audience with suspense, humor, and a surprising finale. Raskin extends her texts with pictures which combine detailed line drawings and bold blocks of color, and demonstrates her book-designing talent by interspersing both words and illustrations with typographical variations.

Critics generally praise Raskin for her prolific imagination and fresh approach to language, illustration, and total book composition. At worst, they call her works confusing; at best, intriguing and distinctive. Admired for her skill in weaving together multiple plots and bringing them to adroit conclusions, Raskin has developed mystery puzzles for children into literature both respected and entertaining.

Raskin has won numerous awards as an author and illustrator. *Figgs and Phantoms* was a Newbery Honor Book in 1975. *The Westing Game* won the *Boston Globe-Horn Book* award in 1978 and the Newbery Medal in 1979.

(See also *CLR*, Vol. 1; *Something about the Author*, Vols. 2, 38; *Contemporary Authors*, Vols. 21-24, rev. ed., Vol. 113 [obituary].)

Courtesy of Dennis Flanagan

AUTHOR'S COMMENTARY

"Creative" is not a word I associate with myself or with my work. Creative is what my mother says I am. When I was growing up, the word was "talented." Talented was playing the piano by ear. Talented was drawing a picture of Uncle Arthur that really looked like Uncle Arthur. Talent came naturally, easily. Talent was a gift inherited from the speaker's side of the family.

Today, the vogue word is creative. Once creative meant making the Heaven and the Earth and the whales and the winged fowl and the things that creep and man and woman—all in six days. Now, creative means finger painting and bread baking and candle dipping. I'm not here to put down crafts. . . . Besides, art is a craft. What I object to in the newer meaning of the word creative is the implication that what is handmade is necessarily beautiful, what is machine-made is ugly and banal. That is not true. Homemade zucchini bread is *not* superior to the Model T Ford or the Chrysler Building.

Creativity, unfortunately, also implies the freedom to express oneself—without discipline, without training, without hard work.

That is not only impossible; it is cruel. Let a child's imagination run wild in the name of creativity, and sooner or later, it will stumble and fall and the child will not have the resources or the will to start over again. When true creativity fades, the imagination dies. I've seen this happen too often among my art students: The one flashy style palls, and the student's ignorance of the fundamentals and discipline of the craft prohibits further experimentation. The student, painfully lost, drops out.

Someone defined creativity as making something that never existed before. Perhaps, so. If I spilled coffee on a white tablecloth that would not be a creative act; it would be my own clumsiness, an accident. But artists are trained to observe and make use of accidents. If an artist took the tablecloth off the table, studied the stains, cut the cloth, and framed it, that design of brown on white would, indeed, be a creative work. Depending on the capabilities of the artist, the design could be a pleasing arrangement, or it could contain the mystery of the universe. Design is an art form. To transform accidental coffee stains into a work of art requires a trained eye and a mastery of the elements of design, scale, texture, color, composition. Ideas, feelings, sensitivities—none can be expressed without a command of language and without the discipline of craft.

Art (all forms of art—literature, drama, music, etc.) holds up a mirror to life. It may be a dark mirror, a distorted mirror, a bright shining mirror, a small mirror, a massive mirror, but life is what the artist knows and feels. Even the most fantastic fantasy, even an imageless painting reflects life, or no one would understand it. Life: we are born, we live and die, but not at the same time. Some are aborning while others are dying. Some are trying to grow up while others are trying not to grow old. Most are working or sleeping or dreaming or making love or eating or laughing or crying or screaming. Life is noisy; life is busy. Life is in constant motion. Life can be an incomprehensible clutter. But individually we are born, we live, and we die; that is a pattern. That is the pattern the artist uses in an attempt to impose order and give meaning to life. That pattern is a beginning, a middle, and an end. (pp. 152-53)

Let's get back to something I know about—myself. Since I have been so opinionated on the subject of discipline and training, you are probably curious about my education and work habits. This brief autobiography is not intended to be an educational model, in either the best or worst sense; it's just what happened.

My midwestern schooling was rigid; it consisted entirely of learning by rote. Being a good memorizer, I did well. Creativity was not a word in use, nor was the word "idea." No thinking for yourself in classroom work. That type of elementary education probably set me back two years. But I had books, which set me ahead three years.

My first love was music, until the finance company took the piano away. I turned to what I thought was art. I colored in coloring books, which was actually a good first step. Color is one of the disciplines in art, a very hard-learned discipline, although I was more concerned about staying within the lines than experimenting with color. I also copied cartoons when I wasn't pestering my mother with: "What should I draw next? I'm finished. What should I draw next?" "The coffee pot," she'd reply, or "this apple, that chair." Later, family members—aunts, uncles, cousins—sat for their portraits, but I never drew from my imagination. Possibly I was not able.

When I entered the University of Wisconsin, I decided to become a writer. I desperately wanted a career, and journalism seemed terribly romantic to a 17-year-old, until the following summer when I visited the Art Institute in Chicago—1946, the year of the first major exhibition of nonobjective art, one of the most acclaimed (and reviled) events in art since the Armory Show some 30 years earlier. I was astounded by what I saw. I was awed. For the first time in my life I understood what an artist was; and I knew that that was what I had always wanted to be.

On returning to college in the fall I switched my major to fine art. I studied anatomy; I drew from casts and models. I studied perspective, drawing arches between arches. I studied light and shade, drawing drapery folds within folds. I studied color and techniques of painting and sculpture. Again, all fundamentals. No thinking. Again, a very disciplined and rigid education—at least it was for me (perhaps I was a perfectionist even then, or perhaps I was scared that I had nothing to say). (pp. 152-54)

I took a job in a commercial art studio where I learned to prepare artwork, other people's artwork, for the printer. . . .

During the time I was learning paste-ups and color-separations on the job at the art studio, I was experimenting with typography at home in the evenings. I bought a bench printing press and ten fonts of type, designed and printed ephemera that combined my woodcuts with type, and put together a sample

book. Two years later I quit my job, made the rounds of advertising agencies and publishing houses, and was quickly launched on a free-lance career. My success had much to do with good timing and dumb luck; somehow my style was right for the period.

Style was important, technique was important; but most important then was the idea. This was the age of communication and graphic ideas, and I was learning to think. Every problem had an answer, and it was up to the illustrator-designer to find that answer, to find the one graphic symbol to best convey the message. This was an exciting time; I was illustrating for the *Saturday Evening Post* and pharmaceutical houses and book publishers. Fifteen years later, on accepting my 1,000th book-jacket assignment, free-lance illustration just didn't seem very exciting anymore. It was time for a change.

It was time to illustrate my own ideas; and, at long last, I had an idea. It developed into the picture book ***Nothing Ever Happens on My Block***. Twenty-five books later, here I am.

Having a keen appreciation of my limitations, I try to say one thing with my work: A book is a wonderful place to be. A book is a package, a gift package, a surprise package—and within the wrappings is a whole new world and beyond. I am an illustrator; I am a writer; and just as important to me, I am a designer. (Creativity isn't the only word that has changed; what I really would like to call myself is a bookmaker.)

Creating a book is a decision-making process. Decisions, millions of decisions, one decision after another—yes or no, yes or no—for ideas, plots, characters, names, colors, the placement of one line next to another, one word after another. It's "yes" or "no" all the way—no "maybe's." I have made 60 sketches for one simple drawing, "yes" or "no" for each line I put down, until all the lines together seem right. They seem right only when my "yes" choices have been consistent with each other. The artist's, the writer's, the designer's decisions are based on training, experience, competence, self-criticism, remembered criticism, luck, a compulsion to do the very best. Hard work. And caring. That is what creativity means to me. Creativity is the art of making constant choices in a consistent manner toward an imagined, perfect, inseparable whole. That is something I have yet to do. Maybe the next book. Or the next. Someday, maybe. (p. 154)

> *Ellen Raskin, in a paper given at the 15th annual symposium on children's literature at the University of California, Berkeley, in* Wilson Library Bulletin, *Vol. 53, No. 2, October, 1978, pp. 152-54.*

Those were hard times, the Depression years; they made me a humorist. Just about anything is funny after that. To a child the Depression was bad enough; even more painful was having to watch that dumb Shirley Temple. Try as I might, I could not convince any adult that Shirley Temple was a midget. Squirming, sinking lower and lower into my seat as she showed off her dimpled talents in movies which should have been X-rated, I learned that the cute, the sweet, the sentimental was for grownups only. Now, any goody-goody darling that dares enter my books will end up the villain. Or the bomber. Or at least get pimples.

I had straight dark hair, tap-danced with two left feet, and had a singing range of three wrong notes; I spilled ink on my best dress, . . . and developed a disgusting nose problem. "Get your nose out of that book, Ellen," my mother would say six dozen times a day, "Go out and play." Sticking one's nose

But nothing ever happens on my block.

From Nothing Ever Happens on My Block, *written and illustrated by Ellen Raskin. Atheneum, 1966.*

in a book seemed even more shameful than sucking one's thumb, if not downright obscene; but I kept on reading. Books were my escape; books were my friends. Besides, how could I go out and play when no one wanted to play with me? I was a failure at hopscotch ("You stepped on the line!" "What line?"); I was a klutz at catch ("You didn't even try for the ball!" "What ball?"). Books were the only things I could relate to because books were the only things I could see.

Then I got my first pair of spectacles. And then, awed by the miraculous revelation of details, I began to draw.

Years passed. "Why don't you write a book for older children?" Ann Durell, editor at E. P. Dutton, suggested. "Write about your childhood in Milwaukee during the Depression." What? After a long career as a free-lance artist, . . . I considered myself an illustrator. "But I'm an illustrator," I replied, sure of my facts. On the other hand. . . .

I began my story with snow on the ground and not enough food for Thanksgiving dinner. Just tomatoes and potatoes. Something about tomatoes and potatoes must have seemed funny at the time, for suddenly my plot kinked and out came *The Mysterious Disappearance of Leon (I Mean Noel)*, which has nothing to do with my childhood or Milwaukee or the Depression. Or does it?

I write where my imagination takes me, I think; but on re-reading the first draft of a manuscript I realize it was memory, not invention, that built the characters that shaped the plot that complicated my once-simple story. "Hi, there," I say to those folks I've known; then I rewrite to clarify and rewrite to polish and rewrite because it's still not right. And rewrite some more.

I was always a fussy child, but it was during the hot summer of 1938 that I became the self-critical, running-scared, compulsive perfectionist I am today. (pp. 620-21)

Fussing and fretting, I struggle for perfection, whether I am making lemonade, drawing a picture, or writing a book.

I still have not made the perfect book, but there is always the next one. In gloomier moments I fear that perfection is im-

possible what with all the characters I have to keep track of. In my latest puzzle-mystery *The Westing Game* . . . sixteen major characters are introduced in the first twenty pages.

As for back as I can remember, I invented characters. My sister and I would spend weeks at a time acting out the lives of at least ten characters each. (p. 622)

I am still inventing characters, but now they cast shadows. . . . Shadows from my mother's family, the funny ones. And shadows from my father's family, deeper and darker. Of the six children born to Bessie and Albert Raskin, my father alone survived. I never knew my father's father. In a tattered photograph a sad-eyed young man in a leather apron poses in his shoe-repair store. I was told three things about Albert Raskin: He died long ago, I was named after him, and he was a Wobbly. A Wobbly? It's no wonder I play with words. For years I thought I was named after a man who died in a drunken stupor. Only later did I learn that a Wobbly was a member of the IWW—Industrial Workers of the World—and that my very sober grandfather was a militant socialist, murdered at the age of thirty-four. Is he Garson in *The Tattooed Potato and Other Clues* . . . , dissolute Garson, with his secrets and disguises? I'm not sure.

The grandfather I knew and loved was my father's stepfather, Grandpa Hersh, a short and pudgy man, who wore garters on his arms to hike up his too-long shirt sleeves. Sam Hersh, an immigrant from Russia, became a wealthy builder in Milwaukee. A marriage was arranged with my grandmother after his first wife died and his children were grown. Grandpa Hersh was a quiet man, a kind and patient man, who never made fun of me when I stumbled over words reading one of my favorite fairy tales to him. He was a religious man—an Orthodox Jew—a charitable man, who in the depths of the Depression walked from door to door of the houses he had built and turned over to the jobless tenants their mortgages marked "Paid in Full." When he died of cancer several years later, all that remained of his wealth was the house on the elm-shaded boulevard. Grandpa Hersh, of course, is Uncle Florence in *Figgs & Phantoms*. . . . But in or out of a role, Grandpa Hersh is there, adding his goodness to my humor when it becomes too brittle, rounding my characters with love.

My grandmother Bessie Raskin Hersh married again. At fifty-eight she was overweight and wore thick rimless glasses, but her Russian peasant's skin was flawless, her heavy hair long and still black. Her third husband was a Spaniard, penniless and fifteen years younger than she. Bessie and Frank Garcia lived in a one-room tenement apartment in Chicago. They spoke English with accents, different accents. They worked hard—Frank in a cigar factory, my grandmother as a nursemaid.

I met Frank Garcia only once, at my grandmother's funeral. I was a nineteen-year-old college student; he was forty-four. Tall, lean, strikingly handsome, with fine lips, high cheekbones, and dark eyes, he talked to me about the blue of the Mediterranean sky, of olives, and of the sea. The following year I looked for him in Chicago, but Frank Garcia had left no trace. Then, on rereading *Figgs & Phantoms* I found him again: The Spanish pirate lives forever in a castle in Capri. Brief encounters can be lasting.

I met the boy I call Chris in *The Westing Game* only three times: as an active ten-year-old with an occasional hint of awkwardness; as a grimacing twelve-year-old hobbling on twisted feet; as a tortured fifteen-year-old, knotted by spasms, in a wheelchair. When he came to New York with his father for yet another consultation with yet another specialist, my husband and I took them out to dinner; the third restaurant let us in. Chris and I had a long chat; though he was barely intelligible, I understood him. He was smiling the same smile that he smiles in my book, but in that happier place he has found love and hope and his share of fame. That's how I want it to be. I like happy endings.

I cannot identify all the characters in my books; perhaps I haven't looked hard enough, but my parents are there. My mother came from the era of the flapper. She was sixteen years old when I was born, Sissie Figg Newton was. My father (Newt Newton, Jake Wexler) was a pharmacist, a gambler, a dreamer, who even after the Depression managed to go broke.

My sister is there, all over the place, somehow merged with my daughter Susan. And I'm there, too. I am Iris Fogel and Dickory Dock and Chester Filbert and Angela Wexler—believe it or not; but most of all I am Mona. I am Mona, the moaner; Mona, the searcher. I am Mona who discovers the world of books, who opens a book (within the book) and finds herself in an uncharted land, in a world in a different dimension.

They're all there, recreated in that different dimension—the people I have known, the times I have shared, the strangers who touched me, the child that I was. They come of their own accord, those threads of memory spun with wishes. All I am trying to do is weave an intricate web in which to trap some young and happy noses. (pp. 623-25)

Ellen Raskin, "Characters and Other Clues," in The Horn Book Magazine, *Vol. LIV, No. 6, December, 1978, pp. 620-25.*

GENERAL COMMENTARY

ALICE BACH

Each page of an Ellen Raskin book bears her unique signature and reflects her involvement with both design and language. There is usually a menagerie of some sly, some wistful beasts,

an intriguing combination of organic and geometric forms; and an enjoyment of puns and word play that is contagious. Obviously I'm a fan. Unfortunately in *Moose, Goose and Little Nobody* . . . . these elements are missing or faulted. We don't get the pepper and pizzazz of the earlier books, notably of *And It Rained, Franklin Stein* and *Spectacles*.

Alice Bach, "Mostly for Looking," in The New York Times Book Review, *February 2, 1975, p. 8.*

ALICE BACH

Ellen Raskin, designer of more than a thousand book jackets, author-artist of a dozen picture books, wrote her first novel in 1971. *The Mysterious Disappearance of Leon (I Mean Noel)* has a plot reminiscent of some Gilbert and Sullivan operettas. It's a convoluted story dependent on word play—anagrams, synonyms, acronyms, all manner of verbal trickery—to reach its conclusion. A puzzle as well as a mystery, all the missing words miraculously fall into place on the last page for those who haven't already filled them in.

Miss Raskin, not as wily as the detectives she creates, really tipped her hand in *Figgs & Phantoms*, a 1974 Newbery Honor Book. This Raskin extravaganza is filled with exotic hand lettering, graceful swash chapter openings, beautiful type fonts, and a cast of funny, punny characters. Underneath the swagger and intricacies of a mystery salted with book-lined clues the author has written an elegant romance, extended a Victorian bouquet to all bibliophiles.

In *The Tattooed Potato* Miss Raskin has not included any graphics or unusual typography. The visual images are drawn verbally from the endless costumes and disguises worn by her cast of characters, an outrageous bunch—Manny Mallomar (possibly Mob-connected); his sleazy sidekick Shrimps Marinara; our heroine Dickory Dock (honestly); and the main orchestrator (or perpetrator, according to Chief of Detectives Quinn) Garson, master of disguises, blessed with insights and perceptions that have riddled him with guilt. For Garson possesses the special artist's eye that forces him to see people as they really are, not as they present themselves. Because he fears the pain his genius might inflict on others, he has chosen to disguise himself as a slick portrait painter who perverts his art to please his patrons.

Garson has hired Dickory as his trusty assistant. Her job immediately becomes more than capping tubes of cadmium yellow and washing brushes because the complex and often erratic Garson (Inspector Noserag when he dons his deerstalker) has rented out a first-floor apartment to Manny and Shrimps and is oddly protective toward a hideously mangled deaf mute who lives in the basement making exquisite frames for Garson's paintings. Then there are the visits of Quinn and his boys. . . .

In a denouement few writers possess the panache to pull off, Miss Raskin strips each character of his disguise. We discover that very little is what we thought it was. We have seen what someone *wanted* us to see, like the blind beggar on the corner or the drunken derelict sprawled on the stoop. At the end of her roller-coaster-paced novel, Ellen Raskin unmasks all her characters gently. And as she unpeels them she shows us that the person underneath the disguise is to be loved too. (Except for Manny Mallomar.) (pp. 34-5)

Alice Bach, in a review of "The Tattooed Potato and Other Clues," in The New York Times Book Review, *May 4, 1975, pp. 34-5.*

BARBARA BADER

Before she did a picturebook independently, Ellen Raskin was the artist of a thousand jackets and the illustrator of Dylan Thomas, Ruth Krauss, Edgar Allan Poe; the year that *Nothing Ever Happens On My Block* came out, she illustrated Blake's *Songs of Innocence*. But with the appearance of Chester Filbert she was a cartoonist with a spirit-world of her own.

So to Chester sitting on the curb; sitting on the curb complaining, "Some places have marching bands or haunted houses, courageous hunters hunting ferocious lions and tigers . . ." while behind him, bit by bit, all hell breaks loose. At the first house the window-washer has been moving from window to window; at the second the children have twice rung the doorbell and hidden (when the postman rings, he'll suffer for it); in front of the third the man digging a hole has pulled up first a boot, now a chest; at the last a workman is repairing the ravages of a fire that destroyed the top story before the fire engine arrived. (It passed right in front of the unseeing Chester.) Still to come are a paddy wagon to take the thief away, a parachutist shouting "GERONIMO!", assorted accidents, a rainstorm, and a flurry of greenbacks—but Chester, all unawares, concludes "nothing ever happens on my block. When I grow up I'm going to move."

The great fun of seeing what Chester doesn't is a little like finding what the frantic husband is searching for in *A Good Man and His Good Wife*; and the story playing itself out in contraposition to the text is incipient in *Hector Protector*. What Raskin does—and this is not to suggest that she had either in mind—is to pit visual hijinks against a deadpan text and the effect, by itself, is comic opera. No more than the doings of little blue, moreover, or Charlip's quick saves, does *Nothing Ever Happens,* once seen, call for explanation; but it must be seen in color, as they must: getting away from words meant that color, as well, would have something to say.

Subsequent Raskin books are talkier, trickier, more complex, very complex. She is good enough to be simple. At house number five a witch appears now at one window, now at another, and suddenly there is a witch at every window; during the rainstorm the weathercock flies from house number four to house number two. Robbers and parachutists and firemen spell excitement, adventure; but a migrating weathervane is a discovery and a marvel. (pp. 538-39)

Barbara Bader, "Away from Words," in her American Picture Books from Noah's Ark to the Beast Within, *Macmillan Publishing Company, 1976, pp. 525-43.*

PUBLISHERS WEEKLY

Raskin's highly original novels include pacesetters like *The Mysterious Disappearance of Leon (I Mean Noel)* and *Figgs and Phantoms*. In her latest work [*The Westing Game*], the author shows once more that no one can beat her at intrigue, at concocting marvelous absurdities.

A review of "The Westing Game," in Publishers Weekly, *Vol. 213, No. 18, May 1, 1978, p. 85.*

MAE DURHAM ROGER

I like humor that reaches me, but like it even more if it jolts me, causes me to stop and think a bit. This is an uncommon quality of Ellen Raskin's writing and illustration. Her inventiveness, freshness, are apparent and can satisfy the reader who wants only that. The observant person will detect something more.

Ellen Raskin's humor reaches and *teaches*. She does not repeat. What she says in words is not depicted in her illustrations. The latter extend and complement her text. Raskin gives us humor, but she also offers us insight into ourselves.

Mae Durham Roger, in an introduction to a paper by Ellen Raskin, in Wilson Library Bulletin, *Vol. 53, No. 2, October, 1978, p. 152.*

ALICE BACH

Over the years Ellen Raskin and I had lunch in countless restaurants in New York. As the food fashions changed, so did the lunches. There were the years of chocolate fondue, pasta, and yogurt-dressed salads. We were sitting in a Greenwich Village restaurant eating apple-stuffed crepes last year when Ellen leaned across the table and confided, "I've been asked to manage a mutual fund. It's so tempting, but it would gobble up all my time. The best thing was I was asked." This conversation might have been surprising coming from any other children's book writer and illustrator, but from Ellen Raskin it was par for the course. One of Ellen's longstanding passions was the stock market. She kept thick black ledgers filled with columns of mysterious symbols and had an uncanny ability to analyze stock performance. With nerves of steel she tested investment strategies and guessed right.

One could become fuzzy-headed observing Ellen and her projects. While others raise a few rows of tomatoes and beans in the summer, Ellen, in the sandy soil of a Long Island beach community, raised almost a hundred varieties of vegetables. She wrote books the way she did everything else, with heat and with ease. That gleeful intensity created intricately plotted novels with old-fashioned heroes. Her eccentric characters possessed a kind of noble purity, trying passionately to do the right thing while succumbing to the pitfalls of daily life—loneliness, bravado, grouchiness. They were not often folks judged to be the winners in life. But when all the chips were down, each of those apparent weirdoes managed to triumph, to set things right. Put another way, in solving the overt mystery in each novel, the characters solved their own deeper problems.

Ellen's endings satisfied her readers, assuring them of a universe in which puzzles are solved in the end. Not that Ellen was a sentimentalist; she was far too tough-minded and pragmatic for that. But hope and a fundamental belief that things do work out were natural to her. Accepting the dark side of life, she led her characters into the light.

Ellen herself was as much a heroine as Turtle or Mona or Dickory Dock. From the age of fifteen she suffered from a connective-tissue disease. In the simplest terms, her body was allergic to itself. Her immune system made antibodies against her own tissues. Variously diagnosed as lupus erythematosus and scleroderma, it was a condition similar in etiology to multiple sclerosis and rheumatoid arthritis. When she experienced an acute flare-up of her illness, her tissues became inflamed, and she suffered great pain. (pp. 162-63)

When the disease was in remission, Ellen had the energy of ten people. Running up and down the stairs of her Greenwich Village house, she made it easy to forget the shadow of her illness. Ellen had a buoyant joy for living, a belief in her own talents, and a desire to succeed, to win, to continue to push herself to conquer new fields. . . . Like the crew of her favorite TV fantasy "Star Trek," she accepted her mission to go where no others had gone before. Writing mysteries filled with subtle word play, novels in which every literary and lexigraphic al-

From The Mysterious Disappearance of Leon (I Mean Noel), *written and illustrated by Ellen Raskin. Dutton, 1971. Text and illustrations copyright © 1971 by Ellen Raskin. All rights reserved. Reprinted by permission of the publisher, E. P. Dutton, a division of New American Library.*

lusion might not be understood by every child reader, was a risk. Again, Ellen made it work.

Ellen had a compelling need to be the best. We respect and reward this single-mindedness in business executives; we expect it in our athletes; but we are unsettled by it in writers, who are supposed to be plying their craft for artistic fulfillment. We've all heard dozens of writers insist that they are not interested in sales and that they only write for themselves. They are usually the ones who furtively check royalty statements with grim-lipped dedication and best-seller lists with malice. Ellen openly declared herself to be in competition. Her spirit was bursting to win.

She had wanted to win the Newbery Medal, not shyly, privately wishing, but admitting the Newbery was in the back of her mind as she wrote her novels. Fortunately for her readers, her desire for success resulted in vivid, delightful novels that did not pander to the ghost of Newberys past or present. The morning after the midnight congratulatory call came, she phoned me, laughing, ''I did it; I won!'' She might have been an Olympian, setting a new world's record, so dedicated was she to gathering up her talents and forcing herself to work out daily at her craft—regardless of the pain.

As a Newbery Medalist, Ellen was good for the field of children's books. She was a statesman among writers, teachers, librarians, and editors—many of whom had lost heart in a field overpowered by TV, video games, gimmick-books. She loved the librarians, the meetings and seminars, the letters from children. An introspective child herself, Ellen valued libraries and books all during her life, and she was genuinely grateful to be

able to give something back to the people and profession which had meant so much to her. Whenever she was able, she accepted speaking engagements. Whenever possible, she traveled, speaking of the craft she loved. As many times as she lectured, as many awards as she won, she never developed the habit of flashy talk.

She was important also to other writers, although she rarely talked about her own work. It was the novels of Joseph Conrad she'd discuss, the poems of William Blake. She saw no difference between what Conrad spread before his readers and what she wished to give her own. She was undaunted by the over-cautious who suggested that children might not understand her literary allusions, her verbal gymnastics. No matter, she wanted to share these pleasures. Whenever my own ambition flagged, she rekindled my desire to share ''the good stuff'' with children. (pp. 164-66)

Ellen who worked so hard to hide her pain from her friends was also a master of disguises in her books. In her novels things are not as they seem. That giant who swoops and stumbles through the streets of Pineapple in *Figgs & Phantoms* is really Mona Lisa Newton standing on the shoulders of her beloved Uncle Florence Italy Figg. Together, of course, they are the cosmic Figg-Newton, another Raskin trademark: indefatigable word play, puns, and games.

Toying with words while playing down her enormous erudition was typical of Ellen's inherent modesty. Ellen collected first editions of her favorite writers, Joseph Conrad and Henry James. All the books mentioned in *Figgs & Phantoms* were actually owned by book-collector Ellen Raskin. All except the elusive book that taught Mona Figg about faith and belief, about a special island, Capri—a land beyond the eye.

A superb mystery writer, Ellen left clues. In *The Westing Game* . . . death is outwitted three times. The novel is the optimist's fable: With deceptive simplicity its author tells us about life. Looking back, we can see that even the things that seemed like mistakes, misreading the clues, were not mistakes; they were part of our lives until now. Perhaps the most telling of Ellen's clues is found in Uncle Florence's diary: ''I dream of a gentle world, peopled with good people and filled with simple and quiet things. . . . From books I built my dream; in a book I found Capri.''

Ellen's death has left me sadder than I should have supposed. . . . But then I think of Ellen's hope in the face of despair, her deep capacity for love and joy where others would have dwelt in sadness and misery, and I believe that her work here was done. I know that like Mona Figg's dear Uncle Florence, Ellen has found peace in Capri. (pp. 166-67)

Alice Bach, ''Ellen Raskin: Some Clues about Her Life,'' in The Horn Book Magazine, *Vol. LXI, No. 2, March-April, 1985, pp. 162-67.*

FIGGS AND PHANTOMS (1974)

Except for her beloved Uncle Florence Italy Figg, a 4'6'' mail order book dealer who with his niece forms the Figg-Newton monster (a stunt that enables them to reach the rare and unusual books on Ebenezer Bargain's top shelf), Mona Lisa Newton has no use for her kooky relatives. All former performers except for Mona's mother (Sis) who makes up for it by tap-tappity-tap-tapping around the house, the Figgs are without doubt an unusual family, well deserving both the scorn and the attention their fellow citizens of Pineapple express in italicized inserts.

Take their ritual of Caprification, based on an ancestor's vision of heaven. As "each one must find his own Capri," Romulus Figg intends to look under the Niagara Falls but his twin Remus thinks Capri is not a place at all but lies in numbers, and Truman Figg the human pretzel expects to get there as soon as he can twist his body into a Moebius band ("I've got it just about worked out except for one elbow"). But Uncle Flo insists that the answer is in books (Read, Mona, read!), and it is indeed through a book, *Las Hazanas Fantasticas* by one Pirata Supuesto, that he finds his Capri—for Uncle Flo dies, leaving Mona bereft and more withdrawn now than ever. It is not until she follows him to the imaginary island of Caprichos ("floating through swirling nothingness") that Mona realizes that she has "a lot of remembering to do, a lot of living and learning and loving to do"—and is somehow able to return to life, aided no doubt by the unique bedside encouragements (Sis' tap dancing, Truman's contortions, Remus' fractions, cousin Fido's guilty sympathy) of her frantic relations. As must be evident this is even crazier than Raskin's *Mysterious Disappearance of Leon* . . . , but the zaniness here seems more often forced than inspired, and though the answer to the puzzle is made clear when the time comes, the question remains elusive. Still a juvenile novel—however unstrung—that takes such farcical liberties with death, grief and readers' expectations is rare enough to rate a hearing, and the Figgs—all mask and gesture though they are—do come up with a few show-stopping lines. (pp. 425-26)

A review of "Figgs & Phantoms," in Kirkus Reviews, *Vol. XLII, No. 8, April 15, 1974, pp. 425-26.*

As preposterous and funny as the author's *The Mysterious Disappearance of Leon* (*I Mean Noel*). . . . When Florence dies, Mona embarks on a clue-solving search for Capri, takes a wild mind trip, and returns a wiser and happier person. Although this anticlimactic fantasy may seem to cap just a series of internally logical inanities and Capri to appear merely an idle exercise in agnosticism, Raskin's reckless imagination and unusual sense of humor save the day.

Judy Goldberger and Denise M. Wilms, in a review of "Figgs & Phantoms," in The Booklist, *Vol. 71, No. 1, September 1, 1974, p. 46.*

The author's first full-length story [*The Mysterious Disappearance of Leon* (*I Mean Noel*)] began on a note of light-hearted madness, which continued, unabated, until the end of the book. Her second novel—just as brilliantly inventive—has less unity and more ambiguity; and it is certainly less accessible to children. . . . Readers may find the book a mystery, or an allegory, or a philosophical story—or possibly a spoof on all three. (pp. 138-39)

Ethel L. Heins, in a review of "Figgs and Phantoms," in The Horn Book Magazine, *Vol. L, No. 5, October, 1974, pp. 138-39.*

When an original mind like Ellen Raskin's is let loose, anything can happen. . . . A fantastical novel with dazzling graphics and equally awesome spelling mistakes, plus some clever word play and clues threaded into the highly structured plot. Oh yes, Joseph Conrad plays a part in both the dreams and reality of this funny, fresh book. (p. 114)

Amy Kellman, "Ghosts and Goblins," in Teacher, *Vol. 92, No. 2, October, 1974, pp. 110, 112, 114.*

The book is filled with delightful invention and easy-to-understand humor. One example is the nine foot tall Figg-Newton giant which strides about Pineapple. The giant consists of Mona balancing on her Uncle Flo's shoulders; a long black cloak conceals the giant's trunk and legs. The story is also intricate and, at times, confusing. The enigmatic references made to composers, artists, and authors in the Capri section would be difficult for children to comprehend. Truman Figg's misspelled signs contribute humor. Five of the seven black and white full-page illustrations at the beginning of each chapter show Mona. She is sullen and unattractive in the first four, serene and pretty in the last. The other two illustrations show the leopard and the pirate.

A problem remains in regard to the audience for which the book was intended. The choice of names for characters borders on slapstick comedy, which might be enjoyed by the younger child, while numerous references to the details of the rare book business would be lost on children of any age. (p. 204)

Marilyn Leathers Solt, "The Newbery Medal and Honor Books, 1922-1981: 'Figgs and Phantoms'," in Newbery and Caldecott Medal and Honor Books *by Linda Kauffman Peterson and Marilyn Leathers Solt, G. K. Hall & Co., 1982, pp. 203-04.*

Ellen Raskin won the 1979 Newbery Medal and the *Boston Globe-Horn Book* fiction award for *The Westing Game*, a book which has won a good deal of lavish praise. Although her earlier *Figgs & phantoms* has slipped by with much less notice (two relatively minor awards), it is, in fact, a work of considerably greater depth and resonance.

Raskin generally describes her books as mysteries, and *Figgs & phantoms* is so subtitled. But a Raskin mystery is not of the common or garden variety. All of them offer more than the simple appeal of what Graham Greene calls "an entertainment." While *Figgs & phantoms* indeed has many elements of the "puzzle mystery," the term Raskin used for *The Westing Game*, those readers are misled who think that the "mystery" lies in whether certain events described as taking place in "Capri" (the Figg family's eccentric version of heaven) really happened or are to be understood as a sort of dream sequence. In fact, the central mysteries of this book are of a different and more serious nature.

At first glance, it may seem preposterous to consider a book "serious" when its characters bear names as Mona Lisa Newton, Florence Italy Figg, and Sissie Figg Newton. Sissie's tap-dancing classes hardly seem meant to suggest eternal verities: how can we do anything but laugh at the high school ball team tapping to the sound of "Take Me Out to the Ballgame," the sanitation department practicing a highland fling, and the Horticultural Society tiptoeing through the tulips? Reason tells us that a used-car dealer like Newt Newton could not support a wife and child (even in a house where the sofa has broken springs) if he is so impractical as to trade a blue Buick for a raspberry-red Edsel and a black Cadillac for a sky-blue Studebaker. This slapstick comedy appears to undercut the "realism" of Raskin's characters. And typographical jokes abound throughout the book: there is always something wrong in the signs which punctuate the story (except for the old, presumably genuine, theatrical posters), as we note advertisements for out-of-prin*k* books, 2*r*d-hand cars, and lessons in baton-twir*p*ing. Even the signpainter's own name is mislettered (Tru*nam*) in one of them. In fact, though, these "errors" challenge the reader, establish a cadre of initiates, and actually advertise the importance of rereading and revising interpretations.

While Raskin certainly enjoys buffoonery, those who assume her subject matter therefore has no genuine significance are making the mistake of the book's heroine. Mona, daughter of the manically cheerful Newt and Sissie and niece of such eccentrics as Gracie Jo and Kadota Figg (who have named their only child after a favorite bull terrier), is acutely aware of the ridiculousness of it all and rejects her family as too absurd to be borne. Overweight and resentful of what "the people" of her hometown, Pineapple, may be saying of her unattractive appearance, she rudely cuts off an uncle who inquires about her diet. All but the most superficial readers ought to be able to see that Mona is not doing herself any good by wallowing in self-pity, and when a real crisis occurs, her very life is at stake. That is, when the one member of the family she respects, her uncle Florence, dies and passes on to "Capri," Mona is determined to follow him—ostensibly to share his "dream," but logically she must also share his death. "Capri" is not really very funny after all.

A truer estimate of Raskin's intentions may be gained by seeing *Figgs & phantoms* in the light of serious traditions of literary burlesque—as in the works of Charles Dickens or in books for children such as those by Louise Fitzhugh. *Harriet the Spy*, in fact, provides a number of illuminating parallels and contrasts to *Figgs & phantoms*. It is also a novel about a young girl's development and need for understanding of social relationships. Both books center on very bright but not exactly likeable little girls, each of whom is dependent on an adult who is removed from the scene fairly early in the action. In both cases, the little girl's imperceptiveness leads her to near disaster before she learns to understand others well enough to get along in the world on her own.

But an apparent difference between these two novels may be perceived in the degree to which each is presented from the central character's point of view. *Harriet the Spy* is absolutely limited to Harriet's point of view: nothing whatsoever is divulged to the reader that is not known to Harriet. The few brief instances in which we hear remarks made by Harriet's parents not intended for her ears actually occur at moments when Harriet is at the edge of the scene and is clearly stated to be eavesdropping. . . . *Figgs & phantoms*, on the other hand, has a few scenes in which Mona is not present at all . . . , others in which we presume she is out of earshot . . . , and a number of instances in which we are told what another character is actually thinking. . . . Thus the third-person narrator here is a good deal more omniscient than in *Harriet the Spy*. Raskin's narrator also appears to be more detached than the narrator of *Harriet the Spy*, whose remarks often actually convey Harriet's viewpoint. . . . (pp. 128-30)

Since the narrator of *Figgs & phantoms* is not limited to Mona's point of view, are we to take as objective reporting the italicized passages set off by stars which tell us "what the people of Pineapple said"? This technical issue is pertinent not only to the scope of the narrator's vision but also to the problem of Mona's development. As astute a critic as Jean Stafford, who found this book "excellent" and well worth rereading, interpreted the italics as a chorus. She said, "From the sidelines, the people of Pineapple judge and denounce the Figgs. . . . In time, however, after a series of most wondrous adventures and tragedies, the family is accepted by the citizenry." Confirmation and/or denial that Pineapple holds such a general view of the Figgs may be found in remarks made by some of the

other characters. We may dismiss Newt Newton's disbelief that the people of Pineapple are saying such things . . . as yet another instance of Newt's sunny optimism (and total lack of astute observation). But at the same time, we may ask ourselves whether Mona, who prompts Newt's protest by telling him what "people are saying" about her uncle Truman, is any more qualified to know exactly what is said and thought by others. To resolve this question, we should examine the passages in italics reporting "public opinion" to determine their objectivity and narrative status.

In the first half of the book, every one of these passages is inserted at a moment in which Mona is feeling acute embarrassment or resentment, and the chorus of "the people of Pineapple" can be seen to mirror accurately her own concerns. The first, suggesting Pineapple's low opinion of Mona herself, comes when she has been roundly scolded by Mrs. Lumpholz, the only other person present. The italicized passage reads, "*Just look at her balancing up there like Truman the Human Pretzel.*" . . . In fact, there is no one but Mrs. Lumpholz there to look at her. A comment about her uncle Florence reflects Mona's own feeling that he is "the best of the lot, by far" and comes directly after we have heard, "That's all the people of Pineapple did these days was laugh and gossip about Figgs, she thought." . . . The third of these passages criticizes her mother as "that tap-dancing Sister Figg" and Mona herself as a "misfit." . . . Immediately following Mona's arrival home, this passage mirrors her "inner fury" at being greeted by Sissie's "tap-tappity-tap-tap." . . .

The other passages of this type are all equally tied to Mona's preoccupations of the moment. Like Mona, the italicized voice appreciates her uncle as "a real star." But when Sissie has just explained that she has been teaching the volunteer fire department a double-time step for the Founder's Day parade, we hear that "the people of Pineapple said" Sissie was "making a fool of herself and the volunteer fire department to boot." . . . Oddly, though, almost everyone in town seems to be taking those tap-dancing lessons, including the Chamber of Commerce ("tapping to 'There's No Business like Show Business'"). In fact, the only remarks critical of Figgs that we actually hear, aside from the italicized passages . . . , are exclamations from Mrs. Lumpholz—with whom we may well sympathize.

Mrs. Lumpholz may offer the key to the puzzle of objectivity. It is obvious that Mona misinterprets Mrs. Lumpholz's motives all along. While she presumes Mrs. Lumpholz is being mean and vindictive in the first episode, we can gather that the protest was, at least in part, generated by concern for aging, ailing Florence, staggering under the weight of the plump niece perched on his shoulders to constitute the "Figg-Newton giant": Mona has indeed grown to be too heavy a burden. The next time we see Mrs. Lumpholz (Mona is conspicuously absent from the scene), she is concerned to see Florence walking in the car lot in the early morning in his bathrobe and with bare feet. . . . The bare feet prepare the reader for the contents of the shoebox Mrs. Lumpholz later tries to present to Florence; tellingly, however, Mona thinks it must contain a bomb: "'It's probably a bomb,' Mona said. Newt and Sissie laughed, but she had not meant to be clever." . . . She still apparently harbors such paranoiac suspicions when Mrs. Lumpholz brings the same box to her hospital room. . . . Mrs. Lumpholz may be something of a busybody, but she is clearly harmless—in everyone's eyes but Mona's.

From Figgs & Phantoms, *written and illustrated by Ellen Raskin. Dutton, 1974. Text and illustrations copyright © 1974 by Ellen Raskin. All rights reserved. Reprinted by permission of the publisher, E. P. Dutton, a division of New American Library.*

Bump Popham, another person whose perfectly normal jesting greeting is interpreted as an insult by Mona, has also been shown to be friendly and concerned about Florence's well-being in the scene which leads up to Florence's going into Bargain's bookshop to "dicker over the price of a book he just happened to find on the third shelf." . . . Florence's relationship with Eb Bargain is another matter about which Mona is profoundly mistaken. She thinks Bargain does not know about the Figg-Newton giant's inspections of the upper shelves of the bookshop, and she therefore is alarmed when an item about the "giant" appears in the local newspaper. . . . In the end, it is obvious that Bargain knew about the giant all along. At a later point, when Fido loses his balance in the bookshop and leaves Mona hanging from the top shelf, we hear that "old man Bargain had raised his head and was waving a notebook at her threateningly." . . . This threat is not the objective observation of an omniscient narrator, but another instance of Mona's fears, in this case blending into the third-person (nonitalicized) narration.

Of course, the fact that Mona *is* quite mistaken does not become clear until the last section of the book, in which we observe the entire population of Pineapple enjoying Sissie's Founders'

Day extravaganza, either as participants or on the sidelines. Does this mean the town has finally accepted the Figgs, after much denunciation, as Jean Stafford thinks? I have already noted that the only suggestion of such general denunciation comes in the italicized passages in the first half of the book. There are no italicized passages in the "Capri" sequence, in which Pineapple is almost entirely absent from Mona's consciousness, and the italicized passages in the final section . . . are of an entirely different nature. These recount what Mona actually sees and hears for herself: and that is a scene which is, as she finally realizes, a "happy scene." . . . (pp. 130-32)

Typographical distinctions are part of Raskin's strategy, not mere jokes or the invention of a publisher's book designer. In the final argument between the author and Truman at the end of the book, our attention is called to the fact that the book ends with an ampersand. If we then turn back to the beginning, we can see that it also *begins* with an ampersand. As in *Finnegans Wake,* where the first sentence finishes the incomplete last sentence, this device symbolizes the cyclical or continuous nature of human life. But if typography is so important to Raskin, we must ask why the early italicized passages are set off by a single introductory star, whereas the final section uses rows of stars, both for italicized and nonitalicized passages.

The answer appears to be that the early italicized passages signalled by a single star and usually placed in the midst of a continuing scene (that is, not divided from what precedes or follows by a chapter break or a spaced row of five stars) represent what Mona *imagines* others may be saying about her family and herself. We cannot assume that Mona is right when one such passage . . . echoes Mona's own earlier words in calling her uncle Truman "a double-jointed idiot." . . . When Mona is recovering, the "hearsay" passages cease in favor of objective reporting, set off by the rows of stars used throughout to indicate normal narrative divisions. Those earlier "one-star" passages, then, function like the excerpts from Harriet's notebook in *Harriet the Spy:* that is, they give us more direct information about what is going on in the mind of the central figure, in her *own* words, than is possible for the third-person narration, no matter how centered the point of view is on what Harriet (or Mona) observes. Thus the italicized passages in the first half of the book form the central "mystery" of *Figgs & phantoms.* To grasp what is going on in the mind of the central character fully, we must (like Mona) sharpen our perceptions and look below the surface, weighing all sorts of evidence— including what appears to be merely comic typesetting.

If we do not do this, we are in danger of sympathizing with Mona for all the wrong reasons and likely to miss one of the book's most significant concerns. To see why this is so, let us consider the first statement on the back cover of the paperback edition: "If the Figgs in *your* family were a Tap Dancing Mother, a cousin named Fido the Second, and Nine Performing Canines, you'd be miserable, too." Perhaps so. Most of us live through times when we find our families embarrassing— especially, although by no means exclusively, at about Mona's age. And no doubt there is more to find embarrassing in this family than in a more "average" one. But rejection of one's own family is a serious matter. To reject one's background is to reject an important part of oneself, as Alan Garner suggests through the character of Gwyn in *The Owl Service.*

Mona's descent into deepening alienation and her eventual recovery are shown both literally and symbolically in Raskin's splendid illustrations, which, like the typographical eccentricities, provide keys to the structure and meaning of the book.

The frontispiece shows us a "phantom": a panther in a palm tree, an image which contributes to the nightmare quality of the dream sequence in which Mona finds herself in someone else's dream. The illustrations to parts 1 through 4 show Mona's face: scowling, sulky, distraught, and associated with a progression of images of figs and pineapples. These pictures trace Mona's worsening state, and in the same way the last one indicates her restoration to physical and mental health as a result of the salutory shocks she has received in the dream world of "Capri."

To look at the sequence more closely, we first see her enclosed in a fig-shaped space—but dropping from the fig tree, not firmly attached, which points to her wish to disassociate herself from her family. Then we see the fig planted within a pineapple: Mona feels hemmed in, not only by her family but by the town of Pineapple, which she sees as scorning her as one of the ridiculous Figgs. Next we see the pineapple expand and become vacant space itself, at the same time that it begins to show an expansion of wildly growing foliage, at the beginning of the chapter in which we hear about the Figg family "Capri" ritual—an exotic growth which has nothing to do with the other residents of Pineapple. At the beginning of part 4, which takes up events after Florence's death, a vacant, not fully materialized palm tree sprouts from the vacant (except for Mona's face) pineapple. This is appropriate because in this section Mona's thoughts turn from "the people of Pineapple" almost completely and there is only a single "one-star" italicized passage (the last in the book). At this stage, Mona is searching for clues to lead her to her uncle's "Capri," and one of the most important of these is a picture of a pink palm tree. Part 5, the dream sequence, is linked to the earlier sequence *only* by the palm tree, now with the head of the would-be pirate materializing in it and dominating the scene: as indeed it should, for this particular "Capri" is the pirate's own dream.

The last section, part 6, begins with an illustration which carries over none of the fig-pineapple-palm images. In fact, we see there nothing that has been seen before at all except the decorative and exuberant foliage, a vacant space, and Mona's head, all three of which are as transformed as the Mona we read about in this section. Mona is smiling and clear-eyed for the first time, looking out rather than into herself, and the foliage trained about a window bears flowers. Mona, now come into "bloom," is able to look outward because the pirate has helped to heal her by telling her the painful truth: that she is "a selfish, stubborn, self-centered child." . . . He has revealed her ignorance—both of other people, including her beloved uncle, and of books. One of many instances which prove the former is her encounter on "Capri" with the woman with the head of a pig . . . , whose picture she had seen in a book that she "quickly decided . . . had found its way into [Florence's] trunk by accident." . . . And her ignorance of books, despite her "professional" expertise, is depicted with splendid symbolism when she is unable to conjure up the contents of Conrad's *Typhoon:* as the pirate says, to her a book is a package.

The connection between Mona's inability to recognize her uncle's separate existence and needs and her ignorance of Conrad's words is an important one. While not the only author alluded to or echoed in this book, Conrad is a vital key for a full understanding of the "mysteries" involved. A first quotation, from *Heart of Darkness*, frightens Mona: "We live, as we dream—alone." . . . Mona "refused to believe it had anything to do with Capri": but of course it is exactly the lesson she has to learn in her invasion of "Capri," someone else's dream. It is only through books that we can live in the dreams of others. The other quotations from Conrad are one-word summaries which are likely to be puzzling to readers who do not know Conrad's works. Fido's summary of *Lord Jim*—"Jump" . . .—is potentially hilarious to those familiar with Conrad. Whatever Fido may think it means, Mona takes the message literally in a sense central to the great disaster of Lord Jim's life: "Abandon ship." Even readers who do not know this should be able to see that "Jump" might be disastrous advice for Mona, suggesting suicide. Fido appears to sense the danger and returns with another one-word summary of a work by Conrad just as Mona slips into a coma: "Wait." . . . Wait is the name of a principal character in *The Nigger of the Narcissus* and conveys a message Fido rightly sees as appropriate for Mona.

Mona is not only trying to invade someone else's dream, she has been trying to read by proxy, through Fido. If she had finished *Heart of Darkness*, she might eventually have realized that it had some interesting parallels to her own experience. Albert J. Guerard remarks that both *Heart of Darkness* and *The Secret Sharer* are "in fact the same story, and have the same mythical theme—the theme of initiation and moral education, the theme of progress through temporary reversion and achieved self-knowledge, the theme of man's exploratory descent into the primitive sources of being." They also share the motif of the double, the other human being with whom the narrator identifies, but who he must learn is actually other.

Something like this is also Mona's experience: she has regarded her uncle as part of herself, the other half of the Figg-Newton giant. She must learn that he is himself and leave him to his own identity before she is finally released to find her own. And as it happens, her progress towards common humanity is signified in a gesture which comes right out of *Heart of Darkness*. Readers of that work will recall that the narrator, Marlow, has identified himself with the terrible Kurtz, who represents what he, or any of us, could, at our worst, become. After the death of Kurtz, Marlow returns to Europe and, in an act of kindness, tells Kurtz's fiancée what she wants to hear: that the last words Kurtz had spoken were her name. This is a lie, but one necessary to preserve the woman's peace of mind. In exactly the same way, Mona, comforting the tormented Fido, gives him a posthumous message from Florence which is a lie pure and simple, but just what Fido needs to hear.

Mona may not have finished her reading, but she behaves like a Conrad character. The great themes of Conrad's novels are isolation and alienation, and their opposites and remedies, fidelity and human solidarity. What Conrad called the "true lie," as in Marlow's lie to Kurtz's fiancée, is part of the remedy for isolation and alienation. Mona, like Marlow, tells a lie which is "true" in the sense that it affirms the values people must or should live by. As Conrad put it in an essay, "For the great mass of mankind the only saving grace that is needed is steady fidelity to what is nearest to hand and heart in the short moment of each human effort." Fido, and his need, are what are nearest to Mona in her particular moment.

Conrad, then, is a vital clue to those who would read *Figgs & phantoms* as a mystery—or as a puzzle, as the cover illustration for the paperback edition suggests, aptly showing some volumes of Conrad as bits in a jigsaw puzzle. But everything else in the book also fits in as neatly as pieces of a jigsaw puzzle, including the details of names and language, which I am tempted to relate to a crossword puzzle. I cannot help wondering whether it is not likely that Raskin came across *caprifig* in such a puzzle—or, more likely, *caprification*, "to ripen figs by the stinging of a gall insect." The word makes an apt metaphor for Mona's ripening: she is green, immature, bitter, and has to be thoroughly stung before she shows signs of mellowing and sweetening.

Raskin reminds us that buffoonery may camouflage matters which are deadly serious by also interweaving references to *The Yeoman of the Guard*, the only Gilbert and Sullivan operetta which ends tragically for a character with whom we feel real sympathy. The jester Jack Point is not mentioned by name in *Figgs & phantoms,* but a song primarily associated with him is quoted at the crucial moment after Mona slams shut *Heart of Darkness.* . . . And anyone who knows *The Yeoman* (a group likely to loom larger among the readers of Ellen Raskin than do Conrad readers) is likely to recall Jack Point's two songs about the bitter lot of the "private buffoon." The one which seems most appropriate to bear in mind in relation to the art of Ellen Raskin is the song which ends,

> He who'd make his fellow, fellow, fellow creatures wise
> Must always gild the philosophic pill.
>
> (pp. 132-37)

> Constance B. Hieatt, "The Mystery of 'Figgs & Phantoms'," in Children's Literature: Annual of the Modern Language Association Group on Children's Literature and The Children's Literature Association, Vol. 13, 1985, pp. 128-38.

MOOSE, GOOSE, AND LITTLE NOBODY (1974)

"One day a big wind blew. Trees fell and a gas pump flew. From somewhere a red roof spun through the air and came down with a BUMP!" From that relatively straightforward introduction Raskin launches into one of her nonsensical plays on the sound and sight and independent existence of words. The gas pump and red roof (the latter, really a sort of detached attic, inhabited by a young mouse) land effectively in the laps of a moose and a goose—who, reading the sign, decide that their small visitor must be a gas. ("Hello Gas.") Mouse's protests (he thinks he's a Moose, but the others know better) send all three on a search for his mother, his house and his name, and different signs and structures along the way suggest to Moose and Goose that the mouse is a lion, a phone, a bus, a mail and a stop. (This last is Goose's conclusion, though Moose argues, "No, no, his name is Go.") Children, more in touch than literate adults are with words as physical objects, will probably find all this funnier than we do—but it's justified at any level by the turnabout that follows: when the three finally do come to a small, roofless red house complete with waiting mother, Goose and Moose are sure that their friend is a snow— an error easily understood when you see the arrow-shaped sign labeled "mouse" turned upside down, and easily remedied when the now happy mouse, no longer a nobody, turns it right side round. Demonstrating not only the satisfaction of having a home, a mother, and an identity and the importance of words in providing the last of the three, but proving also Raskin's ability (less evident in *Who Said Sue* and *Moe Q. McGlutch*) to inform her silly situations and crisp, witty pictures with some unobtrusive psychological substance.

> A review of "Moose, Goose and Little Nobody," in Kirkus Reviews, Vol. XLII, No. 17, September 1, 1974, p. 940.

Ms. Raskin's new book has just about everything good going for it. The story of the moose and the goose who befriend a lost mouse could wind up a modern "Goldilocks and the Three Bears" since it has believably anthropomorphic star characters, a serious dilemma to be resolved, rhythmical repetitions of key sentences and delightfully sunny pictures. . . . Children will love the nonsense as the animals explore a phone booth, a mailbox and other unlikely prospects before getting to mouse house.

> A review of "Moose, Goose, and Little Nobody," in Publishers Weekly, Vol. 206, No. 10, September 2, 1974, p. 69.

Raskin's characteristic catchy word games, reduced in complexity for this easy-to-read book, are built into repetitive sequences and short sentences full of rhyming sounds. Her four-color illustrations combine open space with sections of intricate pattern; the pictures are invigorated by juxtaposition of black-and-white animal figures and their bright-toned props. Wittier than average easy-reading fare.

> Judy Goldberger and Denise M. Wilms, in a review of "Moose, Goose and Little Nobody," in The Booklist, Vol. 71, No. 4, October 15, 1974, p. 246.

The situation is light; the word game is clear and just involving enough for young children; and the humorous illustrations are a treat (the tiny mouse cries out for "Mommy" each time a new parent is suggested). Less complicated and more fun than Raskin's earlier word based stories such as *Who, Said Sue, Said Whoo?* . . . , this is prime fare for storyhour.

> Carol Chatfield, in a review of "Moose, Goose and Little Nobody," in School Library Journal, an appendix to Library Journal, Vol. 21, No. 3, November, 1974, p. 50.

THE TATTOOED POTATO AND OTHER CLUES (1975)

Raskin's return engagement—her last stop on the magical mystery tour was *Figgs & Phantoms* . . .—could be none but Raskin's alone. Her unfortunate heroine is art student Dickory Dock who, besides being plagued by people's jokes on her name, gets embroiled in an adventure that nets her the murderer of her parents, the blackmailers of a brilliant painter who went into hiding 15 years before, and the big payoff: "She was learning to be a phony." Some of the gadgetry of the earlier books, perhaps largely the product of their illustrations, is gone. A wild, farcical quality remains but is toned down a little, which makes the author appear as involved in telling a good story as she is in devising clever gimmicks. Successful, if disjointed, entertainment.

> Judy Goldberger and Denise M. Wilms, in a review of "The Tattooed Potato and Other Clues," in The Booklist, Vol. 71, No. 18, May 15, 1975, p. 967.

A delightful, zany and compassionate book that defies a brief summary. Dickory Dock the heroine and her eccentric artist employer Garson solve more than mysteries—they uncover human horror stories. But the horror is balanced by wit and the nightmare with the crazy, and the result is a superb, rollicking novel that makes wonderful reading. (The publishers recommend the book for ages 9-12, but they do it an injustice; it's appropriate for any age at all.)

Raskin at her drawing board. Photograph © 1986 Nancy Crampton.

Brigitte Weeks, in a review of "The Tattooed Potato and Other Clues," in Book World—The Washington Post, *June 8, 1975, p. 4.*

After she answers an advertisement for an artist's assistant, Dickory Dock becomes involved in six mysteries each unique and yet ingeniously tied together. Raskin's unusual talent with words, unusual events and unusual situations is played to the hilt, but never overdone. Throughout the reading one is constantly laughing at her puns and yet deeply engrossed in solving each separate and the ultimate mystery concerning Garson and his friends. A must title for all collections serving students grades 4-8 who ask either for a mystery, funny or just good book.

James A. Norsworthy, Jr., in a review of "The Tattooed Potato and Other Clues," in Catholic Library World, *Vol. 47, No. 3, October, 1975, p. 133.*

"A spoof of Sherlock Holmes," states the book's jacket, but this is a spoof of detective fiction in general, and a rollicking good one. A baffled Chief of Detectives in New York City turns repeatedly to the painter Garson, who uses brilliant deductive powers to solve a series of crimes (all ridiculous) while apparently oblivious to the menacing tenants who frighten his assistant, Dickory Dock. . . . And there's a mystery about Garson himself. A bit of murder, which it is hard to take seriously since the whole book is such a rummy soufflé. Humor, action, zany characters, and a blithe style: a palpable hit.

Zena Sutherland, in a review of "The Tattooed Potato and Other Clues," in Bulletin of the Center for Children's Books, *Vol. 29, No. 3, November, 1975, p. 52.*

Ellen Raskin's [*The Tattooed Potato and Other Clues*] is a cookier book altogether [than Stephen Chance's *Septimus and the Stone of Offering*]: quick, allusive, pasticheur and altogether not to be caught out in any old nursery. . . . The scenery and the personae are relentlessly Greenwich Village picturesquerie—drunks, fat cops, art emperors, white-suited blackhearted blackmailers, goofy art-student boyfriend. With much of the charm and funniness of "Sesame Street", Ellen Raskin sugars her pills of art education, and brings together her gleefully confusing scatter of inventiveness with quite a flourish at the end. But she has not quite the heart to give her book a heart, for all its attractiveness.

Fred Inglis, "Private Eyes," in The Times Literary Supplement, *No. 3900, December 10, 1976, p. 1548.*

This grotesque and highly offensive effort suffers from a strained and self-conscious attempt at cuteness. Impairments are used in egregious ways—obvious clues to a thief, disguises, establishing a character as pitiful or repulsive. The badly disfigured and irremediably injured Isaac is presented as a gentle Frankenstein, decent and kind, but barely human: "A loud howl erupted from the crippled mute like a clap of wondrous thunder. He rocked in his chair and threw back his head, uttering cries that echoed through the room. Dickory could hear his 'ung-ung-ung' through the thick glass. Isaac . . . was laughing.'' Obvious and childish name jokes—Dinkel, Finkel and Winkel, the detectives; Shrimps Marinara; Dickory and Donald Dock; Garson-Noserag—seem bizarrely out of place with such violent episodes as murders, kidnappings, and attempted suicide. The central concern of the book seems to be the relationship of illusion and reality. It seems a convoluted and hurtful way to say that things are seldom what they seem. (p. 276)

> *Barbara H. Baskin and Karen H. Harris, "An Annotated Guide to Juvenile Fiction Portraying the Handicapped, 1940-1975: 'The Tattooed Potato and Other Clues'," in their* Notes from a Different Drummer: A Guide to Juvenile Fiction Portraying the Handicapped, *R. R. Bowker Company, 1977, pp. 275-76.*

TWENTY-TWO, TWENTY-THREE (1976)

Unquestionably, Ellen Raskin is a genuine kook. However, that doesn't prevent her originality from lapsing into over-ingenuity, which is what happens here. At the start, the little road signs pointing left to ''front cover'' and ''jacket'' and right to (pages) ''twenty-two, twenty-three'' are appreciably witty touches, but wit turns to manner when the whole book becomes nothing but an overburdened journey to ''twenty-two, twenty-three,'' with the only topic of discussion being a mouse's proper costume for the trip—debated at artificial and tiresome length by her fellow travelers: the bear in his underwear, the frogs in clogs, the cock in the smock, the dove with gloves on his feet, and too many such others. The pictures of course are more clever, but, in the end, too clever. Spiffy and elegant, the animals regroup themselves from page to page in jumbled, confusing arrangements that make no sense at all until, on the climactic double-spread pages twenty-two and twenty-three, they have formed a Christmas tree shape and a red suited Santa (the bear) and spelled out the message ''Merry New Year.'' In our view, it's a head trip that will attract few passengers.

> *A review of ''Twenty-Two, Twenty-Three,'' in* Kirkus Reviews, *Vol. XLIV, No. 13, July 1, 1976, p. 729.*

Ellen Raskin will surely be on everyone's honors list when this uncommonly rewarding flight into wonderland appears. Her dashing pictures of animals, bravely colored, invite the reader to come along on their mysterious pilgrimage. . . . The book has every right to expect a part in Yuletide celebrations in 1976 and for years to come. (pp. 90-1)

> *A review of ''Twenty-Two, Twenty-Three,'' in* Publishers Weekly, *Vol. 210, No. 1, July 5, 1976, pp. 90-1.*

To her special audience who are into her word play and pay close attention to her visual sleight of hand, Ellen Raskin sends *Twenty-Two, Twenty-Three.* . . . Some of the rhymes are forced, and the concept may confuse youngest listeners, but Raskin is never less than original and studiously avoids all the usual Christmas clichés. (p. 87)

> *Matilda R. Kornfeld, "Harvest Holiday (Slim Pickings for '76)," in* School Library Journal, *Vol. 23, No. 2, October, 1976, pp. 85-7.*

In a most ingenious contrivance, Raskin concocts a holiday message with nonsensically dressed animals who speak in a rhyming text and who cumulate on pages 22 and 23 in an imaginative puzzle-pastiche. . . . Imaginative, fresh and amusing, this is both a marvelous encouragement to visual perception and a beautiful piece of bookmaking, with handsome pages, intriguing endpapers, and some graphic information about the construction of a book.

> *Zena Sutherland, in a review of ''Twenty-Two, Twenty-Three,'' in* Bulletin of the Center for Children's Books, *Vol. 30, No. 4, December, 1976, p. 65.*

Imagine a Macy's Thanksgiving parade, an old world mummers' pageant and an animals' costume party staged as a three-ring circus—and you have an idea of *Twenty-two, Twenty-three.* . . . It says ''Happy Christmas'' and ''Merry New Year'' on pages 22 and 23 . . . , and when you've unscrambled what's going on in the hellzapoppin' picture spread across pages 22-23, you find 33 ''properly dressed animals'' in 29 different costumes.

If this seems confusing, so does this book. Like many of Ellen Raskin's picture books, it is a dramatic production number intricately staged and mounted with two, three, four—no, there are many more—story lines unwinding at the same time in word and/or image, all detailed in her inventive, distinctively stylized illustrations. The idea, of course, is to discover what's going on.

This time Miss Raskin has put on a visual fashion show of animals parading in people's dress—asses in glasses, does in hose, a llama in pajamas, a snail in a veil, a bear in his underwear, et al. There is the thinnest of connecting threads about a mouse's pilgrimage around the world.

What's the point of all the frantic festivity? Well, the rhythmic text plus its internal rhyme could be mnemonics for remembering the catalogue of clothing, while the word-sound punning, naturally, is to encourage playing with words—a first step to a child's learning to read. Yet in 24 pages a lot goes on while very little happens. One would have wished for more wit and a little less whimsy.

> *Margaret F. O'Connell, in a review of ''Twenty-Two, Twenty-Three,'' in* The New York Times Book Review, *December 12, 1976, p. 34.*

This is basically an alphabet book with crazy rhymes about even crazier looking animals in a puzzling book which somehow ends with Christmas. In addition, the author/illustrator is supposed to be explaining to kids about color separation and which parts of the book are which. All this ends up in a tremendous mess. I wish she could have taken one thing at a time and then perhaps the reader would have a fighting chance.

> *Ardis Kimzey, in a review of ''Twenty-Two, Twenty-Three,'' in* Children's Book Review Service, *Vol. 5, No. 5, January, 1977, p. 41.*

THE WESTING GAME (1978)

AUTHOR'S COMMENTARY

With deepest gratitude and everlasting astonishment I accept the 1979 John Newbery Medal and the awesome covenant it exacts, on behalf of my young, my dedicated, my loyal readers. (p. 385)

To be honored for my contribution to American literature for children in this year of all years [The International Year of the Child] is cause for wonder. I do write books for children con-

From Twenty-Two, Twenty-Three, *written and illustrated by Ellen Raskin. Atheneum, 1976. Copyright © 1976 by Ellen Raskin. All rights reserved. Reprinted with the permission of Atheneum Publishers.*

sciously and proudly, but now I must ask myself: Why? What? How?

To me, writing for a reading child does *not* mean preaching or teaching (I leave that to the more qualified). It does *not* mean prescriptive formula (if I had the need for formulas I would write for adults). It does *not* mean catering to arbitrary reading levels or age groups; my readers have one thing in common: They are young enough or curious enough to read slowly, and the slower the better for my books.

The one literary concession I do make, one that forces me to eliminate words here and add sentences there, is to the look of the book. I write and design my book to look accessible to the young reader; it will have less than two hundred pages, and there will be no endless seas of gray type. I plan for margins wide enough for the hands to hold, typographic variations for the eyes to rest, decorative breaks for the mind to breathe. I want my children's book to look like a wonderful place to be.

But why? Why, as an adult, do I write books for children? I have thought long and hard about this too-often-asked question, and the only answer I can come up with is: maybe because I'm short.

I may not appear short to some of you; but, believe me, I have spent most of my years looking up people's noses. As a child,

being school-bright was little compensation for being a year younger than my Nordic classmates. Great expectations were had of me when I was skipped to the third grade, but then and there my string of perfect report cards was broken. I flunked posture! A shy child, I lacked the courage to explain that I *was* standing up straight; I was just shorter than everyone else. To add injury to insult, the geography books I had to balance on my head probably squashed me down another two inches. And not having eyes on the top of my flattened skull, I could no longer name the states that border on the Mississippi.

I did have a brief respite from shortness. Having grown up as far as I could, I left the tall state of Wisconsin to launch a successful career as a free-lance illustrator, eye-to-eye with the average-sized natives of New York City. Then one unforgettable afternoon [my daughter] Susie left her house key at school, and I was soon to step back into the frustrations of the undersized. The doorbell rang, I rose from my drawing boards, crossed the room, opened the front door, and looked *up* at my twelve-year-old daughter. Up, not down.

Short again and forevermore, I started my first children's book. With the comfort of hindsight I could look back and smile at my early moping self. Lucky adult that I became, I offered ***Nothing Ever Happens on My Block*** . . . to the right editor—Jean Karl. (pp. 386-87)

Switching from commercial art to picture books is plausible, but what about from picture books to the novel? Simple. All it takes is a brilliant editor, Ann Durell, who in a rare lapse into looniness asked this illustrator to write a long book; and who, a year later when the moon again was full, confronted by the unlikeliest of novels (not-what-she-had-in-mind-at-all, she-may-be-crazy-but-the-author's-even-nuttier) had the courage to publish it. (p. 387)

Had Ann Durell and I had our wits about us, we might not have been so surprised at my funny way with words. Those years of art training, those many years of sketching and drawing sharpened my eye to the out-of-scale, the out-of-proportion. (Everything looks weird if you stare long enough.) The visual artist looks and can see beauty in the absurd, magic in the mundane. What varies from the norm describes the norm, and how much easier it is to tell those meanings in words. In words. With words. Words about words. Words are adaptable tools to a dedicated reader; to the illustrator words become tools as brushes have been, and brush strokes are meant to be visible. (p. 388)

Well, the words kept coming: *The Mysterious Disappearance of Leon (I mean Noel)*, then *Figgs & Phantoms*, then *The Tattooed Potato and Other Clues* . . . ; and then three years ago I sat down at the typewriter with no wisp of an idea, just the urge to write another children's book. It will have a story. It will have a character with whom my readers can relate. And, because of who I am and was, and out of my compassion for the hurts and hazards of childhood, it will have a happy ending. But what shall I write about?

It is 1976, the Bicentennial year. My story will have a historical background; its locale, the place I know best: Milwaukee. I now have my first character: Lake Michigan.

Recalling that Amy Kellman's daughter asked for a puzzle-mystery, I decide that the format of my historical treatise will be a puzzle-mystery (whatever that is). I type out the words of "America the Beautiful" and cut them apart.

Meanwhile on television, between re-created Revolutionary battles blasting and fireworks booming, come reports of the death of an infamous millionaire. Anyone who can spell *Howard Hughes* is forging a will. Good, I'll try it, too.

Now I have Lake Michigan, a jumbled "America the Beautiful," the first draft of a very strange will, and a dead millionaire—a fine beginning for a puzzle-mystery, but where is the historical background? Wisconsin abounds in labor history; therefore, my millionaire will be an industrialist, murdered because—let me see, because he was a notorious strikebreaker. Old man Kohler! I shift the scene sixty miles north to my father's hometown, Sheboygan, which borders on the Kohler company, factory, and town. I cannot use the name Sheboygan (my readers will think I'm trying to be funny), and I certainly cannot use the name Kohler (they're still making toilets up there). Instead, I raise the shore of Lake Michigan, and my industrialist, named Samuel W. Westing, will die in his mansion on the cliff called the Westing house.

Now I need heirs, lots of them. Since my books collect characters, invited or not, I plan for a goodly number at the start. Sixteen seems a goodly number, almost too good; I will pair them: eight pairs of heirs. Imperfect heirs. My characters will be imperfect, each handicapped by some physical, emotional, or moral defect. Defects which will make them easier to remember, imperfect because aren't we all?

And in honor of the Bicentennial, they will be melting-pot characters: Polish, Jewish, German, Greek, Chinese, Black. With the blind arrogance of the possessed, I devise sixteen imperfect ethnics. Ordinary folk: dressmaker, judge, cook, podiatrist, maid, inventor, secretary, student—this is getting boring—a reluctant bride-to-be, a bird watcher in a wheelchair, a thirteen-year-old girl who plays the stock market—still boring—a bookie, a burglar, a bomber—that's better. And the murderer will limp. Out of respect for plodding, rereading readers who never miss a clue, if the murderer limps, I must make most of my characters, at one time or another, limp.

I am off and typing. I still do not know who is the bookie, who is the bomber, who killed Sam Westing, or why everyone is gimping around, but no matter. The characters will shape the action; the action will shape the characters. My characters will show me the way. And so they do.

"'Grownups are so obvious,'" Turtle says in my book. That may be, but I am quick to scoff at others' faults before they scoff at mine. With time I tolerate the imperfections of the stranger; with acquaintance I begin to understand; with caring the faults fall away, and I perceive, in rare times touch, the true being of a friend. So, too, when I write. Those characters, whom I myself create and name, begin as strangers. Slowly, slowly, they take shape and grow and cast shadows on one another and on me. I learn to like them, to love them. Although I rewrite my story many times, I try not to alter this fragile metamorphosis. I would like my readers to share the joy of watching those ridiculous strangers become good friends.

Unfortunately, I end up loving all of my characters. None of them could possibly be a murderer. And mean old Sam Westing isn't so mean after all, once you get to know him. I cannot let him die. Now I really have a problem: How can there be a will if nobody died?

It is rewrite time. The plot thickens and thickens but refuses to jell, and I refuse to give up; two hundred million dollars is at stake, and I want to win. Knitting and unraveling, knotting and unknotting, I rewrite the manuscript again. And again. At last (hallelujah at last!) I find the answer to the question I forgot to ask. The plot comes full circle; all points of the compass are touched; the game is won. My book is done.

Sam Westing, the rascal, almost outwitted me with not one, but four disguises. I almost outwitted myself; my tribute to American labor history ended up a comedy in praise of capitalism. In the larger sense, however, it did turn out to be exactly what I wanted it to be—a children's book.

It is the book that is the important thing, not who I am or how I did it, but the book. Not me, the book. I fear for the book in this age of inflated personalities, in which the public's appetite for an insight into the lives of the famous has been whetted by publicity-puffers and profit-pushers into an insatiable hunger for gossip. I worry that who-the-writer-is has become of more interest than what-the-writer-writes. I am concerned that this dangerous distortion may twist its way into children's literature.

I do understand the attempt to introduce books to children through their authors, and in my travels I have seen it done effectively and well. I salute all efforts to encourage reading. But an author is not a performer; meeting a writer is not a substitute for reading a book. It is the book that lives, not the author. It is not I that is being honored here tonight; it is my book.

What becomes of Ellen Raskin is of little matter on this occasion. What does matter, what we are celebrating here tonight, is that Turtle and Angela and Chris and Sydelle, all sixteen of my beloved characters are alive and well and forevermore will be playing The Westing Game. I hold the Newbery Medal in my hand, but the shinier one is on the book. (pp. 388-91)

Ellen Raskin, "Newbery Medal Acceptance," in The Horn Book Magazine, *Vol. LV, No. 4, August, 1979, pp. 385-91.*

Another mystery puzzle for fans of Raskin's earlier novels. This one centers on the challenge set forth in the will of eccentric multimillionaire Samuel Westing. Sixteen heirs of diverse backgrounds and ages are assembled in the old "Westing house," paired off, and given clues to a puzzle they must solve—apparently in order to inherit. (Not so coincidentally, most of these characters have recently moved into a new luxury apartment building behind the mansion.) So the race is on, intensified by shifting identities and the suspicion that Westing was murdered by one of the heirs. Readers may solve the initial puzzle sooner than the characters, but the central mystery holds until the end. The heroine is 13-year-old Tabitha-Ruth "Turtle" Wexler, and she's the only character that's given more than one dimension—though most are wittily conceived and all serve admirably for this genre. Young readers will be satisfied that Turtle turns out to be the real winner and they will enjoy the process by which she learns—and earns—her reward. (pp. 87-8)

Margaret A. Dorsey, in a review of "The Westing Game," in School Library Journal, *Vol. 24, No. 8, April, 1978, pp. 87-8.*

A supersharp mystery, more a puzzle than a novel, but endowed with a vivid and extensive cast. . . . As Westing had warned, all are not what they seem, and you the reader end up liking them better than you expected to. If Raskin's crazy ingenuity has threatened to run away with her on previous occasions, here the complicated game is always perfectly meshed with character and story. Confoundingly clever, and very funny.

A review of "The Westing Game," in Kirkus Reviews, *Vol. XLVI, No. 8, April 15, 1978, p. 438.*

Raskin is an arch storyteller here, cagily dropping clues and embellishing her intricate plot with the seriocomic foibles of an eminently eccentric cast. The result is amazingly imaginative entertainment with a cutting edge and humane underpinnings that warm the tied-up-tight conclusion.

Denise M. Wilms, in a review of "The Westing Game," in Booklist, *Vol. 74, No. 19, June 1, 1978, p. 1555.*

With the merest nod to traditional devices, Ellen Raskin lures a quirky cast of characters to an apartment building on Lake Michigan, serves up a dead man's will to bind them together, and then bolts for her own literary homestead. Here the terrain is lush with puns and other word play, with comic shrubbery and broadleafed notions. . . .

Raskin's style is pointillist, the narrative formed by brief daubs of action and dialogue. An innovator, she is unafraid to take risks. The plumb line of her plot, once dropped, becomes as tangled as a fishing line. She piles mystery upon mystery, not the least of which is to veil the identity of her protagonist until her allegorical canvas is complete.

With panache, she sweeps story chaff under the carpet, dares to play dramatic action off-stage (as in Turtle's discovery of the cadaver), and at times uses baling wire to repair plot points and motivations. But no matter. Her literary choreography is bouncy, complex and full of surprises. *The Westing Game* is a page turner.

One of the few artist-writers in the children's field successfully to embrace the novel, Raskin hardly need sign her fiction. Like some painters whose signature is in every brush-stroke, hers is on every page. A restaurateur named Hoo runs a place called Hoo's On First. Sam Westing's mansion is referred to as the Westing house. And his will requests that "in place of flowers, donations be sent to Blind Bowlers of America."

While Raskin pins down her characters with very real darts (the social-climbing Grace Wexler refuses to shed her furs at the reading of the will: "She did not want to be taken for one of the poor relatives"), she takes a characteristic slapstick approach to names. In her Newbery honor book, *Figgs & Phantoms,* we met Sister Figg Newton. The heroine of *The Tattooed Potato* is Dickory Dock. In *The Westing Game,* the author virtually boxes the compass: Northrup, Eastman, McSouthers, and of course, Westing.

And in the Raskin Game that's the clue of clues.

Sid Fleischman, "A Raskin Riddle," in Book World—The Washington Post, *June 11, 1978, p. E4.*

Remember pop-up books, those stiff paper confections which, when opened at right angles, produced eleborate scenes of castles, formal gardens or dwarf-inhabited forests? *The Westing Game* reminds me of a pop-up book created by a superior designer (that being, of course, what author Ellen Raskin is in another incarnation). Here she begins with a set of characters as flat as so many flounders—the stuffy young intern, the social-climbing mama, the high-school athlete, the mousy dressmaker, etc. and causes them to pop up into focus one by one.

The story purports to be a mystery in which an eccentric millionaire's will designates a collection of unlikely heirs, moves them into a specially constructed high-rise, and requires them to compete with each other for the inheritance—or is it to discover which one of them is his murderer? The central character appears to be a skinny kid named Turtle Wexler, shin-kicker, witch, stock-market investor and determined detective. I say *purports* and *appears* because not only does the situation turn out to be otherwise than it is represented, but, judged solely according to the canons of the classic whodunit, it is as full of holes as a piece of paper lace. (p. 36)

We would do well to remember, however, that another of Miss Raskin's specialties as an illustrator is *trompe l'oeil*. Clues abound, but the contestants are warned, "It's not what you have, it's what you don't have that counts," and, "It will be up to the other players to discover who you really are." Thus, although many readers will unravel the principal puzzle before the characters (thereby achieving a cozy sense of superiority), author Raskin brings her cut-outs to dimensionality with such deft snips of the scissors that what began as holes in the plot end up as elements of style.

This is not a book for the easily confused, the unsophisticated, or the purist mystery fan, but it's great fun for those who enjoy illusion, word play or sleight of hand and don't mind a small rustle of paper in the background. (pp. 36-7)

Georgess McHargue, in a review of "The Westing Game," in The New York Times Book Review, *June 25, 1978, pp. 36-7.*

Full marks to this 1979 Newbery Medal winner for originality, inventiveness and jigsaw plotting, but it will need an intelligent and determined reader to follow the twists and turns of events, to maintain a continued and perceptive assessment of the sixteen characters and their frequent role playing, to tread a purposeful path through a maze of apparently inconsequential statements and misguided suspicions, and to accept wholeheartedly the ingenious efforts of a thirteen-year-old girl who plays the stock market and out-smarts the adults in a Perry Mason style climax. . . .

Skilfully engineered though this unconventional brain-teaser of a book is, I am afraid many young readers on this side of the Atlantic will find it too slick, too involved and too confusing.

G. Bott, in a review of "The Westing Game," in The Junior Bookshelf, *Vol. 43, No. 5, October, 1979, p. 283.*

José María Sánchez-Silva

1911-

Spanish author of fiction and short stories.

Perhaps the most respected contemporary children's author in Spain, Sánchez-Silva is acclaimed for his skillful blending of fantasy and reality, his poetic writing style, and the universality of his themes. Winner of several national awards for his adult literature and journalism, he is the creator of approximately twenty realistic fantasies and what James Krüss, corecipient with Sánchez-Silva of the Hans Christian Andersen Medal, calls "beautiful sad legends." Sánchez-Silva centers his stories for children and young adults on family life, human relationships, and animals, and often weaves philosophical thoughts and naturalistic facts into his tales. Four of his works have appeared in English. *Marcelino*, also published as *The Miracle of Marcelino*, is the first of a quartet of books about an orphan boy who meets Christ, dies, and goes to heaven. Considered a children's classic and likened to Saint-Exupéry's *The Little Prince*, *Marcelino* exemplifies Sánchez-Silva's penchant for introducing transcendental experiences into everyday life. Noted for its sensitive characterizations, *The Boy and the Whale* tells how the protagonist gradually outgrows his need for an imaginary playmate. *Ladis and the Ant* and *Second Summer with Ladis* depict the adventures of a boy who goes to the country for the summer, shrinks to the size of an ant, and observes the factually described life of these anthropomorphic insects. Sometimes used as Spanish textbooks in Europe and the United States, many of Sánchez-Silva's works have been translated into more than twenty-five languages.

Critics praise Sánchez-Silva for his simple, direct language and his warm, perceptive depiction of both human and animal interactions. Applauded for their charm and unobtrusive combination of real-life situations, scientific facts, and fantasy elements, Sánchez-Silva's books are recognized as major contributions to Spanish children's literature.

Sánchez-Silva was selected by the Hans Christian Andersen committee as a highly commended author in 1966 and received the Hans Christian Andersen Medal in 1968 for his body of work.

(See also *Something about the Author*, Vol. 16 and *Contemporary Authors*, Vols. 73-76.)

GENERAL COMMENTARY

BETTINA HÜRLIMANN

[The following excerpt was originally published in German in 1959.]

Anyone who has given any attention to early children's literature will know that for a while all writing about conduct had no purpose beyond pointing out the easiest way to Heaven; for life did not count for very much, but Heaven counted for everything. An early death, however sad, meant a joyous entry into paradise—especially if the child were courageous in his dying. This idea prevailed in Puritan England, in most of the countries of Europe, and even more so in America. With the

nineteenth century, however, the emphasis on holy dying was largely got rid of, even though the figure of the child destined for an early assumption of celestial glory persisted.

In *Marcelino* (1952) by Sanchez-Silva this subject of what we might call the glad acceptance of death is taken up in a way which is both modern and also rooted in popular tradition. Marcelino is a thoroughly normal orphan who possesses all the virtues and vices of a nine-year-old Spanish boy. He keeps small creatures and displays a love of blood and death in the elaborate way in which he kills them (an expression of the juvenile preliminaries to a passion for bull-fighting). He also tells lies and finally steals in order to bring bread and wine to a figure of Christ. This Christ figure is carved of wood and stands in a room which the child has been forbidden to enter. When he does so the figure comes alive before the child's eyes, holds a conversation with him, and finally takes him with Him into death, which is really the door to true life. The whole thing is very Spanish in conception and the Spaniards are probably affected more nearly than we are by the charming dialogue between Marcelino and Christ.

The most remarkable thing in the story is the character of the little urchin who, as an orphan, has been brought up by the monks. He combines in himself all the features of pulsing everyday life only to shine out suddenly with an inner greatness, a grace and a spirit of sacrifice, which has only been seen before in *The little prince,* and then in a very different fashion.

The story of this boy and of his death in the forbidden attic in the arms of the wooden Christ can well be explained psychologically and thereby intellectually understood. But in doing such a thing we pass over the full meaning of the book which aims to present in real terms a quite supernatural experience. Its effect on the reader, and especially on the simple mind of a child, is deeper than something which is just apprehended by the understanding.

This celebrated story has been filmed and has thereby achieved an international fame. The book itself has become part of the Spanish heritage. Although its origins are entirely Spanish and Catholic, like all truly poetic utterances it breaks through the barriers of creed and has become after very few years a classic of world literature for children.

Sanchez-Silva has written numerous books, including some half-dozen for children. Of these it seems to me that the sadly beautiful *La Burrita Non* (1955) is well worth mentioning, the story of a donkey which, like *Marcelino,* brings a transcendental meaning to everyday life. Although the argument of the book is on the theme of kindness to animals, this is not to be understood simply at such a level. The cruelly treated little donkey Burrita dies without any consolation; there then follows a wonderfully conceived story of a paradise for animals, seen in the form of a dream. The world may not be changed by such things, but every child who reads this book will look with fresh eyes at the poor working-donkeys of Spain. (pp. 86-7)

> *Bettina Hürlimann, "Fantasy and Reality," in her* Three Centuries of Children's Books in Europe, *edited and translated by Brian W. Alderson, Oxford University Press, London, 1967, pp. 76-92.*

BOOKBIRD

Jose María Sánchez-Silva was born . . . into a literary environment: his father was a journalist, and his mother wrote poetry. The child was not yet ten when he was left entirely on his own: his mother died, his father disappeared. From that moment Sánchez-Silva's childhood took on an almost fictional quality, and it remained ever-present to him. . . . The experience of that childhood and his love for young people and understanding of their problems are the basis of his great success.

Thirty years later the critic Enrique Pavón said: "Sánchez-Silva is one of the half-dozen contemporary Spanish authors who have received world-wide acclaim." . . .

"His works"—continue the critics—"are as comprehensive as few others and mirror a depth of feeling and delicate humour expressed with great stylistic clarity. Sánchez-Silva was not influenced by literary trends but always remained himself and steered towards different, more universal currents which were not influenced by the fashion of the day." The critic Antonio Valencia writes: "I know no more independent and personal literature than his, and yet he created works of universal validity. The basic challenge to any writer, that of creating a world and making it habitable for others, is met by Sánchez-Silva as it is by few other contemporary writers."

The author himself says:

> I am 55 years old and have found no more important or dignified life task than the occu-

pation with the education, upbringing and poetic development of children. I believe that the famous concept 'Cherchez la femme' is no longer a possible road for understanding the human predicament. From now on it must be 'Cherchez l'enfant'.

Sánchez-Silva has published approximately 20 books for children and young people within the last twenty years. (p. 18)

After these twenty years one can trace the outline of his works of the past, the present and of the immediate future. Apart from a few exceptions his main themes were the family, human relations, animals and a kind of "magic realism" which he employs to reveal the mainspring of his creations: poetry, action, joy and truth as opposed to trash and violence, morbidity and sensualism.

As a narrator—say the Spanish critics—Sánchez-Silva began with rather individual and personal stories. Only after *Marcelino* he began to write symbolic and universal stories. He developed the theme of the family in a four-volume work, starting with the figure of the mother in the great series *Marcelino.* The second part he called *Historias Menores* (*Little stories*) and the third *Aventura en el cielo* (*Adventures in heaven*); the figure of the father is described in *Adán y el Señor Dios* (*Adán and the Lord*).

The more demanding line in Sánchez-Silva's work is that dealing with human relations. It begins in a few works of lesser importance and finds its pinnacle in *Luiso,* a novel on the insecure social position of a child in a family of merchant marines.

The trilogy *La Burrita Non* (*Little donkey Odd*) which was included in the honour list of the Hans Christian Andersen Award deals with animals. Its aim is to convince the child that animals know no reward other than the kind treatment and love they receive from children. The series is continued in *Un Gran Pequeño* [*Ladis and the Ant*], the story of a child who makes friends with an ant, and *Segundo Verano* [*Second summer with Ladis*].

For José María Sánchez-Silva the magic which makes life great, unpredictable and joyful lies in reality. A further trilogy is based on this idea. It starts with *Adios, Josefina* [*The Boy and the Whale*], the story of a boy who has an imaginary whale. Taking leave of childhood also means taking leave of Josefina. *El Espejo Habitado* (*The lived-in mirror*) followed, the story of a girl who experiences three dreams in a mirror.

Two story books, one for children, *Cuentos de Navidad* (*Christmas stories*), and one for adolescents, *Alrededor de las doce* (*About twelve*), which is slightly humorous, and his *Colasín, Colasón,* an homage to Hans Christian Andersen whom he admires, are remarkable exceptions in Sánchez-Silva's oeuvre.

Sánchez-Silva is the greatest Spanish contemporary writer for children both as regards the quality and the quantity of his work. Theses on him have appeared in Germany and Italy as well as in Spain. Some of his books are used as set texts for students of Spanish in Europe and North-America.

He is convinced that the poetic language which has its origin in love will pave the way for a universal language where one will realize beyond the frontiers of nations and races that it is necessary to destroy at least the artificial evils which oppress mankind. (pp. 18-19)

"Jose Maria Sanchez-Silva," in Bookbird, Vol. VI,
No. 4 (December 15, 1968), pp. 18-19.

ADIÓS, JOSEFINA! [THE BOY AND THE WHALE] (1962)

The Boy and the Whale has a strong element of fantasy. To a
child of six or seven, Santiago's whale will seem just as real
as it seemed to the Spanish boy who had imagined her and
given her a name. But a boy's imagination grows and changes
with his own growth. At the beginning of this brief, entrancing
tale, Josefina was carefully put in a glass of water by Santiago's
bed at night; later, when he went to the seaside, she was sent
off to visit her relatives, but a rendez-vous was arranged for
the next day; at the end of story, the boy went to school and
the whale volunteered a final farewell, at the school gates. The
line of action (for dreams are seen as action) is simple for a
child, double for the adult who sees how the boy is using the
whale as a way of expressing his fears—of the dentist, of
school, of death. But the author has not confused the two
themes in the book. He is in tune with the boy and never
obtrudes his adult attitude or his adult interest in the boy's
feelings.

> Margery Fisher, in a review of "The Boy and the
> Whale," in Growing Point, Vol. 2, No. 6, December,
> 1963, p. 246.

This is the second time that the Spanish author has had one of
his books translated into English. It ought not to be the last.
The story of the Boy's (only well on in the book do we know
his name) progress through the joys and vicissitudes of childhood and adolescence is told with a simplicity, a directness,
and a universality reminiscent of good folk literature. In all
his problems . . . the Boy is helped by the presence of his
imaginary Whale. At the end he can say good-bye with ease
because he has grown up. The essence of reality in this fantasy
will appeal to most children between eight and eleven. It is
also excellent for reading aloud.

> Laurence Adkins, in a review of "The Boy and the
> Whale," in The School Librarian and School Library
> Review, Vol. 12, No. 2, July, 1964, p. 214.

[A] gentle and charming story about a small boy's imaginative
play and the ways in which he translates the events of his real
life into his world of fancy. . . . The style is simple and potent,
the relationships are perceptive—that between The Boy and
his grandmother especially so; The Boy's imaginings are psychologically sound, and the integration of reality and fancy is
wonderfully smooth.

> Zena Sutherland, in a review of "The Boy and the
> Whale," in Bulletin of the Center for Children's Books,
> Vol. XVIII, No. 1, September, 1964, p. 19.

UN GRAN PEQUEÑO [LADIS AND THE ANT] (1967)

A poor boy, Ladis, is sent to live in the country for a while
with a forester. Fantasy now enters the story for Ladis is able
to speak to the ants and Mufra, their queen, takes him into an
ant-hill where he sees the wonderful social life of these insects.
In this miniature country Ladis learns to love and admire the
insect world.

An imaginative and yet informative story which is well written
and absorbing for children of any country.

A review of "Ladis and the Ant," in The Junior
Bookshelf, Vol. 32, No. 5, October, 1968, p. 299.

Ladis from slum sickliness and timidity to alfresco health and
vitality via a share in the life of an anthill is not quite **The Boy
and the Whale** . . . but the conjunction of naturalism and fantasy
is similar, and similarly suspect. . . . And whereas Ladis' home
life is all of a piece (even if all glum, the compleat picture of
poverty), the anthill is sometimes not inappropriately a microcosm of human society, sometimes a substitute—as when Ladis
teaches some of the ants to play football. . . . The book has
moments of some poignance but Ladis' transformation (just
what the doctor predicted) is even less convincing than his
initiation into ant life by Mufra. It is, however, one of the few
contemporary Spanish translations we have, and may be wanted
in large collections for that reason—also because the author
was co-winner of the Hans Christian Andersen Award in 1968.

> A review of "Ladis and the Ant," in Kirkus Reviews,
> Vol. XXXVII, No. 8, April 15, 1969, p. 442.

Into this realistic, essentially ordinary story, the author introduces Ladis' remarkable encounter with the queen ant Mufra,
whose bite reduces Ladis in size so that he can ride on Mufra's
back and visit the ant kingdom. Interesting information is im-
parted about the living habits of insects, but the purpose of the
contrived fantastical episodes is to provide a bridge for the
chasm between the initially lonely, frightened, self-centered
boy who returns home stronger, wiser, and happier. There's
no real excitement here; only a mildly sympathetic story of a
boy who, while retaining his essential bookishness and sensitivity, can grow out of himself and into a world encompassing
more than a one-room tenement. (pp. 93-4)

> Frances M. Postell, in a review of "Ladis and the
> Ant," in School Library Journal, an appendix to Li-
> brary Journal, Vol. 15, No. 9, May, 1969, pp. 93-4.

The scientific information [Ladis] learns on his explorations is
especially memorable, because the insects concerned have been
affectionately endowed with personalities.

Marvelous as these adventures are the real magic is in the
changes summer brings to Ladis. As feebleness and pallor give
way to healthy vigor, his timidity is replaced by curiosity and
appreciation; in the end, he discovers that true involvement
with others is frequently an antidote for fear, and sometimes
the prescription for love.

> Mary Lynne Bird, in a review of "Ladis and the
> Ant," in The New York Times Book Review, July
> 13, 1969, p. 26.

EL SEGUNDO VERANO DE LADIS [SECOND SUMMER WITH LADIS] (1968)

Second summer with Ladis, a sequel to **Ladis and the ant,** is a
poet's tale—concise yet free in tone, making an easy transition
from adventure to exposition and back again. Mufra's didactic
asides to the boy are in a tradition that is rarely revived in
England now; they take us straight back to Jack's insects, and
none the worse for that. The child who is prepared to accept
facts about Argentine ants and their migratory instinct alongside
a sharp description of a battle between these interlopers and
Mufra's people will find yet another dream here—the dream
of being accepted within the natural world. From another angle

the story shows in symbolic terms how a town boy can feel himself into the ambience of the country.

Margery Fisher, in a review of "Second Summer with Ladis," in Growing Point, *Vol. 8, No. 5, November, 1969, p. 1407.*

Second Summer with Ladis maintains the extraordinarily high standard which was set by its predecessor, **Ladis and the Ant.** A short book, . . . it tells how Ladis goes into the country for the second time and is again caught up in the life of the ant community, round his uncle's farm. Señor Sánchez-Silva has two gifts which he combines felicitously. He is a secure fantasist (Ladis changes to ant size without any fuss) and he is a naturalist who refuses, for the sake of a story, to bend his scientific observations. So that when the ant colony, of which Ladis's friend Mufra is head, is threatened by war to the death from the more powerful Argentinian ants, Ladis is put in the terrible position f witnessing its defeat—under oath not to disturb the course of nature. The description of the battle between the rival ant communities is as vivid, as exciting and as moving as an eye-witness account of, say, Glencoe or Ypres: it is with relief that one hears the tiny voice of the wounded Mufra suggesting to poor Ladis that he should take her and a few battered followers home with him in a matchbox to a flower-pot in Madrid, where the life cycle may be completed— and renewed. The Ladis books are minor masterpieces. It is to be hoped that the flower-pot in Madrid will provide a further opportunity for us to meet Ladis the Spanish boy, and Mufra the ant.

"Continuations and Beginnings," in The Times Literary Supplement, *No. 3536, December 4, 1969, p. 1389.*

John (Lewis) Steptoe

1950-

Black American author/illustrator of picture books and fiction, reteller, and illustrator.

Steptoe is recognized as an author whose works reflect the thoughts and feelings of the young as well as his own artistic versatility. One of the first author/illustrators to relate the black experience to a primary grade audience from an authentic perspective, he combines striking art work with realistic and often humorous treatments of such subjects as the interaction between parents and children, school, and brotherhood. At seventeen, Steptoe created *Stevie*, a picture book about overcoming jealousy which is considered a landmark in juvenile literature for its expression of a universal theme through the language, setting, and cultural scope of an urban child. Subsequent works, which also feature black dialogue and inner city settings, provide young readers with positive depictions of urban environment and family life. Several of these books developed from Steptoe's relationship with his family; in *Daddy Is a Monster . . . Sometimes,* for example, he represents his children as the main characters and makes the father an illustrative self-portrait. Steptoe's only novel, *Marcia,* focuses on a young couple who are debating whether or not to enter into a sexual relationship; directed to young adults, it presents viewpoints on romance, sexuality, and birth control through the narratives of several characters. As an illustrator, Steptoe moved from creating powerful and expressionistic art which relies on heavy outline, bright colors, and African motifs to more subtle paintings which reflect such styles as art deco and surrealism. *The Story of Jumping Mouse,* however, marks Steptoe's departure from the subjects and illustration techniques of his previous works. A free adaptation of a native American legend which relates how acts of selflessness transform a mouse into an eagle, *The Story of Jumping Mouse* is illustrated with intricately detailed black-and-white pencil sketches which are often drawn from the mouse's perspective.

Critics praise Steptoe as an innovative author whose works successfully combine positive messages and frankness with a variety of artistic styles. Especially appreciative of his strong characterizations, accurate use of black English, and understanding of children and their perceptions, reviewers also comment favorably on each stage of Steptoe's development as a visual artist. Although his stories are occasionally thought to be weakly constructed and to include intrusive philosophies, Steptoe is usually acclaimed for the universality and optimism of his works as well as for the technical brilliance of his illustrations.

In 1970, the John Steptoe Library was dedicated in Brooklyn, New York. In 1978, *Stevie* received the Lewis Carroll Shelf Award and in 1985 *The Story of Jumping Mouse* was selected as a Caldecott Honor Book. Steptoe has also been honored with several awards for his illustrations.

(See also *CLR,* Vol. 2; *Something about the Author,* Vol. 8; *Contemporary Authors New Revision Series,* Vol. 3; and *Contemporary Authors,* Vols. 49-52.)

Courtesy of John Steptoe

GENERAL COMMENTARY

RAY ANTHONY SHEPARD

What, if any, is the difference between a Black and a non-Black illustrator/writer as each creates picture books set in urban Black communities? Ezra Jack Keats and John Steptoe make for an interesting comparison.

The illustrations of Ezra Jack Keats for *Snowy Day* (1963) received the Caldecott award. The year 1963 was the high point of the integrationist civil rights movement, symbolized in the March on Washington. *Snowy Day,* as a mirror of the times, was a position statement from the liberal literary establishment and set forth a new social idea for the nation's younger readers.

Snowy Day, in presenting a Black kid engulfed in snow, said that there were Black kids in the otherwise White World but that in spite of the color difference, Black kids enjoyed snow and whiteness as well as everyone else. *Snowy Day* said that Black kids were human by presenting them as colored white kids.

The success of *Snowy Day* encouraged *Whistle For Willie* (1964). The story showed Peter's world in bright and happy reds and yellows, where mommy and daddy dressed like a nice middle-class white family, and even a white girl jumped rope with a

Black girl. *Peter's Chair* (1967) took a close look inside Peter's home. The colors became more somber, for after all, they were middle class; the colors provided a happy background for a happy family, nevertheless. White was the predominant color used (ten out of 30 pages). The whiteness emphasized the universality of Peter's family and his story.

By 1968 the civil rights movement had been shot in Memphis, and the Black Power movement moved to the forefront as an ominous storm. *A Letter to Amy* (1968) kept pace with the times. It was significant. The bright and happy colors of Peter's world were replaced by dark and threatening clouds. Even though a white boy, whose parents hadn't escaped, came to Peter's birthday party, the neighborhood took on the appearance of a "slum" or a "ghetto" as seen by an outsider. Mommy was there, dressed like you know who, but middle-class daddy had disappeared.

In 1969 came *Goggles,* and the integration dream was over. Whites were not as welcome as they had been in the Black community. The drawings for *Goggles* show Peter's world as if seen from inside a locked car with windows rolled up tight. Every illustration shouts, "Look, see, we're in a ghetto." By now Peter's mommy has disappeared, and Peter and Archie are fighting to survive against a gang of older boys in an economically deprived world. This view merited the Caldecott runner-up medal.

Hi Cat! (1970) continued the adventures of Archie and Peter in Blackland. There is a retreat from the white gloom of *Goggles;* the drawings and story become lighter. It is still in an underdeveloped setting, but the natives are happy. In 1971 Keats seems willing enough to bring equal time to the slum world. His latest book, *Apt. 3* (1971), shows a non-Black kid's quest in a ghetto apartment house. Perhaps the kid is even white; you are not quite sure—but at least—and at last, he is not Black.

For those who think I'm being unfair, and that my comments have more to do with politics than art, let me ask you: How would any of the Keats books be changed if the characters were white? The stories would be the same, of course, thematically speaking. The color of the characters is irrelevant. It is relevant only in terms of one's understanding of the book-buying market and the political-social times; thus the books were conceived with political awareness.

John Steptoe's *Stevie* (1969), published the same year as *Goggles,* is another story set in Blackland, but this is a work seen through the eyes of an insider. The drawings in the two books—one by Steptoe, the other by Keats—offer sharp contrasts. Steptoe had no need to convince his readers of where he is, so gone are the signs that announce G H E T T O, for *Stevie* is set in a Black community, and although it may be part of the same city shown by Keats, the difference is obvious. Steptoe shows love for his people.

The same sense of love of one's people holds true in *Uptown* (1970) and *Train Ride* (1971). Of course, John Steptoe is not a liberal white, thus he has no need to show human sameness, but instead celebrates the ethnic difference of Blacks. His three books are in harmony; the illustrations, narratives, the settings, and the language sounds feed into each other, creating a harmonious total. He sees his world. Thematically, his books would have to be considerably changed if the characters were made non-Black.

The language gives an indication of different points of view: From *Goggles:* "Footsteps! 'The big boys! They followed me.'" From *Stevie:* "Naw, my Momma said he can't go in the park cause the last time he went he fell and hurt his knee, with his old stupid self."

Stevie, Steptoe's first book—like Keats' *Snowy Day,* was a beginner's success. *Stevie* received the Society of Illustrators Gold Medal, and it was also named an American Library Assn. Notable Children's Book. This is not surprising because the story is about an easily recognizable universal theme of peer jealousy. It is not difficult for all children to find themselves in Stevie. One reviewer called the book *"a convincing story for all children"* (emphasis added). But *Uptown* and *Train Ride,* his best so far, move away from the easily recognizable universal theme and move closer to the particular experience of a Black kid growing up in Harlem. Even though the universal theme is there, as it is in all literature, one senses the critics cooling off in their embrace of Steptoe. In order to love what he has done in his last two books, one must be willing to surrender the idea that in order for there to be equality, there must be similarity. Steptoe pushes one to see equality in terms of our ethnic differences.

It may be unnecessary to have an either/or situation, but it is necessary that Keats' books be recognized as an outside view of Black life. His books may serve a necessary function for those people who need to be convinced of our human similarity, and who can not give up the melting pot myth.

The white reader, if I may engage in the dangers of generalization, will see in Keats' characters children who confirm sameness, but who live in a terrible environment. The reader's emotional response combines a feeling of pity and an attraction to the children's adventures. Thus is created another generation of liberals. In the Steptoe books white readers are exposed to a life style that is foreign to them. The illustrations do not push them into emotional ambivalence: attraction, on the one hand, and sympathy, on the other. Steptoe presents an uncompromised Black world that increases the readers' awareness of ethnic grouping in this country. It makes them realize that the world is not made completely in their image.

For the Black reader, to continue the dangers of generalization, the difference is simple. In Keats there is someone who looks like me, and in Steptoe there is someone who knows what is going on.

> *Ray Anthony Shepard, "Adventures in Blackland with Keats and Steptoe," in* Interracial Books for Children, *Vol. 3, No. 4, Autumn, 1971, p. 3.*

BARBARA BADER

Stevie is above all confident—a bold transposition of Rouault to the nursery. . . . It is as if Steptoe, not knowing that there was a way to illustrate for young children, or being told, went his own way; and in his own way made something fresh of a child's perennial resentment of a newcomer—"his old crybaby self." That Stevie's mother leaves him at Robert's during the working week, that the two boys don't speak schoolbook English, is secondary, surely, to the strong bright intimacy. If *Stevie* is, circumstantially, a 'black' book, it is also, because of the substantiation, the more credible regardless; like [Sue Felt's] *Rosa-Too-Little* it has character, like [Ellen Tarry and Marie Hall Ets's] *My Dog Rinty* verisimilitude. The icon-like intensity is Steptoe's art.

From Stevie, *written and illustrated by John Steptoe. Harper & Row, 1969. Copyright © 1969 by John L. Steptoe. All rights reserved. Reprinted by permission of Harper & Row, Publishers, Inc.*

In *Uptown* and especially in *Train Ride*. . . , the protagonists are older and the narrative—it is hardly a story—is diffuse, itself circumstantial, and topical, reflecting then-current attitudes. To the extent that *Train Ride* reflects chiefly attitudes rather than feelings, and has no 'beyond,' no larger frame of reference, it is limited and indeed exclusionary; but it is limited first. (p. 382)

> *Barbara Bader, "Negro Identification, Black Identity," in her* American Picture Books from Noah's Ark to the Beast Within, *Macmillan Publishing Company, 1976, pp. 373-82.*

MASHA KABAKOW RUDMAN

There is no conflict whatsoever in some stories with siblings as the characters. In John Steptoe's *My Special Best Words,* Bweela, although she is only three years old, lovingly and competently takes care of her younger brother. They do have some verbal quarrels, but the reader recognizes this as part of the fun; the relationship remains strongly positive. (p. 20)

Most books for young children concerned with sex education describe the birth process. They rarely take into consideration the other aspects of sexuality in a child's life. . . . *My Special Best Words* is one of the exceptions. . . . Bweela tries to toilet-train her brother, and the two children romp together in the

bathroom. They are comfortable with their bodies. The illustrations help to convey the sense of joy and comfort with themselves and each other. As usual, Steptoe is educational at the same time that he is disturbing the complacency of some of the reading public. (pp. 152-53)

[The author's] first book, *Stevie,* was published when he was only seventeen years old. Steptoe, a Black, says of himself, "I don't just happen to be Black." His illustrations, reminiscent of Rouault's paintings, convey a sense of black universality that is at once appealing and dramatic. Ray Shepard, in his article "Adventures in Blackland with Keats and Steptoe" [see excerpt above dated 1971] . . . , claims that Keats's characters could be either white or black but that Steptoe "celebrates the ethnic differences of Blacks." He feels that the characters in Steptoe's books could not be white without drastically changing the story. Perhaps this is true in the case of *Uptown,* which is written in contemporary black urban speech. *Uptown* is the story of two boys who wonder what they will do and be when they grow up. They talk about black pride and clothing that sets them off from Whites, but their conversation about how they feel and what their options are is the same as most poor urban children growing up in less than middle-class comfort in a large city.

Stevie . . . could, in this author's opinion, easily have nonblack characters as its main figures. The story is about sibling rivalry, about caring adults, and about a child and his feelings. Steptoe's illustrations combined with the text fit well. There is certainly no sense that Stevie's blackness is inappropriate, but he is not a stereotype and could therefore be a child of almost any ethnic background. He would not be rich or even middle class, but he could be any color.

In Steptoe's books, as in Keats's early ones, the city is a place that is challenging but not punitive. The colors are not pastel, but they are not brash or ugly. Keats's ghetto is littered, depressing, and to be reckoned with; Steptoe's is alive and flourishing. His book *Train Ride* again affirms the city and the children's capability of coping with it and enjoying it. This time the children live in Brooklyn, not Harlem. Again, black urban speech is used. The story is simply that of a group of young black boys who take a forbidden subway ride uptown to Times Square. They arrive home very late after having had a marvelous time. Each is punished by his parents. Though they all agree that their fathers have given them the worst beatings they ever had, they are undaunted and will probably repeat the adventures at a subsequent time.

The city is again presented here as a place in which people can enjoy life and survive adversity. The children in the story all have names; they are recognizable individuals. They all have loving, concerned families; they are not stereotypes of children from broken homes. Their parents all care about their behavior; they are not permitted to run loose. They are bright, capable children who feel good about themselves. It is this sense of positive self-image and underlying optimism that Steptoe conveys. These qualities are part of what makes his books appealing and useful. (pp. 185-86)

> *Masha Kabakow Rudman, in her* Children's Literature: An Issues Approach, *D. C. Heath and Company, 1976, 443 p.*

MYRA POLLACK SADKER AND DAVID MILLER SADKER

John Steptoe, in his picture books for young children, combines black English with bold and striking illustrations. (p. 154)

Stevie deals with a universal situation, a younger child's intrusion into an older child's life. But the book relates this universal situation in a ghetto context through the use of language, environment, and illustrations. The ghetto context is also used in *Uptown* . . . , the story of two black boys as they reminisce about their past and daydream about their future. Their discussions include experiences with junkies, black power, karate experts, and hippies. One boy even considers becoming a policeman but is dissuaded by his friend: "nobody digs cops, you wouldn't have no friends." Finally, they agree. "Guess we'll just hang out together for a while and just dig on everythin' that's goin' on."

Birthday . . . continues the bold illustrations that have marked Steptoe's work, and it relates a strong black theme. Javaka Shatu lives in Yoruba, a small American town, and he is celebrating his eighth birthday. It is a future place, in a distant time, where black pride and brotherhood are all-pervasive. Perhaps the brotherhood theme of *Birthday* may be Steptoe's dream for America. (pp. 154-55)

> *Myra Pollack Sadker and David Miller Sadker, "The Black Experience in Children's Literature," in their* Now Upon a Time: A Contemporary View of Children's Literature, *Harper & Row, Publishers, 1977, pp. 129-62.*

ELLEN TREMPER

Stevie is written in modified Black English (more a transcription of pronunciation than a different grammatical system). This is Steptoe's first book and the language may have been a concession to the traditionalist's views of Black and Standard English. The non-black reader certainly does not feel he is in a different language system, and the story line has universal appeal as well. Sibling rivalry is the subject of the book but with a twist realistically reflective of the situation of the black working class. For Stevie, the sibling in this story, is not a blood relative but a child who is living with the narrator's family during the week while his own mother goes to work. The loss of the "brother," which is the subject of wishful fantasy, becomes real when Stevie's parents move away and the baby sitting arrangement ends. This makes for a neat resolution of the fantasy as Robert, the narrator, must sadly realize his loss.

Robert tells his story in Black English. He is a realistically drawn figure whose language seems an integral part of his character and position in life. And he is sympathetic since we all, in some way, have felt the jealousy and irritation he feels when Stevie comes into his home. The story is so short that he does not spend much time harping on the wrongs done him—the mud on his bedspread, his toys broken up, his being unable to go to the park with his friends since he must mind Stevie—before he is faced with permanent loss of the little boy. He becomes even more sympathetic at this point since we admire his honesty in recognizing that he has grown to love Stevie.

There is no over-sentimentalization in the story except, perhaps, for a line close to the end of the book, "Aw, no! I let my corn flakes get soggy thinkin' about him." But it is quickly forgotten, given the charming simplicity of the very last words.

> He was a nice little guy.
> He was kinda like a little brother.
> Little Stevie. . . .

In fact, the whole story is charming in its simplicity. It is not a book to which one feels Black English has been added in the "appropriate" amounts. And while the language gives the young reader easier access to the story than he or she might have had if it had been written in Standard, all aspects of this book should make a child feel comfortable. (pp. 109-10)

Unlike the language of [Lucille Clifton's] *My Brother Fine With Me,* the language of *Train Ride* by Steptoe does not feel grafted onto the story. As Henry James said of morality, Black English is not something to be measured out and poured into the phial of art like a dose of medicine. It needs to be integral to the story. In this book some boys, probably none older than eleven or twelve, with nothing to do on a warm summer's night, dare each other to sneak onto the West Side train in Harlem and ride down to 42 Street where they take in the flashiness of Times Square, see white people in large numbers, and play the pin ball machines in the arcades. At eleven o'clock they are confronted with reality—no money and the beatings they are going to get from their fathers if and when they get home. They beg the token seller to let them on the train, and then they go home to their just desserts. The next day they decide that whatever they are going to do, they are going to do it in their own neighborhood. But they are charmingly and realistically unrepentant about their escapade. As they sit on the stoop talking about it, Charlie, the narrator, reports:

> We all was tellin' everybody what a good time
> we had, but nobody told about the beatin's we
> got.

"We'll probably do it again," I said.

"Yeah, when?"

"I don't know, but I'll take y'all up there again, cause it was a boss time."

The culture shock the boys experience when they hit Times Square is what enriches the simple story line. Suddenly, the narrow world of these kids is opened up for them as they glimpse a reality undreamt of.

> There was a lot of people walkin' around. There was a lot of white people. There wasn't no white people around where we lived, except maybe our teachers in school. A lot of the men had long hair. [This book was published in 1971.] A lot of men had on suits. Some had on real pretty clothes. There was these boys like us out on the streets shinin' shoes and makin' a lot of money.
>
> We saw a cop ridin' a real horse. And we saw a cowboy walkin' in the street. Around the corner was a lot of tall buildings and more movies. Everybody was movin' real fast.
>
> "Hey, look at them signs up there!" Billy yelled.
>
> They was boss, and real big. There was this big clock. And there was this big iron with steam comin' out of it. There was colored lights and cars and more people. And all that goin' on at night time. There was so much to see. . . .

The language of this description is far from elegant. The repetition of words and the uninteresting and repetitive word order make it unworthy of a college freshman theme. Yet the dazzled senses of these boys eloquently shine through the prosaic style, convincing us of the "felt life" behind the words and the accuracy of the writer's impressions (the need for which are two other Jamesian dicta). In fact, the Black English is what makes the book as good as it is. While one might argue that the theme of sibling rivalry—both in *Stevie* and *My Brother Fine With Me*—might well be presented in Standard English with no great loss, the story of *Train Ride* would be rendered null if delivered in sanitized Standard. While the emotions created by the experiences of the boys may be universal, the experiences themselves are very particularly those of black working class children, and would literally lose in the translation into Standard. (pp. 114-15, 118)

> *Ellen Tremper, "Black English in Children's Literature," in* The Lion and the Unicorn, *Vol. 3, No. 2, Winter, 1979-80, pp. 105-24.*

PATRICIA JEAN CIANCIOLO

[John Steptoe] has illustrated three stories [*Stevie, My Special Best Words*, and Eloise Greenfield's *She Come Bringing Me That Little Baby Girl*] about black children and their responses to various universal experiences. . . . In all three of these picture books, young readers, regardless of their race, nationality, religion, or sex, will probably recognize and empathize with the children's feelings of jealously and rejection when their parents, relatives, and friends fuss over younger children. They will also recognize their own protective and possessive attitudes towards younger children, attitudes portrayed so credibly in these fine picture books. (p. 17)

> *Patricia Jean Cianciolo, in an introduction to her* Picture Books for Children, *revised edition, American Library Association, 1981, pp. 1-30.*

DONNA E. NORTON

The varied relationships between a father and his two children are featured in Steptoe's *Daddy Is a Monster . . . Sometimes*. The illustrations show two different reactions by the same father. While he is nice most of the time, he can turn into a monster with "teeth comin out his mouth" and hair on his face when his son and daughter fight over the teddy bear, play with their food at a restaurant, are extra messy or noisy, and when they have an accident in the house. Daddy concludes that: "I'm probably a monster daddy when I got monster kids." This book has been praised for the strong father/child relationships it develops; literature about a black experience often shows a family without a father.

Steptoe's subjects in his books for young children could be any children who have problems at home, are jealous of another child, or have a father who is sometimes unhappy with their behavior. The language and the illustrations make it a black experience. . . . The dialect follows the criteria for black literature because it rings true and blends naturally with the story. (p. 496)

> *Donna E. Norton, "Multiethnic Literature," in her* Through the Eyes of a Child: An Introduction to Children's Literature, *Charles E. Merrill Publishing Company, 1983, pp. 486-545.*

MARCIA (1976)

The trouble with most of the new YA novels dealing with sex is that seventeen-year-old behavior, presuming seventeen-year-old feelings, is depicted in stories read chiefly by twelve-year-olds—and, in truth, written at their level. Steptoe's thin but pointed first novel is different. Marcia is only fourteen, and though her boyfriend Danny is pushing her to have sex she herself feels unready; you can see other girls her age empathizing totally and those a little younger relating with understanding. Marcia makes two impassioned, soapbox speeches—one on aggression and manhood to her boyfriend, one on birth control to her mother—which express more confusion than she realizes (and perhaps more than Steptoe realizes), and feminists might well fault the author not only for the girls' preoccupation with boys and clothes, but, more important, for his assumption that eventual capitulation is inevitable. (Would it really be worse to lose Danny?) To us, Marcia's mother is a bit too hasty with the same assumption—but no one can fault her alacrity in fixing her daughter up with contraceptives. And, whatever we adults make of its message, *Marcia*—with its modified black English, sassy dialogue, and underlying earnestness—is an issue book attuned to its intended audience.

> *A review of "Marcia," in* Kirkus Reviews, *Vol. XLIV, No. 8, April 15, 1976, p. 484.*

For urban Black teen-age girls, this book deals frankly with male "machismo," responsible sex, and contraception. Unfortunately, impact is limited by cardboard characters and a storyline consisting solely of when and on whose terms will Marcia and Danny screw (yes, that's the word used). Interest is sustained less by plot than by the often lyrical rendition of Black speech. But whenever the message gets "heavy," characters deliver set pieces in standard English. Some messages reflecting a political stance, e.g., contraception is right for

From Daddy Is a Monster . . . Sometimes, *written and illustrated by John Steptoe. Lippincott, 1980.*
Copyright © 1980 by John Steptoe. Reprinted by permission of Harper & Row, Publishers, Inc.

young girls but population control is a plot by the haves against the have-nots, are inappropriate (how many readers will identify—no less identify with—the Viet Cong?). Steptoe's illustrations, which serve story and spirit so well in his picture books, merely decorate. (pp. 73-4)

Joan Scherer Brewer, in a review of "Marcia," in
School Library Journal, *Vol. 22, No. 9, May, 1976,
pp. 73-4.*

This brief, exuberant first junior novel reveals a picture-book author-artist's talent for creating vivid, likeable characters, who, in this case, manage to balance out some provoking sloppiness in story construction and exposition. . . . The events unfold mainly from Marcia's viewpoint, with Danny becoming the narrator for several pertinent sections—a shift made disconcerting by the author's jarring intrusion in the introductory paragraphs of these sections. Also, two lengthy discussions (one between Marcia and Danny on the subject of survival and the other between Marcia and her mother on Marcia's right to make a life for herself) become a platform for Steptoe's philosophy instead of dialogues that organically evolve from the characters' experience. Steptoe needs a lighter hand to become more effective—and affecting. Still, the story, written in black English, is appealing, and its concerns are common ones for young people; Steptoe hasn't flinched from dealing with the

issue head-on. And one note of a practical nature: the book's large print and brevity coupled with its honest treatment of mature subject matter may make it a candidate for reluctant readers.

Denise M. Wilms, in a review of "Marcia," in The
Booklist, *Vol. 72, No. 17, May 1, 1976, p. 1272.*

John Steptoe's first junior novel is an imaginative and frank story. . . . Capturing the nuances of the black urban dialect, Mr. Steptoe's language is both convincing and real, and because it is also easy to read, I would certainly list his book in the high interest-low vocabulary category. Highlighting his text is Mr. Steptoe's bold four-colored illustrations which visually offset this positive book for teenagers.

Patricia A. Spence, in a review of "Marcia," in
Children's Book Review Service, *Vol. 5, No. 1, September, 1976, p. 9.*

The characters are believable although not drawn in depth, the dialogue is brisk, the concerns of Marcia and other teenagers in the story are genuine, but the book is weak in story line: both in the first-person passages by Marcia and in the third person episodes that reflect Danny's viewpoint, there's a great deal of conversation but not much plot development.

Zena Sutherland, in a review of "Marcia," in Bulletin of the Center for Children's Books, *Vol. 30, No. 2, October, 1976, p. 33.*

It all comes down to the question of "Will she or won't she?" and all of the lecturing, talking, and speechifying seem a justification for Marcia's "putting out" to keep her Danny. References to Viet Nam and use of current slang and colloquialisms already date this book-of-the-hour. Steptoe's junior *True Story* is disappointingly shallow, tough with gristle, rather than sinew. On the other hand, the art work, a combination of painting and collage, carries a dramatic impact missing in the text. Steptoe's powerful portraits of the characters—Marcia, Danny, the mother, and another young couple—are revealing and unforgettable, Rouault-like studies with qualities of batik.

Ruth M. Stein, in a review of "Marcia," in Language Arts, *Vol. 54, No. 2, February, 1977, p. 209.*

DADDY IS A MONSTER . . . SOMETIMES (1980)

"I'm probably a monster daddy," Bweela and her brother Javaka's daddy admits at the close, "when I got monster kids." And that, literally, is what we've been seeing: pictures of the kids misbehaving and sprouting whiskers and ears; pictures of Daddy reacting, and turning into a monster too. Some youngsters may not grasp the connection until it's spelled out, since the kids' physical transformations are not accompanied by words, the incidents are not precisely parallel, and the most developed incident is somewhat subtle (Bweela and Javaka accept an ice cream cone from a lady who reproaches their father for only buying one for himself—after he's already treated them). And there's an incongruence here between the elaborate illustrational style and the simple lesson, and even between the aforementioned incident and the other, very routine instances of nuisance behavior (a messy room, delaying tactics at bedtime, etc.). But in themselves the illustrations are forceful and compelling, with Daddy's shifts from reasonableness to irritation to glowering anger strikingly put across. So, though it's a weak vehicle for a lot of emotion, the authenticity of that emotion is not to be lightly dismissed.

A review of "Daddy Is a Monster . . . Sometimes," in Kirkus Reviews, *Vol. XLVIII, No. 7, April 1, 1980, p. 437.*

There's love underneath it all on both sides, and daddy's humor isn't to be missed. . . . Steptoe's art has developed enormously. Heavy outlines are still a trademark, but neon colors have been abandoned for low-key earthy tones; style has shifted from muted, soft-smudged shapes of *Stevie* and *Train Ride* days to an art deco-like, electrified-looking chatter of lines to describe the faces and the world of father and children. The story is slightly fragmented, but the combination of fresh art and affectionate family interaction is still a winning one; the whole is a very easy scene with which to identify.

Denise M. Wilms, in a review of "Daddy Is a Monster . . . Sometimes," in Booklist, *Vol. 76, No. 16, April 15, 1980, p. 1210.*

It's nice to have a book about a father and children who form a family; it's nice to feel the warm love that permeates the relationship despite the flares of irritation. The writing style (mostly dialogue, partly Black idiom) is adequate, the pictures are technically brilliant but may be limited in appeal for close viewing because the lines and shapes that give the faces expression when viewed at a distance have an almost scrofulous look at close range.

Zena Sutherland, in a review of "Daddy Is a Monster . . . Sometimes," in Bulletin of the Center for Children's Books, *Vol. 34, No. 1, September, 1980, p. 22.*

This book focuses on the tensions between parent and child that occur in every family, and Steptoe has used his own Black urban family to demonstrate them. Better than most books for young children that have concentrated on feelings and personal relationships rather than on plot, Steptoe's book goes into some detail about the incidents that make Daddy seem a monster. Daddy's behavior is balanced with universal provocations like "just wanting to make a little noise" (even when Daddy is on the phone). Another factor to recommend the book is unstereotyped characters. The presentation, however, is too difficult for most children in the early grades to handle. Much of the text consists of dialogue between Bweela and her brother Javaka, unrelieved at times for several pages with no third-person commentary. To his credit, Steptoe has Bweela and Javaka call each other by name—at least where the identity of the speaker makes a real difference. Even so, the numerous subquotes and the use, however sparing, of black dialect contributes to the problem. The illustrations, although of a very high artistic quality, consistently use light and surrealism that is so sophisticated that an unaided child would find some of the illustrations difficult to understand.

Richard Morrissey, in a review of "Daddy Is a Monster . . . Sometimes," in School Library Journal, *Vol. 27, No. 6, February, 1981, p. 60.*

The humor in the children's being unaware of their sometimes monstrous behavior is made even more appealing when you learn that their father does not think of himself as a monster either. At the end of the story, Bweela and Javaka ask their father why he is a monster sometimes. He at first does not understand what they are talking about. When he does understand, he says "Well, I'm probably a monster daddy when I got monster kids." Since Bweela and Javaka know there are not any monster children in the house, they just laugh and say, "Daddy, you crazy."

This story is a must for children's enjoyment. The pictures are wonderfully colorful and the more you look at them, the more you see in them.

Also, this book will certainly be thought-provoking for adults. It's a reminder of how creative children are in understanding and expressing their perceptions of people they interact with. In addition, it depicts a parent who does many of the things parents/guardians do without a second thought. We enforce children's bedtime, make sure children have enough of the foods they need to stay healthy, teach children not to be destructive and we try to make children aware of other people's needs. These are a part of taking care of children, right? Well, have you thought of how children may perceive *you* in some of these situations?

The title of this book may put some people off. Don't let it.

A review of "Daddy Is a Monster . . . Sometimes," in Interracial Books for Children Bulletin, *Vol. 12, Nos. 7 & 8, 1981, p. 20.*

Most children find their parents to be monsters sometimes. These feelings find humorous and loving expression here as

Javaka and Bweela discuss and recall several transformations of their usually quite human father. The idea that children can be monsters too will interest the young reader or listener, and the familiar, everyday occurrences and realistic relationships will appeal. Exceptional, surrealistic illustrations give the book special artistic value for children.

> *Sharon Spredemann Dreyer, "Annotations: 'Daddy Is a Monster . . . Sometimes'," in her* The Bookfinder, When Kids Need Books: Annotations of Books Published 1979 through 1982, *American Guidance Service, 1985, p. 356.*

JEFFREY BEAR CLEANS UP HIS ACT (1983)

The idea behind that slangy title is pretty crude too—but in an almost prissy way. Second grader Jeffrey Bear reacts to a boring classroom lecture from sanitation-man Mr. Polar, and the stern vigilance of teacher Ms. Gloria ("Grizzly") Bearfacts, by imagining himself the teacher, and the two of them "taking lessons" from *him.* But whether he screams, jokes, or lectures, the kids deride him; so, when Ms. Bearfacts wakes him up by asking sarcastically if he'd like to exchange places, he quietly and meekly declines. The sanitation-man is a bore, the teacher is a horror—and if the lesson's supposed to be that kids can't do better, it's not much of one.

> *A review of "Jeffrey Bear Cleans Up His Act," in* Kirkus Reviews, *Vol. LI, No. 9, May 1, 1983, p. 521.*

The story has some appeal in its imagining of power, but is improbable in presenting a daydream in which the dreamer loses control of the situation—unless the implication is that Jeffrey falls asleep, which is not made clear. The characters are all bears, but only from the neck up; the teacher is presented as a grim disciplinarian. Steptoe's paintings have power and vigor, but they do not combine attractively with balloon captions.

> *Zena Sutherland, in a review of "Jeffrey Bear Cleans Up His Act," in* Bulletin of the Center for Children's Books, *Vol. 37, No. 1, September, 1983, p. 18.*

Steptoe's humor effortlessly captures the frustration of a young child (albeit a bear child) learning to cope with school, and his illustrations (which are softer than *Stevie* or *Birthday*) are bear-like caricatures of humans that are strikingly expressive (one illustration of Ms. Bearfacts standing against a poster is very reminiscent of da Vinci's *Mona Lisa*).

> *Joe Bearden, in a review of "Jeffrey Bear Cleans Up His Act," in* School Library Journal, *Vol. 30, No. 1, September, 1983, p. 112.*

THE STORY OF JUMPING MOUSE: A NATIVE AMERICAN LEGEND (1984)

Whatever the authenticity of Steptoe's Plains Indian legend of a seeking, selfless mouse who turns into an eagle, his powerful, over-scale picturization is apt to evoke a response—at least the first time around. After that, the impact wears off, and the bathos intervenes. But there is still the pull of being down on the mouse's level, and being drawn into his world by the magic-realism of the gray-toned, double-page bleeds. Alongside, the text is prolix, the story-elements commonplace. A young mouse, hearing tell "of the far-off land," sets forth. Stopped by a river, he meets a frog—Magic Frog, she tells him—who turns him into Jumping Mouse. Also: "You will encounter hardships . . . but don't despair. You will reach the far-off land if you keep hope alive within you." He lingers for a time with a fat old mouse, who falls prey to a snake in his lassitude. Going on, he comes across a dying, blind bison—to whom he gives his sight. He comes across a helpless, unsniffing wolf—to whom he gives his sense of smell. At last, having reached the far-off land, he weeps (that piteous, blind visage filling the page): "I feel the earth beneath my paws. I hear the wind rustling leaves on the trees . . . but I'll never be as I was. How will I ever manage?" Magic Frog appears, praises him, tells him to "Jump high"—and, by gosh (but not without further words), we see him outlined against the bright sky . . . and, overleaf, the bright-eyed, fierce-beaked head of an eagle. Think of it perhaps as a demonstration of art's transforming power, the weaknesses of the tale (and the telling) notwithstanding.

> *A review of "The Story of Jumping Mouse," in* Kirkus Reviews, *Juvenile Issue, Vol. LII, Nos. 1-5, March 1, 1984, p. J-10.*

This is a free adaptation of a Native American "why" story that explains how the eagle came to be; the tribal source is not provided. On oversize pages, the artist has used black and white to good dramatic effect, with handsome (occasionally crowded) pictures that show a world scaled to the size of a small mouse, with a surer touch in the draughtsmanship than is found in most of Steptoe's earlier work. . . . [*The Story of Jumping Mouse* has] a pleasing ending, rather abrupt but dramatic.

> *Zena Sutherland, in a review of "The Story of Jumping Mouse," in* Bulletin of the Center for Children's Books, *Vol. 37, No. 8, April, 1984, p. 156.*

[This] is both a departure and a risk for Steptoe; most of his work has featured city settings and black protagonists, and Steptoe's identity has principally been that of a black artist and writer. Now he's left those parameters behind with art that breaks out of his earlier style and a story drawn from a northern Plains Indian legend that meditates on the renewing power of sacrifice. The extensive, complex black-and-white pictures have a raw power and presence, even though their shadings and textures are roughened. They enlarge the story. . . . Although this is a picture book, there is a great deal of text. The philosophical bent of the story makes it suitable for an older audience, who might well find it a springboard to fruitful discussion. (pp. 1486, 1488)

> *Denise M. Wilms, in a review of "The Story of Jumping Mouse" in* Booklist, *Vol. 80, No. 20, June 15, 1984, pp. 1486, 1488.*

The artist has forsaken color work, yet the large illustrations, carefully detailed in their depiction of the animals and the vistas of river, forest, and desert lands, are unmistakably his; meeting the demands of a new medium, he has used black, white, and shades of gray like a full palette, with subtle gradations and nuances defining the forms and figures in the striking pictures.

> *Ethel L. Heins, in a review of "The Story of Jumping Mouse," in* The Horn Book Magazine, *Vol. LX, No. 4, August, 1984, p. 462.*

This character bears some resemblance to the "Christ figure" in Christian literary tradition. . . .

The text is succinct, although Steptoe uses dignified and somewhat elaborate dialogue, as befits the magical setting. The beauties of nature have been evoked intermittently, as when the narrator describes "cool breezes that blew down from the mountain peaks," and "the rhythm of the wolf's padding paws."

As the book's illustrator, Steptoe draws upon a style that he used with great brilliance in [Birago Diop's] *Mother Crocodile* (Delacorte, 1981). Yet he is also moving in an entirely new direction. He creates mixtures of black and white, and is able to animate the surfaces and depict a rich environment with more success than most artists can achieve with a full range of color. He also designs arrangements that are handsome, asymmetrical, and unusual in their intricate weaving of negative and positive spaces.

Steptoe's style calls for a special kind of looking. While his basic drawings are simple and realistic, initially appearing to be almost photographic, he nonetheless produces a unique quality of organic growth in his landscapes. Tonality, space, and surface effects are used for intense, dynamic renderings of nature. (pp. 50-1)

> *Donnarae MacCann and Olga Richard, in a review of "The Story of Jumping Mouse," in* Wilson Library Bulletin, *Vol. 59, No. 1, September, 1984, pp. 50-1.*

The author is sensitive to the reality of the creatures, respecting their natural instincts, yet the smooth flow of events grips the imagination of the reader. John Steptoe's powerful pencil sketches, exuding a batik-like nature, provide an emotional empathy with the animals. Their impact is heightened by both the increased size of the book and the skillful use of black/white reversals for emphasis, focus, and effect. Dramatic close-up perspectives heighten the poignant sensitivity of the artist to portray the spiritual qualities in the dreamer's search. (p. 632)

> *Ronald A. Jobe, in a review of "The Story of Jumping Mouse," in* Language Arts, *Vol. 61, No. 6, October, 1984, pp. 631-32.*

APPENDIX

The following is a listing of all sources used in Volume 12 of *Children's Literature Review*. Included in this list are all copyright and reprint rights and acknowledgments for those essays for which permission was obtained. Every effort has been made to trace copyright, but if omissions have been made, please let us know.

THE EXCERPTS IN CLR, VOLUME 12, WERE REPRINTED FROM THE FOLLOWING PERIODICALS:

Arbuthnot, May Hill. From *Children and Books*. Third edition. Scott, Foresman, 1964. Copyright © 1964 by Scott, Foresman and Company, Glenview, IL 60025. All rights reserved. Reprinted by permission.

Arbuthnot, May Hill. From *Children's Reading in the Home*. Scott, Foresman, 1969. Copyright © 1969 by Scott, Foresman and Company. All rights reserved. Reprinted by permission.

Arbuthnot, May Hill and others. From *Children's Books Too Good to Miss*. Seventh edition. University Press Books, 1979. Copyright 1948, © 1963, 1966, 1971. Copyright © 1979 by UPBS, Inc. Reprinted by permission of the publisher.

Bader, Barbara. From *American Picture Books from Noah's Ark to the Beast Within*. Macmillan, 1976. Copyright © 1976 by Barbara Bader. All rights reserved. Reprinted with permission of Macmillan Publishing Company.

Baskin, Barbara H. and Karen H. Harris. From *Notes from a Different Drummer: A Guide to Juvenile Fiction Portraying the Handicapped*. Bowker, 1977. Copyright © 1977 by Barbara H. Baskin and Karen H. Harris. All rights reserved. Reprinted with permission of R. R. Bowker, Division of Reed Publishing, USA.

Broderick, Dorothy M. From *An Introduction to Children's Work in Public Libraries*. The H. W. Wilson Company, 1965. Copyright © 1965 by Dorothy M. Broderick. Reprinted by permission of the publisher.

Brown, Marcia. From *Lotus Seeds: Children, Pictures, and Books*. Charles Scribner's Sons, 1986. Copyright 1949, © 1955, 1962, 1967, 1968, 1972, 1974, 1977, 1982, 1983, 1984, 1986 Marcia Brown. All rights reserved. Reprinted with the permission of Charles Scribner's Sons.

Campbell, Patricia J. From *Presenting Robert Cormier*. Twayne, 1985. Copyright 1985 G. K. Hall & Co. All rights reserved. Reprinted with the permission of G. K. Hall & Co., Boston.

Cianciolo, Patricia. From *Illustrations in Children's Books*. Second edition. Brown, 1976. Copyright © 1970, 1976 by Wm. C. Brown Company Publishers. All rights reserved. Reprinted by permission of the author.

Cianciolo, Patricia Jean. From *Picture Books for Children*. Revised edition. American Library Association, 1981. Copyright © 1981 by the American Library Association. All rights reserved. Reprinted by permission.

Crouch, Marcus. From *The Nesbit Tradition: The Children's Novel in England 1945-1970*. Ernest Benn Limited, 1972. © Marcus Crouch 1972. Reprinted by permission of the author.

Dreyer, Sharon Spredemann. From *The Bookfinder, When Kids Need Books: Annotations of Books Published 1979 through 1982*. American Guidance Service, 1985. © 1985 American Guidance Service, Inc. All rights reserved. Reprinted by permission.

Fiedler, Jean and Jim Mele. From *Isaac Asimov*. Ungar, 1982. Copyright © 1982 by Frederick Ungar Publishing Co., Inc. Reprinted by permission.

Fisher, Margery. From *Matters of Fact: Aspects of Non-Fiction for Children*. Brockhampton Press, 1972. Copyright © 1972 by Margery Fisher. All rights reserved. Reprinted by permission of Hodder & Stoughton Limited.

Fisher, Margery. From *Who's Who in Children's Books: A Treasury of the Familiar Characters of Childhood*. Weidenfeld & Nicolson, 1975. Copyright © 1975 by Margery Fisher. All rights reserved. Reprinted by permission.

Gardam, Jane. From *A Long Way from Verona*. Macmillan, 1971, Hamish Hamilton, 1971. Copyright © 1971 Jane Gardam. All rights reserved. Reprinted with permission of Macmillan Publishing Company. In Canada by Hamish Hamilton Ltd.

Gardam, Jane. From "Mrs. Hookaneye and I," in *The Thorny Paradise: Writers on Writing for Children*. Edited by Edward Blishen. Kestrel Books, 1975. Collection copyright © 1975 by Edward Blishen. All rights reserved. Reprinted by permission of the author.

Georgiou, Constantine. From *Children and Their Literature*. Prentice-Hall, 1969. © 1969 by Prentice-Hall, Inc. All rights reserved. Reprinted by permission of the author.

Gillespie, John and Diana Lembo. From *Juniorplots: A Book Talk Manual for Teachers and Librarians*. R. R. Bowker, 1967. Copyright © 1967 by Reed Publishing, USA, Division of Reed Holdings, Inc. All rights reserved. Reprinted with permission of the publisher.

Gunn, James. From *Isaac Asimov: The Foundations of Science Fiction*. Oxford University Press, 1982. Copyright © 1982 by Oxford University Press, Inc. Reprinted by permission.

Huck, Charlotte S. and Doris Young Kuhn. From *Children's Literature in the Elementary School*. Second edition. Holt, Rinehart and Winston, 1968. Copyright © 1961, 1968 by Holt, Rinehart and Winston, Inc. All rights reserved. Reprinted by permission of CBS College Publishing.

Hürlimann, Bettina. From *Three Centuries of Children's Books in Europe*. Edited and translated by Brian W. Alderson. Oxford University Press, London, 1967. © Oxford University Press 1967. Reprinted by permission of the publisher.

Inglis, Fred. From *The Promise of Happiness: Value and Meaning in Children's Fiction*. Cambridge University Press, 1981. © Cambridge University Press, 1981. Reprinted by permission of the publisher.

Kimmel, Margaret Mary and Elizabeth Segel. From *For Reading Out Loud! A Guide to Sharing Books with Children*. Dell, 1983. Copyright © 1983 by Margaret Mary Kimmel and Elizabeth Segel. All rights reserved. Reprinted by permission of Delacorte Press.

Kingston, Carolyn T. From *The Tragic Mode in Children's Literature*. New York: Teachers College Press, 1974. Copyright © 1974 by Teachers College, Columbia University. Reprinted by permission of the publisher.

MacCann, Donnarae and Olga Richard. From *The Child's First Books: A Critical Study of Pictures and Texts*. Wilson, 1973. Copyright © 1973 by Donnarae MacCann and Olga Richard. Reprinted by permission of The H. W. Wilson Company.

Moss, Elaine. From *Children's Books of the Year: 1974*. Hamish Hamilton, 1975. © Elaine Moss 1975. All rights reserved. Reprinted by permission of the author.

Norton, Donna E. From *Through the Eyes of a Child: An Introduction to Children's Literature*. Revised second edition. Merrill, 1987. Copyright © 1983, 1987 by Merrill Publishing Company, a Bell & Howell Company. All rights reserved. Reprinted by permission of Merrill Publishing Company, Columbus, OH.

Patrouch, Joseph F., Jr. From *The Science Fiction of Isaac Asimov*. Doubleday, 1974. Copyright © 1974 by Joseph F. Patrouch, Jr. All rights reserved. Reprinted by permission of Doubleday & Company, Inc.

Peet, Bill. From ''Bill Peet,'' a promotional piece. Houghton Mifflin, 1983. Reprinted by permission of Houghton Mifflin Company.

Perkins, Agnes. From ''Romantic, Fantastic and Realistic Stories for Children: What Books Should Be Sent to Coventry?'' in *Children and Their Literature: A Readings Book*. Edited by Jill P. May. ChLA Publications, 1983. Copyright © 1983 by The Children's Literature Association. All rights reserved. Reprinted by permission of the publisher.

Peterson, Linda Kauffman. From ''The Caldecott Medal and Honor Books, 1938-1981: 'Stone Soup: An Old Tale', 'Henry Fisherman', 'Dick Whittington and His Cat', 'Skipper John's Cook', 'Puss in Boots', 'Cinderella: or, The Little Glass Slipper','' in *Newbery and Caldecott Medal and Honor Books: An Annotated Bibliography*. By Linda Kauffman Peterson and Marilyn Leathers Solt. Hall, 1982. Copyright 1982 by G. K. Hall & Co. Reprinted with the permission of G. K. Hall & Co., Boston.

Rees, David. From *The Marble in the Water: Essays on Contemporary Writers of Fiction for Children and Young Adults*. The Horn Book, Inc., 1980. Copyright © 1979, 1980 by David Rees. All rights reserved. Reprinted by permission of the publisher.

Rudman, Masha Kabakow. From *Children's Literature: An Issues Approach*. Heath, 1976. Copyright © 1976 by D. C. Heath and Company. All rights reserved. Reprinted by permission of Longman, Inc.

Sadker, Myra Pollack and David Miller Sadker. From *Now Upon a Time: A Contemporary View of Children's Literature*. Harper & Row, 1977. Copyright © 1977 by Myra Pollack Sadker and David Miller Sadker. All rights reserved. Reprinted by permission of Harper & Row, Publishers, Inc.

Sebesta, Sam Leaton and William J. Iverson. From *Literature for Thursday's Child*. Science Research Associates, 1975. © 1975, Science Research Associates, Inc. All rights reserved. Reprinted by permission of the authors.

Solt, Marilyn Leathers. From ''The Newbery Medal and Honor Books, 1922-1981: 'Figgs and Phantoms','' in *Newbery and Caldecott Medal and Honor Books: An Annotated Bibliography*. By Linda Kauffman Peterson and Marilyn Leathers Solt. Hall, 1982. Copyright 1982 by G. K. Hall & Co. Reprinted with the permission of G. K. Hall & Co., Boston.

Steele, Mary. From "Fiction 6 to 9: 'Kit'," in *The Signal Review of Children's Books 2: A Selective Guide to Picture Books, Fiction, Plays, Poetry, Information Books, Published during 1983*. Edited by Nancy Chambers. Thimble Press, 1984. Copyright © 1984 The Thimble Press. Reprinted by permission of the publisher.

Sutherland, Zena, May Hill Arbuthnot, and Dianne L. Monson. From *Children and Books*. Seventh edition. Scott, Foresman, 1986. Copyright © 1986, 1981, 1977, 1972, 1964, 1957, 1947 Scott, Foresman and Company. All rights reserved. Reprinted by permission.

Townsend, John Rowe. From *Written for Children: An Outline of English-Language Children's Literature*. Second revised edition. J. B. Lippincott, Publishers, 1983, Penguin Books, 1983. Copyright © 1965, 1974, 1983 by John Rowe Townsend. All rights reserved. Reprinted by permission of Harper & Row, Publishers, Inc. In Canada by Penguin Books Ltd.

Ward, Lynd. From "The Book Artist: Ideas and Techniques," in *Illustrators of Children's Books: 1946-1956*. Ruth Hill Viguers, Marcia Dalphin, and Bertha Mahoney Miller, eds. Horn Book, 1958. Copyright © 1958 by the Horn Book, Inc. Reprinted by permission of the publisher.

CUMULATIVE INDEX TO AUTHORS

This index lists all author entries in *Children's Literature Review* and includes cross-references to them in other Gale sources. References in the index are identified as follows:

AITN: *Authors in the News*, Volumes 1-2

CA: *Contemporary Authors* (original series), Volumes 1-118

CANR: *Contemporary Authors New Revision Series*, Volumes 1-19

CAP: *Contemporary Authors Permanent Series*, Volumes 1-2

CA-R: *Contemporary Authors* (revised editions), Volumes 1-44

CLC: *Contemporary Literary Criticism*, Volumes 1-40

CLR: *Children's Literature Review*, Volumes 1-12

DLB: *Dictionary of Literary Biography*, Volumes 1-54

DLB-DS: *Dictionary of Literary Biography Documentary Series*, Volumes 1-4

DLB-Y: *Dictionary of Literary Biography Yearbook*, Volumes 1980-1985

NCLC: *Nineteenth-Century Literature Criticism*, Volumes 1-13

SAAS: *Something about the Author Autobiography Series*, Volume 1-3

SATA: *Something about the Author*, Volumes 1-46

TCLC: *Twentieth-Century Literary Criticism*, Volumes 1-21

YABC: *Yesterday's Authors of Books for Children*, Volumes 1-2

Adkins, Jan 1944-.....................7
See also SATA 8
See also CA 33-36R

Adoff, Arnold 1935-...................7
See also SATA 5
See also CA 41-44R
See also AITN 1

Aiken, Joan (Delano) 1924-..............1
See also CLC 35
See also SAAS 1
See also SATA 2, 30
See also CANR 4
See also CA 9-12R

Alcott, Louisa May 1832-1888..........1
See also NCLC 6
See also YABC 1
See also DLB 1, 42

Alexander, Lloyd (Chudley) 1924-.....**1, 5**
See also CLC 35
See also SATA 3
See also CANR 1
See also CA 1-4R
See also DLB 52

Aliki (Liacouras Brandenberg) 1929-.....9
See also Brandenberg, Aliki (Liacouras)

Andersen, Hans Christian 1805-1875.....6
See also NCLC 7
See also YABC 1

Anglund, Joan Walsh 1926-..............1
See also SATA 2
See also CANR 15
See also CA 5-8R

Anno, Mitsumasa 1926-................2
See also SATA 5, 38
See also CANR 4
See also CA 49-52

Ardizzone, Edward (Jeffrey Irving)
1900-1979........................3
See also SATA 1, 28
See also obituary SATA 21
See also CANR 8
See also CA 5-8R
See also obituary CA 89-92

Armstrong, William H(oward) 1914-......1
See also SATA 4
See also CANR 9
See also CA 17-20R
See also AITN 1

Aruego, Jose 1932-....................5
See also SATA 6
See also CA 37-40R

Ashley, Bernard 1935-.................4
See also SATA 39
See also CA 93-96

Asimov, Isaac 1920-...................12
See also CLC 1, 3, 9, 19, 26
See also SATA 1, 26
See also CANR 2, 19
See also CA 1-4R
See also DLB 8

Aylesworth, Thomas G(ibbons) 1927-.....6
See also SATA 4
See also CANR 10
See also CA 25-28R

Babbitt, Natalie 1932-..................2
See also SATA 6
See also CANR 2, 19
See also CA 49-52
See also DLB 52

Bacon, Martha (Sherman) 1917-1981 3
See also SATA 18
See also obituary SATA 27
See also CA 85-88
See also obituary CA 104

Bang, Garrett 1943-
See Bang, Molly (Garrett)

Bang, Molly (Garrett) 1943-.............8
See also SATA 24
See also CA 102

Bawden, Nina 1925-....................2
See also Kark, Nina Mary (Mabey)
See also DLB 14

Baylor, Byrd 1924-....................3
See also SATA 16
See also CA 81-84

Bemelmans, Ludwig 1898-1962...........6
See also SATA 15
See also CA 73-76
See also DLB 22

Benary, Margot 1889-1979
See Benary-Isbert, Margot

Benary-Isbert, Margot 1889-1979........12
See also CLC 12
See also SATA 2
See also obituary SATA 21
See also CANR 4
See also CA 5-8R
See also obituary CA 89-92

Bendick, Jeanne 1919-.................5
See also SATA 2
See also CANR 2
See also CA 5-8R

Bethancourt, T(homas) Ernesto 1932-.....3
See also Paisley, Tom
See also SATA 11

Bland, Edith Nesbit 1858-1924
  See Nesbit, E(dith)

Blume, Judy (Sussman Kitchens)
  1938- 2
  See also CLC 12, 30
  See also SATA 2, 31
  See also CANR 13
  Sec also CA 29-32R
  See also DLB 52

Bond, (Thomas) Michael 1926- 1
  See also SAAS 3
  See also SATA 6
  See also CANR 4
  See also CA 5-8R

Bond, Nancy (Barbara) 1945- 11
  See also SATA 22
  See also CANR 9
  See also CA 65-68

Bontemps, Arna (Wendell) 1902-1973 6
  See also CLC 1, 18
  See also SATA 2, 44
  See also obituary SATA 24
  See also CANR 4
  See also CA 1-4R
  See also obituary CA 41-44R
  See also DLB 48, 51

Boston, L(ucy) M(aria Wood) 1892-.......3
  See also SATA 19
  See also CA 73-76

Bova, Ben(jamin William) 1932-..........3
  See also SATA 6
  See also CANR 11
  See also CA 5-8R
  See also DLB-Y 81

Brandenberg, Aliki (Liacouras) 1929-
  See Aliki (Liacouras Brandenberg)
  See also SATA 2, 35
  See also CANR 4, 12
  See also CA 1-4R

Briggs, Raymond (Redvers) 1934- 10
  See also SATA 23
  See also CA 73-76

Brown, Marcia (Joan) 1918- 12
  See also SATA 7
  See also CA 41-44R

Brown, Margaret Wise 1910-1952 10
  See also YABC 2
  See also CA 108
  See also DLB 22

Bruna, Dick 1927-.....................7
  See also SATA 30, 43
  See also CA 112

Brunhoff, Jean de 1899-1937............4
  See also SATA 24
  See also CA 118

Brunhoff, Jean de 1899-1937 and
  Laurent de Brunhoff 1925-..........4

Brunhoff, Laurent de 1925-.............4
  See also SATA 24
  See also CA 73-76

Brunhoff, Laurent de 1925- and
  Jean de Brunhoff 1899-1937........4

Burnford, Sheila 1918-1984...........2
  See also SATA 3
  See also obituary SATA 38
  See also CANR 1
  See also CA 1-4R
  See also obituary CA 112

Burningham, John (Mackintosh)
  1936-............................9
  See also SATA 16
  See also CA 73-76

Burton, Hester (Wood-Hill) 1913-........1
  See also SATA 7
  See also CANR 10
  See also CA 9-12R

Burton (Demetrios), Virginia Lee
  1909-1968.......................11
  See also SATA 2
  See also CAP 1
  See also CA 13-14
  See also obituary CA 25-28R
  See also DLB 22

Byars, Betsy (Cromer) 1928-.............1
  See also CLC 35
  See also SAAS 1
  See also SATA 4, 46
  See also CANR 18
  See also CA 33-36R
  See also DLB 52

Cameron, Eleanor (Butler) 1912-.........1
  See also SATA 1, 25
  See also CANR 2
  See also CA 1-4R
  See also DLB 52

Carle, Eric 1929-.....................10
  See also SATA 4
  See also CANR 10
  See also CA 25-28R

Carroll, Lewis 1832-1898...............2
  See also Dodgson, Charles Lutwidge
  See also NCLC 2
  See also DLB 18

Charlip, Remy 1929-...................8
  See also SATA 4
  See also CA 33-36R

Chauncy, Nan(cen Beryl Masterman)
  1900-1970.......................6
  See also SATA 6
  See also CANR 4
  See also CA 1-4R

Christie, (Ann) Philippa (Pearce) 1920-
  See Pearce (Christie), (Ann) Philippa
  See also CANR 4

Christopher, John 1922-................2
  See also Youd, (Christopher) Samuel

Cleary, Beverly (Atlee Bunn) 1916- 2, 8
  See also SATA 2, 43
  See also CANR 2, 19
  See also CA 1-4R
  See also DLB 52

Cleaver, Bill 1920-1981 6
  See also SATA 22
  See also obituary SATA 27
  See also CA 73-76
  See also DLB 52

Cleaver, Bill 1920-1981 and
  Vera Cleaver 1919-...............6
  See also DLB 52

Cleaver, Vera 1919- 6
  See also SATA 22
  See also CA 73-76
  See also DLB 52

Cleaver, Vera 1919- and
  Bill Cleaver 1920-1981.............6
  See also DLB 52

Clifton, Lucille 1936- 5
  See also CLC 19
  See also SATA 20
  See also CANR 2
  See also CA 49-52
  See also DLB 5, 41

Coatsworth, Elizabeth 1893-1986........2
  See also SATA 2
  See also CANR 4
  See also CA 5-8R
  See also DLB 22

Cobb, Vicki 1938-.....................2
  See also SATA 8
  See also CANR 14
  See also CA 33-36R

Cohen, Daniel 1936-....................3
  See also SATA 8
  See also CANR 1
  See also CA 45-48

Cole, Joanna 1944-....................5
  See also SATA 37
  See also CA 115

Collier, James Lincoln 1928-.............3
  See also CLC 30
  See also SATA 8
  See also CANR 4
  See also CA 9-12R

Collodi, Carlo 1826-1890 5
  See also Lorenzini, Carlo

Conford, Ellen (Schaffer) 1942- 10
  See also SATA 6
  See also CANR 13
  See also CA 33-36R

Conly, Robert L(eslie) 1918-1973
  See O'Brien, Robert C.
  See also SATA 23
  See also CA 73-76
  See also obituary CA 41-44R

Cooper, Susan 1935-....................4
  See also SATA 4
  See also CANR 15
  See also CA 29-32R

Corbett, Scott 1913-....................1
  See also SAAS 2
  See also SATA 2, 42
  See also CANR 1
  See also CA 1-4R

Cormier, Robert (Edmund) 1925-........12
  See also CLC 12, 30
  See also SATA 10, 45
  See also CANR 5
  See also CA 1-4R
  See also DLB 52

Crews, Donald 1938-....................7
  See also SATA 30, 32
  See also CA 108

Dahl, Roald 1916-................... 1, 7
  See also CLC 1, 6, 18
  See also SATA 1, 26
  See also CANR 6
  See also CA 1-4R

de Angeli, Marguerite 1889- 1
  See also SATA 1, 27
  See also CANR 3
  See also CA 5-8R
  See also DLB 22
  See also AITN 2

DeJong, Meindert 1906- 1
   See also SATA 2
   See also CA 13-16R
   See also DLB 52

de Paola, Thomas Anthony 1934-
   See de Paola, Tomie
   See also SATA 11
   See also CANR 2
   See also CA 49-52

de Paola, Tomie 1934- 4
   See also de Paola, Thomas Anthony

Dodgson, Charles Lutwidge 1832-1898
   See Carroll, Lewis
   See also YABC 2

Donovan, John 1928- 3
   See also CLC 35
   See also SATA 29
   See also CA 97-100

du Bois, William (Sherman) Pène
   1916- 1
   See also SATA 4
   See also CANR 17
   See also CA 5-8R

Emberley, Barbara (Anne) 1932- 5
   See also SATA 8
   See also CANR 5
   See also CA 5-8R

Emberley, Barbara (Anne) 1932- and
   Ed(ward Randolph) Emberley
   1931- 5

Emberley, Ed(ward Randolph) 1931- 5
   See also SATA 8
   See also CANR 5
   See also CA 5-8R

Emberley, Ed(ward Randolph) 1931- and
   Barbara (Anne) Emberley 1932- 5

Engdahl, Sylvia Louise 1933- 2
   See also SATA 4
   See also CANR 14
   See also CA 29-32R

Enright, Elizabeth 1909-1968 4
   See also SATA 9
   See also CA 61-64
   See also obituary CA 25-28R
   See also DLB 22

Estes, Eleanor 1906- 2
   See also SATA 7
   See also CANR 5
   See also CA 1-4R
   See also DLB 22

Farmer, Penelope (Jane) 1939- 8
   See also SATA 39, 40
   See also CANR 9
   See also CA 13-16R

Feelings, Muriel (Grey) 1938-
   See Feelings, Muriel L.
   See also SATA 16
   See also CA 93-96

Feelings, Muriel L. 1938- 5
   See also Feelings, Muriel (Grey)

Feelings, Muriel L. 1938- and
   Tom Feelings 1933- 5

Feelings, Thomas 1933-
   See Feelings, Tom
   See also SATA 8
   See also CA 49-52

Feelings, Tom 1933- 5
   See also Feelings, Thomas

Feelings, Tom 1933- and
   Muriel L. Feelings 1938- 5

Fitzgerald, John D(ennis) 1907- 1
   See also SATA 20
   See also CA 93-96

Fitzhardinge, Joan Margaret 1912-
   See Joan Phipson
   See also SATA 2
   See also CANR 6
   See also CA 13-16R

Fitzhugh, Louise (Perkins) 1928-1974 1
   See also SATA 1, 45
   See also obituary SATA 24
   See also CAP 2
   See also CA 29-32
   See also obituary CA 53-56
   See also DLB 52

Fleischman, (Albert) Sid(ney) 1920- 1
   See also SATA 8
   See also CANR 5
   See also CA 1-4R

Foster, Genevieve (Stump) 1893-1979 7
   See also SATA 2
   See also obituary SATA 23
   See also CANR 4
   See also CA 5-8R
   See also obituary CA 89-92

Fox, Paula 1923- 1
   See also CLC 2, 8
   See also SATA 17
   See also CA 73-76
   See also DLB 52

French, Paul 1920-
   See Asimov, Isaac

Fritz, Jean (Guttery) 1915- 2
   See also SAAS 2
   See also SATA 1, 29
   See also CANR 5, 16
   See also CA 1-4R
   See also DLB 52

Gág, Wanda (Hazel) 1893-1946 4
   See also YABC 1
   See also CA 113
   See also DLB 22

Gardam, Jane (Mary Pearson)
   1928- 12
   See also SATA 28, 39
   See also CANR 2, 18
   See also CA 49-52
   See also DLB 14

Geisel, Theodor Seuss 1904- 1
   See Seuss, Dr.
   See also SATA 1, 28
   See also CANR 13
   See also CA 13-16R

George, Jean Craighead 1919- 1
   See also CLC 35
   See also SATA 2
   See also CA 5-8R
   See also DLB 52

Gibbons, Gail (Gretchen) 1944- 8
   See also SATA 23
   See also CANR 12
   See also CA 69-72

Giovanni, Nikki 1943- 6
   See also CLC 2, 4, 19
   See also SATA 24
   See also CANR 18
   See also CA 29-32R
   See also DLB 5, 41
   See also AITN 1

Glubok, Shirley (Astor) 1933- 1
   See also SATA 6
   See also CANR 4
   See also CA 5-8R

Goffstein, M(arilyn) B(rooke) 1940- 3
   See also SATA 8
   See also CANR 9
   See also CA 21-24R

Graham, Lorenz B(ell) 1902- 10
   See also SATA 2
   See also CA 9-12R

Grahame, Kenneth 1859-1932 5
   See also YABC 1
   See also CA 108
   See also DLB 34

Greenaway, Catherine 1846-1901
   See Greenaway, Kate
   See also CA 113

Greenaway, Kate 1846-1901 6
   See also Greenaway, Catherine
   See also YABC 2

Greene, Bette 1934- 2
   See also CLC 30
   See also SATA 8
   See also CANR 4
   See also CA 53-56

Greenfield, Eloise 1929- 4
   See also SATA 19
   See also CANR 1, 19
   See also CA 49-52

Gripe, Maria (Kristina) 1923- 5
   See also SATA 2
   See also CANR 17
   See also CA 29-32R

Hamilton, Virginia (Esther) 1936- 1, 11
   See also CLC 26
   See also SATA 4
   See also CA 25-28R
   See also DLB 33, 52

Haskins, James 1941- 3
   See also SATA 9
   See also CA 33-36R

Haugaard, Erik Christian 1923- 11
   See also SATA 4
   See also CANR 3
   See also CA 7-8R

Hay, Timothy 1910-1952
   See Brown, Margaret Wise

Henry, Marguerite 1902- 4
   See also SATA 11
   See also CANR 9
   See also CA 17-20R
   See also DLB 22

Hentoff, Nat(han Irving) 1925- 1
   See also CLC 26
   See also SATA 27, 42
   See also CANR 5
   See also CA 1-4R

Hergé 1907-1983 6
   See also Rémi, Georges

Author Index

Hinton, S(usan) E(loise) 1950-............3
See also CLC 30
See also SATA 19
See also CA 81-84

Hoban, Russell (Conwell) 1925- 3
See also CLC 7, 25
See also SATA 1, 40
See also CA 5-8R
See also DLB 52

Hogrogian, Nonny 1932-................2
See also SAAS 1
See also SATA 7
See also CANR 2
See also CA 45-48

Houston, James A(rchibald) 1921-........3
See also SATA 13
See also CA 65-68

Howe, James 1946-....................9
See also SATA 29
See also CA 105

Hughes, Monica (Ince) 1925-............9
See also SATA 15
See also CA 77-80

Hughes, Ted 1930-....................3
See also CLC 2, 4, 9, 14, 37
See also SATA 27
See also CANR 1
See also CA 1-4R
See also DLB 40

Hunt, Irene 1907- 1
See also SATA 2
See also CANR 8
See also CA 17-20R
See also DLB 52

Hunter, Kristin (Eggleston) 1931-........3
See also CLC 35
See also SATA 12
See also CANR 13
See also CA 13-16R
See also DLB 33
See also AITN 1

Isadora, Rachel 1953(?)- 7
See also SATA 32
See also CA 111

Iwamatsu, Jun Atsushi 1908-
See Yashima, Taro
See also SATA 14
See also CA 73-76

Jansson, Tove (Marika) 1914-...........2
See also SATA 3, 41
See also CA 17-20R

Jarrell, Randall 1914-1965............6
See also CLC 1, 2, 6, 9, 13
See also SATA 7
See also CANR 6
See also CA 5-8R
See also obituary CA 25-28R
See also DLB 48, 52

Jonas, Ann 1932-....................12
See also SATA 42
See also CA 118

Jordan, June 1936-...................10
See also CLC 5, 11, 23
See also SATA 4
See also CA 33-36R
See also DLB 38

Kark, Nina Mary (Mabey) 1925-
See Bawden, Nina
See also SATA 4
See also CANR 8
See also CA 17-20R

Kästner, Erich 1899-1974 4
See also SATA 14
See also CA 73-76
See also obituary CA 49-52

Keats, Ezra Jack 1916-1983 1
See also SATA 14
See also obituary SATA 34
See also CA 77-80
See also obituary CA 109
See also AITN 1

Kellogg, Steven 1941-..................6
See also SATA 8
See also CANR 1
See also CA 49-52

Klein, Norma 1938-...................2
See also CLC 30
See also SAAS 1
See also SATA 7
See also CANR 15
See also CA 41-44R

Konigsburg, E(laine) L(obl) 1930- 1
See also SATA 4
See also CANR 17
See also CA 21-24R
See also DLB 52

Korinetz, Yuri (Iosifovich) 1923- 4
See also SATA 9
See also CANR 11
See also CA 61-64

Kotzwinkle, William 1938-..............6
See also CLC 5, 14, 35
See also SATA 24
See also CANR 3
See also CA 45-48

Krahn, Fernando 1935- 3
See also SATA 31
See also CANR 11
See also CA 65-68

Krementz, Jill 1940-...................5
See also SATA 17
See also CA 41-44R
See also AITN 1, 2

Krüss, James (Jacob Hinrich) 1926-.......9
See also SATA 8
See also CANR 5
See also CA 53-56

Kurelek, William 1927-1977 2
See also SATA 8
See also obituary SATA 27
See also CANR 3
See also CA 49-52

Kuskin, Karla (Seidman) 1932-..........4
See also SAAS 3
See also SATA 2
See also CANR 4
See also CA 1-4R

Lagerlöf, Selma (Ottiliana Lovisa)
1858-1940.......................7
See also TCLC 4
See also SATA 15
See also CA 108

Langstaff, John (Meredith) 1920-........3
See also SATA 6
See also CANR 4
See also CA 1-4R

Lasky (Knight), Kathryn 1944-.........11
See also SATA 13
See also CANR 11
See also CA 69-72

Lawson, Robert 1892-1957 2
See also YABC 2
See also CA 118
See also DLB 22

Lear, Edward 1812-1888 1
See also NCLC 3
See also SATA 18
See also DLB 32

Lee, Dennis (Beynon) 1939-.............3
See also SATA 14
See also CANR 11
See also CA 25-28R
See also DLB 53

Le Guin, Ursula K(roeber) 1929-.........3
See also CLC 8, 13, 22
See also SATA 4
See also CANR 9
See also CA 21-24R
See also DLB 8, 52
See also AITN 1

L'Engle, Madeleine 1918-...............1
See also CLC 12
See also SATA 1, 27
See also CANR 3
See also CA 1-4R
See also AITN 2
See also DLB 52

LeShan, Eda J(oan) 1922- 6
See also SATA 21
See also CA 13-16R

LeSieg, Theo 1904-
See Seuss, Dr.

Lester, Julius B. 1939-.................2
See also SATA 12
See also CANR 8
See also CA 17-20R

Lewin, Hugh (Francis) 1939-............9
See also SATA 40
See also CA 113

Lewis, C(live) S(taples) 1898-1963 3
See also CLC 1, 3, 6, 14, 27
See also SATA 13
See also CA 81-84
See also DLB 15

Lindgren, Astrid 1907-.................1
See also SATA 2, 38
See also CA 13-16R

Lindsay, Norman (Alfred William)
1879-1969.......................8
See also CA 102

Lionni, Leo(nard) 1910-................7
See also SATA 8
See also CA 53-56

Little, (Flora) Jean 1932-...............4
See also SATA 2
See also CA 21-24R

Lively, Penelope (Margaret) 1933-........7
See also CLC 32
See also SATA 7
See also CA 41-44R
See also DLB 14

Livingston, Myra Cohn 1926- 7
  See also SAAS 1
  See also SATA 5
  See also CANR 1
  See also CA 1-4R

Lobel, Arnold (Stark) 1933- 5
  See also SATA 6
  See also CANR 2
  See also CA 1-4R
  See also AITN 1

Lorenzini, Carlo 1826-1890
  See Collodi, Carlo
  See also SATA 29

Lowry, Lois 1937- 6
  See also SAAS 3
  See also SATA 23
  See also CANR 13
  See also CA 69-72
  See also DLB 52

Macaulay, David (Alexander) 1946- 3
  See also SATA 27, 46
  See also CANR 5
  See also CA 53-56

MacDonald, Golden 1910-1952
  See Brown, Margaret Wise

Mahy, Margaret (May) 1936- 7
  See also SATA 14
  See also CANR 13
  See also CA 69-72

Major, Kevin 1949- 11
  See also CLC 26
  See also SATA 32
  See also CA 97-100

Manley, Seon 1921- 3
  See also SAAS 2
  See also SATA 15
  See also CA 85-88

Mark, Jan(et Marjorie Brisland)
  1943- 11
  See also SATA 22
  See also CANR 17
  See also CA 93-96

Mathis, Sharon Bell 1937- 3
  See also SAAS 3
  See also SATA 7
  See also CA 41-44R
  See also DLB 33

Mayer, Mercer 1943- 11
  See also SATA 16, 32
  See also CA 85-88

McCloskey, (John) Robert 1914- 7
  See also SATA 2, 39
  See also CA 9-12R
  See also DLB 22

McClung, Robert M(arshall) 1916- 11
  See also SATA 2
  See also CANR 6
  See also CA 13-14R
  See also AITN 2

McCord, David (Thompson Watson)
  1897- 9
  See also SATA 18
  See also CA 73-76

McDermott, Gerald (Edward) 1941- 9
  See also SATA 16
  See also CA 85-88
  See also AITN 2

McHargue, Georgess 1941- 2
  See also SATA 4
  See also CA 25-28R

McKinley, (Jennifer Carolyn) Robin
  1952- 10
  See also SATA 32
  See also CA 107
  See also DLB 52

Milne, A(lan) A(lexander) 1882-1956 1
  See also TCLC 6
  See also YABC 1
  See also CA 104
  See also DLB 10

Mitsumasa Anno 1926-
  See Anno, Mitsumasa

Monjo, F(erdinand) N(icolas, III)
  1924-1978 2
  See also SATA 16
  See also CA 81-84

Montgomery, L(ucy) M(aud)
  1874-1942 8
  See also YABC 1
  See also CA 108

Mukerji, Dhan Gopal 1890-1936 10
  See also SATA 40

Myers, Walter Dean 1937- 4
  See also CLC 35
  See also SAAS 2
  See also SATA 27, 41
  See also CA 33-36R
  See also DLB 33

Nesbit, E(dith) 1858-1924 3
  See also YABC 1
  See also CA 118

Ness, Evaline (Michelow) 1911-1986 6
  See also SAAS 1
  See also SATA 1, 26
  See also CANR 5
  See also CA 5-8R

North, Captain George 1850-1894
  See Stevenson, Robert Louis (Balfour)

Norton, Mary 1903- 6
  See also SATA 18
  See also CA 97-100

Nöstlinger, Christine 1936- 12
  See also SATA 37
  See also CA 115

Oakley, Graham 1929- 7
  See also SATA 30
  See also CA 106

O'Brien, Robert C. 1918-1973 2
  See also Conly, Robert L(eslie)

O'Connor, Patrick 1915-
  See Wibberley, Leonard

O'Dell, Scott 1903- 1
  See also CLC 30
  See also SATA 12
  See also CANR 12
  See also CA 61-64
  See also DLB 52

Paisley, Tom 1932-
  See Bethancourt, T(homas) Ernesto
  See also CANR 15
  See also CA 61-64

Paterson, Katherine (Womeldorf)
  1932- 7
  See also CLC 12, 30
  See also SATA 13
  See also CA 21-24R
  See also DLB 52

Pearce (Christie), (Ann) Philippa
  1920- 9
  See also Christie, (Ann) Philippa (Pearce)
  See also CLC 21
  See also SATA 1
  See also CA 5-8R

Peet, Bill 1915- 12
  See also Peet, William Bartlett

Peet, William Bartlett 1915-
  See Peet, Bill
  See also SATA 2, 41
  See also CA 17-20R

Petry, Ann (Lane) 1908- 12
  See also CLC 1, 7, 18
  See also SATA 5
  See also CANR 4
  See also CA 5-8R

Peyton, K. M. 1929- 3
  See also Peyton, Kathleen (Wendy)

Peyton, Kathleen (Wendy) 1929-
  See Peyton, K. M.
  See also SATA 15
  See also CA 69-72

Pfeffer, Susan Beth 1948- 11
  See also SATA 4
  See also CA 29-32R

Phipson, Joan 1912- 5
  See also Fitzhardinge, Joan Margaret

Pienkowski, Jan 1936- 6
  See also SATA 6
  See also CANR 11
  See also CA 65-68

Pinkwater, D(aniel) Manus 1941- 4
  See also SAAS 3
  See also SATA 46
  See also CLC 35
  See also CANR 12
  See also CA 29-32R

Pinkwater, Manus 1941-
  See Pinkwater, D(aniel) Manus
  See also SATA 8

Polder, Markus 1926-
  See Krüss, James (Jacob Hinrich)

Potter, (Helen) Beatrix 1866-1943 1
  See also YABC 1
  See also CA 108

Pringle, Laurence P. 1935- 4
  See also SATA 4
  See also CANR 14
  See also CA 29-32R

Provensen, Alice (Rose Twitchell)
  1918- 11
  See also SATA 9
  See also CANR 5
  See also CA 53-56

Provensen, Martin (Elias) 1916- 11
  See also SATA 9
  See also CANR 5
  See also CA 53-56

Author Index

Ransome, Arthur (Michell)
    1884-1967.........................8
    See also SATA 22
    See also CA 73-76

Raskin, Ellen 1928-1984............ **1, 12**
    See also SATA 2, 38
    See also CA 21-24R
    See also obituary CA 113
    See also DLB 52

Rau, Margaret (Wright) 1913- 8
    See also SATA 9
    See also CANR 8
    See also CA 61-64

Rémi, Georges 1907-1983
    See Hergé
    See also SATA 13
    See also obituary SATA 32
    See also CA 69-72
    See also obituary CA 109

Rey, H(ans) A(ugusto) 1898-1977........5
    See also SATA 1, 26
    See also CANR 6
    See also CA 5-8R
    See also obituary CA 73-76
    See also DLB 22

Rey, H(ans) A(ugusto) 1898-1977 and
    Margret (Elisabeth) Rey 1906-.......5

Rey, Margret (Elisabeth) 1906-..........5
    See also SATA 26
    See also CA 105

Rey, Margret (Elisabeth) 1906- and
    H(ans) A(ugusto) Rey 1898-1977.....5

Rockwell, Thomas 1933-.................6
    See also SATA 7
    See also CA 29-32R

Rodman, Maia 1927-
    See Wojciechowska, Maia

Sachs, Marilyn (Stickle) 1927-............2
    See also CLC 35
    See also SAAS 2
    See also SATA 3
    See also CANR 13
    See also CA 17-20R

Sage, Juniper 1910-1952
    See Brown, Margaret Wise

**Saint-Exupéry, Antoine (Jean Baptiste Marie
    Roger) de** 1900-1944 10
    See also TCLC 2
    See also SATA 20
    See also CA 108

Sánchez-Silva, José María 1911-.........12
    See also SATA 16
    See also CA 73-76

Sasek, M(iroslav) 1916-1980 4
    See also SATA 16
    See also obituary SATA 23
    See also CA 73-76
    See also obituary CA 101

Scarry, Richard (McClure) 1919-.........3
    See also SATA 2, 35
    See also CANR 18
    See also CA 17-20R

Schwartz, Alvin 1927-...................3
    See also SATA 4
    See also CANR 7
    See also CA 13-16R

Schweitzer, Byrd Baylor 1924-
    See Baylor, Byrd

Selden (Thompson), George 1929- 8
    See also Thompson, George Selden
    See also DLB 52

Selsam, Millicent E(llis) 1912-............1
    See also SATA 1, 29
    See also CANR 5
    See also CA 9-12R

Sendak, Maurice (Bernard) 1928-.........1
    See also SATA 1, 27
    See also CANR 11
    See also CA 5-8R

Seredy, Kate 1899-1975 10
    See also SATA 1
    See also obituary SATA 24
    See also CA 5-8R
    See also obituary CA 57-60
    See also DLB 22

Serraillier, Ian (Lucien) 1912-............2
    See also SAAS 3
    See also SATA 1
    See also CANR 1
    See also CA 1-4R

Seuss, Dr. 1904-.......................9
    See also Geisel, Theodor Seuss

Showers, Paul C. 1910- 6
    See also SATA 21
    See also CANR 4
    See also CA 1-4R

Shulevitz, Uri 1935-....................5
    See also SATA 3
    See also CANR 3
    See also CA 9-12R

Silverstein, Shel(by) 1932- 5
    See also SATA 27, 33
    See also CA 107

Simon, Seymour 1931- 9
    See also SATA 4
    See also CANR 11
    See also CA 25-28R

Singer, Isaac Bashevis 1904- 1
    See also CLC 1, 3, 6, 9, 11, 15, 23, 38
    See also SATA 3, 27
    See also CANR 1
    See also CA 1-4R
    See also DLB 6, 28, 52
    See also AITN 1, 2

Slote, Alfred 1926-.....................4
    See also SATA 8

Smucker, Barbara (Claassen) 1915-......10
    See also SATA 29
    See also CA 106

Sneve, Virginia Driving Hawk 1933- 2
    See also SATA 8
    See also CANR 3
    See also CA 49-52

Sobol, Donald J. 1924- 4
    See also SATA 1, 31
    See also CANR 1, 18
    See also CA 1-4R

Southall, Ivan (Francis) 1921-............2
    See also SAAS 3
    See also SATA 3
    See also CANR 7
    See also CA 9-12R

Speare, Elizabeth George 1908- 8
    See also SATA 5
    See also CA 1-4R

Spier, Peter (Edward) 1927- 5
    See also SATA 4
    See also CA 5-8R

Steig, William 1907- 2
    See also SATA 18
    See also CA 77-80
    See also AITN 1

Steptoe, John (Lewis) 1950-......... **2, 12**
    See also SATA 8
    See also CANR 3
    See also CA 49-52

Sterling, Dorothy 1913- 1
    See also SAAS 2
    See also SATA 1
    See also CANR 5
    See also CA 9-12R

Stevenson, Robert Louis (Balfour)
    1850-1894.................... **10, 11**
    See also NCLC 5
    See also YABC 2
    See also DLB 18

Strasser, Todd 1950-...................11
    See also SATA 41, 45
    See also CA 117

Stren, Patti 1949-......................5
    See also SATA 41
    See also CA 117

Suhl, Yuri 1908- 2
    See also SAAS 1
    See also SATA 8
    See also CANR 2
    See also CA 45-48

Sutcliff, Rosemary 1920- 1
    See also CLC 26
    See also SATA 6, 44
    See also CA 5-8R

Taylor, Mildred D(elois) 19??-............9
    See also CLC 21
    See also SATA 15
    See also CA 85-88
    See also DLB 52

Thomas, Ianthe 1951-...................8
    See also SATA 42

Thompson, George Selden 1929-
    See Selden (Thompson), George
    See also SATA 4
    See also CA 5-8R
    See also DLB 52

Tobias, Tobi 1938-.....................4
    See also SATA 5
    See also CANR 16
    See also CA 29-32R

Townsend, John Rowe 1922-.............2
    See also SAAS 2
    See also SATA 4
    See also CA 37-40R

Travers, P(amela) L(yndon) 1906-........2
    See also SAAS 2
    See also SATA 4
    See also CA 33-36R

Treece, Henry 1911-1966 2
  See also SATA 2
  See also CANR 6
  See also CA 1-4R
  See also obituary CA 25-28R

Tunis, Edwin (Burdett) 1897-1973 2
  See also SATA 1, 28
  See also obituary SATA 24
  See also CANR 7
  See also CA 5-8R
  See also obituary CA 45-48

Uchida, Yoshiko 1921- 6
  See also SAAS 1
  See also SATA 1
  See also CANR 6
  See also CA 13-16R

Uncle Gus 1898-1977
  See Rey, H(ans) A(ugusto)

Uncle Shelby 1932-
  See Silverstein, Shel(by)

Ungerer, Jean Thomas 1931-
  See Ungerer, Tomi
  See also SATA 5, 33
  See also CA 41-44R

Ungerer, Tomi 1931-....................3
  See also Ungerer, Jean Thomas

Van Allsburg, Chris 1949-...............5
  See also SATA 37
  See also CA 113, 117

Viorst, Judith 1931- 3
  See also SATA 7
  See also CANR 2
  See also CA 49-52
  See also DLB 52

Walsh, Gillian Paton 1939-
  See Walsh, Jill Paton
  See also SATA 4
  See also CA 37-40R

Walsh, Jill Paton 1939-.................2
  See also Walsh, Gillian Paton
  See also CLC 35

Watanabe, Shigeo 1928-.................8
  See also SATA 32, 39
  See also CA 112

Watson, Clyde 1947-....................3
  See also SATA 5
  See also CANR 4
  See also CA 49-52

Weiss, Harvey 1922-....................4
  See also SATA 1, 27
  See also CANR 6
  See also CA 5-8R

Wersba, Barbara 1932- 3
  See also CLC 30
  See also SAAS 2
  See also SATA 1
  See also CANR 16
  See also CA 29-32R
  See also DLB 52

White, E(lwyn) B(rooks) 1899-1985 1
  See also CLC 10, 34, 39
  See also SATA 2, 29
  See also obituary SATA 44
  See also CANR 16
  See also CA 13-16R
  See also obituary CA 116
  See also DLB 11, 22
  See also AITN 2

White, Robb 1909- 3
  See also SAAS 1
  See also SATA 1
  See also CANR 1
  See also CA 1-4R

Wibberley, Leonard (Patrick O'Connor) 1915-1983.......................3
  See also SATA 2, 45
  See also obituary SATA 36
  See also CANR 3
  See also CA 5-8R
  See also obituary CA 111

Wilder, Laura Ingalls 1867-1957 2
  See also SATA 15, 29
  See also CA 111
  See also DLB 22

Wildsmith, Brian 1930- 2
  See also SATA 16
  See also CA 85-88

Willard, Barbara (Mary) 1909-...........2
  See also SATA 17
  See also CANR 15
  See also CA 81-84

Willard, Nancy 1936- 5
  See also CLC 7, 37
  See also SATA 30, 37
  See also CANR 10
  See also CA 89-92
  See also DLB 5, 52

Williams, Jay 1914-1978 8
  See also SATA 3, 41
  See also obituary SATA 24
  See also CANR 2
  See also CA 1-4R
  See also obituary CA 81-84

Williams, Kit 1948-....................4
  See also SATA 44
  See also CA 107

Williams, Vera B. 1927-.................9
  See also SATA 33

Wojciechowska, Maia (Teresa) 1927-......1
  See also CLC 26
  See also SAAS 1
  See also SATA 1, 28
  See also CANR 4
  See also CA 9-12R

Wrightson, Patricia 1921- 4
  See also SATA 8
  See also CANR 3, 19
  See also CA 45-48

Yashima, Taro 1908-....................4
  See also Iwamatsu, Jun Atsushi

Yep, Laurence (Michael) 1948-...........3
  See also CLC 35
  See also SATA 7
  See also CANR 1
  See also CA 49-52
  See also DLB 52

Yolen, Jane H(yatt) 1939- 4
  See also SAAS 1
  See also SATA 4, 40
  See also CANR 11
  See also CA 13-16R
  See also DLB 52

Youd, (Christopher) Samuel 1922-
  See Christopher, John
  See also SATA 30
  See also CA 77-80

Zei, Alki 1928-.........................6
  See also SATA 24
  See also CA 77-80

Zim, Herbert S(pencer) 1909-............2
  See also SAAS 2
  See also SATA 1, 30
  See also CANR 17
  See also CA 13-16R

Zimnik, Reiner 1930- 3
  See also SATA 36
  See also CA 77-80

Zindel, Paul 1936-.....................3
  See also CLC 6, 26
  See also SATA 16
  See also CA 73-76
  See also DLB 7, 52

Zolotow, Charlotte (Shapiro) 1915- 2
  See also SATA 1, 35
  See also CANR 3, 18
  See also CA 5-8R
  See also DLB 52

Author Index

CUMULATIVE INDEX TO NATIONALITIES

AMERICAN

Adkins, Jan **7**
Adoff, Arnold **7**
Alcott, Louisa May **1**
Alexander, Lloyd **1, 5**
Aliki **9**
Anglund, Joan Walsh **1**
Armstrong, William H. **1**
Aruego, Jose **5**
Asimov, Isaac **12**
Aylesworth, Thomas G. **6**
Babbitt, Natalie **2**
Bacon, Martha **3**
Bang, Molly **8**
Baylor, Byrd **3**
Bemelmans, Ludwig **6**
Benary-Isbert, Margot **12**
Bendick, Jeanne **5**
Bethancourt, T. Ernesto **3**
Blume, Judy **2**
Bond, Nancy **11**
Bontemps, Arna **6**
Bova, Ben **3**
Brown, Marcia **12**
Brown, Margaret Wise **10**
Burton, Virginia Lee **11**
Byars, Betsy **1**
Cameron, Eleanor **1**
Carle, Eric **10**
Charlip, Remy **8**
Cleary, Beverly **2, 8**
Cleaver, Bill **6**
Cleaver, Vera **6**
Clifton, Lucille **5**
Coatsworth, Elizabeth **2**
Cobb, Vicki **2**
Cohen, Daniel **3**
Cole, Joanna **5**
Collier, James Lincoln **3**

Conford, Ellen **10**
Corbett, Scott **1**
Cormier, Robert **12**
Crews, Donald **7**
de Angeli, Marguerite **1**
DeJong, Meindert **1**
de Paola, Tomie **4**
Donovan, John **3**
du Bois, William Pène **1**
Emberley, Barbara **5**
Emberley, Ed **5**
Engdahl, Sylvia Louise **2**
Enright, Elizabeth **4**
Estes, Eleanor **2**
Feelings, Muriel L. **5**
Feelings, Tom **5**
Fitzgerald, John D. **1**
Fitzhugh, Louise **1**
Fleischman, Sid **1**
Foster, Genevieve **7**
Fox, Paula **1**
Fritz, Jean **2**
Gág, Wanda **4**
Geisel, Theodor Seuss **1**
George, Jean Craighead **1**
Gibbons, Gail **8**
Giovanni, Nikki **6**
Glubok, Shirley **1**
Goffstein, M. B. **3**
Graham, Lorenz B. **10**
Greene, Bette **2**
Greenfield, Eloise **4**
Hamilton, Virginia **1, 11**
Haskins, James **3**
Henry, Marguerite **4**
Hentoff, Nat **1**
Hinton, S. E. **3**
Hoban, Russell **3**
Hogrogian, Nonny **2**

Howe, James **9**
Hunt, Irene **1**
Hunter, Kristin **3**
Isadora, Rachel **7**
Jarrell, Randall **6**
Jonas, Ann **12**
Jordan, June **10**
Keats, Ezra Jack **1**
Kellogg, Steven **6**
Klein, Norma **2**
Konigsburg, E. L. **1**
Kotzwinkle, William **6**
Krementz, Jill **5**
Kuskin, Karla **4**
Langstaff, John **3**
Lasky, Kathryn **11**
Lawson, Robert **2**
Le Guin, Ursula K. **3**
L'Engle, Madeleine **1**
LeShan, Eda J. **6**
Lester, Julius **2**
Lionni, Leo **7**
Livingston, Myra Cohn **7**
Lobel, Arnold **5**
Lowry, Lois **6**
Manley, Seon **3**
Mathis, Sharon Bell **3**
Mayer, Mercer **11**
McCloskey, Robert **7**
McClung, Robert M. **11**
McCord, David **9**
McDermott, Gerald **9**
McHargue, Georgess **2**
McKinley, Robin **10**
Monjo, F. N. **2**
Mukerji, Dhan Gopal **10**
Myers, Walter Dean **4**
Ness, Evaline **6**
O'Brien, Robert C. **2**

O'Dell, Scott **1**
Paterson, Katherine **7**
Peet, Bill **12**
Petry, Ann **12**
Pfeffer, Susan Beth **11**
Pinkwater, D. Manus **4**
Pringle, Laurence **4**
Provensen, Alice **11**
Provensen, Martin **11**
Raskin, Ellen **1, 12**
Rau, Margaret **8**
Rey, H. A. **5**
Rey, Margret **5**
Rockwell, Thomas **6**
Sachs, Marilyn **2**
Scarry, Richard **3**
Schwartz, Alvin **3**
Selden, George **8**
Selsam, Millicent E. **1**
Sendak, Maurice **1**
Seredy, Kate **10**
Seuss, Dr. **9**
Showers, Paul **6**
Shulevitz, Uri **5**
Silverstein, Shel **5**
Simon, Seymour **9**
Singer, Isaac Bashevis **1**
Slote, Alfred **4**
Smucker, Barbara **10**
Sneve, Virginia Driving
  Hawk **2**
Sobol, Donald J. **4**
Speare, Elizabeth George **8**
Spier, Peter **5**
Steig, William **2**
Steptoe, John **2, 12**
Sterling, Dorothy **1**
Strasser, Todd **11**
Suhl, Yuri **2**

Taylor, Mildred D. 9
Thomas, Ianthe 8
Tobias, Tobi 4
Tunis, Edwin 2
Uchida, Yoshiko 6
Van Allsburg, Chris 5
Viorst, Judith 3
Watson, Clyde 3
Weiss, Harvey 4
Wersba, Barbara 3
White, E. B. 1
White, Robb 3
Wibberley, Leonard 3
Wilder, Laura Ingalls 2
Willard, Nancy 5
Williams, Jay 8
Williams, Vera B. 9
Wojciechowska, Maia 1
Yashima, Taro 4
Yep, Laurence 3
Yolen, Jane 4
Zim, Herbert S. 2
Zindel, Paul 3
Zolotow, Charlotte 2

AUSTRALIAN
Chauncy, Nan 6
Lindsay, Norman 8
Phipson, Joan 5
Southall, Ivan 2
Travers, P. L. 2
Wrightson, Patricia 4

AUSTRIAN
Bemelmans, Ludwig 6
Nöstlinger, Christine 12

BELGIAN
Hergé 6

CANADIAN
Burnford, Sheila 2
Houston, James 3
Hughes, Monica 9
Kurelek, William 2
Lee, Dennis 3

Little, Jean 4
Major, Kevin 11
Montgomery, L. M. 8
Smucker, Barbara 10
Stren, Patti 5

CHILEAN
Krahn, Fernando 3

CZECHOSLOVAKIAN
Sasek, M. 4

DANISH
Andersen, Hans Christian 6
Haugaard, Erik Christian 11

DUTCH
Bruna, Dick 7
DeJong, Meindert 1
Lionni, Leo 7
Spier, Peter 5

ENGLISH
Aiken, Joan 1
Ardizzone, Edward 3
Ashley, Bernard 4
Bawden, Nina 2
Bond, Michael 1
Boston, L. M. 3
Briggs, Raymond 10
Burningham, John 9
Burton, Hester 1
Carroll, Lewis 2
Chauncy, Nan 6
Christopher, John 2
Cooper, Susan 4
Dahl, Roald 1, 7
Farmer, Penelope 8
Gardam, Jane 12
Greenaway, Kate 6
Grahame, Kenneth 5
Hughes, Monica 9
Hughes, Ted 3
Lear, Edward 1
Lewis, C. S. 3
Lively, Penelope 7

Macaulay, David 3
Mark, Jan 11
Milne, A. A. 1
Nesbit, E. 3
Norton, Mary 6
Oakley, Graham 7
Pearce, Philippa 9
Peyton, K. M. 3
Pieńkowski, Jan 6
Potter, Beatrix 1
Ransome, Arthur 8
Serraillier, Ian 2
Sutcliff, Rosemary 1
Townsend, John Rowe 2
Travers, P. L. 2
Treece, Henry 2
Walsh, Jill Paton 2
Wildsmith, Brian 2
Willard, Barbara 2
Williams, Kit 4

FILIPINO
Aruego, Jose 5

FINNISH
Jansson, Tove 2

FRENCH
Brunhoff, Jean de 4
Brunhoff, Laurent de 4
Saint-Exupéry, Antoine de 10
Ungerer, Tomi 3

GERMAN
Benary-Isbert, Margot 12
Kästner, Erich 4
Krüss, James 9
Rey, H. A. 5
Rey, Margret 5
Zimnik, Reiner 3

GREEK
Zei, Alki 6

HUNGARIAN
Seredy, Kate 10

INDIAN
Mukerji, Dhan Gopal 10

ISRAELI
Shulevitz, Uri 5

ITALIAN
Collodi, Carlo 5
Munari, Bruno 9

JAPANESE
Anno, Mitsumasa 2
Watanabe, Shigeo 8
Yashima, Taro 4

NEW ZEALAND
Mahy, Margaret 7

POLISH
Pieńkowski, Jan 6
Shulevitz, Uri 5
Singer, Isaac Bashevis 1
Suhl, Yuri 2
Wojciechowska, Maia 1

RUSSIAN
Korinetz, Yuri 4

SCOTTISH
Burnford, Sheila 2
Stevenson, Robert Louis 10,
11

SOUTH AFRICAN
Lewin, Hugh 9

SPANISH
Sánchez-Silva, José María 12

SWEDISH
Gripe, Maria 5
Lagerlöf, Selma 7
Lindgren, Astrid 1

WELSH
Dahl, Roald 1, 7

CUMULATIVE INDEX TO TITLES

A and THE; or, William T. C. Baumgarten Comes to Town (Raskin) **1**:155
A Apple Pie (Greenaway) **6**:134
ABC (Burningham) **9**:39
ABC (Lear) **1**:126
ABC (Munari) **9**:125
ABC (Pieńkowski) **6**:233
The ABC Bunny (Gág) **4**:90
ABCDEFGHIJKLMNOP-QRSTUVWXYZ (Kuskin) **4**:138
ABC's of Ecology (Asimov) **12**:47
ABC's of Space (Asimov) **12**:45
ABC's of the Earth (Asimov) **12**:46
ABC's of the Ocean (Asimov) **12**:45
A Is for Always (Anglund) **1**:19
About David (Pfeffer) **11**:201
About the B'nai Bagels (Konigsburg) **1**:119
About the Foods You Eat (Simon) **9**:215
About the Sleeping Beauty (Travers) **2**:176
Abraham Lincoln (Foster) **7**:94
Abraham Lincoln's World (Foster) **7**:92
The Acorn Quest (Yolen) **4**:268
Across Five Aprils (Hunt) **1**:109
Across the Sea (Goffstein) **3**:57
Adam Clayton Powell: Portrait of a Marching Black (Haskins) **3**:63
Adiós, Josefina! (Sánchez-Silva) **12**:232
Adler und Taube (Krüss) **9**:86

Adventures in Making: The Romance of Crafts around the World (Manley) **3**:145
The Adventures of Pinocchio (Collodi) **5**:69
Africa Dream (Greenfield) **4**:100
After the First Death (Cormier) **12**:143
The Age of Giant Mammals (Cohen) **3**:37
Ah-Choo (Mayer) **11**:170
Air in Fact and Fancy (Slote) **4**:199
Akavak: An Eskimo Journey (Houston) **3**:84
Alan Mendelsohn, the Boy from Mars (Pinkwater) **4**:169
Album of Dogs (Henry) **4**:112
Album of Horses (Henry) **4**:112
The Alchemists: Magic into Science (Aylesworth) **6**:50
Alexander and the Terrible, Horrible, No Good, Very Bad Day (Viorst) **3**:207
Alexander and the Wind-Up Mouse (Lionni) **7**:133
Alexander Soames: His Poems (Kuskin) **4**:137
The Alfred G. Graebner Memorial High School Handbook of Rules and Regulations: A Novel (Conford) **10**:94
Alice's Adventures in Wonderland (Carroll) **2**:31
All about Arthur (An Absolutely Absurd Ape) (Carle) **10**:78
All about Horses (Henry) **4**:114
All Around You (Bendick) **5**:36

All Butterflies: An ABC (Brown) **12**:105
All Day Long: Fifty Rhymes of the Never Was and Always Is (McCord) **9**:100
All in the Woodland Early (Yolen) **4**:265
All My Men (Ashley) **4**:15
All Sizes of Noises (Kuskin) **4**:137
All the Colors of the Race: Poems (Adoff) **7**:37
All upon a Stone (George) **1**:89
All Us Come cross the Water (Clifton) **5**:54
The Alley (Estes) **2**:73
The Alligator Case (du Bois) **1**:62
Alligator Pie (Lee) **3**:115
Alligators All Around (Sendak) **1**:167
Alligators and Crocodiles (Zim) **2**:225
All-of-a-Sudden Susan (Coatsworth) **2**:53
Allumette: A Fable, with Due Respect to Hans Christian Andersen, the Grimm Brothers, and the Honorable Ambrose Bierce (Ungerer) **3**:199
The Almost All-White Rabbity Cat (DeJong) **1**:55
Alone in the Wild Forest (Singer) **1**:173
Along Came a Dog (DeJong) **1**:56
Alpha Centauri: The Nearest Star (Asimov) **12**:54
The Alphabet Tree (Lionni) **7**:133

Altogether, One at a Time (Konigsburg) **1**:119
Always Reddy (Henry) **4**:110
Amanda, Dreaming (Wersba) **3**:215
The Amazing Egg (McClung) **11**:192
The Amazing Laser (Bova) **3**:31
American Colonial Paper House: To Cut Out and Color (Ness) **6**:208
America's Endangered Birds: Programs and People Working to Save Them (McClung) **11**:191
Amifika (Clifton) **5**:58
Amish Adventure (Smucker) **10**:191
Amos and Boris (Steig) **2**:158
Amy and Laura (Sachs) **2**:131
Amy Moves In (Sachs) **2**:131
Anansi the Spider: A Tale from the Ashanti (McDermott) **9**:110
Anastasia Again! (Lowry) **6**:195
Anastasia at Your Service (Lowry) **6**:196
Anastasia Krupnik (Lowry) **6**:194
Ancient Monuments and How They Were Built (Cohen) **3**:37
The Ancient Visitors (Cohen) **3**:38
And It Rained (Raskin) **1**:155
And So My Garden Grows (Spier) **5**:219
And Then What Happened, Paul Revere? (Fritz) **2**:79
And This Is Laura (Conford) **10**:94

And to Think That I Saw It on Mulberry Street (Seuss) **1**:84; **9**:172

Andrew Jackson (Foster) **7**:95

Andy (That's My Name) (de Paola) **4**:55

Angel Dust Blues: A Novel (Strasser) **11**:246

Angels and Other Strangers: Family Christmas Stories (Paterson) **7**:237

Angie's First Case (Sobol) **4**:212

Animal Fact/Animal Fable (Simon) **9**:213

The Animal Fair (Provensen and Provensen) **11**:209

The Animal Family (Jarrell) **6**:162

Animal Superstitions (Aylesworth) **6**:56

Animal Territories (Cohen) **3**:38

The Animals and the Ark (Kuskin) **4**:135

Animals and Their Babies (Carle) **10**:79

Animals and Their Niches: How Species Share Resources (Pringle) **4**:183

Animals as Parents (Selsam) **1**:159

The Animals' Conference (Kästner) **4**:125

Animals for Sale (Munari) **9**:124

Animals in Field and Laboratory: Science Projects in Animal Behavior (Simon) **9**:201

Animals in Your Neighborhood (Simon) **9**:211

Animals of the Bible (Asimov) **12**:56

Annaluise and Anton (Kästner) **4**:123

Anne of Avonlea (Montgomery) **8**:134

Anne of Green Gables (Montgomery) **8**:131

Anne of Ingleside (Montgomery) **8**:139

Anne of the Island (Montgomery) **8**:137

Annegret und Cara (Benary-Isbert) **12**:73

Anno's Alphabet: An Adventure in Imagination (Anno) **2**:1

The Ants Who Took Away Time (Kotzwinkle) **6**:183

Any Me I Want to Be: Poems (Kuskin) **4**:140

Anything for a Friend (Conford) **10**:95

Apt. 3 (Keats) **1**:113

Appelard and Liverwurst (Mayer) **11**:173

The Apple and Other Fruits (Selsam) **1**:160

Apples (Hogrogian) **2**:87

April Fools (Krahn) **3**:103

Aquarius (Mark) **11**:152

Aquatic Insects and How They Live (McClung) **11**:186

Arabel's Raven (Aiken) **1**:2

Die Arche Noah (Benary-Isbert) **12**:70

Archimedes and the Door of Science (Bendick) **5**:40

Are All the Giants Dead? (Norton) **6**:225

Are You There God? It's Me, Margaret (Blume) **2**:15

Arilla Sun Down (Hamilton) **11**:76

The Ark (Benary-Isbert) **12**:70

Arm in Arm: A Collection of Connections, Endless Tales, Reiterations, and Other Echolalia (Charlip) **8**:28

The Arm of the Starfish (L'Engle) **1**:129

Armitage, Armitage, Fly Away Home (Aiken) **1**:2

Armored Animals (Zim) **2**:225

The Armourer's House (Sutcliff) **1**:183

Around Fred's Bed (Pinkwater) **4**:165

Around the World in Eighty Days (Burningham) **9**:44

Arrow to the Sun: A Pueblo Indian Tale (McDermott) **9**:111

Art and Archaeology (Glubok) **1**:95

The Art and Industry of Sandcastles: Being an Illustrated Guide to Basic Constructions along with Divers Information Devised by One Jan Adkins, a Wily Fellow (Adkins) **7**:18

The Art of America from Jackson to Lincoln (Glubok) **1**:95

The Art of America in the Gilded Age (Glubok) **1**:95

The Art of Ancient Mexico (Glubok) **1**:96

The Art of Ancient Peru (Glubok) **1**:96

The Art of China (Glubok) **1**:97

The Art of India (Glubok) **1**:97

The Art of Japan (Glubok) **1**:97

The Art of Lands in the Bible (Glubok) **1**:98

The Art of the Etruscans (Glubok) **1**:98

The Art of the New American Nation (Glubok) **1**:99

The Art of the North American Indian (Glubok) **1**:99

The Art of the Northwest Coast Indians (Glubok) **1**:99

The Art of the Spanish in the United States and Puerto Rico (Glubok) **1**:100

Arthur Mitchell (Tobias) **4**:215

Arts and Crafts You Can Eat (Cobb) **2**:64

Ash Road (Southall) **2**:147

Asimov's Guide to Halley's Comet: The Awesome Story of Comets (Asimov) **12**:63

Astercote (Lively) **7**:151

Astrology and Foretelling the Future (Aylesworth) **6**:50

At Mary Bloom's (Aliki) **9**:25

At the Beach (Tobias) **4**:217

At the Sign of the Dog and Rocket (Mark) **11**:156

Attar of the Ice Valley (Wibberley) **3**:224

August the Fourth (Farmer) **8**:86

Augustus Caesar's World, a Story of Ideas and Events from B.C. 44 to 14 A.D. (Foster) **7**:93

Auno and Tauno: A Story of Finland (Henry) **4**:109

Das Austauschkind (Nöstlinger) **12**:189

Autumn Street (Lowry) **6**:195

Avocado Baby (Burningham) **9**:50

Away and Ago: Rhymes of the Never Was and Always Is (McCord) **9**:102

Awful Evelina (Pfeffer) **11**:200

The BFG (Dahl) **7**:82

B is een beer (Bruna) **7**:50

B Is for Bear: An ABC (Bruna) **7**:50

Babar and Father Christmas (Brunhoff) **4**:32

Babar and His Children (Brunhoff) **4**:32

Babar and the Old Lady (Brunhoff) **4**:37

Babar and the Professor (Brunhoff) **4**:34

Babar and the Wully-Wully (Brunhoff) **4**:39

Babar at Home (Brunhoff) **4**:32

Babar at the Seashore (Brunhoff) **4**:38

Babar at the Seaside (Brunhoff) **4**:38

Babar Comes to America (Brunhoff) **4**:36

Babar Goes on a Picnic (Brunhoff) **4**:38

Babar Goes Skiing (Brunhoff) **4**:38

Babar in the Snow (Brunhoff) **4**:38

Babar Loses His Crown (Brunhoff) **4**:37

Babar the Gardener (Brunhoff) **4**:38

Babar the King (Brunhoff) **4**:31

Babar Visits Another Planet (Brunhoff) **4**:38

Babar's Birthday Surprise (Brunhoff) **4**:38

Babar's Castle (Brunhoff) **4**:35

Babar's Childhood (Brunhoff) **4**:37

Babar's Coronation (Brunhoff) **4**:37

Babar's Cousin: That Rascal Arthur (Brunhoff) **4**:33

Babar's Day Out (Brunhoff) **4**:38

Babar's Fair (Brunhoff) **4**:34

Babar's French Lessons (Brunhoff) **4**:35

Babar's Mystery (Brunhoff) **4**:39

Babar's Picnic (Brunhoff) **4**:34

Babar's Trunk (Brunhoff) **4**:38

Babar's Visit to Bird Island (Brunhoff) **4**:34

The Baby (Burningham) **9**:46

A Baby for Max (Lasky) **11**:121

A Baby Sister for Frances (Hoban) **3**:75

A Baby Starts to Grow (Showers) **6**:244

Backbone of the King: The Story of Paka'a and His Son Ku (illus. Brown) **12**:102

Backstage (Isadora and Maiorano) **7**:104

The Bad Island (Steig) **2**:158

The Bad Little Duckhunter (Brown) **10**:54

The Bad Speller (Steig) **2**:159

The Bad-Tempered Ladybird (Carle) **10**:81

The Baker and the Basilisk (McHargue) **2**:117

The Bakers: A Simple Book about the Pleasures of Baking Bread (Adkins) **7**:22

The Ballad of St. Simeon (Serraillier) **2**:135

The Ballad of the Pilgrim Cat (Wibberley) **3**:224

Bang Bang You're Dead (Fitzhugh and Scoppettone) **1**:71

Barefoot in the Grass (Armstrong) **1**:22

A Bargain for Frances (Hoban) **3**:75

Bartholomew and the Oobleck (Seuss) **9**:177

The Baseball Trick (Corbett) **1**:42

Bass and Billy Martin (Phipson) **5**:182

The Bastable Children (Nesbit) **3**:161

The Bat-Poet (Jarrell) **6**:158

The Battle for the Atlantic (Williams) **8**:223

The Battle of Bubble and Squeak (Pearce) **9**:156

Battleground: The United States Army in World War II (Collier) **3**:44

The Bear and the People (Zimnik) **3**:242

A Bear Called Paddington (Bond) **1**:27

Bear Circus (du Bois) **1**:62

The Bear Who Saw the Spring (Kuskin) **4**:136

The Bear's House (Sachs) **2**:131

The Bears of the Air (Lobel) **5**:164

Bear's Picture (Pinkwater) **4**:162

The Beast of Monsieur Racine (Ungerer) **3**:200

The Beast with the Magical Horn (Cameron) **1**:39

The Beasts of Never (McHargue) **2**:117

Beauty: A Retelling of the Story of Beauty and the Beast (McKinley) **10**:121

Beauty and the Beast
(Pearce) **9**:154
The Beauty Queen
(Pfeffer) **11**:198
The Beckoning Lights
(Hughes) **9**:77
Bed-knob and Broomstick
(Norton) **6**:222
Bedtime for Frances
(Hoban) **3**:75
*Bees, Wasps, and Hornets, and
How They Live*
(McClung) **11**:187
The Beethoven Medal
(Peyton) **3**:171
Beezus and Ramona
(Cleary) **2**:45; **8**:47
Before You Came This Way
(Baylor) **3**:13
Before You Were a Baby
(Showers and Showers) **6**:244
Beneath Your Feet
(Simon) **9**:211
*Benjamin West and His Cat
Grimalkin* (Henry) **4**:110
Ben's Dream (Van
Allsburg) **5**:240
Ben's Trumpet (Isadora) **7**:104
Benson Boy (Southall) **2**:148
Beowulf (Sutcliff) **1**:183
Beowulf the Warrior
(Serraillier) **2**:135
Bertie's Escapade
(Grahame) **5**:135
Bess and the Sphinx
(Coatsworth) **2**:53
The Best New Thing
(Asimov) **12**:46
The Best of Enemies
(Bond) **11**:28
Best Word Book Ever
(Scarry) **3**:182
Betje Big gaat naar de markt
(Bruna) **7**:52
Betrayed (Sneve) **2**:143
Better Than All Right
(Pfeffer) **11**:197
Beyond the Burning Lands
(Christopher) **2**:37
Beyond the Chocolate War
(Cormier) **12**:151
Beyond the Dark River
(Hughes) **9**:71
Beyond the Divide
(Lasky) **11**:119
Beyond the Tomorrow Mountains
(Engdahl) **2**:69
Beyond the Weir Bridge
(Burton) **1**:30
Big Anthony and the Magic Ring
(de Paola) **4**:62
Big Bad Bruce (Peet) **12**:203
The Big Cleanup (Weiss) **4**:224
Big Dog, Little Dog
(Brown) **10**:51
The Big Joke Game
(Corbett) **1**:43
The Big Orange Splot
(Pinkwater) **4**:166
Big Red Barn (Brown) **10**:66
*Big Sister Tells Me That I'm
Black* (Adoff) **7**:33
The Big Six (Ransome) **8**:180

The Biggest House in the World
(Lionni) **7**:132
Bilgewater (Gardam) **12**:167
Bill and Pete (de Paola) **4**:61
*Bill Bergson and the White Rose
Rescue* (Lindgren) **1**:135
Bill Bergson Lives Dangerously
(Lindgren) **1**:135
Bill Bergson, Master Detective
(Lindgren) **1**:135
Bill's Garage (Spier) **5**:228
Bill's Service Station
(Spier) **5**:228
*Billy Goat and His Well-Fed
Friends* (Hogrogian) **2**:87
Billy's Balloon Ride
(Zimnik) **3**:242
Billy's Picture (Rey) **5**:196
Binary Numbers (Watson) **3**:211
The Bird and the Stars
(Showers) **6**:246
The Bird Smugglers
(Phipson) **5**:184
Birds at Home (Henry) **4**:109
Birds on Your Street
(Simon) **9**:208
Birds: Poems (Adoff) **7**:37
Birkin (Phipson) **5**:180
Birth of a Forest (Selsam) **1**:160
Birth of an Island
(Selsam) **1**:160
The Birth of the United States
(Asimov) **12**:50
Birthday (Steptoe) **2**:162
The Birthday Present
(Munari) **9**:125
The Birthday Visitor
(Uchida) **6**:257
A Birthday Wish
(Emberley) **5**:100
*Birthdays of Freedom: America's
Heritage from the Ancient
World* (Foster) **7**:95
*Birthdays of Freedom: From the
Fall of Rome to July 4, 1776,
Book Two* (Foster) **7**:97
The Bishop and the Devil
(Serraillier) **2**:136
Black and White (Brown) **10**:52
The Black BC's (Clifton) **5**:53
The Black Cauldron
(Alexander) **1**:11; **5**:18
The Black Death, 1347-1351
(Cohen) **3**:39
Black Folktales (Lester) **2**:112
Black Gold (Henry) **4**:113
Black Hearts in Battersea
(Aiken) **1**:2
Black Is Brown Is Tan
(Adoff) **7**:32
The Black Island (Hergé) **6**:148
*Black Jack: Last of the Big
Alligators* (McClung) **11**:185
The Black Pearl (O'Dell) **1**:145
Black Pilgrimage
(Feelings) **5**:106
The Blanket (Burningham) **9**:47
*Blaze: The Story of a Striped
Skunk* (McClung) **11**:186
The Blonk from Beneath the Sea
(Bendick) **5**:38
Blood (Zim) **2**:225

The Bloody Country (Collier and
Collier) **3**:44
Blowfish Live in the Sea
(Fox) **1**:76
Blubber (Blume) **2**:16
The Blue Jackal (illus.
Brown) **12**:106
Blue Moose (Pinkwater) **4**:163
Blue Mystery (Benary-
Isbert) **12**:73
The Blue Sword
(McKinley) **10**:123
The Blue Thing
(Pinkwater) **4**:166
Blue Trees, Red Sky
(Klein) **2**:97
Blueberries for Sal
(McCloskey) **7**:205
Bo the Constrictor That Couldn't
(Stren) **5**:231
Boat Book (Gibbons) **8**:95
Body Sense/Body Nonsense
(Simon) **9**:217
The Body Snatchers
(Cohen) **3**:39
Boek zonder woorden
(Bruna) **7**:51
Bones (Zim) **2**:226
Bonhomme and the Huge Beast
(Brunhoff) **4**:39
The Book of Dragons
(Nesbit) **3**:162
*The Book of Nursery and Mother
Goose Rhymes* (de
Angeli) **1**:52
A Book of Scary Things
(Showers) **6**:247
A Book of Seasons (Provensen
and Provensen) **11**:212
The Book of Three
(Alexander) **1**:12; **5**:18
Border Hawk: August Bondi
(Alexander) **5**:17
Bored—Nothing to Do!
(Spier) **5**:226
*Borka: The Adventures of a
Goose with No Feathers*
(Burningham) **9**:38
Born to Trot (Henry) **4**:111
The Borrowers (Norton) **6**:220
The Borrowers Afield
(Norton) **6**:221
The Borrowers Afloat
(Norton) **6**:222
The Borrowers Aloft
(Norton) **6**:223
The Borrowers Avenged
(Norton) **6**:226
Boss Cat (Hunter) **3**:97
The Boundary Riders
(Phipson) **5**:178
A Box Full of Infinity
(Williams) **8**:231
*A Boy, a Frog, and a
Friend* (Mayer and
Mayer) **11**:166
A Boy, a Dog, and a Frog
(Mayer) **11**:159
The Boy and the Whale (Sánchez-
Silva) **12**:232
*A Boy Had a Mother Who Bought
Him a Hat* (Kuskin) **4**:141

*The Boy Who Didn't Believe in
Spring* (Clifton) **5**:54
The Boy Who Spoke Chimp
(Yolen) **4**:268
*The Boy Who Was Followed
Home* (Mahy) **7**:183
Boy without a Name
(Lively) **7**:159
A Boy's Will (Haugaard) **11**:110
Brady (Fritz) **2**:79
Brainbox Sorts It Out
(Nöstlinger) **12**:188
Brainstorm (Myers) **4**:157
A Brand-New Uncle
(Seredy) **10**:181
Brave Buffalo Fighter (*Waditaka
Tatanka Kisisohitika*)
(Fitzgerald) **1**:69
The Brave Cowboy
(Anglund) **1**:19
Bread and Honey
(Southall) **2**:149
Bread and Jam for Frances
(Hoban) **3**:76
Break in the Sun (Ashley) **4**:17
Breakthroughs in Science
(Asimov) **12**:34
*Brer Rabbit: Stories from Uncle
Remus* (Brown) **10**:50
Brian Wildsmith's ABC
(Wildsmith) **2**:208
Brian Wildsmith's Birds
(Wildsmith) **2**:208
Brian Wildsmith's Circus
(Wildsmith) **2**:209
Brian Wildsmith's Fishes
(Wildsmith) **2**:210
*Brian Wildsmith's Mother Goose:
A Collection of Nursery
Rhymes* (Wildsmith) **2**:210
Brian Wildsmith's 1, 2, 3's
(Wildsmith) **2**:211
Brian Wildsmith's Puzzles
(Wildsmith) **2**:211
*Brian Wildsmith's The Twelve
Days of Christmas*
(Wildsmith) **2**:212
Brian Wildsmith's Wild Animals
(Wildsmith) **2**:212
Bridge to Terabithia
(Paterson) **7**:232
Bridget and William
(Gardam) **12**:168
Briefe an Pauline (Krüss) **9**:87
Brighty of the Grand Canyon
(Henry) **4**:112
The Bronze Bow (Speare) **8**:208
Brother Dusty-Feet
(Sutcliff) **1**:184
Brothers of the Wind
(Yolen) **4**:268
Bruno Munari's ABC
(Munari) **9**:125
Bruno Munari's Zoo
(Munari) **9**:127
Bubble, Bubble (Mayer) **11**:167
Bubbles (Greenfield) **4**:96
Bufo: The Story of a Toad
(McClung) **11**:179
Buford the Little Bighorn
(Peet) **12**:198
*The Bug That Laid the Golden
Eggs* (Selsam) **1**:160

Building Blocks of the Universe (Asimov) **12**:32

A Building on Your Street (Simon) **9**:207

Bulbs, Corms, and Such (Selsam) **1**:161

The Bumblebee Flies Anyway (Cormier) **12**:149

The Bun: A Tale from Russia (illus. Brown) **12**:104

Bunnicula: A Rabbit-Tale of Mystery (Howe and Howe) **9**:56

Bunny, Hound, and Clown (Mukerji) **10**:135

The Burglar Next Door (Williams) **8**:235

The Buried Moon and Other Stories (Bang) **8**:19

The Burning of Njal (Treece) **2**:182

Burt Dow, Deep-Water Man: A Tale of the Sea in the Classic Tradition (McCloskey) **7**:210

The Bus under the Leaves (Mahy) **7**:182

Busiest People Ever (Scarry) **3**:183

But Jasper Came Instead (Nöstlinger) **12**:189

The Butter Battle Book (Seuss) **9**:194

By the Great Horn Spoon! (Fleischman) **1**:73

By the Shores of Silver Lake (Wilder) **2**:205

CDB! (Steig) **2**:159

C.O.L.A.R.: A Tale of Outer Space (Slote) **4**:203

The Caboose Who Got Loose (Peet) **12**:202

A Calf Is Born (Cole) **5**:64

Calico Captive (Speare) **8**:205

Calico, the Wonder Horse; or, The Saga of Stewy Slinker (Burton) **11**:45

Call Me Bandicoot (du Bois) **1**:63

Camilla (L'Engle) **1**:129

Can I Keep Him? (Kellogg) **6**:170

Candy (White) **3**:220

Cannonball Simp (Burningham) **9**:41

The Capricorn Bracelet (Sutcliff) **1**:184

Captain Kidd's Cat (Lawson) **2**:109

Captain of the Planter: The Story of Robert Smalls (Sterling) **1**:177

Capyboppy (Peet) **12**:198

Cargo Ships (Zim and Skelly) **2**:226

Carousel (Crews) **7**:61

Carrie's War (Bawden) **2**:10

Cars, Boats, Trains, and Planes of Today and Tomorrow (Aylesworth) **6**:52

The Case of the Gone Goose (Corbett) **1**:43

The Case of the Silver Skull (Corbett) **1**:43

The Castle Number Nine (Bemelmans) **6**:65

A Castle of Bone (Farmer) **8**:80

The Castle of Llyr (Alexander) **1**:12; **5**:19

The Castle of Yew (Boston) **3**:26

Castle on the Border (Benary-Isbert) **12**:75

Castors Away (Burton) **1**:30

The Cat and the Captain (Coatsworth) **2**:54

The Cat in the Hat (Seuss) **1**:84; **9**:182

The Cat in the Hat Beginner Book Dictionary, by the Cat Himself and P. D. Eastman (Seuss and Eastman) **9**:188

The Cat in the Hat Comes Back! (Seuss) **9**:184

The Cat Who Went to Heaven (Coatsworth) **2**:54

The Cat Who Wished to Be a Man (Alexander) **1**:12; **5**:22

Catch the Ball! (Carle) **10**:85

Caterpillars (Sterling) **1**:178

Caterpillars and How They Live (McClung) **11**:183

Cathedral: The Story of Its Construction (Macaulay) **3**:140

The Cats (Phipson) **5**:184

A Cat's Body (Cole) **5**:68

The Cat's Quizzer (Seuss) **9**:193

The Cave above Delphi (Corbett) **1**:43

Cecily G. and the Nine Monkeys (Rey) **5**:192

The Celery Stalks at Midnight (Howe) **9**:59

Cells: The Basic Structure of Life (Cobb) **2**:64

Centerburg Tales (McCloskey) **7**:207

Central City/Spread City: The Metropolitan Regions Where More and More of Us Spend Our Lives (Schwartz) **3**:188

The Centurion (Treece) **2**:183

Ceramics: From Clay to Kiln (Weiss) **4**:223

Chains, Webs, and Pyramids: The Flow of Energy in Nature (Pringle) **4**:179

A Chair for My Mother (Williams) **9**:232

The Challenge of the Green Knight (Serraillier) **2**:136

Chancy and the Grand Rascal (Fleischman) **1**:73

The Changing Earth (Viorst) **3**:207

Chariot in the Sky: A Story of the Jubilee Singers (Bontemps) **6**:82

Charity at Home (Willard) **2**:216

Charlie and the Chocolate Factory (Dahl) **1**:49; **7**:69

Charlie and the Great Glass Elevator: The Further Adventures of Charlie Bucket and Willy Wonka, Chocolate-Maker Extraordinary (Dahl) **1**:50; **7**:73

"Charlie Needs a Cloak" (de Paola) **4**:55

Charlotte Sometimes (Farmer) **8**:78

Charlotte's Web (White) **1**:193

Chase Me, Catch Nobody! (Haugaard) **11**:109

Chasing the Goblins Away (Tobias) **4**:216

Chaucer and His World (Serraillier) **2**:137

The Chemicals of Life: Enzymes, Vitamins, Hormones (Asimov) **12**:31

Chemistry in the Kitchen (Simon) **9**:203

Cherokee Run (Smucker) **10**:189

Chester Cricket's New Home (Selden) **8**:202

Chester Cricket's Pigeon Ride (Selden) **8**:201

Chester the Worldly Pig (Peet) **12**:196

The Chestry Oak (Seredy) **10**:178

The Chewing-Gum Rescue and Other Stories (Mahy) **7**:186

The Chichi Hoohoo Bogeyman (Sneve) **2**:144

A Chick Hatches (Cole) **5**:64

Chicken Soup with Rice (Sendak) **1**:167

The Chief of the Herd (Mukerji) **10**:133

Child of the Owl (Yep) **3**:235

The Children Come Running (Coatsworth) **2**:54

The Children of Green Knowe (Boston) **3**:26

The Children of Noisy Village (Lindgren) **1**:135

The Children of the House (Pearce and Fairfax-Lucy) **9**:152

A Child's Garden of Verses (Stevenson) **11**:222

A Child's Good Morning (Brown) **10**:62

A Child's Good Night Book (Brown) **10**:51

Childtimes: A Three-Generation Memoir (Greenfield and Little) **4**:101

The China People (Farmer) **8**:76

Chinaman's Reef Is Ours (Southall) **2**:149

Chip Rogers, Computer Whiz (Simon) **9**:221

Chipmunks on the Doorstep (Tunis) **2**:191

The Chocolate War (Cormier) **12**:130

Choo Choo: The Story of a Little Engine Who Ran Away (Burton) **11**:44

The Christmas Book (Bruna) **7**:49

Christmas in Noisy Village (Lindgren) **1**:136

Christmas in the Barn (Brown) **10**:62

Christmas in the Stable (Lindgren) **1**:136

Christmas Is a Time of Giving (Anglund) **1**:19

Christmas Manger (Rey) **5**:194

Christmas Time (Gibbons) **8**:94

Chronicles of Avonlea, in Which Anne Shirley of Green Gables and Avonlea Plays Some Part (Montgomery) **8**:136

The Chronicles of Narnia (Lewis) **3**:126

The Church Cat Abroad (Oakley) **7**:215

The Church Mice Adrift (Oakley) **7**:217

The Church Mice and the Moon (Oakley) **7**:216

The Church Mice at Bay (Oakley) **7**:218

The Church Mice at Christmas (Oakley) **7**:220

The Church Mice in Action (Oakley) **7**:223

The Church Mice Spread Their Wings (Oakley) **7**:217

The Church Mouse (Oakley) **7**:213

Les Cigares du Pharaon (Hergé) **6**:148

The Cigars of the Pharaoh (Hergé) **6**:148

Cinderella; or, The Little Glass Slipper (illus. Brown) **12**:98

Cinnabar, the One O'Clock Fox (Henry) **4**:113

A Circle of Seasons (Livingston) **7**:174

The Circus in the Mist (Munari) **9**:128

City: A Story of Roman Planning and Construction (Macaulay) **3**:142

City and Suburb: Exploring an Ecosystem (Pringle) **4**:180

City of Darkness (Bova) **3**:32

The City of Gold and Lead (Christopher) **2**:38

City Seen from A to Z (Isadora) **7**:108

Clancy's Cabin (Mahy) **7**:183

The Clashing Rocks: The Story of Jason (Serraillier) **2**:137

Clay, Wood, and Wire: A How-To-Do-It Book of Sculpture (Weiss) **4**:220

The Clock We Live On (Asimov) **12**:33

Clocks and How They Go (Gibbons) **8**:90

The Cloud Book: Words and Pictures (de Paola) **4**:57

The Clown of God: An Old Story (de Paola) **4**:61

Cluck Baa (Burningham) **9**:51

The Coat-Hanger Christmas Tree (Estes) **2**:73

Cockroaches (Cole) **5**:61

Cockroaches: Here, There, and Everywhere (Pringle) **4**:176

A Cold Wind Blowing (Willard) **2**:216

Coll and His White Pig (Alexander) **1**:13; **5**:19

Collage and Construction
(Weiss) **4**:225
*Colonial Craftsmen and the
Beginnings of American
Industry* (Tunis) **2**:192
Colonial Living (Tunis) **2**:192
The Color Kittens
(Brown) **10**:59
A Color of His Own
(Lionni) **7**:137
Colors (Pieńkowski) **6**:230
A Colour of His Own
(Lionni) **7**:137
Colours (Pieńkowski) **6**:230
Come Away (Livingston) **7**:170
*Come Away from the Water,
Shirley* (Burningham) **9**:47
Comet in Moominland
(Jansson) **2**:93
*The Comical Tragedy or Tragical
Comedy of Punch and Judy*
(Brown) **10**:49
*Coming Home from the War: An
Idyll* (Krüss) **9**:87
Commercial Fishing (Zim and
Krantz) **2**:226
*The Complete Adventures of
Charlie and Mr. Willy Wonka*
(Dahl) **7**:77
The Complete Book of Dragons
(Nesbit) **3**:162
*The Complete Computer
Popularity Program*
(Strasser) **11**:251
*Computer Sense, Computer
Nonsense* (Simon) **9**:221
Confessions of an Only Child
(Klein) **2**:97
Conrad: The Factory-Made Boy
(Nöstlinger) **12**:187
*The Controversial Coyote:
Predation, Politics, and
Ecology* (Pringle) **4**:182
The Cookie Tree
(Williams) **8**:229
Coot Club (Ransome) **8**:176
Corals (Zim) **2**:226
*Corn Is Maize: The Gift of the
Indians* (Aliki) **9**:24
Cornelius (Lionni) **7**:140
Count Up: Learning Sets
(Burningham) **9**:50
The Counterfeit African
(Williams) **8**:221
Country Noisy Book
(Brown) **10**:49
Country of Broken Stone
(Bond) **11**:28
The Country of the Heart
(Wersba) **3**:215
Courage, Dana (Pfeffer) **11**:203
The Court of the Stone Children
(Cameron) **1**:39
The Courtship of Animals
(Selsam) **1**:161
Cowardly Clyde (Peet) **12**:205
Cowboy and His Friend
(Anglund) **1**:19
The Cowboy's Christmas
(Anglund) **1**:20
Cowboy's Secret Life
(Anglund) **1**:20
Coyote Cry (Baylor) **3**:14

Coyote in Manhattan
(George) **1**:89
Crabs (Zim and Krantz) **2**:227
The Craft of Sail (Adkins) **7**:20
The Crane (Zimnik) **3**:242
Crash! Bang! Boom!
(Spier) **5**:221
A Crazy Flight and Other Poems
(Livingston) **7**:169
*The Creoles of Color of New
Orleans* (Haskins) **3**:63
The Cricket in Times Square
(Selden) **8**:196
Crisis on Conshelf Ten
(Hughes) **9**:69
*A Crocodile's Tale: A Philippine
Folk Tale* (Aruego and
Aruego) **5**:30
Cromwell's Boy
(Haugaard) **11**:108
The Crooked Snake
(Wrightson) **4**:240
*Cross Your Fingers, Spit in Your
Hat: Superstitions and Other
Beliefs* (Schwartz) **3**:188
Crow Boy (Yashima) **4**:251
The Cruise of the Arctic Star
(O'Dell) **1**:145
The Cuckoo Tree (Aiken) **1**:3
*The Cucumber King: A Story with
a Beginning, a Middle, and an
End, in which Wolfgang
Hogelmann Tells the Whole
Truth* (Nöstlinger) **12**:184
The Cupboard
(Burningham) **9**:47
Curious George (Rey) **5**:193
Curious George Flies a Kite
(Rey) **5**:198
Curious George Gets a Medal
(Rey) **5**:198
*Curious George Goes to the
Hospital* (Rey) **5**:199
*Curious George Learns the
Alphabet* (Rey) **5**:199
Curious George Rides a Bike
(Rey) **5**:196
Curious George Takes a Job
(Rey) **5**:196
The Curse of Cain
(Southall) **2**:150
Cutlass Island (Corbett) **1**:44
Cyrus the Unsinkable Sea Serpent
(Peet) **12**:203
Da lontano era un'isola
(Munari) **9**:129
*Daddy Is a
Monster . . . Sometimes*
(Steptoe) **12**:240
Daedalus and Icarus
(Farmer) **8**:79
Daisy (Coatsworth) **2**:54
Daisy Summerfield's Style
(Goffstein) **3**:58
Dance in the Desert
(L'Engle) **1**:130
The Dancing Camel
(Byars) **1**:35
*The Dancing Kettle and Other
Japanese Folk Tales*
(Uchida) **6**:250
*Danger from Below:
Earthquakes, Past, Present,
and Future* (Simon) **9**:213

*Danger Point: The Wreck of the
Birkenhead* (Corbett) **1**:44
Dangerous Spring (Benary-
Isbert) **12**:77
*Danny Dunn and the Anti-Gravity
Paint* (Williams and
Abrashkin) **8**:222
*Danny Dunn and the Automatic
House* (Williams and
Abrashkin) **8**:227
Danny Dunn and the Fossil Cave
(Williams and
Abrashkin) **8**:225
Danny Dunn and the Heat Ray
(Williams and
Abrashkin) **8**:225
*Danny Dunn and the Homework
Machine* (Williams and
Abrashkin) **8**:223
*Danny Dunn and the Smallifying
Machine* (Williams and
Abrashkin) **8**:230
*Danny Dunn and the Swamp
Monster* (Williams and
Abrashkin) **8**:232
*Danny Dunn and the Universal
Glue* (Williams and
Abrashkin) **8**:236
*Danny Dunn and the Voice from
Space* (Williams and
Abrashkin) **8**:229
*Danny Dunn and the Weather
Machine* (Williams and
Abrashkin) **8**:223
Danny Dunn, Invisible Boy
(Williams and
Abrashkin) **8**:233
Danny Dunn on a Desert Island
(Williams and
Abrashkin) **8**:223
Danny Dunn on the Ocean Floor
(Williams and
Abrashkin) **8**:224
Danny Dunn, Scientific Detective
(Williams and
Abrashkin) **8**:234
Danny Dunn, Time Traveler
(Williams and
Abrashkin) **8**:226
Danny Goes to the Hospital
(Collier) **3**:44
*Danny: The Champion of the
World* (Dahl) **7**:74
The Dark Ages (Asimov) **12**:42
The Dark Bright Water
(Wrightson) **4**:246
The Dark Canoe (O'Dell) **1**:146
The Dark Is Rising
(Cooper) **4**:44
*The Dark Wood of the Golden
Birds* (Brown) **10**:59
Darlene (Greenfield) **4**:103
*Daughter of Earth: A Roman
Myth* (McDermott) **9**:119
David He No Fear
(Graham) **10**:109
David Starr, Space Ranger
(Asimov) **12**:30
David's Little Indian: A Story
(Brown) **10**:66
David's Witch Doctor
(Mahy) **7**:184
Dawn (Bang) **8**:23

Dawn (Shulevitz) **5**:206
*Dawn from the West: The Story
of Genevieve Caulfield*
(Rau) **8**:185
*A Dawn in the Trees: Thomas
Jefferson, the Years 1776 to
1789* (Wibberley) **3**:224
Dawn of Fear (Cooper) **4**:43
*A Day of Pleasure: Stories of a
Boy Growing Up in Warsaw*
(Singer) **1**:173
The Day the Gang Got Rich
(Kotzwinkle) **6**:181
*The Day the Numbers
Disappeared* (Bendick and
Simon) **5**:40
*The Day the Teacher Went
Bananas* (Howe) **9**:59
Daydreamers (Greenfield) **4**:103
Daylight Robbery
(Williams) **8**:235
Days of Terror
(Smucker) **10**:190
Days with Frog and Toad
(Lobel) **5**:173
The Dead Bird (Brown) **10**:66
The Dead Letter Box
(Mark) **11**:154
Dead Man's Light
(Corbett) **1**:44
Deadly Ants (Simon) **9**:214
Deadmen's Cave
(Wibberley) **3**:225
Dear Lovey Hart: I Am Desperate
(Conford) **10**:93
Dear Mr. Henshaw
(Cleary) **8**:59
Dear Readers and Riders
(Henry) **4**:115
Death Is Natural (Pringle) **4**:181
Deathwatch (White) **3**:221
Deenie (Blume) **2**:16
Delpha Green and Company
(Cleaver and Cleaver) **6**:108
Der Denker Greift Ein
(Nöstlinger) **12**:188
Department Store
(Gibbons) **8**:98
Desert Dan (Coatsworth) **2**:55
The Desert Is Theirs
(Baylor) **3**:14
Devil on My Back
(Hughes) **9**:78
*The Devil Rides with Me and
Other Fantastic Stories*
(Slote) **4**:203
Devil's Hill (Chauncy) **6**:90
The Devil's Storybook
(Babbitt) **2**:5
Dick Bruna's Animal Book
(Bruna) **7**:51
Dick Bruna's Word Book
(Bruna) **7**:53
Dick Foote and the Shark
(Babbitt) **2**:5
Dick Whittington and His Cat
(illus. Brown) **12**:95
*Did I Ever Tell You How Lucky
You Are?* (Geisel) **1**:85
Died on a Rainy Sunday
(Aiken) **1**:3
Dierenboek (Bruna) **7**:51

Title Index

The Diggers (Brown) 10:67

Digging Up Dinosaurs (Aliki) 9:28

Dinner Ladies Don't Count (Ashley) 4:18

Dinner Time (Pieńkowski) 6:231

The Dinosaur Is the Biggest Animal That Ever Lived and Other Wrong Ideas You Thought Were True (Simon) 9:220

Dinosaur Story (Cole) 5:63

Dinosaurs (Zim) 2:227

Dinosaurs and People: Fossils, Facts, and Fantasies (Pringle) 4:184

Dinosaurs and Their World (Pringle) 4:174

Diogenes: The Story of the Greek Philosopher (Aliki) 9:21

The Disappearing Dog Trick (Corbett) 1:44

Disaster (Sobol) 4:211

Discovering the Royal Tombs at Ur (Glubok) 1:100

Discovering What Earthworms Do (Simon) 9:202

Discovering What Frogs Do (Simon) 9:202

Discovering What Gerbils Do (Simon) 9:204

Discovering What Goldfish Do (Simon) 9:202

Divide and Rule (Mark) 11:148

Do Tigers Ever Bite Kings? (Wersba) 3:216

Do You Have the Time, Lydia? (Ness) 6:207

Do You Want to Be My Friend? (Carle) 10:74

Dr. Anno's Magical Midnight Circus (Anno) 2:2

Dr. Merlin's Magic Shop (Corbett) 1:45

Dr. Seuss's ABC (Seuss) 1:85; 9:187

Dr. Seuss's Sleep Book (Seuss) 1:85; 9:187

The Dog (Burningham) 9:47

A Dog and a Half (Willard) 2:217

The Dog Days of Arthur Cane (Bethancourt) 3:18

A Dog So Small (Pearce) 9:149

The Dog That Could Swim under Water: Memoirs of a Springer Spaniel (Selden) 8:196

Dogs and Dragons, Trees and Dreams: A Collection of Poems (Kuskin) 4:144

Dollmaker: The Eyelight and the Shadow (Lasky) 11:116

The Dolphin Crossing (Walsh) 2:197

Dom and Va (Christopher) 2:39

Dominic (Steig) 2:159

The Dong with the Luminous Nose (Lear) 1:127

"Don't Play Dead Before You Have To" (Wojciechowska) 1:196

Don't You Remember? (Clifton) 5:55

The Door in the Hedge (McKinley) 10:122

The Door in the Wall (de Angeli) 1:53

Door to the North (Coatsworth) 2:55

Dorrie's Book (Sachs) 2:132

A Double Discovery (Ness) 6:203

The Double Planet (Asimov) 12:34

The Double Quest (Sobol) 4:206

Down Half the World (Coatsworth) 2:55

Down to Earth (Wrightson) 4:242

Dragon Night and Other Lullabies (Yolen) 4:266

The Dragon of an Ordinary Family (Mahy) 7:179

The Dragon Takes a Wife (Myers) 4:156

Dragonfly Summer (Farmer) 8:79

Dragonwings (Yep) 3:236

The Dream Book: First Comes the Dream (Brown) 10:59

Dream Days (Grahame) 5:128

Dream of Dark Harbor (Kotzwinkle) 6:183

The Dream Time (Treece) 2:183

The Dream Watcher (Wersba) 3:216

Dream Weaver (Yolen) 4:265

Dreams (Keats) 1:114

Dreams of Victory (Conford) 10:90

Dreams, Visions, and Drugs: A Search for Other Realities (Cohen) 3:39

Drei Mal Drei: An Einem Tag (Krüss) 9:85

The Driftway (Lively) 7:154

The Drinking Gourd (Monjo) 2:120

A Drop of Blood (Showers) 6:243

The Drugstore Cat (Petry) 12:210

Drummer Hoff (Emberley) 5:94

Dry Victories (Jordan) 10:118

Duck on a Pond (Willard) 2:217

The Dueling Machine (Bova) 3:32

The Dunkard (Selden) 8:199

Dust of the Earth (Cleaver and Cleaver) 6:110

Dustland (Hamilton) 11:80

ESP (Aylesworth) 6:50

E.T.! The Extra-Terrestrial (Kotzwinkle) 6:184

E.T.! The Extra-Terrestrial Storybook (Kotzwinkle) 6:185

Eagle and Dove (Krüss) 9:86

Eagle Mask: A West Coast Indian Tale (Houston) 3:85

The Eagle of the Ninth (Sutcliff) 1:185

Early Thunder (Fritz) 2:80

Earth: Our Planet in Space (Simon) 9:220

Earthdark (Hughes) 9:69

The Earthsea Trilogy (Le Guin) 3:118

East of the Sun and West of the Moon (Mayer) 11:174

The Easter Cat (DeJong) 1:56

An Easy Introduction to the Slide Rule (Asimov) 12:39

Eats: Poems (Adoff) 7:35

Der Ebereschenhof (Benary-Isbert) 12:72

Ecology (Bendick) 5:48

Ecology: Science of Survival (Pringle) 4:175

Ed Emberley's A B C (Emberley) 5:100

Ed Emberley's Amazing Look Through Book (Emberley) 5:101

Ed Emberley's Big Green Drawing Book (Emberley) 5:102

Ed Emberley's Big Orange Drawing Book (Emberley) 5:102

Ed Emberley's Big Purple Drawing Book (Emberley) 5:103

Ed Emberley's Crazy Mixed-Up Face Game (Emberley) 5:103

Ed Emberley's Drawing Book: Make a World (Emberley) 5:98

Ed Emberley's Drawing Book of Animals (Emberley) 5:97

Ed Emberley's Drawing Book of Faces (Emberley) 5:99

Ed Emberley's Great Thumbprint Drawing Book (Emberley) 5:100

The Edge of the Cloud (Peyton) 3:172

Egg Thoughts and Other Frances Songs (Hoban) 3:76

Egg to Chick (Selsam) 1:161

The Eggs: A Greek Folk Tale (Aliki) 9:20

Ego-Tripping and Other Poems for Young People (Giovanni) 6:116

The Egyptians (Asimov) 12:41

Eight for a Secret (Willard) 2:217

Eight Plus One: Stories (Cormier) 12:148

The Eighteenth Emergency (Byars) 1:35

Einstein Anderson Goes to Bat (Simon) 9:218

Einstein Anderson Lights Up the Sky (Simon) 9:219

Einstein Anderson Makes Up for Lost Time (Simon) 9:216

Einstein Anderson, Science Sleuth (Simon) 9:216

Einstein Anderson Sees Through the Invisible Man (Simon) 9:219

Einstein Anderson Shocks His Friends (Simon) 9:216

Einstein Anderson Tells a Comet's Tale (Simon) 9:217

Electronics for Boys and Girls (Bendick) 5:34

Elephant Boy: A Story of the Stone Age (Kotzwinkle) 6:180

The Elephant's Wish (Munari) 9:125

Eli (Peet) 12:204

Elidor and the Golden Ball (McHargue) 2:117

Elijah the Slave (Singer) 1:174

Elisabeth the Cow Ghost (du Bois) 1:63

Elizabite: The Adventures of a Carnivorous Plant (Rey) 5:194

Eliza's Daddy (Thomas) 8:213

Ellen Dellen (Gripe) 5:148

Ellen Grae (Cleaver and Cleaver) 6:101

Ellen Tebbits (Cleary) 2:45; 8:45

The Elm Street Lot (Pearce) 9:153

Eloquent Crusader: Ernestine Rose (Suhl) 2:165

Elvis and His Friends (Gripe) 5:148

Elvis and His Secret (Gripe) 5:148

Elvis! Elvis! (Gripe) 5:148

Elvis Karlsson (Gripe) 5:148

The Emergency Book (Bendick) 5:41

Emil and Piggy Beast (Lindgren) 1:136

Emil and the Detectives (Kästner) 4:121

Emil's Pranks (Lindgren) 1:136

Emily of New Moon (Montgomery) 8:138

Emily's Runaway Imagination (Cleary) 2:45; 8:50

Emma in Winter (Farmer) 8:78

Emmet Otter's Jug-Band Christmas (Hoban) 3:76

The Emperor and the Kite (Yolen) 4:257

The Emperor's New Clothes (Burton) 11:50

The Emperor's Winding Sheet (Walsh) 2:197

The Enchanted: An Incredible Tale (Coatsworth) 2:56

The Enchanted Castle (Nesbit) 3:162

The Enchanted Island: Stories from Shakespeare (Serraillier) 2:137

Enchantress from the Stars (Engdahl) 2:69

Encore for Eleanor (Peet) 12:205

Encounter Near Venus (Wibberley) 3:225

Encyclopedia Brown and the Case of the Dead Eagles (Sobol) 4:210

Encyclopedia Brown and the Case of the Midnight Visitor (Sobol) 4:211

Encyclopedia Brown and the Case of the Secret Pitch (Sobol) 4:207

Encyclopedia Brown, Boy Detective (Sobol) 4:207

Encyclopedia Brown Carries On (Sobol) **4**:212

Encyclopedia Brown Finds the Clues (Sobol) **4**:208

Encyclopedia Brown Gets His Man (Sobol) **4**:208

Encyclopedia Brown Lends a Hand (Sobol) **4**:210

Encyclopedia Brown Saves the Day (Sobol) **4**:209

Encyclopedia Brown Shows the Way (Sobol) **4**:209

Encyclopedia Brown Solves Them All (Sobol) **4**:208

Encyclopedia Brown Takes the Case (Sobol) **4**:209

Encyclopedia Brown's Record Book of Weird and Wonderful Facts (Sobol) **4**:211

End of Exile (Bova) **3**:32

The Ends of the Earth: The Polar Regions of the World (Asimov) **12**:52

An Enemy at Green Knowe (Boston) **3**:27

Energy: Power for People (Pringle) **4**:179

The Ennead (Mark) **11**:147

The Enormous Crocodile (Dahl) **7**:77

Environments Out There (Asimov) **12**:42

The Epics of Everest (Wibberley) **3**:226

Eric Carle's Storybook: Seven Tales by the Brothers Grimm (Carle) **10**:80

The Erie Canal (Spier) **5**:220

Estuaries: Where Rivers Meet the Sea (Pringle) **4**:178

Eugene the Brave (Conford) **10**:95

Ever Ride a Dinosaur? (Corbett) **1**:45

Everett Anderson's Christmas Coming (Clifton) **5**:54

Everett Anderson's Friend (Clifton) **5**:57

Everett Anderson's Nine Month Long (Clifton) **5**:59

Everett Anderson's 1-2-3 (Clifton) **5**:58

Everett Anderson's Year (Clifton) **5**:55

Every Man Heart Lay Down (Graham) **10**:108

Every Time I Climb a Tree (McCord) **9**:100

Everybody Needs a Rock (Baylor) **3**:15

Everyone Knows What a Dragon Looks Like (Williams) **8**:235

Everything Moves (Simon) **9**:210

Exactly Alike (Ness) **6**:201

Exiled from Earth (Bova) **3**:33

The Expeditions of Willis Partridge (Weiss) **4**:222

The Exploits of Moominpappa (Jansson) **2**:93

Explorers on the Moon (Hergé) **6**:148

Exploring Fields and Lots: Easy Science Projects (Simon) **9**:212

Extraterrestrial Civilizations (Asimov) **12**:57

Fables (Lobel) **5**:174

Facts, Frauds, and Phantasms: A Survey of the Spiritualist Movement (McHargue) **2**:118

A Fall from the Sky: The Story of Daedalus (Serraillier) **2**:138

Fall Is Here! (Sterling) **1**:178

Family (Donovan) **3**:51

The Family Christmas Tree Book (de Paola) **4**:65

The Family Conspiracy (Phipson) **5**:179

The Family Tower (Willard) **2**:217

Famous Negro Athletes (Bontemps) **6**:84

Fannie Lou Hamer (Jordan) **10**:119

Fanny and the Battle of Potter's Piece (Lively) **7**:163

Fanny's Sister (Lively) **7**:161

Fantastic Mr. Fox (Dahl) **1**:51; **7**:73

Fantasy Summer (Pfeffer) **11**:204

Far and Few: Rhymes of the Never Was and Always Is (McCord) **9**:98

Far from Shore (Major) **11**:130

Far Out the Long Canal (DeJong) **1**:57

The Far Side of Evil (Engdahl) **2**:70

Farewell to Shady Glade (Peet) **12**:196

Farmer Palmer's Wagon Ride (Steig) **2**:160

The Farthest Shore (Le Guin) **3**:123

Fast Sam, Cool Clyde, and Stuff (Myers) **4**:156

The Fast Sooner Hound (Bontemps and Conroy) **6**:79

Fast-Slow, High-Low: A Book of Opposites (Spier) **5**:222

Fat Elliot and the Gorilla (Pinkwater) **4**:162

Fat Men from Space (Pinkwater) **4**:168

Father Christmas (Briggs) **10**:24

Father Christmas Goes on Holiday (Briggs) **10**:25

Father Fox's Pennyrhymes (Watson) **3**:211

A Father Like That (Zolotow) **2**:233

The Fearsome Inn (Singer) **1**:174

The Feather Star (Wrightson) **4**:241

Feelings (Aliki) **9**:32

Feet and Other Stories (Mark) **11**:154

Felice (Brown) **12**:100

Felicia the Critic (Conford) **10**:91

A Few Fair Days (Gardam) **12**:161

Fiddlestrings (de Angeli) **1**:53

Fierce: The Lion (Ness) **6**:209

Fierce-Face, the Story of a Tiger (Mukerji) **10**:135

Fifteen (Cleary) **2**:46; **8**:48

Figgs and Phantoms (Raskin) **12**:218

Fighting Men: How Men Have Fought through the Ages (Treece and Oakeshott) **2**:184

Fighting Shirley Chisholm (Haskins) **3**:64

Fin M'Coul: The Giant of Knockmany Hill (de Paola) **4**:66

Find a Stranger, Say Goodbye (Lowry) **6**:193

Find Out by Touching (Showers) **6**:241

Find the Constellations (Rey) **5**:196

Find the Hidden Insect (Cole) **5**:66

Finding Out about Jobs: TV Reporting (Bendick and Bendick) **5**:48

Finn Family Moomintroll (Jansson) **2**:93

Finn's Folly (Southall) **2**:150

Fire! Fire! (Gibbons) **8**:98

The Fire Station (Spier) **5**:228

The Firehouse (Spier) **5**:228

The Firemen (Kotzwinkle) **6**:180

Fireweed (Walsh) **2**:198

The First ABC (Lear) **1**:127

First Adventure (Coatsworth) **2**:56

The First Book of Airplanes (Bendick) **5**:37

The First Book of Fishes (Bendick) **5**:41

The First Book of How to Fix It (Bendick and Berk) **5**:39

The First Book of Medieval Man (Sobol) **4**:206

The First Book of Ships (Bendick) **5**:38

The First Book of Space Travel (Bendick) **5**:37

The First Book of Supermarkets (Bendick) **5**:37

The First Book of Time (Bendick) **5**:40

The First Four Years (Wilder) **2**:205

A First Look at Birds (Selsam and Hunt) **1**:162

A First Look at Leaves (Selsam) **1**:162

A First Look at Mammals (Selsam and Hunt) **1**:162

The First Margaret Mahy Story Book: Stories and Poems (Mahy) **7**:181

The First Peko-Neko Bird (Krahn and Krahn) **3**:103

First Pink Light (Greenfield) **4**:99

The First Story (Brown) **10**:55

The First Two Lives of Lukas-Kasha (Alexander) **5**:24

First Words (Burningham) **9**:51

The Fish (Bruna) **7**:49

Fish for Supper (Goffstein) **3**:58

A Fish Hatches (Cole) **5**:65

Fish Head (Fritz) **2**:80

Fish Is Fish (Lionni) **7**:133

The Fish with the Deep Sea Smile (Brown) **10**:48

Five Children and It (Nesbit) **3**:163

Five Down: Numbers as Signs (Burningham) **9**:50

The 500 Hats of Bartholomew Cubbins (Seuss) **9**:172

Flambards (Peyton) **3**:172

Flambards in Summer (Peyton) **3**:173

The Flambards Trilogy (Peyton) **3**:173

Fleas (Cole) **5**:62

Flicks (de Paola) **4**:63

Flight of Exiles (Bova) **3**:33

Flight 714 (Hergé) **6**:149

Flight to the Forest (Willard) **2**:218

Flint's Island (Wibberley) **3**:226

Flocks of Birds (Zolotow) **2**:234

The Flood at Reedsmere (Burton) **1**:31

A Flower with Love (Munari) **9**:130

Fly Away Home (Nostlinger) **12**:185

Fly by Night (Jarrell) **6**:165

Fly Homer Fly (Peet) **12**:199

Fly into Danger (Phipson) **5**:184

Fly-by-Night (Peyton) **3**:176

The Flying Carpet (illus. Brown) **12**:98

A Flying Saucer Full of Spaghetti (Krahn) **3**:104

Follow a Fisher (Pringle) **4**:178

The Food Market (Spier) **5**:228

The Fool of the World and the Flying Ship: A Russian Tale (Ransome) **8**:184

The Fools of Chelm and Their History (Singer) **1**:174

For Me to Say: Rhymes of the Never Was and Always Is (McCord) **9**:101

Forest of the Night (Townsend) **2**:169

Forever (Blume) **2**:17

The Forever Christmas Tree (Uchida) **6**:253

Forever Free: The Story of the Emancipation Proclamation (Sterling) **1**:178

Forgetful Fred (Williams) **8**:233

Fortunately (Charlip) **8**:27

A Fortune for the Brave (Chauncy) **6**:89

Fossils Tell of Long Ago (Aliki) **9**:21

The Foundling and Other Tales of Prydain (Alexander) **1**:13; **5**:22

Four Days in the Life of Lisa (Nöstlinger) **12**:187

The Four Donkeys (Alexander) **1**:14

Four Fur Feet (Brown) **10**:67

Four Rooms from the Metropolitan Museum of Art (Ness) **6**:208

Four Stories for Four Seasons (de Paola)   **4**:59
The Four-Story Mistake (Enright)   **4**:74
4-Way Stop and Other Poems (Livingston)   **7**:172
Fox Eyes (Brown)   **10**:61
The Fox Friend (Coatsworth)   **2**:57
The Fox Hole (Southall)   **2**:151
Fox in Socks (Seuss)   **1**:85; **9**:188
The Fox Went Out on a Chilly Night: An Old Song (Spier)   **5**:217
Frankie's Hat (Mark)   **11**:157
Franklin Stein (Raskin)   **1**:155
Frederick (Lionni)   **7**:131
Frederick Douglass: Slave-Fighter-Freeman (Bontemps)   **6**:83
Freedom Train: The Story of Harriet Tubman (Sterling)   **1**:179
Freight Train (Crews)   **7**:56
The Friend (Burningham)   **9**:47
Friend Dog (Adoff)   **7**:36
A Friend Is Someone Who Likes You (Anglund)   **1**:20
Friend Monkey (Travers)   **2**:177
Friend: The Story of George Fox and the Quakers (Yolen)   **4**:259
Friends till the End: A Novel (Strasser)   **11**:247
Frog and Toad All Year (Lobel)   **5**:170
Frog and Toad Are Friends (Lobel)   **5**:165
Frog and Toad Together (Lobel)   **5**:167
Frog Goes to Dinner (Mayer)   **11**:168
Frog Went A-Courtin' (Langstaff)   **3**:109
Frog, Where Are You? (Mayer)   **11**:165
The Frogmen (White)   **3**:221
A Frog's Body (Cole)   **5**:66
From Afar It Is an Island (Munari)   **9**:129
From Anna (Little)   **4**:151
From Lew Alcindor to Kareem Abdul Jabbar (Haskins)   **3**:64
From Pond to Prairie: The Changing World of a Pond and Its Life (Pringle)   **4**:176
From Shore to Ocean Floor: How Life Survives in the Sea (Simon)   **9**:207
From the Mixed-Up Files of Mrs. Basil E. Frankweiler (Konigsburg)   **1**:120
Frontier Living (Tunis)   **2**:192
Fungus the Bogeyman (Briggs)   **10**:26
Fungus the Bogeyman Plop-Up Book (Briggs)   **10**:33
Funniest Storybook Ever (Scarry)   **3**:183
Funny Bananas (McHargue)   **2**:118
The Funny Thing (Gág)   **4**:89

The Further Adventures of Nils (Lagerlöf)   **7**:110
The Further Adventures of Robinson Crusoe (Treece)   **2**:184
The Gadget Book (Weiss)   **4**:226
The Gales of Spring: Thomas Jefferson, the Years 1789-1801 (Wibberley)   **3**:226
Games and Puzzles You Can Make Yourself (Weiss)   **4**:228
The Garden of Abdul Gasazi (Van Allsburg)   **5**:238
The Garden under the Sea (Selden)   **8**:196
Gases (Cobb)   **2**:65
The Gathering (Hamilton)   **11**:82
The Gats! (Goffstein)   **3**:59
Gaudenzia, Pride of the Palio (Henry)   **4**:113
Gay-Neck, the Story of a Pigeon (Mukerji)   **10**:131
The Genie of Sutton Place (Selden)   **8**:200
The Gentle Desert: Exploring an Ecosystem (Pringle)   **4**:183
Gentleman Jim (Briggs)   **10**:30
Geological Disasters: Earthquakes and Volcanoes (Aylesworth)   **6**:55
(George) (Konigsburg)   **1**:120
George and Red (Coatsworth)   **2**:57
George and the Cherry Tree (Aliki)   **9**:18
George Washington (Foster)   **7**:93
George Washington's Breakfast (Fritz)   **2**:81
George Washington's World (Foster)   **7**:91
George's Marvelous Medicine (Dahl)   **7**:80
Georgie Has Lost His Cap (Munari)   **9**:125
Geraldine, the Music Mouse (Lionni)   **7**:138
Get Set! Go! Overcoming Obstacles (Watanabe)   **8**:216
Ghond, the Hunter (Mukerji)   **10**:132
The Ghost Dance Caper (Hughes)   **9**:70
Ghost in a Four-Room Apartment (Raskin)   **1**:156
The Ghost in the Noonday Sun (Fleischman)   **1**:74
The Ghost of Thomas Kempe (Lively)   **7**:154
Ghost Paddle: A Northwest Coast Indian Tale (Houston)   **3**:85
The Giant (du Bois)   **1**:63
The Giant Golden Book of Cat Stories (Coatsworth)   **2**:57
Giant John (Lobel)   **5**:163
The Giant Panda at Home (Rau)   **8**:188
The Giants' Farm (Yolen)   **4**:263
The Giants Go Camping (Yolen)   **4**:265
A Gift for Sula Sula (Ness)   **6**:201

The Gift of Sarah Barker (Yolen)   **4**:267
Gigi cerca il suo berretto (Munari)   **9**:125
Ginger Pye (Estes)   **2**:73
The Gingerbread Rabbit (Jarrell)   **6**:158
A Giraffe and a Half (Silverstein)   **5**:209
The Girl and the Goatherd; or, This and That and Thus and So (Ness)   **6**:205
The Girl Called Moses: The Story of Harriet Tubman (Petry)   **12**:210
Girl Missing: A Novel (Nöstlinger)   **12**:186
The Girl Who Cried Flowers and Other Tales (Yolen)   **4**:260
The Girl Who Loved the Wind (Yolen)   **4**:260
Girls Can Be Anything (Klein)   **2**:98
Give Dad My Best (Collier)   **3**:45
The Giving Tree (Silverstein)   **5**:209
Glasblasarns Barn (Gripe)   **5**:144
The Glassblower's Children (Gripe)   **5**:144
Glimpses of Louisa (Alcott)   **1**:9
The Glorious Flight: Across the Channel with Louis Blériot July 25, 1909 (Provensen and Provensen)   **11**:215
Die Glücklichen Inseln Hinter dem Winde (Krüss)   **9**:83
Die Glücklichen Inseln Hinter dem Winde Bd. 2 (Krüss)   **9**:84
The Gnats of Knotty Pine (Peet)   **12**:203
Go and Hush the Baby (Byars)   **1**:35
Gobble, Growl, Grunt (Spier)   **5**:220
The Goblins Giggle and Other Stories (Bang)   **8**:17
God Wash the World and Start Again (Graham)   **10**:109
Goggles! (Keats)   **1**:114
Going Back (Lively)   **7**:159
Gold: The Fascinating Story of the Noble Metal through the Ages (Cohen)   **3**:40
The Golden Age (Grahame)   **5**:126
The Golden Basket (Bemelmans)   **6**:64
The Golden Bunny and 17 Other Stories and Poems (Brown)   **10**:63
The Golden Door: The United States from 1865 to 1918 (Asimov)   **12**:54
The Golden Egg Book (Brown)   **10**:55
The Golden One (Treece)   **2**:185
The Golden Road (Montgomery)   **8**:136
The Golden Serpent (Myers)   **4**:160

Goldengrove (Walsh)   **2**:199
Gold-Fever Trail: A Klondike Adventure (Hughes)   **9**:68
Goldie, the Dollmaker (Goffstein)   **3**:59
Golly Gump Swallowed a Fly (Cole)   **5**:68
A Gondola for Fun (Weiss)   **4**:220
Gone Is Gone; or, The Story of a Man Who Wanted to Do Housework (Gág)   **4**:90
Gone-Away Lake (Enright)   **4**:75
Good Ethan (Fox)   **1**:77
The Good Knight Ghost (Bendick)   **5**:38
Good Luck Duck (DeJong)   **1**:57
Good Luck to the Rider (Phipson)   **5**:177
The Good Master (Seredy)   **10**:171
Good Morning (Bruna)   **7**:53
Good News (Greenfield)   **4**:96
Good Night, Prof, Dear (Townsend)   **2**:170
Good Old James (Donovan)   **3**:51
Good, Says Jerome (Clifton)   **5**:55
Good-bye to the Jungle (Townsend)   **2**:171
The Good-for-Nothing Prince (Williams)   **8**:230
Goodnight (Hoban)   **3**:77
Goodnight Moon (Brown)   **10**:55
Goody Hall (Babbitt)   **2**:6
The Gorgon's Head: The Story of Perseus (Serraillier)   **2**:138
Gorilla (McClung)   **11**:194
Graham Oakley's Magical Changes (Oakley)   **7**:219
Un gran pequeño (Sánchez-Silva)   **12**:232
Grand Papa and Ellen Aroon (Monjo)   **2**:121
Grandfather Learns to Drive (Krüss)   **9**:88
Grandmother Cat and the Hermit (Coatsworth)   **2**:58
Granpa (Burningham)   **9**:52
Graphology: A Guide to Handwriting Analysis (Aylesworth)   **6**:53
Grasshopper on the Road (Lobel)   **5**:172
The Gray Kangaroo at Home (Rau)   **8**:189
The Great Blueness and Other Predicaments (Lobel)   **5**:165
The Great Brain (Fitzgerald)   **1**:69
The Great Brain at the Academy (Fitzgerald)   **1**:69
The Great Brain Reforms (Fitzgerald)   **1**:69
The Great Flood (Spier)   **5**:224
The Great Gilly Hopkins (Paterson)   **7**:235
Great Ideas of Science: The Men and the Thinking behind Them (Asimov)   **12**:45
The Great Millionaire Kidnap (Mahy)   **7**:184

Great Northern?
(Ransome) **8**:182
The Great Piratical
Rumbustification & The
Librarian and the Robbers
(Mahy) **7**:185
The Great Watermelon Birthday
(Williams) **9**:231
The Great Wheel
(Lawson) **2**:109
The Greeks: A Great Adventure
(Asimov) **12**:38
The Green Coat (Gripe) **5**:148
Green Darner: The Story of a
Dragonfly (McClung) **11**:180
Green Eggs and Ham
(Seuss) **1**:86; **9**:185
The Green Flash and Other Tales
of Horror, Suspense, and
Fantasy (Aiken) **1**:4
Green Grass and White Milk
(Aliki) **9**:23
Green Says Go (Emberley) **5**:96
The Greentail Mouse
(Lionni) **7**:135
Greenwitch (Cooper) **4**:45
Gregory Griggs and Other
Nursery Rhyme People
(Lobel) **5**:172
The Gremlins (Dahl) **7**:68
Greta the Strong (Sobol) **4**:209
The Grey King (Cooper) **4**:47
The Grey Lady and the
Strawberry Snatcher
(Bang) **8**:20
Greyling: A Picture Story from
the Islands of Shetland
(Yolen) **4**:257
The Groober (Byars) **1**:36
Grossvater Lerner auf Fahren
(Krüss) **9**:88
The Grouchy Ladybug
(Carle) **10**:81
The Grove of Green Holly
(Willard) **2**:218
Grover (Cleaver and
Cleaver) **6**:104
Growing Pains: Diaries and
Drawings for the Years 1908-
1917 (Gág) **4**:91
The Guardian of Isis
(Hughes) **9**:73
The Guardians
(Christopher) **2**:39
Guarneri: Story of a Genius
(Wibberley) **3**:227
Guests in the Promised Land
(Hunter) **3**:98
Gull Number 737 (George) **1**:89
Gypsy (Seredy) **10**:179
Gypsy Moth: Its History in
America (McClung) **11**:188
Hadassah: Esther the Orphan
Queen (Armstrong) **1**:22
Hairs in the Palm of the Hand
(Mark) **11**:151
Hakon of Rogen's Saga
(Haugaard) **11**:102
Hakon's Saga
(Haugaard) **11**:102
Half a World Away
(Chauncy) **6**:91
Halloween (Gibbons) **8**:99

The Hand of Apollo
(Coatsworth) **2**:58
A Handful of Thieves
(Bawden) **2**:11
Handles (Mark) **11**:155
Handtalk: An ABC of Finger
Spelling and Sign Language
(Charlip, Mary Beth, and
Ancona) **8**:31
Hang Tough, Paul Mather
(Slote) **4**:200
Hansi (Bemelmans) **6**:63
Happy Birthday to You!
(Seuss) **9**:185
The Happy Islands behind the
Winds (Krüss) **9**:83
The Happy Place
(Bemelmans) **6**:69
Happy Times in Noisy Village
(Lindgren) **1**:137
Harbor (Crews) **7**:60
Harbour (Crews) **7**:60
The Hard Life of the Teenager
(Collier) **3**:45
The Hare and the Tortoise
(Wildsmith) **2**:212
The Hare and the Tortoise & The
Tortoise and the Hare / La
Liebre y la Tortuga & La
Tortuga y la Liebre (du Bois
and Lee Po) **1**:63
Hari, the Jungle Lad
(Mukerji) **10**:131
Harlequin and the Gift of Many
Colors (Charlip and
Supree) **8**:29
Harquin: The Fox Who Went
Down to the Valley
(Burningham) **9**:41
Harriet the Spy (Fitzhugh) **1**:71
Harriet Tubman, Conductor on
the Underground Railroad
(Petry) **12**:210
Harry Cat's Pet Puppy
(Selden) **8**:200
The Hat (Ungerer) **3**:200
The Hating Book
(Zolotow) **2**:234
Haunted House
(Pieńkowski) **6**:230
The Haunting (Mahy) **7**:187
Have a Happy Measle, a Merry
Mumps, and a Cheery
Chickenpox (Bendick, Bendick,
and Bendick) **5**:38
Have You Seen My Cat?
(Carle) **10**:77
Havelok the Dane
(Serraillier) **2**:139
Hawk, I'm Your Brother
(Baylor) **3**:15
The Hawkstone
(Williams) **8**:231
Hazel Rye (Cleaver and
Cleaver) **6**:114
Head in the Clouds
(Southall) **2**:152
Hear Your Heart
(Showers) **6**:243
Heat (Cobb) **2**:65
Heat and Temperature
(Bendick) **5**:47

Heather, Oak, and Olive: Three
Stories (Sutcliff) **1**:185
The Heavenly Host
(Asimov) **12**:51
Heavy Equipment (Adkins) **7**:26
Heb jij een hobbie?
(Bruna) **7**:52
Hector Protector and As I Went
over the Water
(Sendak) **1**:167
Heiligenwald (Benary-
Isbert) **12**:73
Heimkehr aus dem Kriege
(Krüss) **9**:87
Heinrich Schliemann, Discoverer
of Buried Treasure
(Selden) **8**:198
Helga's Dowry: A Troll Love
Story (de Paola) **4**:59
Hell's Edge (Townsend) **2**:172
Helping Horse (Phipson) **5**:183
The Henchmans at Home
(Burton) **1**:31
Hengest's Tale (Walsh) **2**:200
Henry and Beezus (Cleary) **8**:46
Henry and Ribsy (Cleary) **2**:46;
8:47
Henry and the Clubhouse
(Cleary) **8**:50
Henry and the Paper Route
(Cleary) **2**:47; **8**:48
Henry Huggins (Cleary) **2**:47;
8:44
Henry-Fisherman: A Story of the
Virgin Islands (Brown) **12**:94
Henry's Red Sea
(Smucker) **10**:188
Heracles the Strong
(Serraillier) **2**:139
Herbert Hated Being Small
(Kuskin) **4**:143
Here Comes Thursday!
(Bond) **1**:27
Here I Stay (Coatsworth) **2**:58
Heritage of the Star
(Engdahl) **2**:70
Herman the Loser (Hoban) **3**:77
The Hermit and Harry and Me
(Hogrogian) **2**:88
The Hero and the Crown
(McKinley) **10**:125
The Hero from Otherwhere
(Williams) **8**:232
Heroes and History
(Sutcliff) **1**:186
Hetty (Willard) **2**:218
Hetty and Harriet
(Oakley) **7**:221
Hey, Lover Boy
(Rockwell) **6**:240
"Hey, What's Wrong with This
One?"
(Wojciechowska) **1**:196
Hi, Cat! (Keats) **1**:114
Hi! Ho! The Rattlin' Bog and
Other Folk Songs for Group
Singing (Langstaff) **3**:109
Hi, Mrs. Mallory!
(Thomas) **8**:214
Hiccup (Mayer) **11**:172
Hickory Stick Rag
(Watson) **3**:212

The Hidden House
(Brown) **10**:63
The Hidden World: Life under a
Rock (Pringle) **4**:181
Hidden Worlds: Pictures of the
Invisible (Simon) **9**:220
Hide and Seek
(Coatsworth) **2**:59
Hiding Out (Rockwell) **6**:238
Higglety Pigglety Pop! or, There
Must Be More to Life
(Sendak) **1**:168
High and Haunted Island
(Chauncy) **6**:92
The High Deeds of Finn MacCool
(Sutcliff) **1**:186
High Elk's Treasure
(Sneve) **2**:144
The High King
(Alexander) **1**:14; **5**:21
The High World
(Bemelmans) **6**:72
The Highest Hit (Willard) **5**:248
Hildegarde and Maximilian
(Krahn) **3**:104
Hills End (Southall) **2**:152
Hindu Fables, for Little Children
(Mukerji) **10**:133
His Own Where (Jordan) **10**:116
Hisako's Mysteries
(Uchida) **6**:255
Hobo Toad and the Motorcycle
Gang (Yolen) **4**:259
The Hoboken Chicken Emergency
(Pinkwater) **4**:167
Hoists, Cranes, and Derricks
(Zim) **2**:227
Hold Fast (Major) **11**:127
Hold Zero! (George) **1**:90
Holding Up the Sky: Young
People in China (Rau) **8**:194
Holes and Peeks (Jonas) **12**:174
The Hollow Land
(Gardam) **12**:169
The Hollywood Kid
(Wojciechowska) **1**:197
Home for a Bunny
(Brown) **10**:66
Home Free (Lasky) **11**:121
Home from Far (Little) **4**:147
The Home Run Trick
(Corbett) **1**:45
Homer Price
(McCloskey) **7**:203
The Homework Machine
(Williams and
Abrashkin) **8**:223
The Honeybee and the Robber: A
Moving / Picture Book
(Carle) **10**:84
Hongry Catch the Foolish Boy
(Graham) **10**:110
Honker: The Story of a Wild
Goose (McClung) **11**:183
Hooray for Me! (Charlip and
Moore) **8**:31
Hop on Pop (Seuss) **1**:86; **9**:187
The Horn of Roland
(Williams) **8**:229
Horned Helmet (Treece) **2**:185
Horse (Gardam) **12**:170
A Horse and a Hound, a Goat
and a Gander (Provensen and
Provensen) **11**:213

The Horse and His Boy (Lewis) **3**:134

A Horse Came Running (DeJong) **1**:57

The Horse in the Camel Suit (du Bois) **1**:64

Horse with Eight Hands (Phipson) **5**:183

Horses (Brown) **10**:53

A Horse's Body (Cole) **5**:66

Horseshoe Crab (McClung) **11**:184

Horton Hatches the Egg (Seuss) **9**:174

Horton Hears a Who! (Seuss) **1**:86; **9**:179

The Hospital Book (Howe) **9**:57

The Hotshot (Slote) **4**:202

The Hound of Ulster (Sutcliff) **1**:186

The House in Norham Gardens (Lively) **7**:158

The House of a Hundred Windows (Brown) **10**:53

The House of Dies Drear (Hamilton) **1**:103

The House of Secrets (Bawden) **2**:12

The House of Sixty Fathers (DeJong) **1**:58

The House of Wings (Byars) **1**:36

The House with Roots (Willard) **2**:218

How a House Happens (Adkins) **7**:19

How Animals Behave (Bendick) **5**:48

How Animals Live Together (Selsam) **1**:162

How Animals Tell Time (Selsam) **1**:163

How Beastly! (Yolen) **4**:266

How Did We Find Out about Atoms? (Asimov) **12**:53

How Did We Find Out about Black Holes? (Asimov) **12**:56

How Did We Find Out about Coal? (Asimov) **12**:58

How Did We Find Out about Comets? (Asimov) **12**:52

How Did We Find Out about Computers? (Asimov) **12**:63

How Did We Find Out about Dinosaurs? (Asimov) **12**:50

How Did We Find Out about DNA? (Asimov) **12**:64

How Did We Find Out about Earthquakes? (Asimov) **12**:56

How Did We Find Out about Electricity? (Asimov) **12**:49

How Did We Find Out about Energy? (Asimov) **12**:52

How Did We Find Out about Genes? (Asimov) **12**:62

How Did We Find Out about Life in the Deep Sea? (Asimov) **12**:60

How Did We Find Out about Nuclear Power? (Asimov) **12**:53

How Did We Find Out about Numbers? (Asimov) **12**:50

How Did We Find Out about Oil? (Asimov) **12**:58

How Did We Find Out about Our Human Roots? (Asimov) **12**:58

How Did We Find Out about Outer Space? (Asimov) **12**:55

How Did We Find Out about Solar Power? (Asimov) **12**:59

How Did We Find Out about the Atmosphere? (Asimov) **12**:64

How Did We Find Out about the Beginning of Life? (Asimov) **12**:60

How Did We Find Out about the Universe? (Asimov) **12**:61

How Did We Find Out about Vitamins? (Asimov) **12**:51

How Did We Find Out the Earth Is Round? (Asimov) **12**:48

How Do I Eat It? (Watanabe) **8**:216

How Do I Put It On? Getting Dressed (Watanabe) **8**:216

How Droofus the Dragon Lost His Head (Peet) **12**:201

How God Fix Jonah (Graham) **10**:104

How Heredity Works: Why Living Things Are as They Are (Bendick) **5**:47

How, Hippo! (Brown) **12**:104

How It Feels When a Parent Dies (Krementz) **5**:155

How Many Miles to Babylon? (Fox) **1**:77

How Many Teeth? (Showers) **6**:242

How Much and How Many: The Story of Weights and Measures (Bendick) **5**:35

How Puppies Grow (Selsam) **1**:163

How Santa Claus Had a Long and Difficult Journey Delivering His Presents (Krahn) **3**:104

How the Doctor Knows You're Fine (Cobb) **2**:65

How the Grinch Stole Christmas (Seuss) **1**:86; **9**:184

How the Whale Became (Hughes) **3**:92

How to Be a Hero (Weiss) **4**:225

How to Be a Space Scientist in Your Own Home (Simon) **9**:218

How to Be an Inventor (Weiss) **4**:230

How to Eat Fried Worms (Rockwell) **6**:236

How to Eat Fried Worms and Other Plays (Rockwell) **6**:239

How to Make a Cloud (Bendick) **5**:44

How to Make Your Own Books (Weiss) **4**:227

How to Make Your Own Movies: An Introduction to Filmmaking (Weiss) **4**:227

How to Run a Railroad: Everything You Need to Know about Model Trains (Weiss) **4**:228

How Tom Beat Captain Najork and His Hired Sportsmen (Hoban) **3**:78

How We Found Out about Vitamins (Asimov) **12**:51

How We Got Our First Cat (Tobias) **4**:218

How You Talk (Showers) **6**:242

How Your Mother and Father Met, and What Happened After (Tobias) **4**:217

Howliday Inn (Howe) **9**:58

Hubert's Hair-Raising Adventure (Peet) **12**:193

Hug Me (Stren) **5**:230

Huge Harold (Peet) **12**:194

Hugo (Gripe) **5**:142

Hugo and Josephine (Gripe) **5**:143

Hugo och Josefin (Gripe) **5**:143

The Hullabaloo ABC (Cleary) **2**:47

The Human Body: Its Structure and Operation (Asimov) **12**:37

Human Nature-Animal Nature: The Biology of Human Behavior (Cohen) **3**:40

Humbert, Mister Firkin, and the Lord Mayor of London (Burningham) **9**:40

Hunches in Bunches (Seuss) **9**:194

The Hundred Penny Box (Mathis) **3**:149

The Hundredth Dove and Other Tales (Yolen) **4**:264

Hunted in Their Own Land (Chauncy) **6**:92

Hunted Mammals of the Sea (McClung) **11**:191

Hunter in the Dark (Hughes) **9**:74

The Hunting of the Snark: An Agony in Eight Fits (Carroll) **2**:34

Hurrah, We're Outward Bound! (Spier) **5**:219

Hurry Home, Candy (DeJong) **1**:58

I, Adam (Fritz) **2**:81

I Am a Clown (Bruna) **7**:52

I Am a Hunter (Mayer) **11**:165

I Am Papa Snap and These Are My Favorite No Such Stories (Ungerer) **3**:201

I Am the Cheese (Cormier) **12**:139

I Am the Running Girl (Adoff) **7**:35

I Can Build a House! (Watanabe) **8**:217

I Can Count More (Bruna) **7**:51

I Can Do It! (Watanabe) **8**:217

I Can Read (Bruna) **7**:50

I Can Ride It! Setting Goals (Watanabe) **8**:217

I Can Take a Walk! (Watanabe) **8**:217

I Go by Sea, I Go by Land (Travers) **2**:178

I Had Trouble in Getting to Solla Sollew (Seuss) **9**:189

I Have Four Names for My Grandfather (Lasky) **11**:114

I Klockornas Tid (Gripe) **5**:145

I Love My Mother (Zindel) **3**:248

I, Momolu (Graham) **10**:106

I Never Loved Your Mind (Zindel) **3**:248

I Own the Racecourse! (Wrightson) **4**:242

I See a Song (Carle) **10**:76

I See What I See! (Selden) **8**:197

I Want to Stay Here! I Want to Go There! A Flea Story (Lionni) **7**:137

I Wish That I Had Duck Feet (Seuss) **1**:87; **9**:189

I Would Rather Be a Turnip (Cleaver and Cleaver) **6**:106

The Ice Is Coming (Wrightson) **4**:245

If All the Swords in England (Willard) **2**:219

If I Had . . . (Mayer) **11**:164

If I Had My Way (Klein) **2**:98

If I Ran the Circus (Seuss) **1**:87; **9**:181

If I Ran the Zoo (Seuss) **1**:87; **9**:178

If It Weren't for You (Zolotow) **2**:234

If This Is Love, I'll Take Spaghetti (Conford) **10**:98

Iggie's House (Blume) **2**:17

Ik ben een clown (Bruna) **7**:52

Ik kan lezen (Bruna) **7**:50

I'll Get There. It Better Be Worth the Trip. (Donovan) **3**:52

The Illustrated Marguerite Henry (Henry) **4**:116

Ilse Janda, 14 (Nöstlinger) **12**:186

I'm Hiding (Livingston) **7**:168

I'm Only Afraid of the Dark (At Night!) (Stren) **5**:235

I'm Really Dragged but Nothing Gets Me Down (Hentoff) **1**:107

I'm the King of the Castle! Playing Alone (Watanabe) **8**:217

I'm Trying to Tell You (Ashley) **4**:18

I'm Waiting (Livingston) **7**:169

The Important Book (Brown) **10**:57

The Impossible People: A History Natural and Unnatural of Beings Terrible and Wonderful (McHargue) **2**:118

Impossible, Possum (Conford) **10**:90

In a Beaver Valley: How Beavers Change the Land (Pringle) **4**:175

In a People House (Seuss) **9**:192

In My Garden (Zolotow) **2**:235

In Search of Ghosts (Cohen) **3**:40

In Spite of All Terror (Burton) **1**:32

In the Company of Clowns: A Commedia (Bacon)   3:11
In the Country of Ourselves (Hentoff)   1:108
In the Flaky Frosty Morning (Kuskin)   4:140
In the Middle of the Trees (Kuskin)   4:135
In the Middle of the World (Korinetz)   4:130
In the Night Kitchen (Sendak)   1:168
In the Rabbitgarden (Lionni)   7:136
In the Time of the Bells (Gripe)   5:145
In-Between Miya (Uchida)   6:255
Inch by Inch (Lionni)   7:128
The Incredible Journey (Burnford)   2:19
The Incredible Television Machine (LeShan and Polk)   6:189
Indian Encounters: An Anthology of Stories and Poems (Coatsworth)   2:59
Indian Festivals (Showers)   6:245
Indian Mound Farm (Coatsworth)   2:59
Indian Summer (Monjo)   2:121
Indians (Tunis)   2:193
Inside Jazz (Collier)   3:45
Inside: Seeing Beneath the Surface (Adkins)   7:21
Inside the Atom (Asimov)   12:31
Intelligence: What Is It? (Cohen)   3:41
Into the Woods: Exploring the Forest Ecosystem (Pringle)   4:178
The Intruder (Townsend)   2:172
The Invaders: Three Stories (Treece)   2:185
The Inway Investigators; or, The Mystery at McCracken's Place (Yolen)   4:258
Irma and Jerry (Selden)   8:201
The Iron Giant: A Story in Five Nights (Hughes)   3:92
The Iron Lily (Willard)   2:220
Is This a Baby Dinosaur? (Selsam)   1:163
Isabel's Noel (Yolen)   4:257
Isamu Noguchi: The Life of a Sculptor (Tobias)   4:214
The Isis Pedlar (Hughes)   9:75
Island of the Blue Dolphins (O'Dell)   1:146
The Island of the Grass King: The Further Adventures of Anatole (Willard)   5:248
The Island of the Skog (Kellogg)   6:172
L'Isle noire (Hergé)   6:148
It Ain't All for Nothin' (Myers)   4:158
It Happened One Summer (Phipson)   5:178
It Looks Like Snow: A Picture Book (Charlip)   8:26
It's a Gingerbread House: Bake It! Build It! Eat It! (Williams)   9:230

It's Not the End of the World (Blume)   2:17
It's Not What You Expect (Klein)   2:98
Jacob Have I Loved (Paterson)   7:238
Jafta (Lewin)   9:90
Jafta—My Father (Lewin)   9:90
Jafta—My Mother (Lewin)   9:90
Jafta—The Journey (Lewin)   9:92
Jafta—The Town (Lewin)   9:92
Jafta—The Wedding (Lewin)   9:90
Jahdu (Hamilton)   11:82
Jake (Slote)   4:199
Jambo Means Hello: Swahili Alphabet Book (Feelings)   5:107
James and the Giant Peach (Dahl)   1:51; 7:68
James and the Rain (Kuskin)   4:134
Jane, Wishing (Tobias)   4:216
Janey (Zolotow)   2:235
Jangle Twang (Burningham)   9:51
A Jar of Dreams (Uchida)   6:259
Jazz Country (Hentoff)   1:108
Jean and Johnny (Cleary)   2:48; 8:49
Jeffrey Bear Cleans Up His Act (Steptoe)   12:241
Jem's Island (Lasky)   11:117
Jennie's Hat (Keats)   1:115
Jennifer and Josephine (Peet)   12:199
Jennifer, Hecate, Macbeth, William McKinley, and Me, Elizabeth (Konigsburg)   1:121
Jesse and Abe (Isadora)   7:108
Jethro and the Jumbie (Cooper)   4:49
The Jezebel Wolf (Monjo)   2:122
Jim Along, Josie: A Collection of Folk Songs and Singing Games for Young Children (Langstaff and Langstaff)   3:110
Jim and the Beanstalk (Briggs)   10:23
Jimmy Has Lost His Cap: Where Can It Be? (Munari)   9:125
Jimmy of Cherry Valley (Rau)   8:186
Jimmy Yellow Hawk (Sneve)   2:145
Jingo Django (Fleischman)   1:74
Joan of Arc (Williams)   8:225
Jock's Island (Coatsworth)   2:59
Joe and the Snow (de Paola)   4:54
John Brown: A Cry for Freedom (Graham)   10:111
John Burningham's ABC (Burningham)   9:39
John Henry: An American Legend (Keats)   1:115
Johnny the Clockmaker (Ardizzone)   3:4
Jokes from Black Folks (Haskins)   3:65
Jonah, the Fisherman (Zimnik)   3:243

Josefin (Gripe)   5:142
Josefina February (Ness)   6:200
Josephine (Gripe)   5:142
Josh (Southall)   2:153
Journey behind the Wind (Wrightson)   4:247
Journey between Worlds (Engdahl)   2:70
Journey from Peppermint Street (DeJong)   1:58
Journey Home (Uchida)   6:258
Journey to Jericho (O'Dell)   1:147
Journey to Topaz: A Story of the Japanese-American Evacuation (Uchida)   6:256
Journey to Untor (Wibberley)   3:228
The Journey with Jonah (L'Engle)   1:130
Journeys of Sebastian (Krahn)   3:105
Juan and the Asuangs (Aruego)   5:28
Julia's House (Gripe)   5:147
Julias Hus och Nattpappan (Gripe)   5:147
Julie of the Wolves (George)   1:90
Jumanji (Van Allsburg)   5:239
June Anne June Spoon and Her Very Adventurous Search for the Moon (Kuskin)   4:139
June 7! (Aliki)   9:23
Jungle Beasts and Men (Mukerji)   10:130
The Juniper Tree and Other Tales from Grimm (Sendak)   1:169
Junius Over Far (Hamilton)   11:92
Jupiter, the Largest Planet (Asimov)   12:49
Just between Us (Pfeffer)   11:200
Just Cats: Learning Groups (Burningham)   9:50
Just Like Everyone Else (Kuskin)   4:135
Just Me and My Dad (Mayer)   11:172
Just Morgan (Pfeffer)   11:196
Just the Thing for Geraldine (Conford)   10:92
Justice and Her Brothers (Hamilton)   11:79
Justin Morgan Had a Horse (Henry)   4:109
To kaplani tis Vitrinas (Zei)   6:260
Karen's Curiosity (Provensen and Provensen)   11:209
Karen's Opposites (Provensen and Provensen)   11:209
Kate (Little)   4:150
The Kate Greenaway Treasury: An Anthology of the Illustrations and Writings of Kate Greenaway (Greenaway)   6:135
Kate Greenaway's Book of Games (Greenaway)   6:135
Kate Greenaway's Language of Flowers (Greenaway)   6:133

Kate Rider (Burton)   1:32
Katy and the Big Snow (Burton)   11:49
Keep Calm (Phipson)   5:185
Keep Your Mouth Closed, Dear (Aliki)   9:19
The Keeper of the Isis Light (Hughes)   9:72
Kenny's Window (Sendak)   1:170
Kermit the Hermit (Peet)   12:196
Kerstmis (Bruna)   7:49
The Kestrel (Alexander)   5:25
The Key Word and Other Mysteries (Asimov)   12:55
Kid Power (Pfeffer)   11:199
Kid Power Strikes Back (Pfeffer)   11:205
The Kids' Cat Book (de Paola)   4:63
Killer Whales (Simon)   9:212
Kilmeny of the Orchard (Montgomery)   8:135
Kimako's Story (Jordan)   10:120
A Kind of Wild Justice (Ashley)   4:16
The King and His Friends (Aruego)   5:27
King George's Head Was Made of Lead (Monjo)   2:122
King Grisly-Beard (Sendak)   1:171
King of the Wind (Henry)   4:111
The Kingdom and the Cave (Aiken)   1:4
A Kingdom in a Horse (Wojciechowska)   1:197
The Kingdom of the Sun (Asimov)   12:34
The King's Beard (Wibberley)   3:228
The King's Falcon (Fox)   1:78
The King's Fifth (O'Dell)   1:148
The King's Fountain (Alexander)   1:15; 5:22
The King's Stilts (Seuss)   9:174
Kintu: A Congo Adventure (Enright)   4:71
The Kissimmee Kid (Cleaver and Cleaver)   6:113
Kit (Gardam)   12:171
The Kite That Won the Revolution (Asimov)   12:37
Kiviok's Magic Journey: An Eskimo Legend (Houston)   3:86
Klippity Klop (Emberley)   5:98
The Knee-High Man and Other Tales (Lester)   2:112
Kneeknock Rise (Babbitt)   2:6
The Knight and the Dragon (de Paola)   4:64
The Knight of the Lion (McDermott)   9:117
Knight's Fee (Sutcliff)   1:187
Knights in Armor (Glubok)   1:100
Knights of the Crusades (Williams)   8:225
Konrad: Oder, das Kind aus der Konservenbüchs (Nöstlinger)   12:187
Konta stis ragies (Zei)   6:262

The Kweeks of Kookatumdee (Peet) **12**:207
Ladies of the Gothics: Tales of Romance and Terror by the Gentle Sex (Manley and Lewis) **3**:145
Ladis and the Ant (Sánchez-Silva) **12**:232
Lady Ellen Grae (Cleaver and Cleaver) **6**:102
The Lady of Guadalupe (de Paola) **4**:63
Ladybug (McClung) **11**:184
Lafcadio, the Lion Who Shot Back (Silverstein) **5**:208
The Land Beyond (Gripe) **5**:145
The Land of Black Gold (Hergé) **6**:148
The Land of Canaan (Asimov) **12**:46
The Land of Forgotten Beasts (Wersba) **3**:217
Landet Utanfor (Gripe) **5**:145
The Lantern Bearers (Sutcliff) **1**:187
The Lark and the Laurel (Willard) **2**:220
The Last Battle (Lewis) **3**:135
The Last Battle (Wibberley) **3**:228
The Last Guru (Pinkwater) **4**:168
The Last Little Cat (DeJong) **1**:59
The Last Viking (Treece) **2**:186
Laura's Luck (Sachs) **2**:132
The Lazy Bear (Wildsmith) **2**:213
Lazy Tinka (Seredy) **10**:182
Lazy Tommy Pumpkinhead (du Bois) **1**:64
Leaper: The Story of an Atlantic Salmon (McClung) **11**:181
Learning to Say Good-By: When a Parent Dies (LeShan) **6**:188
The Legend of New Amsterdam (Spier) **5**:226
The Legend of Old Befana: An Italian Christmas Story (de Paola) **4**:65
Legends of the Saints (Petry) **12**:212
Leif the Unlucky (Haugaard) **11**:109
The Lemonade Trick (Corbett) **1**:46
Lenny Kandell, Smart Aleck (Conford) **10**:99
Lens and Shutter: An Introduction to Photography (Weiss) **4**:226
Lentil (McCloskey) **7**:200
Leonardo da Vinci (Williams) **8**:226
Leonardo da Vinci: The Artist, Inventor, Scientist in Three-Dimensional, Movable Pictures (Provensen and Provensen) **11**:218
Leopard's Prey (Wibberley) **3**:229
The Leopard's Tooth (Kotzwinkle) **6**:182

Let Me Fall Before I Fly (Wersba) **3**:218
Let the Balloon Go (Southall) **2**:153
Let the Circle Be Unbroken (Taylor) **9**:228
Let's Make Rabbits: A Fable (Lionni) **7**:139
Let's Paint a Rainbow (Carle) **10**:85
Let's Try It Out: Hot and Cold (Simon) **9**:206
A Letter to Amy (Keats) **1**:115
Letterbox: The Art and History of Letters (Adkins) **7**:27
Letters to Horseface: Being the Story of Wolfgang Amadeus Mozart's Journey to Italy, 1769-1770, When He Was a Boy of Fourteen (Monjo) **2**:123
Letters to Pauline (Krüss) **9**:87
Der Leuchtturm auf den Hummer-Klippen (Krüss) **9**:82
La Liebre y la Tortuga & La Tortuga y la Liebre / The Hare and the Tortoise & The Tortoise and the Hare (du Bois and Lee Po) **1**:63
Life and Death (Zim and Bleeker) **2**:228
Life and Death in Nature (Simon) **9**:211
The Life and Death of a Brave Bull (Wojciechowska) **1**:198
The Life and Death of Martin Luther King, Jr. (Haskins) **3**:65
Life in Colonial America (Speare) **8**:210
Life in the Dark: How Animals Survive at Night (Simon) **9**:208
Life in the Middle Ages (Williams) **8**:227
The Life of Winston Churchill (Wibberley) **3**:229
Life on Ice: How Animals Survive in the Arctic (Simon) **9**:210
Life Story (Burton) **11**:51
Lift Every Voice (Sterling and Quarles) **1**:179
Light (Crews) **7**:58
A Light in the Attic (Silverstein) **5**:212
Lighthouse Island (Coatsworth) **2**:60
The Lighthouse Keeper's Son (Chauncy) **6**:94
The Lighthouse on the Lobster Cliffs (Krüss) **9**:82
Lightning (Bendick) **5**:39
Lightning and Thunder (Zim) **2**:228
A Likely Place (Fox) **1**:78
Limericks by Lear (Lear) **1**:127
Lines Scribbled on an Envelope and Other Poems (L'Engle) **1**:131
A Lion in the Meadow (Mahy) **7**:178
The Lion, the Witch, and the Wardrobe (Lewis) **3**:135

Lisa and Lottie (Kästner) **4**:124
Listen for the Fig Tree (Mathis) **3**:149
Listen for the Singing (Little) **4**:152
Listen to a Shape (Brown) **12**:107
Listen to the Crows (Pringle) **4**:180
Listening (Seredy) **10**:172
The Listening Walk (Showers) **6**:242
Little Babar Books (Brunhoff) **4**:37, 38
Little Blue and Little Yellow: A Story for Pippo and Ann and Other Children (Lionni) **7**:127
Little Books (Burningham) **9**:46, 47
The Little Brass Band (Brown) **10**:65
The Little Brute Family (Hoban) **3**:78
The Little Carousel (Brown) **12**:93
Little Chicken (Brown) **10**:52
The Little Cow and the Turtle (DeJong) **1**:59
The Little Cowboy (Brown) **10**:56
A Little Destiny (Cleaver and Cleaver) **6**:112
The Little Drummer Boy (Keats) **1**:116
The Little Farmer (Brown) **10**:56
The Little Fir Tree (Brown) **10**:64
The Little Fisherman, a Fish Story (Brown) **10**:53
The Little Fishes (Haugaard) **11**:105
Little Frightened Tiger (Brown) **10**:63
Little Fur Family (Brown) **10**:53
Little Giants (Simon) **9**:219
The Little House (Burton) **11**:47
Little House in the Big Woods (Wilder) **2**:205
Little House on the Prairie (Wilder) **2**:206
The Little Island (Brown) **10**:54
Little Lost Lamb (Brown) **10**:53
A Little Love (Hamilton) **11**:91
The Little Man (Kästner) **4**:127
The Little Man and the Big Thief (Kästner) **4**:127
The Little Man and the Little Miss (Kästner) **4**:127
Little Monster at Home (Mayer) **11**:173
Little Monster at School (Mayer) **11**:173
Little Monster at Work (Mayer) **11**:173
Little Monster's Alphabet Book (Mayer) **11**:173
Little Monster's Bedtime Book (Mayer) **11**:173
Little Monster's Counting Book (Mayer) **11**:173
Little Monster's Mother Goose (Mayer) **11**:173

Little Monster's Neighborhood (Mayer) **11**:173
Little Monster's Word Book (Mayer) **11**:172
A Little Oven (Estes) **2**:74
The Little Prince (Saint-Exupéry) **10**:137
The Little Roaring Tiger (Zimnik) **3**:243
A Little Schubert (Goffstein) **3**:59
The Little Spotted Fish (Yolen) **4**:261
Little Tim and the Brave Sea Captain (Ardizzone) **3**:5
Little Town on the Prairie (Wilder) **2**:206
The Little Witch (Mahy) **7**:180
Little Women (Alcott) **1**:10
The Little Wood Duck (Wildsmith) **2**:213
Liverwurst Is Missing (Mayer) **11**:175
Lives at Stake: The Science and Politics of Environmental Health (Pringle) **4**:185
Living Things (Bendick) **5**:42
Liza Lou and the Yeller Belly Swamp (Mayer) **11**:170
Lizard Music (Pinkwater) **4**:164
Lizzie Lights (Chauncy) **6**:93
Lock, Stock, and Barrel (Sobol) **4**:207
Locks and Keys (Gibbons) **8**:91
Lollipop: Kinderroman (Nöstlinger) **12**:188
The Lollipop Princess: A Play for Paper Dolls in One Act (Estes) **2**:74
A Lollygag of Limericks (Livingston) **7**:173
London Bridge Is Falling Down (Emberley) **5**:96
London Bridge Is Falling Down! (Spier) **5**:217
Lonesome Boy (Bontemps) **6**:83
Long Ago When I Was Young (Nesbit) **3**:164
The Long and Short of Measurement (Cobb) **2**:66
Long, Broad, and Quickeye (Ness) **6**:205
The Long Journey from Space (Simon) **9**:219
Long Journey Home: Stories from Black History (Lester) **2**:113
The Long Lost Coelacanth and Other Living Fossils (Aliki) **9**:23
The Long Secret (Fitzhugh) **1**:72
The Long View into Space (Simon) **9**:214
A Long Way from Verona (Gardam) **12**:162
The Long Way Home (Benary-Isbert) **12**:76
The Long Winter (Wilder) **2**:206
Look at Your Eyes (Showers) **6**:242
Look Through My Window (Little) **4**:149
Look to the Night Sky: An Introduction to Star Watching (Simon) **9**:212

Look What I Can Do
  (Aruego) **5**:29
The Lorax (Seuss) **1**:87; **9**:192
Lordy, Aunt Hattie
  (Thomas) **8**:212
Lorry Driver (Munari) **9**:125
*The Lost Dispatch: A Story of
  Antietam* (Sobol) **4**:206
*Lost Wild America: The Story of
  Our Extinct and Vanishing
  Wildlife* (McClung) **11**:185
*Lost Wild Worlds: The Story of
  Extinct and Vanishing Wildlife
  of the Eastern Hemisphere*
  (McClung) **11**:190
Lotta on Troublemaker Street
  (Lindgren) **1**:137
Lottie and Lisa (Kästner) **4**:124
The Lotus Caves
  (Christopher) **2**:40
Love and Tennis (Slote) **4**:202
Love Is a Special Way of Feeling
  (Anglund) **1**:20
The Luck of Pokey Bloom
  (Conford) **10**:93
The Luckiest Girl (Cleary) **2**:48
The Luckiest One of All
  (Peet) **12**:206
Lucky Chuck (Cleary) **8**:61
*Lucky Starr and the Big Sun of
  Mercury* (Asimov) **12**:31
*Lucky Starr and the Moons of
  Jupiter* (Asimov) **12**:32
*Lucky Starr and the Oceans of
  Venus* (Asimov) **12**:31
*Lucky Starr and the Pirates of the
  Asteroids* (Asimov) **12**:30
*Lucky Starr and the Rings of
  Saturn* (Asimov) **12**:32
The Lucky Stone (Clifton) **5**:59
Lucretia Mott, Gentle Warrior
  (Sterling) **1**:179
Lucy Brown and Mr. Grimes
  (Ardizzone) **3**:5
Luke and Angela
  (Nöstlinger) **12**:188
Luki-Live (Nöstlinger) **12**:188
Lumberjack (Kurelek) **2**:101
Luna: The Story of a Moth
  (McClung) **11**:181
Luther Tarbox (Adkins) **7**:22
M. C. Higgins, the Great
  (Hamilton) **1**:104; **11**:71
MA nDA LA (Adoff) **7**:31
Machine Tools (Zim and
  Skelly) **2**:229
The MacLeod Place
  (Armstrong) **1**:22
Madeline (Bemelmans) **6**:66
Madeline and the Bad Hat
  (Bemelmans) **6**:73
Madeline and the Gypsies
  (Bemelmans) **6**:74
Madeline in London
  (Bemelmans) **6**:76
Madeline's Rescue
  (Bemelmans) **6**:69
*The Magic Bed-knob; or, How to
  Become a Witch in Ten Easy
  Lessons* (Norton) **6**:219
Magic Camera
  (Pinkwater) **4**:162
The Magic City (Nesbit) **3**:164

The Magic Finger (Dahl) **1**:52;
  7:72
Magic for Marigold
  (Montgomery) **8**:139
The Magic Gate
  (Williams) **8**:222
The Magic Grandfather
  (Williams) **8**:237
*The Magic Listening Cap: More
  Folk Tales from Japan*
  (Uchida) **6**:251
The Magic Moscow
  (Pinkwater) **4**:171
*The Magic Pudding: Being the
  Adventures of Bunyip Bluegum
  and His Friends Bill Barnacle
  and Sam Sawnoff*
  (Lindsay) **8**:101
The Magic Stone (Farmer) **8**:77
*The Magic Tree: A Tale from the
  Congo* (McDermott) **9**:110
*The Magical Adventures of Pretty
  Pearl* (Hamilton) **11**:86
The Magician (Shulevitz) **5**:205
The Magician's Nephew
  (Lewis) **3**:135
*The Magnificent Morris Mouse
  Clubhouse* (Gibbons) **8**:92
Mai contenti (Munari) **9**:125
*Maikäfer Flieg!: Mein Vater, das
  Kriegsende, Cohn und Ich*
  (Nöstlinger) **12**:185
Major: The Story of a Black Bear
  (McClung) **11**:180
*Make a Circle, Keep Us In:
  Poems for a Good Day*
  (Adoff) **7**:32
Make Way for Ducklings
  (McCloskey) **7**:200
Making Music for Money
  (Collier) **3**:46
*The Making of an Afro-American:
  Martin Robison Delaney, 1812-
  1885* (Sterling) **1**:180
*The Making of Man: The Story of
  Our Ancient Ancestors*
  (Collier) **3**:46
Making Sense of Money
  (Cobb) **3**:66
Making the Movies
  (Bendick) **5**:34
*Makoto, the Smallest Boy: A
  Story of Japan* (Uchida) **6**:256
Malcolm X (Adoff) **7**:31
The Malibu and Other Poems
  (Livingston) **7**:170
Mammals and How They Live
  (McClung) **11**:182
Man Changes the Weather
  (Bova) **3**:34
*The Man in the Manhole and the
  Fix-It Men* (Brown and
  Hurd) **10**:54
*The Man Who Played Accordion
  Music* (Tobias) **4**:218
The Man Who Talked to a Tree
  (Baylor) **3**:15
*The Man Who Took the Indoors
  Out* (Lobel) **5**:168
*The Man Whose Mother Was a
  Pirate* (Mahy) **7**:180
Man with a Sword
  (Treece) **2**:186

The Man with the Purple Eyes
  (Zolotow) **2**:235
Ein Mann für Mama
  (Nöstlinger) **12**:185
*The Many Lives of Benjamin
  Franklin* (Aliki) **9**:25
The Many Mice of Mr. Brice
  (Seuss) **9**:193
The Maplin Bird (Peyton) **3**:177
Marcella's Guardian Angel
  (Ness) **6**:208
*Margaret Wise Brown's
  Wonderful Story Book*
  (Brown) **10**:56
Maria Tallchief (Tobias) **4**:213
Marian Anderson (Tobias) **4**:213
Marcia (Steptoe) **12**:238
The Mark of the Horse Lord
  (Sutcliff) **1**:188
Marly the Kid (Pfeffer) **11**:198
Marra's World
  (Coatsworth) **2**:60
Marrying Off Mother
  (Nöstlinger) **12**:185
Mars, the Red Planet
  (Asimov) **12**:55
Martha, the Movie Mouse
  (Lobel) **5**:164
*The Marvelous Misadventures of
  Sebastian* (Alexander) **1**:16;
  5:21
*Marvin K. Mooney Will You
  Please Go Now* (Geisel) **1**:88
Mary Jane (Sterling) **1**:180
Mary McLeod Bethune
  (Greenfield) **4**:99
Mary Poppins (Travers) **2**:178
Mary Poppins from A to Z
  (Travers) **2**:179
Mary Poppins in the Park
  (Travers) **2**:179
The Marzipan Moon
  (Willard) **5**:249
Masquerade (Williams) **4**:231
The Master Monkey
  (Mukerji) **10**:135
The Master Puppeteer
  (Paterson) **7**:231
Mathinna's People
  (Chauncy) **6**:92
De matroos (Bruna) **7**:50
Matt and Jo (Southall) **2**:155
Matt Gargan's Boy
  (Slote) **4**:201
A Matter of Principle: A Novel
  (Pfeffer) **11**:202
Maurice's Room (Fox) **1**:79
Max (Isadora) **7**:102
*Maybe You Should Fly a Jet!
  Maybe You Should Be a Vet!*
  (Seuss) **9**:194
Maybelle, the Cable Car
  (Burton) **11**:51
*Mazel and Shlimazel; or, The
  Milk of the Lioness*
  (Singer) **1**:175
McBroom Tells the Truth
  (Fleischman) **1**:75
McBroom's Ghost
  (Fleischman) **1**:75
McBroom's Zoo
  (Fleischman) **1**:75
McElligot's Pool (Seuss) **9**:175

Me and My Captain
  (Goffstein) **3**:60
Me and My Family Tree
  (Showers) **6**:247
Me and My Little Brain
  (Fleischman) **1**:70
Me and Neesie (Greenfield) **4**:99
Me and the Terrible Two
  (Conford) **10**:92
*Me and Willie and Pa: The Story
  of Abraham Lincoln and His
  Son Tad* (Monjo) **2**:124
Me Too (Cleaver and
  Cleaver) **6**:109
The Measure of the Universe
  (Asimov) **12**:61
Measuring (Bendick) **5**:45
Medicine (Zim) **2**:229
A Medieval Feast (Aliki) **9**:30
Meet My Folks! (Hughes) **3**:93
Meet the Austins
  (L'Engle) **1**:131
Meet the Giant Snakes
  (Simon) **9**:214
Ho megalos peripatos tou Petrou
  (Zei) **6**:261
*Mein Urgrossvater, die Helden
  und Ich* (Krüss) **9**:87
Mein Urgrossvater und Ich
  (Krüss) **9**:83
The Mellops' Go Spelunking
  (Ungerer) **3**:202
*Men from the Village Deep in the
  Mountains and Other Japanese
  Folk Tales* (Bang) **8**:18
Men of the Hills (Treece) **2**:187
Merle the High Flying Squirrel
  (Peet) **12**:202
The Mermaid and the Whale
  (McHargue) **2**:119
The Merrymaker (Suhl) **2**:165
A Messenger for Parliament
  (Haugaard) **11**:107
*Mice, Moose, and Men: How
  Their Populations Rise and
  Fall* (McClung) **11**:188
Michael Bird-Boy (de
  Paola) **4**:57
Microbes at Work
  (Selsam) **1**:163
The Middle Moffat (Estes) **2**:74
Midnight Adventure
  (Briggs) **10**:23
The Midnight Fox (Byars) **1**:36
Midnight Is a Place (Aiken) **1**:4
Miffy in the Hospital
  (Bruna) **7**:52
Miffy's Dream (Bruna) **7**:52
The Mighty Ones (DeJong) **1**:59
Mik and the Prowler
  (Uchida) **6**:253
*Mike Mulligan and His Steam
  Shovel* (Burton) **11**:44
Milkweed (Selsam) **1**:164
*The Milky Way Galaxy: Man's
  Exploration of the Stars*
  (Bova) **3**:34
Millions of Cats (Gág) **4**:87
The Mills of God
  (Armstrong) **1**:23
The Mimosa Tree (Cleaver and
  Cleaver) **6**:105
Mine (Mayer and Mayer) **11**:166

Mine for Keeps (Little) **4**:147
Ming Lo Moves the Mountain (Lobel) **5**:176
The Minnow Family—Chubs, Dace, Minnows, and Shiners (Pringle) **4**:180
The Minnow Leads to Treasure (Pearce) **9**:143
Minnow on the Say (Pearce) **9**:143
The Minority Peoples of China (Rau) **8**:193
The Minstrel and the Mountain (Yolen) **4**:257
Miranda the Great (Estes) **2**:74
Mirror Magic (Simon) **9**:215
Missee Lee (Ransome) **8**:180
The Missing Maple Syrup Sap Mystery; or, How Maple Syrup Is Made (Gibbons) **8**:90
The Missing Piece (Silverstein) **5**:211
The Missing Piece Meets the Big O (Silverstein) **5**:212
Mr. Bass' Planetoid (Cameron) **1**:40
Mr. Bat's Great Invention (Nöstlinger) **12**:184
Mr. Bats Meisterstück; oder, die Total Verjüngte Oma (Nöstlinger) **12**:184
Mr Bidery's Spidery Garden (McCord) **9**:101
Mr Gumpy's Motor Car (Burningham) **9**:45
Mr Gumpy's Outing (Burningham) **9**:43
Mr. Kelso's Lion (Bontemps) **6**:84
Mr. Mysterious and Company (Fleischman) **1**:75
Mr. Noah and the Second Flood (Burnford) **2**:20
Mr. Revere and I (Lawson) **2**:110
Mrs. Beggs and the Wizard (Mayer) **11**:167
Mrs. Cockle's Cat (Pearce) **9**:149
Mrs Discombobulous (Mahy) **7**:179
Mrs. Frisby and the Rats of NIMH (O'Brien) **2**:127
Mistresses of Mystery: Two Centuries of Suspense Stories by the Gentle Sex (Manley and Lewis) **3**:145
Misty of Chincoteague (Henry) **4**:110
Mitch and Amy (Cleary) **2**:48; **8**:52
The Mixed-Up Chameleon (Carle) **10**:79
The Mock Revolt (Cleaver and Cleaver) **6**:107
Model Buildings and How to Make Them (Weiss) **4**:229
Model Cars and Trucks and How to Build Them (Weiss) **4**:227
Moe Q. McGlutch, He Smoked Too Much (Raskin) **1**:156
The Moffats (Estes) **2**:75

Mog at the Zoo (Pieńkowski and Nicoll) **6**:233
Mog's Mumps (Pieńkowski and Nicoll) **6**:230
Moja Means One: Swahili Counting Book (Feelings) **5**:105
Mojo and the Russians (Myers) **4**:157
Mom, the Wolf Man, and Me (Klein) **2**:99
Momo's Kitten (Yashima and Yashima) **4**:253
Monkeys (Zim) **2**:229
The Monsters' Ball (de Paola) **4**:54
Monsters from the Movies (Aylesworth) **6**:49
Moominpappa at Sea (Jansson) **2**:94
Moominsummer Madness (Jansson) **2**:94
Moominvalley in November (Jansson) **2**:94
The Moon (Asimov) **12**:40
The Moon and a Star and Other Poems (Livingston) **7**:168
The Moon by Night (L'Engle) **1**:132
The Moon in Fact and Fancy (Slote) **4**:198
Moon Man (Ungerer) **3**:202
The Moon Ribbon and Other Tales (Yolen) **4**:262
The Moon Walker (Showers) **6**:247
The Mooncusser's Daughter (Aiken) **1**:5
Moon-Whales and Other Moon Poems (Hughes) **3**:93
Moose, Goose, and Little Nobody (Raskin) **12**:223
More Adventures of the Great Brain (Fitzgerald) **1**:70
More Tales from Grimm (Gág) **4**:94
More Words of Science (Asimov) **12**:48
Morgan's Zoo (Howe) **9**:60
Morning Is a Little Child (Anglund) **1**:21
The Mortal Instruments (Bethancourt) **3**:18
Mother Goose; or, The Old Nursery Rhymes (Greenaway) **6**:132
Mother, Mother, I Feel Sick, Send for the Doctor Quick, Quick, Quick: A Picture Book and Shadow Play (Charlip and Supree) **8**:27
Moths and Butterflies and How They Live (McClung) **11**:184
Motion and Gravity (Bendick) **5**:45
Motors and Engines and How They Work (Weiss) **4**:225
Mountain Rose (Stren) **5**:234
The Mouse and His Child (Hoban) **3**:78
The Mouse and the Motorcycle (Cleary) **2**:48; **8**:51

Mouse Days: A Book of Seasons (Lionni) **7**:139
Mouse Soup (Lobel) **5**:171
Mouse Tales (Lobel) **5**:168
Movie Monsters (Aylesworth) **6**:51
Moving Day (Tobias) **4**:215
Moving Heavy Things (Adkins) **7**:25
Much Bigger than Martin (Kellogg) **6**:174
Muley-Ears, Nobody's Dog (Henry) **4**:113
Mummies (McHargue) **2**:119
Mummies Made in Egypt (Aliki) **9**:27
The Muppet Guide to Magnificent Manners: Featuring Jim Henson's Muppets (Howe) **9**:60
Museum: The Story of America's Treasure Houses (Schwartz) **3**:189
Music, Music for Everyone (Williams) **9**:235
Musk Oxen: Bearded Ones of the Arctic (Rau) **8**:188
Mustang, Wild Spirit of the West (Henry) **4**:115
My Ballet Class (Isadora) **7**:105
My Book about Me: By Me, Myself. I Wrote It! I Drew It! With a Little Help from My Friends Dr. Seuss and Roy McKie (Seuss and McKie) **9**:191
My Brother Fine with Me (Clifton) **5**:56
My Brother Sam Is Dead (Collier and Collier) **3**:47
My Crazy Sister (Goffstein) **3**:60
My Darling, My Hamburger (Zindel) **3**:249
My Father, the Coach (Slote) **4**:200
My Friend Jacob (Clifton) **5**:60
My Friend John (Zolotow) **3**:236
My Great-Grandfather and I: Useful and Amusing Occurrences and Inspirations from the Lobster Shack on Helgoland Told to the "Leathery Lisbeth" and Embellished with Verses from My Great-Grandfather and Me, Carefully Put on Paper for Children of All Ages (Krüss) **9**:83
My Great-Grandfather, the Heroes, and I: A Brief Study of Heroes in Verse and Prose, Made Up and Told in Several Attic Rooms by My Great-Grandfather and Myself (Krüss) **9**:87
My Heart's in Greenwich Village (Manley) **3**:146
My Heart's in the Heather (Manley) **3**:146
My Island Grandma (Lasky) **11**:115

My Little Hen (Provensen and Provensen) **11**:211
My Mama Says There Aren't Any Zombies, Ghosts, Vampires, Creatures, Demons, Monsters, Fiends, Goblins, or Things (Viorst) **3**:208
My Name Is Paula Popowich! (Hughes) **9**:77
My Puppy Is Born (Cole) **5**:63
My Robot Buddy (Slote) **4**:201
My School (Spier) **5**:228
My Side of the Mountain (George) **1**:91
My Special Best Words (Steptoe) **2**:163
My Street's a Morning Cool Street (Thomas) **8**:213
My Trip to Alpha I (Slote) **4**:202
My Very First Book of Colors (Carle) **10**:77
My Very First Book of Numbers (Carle) **10**:77
My Very First Book of Shapes (Carle) **10**:77
My Very First Book of Words (Carle) **10**:77
My Very First Library (Carle) **10**:77
My Visit to the Dinosaurs (Aliki) **9**:21
My World (Brown) **10**:58
Mysteries of Migration (McClung) **11**:194
The Mysterious Disappearance of Leon (I Mean Noel) (Raskin) **1**:156
The Mysterious Tadpole (Kellogg) **6**:175
The Mystery Beast of Ostergeest (Kellogg) **6**:170
The Mystery of the Flying Orange Pumpkin (Kellogg) **6**:177
The Mystery of the Giant Footsteps (Krahn) **3**:105
The Mystery of the Loch Ness Monster (Bendick) **5**:49
The Mystery of the Magic Green Ball (Kellogg) **6**:175
The Mystery of the Missing Red Mitten (Kellogg) **6**:172
The Mystery of the Stolen Blue Paint (Kellogg) **6**:178
Names, Sets, and Numbers (Bendick) **5**:43
Nana Upstairs and Nana Downstairs (de Paola) **4**:54
Naomi in the Middle (Klein) **2**:100
The Nap Master (Kotzwinkle) **6**:183
The Nargun and the Stars (Wrightson) **4**:244
Nathaniel Hawthorne: Captain of the Imagination (Manley) **3**:147
Nattpappan (Gripe) **5**:146
Natural Fire: Its Ecology in Forests (Pringle) **4**:184
The Near East: 10,000 Years of History (Asimov) **12**:42
Near the Window Tree: Poems and Notes (Kuskin) **4**:142

A Near Thing for Captain Najork (Hoban) **3**:81

A Necklace of Raindrops (Aiken) **1**:6

The Neighbors (illus. Brown) **12**:103

Nella nebbia di Milano (Munari) **9**:128

The Neon Motorcycle (Rockwell) **6**:237

Nessie the Monster (Hughes) **3**:94

New Friends for Susan (Uchida) **6**:251

New Life: New Room (Jordan) **10**:119

New Road! (Gibbons) **8**:96

New Year's Day (Aliki) **9**:20

New York City Too Far from Tampa Blues (Bethancourt) **3**:19

New Zealand: Yesterday and Today (Mahy) **7**:184

Nibble, Nibble: Poems for Children (Brown) **10**:67

Nicholas and the Fast Moving Diesel (Ardizzone) **3**:6

Nicholas Knock and Other People (Lee) **3**:116

Nicky Goes to the Doctor (Scarry) **3**:184

Night Again (Kuskin) **4**:144

Night and Day (Brown) **10**:50

Night Birds on Nantucket (Aiken) **1**:6

The Night Daddy (Gripe) **5**:146

Night Fall (Aiken) **1**:6

The Night Journey (Lasky) **11**:116

A Night without Stars (Howe) **9**:58

Night's Nice (Emberley) **5**:92

Nijntje in het ziekenhuis (Bruna) **7**:52

Nijntje's droom (Bruna) **7**:52

Nils Holgerssons underbara resa genom Sverige (Lagerlöf) **7**:110

Nine Lives (Alexander) **5**:18

No, Agatha! (Isadora) **7**:106

No Bath Tonight (Yolen) **4**:265

No Beat of Drum (Burton) **1**:32

No Kiss for Mother (Ungerer) **3**:202

No Measles, No Mumps for Me (Showers) **6**:248

No Promises in the Wind (Hunt) **1**:109

No Such Things (Peet) **12**:206

No Way of Knowing: Dallas Poems (Livingston) **7**:174

Noah's Ark (Spier) **5**:224

The Noble Doll (Coatsworth) **2**:60

Nobody Plays with a Cabbage (DeJong) **1**:60

Nobody's Family Is Going to Change (Fitzhugh) **1**:73

The Noisy Bird Book (Brown) **10**:51

Noisy Book (Brown) **10**:48

Noisy Words (Burningham) **9**:51

Nonsense Book (Lear) **1**:127

Nonstop Nonsense (Mahy) **7**:184

The Noon Balloon (Brown) **10**:62

Norby and the Invaders (Asimov and Asimov) **12**:64

Norby and the Lost Princess (Asimov and Asimov) **12**:63

Norby, the Mixed-Up Robot (Asimov) **12**:62

Norby's Other Secret (Asimov and Asimov) **12**:62

North Town (Graham) **10**:105

Not What You Expected (Aiken) **1**:7

Notes to a Science Fiction Writer (Bova) **3**:35

Nothing at All (Gág) **4**:92

Nothing Ever Happens on My Block (Raskin) **1**:157

Nothing Like a Fresh Coat of Paint (Spier) **5**:225

Nothing to Be Afraid Of (Mark) **11**:150

Now One Foot, Now the Other (de Paola) **4**:65

Now We Can Go (Jonas) **12**:177

Nuclear Power: From Physics to Politics (Pringle) **4**:185

Number Play (Burningham) **9**:50

The Nursery "Alice" (Carroll) **2**:35

Nutshell Library (Sendak) **1**:171

O Sliver of Liver: Together with Other Triolets, Cinquains, Haiku, Verses, and a Dash of Poems (Livingston) **7**:173

Observation (Bendick) **5**:45

Odyssey of Courage: The Story of Alvar Nunez Cabeza de Vaca (Wojciechowska) **1**:198

Of Course Polly Can Ride a Bike (Lindgren) **1**:137

Of Dikes and Windmills (Spier) **5**:219

Of Nightingales That Weep (Paterson) **7**:230

Oh, A-Hunting We Will Go (Langstaff) **3**:110

Oh, Say Can You Say? (Seuss) **9**:193

Oh, Were They Ever Happy! (Spier) **5**:225

Oh What a Noise! (Shulevitz) **5**:204

Ol' Dan Tucker (Langstaff) **3**:110

Old Mrs. Twindlytart and Other Rhymes (Livingston) **7**:169

Old Peter's Russian Tales (Ransome) **8**:170

The Old Testament (de Angeli) **1**:53

An Older Kind of Magic (Wrightson) **4**:244

The Oldest Man and Other Timeless Stories (Kotzwinkle) **6**:181

An Old-Fashioned Thanksgiving (Alcott) **1**:11

Oliver Button Is a Sissy (de Paola) **4**:62

On a marche sur la lune (Hergé) **6**:148

On Beyond Zebra (Seuss) **1**:88; **9**:180

On Christmas Day in the Morning! (Langstaff) **3**:110

On Christmas Eve (Brown) **10**:68

On the Day Peter Stuyvesant Sailed into Town (Lobel) **5**:166

On the Other Side of the Gate (Suhl) **2**:165

On the Way Home (Wilder) **2**:206

Once a Mouse . . . A Fable Cut in Wood (illus. Brown) **12**:101

Once on a Time (Milne) **1**:142

Once upon a Time in a Pigpen and Three Other Margaret Wise Brown Books (Brown) **10**:68

One at a Time: His Collected Poems for the Young (McCord) **9**:103

The One Bad Thing about Father (Monjo) **2**:124

One Big Wish (Williams) **8**:237

One by Sea (Corbett) **1**:46

One Earth, Many People: The Challenge of Human Population Growth (Pringle) **4**:175

One Fine Day (Hogrogian) **2**:88

One Fish, Two Fish, Red Fish, Blue Fish (Seuss) **1**:88; **9**:185

One Frog Too Many (Mayer and Mayer) **11**:169

One I Love, Two I Love, and Other Loving Mother Goose Rhymes (Hogrogian) **2**:88

One Monday Morning (Shulevitz) **5**:202

One Monster after Another (Mayer) **11**:168

One Morning in Maine (McCloskey) **7**:207

The One Pig with Horns (Brunhoff) **4**:40

One Small Blue Bead (Baylor) **3**:16

One to Grow On (Little) **4**:149

1, 2, 3 to the Zoo (Carle) **10**:71

One Was Johnny: A Counting Book (Sendak) **1**:172

One Wide River to Cross (Emberley) **5**:93

The Only Earth We Have (Pringle) **4**:174

The Open Gate (Seredy) **10**:178

The Optical Illusion Book (Simon) **9**:210

The Orchard Cat (Kellogg) **6**:171

Orlando, the Brave Vulture (Ungerer) **3**:203

Orphans of the Wind (Haugaard) **11**:103

Oscar Lobster's Fair Exchange (Selden) **8**:196

Otherwise Known as Sheila the Great (Blume) **2**:17

Otis Spofford (Cleary) **8**:46

Otto and the Magic Potatoes (du Bois) **1**:64

Otto at Sea (du Bois) **1**:65

Otto in Texas (du Bois) **1**:65

Otus: The Story of a Screech Owl (McClung) **11**:182

Our Animal Friends at Maple Hill Farm (Provensen and Provensen) **11**:211

Our Federal Union: The United States from 1816-1865 (Asimov) **12**:51

Our Hungry Earth: The World Food Crisis (Pringle) **4**:181

Our World: The People's Republic of China (Rau) **8**:187

Outcast (Sutcliff) **1**:189

OUTside INside Poems (Adoff) **7**:36

The Outsiders (Hinton) **3**:70

Over Sea, Under Stone (Cooper) **4**:42

The Owl and the Pussycat (Lear) **1**:127

The Owl and the Woodpecker (Wildsmith) **2**:213

An Owl and Three Pussycats (Provensen and Provensen) **11**:214

Owl at Home (Lobel) **5**:169

Paddington Abroad (Bond) **1**:28

Paddington at Large (Bond) **1**:28

Paddington at Work (Bond) **1**:28

Paddington Bear (Bond) **1**:28

Paddington Helps Out (Bond) **1**:29

Paddington Marches On (Bond) **1**:29

Paddington Takes the Air (Bond) **1**:29

Paint, Brush, and Palette (Weiss) **4**:223

Palmistry (Aylesworth) **6**:53

Pamela Camel (Peet) **12**:206

Pancakes for Breakfast (de Paola) **4**:60

Pancakes, Pancakes! (Carle) **10**:74

Papagayo, the Mischief Maker (McDermott) **9**:119

The Paper Airplane Book (Simon) **9**:204

Paper Dolls (Pfeffer) **11**:204

Paper, Ink, and Roller: Print-Making for Beginners (Weiss) **4**:220

Paper, Paper Everywhere (Gibbons) **8**:95

Pappa Pellerin's Daughter (Gripe) **5**:143

Pappa Pellerins Dotter (Gripe) **5**:143

Parade (Crews) **7**:62

The Parade Book (Emberley) **5**:91

Pardon Me, You're Stepping on My Eyeball! (Zindel) **3**:250

Parker Pig, Esquire (de Paola) **4**:54

Parrakeets (Zim) **2**:229

Parsley (Bemelmans) **6**:72

A Pattern of Roses
    (Peyton) **3**:177

Paul Robeson (Greenfield) **4**:98

*Paul Robeson: The Life and
    Times of a Free Black Man*
    (Hamilton) **1**:104

*Pauline and the Prince of the
    Wind* (Krüss) **9**:86

Pauline und der Prinz im Wind
    (Krüss) **9**:86

Paul's Horse, Herman
    (Weiss) **4**:221

Pavo and the Princess
    (Ness) **6**:202

The Peaceable Kingdom
    (Coatsworth) **2**:60

*The Pedaling Man and Other
    Poems* (Hoban) **3**:81

Peeper: First Voice of Spring
    (McClung) **11**:190

*Pencil, Pen, and Brush Drawing
    for Beginners* (Weiss) **4**:222

The Penguin Book (Rau) **8**:186

Pennington's Heir
    (Peyton) **3**:178

Pennington's Last Term
    (Peyton) **3**:178

People (Spier) **5**:227

*The People Could Fly: American
    Black Folk Tales*
    (Hamilton) **11**:93

The People of New China
    (Rau) **8**:189

The People of the Ax
    (Williams) **8**:234

*The People's Choice: The Story
    of Candidates, Campaigns, and
    Elections* (Schwartz) **3**:190

The People's Republic of China
    (Rau) **8**:187

The Peppermint Family
    (Brown) **10**:60

The Peppermint Pig
    (Bawden) **2**:12

Perilous Pilgrimage
    (Treece) **2**:187

Pet Show! (Keats) **1**:116

The Pet Store (Spier) **5**:228

Peter and Butch (Phipson) **5**:181

Peter and Veronica
    (Sachs) **2**:132

Peter Duck (Ransome) **8**:174

Peter Graves (du Bois) **1**:65

*Peter Piper's Alphabet: Peter
    Piper's Practical Principles of
    Plain and Perfect
    Pronunciation* (illus.
    Brown) **12**:100

Peter Treegate's War
    (Wibberley) **3**:229

Peter's Chair (Keats) **1**:116

Petey (Tobias) **4**:217

Le Petit Prince (Saint-
    Exupéry) **10**:137

Petronella (Williams) **8**:233

Petros' War (Zei) **6**:261

*Pets in a Jar: Collecting and
    Caring for Small Wild Animals*
    (Simon) **9**:209

Pezzettino (Lionni) **7**:137

Philbert the Fearful
    (Williams) **8**:227

*Philip Hall Likes Me. I Reckon
    Maybe* (Greene) **2**:85

Philomena (Seredy) **10**:180

Phoebe's Revolt (Babbitt) **2**:6

Pickle Creature
    (Pinkwater) **4**:169

Picnic at Babar's
    (Brunhoff) **4**:34

*The Picts and the Martyrs; or,
    Not Welcome at All*
    (Ransome) **8**:181

*A Piece of the Power: Four Black
    Mayors* (Haskins) **3**:65

Pierre: A Cautionary Tale
    (Sendak) **1**:172

Pigeon Post (Ransome) **8**:177

The Pigman (Zindel) **3**:251

Pigs Plus: Learning Addition
    (Burningham) **9**:50

The Pig-Tale (Carroll) **2**:35

Pilyo the Piranha (Aruego) **5**:29

Pinkerton, Behave!
    (Kellogg) **6**:176

Pinky Pye (Estes) **2**:75

Pipes and Plumbing Systems (Zim
    and Skelly) **2**:230

Pippa Passes (Corbett) **1**:46

Pippi Goes on Board
    (Lindgren) **1**:138

Pippi in the South Sea
    (Lindgren) **1**:138

Pippi Longstocking
    (Lindgren) **1**:138

The Pirate Uncle (Mahy) **7**:185

Pirate's Island
    (Townsend) **2**:173

The Place (Coatsworth) **2**:61

A Place to Come Back To
    (Bond) **11**:30

A Place to Live (Bendick) **5**:43

The Plan for Birdsmarsh
    (Peyton) **3**:180

The Planet of Junior Brown
    (Hamilton) **1**:104

*The Planet-Girded Suns: Man's
    View of Other Solar Systems*
    (Engdahl) **2**:71

Plants in Winter (Cole) **5**:63

Play on Words (Provensen and
    Provensen) **11**:210

Plenty of Fish (Selsam) **1**:164

Plink, Plink, Plink (Baylor) **3**:16

A Pocket Full of Seeds
    (Sachs) **2**:133

The Pocket Mouse
    (Willard) **2**:221

Poems of Lewis Carroll
    (Carroll) **2**:35

Poetry Is (Hughes) **3**:94

Poisonous Snakes (Simon) **9**:216

The Polite Penguin
    (Brown) **10**:50

Polly's Tiger (Phipson) **5**:183

The Pooh Story Book
    (Milne) **1**:142

The Pool of Fire
    (Christopher) **2**:41

Poor Richard in France
    (Monjo) **2**:129

*Poor Stainless: A New Story
    about the Borrowers*
    (Norton) **6**:224

The Popcorn Book (de
    Paola) **4**:60

*Popo and Fifina, Children of
    Haiti* (Bontemps and
    Hughes) **6**:78

*Popol et Virginie au pays des
    lapinos* (Hergé) **6**:149

Popol Out West (Hergé) **6**:149

Poppy Pig Goes to Market
    (Bruna) **7**:52

Porko Von Popbutton (du
    Bois) **1**:65

Portfolio of Horse Paintings
    (Henry) **4**:112

Portfolio of Horses
    (Henry) **4**:112

The Portmanteau Book
    (Rockwell) **6**:237

Portrait of Ivan (Fox) **1**:79

*The Post Office Book: Mail and
    How It Moves* (Gibbons) **8**:93

The Potters' Kitchen
    (Isadora) **7**:103

*Practical Music Theory: How
    Music Is Put Together from
    Bach to Rock* (Collier) **3**:48

The Practical Princess
    (Williams) **8**:230

*The Practical Princess and Other
    Liberating Fairy Tales*
    (Williams) **8**:236

A Prairie Boy's Summer
    (Kurelek) **2**:103

A Prairie Boy's Winter
    (Kurelek) **2**:103

Prank (Lasky) **11**:120

Pretty Pretty Peggy Moffitt (du
    Bois) **1**:66

Pretzel (Rey) **5**:195

Pretzel and the Puppies
    (Rey) **5**:195

Prime Time (Pfeffer) **11**:205

Prince Bertram the Bad
    (Lobel) **5**:163

*Prince Caspian: The Return to
    Narnia* (Lewis) **3**:136

The Prince in Waiting
    (Christopher) **2**:41

*The Prince of the Dolomites: An
    Old Italian Tale* (de
    Paola) **4**:64

*Prince Rabbit and the Princess
    Who Could Not Laugh*
    (Milne) **1**:143

The Princess and the Clown
    (Mahy) **7**:180

The Procession (Mahy) **7**:179

*Professor Wormbog in Search for
    the Zipperump-a-Zoo*
    (Mayer) **11**:172

Profiles in Black Power
    (Haskins) **3**:66

Projects with Air (Simon) **9**:209

Projects with Plants
    (Simon) **9**:207

The Promised Year
    (Uchida) **6**:252

The Proud Circus Horse
    (Zimnik) **3**:244

*A Proud Taste for Scarlet and
    Miniver* (Konigsburg) **1**:122

The Proud Wooden Drummer
    (Krüss) **9**:88

The Prydain Chronicles
    (Alexander) **1**:16

Psst! Doggie— (Keats) **1**:117

*Puddin' Poems: Being the Best of
    the Verse from "The Magic
    Pudding"* (Lindsay) **8**:106

Punch and Judy
    (Emberley) **5**:92

Puppeteer (Lasky) **11**:121

Puppy Summer (DeJong) **1**:60

Puss in Boots (illus.
    Brown) **12**:96

Pussy Willow (Brown) **10**:61

A Pussycat's Christmas
    (Brown) **10**:59

Putting the Sun to Work
    (Bendick) **5**:49

Pyramid (Macaulay) **3**:143

Python's Party
    (Wildsmith) **2**:214

The Quangle Wangle's Hat
    (Lear) **1**:127

The Quarreling Book
    (Zolotow) **2**:236

*The Queen Always Wanted to
    Dance* (Mayer) **11**:166

The Queen Elizabeth Story
    (Sutcliff) **1**:189

Queen of Hearts (Cleaver and
    Cleaver) **6**:111

The Quest of Captain Cook
    (Selsam) **1**:164

The Question Box
    (Williams) **8**:226

*Questions and Answers about
    Ants* (Selsam) **1**:165

*Questions and Answers about
    Horses* (Selsam) **1**:165

The Quicksand Book (de
    Paola) **4**:59

The Quiet Noisy Book
    (Brown) **10**:60

The Quilt (Jonas) **12**:175

Quips and Quirks
    (Watson) **3**:213

Quito Express
    (Bemelmans) **6**:66

The Quitting Deal
    (Tobias) **4**:215

The Rabbit (Burningham) **9**:46

Rabbit Hill (Lawson) **2**:110

A Racecourse for Andy
    (Wrightson) **4**:242

Rackety-Bang and Other Verses
    (Rockwell) **6**:235

Raffy and the Nine Monkeys
    (Rey) **5**:192

Raging Robots and Unruly Uncles
    (Mahy) **7**:186

The Railway Children
    (Nesbit) **3**:164

*The Railway Engine and the
    Hairy Brigands* (Mahy) **7**:181

Rain (Spier) **5**:228

Rain Rain Rivers
    (Shulevitz) **5**:203

Rainbow Valley
    (Montgomery) **8**:137

Rainbows and Fireworks
    (Pfeffer) **11**:197

Rajpur: Last of the Bengal Tigers
    (McClung) **11**:193

Ralph Bunche: A Most Reluctant Hero (Haskins) **3**:66
Ralph S. Mouse (Cleary) **8**:58
Rama, the Hero of India: Valmiki's "Ramayana" Done into a Short English Version for Boys and Girls (Mukerji) **10**:134
Ramona and Her Father (Cleary) **8**:55
Ramona and Her Mother (Cleary) **8**:56
Ramona Forever (Cleary) **8**:62
Ramona Quimby, Age 8 (Cleary) **8**:57
Ramona the Brave (Cleary) **2**:49; **8**:55
Ramona the Pest (Cleary) **2**:49; **8**:52
Randy's Dandy Lions (Peet) **12**:195
Rasmus and the Vagabond (Lindgren) **1**:139
Ray Charles (Mathis) **3**:151
Read One: Numbers as Words (Burningham) **9**:50
Ready, Steady, Go! (Watanabe) **8**:216
The Real Hole (Cleary) **2**:50; **8**:49
The Real Thief (Steig) **2**:160
Realm of Algebra (Asimov) **12**:36
Realm of Measure (Asimov) **12**:34
Realm of Numbers (Asimov) **12**:33
The Rebel (Burton) **1**:33
Rebels of the Heavenly Kingdom (Paterson) **7**:242
Recycling Resources (Pringle) **4**:179
Red Earth, Blue Sky: The Australian Outback (Rau) **8**:191
Red Light, Green Light (Brown) **10**:52
Red Pawns (Wibberley) **3**:229
The Red Room Riddle (Corbett) **1**:46
Redbird: The Story of a Cardinal (McClung) **11**:185
Religions (Haskins) **3**:66
The Reluctant Dragon (Grahame) **5**:135
Remove Protective Coating a Little at a Time (Donovan) **3**:53
The Renowned History of Little Red Riding-Hood (Hogrogian) **2**:89
The Return of the Great Brain (Fitzgerald) **1**:70
Return of the Moose (Pinkwater) **4**:169
Return to Gone-Away (Enright) **4**:76
Return to South Town (Graham) **10**:111
Return to the Happy Islands (Krüss) **9**:84
The Revenge of Samuel Stokes (Lively) **7**:163

The Revenge of the Incredible Dr. Rancid and His Youthful Assistant, Jeffrey (Conford) **10**:97
Revolutionaries: Agents of Change (Haskins) **3**:67
The Reward Worth Having (Williams) **8**:235
Ribsy (Cleary) **2**:50; **8**:51
Rich and Famous: The Future Adventures of George Stable (Collier) **3**:48
Richard Scarry's Animal Nursery Tales (Scarry) **3**:185
Richard Scarry's Color Book (Scarry) **3**:185
Richard Scarry's Great Big Air Book (Scarry) **3**:185
The Richleighs of Tantamount (Cleary) **3**:221
Ride into Danger (Treece) **2**:188
Ride Off: Learning Subtraction (Burningham) **9**:50
The Rider and His Horse (Haugaard) **11**:106
Riders of the Storm (Burton) **1**:34
Rilla of Ingleside (Montgomery) **8**:138
Ring Out! A Book of Bells (Yolen) **4**:261
Ring-Rise, Ring-Set (Hughes) **9**:75
The River and the Forest (Korinetz) **4**:131
River Winding (Zolotow) **2**:236
A Road Down in the Sea (Graham) **10**:109
The Road to Miklagard (Treece) **2**:188
Roald Dahl's Revolting Rhymes (Dahl) **7**:81
Roar and More (Kuskin) **4**:134
The "Roaring 40" (Chauncy) **6**:92
Robert Fulton, Boy Craftsman (Henry) **4**:109
Robin and His Merry Men (Serraillier) **2**:139
Robin in the Greenwood: Ballads of Robin Hood (Serraillier) **2**:140
Robot (Pieńkowski) **6**:232
The Robot and Rebecca and the Missing Owser (Yolen) **4**:268
The Robot and Rebecca: The Mystery of the Code-Carrying Kids (Yolen) **4**:266
Rock 'n' Roll Nights: A Novel (Strasser) **11**:249
Rock Star (Collier) **3**:48
The Rocks of Honey (Wrightson) **4**:241
Roland the Minstrel Pig (Steig) **2**:161
Roll of Thunder, Hear My Cry (Taylor) **9**:226
The Roman Empire (Asimov) **12**:40
The Roman Moon Mystery (Williams) **8**:221
The Roman Republic (Asimov) **12**:39

A Room Made of Windows (Cameron) **1**:40
Rooster Brother (Hogrogian) **2**:89
Rooster Sets Out to See the World (Carle) **10**:76
The Rooster Who Set Out to See the World (Carle) **10**:76
The Rooster Who Understood Japanese (Uchida) **6**:258
Rosa Parks (Greenfield) **4**:97
A Rose for Pinkerton (Kellogg) **6**:177
The Rose on My Cake (Kuskin) **4**:138
Rosebud (Bemelmans) **6**:67
Rosebud (Emberley) **5**:93
Rosie and Michael (Viorst) **3**:208
The Rotten Years (Wojciechowska) **1**:198
Round Trip (Jonas) **12**:173
Rowan Farm (Benary-Isbert) **12**:72
Ruby Throat: The Story of a Humming Bird (McClung) **11**:178
Rudi and the Distelfink (Monjo) **2**:125
Rudyard Kipling: Creative Adventurer (Manley) **3**:147
Rufus M. (Estes) **2**:75
Rumble Fish (Hinton) **3**:71
Run for the Money (Corbett) **1**:47
Run Softly, Go Fast (Wersba) **3**:218
The Runaway Bunny (Brown) **10**:50
Runaway Ralph (Cleary) **8**:54
Runaway to Freedom: A Story of the Underground Railway (Smucker) **10**:189
The Runaway Train (Farmer) **8**:87
Saber-Toothed Tiger and Other Ice Age Mammals (Cole) **5**:65
Sad-Faced Boy (Bontemps) **6**:79
The Sailing Hatrack (Coatsworth) **2**:61
Sailing Small Boats (Weiss) **4**:224
Sailing to Cythera and Other Anatole Stories (Willard) **5**:245
The Sailor (Bruna) **7**:50
The Sailor Dog (Brown) **10**:63
Sailor Jack and the 20 Orphans (Mahy) **7**:179
Saint George and the Dragon: A Mummer's Play (Langstaff) **3**:111
Salvador and Mister Sam: A Guide to Parakeet Care (Gibbons) **8**:88
Sam, Bangs, and Moonshine (Ness) **6**:203
Sam Patch: The High, Wide, and Handsome Jumper (Bontemps and Conroy) **6**:81
Samson: Last of the California Grizzlies (McClung) **11**:188

Samurai of Gold Hill (Uchida) **6**:257
The Samurai's Tale (Haugaard) **11**:110
San Domingo: The Medicine Hat Stallion (Henry) **4**:116
San Francisco (Fritz) **2**:81
Sand and Snow (Kuskin) **4**:139
Satellites in Outer Space (Asimov) **12**:35
The Saturdays (Enright) **4**:73
Saturn and Beyond (Asimov) **12**:57
Schloss an der Grenze (Benary-Isbert) **12**:75
The School (Burningham) **9**:46
School for Sillies (Williams) **8**:230
Science at the Ball Game (Aylesworth) **6**:53
Science at Work: Projects in Oceanography (Simon) **9**:206
Science at Work: Projects in Space Science (Simon) **9**:204
Science Experiments You Can Eat (Cobb) **2**:66
Science in a Vacant Lot (Simon) **9**:203
Science Looks at Mysterious Monsters (Aylesworth) **6**:56
Science Projects in Ecology (Simon) **9**:204
Science Projects in Pollution (Simon) **9**:206
Scoop: Last of the Brown Pelicans (McClung) **11**:187
Scrambled Eggs Super! (Seuss) **9**:178
The Sea Egg (Boston) **3**:28
Sea Gull (Farmer) **8**:77
The Sea Is All Around (Enright) **4**:72
The Sea of Gold and Other Tales from Japan (Uchida) **6**:254
Sea So Big, Ship So Small (Bendick) **5**:40
Sea Star (McClung) **11**:189
Sea Star, Orphan of Chincoteague (Henry) **4**:111
The Sea-Beggar's Son (Monjo) **2**:125
Seacrow Island (Lindgren) **1**:139
The Seagull (Farmer) **8**:77
Search for a Stone (Munari) **9**:129
The Search for Delicious (Babbitt) **2**:7
The Search for Life (Aylesworth) **6**:52
Seashore Story (Yashima) **4**:254
Season Songs (Hughes) **3**:95
Seasons (Burningham) **9**:43
The Seasons for Singing: American Christmas Songs and Carols (Langstaff) **3**:111
The Sea-Thing Child (Hoban) **3**:82
The Second Margaret Mahy Story Book: Stories and Poems (Mahy) **7**:181
Second Summer with Ladis (Sánchez-Silva) **12**:232

The Secret (Coatsworth)   2:61
Secret Agents Four (Sobol)   4:208
The Secret Birthday Message (Carle)   10:75
The Secret Box (Cole)   5:61
The Secret Clocks: Time Senses of Living Things (Simon)   9:213
The Secret Friends (Chauncy)   6:91
Secret of the Hawk (Wibberley)   3:230
The Secret of the Sachem's Tree (Monjo)   2:125
Secret Sea (White)   3:222
Secret Water (Ransome)   8:179
See the Circus (Rey)   5:198
See through the Sea (Selsam and Morrow)   1:165
See What I Found (Livingston)   7:168
The Seeing Stick (Yolen)   4:264
El segundo verano de Ladis (Sánchez-Silva)   12:232
The Self-Made Snowman (Krahn)   3:105
Sense of Direction: Up and Down and All Around (Cobb)   2:67
Serafina the Giraffe (Brunhoff)   4:35
The Serpent's Teeth: The Story of Cadmus (Farmer)   8:80
Servants of the Devil (Aylesworth)   6:49
Seven Days to a Brand-New Me (Conford)   10:97
Seven Stories about a Cat Named Sneakers (Brown)   10:65
Seven Stories by Hans Christian Andersen (Carle)   10:82
Seventeen Kings and Forty-Two Elephants (Mahy)   7:181
Seventeen Seconds (Southall)   2:155
The Seventh Mandarin (Yolen)   4:259
Shadow (illus. Brown)   12:107
Shadow of a Bull (Wojciechowska)   1:199
The Shadow-Cage and Other Tales of the Supernatural (Pearce)   9:155
Shadrach (DeJong)   1:60
Shag: Last of the Plains Buffalo (McClung)   11:182
Shaka, King of the Zulus: A Biography (Cohen)   3:42
Shaker Paper House: To Cut Out and Color (Ness)   6:209
Shapes (Bendick)   5:42
The Shaping of England (Asimov)   12:43
The Shaping of North America from Earliest Times to 1763 (Asimov)   12:48
Sharks (Zim)   2:230
Shaw's Fortune: The Picture Story of a Colonial Plantation (Tunis)   2:194
She Come Bringing Me That Little Baby Girl (Greenfield)   4:97

SHHhhhh......Bang, a Whispering Book (Brown)   10:51
The Shield Ring (Sutcliff)   1:189
Shimmy Shimmy Coke-Ca-Pop! A Collection of City Children's Street Games and Rhymes (Langstaff and Langstaff)   3:112
Ship Models and How to Build Them (Weiss)   4:227
The Ship That Came Down the Gutter (Kotzwinkle)   6:181
Shirlick Holmes and the Case of the Wandering Wardrobe (Yolen)   4:267
The Shooting Star (Benary-Isbert)   12:74
The Shopping Basket (Burningham)   9:49
The Short Voyage of the 'Albert Ross' (Mark)   11:150
Sia Lives on Kilimanjaro (Lindgren)   1:140
Sidewalk Story (Mathis)   3:151
The Sign of the Beaver (Speare)   8:210
The Sign of the Chrysanthemum (Paterson)   7:230
Silent Ship, Silent Sea (White)   3:222
Silky: An Incredible Tale (Coatsworth)   2:61
The Silver Branch (Sutcliff)   1:190
The Silver Chair (Lewis)   3:136
The Silver Crown (O'Brien)   2:128
Silver on the Tree (Cooper)   4:47
The Silver Sword (Serraillier)   2:141
The Silver Whistle (Williams)   8:231
Simon (Sutcliff)   1:190
Simon Boom Gives a Wedding (Suhl)   2:166
Simon's Song (Emberley)   5:97
Simple Gifts: The Story of the Shakers (Yolen)   4:263
Simple Pictures Are Best (Willard)   5:247
The Simple Prince (Yolen)   4:264
Sing Down the Moon (O'Dell)   1:148
The Singing Hill (DeJong)   1:61
The Singing Tree (Seredy)   10:176
A Single Light (Wojciechowska)   1:199
Sir Arthur Evans, Discoverer of Knossos (Selden)   8:198
Sister (Greenfield)   4:97
Sister of the Bride (Cleary)   8:50
Six and Silver (Phipson)   5:178
Skates! (Keats)   1:117
Skip Trip (Burningham)   9:51
Skipper John's Cook (Brown)   12:96
The Sky Was Blue (Zolotow)   2:236
Slam Bang (Burningham)   9:51
Slappy Hooper, the Wonderful Sign Painter (Bontemps and Conroy)   6:80

Slater's Mill (Monjo)   2:126
The Slave Dancer (Fox)   1:79
A Slave's Tale (Haugaard)   11:103
Sledges to the Rescue (Briggs)   10:23
Sleep Is for Everyone (Showers)   6:246
The Sleeping Beauty (Mayer)   11:175
Sleepy ABC (Brown)   10:62
Sleepy People (Goffstein)   3:61
Sloan and Philamina; or, How to Make Friends with Your Lunch (Stren)   5:231
The Sly Old Cat (Potter)   1:153
Small Pig (Lobel)   5:164
The Smallest Dinosaurs (Simon)   9:218
Smeller Martin (Lawson)   2:111
Smoke from Cromwell's Time (Aiken)   1:7
Smokey (Peet)   12:195
Snail, Where Are You? (Ungerer)   3:203
Snails (Zim and Krantz)   2:230
A Snake's Body (Cole)   5:67
Snakes: Their Place in the Sun (McClung)   11:192
Sneakers: Seven Stories about a Cat (Brown)   10:65
The Sneetches and Other Stories (Seuss)   9:186
Sniff Shout (Burningham)   9:51
Snippy and Snappy (Gág)   4:89
The Snow (Burningham)   9:46
The Snow Monkey at Home (Rau)   8:190
Snow Tracks (George)   1:92
The Snowman (Briggs)   10:29
The Snowy Day (Keats)   1:117
Snuffie (Bruna)   7:51
Snuffy (Bruna)   7:51
Social Welfare (Myers)   4:157
Socks (Cleary)   2:51; 8:54
The Solar System (Asimov)   12:53
The Soldier and Death: A Russian Folk Tale Told in English (Ransome)   8:171
Soldier and Tsar in the Forest: A Russian Tale (Shulevitz)   5:205
Soldier, Soldier, Won't You Marry Me? (Langstaff)   3:112
Solids, Liquids, and Gases (Bendick)   5:47
Some of the Days of Everett Anderson (Clifton)   5:53
The Something (Babbitt)   2:8
Something Special for Me (Williams)   9:234
Sometimes I Dance Mountains (Baylor)   3:16
The Song in My Drum (Hoban)   3:82
Song of the Boat (Graham)   10:110
Song of the Trees (Taylor)   9:225
Songs of the Dream People: Chants and Images from the Indians and Eskimos of North America (Houston)   3:86

Songs of the Fog Maiden (de Paola)   4:62
Sonora Beautiful (Clifton)   5:60
Sophia Scrooby Preserved (Bacon)   3:11
The Sorely Trying Day (Hoban)   3:82
The Soul Brothers and Sister Lou (Hunter)   3:99
The Sound of the Dragon's Feet (Zei)   6:262
Sounder (Armstrong)   1:23
Sour Land (Armstrong)   1:24
South Swell (Wibberley)   3:230
South Town (Graham)   10:105
Space and Time (Bendick)   5:42
A Space Story (Kuskin)   4:143
Space Trap (Hughes)   9:77
The Spanish Armada (Williams)   8:228
The Sparrow Bush (Coatsworth)   2:62
Sparrow Socks (Selden)   8:198
Speak Out in Thunder Tones: Letters and Other Writings by Black Northerners, 1787-1865 (Sterling)   1:181
Speak Up: More Rhymes of the Never Was and Always Is (McCord)   9:104
A Special Trick (Mayer)   11:165
A Spell Is Cast (Cameron)   1:41
Sphinx: The Story of a Caterpillar (McClung)   11:178
Spiderweb for Two: A Melendy Maze (Enright)   4:75
Spike: The Story of a Whitetail Deer (McClung)   11:179
Spin a Soft Black Song: Poems for Children (Giovanni)   6:115
The Spirit of the Lord: Revivalism in America (Cohen)   3:42
The Splintered Sword (Serraillier)   2:188
The Spooky Tail of Prewitt Peacock (Peet)   12:202
Spotted Salamander (McClung)   11:182
Spotty (Rey)   5:195
Die Sprechmachine (Krüss)   9:86
The Sprig of Broom (Willard)   2:222
Spring Begins in March (Little)   4:148
Spring Comes to the Ocean (George)   1:92
Spring Is a New Beginning (Anglund)   1:21
Spring Is Here! (Sterling)   1:181
Square as a House (Kuskin)   4:136
Squawwk! (Rockwell)   6:236
Squib (Bawden)   2:13
The Squirrel Wife (Pearce)   9:153
Squirrels (Wildsmith)   2:214
The Stained Glass Window (Lively)   7:161
Stand in the Wind (Little)   4:151
The Star in the Pail (McCord)   9:102
Star of Night: Stories for Christmas (Paterson)   7:237

Starring Peter and Leigh: A Novel (Pfeffer) **11**:199

The Star-Spangled Banner (Spier) **5**:222

Starting with Melodie (Pfeffer) **11**:203

The Steadfast Tin Soldier (illus. Brown) **12**:97

The Steamroller: A Fantasy (Brown) **10**:68

Stepmother (Mahy) **7**:182

Steven Kellogg's Yankee Doodle (Kellogg) **6**:174

Stevie (Steptoe) **2**:163

Sticks, Spools, and Feathers (Weiss) **4**:223

A Stitch in Time (Lively) **7**:160

The Stolen Oracle (Williams) **8**:221

The Stone Doll of Sister Brute (Hoban) **3**:83

Stone Soup: An Old Tale (illus. Brown) **12**:94

The Stonecutter: A Japanese Folk Tale (McDermott) **9**:115

The Stone-Faced Boy (Fox) **1**:81

Stoneflight (McHargue) **2**:120

The Stones of Green Knowe (Boston) **3**:28

Storie di tre uccellini (Munari) **9**:124

Storm Alert: Understanding Weather Disasters (Aylesworth) **6**:55

Storm from the West (Willard) **2**:222

A Storm without Rain (Adkins) **7**:28

Stormy, Misty's Foal (Henry) **4**:114

The Story Girl (Montgomery) **8**:135

The Story of a Puppet (Collodi) **5**:69

The Story of Babar, the Little Elephant (Brunhoff) **4**:30

The Story of George Washington Carver (Bontemps) **6**:82

The Story of Johnny Appleseed (Aliki) **9**:17

The Story of Jumping Mouse: A Native American Legend (Steptoe) **12**:241

The Story of Paul Bunyan (Emberley) **5**:92

The Story of Persephone (Farmer) **8**:85

The Story of Ruth (Asimov) **12**:47

The Story of Stevie Wonder (Haskins) **3**:67

The Story of the Amulet (Nesbit) **3**:165

Story of the Negro (Bontemps) **6**:80

The Story of Vampires (Aylesworth) **6**:53

The Story of Werewolves (Aylesworth) **6**:54

The Story of William Penn (Aliki) **9**:18

The Story of William Tell (Aliki) **9**:17

The Story of Witches (Aylesworth) **6**:54

A Story to Tell (Bruna) **7**:51

Storybook Dictionary (Scarry) **3**:186

A Storybook from Tomi Ungerer (Ungerer) **3**:203

The Stowaway to the Mushroom Planet (Cameron) **1**:41

Strange Creatures (Simon) **9**:217

Strange Mysteries from Around the World (Simon) **9**:215

A Stranger at Green Knowe (Boston) **3**:29

Stranger on the Ball Club (Slote) **4**:199

Strangers' Bread (Willard) **5**:247

The Streamlined Pig (Brown) **10**:48

Street Gangs: Yesterday and Today (Haskins) **3**:68

Strega Nona: An Old Tale (de Paola) **4**:57

Strictly for Laughs (Conford) **10**:100

A String in the Harp (Bond) **11**:26

Stripe: The Story of a Chipmunk (McClung) **11**:179

Stuart Little (White) **1**:195

Studenplan: Roman (Nöstlinger) **12**:187

Sugaring Time (Lasky) **11**:117

The Sultan's Perfect Tree (Yolen) **4**:263

Sumi and the Goat and the Tokyo Express (Uchida) **6**:256

Sumi's Prize (Uchida) **6**:253

Sumi's Special Happening (Uchida) **6**:254

The Summer after the Funeral (Gardam) **12**:166

The Summer Birds (Farmer) **8**:76

The Summer Book (Jansson) **2**:95

The Summer Night (Zolotow) **2**:237

The Summer Noisy Book (Brown) **10**:60

Summer of My German Soldier (Greene) **2**:86

The Summer of the Falcon (George) **1**:93

The Summer of the Swans (Byars) **1**:37

The Summer People (Townsend) **2**:174

A Summer to Die (Lowry) **6**:192

The Summer with Spike (Willard) **2**:223

The Sun (Zim) **2**:231

Sun Flight (McDermott) **9**:118

Sun Up, Sun Down (Gibbons) **8**:97

Sunday Morning (Viorst) **3**:209

Sunshine (Bemelmans) **6**:68

Super People: Who Will They Be? (Bendick) **5**:50

Superpuppy: How to Choose, Raise, and Train the Best

Possible Dog for You (Pinkwater and Pinkwater) **4**:167

Supersuits (Cobb) **2**:67

Suppose You Met a Witch (Serraillier) **2**:142

The Supreme, Superb, Exalted and Delightful, One and Only Magic Building (Kotzwinkle) **6**:182

Surrender (White) **3**:222

The Survivor (White) **3**:223

The Survivors (Hunter) **3**:101

Susan (Smucker) **10**:189

Swallowdale (Ransome) **8**:174

Swallows and Amazons (Ransome) **8**:171

Sweet Pea: A Black Girl Growing Up in the Rural South (Krementz) **5**:150

Sweet Whispers, Brother Rush (Hamilton) **11**:84

Sweetwater (Yep) **3**:238

The Swift Deer (McClung) **11**:184

Swimmy (Lionni) **7**:129

The Sword and the Scythe (Williams) **8**:221

The Sword of Esau (Southall) **2**:156

The Sword of King Arthur (Williams) **8**:229

The Sword of the Spirits (Christopher) **2**:42

Sword of the Wilderness (Coatsworth) **2**:62

Swords from the North (Treece) **2**:189

Sylvester and the Magic Pebble (Steig) **2**:161

Sylvie and Bruno (Carroll) **2**:36

Symbiosis: A Book of Unusual Friendships (Aruego) **5**:28

Symbols: A Silent Language (Adkins) **7**:24

The Tailor and the Giant (Krüss) **9**:88

The Tailor of Gloucester (Potter) **1**:153

Takao and Grandfather's Sword (Uchida) **6**:252

Take a Number (Bendick and Levin) **5**:39

Take Sky: More Rhymes of the Never Was and Always Is (McCord) **9**:99

Take Two and . . . Rolling! (Pfeffer) **11**:205

Take Wing (Little) **4**:148

Taking Care of Terrific (Lowry) **6**:197

Taking Sides (Klein) **2**:100

The Tale of the Faithful Dove (Potter) **1**:153

The Tale of Three Landlubbers (Serraillier) **2**:143

The Tale of Tuppenny (Potter) **1**:154

Tales from Grimm (Gág) **4**:91

Tales from The Jungle Book (McKinley) **10**:126

Tales of a Fourth Grade Nothing (Blume) **2**:18

Tales of Momolu (Graham) **10**:104

The Tales of Olga da Polga (Bond) **1**:29

Talk about a Family (Greenfield) **4**:101

The Talking Machine: An Extraordinary Story (Krüss) **9**:86

Talking with the Animals (Cohen) **3**:42

Tall Ships (Lasky) **11**:114

Tallyho, Pinkerton! (Kellogg) **6**:178

Tamarindo! (Brown) **12**:101

Tamar's Wager (Coatsworth) **2**:62

Tangara: "Let Us Set Off Again" (Chauncy) **6**:91

Taran Wanderer (Alexander) **1**:17; **5**:20

Tatsinda (Enright) **4**:76

The Tattooed Potato and Other Clues (Raskin) **12**:223

The Tavern at the Ferry (Tunis) **2**:194

Teacup Full of Roses (Mathis) **3**:151

Tear Down the Walls! (Sterling) **1**:181

The Teddy Bear Habit; or, How I Became a Winner (Collier) **3**:49

Teddy Bear's Scrapbook (Howe and Howe) **9**:57

Teen-Age Treasury of Good Humor (Manley) **3**:148

Teen-Age Treasury of Our Science World (Manley and Lewis) **3**:148

Teen-Age Treasury of the Arts (Manley and Lewis) **3**:148

TEEP and BEEP Go to Sleep (Mayer) **11**:176

Telboek no. 2 (Bruna) **7**:51

Telephone Systems (Zim and Skelly) **8**:231

Television Works Like This (Bendick and Bendick) **5**:36

Ten Apples Up on Top! (Seuss) **9**:187

Ten Black Dots (Crews) **7**:56

Ten, Nine, Eight (Bang) **8**:22

The Tenement Tree (Seredy) **10**:180

The Tenth Good Thing about Barney (Viorst) **3**:209

The Terrible Churnadryne (Cameron) **1**:41

The Terrible Roar (Pinkwater) **4**:161

Terrible Troll (Mayer) **11**:165

Terry and the Caterpillars (Selsam) **1**:166

Terry on the Fence (Ashley) **4**:15

Thanksgiving Day (Gibbons) **8**:97

That Was Then, This Is Now (Hinton) **3**:72

Then Again, Maybe I Won't (Blume) **2**:18

Then There Were Five
(Enright) **4**:75
*Theodore and the Talking
Mushroom* (Lionni) **7**:135
*Theodore Roosevelt, an Initial
Biography* (Foster) **7**:97
There, Far Beyond the River
(Korinetz) **4**:129
There Was an Old Woman
(Kellogg) **6**:173
There's a Nightmare in My Closet
(Mayer) **11**:160
*There's a Nightmare in My
Cupboard* (Mayer) **11**:160
There's a Rainbow in My Closet
(Stren) **5**:232
These Happy Golden Years
(Wilder) **2**:207
They Found a Cave
(Chauncy) **6**:89
They Put on Masks
(Baylor) **3**:17
They Walk in the Night
(Coatsworth) **2**:63
Thidwick, the Big-Hearted Moose
(Seuss) **9**:176
The Thief (Rockwell) **6**:239
Thimble Summer (Enright) **4**:71
*Things to Make and Do for
Columbus Day* (Gibbons) **8**:89
*Things to Make and Do for
Halloween* (Gibbons) **8**:89
*Things to Make and Do for
Valentine's Day* (de
Paola) **4**:58
*Things to Make and Do for Your
Birthday* (Gibbons) **8**:89
*The Third Margaret Mahy Story
Book: Stories and Poems*
(Mahy) **7**:183
The Third Road (Bacon) **3**:12
Thirteen (Charlip and
Joyner) **8**:32
The Thirteen Days of Yule
(Hogrogian) **2**:89
The Thirteen Moons
(George) **1**:93
*The 35th of May; or, Conrad's
Ride to the South Seas*
(Kästner) **4**:123
Thirty-Six Exposures
(Major) **11**:132
*This Is a River: Exploring an
Ecosystem* (Pringle) **4**:176
This Is Australia (Sasek) **4**:196
This Is Cape Kennedy
(Sasek) **4**:193
This Is Edinburgh (Sasek) **4**:190
This Is Greece (Sasek) **4**:194
This Is Historic Britain
(Sasek) **4**:196
This Is Hong Kong
(Sasek) **4**:194
This Is Ireland (Sasek) **4**:193
This Is Israel (Sasek) **4**:192
This Is London (Sasek) **4**:188
This Is Munich (Sasek) **4**:191
This Is New York (Sasek) **4**:189
This Is Paris (Sasek) **4**:187
This Is Rome (Sasek) **4**:189
This Is San Francisco
(Sasek) **4**:192
This Is Texas (Sasek) **4**:194

This Is the United Nations
(Sasek) **4**:195
This Is Venice (Sasek) **4**:192
This Is Washington, D.C.
(Sasek) **4**:195
This Star Shall Abide
(Engdahl) **2**:71
Thor: Last of the Sperm Whales
(McClung) **11**:187
Threat to the Barkers
(Phipson) **5**:179
Three and One to Carry
(Willard) **2**:223
Three Big Hogs
(Pinkwater) **4**:164
The Three Billy Goats Gruff
(illus. Brown) **12**:99
*Three by Three: A Picture Book
for All Children Who Can
Count to Three* (Krüss) **9**:85
*Three Days on a River in a Red
Canoe* (Williams) **9**:231
Three Gay Tales from Grimm
(Gág) **4**:93
*Three Gold Pieces: A Greek Folk
Tale* (Aliki) **9**:20
Three on the Run
(Bawden) **2**:14
The Three Robbers
(Ungerer) **3**:204
*3 × 3: A Picture Book for All
Children Who Can Count to
Three* (Krüss) **9**:85
Three Wishes (Clifton) **5**:58
*Through the Broken Mirror with
Alice* (Wojciechowska) **1**:200
*Through the Eyes of Wonder:
Science Fiction and Science*
(Bova) **3**:35
*Through the Looking Glass and
What Alice Found There*
(Carroll) **2**:36
Thunder and Lightnings
(Mark) **11**:145
Thunder in the Sky
(Peyton) **3**:180
Tic, Tac, and Toc
(Munari) **9**:124
Tico and the Golden Wings
(Lionni) **7**:130
A Tide Flowing (Phipson) **5**:186
A Tiger Called Thomas
(Zolotow) **2**:237
Tiger in the Bush
(Chauncy) **6**:89
*Tiger: The Story of a Swallowtail
Butterfly* (McClung) **11**:179
*The Tiger's Bones and Other
Plays for Children*
(Hughes) **3**:96
Tikta'liktak: An Eskimo Legend
(Houston) **3**:86
Till the Break of Day
(Wojciechowska) **1**:200
Tim All Alone (Ardizzone) **3**:6
Tim and Charlotte
(Ardizzone) **3**:6
Tim and Ginger (Ardizzone) **3**:7
Tim in Danger (Ardizzone) **3**:7
Tim to the Lighthouse
(Ardizzone) **3**:7
Tim to the Rescue
(Ardizzone) **3**:8

*Time and Mr. Bass: A Mushroom
Planet Book* (Cameron) **1**:42
*Time Cat: The Remarkable
Journey of Jason and Gareth*
(Alexander) **5**:18
*Time of the Harvest: Thomas
Jefferson, the Years 1801-1826*
(Wibberley) **3**:230
The Time of the Kraken
(Williams) **8**:235
Time of Trial (Burton) **1**:34
Time of Wonder
(McCloskey) **7**:209
*Time to Get Out of the Bath,
Shirley* (Burningham) **9**:48
A Time to Love (Benary-
Isbert) **12**:73
*Time-Ago Lost: More Tales of
Jahdu* (Hamilton) **1**:105
Time-Ago Tales of Jahdu
(Hamilton) **1**:106
The Times They Used to Be
(Clifton) **5**:56
Timm Thaler (Krüss) **9**:85
Tim's Last Voyage
(Ardizzone) **3**:8
Tin Cans (Rockwell) **6**:238
Tin Lizzie (Spier) **5**:223
TINK Goes Fishing
(Mayer) **11**:176
TINKA Bakes a Cake
(Mayer) **11**:176
*The Tin-Pot Foreign General and
the Old Iron Woman*
(Briggs) **10**:33
Tintin au pays de l'or noir
(Hergé) **6**:148
Tintin au Tibet (Hergé) **6**:148
Tintin en Amérique
(Hergé) **6**:147
Tintin in America (Hergé) **6**:147
Tintin in Tibet (Hergé) **6**:148
The Tiny Seed (Carle) **10**:73
*The Tiny Seed and the Giant
Flower* (Carle) **10**:73
Tiny TINK! TONK! Tales
(Mayer) **11**:176
Tituba of Salem Village
(Petry) **12**:211
*To All My Fans, with Love, from
Sylvie* (Conford) **10**:98
To Be a Slave (Lester) **2**:114
To Market! To Market!
(Spier) **5**:218
To the Ends of the Universe
(Asimov) **12**:41
To the Wild Sky (Southall) **2**:156
Toad of Toad Hall
(Milne) **1**:143
Toc, toc, chi è? Apri la porta
(Munari) **9**:124
Today We Are Brother and Sister
(Adoff) **7**:36
Tom and the Two Handles
(Hoban) **3**:83
Tom Fox and the Apple Pie
(Watson) **3**:213
The Tombs of Atuan (Le
Guin) **3**:123
*Tomfoolery: Trickery and Foolery
with Words* (Schwartz) **3**:190
Tommy Helps, Too (Rey) **5**:194

The Tomorrow City
(Hughes) **9**:70
Tom's Midnight Garden
(Pearce) **9**:144
Tony and Me (Slote) **4**:200
The Too-Great Bread Bake Book
(Gibbons) **8**:91
Tool Book (Gibbons) **8**:92
Toolchest: A Primer of Woodcraft
(Adkins) **7**:21
Toolmaker (Walsh) **2**:201
The Tooth Book (Seuss) **9**:194
Tooth-Gnasher Superflash
(Pinkwater) **4**:171
The Toppling Towers
(Willard) **2**:223
*Topsy-Turvies: Pictures to Stretch
the Imagination* (Anno) **2**:2
*The Topsy-Turvy Emperor of
China* (Singer) **1**:175
Tornado! Poems (Adoff) **7**:33
Touch Will Tell (Brown) **12**:107
The Tough Winter
(Lawson) **2**:111
The Tournament of the Lions
(Williams) **8**:224
Town and Country (Provensen
and Provensen) **11**:219
The Town Cats and Other Tales
(Alexander) **5**:23
The Toy Shop (Spier) **5**:228
Tractors (Zim and Skelly) **2**:231
Trail of Apple Blossoms
(Hunt) **1**:110
Train Ride (Steptoe) **2**:164
The Transfigured Hart
(Yolen) **4**:261
The Travels of Babar
(Brunhoff) **4**:31
The Treasure (Shulevitz) **5**:206
Treasure Island
(Stevenson) **10**:193
The Treasure of the Long Sault
(Hughes) **9**:77
The Treasure of Topo-El-Bampo
(O'Dell) **1**:148
The Tree Angel: A Story and Play
(Charlip and Martin) **8**:26
A Tree for Peter
(Seredy) **10**:177
Tree House Island
(Corbett) **1**:47
A Tree on Your Street
(Simon) **9**:208
A Treeful of Pigs (Lobel) **5**:173
The Treegate Series
(Wibberley) **3**:231
Treegate's Raiders
(Wibberley) **3**:231
The Trek (Jonas) **12**:176
Trial Valley (Cleaver and
Cleaver) **6**:111
Tristan and Iseult
(Sutcliff) **1**:190
Der Trommler und die Puppe
(Krüss) **9**:88
Trouble Half-Way
(Mark) **11**:156
Trouble in the Jungle
(Townsend) **2**:175
The Trouble with Donovan Croft
(Ashley) **4**:14

Trubloff: The Mouse Who Wanted to Play the Balalaika (Burningham) **9**:39

Truck (Crews) **7**:57

Trucks (Gibbons) **8**:92

Trucks (Zim and Skelly) **2**:232

The True Adventures of Grizzly Adams (McClung) **11**:194

True Sea Adventures (Sobol) **4**:210

The Trumpet of the Swan (White) **1**:195

Trust a City Kid (Yolen and Huston) **4**:256

The Truth about Mary Rose (Sachs) **2**:133

Truth or Dare (Pfeffer) **11**:204

The Truthful Harp (Alexander) **1**:18; **5**:20

Try It Again, Sam: Safety When You Walk (Viorst) **3**:210

Tuck Everlasting (Babbitt) **2**:8

Tucker's Countryside (Selden) **8**:199

Tugboats Never Sleep (Lasky) **11**:114

TUK Takes a Trip (Mayer) **11**:176

Tuned Out (Wojciechowska) **1**:200

Tunes for a Small Harmonica (Wersba) **3**:220

The Tunnel of Hugsy Goode (Estes) **2**:75

Tunnels (Gibbons) **8**:98

Turkey for Christmas (de Angeli) **1**:54

Turn It Up! A Novel (Strasser) **11**:250

The Turnabout Trick (Corbett) **1**:47

The Twelve Months: A Greek Folktale (Aliki) **9**:26

Twelve Tales from Aesop (Carle) **10**:83

Twentieth Century Discovery (Asimov) **12**:44

Twenty-Four and Stanley (Weiss) **4**:219

The Twenty-Four Days Before Christmas (L'Engle) **1**:132

The Twenty-One Balloons (du Bois) **1**:66

Twenty-Two, Twenty-Three (Raskin) **12**:225

Twins: The Story of Multiple Births (Cole and Edmondson) **5**:62

Twist, Wiggle, and Squirm: A Book about Earthworms (Pringle) **4**:177

A Twister of Twists, a Tangler of Tongues (Schwartz) **3**:190

The Twits (Dahl) **7**:78

Two Bear Cubs (Jonas) **12**:173

Two Dog Biscuits (Cleary) **8**:49

Two Laughable Lyrics (Lear) **1**:128

Two Little Trains (Brown) **10**:58

Two Love Stories (Lester) **2**:115

Two Moral Tales (Mayer) **11**:168

Two More Moral Tales (Mayer) **11**:168

The Two of Them (Aliki) **9**:26

The Two Old Bachelors (Lear) **1**:128

Two Piano Tuners (Goffstein) **3**:61

Tye May and the Magic Brush (Bang) **8**:21

The Ultra-Violet Catastrophe! or, The Unexpected Walk with Great-Uncle Magnus Pringle (Mahy) **7**:183

Umbrella (Yashima) **4**:253

Uncle Elephant (Lobel) **5**:175

Uncle Lemon's Spring (Yolen) **4**:267

Uncle Misha's Partisans (Suhl) **2**:166

Under a Changing Moon (Benary-Isbert) **12**:78

Under the Autumn Garden (Mark) **11**:147

Under the Early Morning Trees: Poems (Adoff) **7**:35

Under the Green Willow (Coatsworth) **2**:63

Under the Window: Pictures and Rhymes for Children (Greenaway) **6**:131

Underground (Macaulay) **3**:144

Underground to Canada (Smucker) **10**:189

The Underside of the Leaf (Goffstein) **3**:61

Understanding Body Talk (Aylesworth) **6**:54

The Unfriendly Book (Zolotow) **2**:237

The Universe (Zim) **2**:232

The Universe: From Flat Earth to Black Holes—and Beyond (Asimov) **12**:39

The Universe: From Flat Earth to Quasar (Asimov) **12**:39

University: The Students, Faculty, and Campus Life at One University (Schwartz) **3**:191

The Untold Tale (Haugaard) **11**:107

L'uomo del camion (Munari) **9**:125

Up a Road Slowly (Hunt) **1**:110

Up Periscope (White) **3**:223

Up the Alley with Jack and Joe (Kotzwinkle) **6**:182

Upside-Downers: More Pictures to Stretch the Imagination (Anno) **2**:2

Uptown (Steptoe) **2**:164

Use Your Brain (Showers) **6**:245

Use Your Head, Dear (Aliki) **9**:31

The Uses of Space (Bova) **3**:36

Vacation Time: Poems for Children (Giovanni) **6**:117

Vaccination and You (Cohen) **3**:43

Vampires and Other Ghosts (Aylesworth) **6**:49

Vanishing Wildlife of Latin America (McClung) **11**:192

Vegetables from Stems and Leaves (Selsam) **1**:166

Il venditore di animali (Munari) **9**:124

Venus, Near Neighbor of the Sun (Asimov) **12**:59

Veronica Ganz (Sachs) **2**:134

The Very Busy Spider (Carle) **10**:85

Very Far Away from Anywhere Else (Le Guin) **3**:123

The Very Hungry Caterpillar (Carle) **10**:72

A Very Long Tail: A Folding Book (Carle) **10**:76

The Very Long Train: A Folding Book (Carle) **10**:76

A Very Touchy Subject (Strasser) **11**:251

A Very Young Circus Flyer (Krementz) **5**:154

A Very Young Dancer (Krementz) **5**:151

A Very Young Gymnast (Krementz) **5**:153

A Very Young Rider (Krementz) **5**:152

A Very Young Skater (Krementz) **5**:154

The Vicksburg Veteran (Monjo) **2**:126

Viking's Dawn (Treece) **2**:189

Viking's Sunset (Treece) **2**:189

Village Books (Spier) **5**:228

The Village Tree (Yashima) **4**:250

De vis (Bruna) **7**:49

A Visit to William Blake's Inn: Poems for Innocent and Experienced Travelers (Willard) **5**:250

Vol 714 pour Sydney (Hergé) **6**:149

The Voyage Begun (Bond) **11**:29

The Voyage of Osiris: A Myth of Ancient Egypt (McDermott) **9**:116

The Voyage of QV 66 (Lively) **7**:162

The Voyage of the Dawn Treader (Lewis) **3**:137

Vulcan: The Story of a Bald Eagle (McClung) **11**:180

W. E. B. DuBois: A Biography (Hamilton) **1**:106

Wagging Tails: An Album of Dogs (Henry) **4**:112

Wait till the Moon Is Full (Brown) **10**:57

Wake Up and Goodnight (Zolotow) **2**:237

Walk a Mile and Get Nowhere (Southall) **2**:157

Walk Home Tired, Billy Jenkins (Thomas) **8**:213

Walk with Your Eyes (Brown) **12**:107

Wall Street: The Story of the Stock Exchange (Sterling) **1**:182

The Wanderers (Coatsworth) **2**:63

The War and the Protest: Viet Nam (Haskins) **3**:68

War Dog (Treece) **2**:190

Warrior Scarlet (Sutcliff) **1**:191

Watch Out! A Giant! (Carle) **10**:82

Watch Out for the Chicken Feet in Your Soup (de Paola) **4**:56

The Watcher in the Garden (Phipson) **5**:186

Watchers in the Wild: The New Science of Ethology (Cohen) **3**:43

The Water of Life (Williams) **8**:238

Water on Your Street (Simon) **9**:209

Water Plants (Pringle) **4**:179

Watson, the Smartest Dog in the U.S.A. (Kuskin) **4**:139

The Wave (Strasser) **11**:248

Waves (Zim) **2**:232

The Way Home (Phipson) **5**:182

The Way of Danger: The Story of Theseus (Serraillier) **2**:143

The Way Things Are and Other Poems (Livingston) **7**:171

The Way to Sattin Shore (Pearce) **9**:158

We Are Best Friends (Aliki) **9**:29

We Didn't Mean to Go to Sea (Ransome) **8**:178

We Have Tomorrow (Bontemps) **6**:80

We Hide, You Seek (Aruego and Dewey) **5**:30

We Interrupt This Semester for an Important Bulletin (Conford) **10**:96

We Read: A to Z (Crews) **7**:55

Weather (Pieńkowski) **6**:230

The Weather Changes Man (Bova) **3**:36

The Weaver's Gift (Lasky) **11**:115

A Weed Is a Flower: The Life of George Washington Carver (Aliki) **9**:18

Welcome Home! (Bemelmans) **6**:75

The Well-Mannered Balloon (Willard) **5**:246

The Westing Game (Raskin) **12**:225

Westmark (Alexander) **5**:24

Westward to Vinland (Treece) **2**:190

What a Good Lunch! Eating (Watanabe) **8**:216

What Can You Do with a Word? (Williams) **8**:227

What Color Is Love? (Anglund) **1**:21

What Did You Bring Me? (Kuskin) **4**:141

What Do People Do All Day? (Scarry) **3**:186

What Do You Do When Your Mouth Won't Open? (Pfeffer) **11**:201

What Do You Think? An Introduction to Public Opinion:

How It Forms, Functions, and Affects Our Lives (Schwartz) **3**:191

What Do You Want to Know about Guppies? (Simon) **9**:211

What Does It Do and How Does It Work? (Hoban) **3**:83

What Happens to a Hamburger (Showers) **6**:245

What Holds It Together (Weiss) **4**:228

What I'd Like to Be (Munari) **9**:125

What Is a Color? (Provensen and Provensen) **11**:209

What Is a Man? (Krahn) **3**:106

What It's All About (Klein) **2**:101

What Made You You? (Bendick) **5**:44

What Makes a Boat Float? (Corbett) **1**:47

What Makes a Light Go On? (Corbett) **1**:48

What Makes a Plane Fly? (Corbett) **1**:48

What Makes Me Feel This Way? Growing Up with Human Emotions (LeShan) **6**:188

What Makes the Sun Shine? (Asimov) **12**:46

What Shall We Do with the Land? (Pringle) **4**:186

What the Neighbours Did and Other Stories (Pearce) **9**:154

What to Do: Everyday Guides for Everyone (Bendick and Warren) **5**:41

Whatever Words You Want to Hear (Pfeffer) **11**:198

What's for Lunch? (Carle) **10**:85

What's Going to Happen to Me? When Parents Separate or Divorce (LeShan) **6**:190

Wheel on the Chimney (Brown and Gergely) **10**:64

The Wheel on the School (DeJong) **1**:61

Wheels: A Pictorial History (Tunis) **2**:194

When Clay Sings (Baylor) **3**:17

When Everyone Was Fast Asleep (de Paola) **4**:57

When I Have a Little Girl (Zolotow) **2**:238

When I Have a Son (Zolotow) **2**:238

When I Was a Boy (Kästner) **4**:126

When I Was a Little Boy (Kästner) **4**:126

When I'm Big (Bruna) **7**:52

When Shlemiel Went to Warsaw and Other Stories (Singer) **1**:176

When the City Stopped (Phipson) **5**:185

When the Pie Was Opened (Little) **4**:148

When the Wind Blew (Brown) **10**:47

When the Wind Blows (Briggs) **10**:30

When the Wind Stops (Zolotow) **2**:238

When Thunders Spoke (Sneve) **2**:145

When You Were a Baby (Jonas) **12**:172

Where Can It Be? (Jonas) **12**:178

Where Does the Day Go? (Myers) **4**:155

Where Does the Garbage Go? (Showers) **6**:245

Where Have You Been? (Brown) **10**:61

Where Is Everybody? (Charlip) **8**:26

Where the Lilies Bloom (Cleaver and Cleaver) **6**:103

Where the Sidewalk Ends (Silverstein) **5**:210

Where the Wild Things Are (Sendak) **1**:172

Where Was Patrick Henry on the 29th of May? (Fritz) **2**:81

Where Wild Willie (Adoff) **7**:34

Where's My Baby? (Rey) **5**:195

Where's My Daddy? (Watanabe) **8**:217

Which Horse Is William? (Kuskin) **4**:136

The Whingdingdilly (Peet) **12**:199

The Whispering Knights (Lively) **7**:152

The Whispering Mountain (Aiken) **1**:8

Whispers and Other Poems (Livingston) **7**:167

Whistle for the Train (Brown) **10**:66

Whistle for Willie (Keats) **1**:118

The White Archer: An Eskimo Legend (Houston) **3**:87

The White Horse Gang (Bawden) **2**:14

The White Marble (Zolotow) **2**:239

The White Mountains (Christopher) **2**:43

The White Mountains Trilogy (Christopher) **2**:43

The White Room (Coatsworth) **2**:64

The White Stag (Seredy) **10**:173

White Stallion of Lipizza (Henry) **4**:114

Whizz! (Lear) **1**:128

Who I Am (Lester) **2**:115

Who Look at Me (Jordan) **10**:115

Who Really Killed Cock Robin? (George) **1**:94

Who, Said Sue, Said Whoo? (Raskin) **1**:157

Who Will Comfort Toffle? (Jansson) **2**:95

Whooping Crane (McClung) **11**:181

Whoppers: Tall Tales and Other Lies (Schwartz) **3**:192

Who's in the Egg? (Provensen and Provensen) **11**:210

Who's Out There? The Search for Extraterrestrial Life (Aylesworth) **6**:51

Who's Seen the Scissors? (Krahn) **3**:106

Who's That Stepping on Plymouth Rock (Fritz) **2**:82

Who's There? Open the Door! (Munari) **9**:124

Whose Town? (Graham) **10**:107

Why Can't I? (Bendick) **5**:43

Why Can't I Be William? (Conford) **10**:90

Why Don't You Get a Horse, Sam Adams? (Fritz) **2**:82

Why Me? (Conford) **10**:100

Why Noah Chose the Dove (Singer) **1**:176

Why Things Change: The Story of Evolution (Bendick) **5**:46

The Whys and Wherefores of Littabelle Lee (Cleaver and Cleaver) **6**:108

The Wicked City (Singer) **1**:176

The Wicked Enchantment (Benary-Isbert) **12**:74

The Wicked Tricks of Tyl Uilenspiegel (Williams) **8**:236

Wide Awake and Other Poems (Livingston) **7**:167

Wiggle to the Laundromat (Lee) **3**:116

Wigwam in the City (Smucker) **10**:189

Wild and Woolly Mammoths (Aliki) **9**:25

Wild Foods: A Beginner's Guide to Identifying, Harvesting, and Cooking Safe and Tasty Plants from the Outdoors (Pringle) **4**:183

The Wild Hunt of Hagworthy (Lively) **7**:153

The Wild Hunt of the Ghost Hounds (Lively) **7**:153

Wild in the World (Donovan) **3**:54

Wild Jack (Christopher) **2**:43

Wildcat under Glass (Zei) **6**:260

The Wildest Horse Race in the World (Henry) **4**:113

Wiley and the Hairy Man: Adapted from an American Folktale (Bang) **8**:19

Willaby (Isadora) **7**:103

William and Mary: A Story (Farmer) **8**:85

William's Doll (Zolotow) **2**:239

Willie Bea and the Time the Martians Landed (Hamilton) **11**:90

Willie Blows a Mean Horn (Thomas) **8**:214

Willie's Adventures: Three Stories (Brown) **10**:63

Willie's Walk to Grandmama (Brown) **10**:52

Willy and His Wheel Wagon (Gibbons) **8**:88

The Wind between the Stars (Mahy) **7**:184

A Wind in the Door (L'Engle) **1**:132

The Wind in the Willows (Grahame) **5**:128

The Windswept City: A Novel of the Trojan War (Treece) **2**:191

The Wing on a Flea: A Book about Shapes (Emberley) **5**:90

The Winged Colt of Casa Mia (Byars) **1**:37

Wingman (Pinkwater) **4**:163

Wings in the Woods (McClung) **11**:178

Winter Holiday (Ransome) **8**:175

The Winter Noisy Book (Brown) **10**:56

Winter Tales from Poland (Wojciechowska) **1**:200

Winterthing (Aiken) **1**:8

Wir Pfeifen auf den Gurkenkönig (Nöstlinger) **12**:184

The Wish Workers (Aliki) **9**:17

The Witch Family (Estes) **2**:76

The Witch in the Cherry Tree (Mahy) **7**:182

The Witch of Blackbird Pond (Speare) **8**:205

The Witch Who Wasn't (Yolen) **4**:256

Witchcraft, Mysticism, and Magic in the Black World (Haskins) **3**:69

The Witches (Dahl) **7**:83

The Witch's Brat (Sutcliff) **1**:191

The Witch's Daughter (Bawden) **2**:15

Witcracks: Jokes and Jests from American Folklore (Schwartz) **3**:192

Wizard Crystal (Pinkwater) **4**:162

The Wizard in the Tree (Alexander) **1**:18; **5**:23

The Wizard Islands (Yolen) **4**:260

A Wizard of Earthsea (Le Guin) **3**:124

The Wizard of Op (Emberley) **5**:99

The Wizard of Washington Square (Yolen) **4**:258

Wobble Pop (Burningham) **9**:51

Wolf Run: A Caribou Eskimo Tale (Houston) **3**:88

The Wolves of Willoughby Chase (Aiken) **1**:8

The Wonderful Adventures of Nils (Lagerlöf) **7**:110

The Wonderful Dragon of Timlin (de Paola) **4**:53

The Wonderful Flight to the Mushroom Planet (Cameron) **1**:42

Wonderful Story Book (Brown) **10**:56

The Wonderful Story of Henry Sugar and Six More (Dahl) **7**:75

Won't Somebody Play with Me? (Kellogg) **6**:171

Wooden Ship (Adkins)　**7**:23
Wordhoard: Anglo-Saxon Stories (Walsh and Crossley-Holland)　**2**:201
Words from History (Asimov)　**12**:43
Words from the Exodus (Asimov)　**12**:37
Words from the Myths (Asimov)　**12**:35
Words in Genesis (Asimov)　**12**:36
Words of Science, and the History behind Them (Asimov)　**12**:33
Words on the Map (Asimov)　**12**:36
Workin' for Peanuts (Strasser)　**11**:250
Working with Cardboard and Paper (Weiss)　**4**:229
The World of Captain John Smith, 1580-1631 (Foster)　**7**:98
The World of Christopher Robin (Milne)　**1**:143
The World of Columbus and Sons (Foster)　**7**:98
The World of Pooh (Milne)　**1**:143
The World of William Penn (Foster)　**7**:100

World on a String: The Story of Kites (Yolen)　**4**:258
World's End Was Home (Chauncy)　**6**:89
The World's Greatest Freak Show (Raskin)　**1**:157
The Worms of Kukumlina (Pinkwater)　**4**:171
Would You Rather. . . (Burningham)　**9**:49
A Wrinkle in Time (L'Engle)　**1**:133
The Wuggie Norple Story (Pinkwater)　**4**:170
The Wump World (Peet)　**12**:200
The Yangtze River (Rau)　**8**:186
The Year at Maple Hill Farm (Provensen and Provensen)　**11**:213
Year of Columbus, 1492 (Foster)　**7**:99
Year of Independence, 1776 (Foster)　**7**:99
Year of Lincoln, 1861 (Foster)　**7**:100
The Year of the Horseless Carriage, 1801 (Foster)　**7**:101
Year of the Pilgrims, 1620 (Foster)　**7**:99
Yeck Eck (Ness)　**6**:208
Yertle the Turtle and Other Stories (Geisel)　**1**:88

Yobgorgle: Mystery Monster of Lake Ontario (Pinkwater)　**4**:170
You Can't Make a Move without Your Muscles (Showers)　**6**:248
You Can't Pet a Possum (Bontemps)　**6**:79
You Never Can Tell (Conford)　**10**:100
The Young Ardizzone: An Autobiographical Fragment (Ardizzone)　**3**:8
Young Booker: Booker T. Washington's Early Days (Bontemps)　**6**:84
Young Kangaroo (Brown)　**10**:65
The Young Landlords (Myers)　**4**:159
Young Man from the Piedmont: The Youth of Thomas Jefferson (Wibberley)　**3**:232
The Young Unicorns (L'Engle)　**1**:134
The Young United States: 1783 to 1830 (Tunis)　**2**:195
Your Brain and How It Works (Zim)　**2**:232
Your Heart and How It Works (Zim)　**2**:233
Your Skin and Mine (Showers)　**6**:242

Your Stomach and Digestive Tract (Zim)　**2**:233
You're the Scaredy-Cat (Mayer)　**11**:169
Z for Zachariah (O'Brien)　**2**:129
Zamani Goes to Market (Feelings)　**5**:105
Zebulon Pike, Soldier and Explorer (Wibberley)　**3**:233
Zeee (Enright)　**4**:77
Zeely (Hamilton)　**1**:106
Zella, Zack, and Zodiac (Peet)　**12**:208
Zeralda's Ogre (Ungerer)　**3**:204
Zlateh the Goat and Other Stories (Singer)　**1**:177
A Zoo for Mister Muster (Lobel)　**5**:163
Zozo (Rey)　**5**:193
Zozo Flies a Kite (Rey)　**5**:198
Zozo Gets a Medal (Rey)　**5**:198
Zozo Goes to the Hospital (Rey)　**5**:199
Zozo Learns the Alphabet (Rey)　**5**:199
Zozo Rides a Bike (Rey)　**5**:196
Zozo Takes a Job (Rey)　**5**:196

Title Index